# GIVE YOUR HORSE
## A CHANCE

# LT. COL. A. L. D'ENDRÖDY

*former member of the Royal Hungarian
Olympic Equestrian Team*

# GIVE YOUR
# — HORSE —
# A CHANCE

## The training of horse and rider for all disciplines including dressage, cross-country and show jumping

J.A. Allen
London

British Library Cataloging in Publication Data
A catalogue record for this book is available from the British Library

First published 1959
Reprinted 1971
Reprinted 1974
Reprinted 1976
Reprinted 1978
Reprinted 1983
Reprinted 1986
Reprinted 1989
Classics Series edition 1999

ISBN 0-85131-741-3

Published by
J. A. Allen & Company Limited,
1 Lower Grosvenor Place, Buckingham Palace Road,
London SW1W 0EL

Printed by Dah Hua International Printing Press Co. Ltd., Hong Kong

# FOREWORD

BY

## HIS GRACE THE DUKE OF BEAUFORT
K.G., G.C.V.O., M.F.H.

I AM most happy to write this foreword, which I hope will encourage many to read this very exceptional book.

Colonel A. L. d'Endrödy has enjoyed a life full of experience of all forms of equestrianism. His methods are most interesting and thorough and he has a power over horses, even those of a most difficult nature, which is in some respects unique.

In this book he gives explanations for preparing a horse for dressage, cross-country and show jumping, a combination which is seldom, if ever, given in one book, but he is the man to do it, because he has excelled at all these. He was champion gentleman race rider in Hungary, he represented Hungary in the 1936 Olympiad, finishing fifth in the three-day event, and he was a member of the Hungarian international show jumping team, winning honours throughout the world.

Since he came to Badminton I have watched him ride many horses, all of which go so well and kindly for him, and I can personally testify how greatly they are improved by his schooling.

He has been most helpful, too, in his suggestions and drawings of obstacles for our three-day event courses.

I can strongly recommend this book to all ambitious riders, of whom, I am pleased to say, there are an ever-increasing and large number.

# PREFACE

BY

## W. C. STEINKRAUS

*Captain of the Olympic Equestrian Team, U.S.A.*

'YOU can't learn how to ride by reading books . . .' Uttered with the conviction usually reserved for the final devastating argument, this statement seems to conclude countless discussions of riding in the course of a year. Since it is sometimes pronounced by 'authorities', and not often contraverted (or even amplified) on the spot, the frightening thought occurs to me that it might be quite widely accepted as valid in terms of its implications as well as in its literal sense.

It is, of course, self-evident that the specific muscular skills of riding—the development of a seat that is sufficiently secure and flexible to enable the rider to communicate with his horse through a comprehensive and articulate 'vocabulary' of aids—must be acquired mounted on the horse rather than in the easy chair. But if we are more interested in practising the art of riding than just in the skills of riding, we have another matter altogether. Intuition and 'muscle knowledge' alone rarely suffice for the art, which generally depends on the human intelligence and comprehension to direct the particular mechanical skills involved. And to say that our comprehension and understanding of horses and of riding technique cannot be developed (and sometimes, unfortunately, led astray) except while we are actually sitting on the horse's back is evident nonsense.

Except on its most elementary level, education is a process of learning rather than of teaching ('good pupils make good teachers'), and learning can and must continue in the absence of the riding master. I hope we can take it for granted that we learn—or try to—from our direct experiences and observations; but there is also much that can be learned vicariously from the distilled experiences and observations of others in the form of advice passed on by word of mouth or of book.

[vii]

It is ironic that so many of the people who have never studied the literature of riding—to which the present volume makes a significant addition—simply 'can't spare the time' to do so. That they should cherish time is reasonable enough, for, after all, time is life; but the only way in which we can truly save time lies in borrowing from the experience (which is to say time) of others. Nothing is more wasteful than the tedious search for a solution to a problem which others have long since solved.

Thus all of us who aspire, in our practice of riding, to something more than an interminable repetition of the same errors of technique or of understanding will find ourselves indebted to Colonel d'Endrödy, who has made available to us in this volume the most precious gift a rider can pass on to his colleagues—his own experience and his understanding of it. His experience has been vast; he has probed it with an exceptionally keen analytical mind for the basic logical and consistent principles that are the only short cuts, and he has set forth these insights in an integrated, systematic form with the most painstaking thoroughness.

No book, no matter how comprehensive, can provide answers to all of the problems that can occur in the infinitely variable relationship between man and horse. Indeed the development of one's riding skill lies not so much in knowing the answers as in understanding the questions. This is to say that the analysis of the problem—the isolation and identification of the impediments to its achievement—will generally suggest the methods of solution. And in this sense we must never deny the horse his final authority as to the appropriateness of our methods, and we must never cease examining his response as the verification of our success or failure in understanding his problem and dealing with it. However, where the nature of the question—represented by the horse's resistance—is not quite clear, or where the response he gives us through his performance seems ambiguous, we will often find within the pages of this book the insights that will enable us to find our way again.

# ACKNOWLEDGEMENTS

THE author desires to express his gratitude to everyone who, by encouragement and assistance, has contributed to the completion of this book.

First of all he wishes to express his deepest gratitude

to His Grace the Duke of Beaufort for his magnanimity, which made the preparation and presentation of the book possible, and for his generous interest in considering it worthy to recommend in his foreword to the riding public;

to Mr. William Steinkraus, captain of the U.S. equestrian team, who has been so kind as to write a preface to the book and has undertaken the great work of refining the 'language' of the text in accordance with the terminology of expert riders;

to his friend, Dr. Ervin Fekete, who has produced from the original Hungarian manuscript the first, raw, but absolutely clear English text. It was an arduous task, requiring enormous time and devotion for the job, which he has offered with utmost cordiality;

to Professor W. Hamilton Whyte for his generous and most valuable assistance in editing the rough translation and thus endowing it with the necessary English idiom;

to his ambitious pupil, Mr. David Somerset, who has been the perfect medium for the author's intense observations on the practical effect of his explanations. In this way Mr. Somerset's rôle became, even if indirectly, an important element of the composition of this work. But his direct contribution by all his endeavours regarding the publication of the book, by taking interest in reading and commenting on the material, and by producing the bulk of the photographs, is not less important;

to Colonel Frank Weldon, captain of the victorious British T.D.E. team in Stockholm, who took intense interest in both the practice and theory of my work. He observed the manner of my riding on the schooling grounds and read the type-script of this book, resulting in his valuable "Appreciation" which, with his kind permission, has been published in the Prospectus of the book and is printed on the inside of its dust-wrapper ;

to Mrs. Pamela Carruthers, Mrs. Rosmary Donner and Lady Violet Vernon, who, by adapting his instructions, have provided opportunity for the extension of his observations. They assisted also by reading the text and making useful suggestions for its clarification;

to Mrs. May Fekete and Miss Marjorie Stoneridge, who have contributed so much work in checking and retyping the translated manuscript;

to Miss Primrose Cumming, the author of so many charming pony stories, who was so kind to make the final check up of the manuscript;

to all experts on the art of riding who, after reading the finished work, have been so kind as to give their criticisms about the value and importance of the book.

Finally, the author may pay special tribute to his devoted friend, the late Count Tony Apponyi, who was a great lover of riding sports and hunting. He it was who, by his friendship with the Duke of Beaufort, enabled the author to settle down in his exile at Badminton.

# CONTENTS

## PART TWO

### METHODS OF COMMUNICATION WITH THE HORSE

#### CHAPTER ONE

*Basic conditions of communication with the horse*

## CHAPTER TWO

### *Stirring the motion of the horse*

## CHAPTER THREE

### *Regulation of the horse's motion*

PART THREE

SCHOOLING THE RIDER AND HORSE IN JUMPING

CHAPTER ONE

*General schooling in jumping and in moving on the country track*

The periods of education and their aims:

## PART FOUR

### *The Three-Day Event*

SPECIAL TRAINING, AND THE PERFORMANCE OF THE TEST

### CHAPTER ONE

### *Subjects of training for the T.D.E.*

# INTRODUCTION

THE excellent works on equitation which appear regularly on the shelves of the world's bookshops happily remind us that even the widespread affection for the motor car cannot alienate sport-loving people from that noble animal, the horse, who willingly becomes the faithful and honest friend of those who trust and care for him.

It is significant that there is such a marked interest in the literature of horsemanship and we who have mastered the art, through the study of the works of past decades and through practical experience, feel it our duty to pass on the knowledge we have acquired to those who wish to carry on this great sport.

The idea of writing a book on riding came to me while I was at Orkenytabor at the Hungarian Academy for riding instructors. The Olympic riding team also trained there and both groups worked closely together to improve the standard of training horses and to develop the art of horsemanship. I was an active member of these two institutions for 14 years and during that time acquired considerable knowledge in the art of riding. In addition, I had many years of riding experience before and after this time. All these years were highlighted by many exciting riding competitions at home and abroad.

I drafted the first outline of my book while in captivity at the foot of the Caucasus Mountains, on the shores of the Black Sea. I was a prisoner of war in Russian hands for three and a half years and during those sad, lonely years the planning of this book was my favourite pastime.

The actual manuscript of this book took shape at Badminton, well known for generations to all lovers of horses and hounds. Fate has indeed been kind to bring me to such a delightful place. Here, thanks to the generosity of His Grace the Duke of Beaufort, of this great huntsman whose interest and experience in horsemanship are universally known, it has been possible for me to write these pages.

I have written this book for riders who have already acquired the skill of sitting firmly on the horse's back, but who desire to acquire a higher knowledge and experience of the art of riding.

First of all, I dedicate it to those who, in combined contests and in show jumping, wish to reach the standard of international competitions. But I should also like to help horsemen who enjoy the thrills of hunting and cross-country riding and who wish to learn how to bring up a horse to be an agreeable comrade who will never deceive or leave him in the lurch and how to increase, by training, its steadiness and endurance.

Bearing in mind this aim, I put stress on the explanation of the practical principles of riding, but to increase their value I also endeavour to acquaint the reader with the necessary theoretical background. I am fully aware of the great *practical advantages of knowledge supported by theories* and therefore shall try to arouse interest in them. The theoretical explanations outlined should not be regarded as an attempt to expose difficulties, but rather as a means for overcoming them.

During discussions about riding problems there often arises the question why do horses perform quite differently according to whether they are mounted by a talented rider or by one of limited natural abilities. Since the clarification of this matter is of great practical importance, and can reduce the margin between the performing capacity of these two groups of riders, I have made great efforts throughout this book towards solving the problems involved.

A thorough analysis of the external features of the functions generally used in practice proves that they can show, regardless of the capacity of the individual rider, a similar picture. Thus, it is obvious that the difference between the functions employed must be hidden in one or another way behind their surface, somewhere in the background. Riders of refined instincts are subconsciously completing their functions with such hidden elements. These are scarcely noticeable to a looker-on, but become much more apparent in the effects produced. I have tried to disclose at least a number of these additional elements and by doing so to fill up the gap which exists particularly in this field of riding instruction.

From the description and the application of these " secret " elements explained in this book, some readers might suppose that the method advocated by me is a strangely " new " one. But, it is by no means so. I have only intended to put the missing dot on the " i ", which " dot ", however, will show the way of overcoming many difficulties encountered during communication with the horse.

Recommendations given in the present work concerning schooling the horse by dressage are governed by the aim of educating horses, the main tasks of which will be jumping and moving in the country. Therefore, explanations of special practices which can eventually be employed during the training of " professional " dressage horses, but are not practicable in connection with jumping and riding at speed, or which could harmfully affect the improvement of the animal's jumping action, are omitted.

Aside from the practical and theoretical treatment of the rider's movements and operations, I may visualise the characteristic sensations and feelings which should accompany them and show how to recognize them. This explanation is obviously an intricate task and most writers and riding instructors tend to avoid it with the simple excuse that each horse, under identical situations, conveys different sensations and creates different feelings, which may also vary from one rider to another. Personally, I have my own opinion about the problem and will try to give practical evidence to support it in this book.

Before starting with the actual theme of the book it should also be mentioned that I have endeavoured to apply in the text the current terms in referring to the various objects and practices of riding. However, for some of them there is no simple term in general use and they could only be indicated by more or less lengthy descriptions. So, in order to avoid their frequent repetitions, which would slow down the narrative, I have, in a few cases, coined simple expressions. Even if at first sight they seem to be strangely new and exaggerated, they should ultimately help towards smoother reading.

PART ONE

# Fundamental
# Objects of Riding

THERE are different methods of schooling horses for
competitions and general riding purposes, but it is difficult
to state which is the best, be it French, German, Italian,
or any other 'national' system.

It is true that all methods which can be regarded as recognized
schools have excellent achievements to prove the success of their
'system', in spite of their different external forms. But when one
examines these methods closely, and especially when one dis-
tinguishes their basic principles from their external techniques,
it is clear that the essentials are the same. In fact, they *have* to
be the same, since the horse, whatever its 'nationality' may be, or
whatever system its schooling is based upon, can perform
effectively only from one particular position, the one which best
suits its construction. Apart from quite rare exceptions, such a
position, for identical tasks, is the same for all horses. Only the
method by which the rider brings his mount into this particular
position may vary, and so only in this sense can one speak of
various systems.

It is my firm conviction that that is the most effective and
practical method of riding which is based on the sensitive
*persuasion* of the horse, i.e. on the attainment of its mental co-
operation, and which, without the use of force, *balances* the
animal during the performance of its physical activities.

To illuminate the meaning of the above statement let us make a
comparison in which the various systems of riding and the
capacity of the horse for understanding them are identified with
languages.

In the various systems there are expressions which comply with
those of the universal language of the horse, others, by their
peculiarity are less understandable by the animal since they are
strange to him.

[1]

By the similarity of the tongue mentioned in the first case, the horse will react without the employment of any compulsion quickly and submissively. In the second case, however, when the rider tends to impose the expressions of his own language on the animal, it will encounter difficulties in understanding them, and consequently its reaction will show signs of resistance. Bearing in mind this consideration for supplying the horse's need, the rider, being the senior partner, has to make all efforts to learn the innate language of the horse, and speak to him by means of this dialect.

This point of view is the issue of the method experienced, composed and practised by me. In this sense I have selected from the various well-tested systems the elements best understandable by the horse, and, as far as possible, excluded those which are based on compulsion.

Furthermore, I have extended the scope for smooth conversation by thorough studies and observations so as to best fit the composition to the horse's mental and physical constitution.

Summing up, I am jointly employing in my method the advantages of the generally known systems with the addition of practices experienced during my career. This eclectic method has great advantages; it is applicable to routine cases and it can also be used successfully for overcoming great difficulties. It keeps the horse supple in its loose state as well in the highest collection. It gives the animal the best chance to perform smoothly the tasks allotted to him, however strenuous they are.

To demonstrate the practical value of the method recommended, I have made a series of pictures (see photographs) taken from seven different horses under my instruction. By studying them you can notice the character of the method which brands its typical mark on the actions and general bearing of the horse in various situations. Under these pictures you will see some in which these horses are ridden by a pupil of mine. According to them you can form an opinion about the applicability of the method to different riders.

The horses in the pictures showing some moments of my international competitions have also been trained by myself. These and some other pictures are the only objects from my 'past' (including all my horses, numerous trophies and other property) which were left to me after my release from captivity.

# General Principles for Schooling the Rider and Training the Horse

## THE SCHOOLING OF THE RIDER

IN every branch of sport, whether it is practised in competitions or just as a pleasant pastime, skilful performance always requires great perseverance in both study and practice. The novice rider is no exception to this rule. He must, in fact, be doubly assiduous, since his endeavour concerns not only himself, but also his mount. He also has to know how to care for his horse. Therefore, the time in which riding, in its real sense, can be mastered is considerably longer than that of any other sport.

Good riding does not mean merely the ability of a rider to sit 'safely' on his horse. It involves some deeply rooted principles which are of basic importance in handling and educating the animal. Good riding starts at the stage when the rider can properly *influence* the horse to obey his will, when he knows how to aid it in overcoming difficulties, how to correct a mistake it has made, and how to overcome its opposition in a constructive manner. Furthermore, it is necessary for the good rider to understand how to use the animal most economically and with the utmost safeguard of its physical fitness, especially when his demands strain the horse to the limit of its abilities.

There are no 'tricks' in riding, only knowledge which has been acquired by hard work carried out with great care. This applies equally to the rider and the horse. 'Tricks' have no place in the art of riding, since in moments of crisis, when effective action is most needed, the superficial 'trick' never succeeds.

All 'recipes' describing various practices on this subject must also be regarded with caution, since they are based upon the special nature of an individual rider and a specific horse. Therefore, 'recipes' are only acceptable when their basic principles are broad enough to be applied successfully to a wide variety of horses and riders.

In short, it is the method of *sound schooling* which should pave the way during the rider's education. By the knowledge thus acquired he will be able to communicate with the horse according to its psychological and physical nature, resulting in success in the most critical cases.

In reaching this aim the advanced education of the rider includes the following tasks:

The attainment of the necessary theoretical knowledge;

the improvement of the rider's ability and skill to influence the horse;

the adoption of the right manner of thinking in exercising his authority over the animal and in selecting the appropriate means of communication;

the development of his capacity to recognize the various sensations produced by the horse, and the evaluation of their importance by horseman-like feeling; and

the improvement of his sense for the horse's physical training.

Now let us consider one by one the general principles characteristic of the above objects.

### Theoretical education of the rider

Theoretical education gives the rider a feeling of certainty in choosing the proper means for influencing the horse; it eliminates tentative experiments and avoids a lot of extra work, since his activities are based not upon guesswork but upon positive knowledge.

The most important advantage of this theoretical knowledge, however, is that, by its application, the art of riding can be simplified. In the light of theory the rider will not only clearly see the movements employed, but he will understand their reasons. When one tries to learn *how* to perform simple actions without knowing *why*, one's movements become routine, and they do not bear essential characteristics. Such actions will always remain awkward and stiff, instead of becoming simple.

### The improvement of the rider's skill

In order to acquire a high degree of performance in riding, it is not enough to understand the theories. It is necessary to master the skill by frequent practice of the suggested movements, actions and exercises.

The rider should not become discouraged, lose his patience, or blame himself or his horse if his first attempts are not successful, and the animal does not react as soon as he expects. Guided by the horse's actual response, he should persistently correct and refine his actions until the animal, by the desired response, gives evidence that their execution is correct.

The activities by which the rider influences the horse are described in the following chapters. The schooling of the pupil should be directed right from the beginning according to these principles. They should be employed also by the schooled rider during training and at any time during his co-operation with the horse.

In addition it should be noted that the rider's capacity for performing his activities may be improved by practice up to a stage when—without being automatic—they become quite instinctive. There is a big difference between 'instinctive' and 'automatic'. In the former actions the 'feeling' dominates the physical movements, and in the latter pure movements are performed only. Instinctive actions are *sensitive*, and automatic ones *mechanical*. What is mechanical in riding upsets the horse, since it is not an engine but a living being.

In opposition to this, the reaction of the horse—reflecting complete subordination to the rider's actions—should become by schooling quite automatic.

*The adoption of thinking in a horsemanship-like manner*

During the process of schooling, or in connection with any other riding exercise, the rider should bear in mind that the horse is a living organism, governed by a brain and a nervous system, and consequently in possession of a will. It is also subject to moods, perhaps of joy and sorrow. Therefore, it is a necessary qualification of a good rider to understand the horse psychologically. He has to know how to bring his mount to respond mentally to his wishes, how to give the horse the chance of expressing its joy, how to recognize its pains (e.g. when it is muscle-bound, etc.).

The mental attitude which the rider ought to adopt in all riding problems can be more clearly demonstrated by two examples.

The first shows the train of thought in the case of a horse who has developed the habit of fright.* The correct way to cure this is by taking measures based on the animal's psychological nature.

When the horse notices something which, in its imagination, gives some cause for fright, it shows certain irregularities in its movements. These irregularities are the signs of fright, and they consist of wincing, starting, side-jumping or sudden stopping, and eventually rearing.

If the rider should chastise the horse for this behaviour, the animal will attribute the resulting pain not to the punishment, but to the cause of fright (because it has been felt at the same time). As a logical consequence of this, the cause of fright—identified in its mind with the punishment—will seem to be even more frightening on the next occasion. But, on the other hand, if, in the moment of fright, the rider employs calming measures (mainly by giving long reins) instead of punishment, the animal will realize that its imagined fears are unfounded. In time (it may last for a considerable period because of its atavistic origin), the frequency and intensity of its fright reactions will gradually decrease and eventually disappear.

The second example may illustrate the rider's way of thinking in a case when the horse is opposed to fulfilling any of his demands.

When the opposition is not the result of pain, muscle fever, or fatigue, then it indicates that the applied signals or aids were not the right ones. Therefore, the rider should consider first of all the alteration of his activities for correcting the situation.

For this purpose, if he is at a loss regarding the signals to be used, the best course is to apply exactly the opposite to those which he has previously employed and thought to be the right ones. The radical change of signals or aids will, perhaps, be too drastic, but it will show the trend to be taken as it will reflect the willingness of the horse to obey. Thus the correction of the rider's own mistakes will improve the animal.

At this juncture it should be mentioned that if the rider conducts his mount in a balancing manner (see page 88) he will generally prevent opposition. His activities alternate not only in their immediate execution, but also between main and counter movements, and in this way he never gets an absolutely faulty conception. In order to master the situation the rider has only to

---

*Fright should not be misjudged for the horse's opposition expressed by a behaviour similar to fright (see page 174).

make the involved levelling functions (see page 78) more expressed, and to perform the yielding movements, coupled with his active or passive functions, more substantially.

The rider who tries to overcome difficulties by understanding the mentality of the horse and using measures which influence its willingness as in the above examples, will save both himself and the horse much trouble, worry and pain. Thus, whenever it is felt that the horse is opposed to fulfilling the demand or gets stuck during its work, the rider should *educate* it and not lose his head by trying to bring the poor animal to its senses by force.

A malicious or stubborn opposition is rather rare in horses, but in the case of such behaviour punishment is justified. However, it can be stated as a generality, that riders have a recourse to abusive methods often when they have exhausted their knowledge. This can be taken as an excellent yardstick in measuring the rider's knowledge of riding. The good rider applies a punishment very rarely, while the bad one is always jogging with the reins and striking with the whip.

*Development of the rider's capacity for recognizing the various sensations, and the evaluation of their importance by 'feeling'*

Sensations and feelings are very important features during the course of riding. They form the basis of the refined communication with the horse.

'Sensations' are the rider's physical reactions caused by certain actions of the horse, by his own actions, or by the response of the animal to the rider's activities. These are, in their various forms, uniform in *character*, both in giving and receiving; only one must be able to evaluate them. Just as the effect of a blow, push, jerk, pressure, etc., is felt similarly by everybody (a blow cannot be regarded as pressure, or a jerk as pulling), the effects conveyed by the horse also give the same sensations to everybody. It is true, however, that some horses display stronger actions than others, and that one person may be more sensitive than another, and so on. Consequently, the actions and the inherent sensations will differ in their intensity. But the difference will never be so great as to alter their character altogether.

By 'feelings', I mean the rider's mental attitude which determines the decisions he makes and the consideration he shows to his horse. But this term should also characterize the *manner* of the rider's activities by which he conveys his decisions to the animal. The acquisition of the proper feelings is a more delicate matter than that of the sensations, because their manifestations are influenced to a high degree by the rider's personal sensitivity. Fortunately, this can be developed successfully in most riders with suitable guidance.

The rider can acquire appreciation of sensations and feelings by persevering observation. To facilitate his task I may show in many cases the characteristic feature of the sensation connected with them, on what the observation should be concentrated, and what exercises have to be done to bring about more clearly the particular sensation or feeling.

It is possible that in the early stages there is no noticeable sensation, or that the rider cannot perceive the necessary feeling. In spite of this he should persevere with observations since they are improving in his subconsciousness. Later on, as a result of this subconscious improvement, the sensations and feelings may suddenly emerge one by one, taking the rider completely by surprise. The main point is that the rider should not lose patience while waiting for these moments, for they will surely turn up sooner or later.

*The improvement of the rider's sense for the arrangement of the horse's training*

By the proper arrangement of the training the rider can save his own and the horse's energy, and speed up the progress of the animal without the danger of overstraining it, or failing to complete its mental and physical culture.

The various distributions of time and work included in this book are examples of the method to be followed.

It is true to say that the schooling of the rider according to the principles described is *at the beginning* somewhat aggravated. But by his effort in acquiring the necessary knowledge he will later on, during his live-long co-operation with the horse, facilitate the task of his mount. This must be the main object of a real horseman! Consequently the rider must not try to make the work easier for his own sake at the expense of the animal's correct treatment. The relief will come from the horse when it submits with pleasure and reacts as intended.

The distribution of the rider's schooling should be built up in the following stages:

The skill of sitting safely in the saddle (this subject does not belong to the scope of this book);

basic knowledge of how to conduct the horse; and

more refined communication between the rider and horse.

The rider becomes acquainted with the basic knowledge in the course of elementary training. This consists of a period of learning principles, and a period of consolidation of this knowledge through practice.

During this latter period, when the rider has learned the elementary methods by which he can exert some influence on the horse, he should begin to observe the sensations caused by the horse's movements, and its willingness to submit to the rider's will. These have an important bearing upon the horseman's conduct. Once attuned to these, he can decide what kind of aid to apply and when.

It takes the beginner from one to one and a half years of learning and daily practice to master the basic techniques of riding. If the pupil should try to shorten this time, it is doubtful if he will ever become a successful rider. The reason for this long training period lies in the fact that the whole muscular system of the rider has to be adjusted to riding. In curtailing the period, the rider's style will always be marked by stiffness, which, naturally, will also adversely affect the horse. But those who are prepared to devote the necessary time to the basic training patiently and wholeheartedly will find that it pays good dividends in the end.

During the period of learning basic principles, the pupil should, if possible, ride a calm and well-educated horse. Thus he will not be concerned with the animal, but only with the act of riding itself, and he can physically adapt himself to it.

This thorough basic training is indispensable even for riders who, as 'naturals', ride frequently, and who decide to embark upon riding as a competitive sport. However, they should not be disheartened if they have to abandon a number of well-established but useless habits.

During the year following his basic training, the rider's principal aim should be to *consolidate* everything that he has learned so that the activities involved become natural to him. He should also try to apply the signals and aids already familiar to him, to a less experienced horse.

It is also recommended that, during this year, the progressing rider should frequently jump in succession a number of small obstacles (say 25 to 30, at a height of about 2 ft. 6 ins. or 0.75 m.). This will help to consolidate his seat in the forward position and in jumping.

Already at this stage of training, the rider should try to develop his sense of judgment in jumping, so that later on he will be able to determine the accurate take-off point well in advance. However, he should *not yet try* to make any corrections, but let the horse take off on its own accord.

After completing his basic training, the young rider can gradually undertake more and more advanced methods of riding, as well as the schooling of young horses, and his own preparation for competitions.

The most important aim in this stage of the rider's schooling is to develop and refine his intellectual (as opposed to physical) riding technique. The aids and signals first performed only mechanically should from now on be given with feeling.

### THE PURPOSE AND AIMS OF THE HORSE'S SCHOOLING

The schooling of the horse yields many rewards. First of all it develops the horse's mentality and its willingness to obey. It also accustoms the animal to using its body correctly, which enables it to fulfil the demands pleasantly both for the rider's and its own sake. Furthermore, schooling is bound greatly to increase the performing capacity of the horse and help it to become a dependable partner in most difficult situations. Last, but not least, schooling considerably lengthens the faithful services of the animal, and thus gives generous recompense for the time spent on the wearisome process. The best reward of all is undoubtedly the many years of successful and agreeable sport offered by a well-schooled mount.

Generally speaking, the education (i.e. the dressage-like schooling) of the horse up to a fairly high level is almost identical for any horse. By a 'fairly high level', I mean a degree of training considerably exceeding the usual standards of elementary schooling.

This particular level should serve as a starting point from

which advanced schooling should commence. From this basis, the teaching of horses to perform special duties in the branch of riding for which they have been selected will not offer any difficulty.

The work of education is composed of two parts, the actual teaching and the accustoming.

In the course of *teaching* the aim is systematically to develop the animal's intelligence, so that it will react to the rider's demands willingly by effective actions expressed in motion and in the display of strength.

The *accustoming* of the horse comprises only that part of the education which aims at making the animal *accept* certain situations, objects, or events without requiring any particular exertion on its part (e.g. road traffic, noise, frightening objects, hounds, croup, etc.).

In both the above parts of training, great demands are placed upon the psychological feeling of the rider and on his patience. While the teaching requires a high standard of riding knowledge, the accustoming work has no such limitations. The actual problems of riding are chiefly connected with those of the first group of tasks, the problems in the second group generally solve themselves automatically in due time.

The length of the schooling period depends mainly upon the physical strength, intelligence, skill and nature of the horse, and to a certain degree on the knowledge of the instructor.

The horse can adopt the external forms of schooled movements in a relatively short time, but it is the improvement of its body in the performances which ultimately determines the length of the schooling period. This must be especially taken into account in the case of young horses which are still in their phase of *natural development*. If their artificial improvement by schooling is not sufficiently gradual, the organism of the animal will not be able to endure the double demand.

In any case plenty of time must be allowed for the horse to become perfectly at ease, physically and mentally, in accomplishing the tasks. A hurried or unthorough schooling is bound to result in difficulties of one kind or another. Any forcible attempt to eliminate these difficulties will only confuse the horse and create a serious setback by overstraining it.

In order to illustrate the length of time required for the schooling recommended in this book, I have taken as an example a four-year-old horse of good average quality. (Generally, the period of natural development is reached by the end of the animal's fifth year.) Thus the training time which is required to reach the level of a sound general education can be set at about one and a half years. Continued schooling, thoroughly to 'fix' the horse's general knowledge, needs an additional year.

In setting the above time limits, my estimates—with regard to the experience of the horseman—apply to a rider of good average knowledge.

Although an experienced rider may find it possible to reduce the time of the actual instruction given, the time which the horse needs for its physical development is just as long whether it is schooled by the best master or by a mere beginner.

In the most favourable circumstances, mainly when dealing with early improved or older horses (over four years), it is possible to curtail the schooling period by one-third, and, very rarely, by half the time I have suggested. But these cases are exceptional.

As a general principle, it is safe to say that the more the horse shows a special gift in a certain direction, e.g. jumping, dressage, etc., and the more responsive it is to education, the more advisable it is to give it enough time and the very best instruction. Such an animal should be treated as a potentially great horse, and deserves all the care and time necessary to develop its physical system and to acquire a well-balanced and elastic movement. It is quite possible to achieve some success with such a horse even by a curtailed schooling course, for it will try hard—especially at the beginning, when it is driven by its natural talent coupled with good will—to fulfil the demands imposed upon it. But the inevitable result of this careless exploitation is that the horse will soon break down or become sour, because of its immaturity. A less intelligent or an unwilling horse does not present such a problem, since nobody would be tempted to introduce it to the critical public after an abridged schooling period.

The treatment of unbroken horses during the earliest period of their education (accustoming to the saddle, mounting, weight of the rider, as well as its piloted riding) is not included in the present work. Here, it is assumed that the novice has already received this introductory education.

EASINESS OF THE RIDER AND HORSE

Creation of easiness is one of the most important tasks both of the rider's and the horse's schooling. It should be improved to the highest possible standard by painstaking exercises in accordance with the innate dexterity and inclination of the partners.

The term 'easiness' in general parlance is mainly used. in a fairly restricted sense, to express a certain physical lightness in the functions of the rider and horse. It has, however, a more deeply rooted meaning which consists of mental and physical elements. In this sense:

Easiness is that quality of the rider by which he facilitates the smooth performance of the horse under any circumstances and on the part of the horse it means the degree of willingness and readiness with which it obeys the rider's demands.

Easiness of the rider is the issue of the horse's easiness, i.e. its suppleness in general bearing and reactions. It does not mean detachment from the horse, cessation of a created contact, or inactivity in his conduct.

Easiness must not be mistaken for 'lightness' which is only a certain manifestation of this easiness.

'Lightness' is the yardstick of that effect of strength which is produced by the rider or the horse in keeping contact, conveying and receiving signals or aids. That which is light is not necessarily ease, and lightness without easiness has no value in riding.

The higher the rider's capacity in combining lightness with easiness, the more energetic actions can he employ during the course of communication with the horse without endangering this easiness. Thus at first lightness has to be improved before energetic actions can be used!

The various functions, procedures and exercises described in this book are composed with special regard to ensuring easiness while the rider is employing them. Thus, during the study of the various paragraphs the reader will get an answer also to the question as to how the horse's and his own easiness can be achieved.

Additionally it is still necessary to examine some details about the physical culture of the rider by which his activities can be endowed with easiness.

To become easy in his activities the rider should make good use of any opportunity, and perform exercises both on horse-back and on the ground which promote the lightness of his movements, flexibility of his body, and the refined control of his muscles. He should acquire the skill to perform movements in complete relaxation like a lightly waving silk cloth, but also with strength like an elastic steel spring. He should be able to change over between these two extremes with equally smooth transitions while increasing as well as decreasing the strength. Furthermore, it is necessary for the rider to become skilled in exercising functions independently, and in employing different strengths in performing them simultaneously.

Lack of easiness in the hands is the greatest disadvantage of riding, and it causes a high percentage of the difficulties encountered by the rider. Therefore it is of utmost importance to free the hands from the least rigidity.

In making them easy the procedure should start with relaxing the shoulders, *elbows*, wrists, and all joints of the hands (fingers). Relaxation of the elbows has a special importance, since by it the relaxation of the arms and hands is considerably promoted. Think often on it!

For this purpose perform smooth, wavy movements in which the shoulders, upper and under-arms, the hands up to the tip of the fingers participate simultaneously with, but independently from, each other, e.g., make Swedish arm exercises (also on horse-back), balance a cane on the tip of one of the fingers (alternating hands), change over repeatedly the whip from one hand to the other with open, smoothly rounded movements.

In order to relax the hands themselves practise the following exercises.

Write with a pencil with a very long point (about half an inch, 12 mm.), until you are able to use it easily without breaking the point. Do this with both hands, and also simultaneously.

Take in one hand a soft rubber ball and in the other a harder one, and exercise, sometimes only on the one and sometimes on both of them, short or prolonged pressures in rotation. Take care when relaxing the pressure that 'contact' is maintained. Change the balls from time to time and repeat the exercise.

Combine the above two exercises, and write with the one hand while pressing the ball with the other.

During riding (in all paces, and also on undulating surfaces) let loose the reins, and imitate writing (normal small letters) simultaneously with both hands.

Play with the fingers on the withers of the horse (see page 61).

The easiness of the seat in its whole constitution is the basis for perceiving sensations conveyed by the horse's back, and for exercising proper influence on it. Therefore it is also an important task of self-education to improve and refine the sensibility and efficiency of the seat (see details in the various paragraphs).

The motional part of self-education should start with suppling the upper body by smooth gymnastic exercises (also on the ground). Then make frequent series of moderate oscillating movements with the upper body in lateral and longitudinal directions without, however, *shifting* the seat from its original posture.

During the next exercises interchange in series the normal and action-ready position of the seat; the pressure by the seat with that of the thighs, and both of them with the pressure, respectively with relaxation, on the stirrups (see also page 81).

The easiness shown by the legs manifests itself most characteristically in the smoothness with which the rider keeps them in a relaxed state on the horse's sides. They must cleave there without clasping, and retain the contact independently from the motion of the animal.

To acquire the skill and feeling, ride in the beginning without stirrups, if possible, on a quiet, rather fat horse of comfortable paces and keep at first the legs motionless on the girth; then, during this exercise, single breathing-like pressures with alternate legs, at the same time taking care that the leg does not lose contact with the horse's side during the moments of relaxation. Exercise slight knocks alternately with the legs; later on perform the above exercises with the use of stirrups, both in the sitting and in forward position.

In order to improve the general easiness, ride often on undulating ground, and practise the recommended exercises up and down hill. The improving quality of this combined exercise lies in the fact that the rider, in order to follow the changing movements of the horse, is obliged to interchange the functions of the engaged muscles in rotation, while he performs also movements producing lightness.

The rider must also learn how to remain steady, i.e. motionless

on the horse's back.  This steadiness should not be mistaken for
a bearing in which the body or parts of it are fixed rigidly into a
certain position, since such a position will always become stiff.
If, however, the rider's bearing is relaxed and easy such stiffness
will automatically disappear.

All exercises which produce easiness and lightness in the rider's
bearing, promote at the same time his skill in adopting the correct
steadiness of his hands, seat, upper body and legs.  By starting
the exercises with ample movements, one should gradually reduce
the magnitude of them until they are performed by the invisible
inner vibration of the engaged muscles only.  It must be stressed
that if the rider is instructed to adopt steadiness before he has
become mobile, flexible and completely relaxed, he will never
lose his initial stiffness.

It is self-evident that the animal's training should also be
carried out in a similar manner, by employing at first comprehensive guiding movements which should be reduced later on
in accordance with its development.

Achievement of the capacity for invisible guidance, being the
result of the rider's easiness and the horse's suppleness, must be
a most important aim of their education.  By this means the rider
will be able to direct the horse by his 'thoughts', which will
react to him smoothly, and with complete readiness.

The rider should never be too 'cautious' in his activities, since
such behaviour can easily make him stiff.  He should concentrate
attention on the easiness of his activities and by remaining
'natural' changing them often.  Such conduct is much more
conducive to good and refined riding than one which is spoilt by
the fear of making a mistake.

In order to promote and safeguard the ease of the horse, the
rider should continuously 'talk' to him.  The media of this conversation are the rider's check upon the animal's attention and
obedience to his driving and retarding signals (half-halts, see
page 133) and to those by which he frequently reminds it on retaining its shoulder mobility (see page 100).  The combination of
these repeated longitudinal and lateral functions attracts the
horse's attention to its master, preserves its suppleness by the
produced easiness and prevents it from adopting irregularities.

# CHAPTER TWO

# The Horse's System of Locomotion and the Sensations Given by its Strides

THE rider's foremost aim is to exploit the animal's locomotion for his own benefit in the most advantageous manner, and most of his action should be designed to achieve this aim. In order to practise his actions in harmony with the horse's movements, to constantly follow the trend of these movements, and to be able to grasp the horse's mentality, it is essential that the rider understands its system of locomotion. The importance of this understanding makes it necessary—even though it may seem tedious—to explore the fundamental features of locomotion (sequence of strides), and to describe the characteristic sensations derived from the animal's pace-movements.

In order to enable the rider to distinguish the various movements of the horse before he can recognize them instinctively, he should

    study the movements of the horse's shoulders; and

    examine the animal's shadow in profile while in motion.

Observation of the horse's shoulders can lead to the following conclusions:

When the horse is performing a forward-swinging action with one of its forelegs, then its shoulder on the same side also makes a forward-directed movement.

When this leg enters into the phase of support, the shoulder on the same side will start to make a backward-directed movement.

By observing this motion of the forelegs and the shoulders, and possessing a knowledge of the horse's system of locomotion, one can deduce with certainty from step to step the kind of movements the hind legs are making.

The other way of obtaining visual impressions of the horse's motion is by watching its shadow. This method of observation affords a visual account, like a film, of the entire system of locomotion. In contrast to the shoulder method, it has the advantage of also showing clearly the movements of the hind legs.

Once the rider has become fully aware of the horse's movements with the aid of one of the above methods, he should extend his observations to himself, carefully noting what he feels in his seat, legs, etc., while the animal performs the observed movement.

When he is able to identify his own sensations with the particular movement of the horse, he should try to deduce by feeling what the animal is doing with its legs from time to time.

The sensations involved are caused by the following movements of the horse:

The horse, while moving its legs in commencing and completing the steps, also raises and sinks its croup and forehand slightly (observe its shadow). The effect of this motion may appear to the rider in different forms, but it will always be accompanied by distinct push-strokes which he is bound to feel in his seat.

The push-strokes produced by the movements of the hind legs are more apparent than those of the forelegs. Therefore, it is advisable to try first of all to recognize the croup-movements and evaluate their significance.

When the rider is able to identify by his sensations the movements of the horse's legs, he will also be capable of judging their quality, and it will be easier for him to find out the most suitable moments when signals and aids can most effectively be applied in co-ordination with the horse's locomotion.

## THE WALK

The pace at which the horse moves most conveniently and with the least exertion is the walk. In this pace the animal uses all four legs separately, so that each leg moves independently of the others, and in comparison with the other paces, the cadence shows little natural swing.

The relatively long intervals between the movements offer plenty of opportunity to the rider to exercise his instructive influence on the horse, and to the animal to appreciate all that it has been taught. But the fact that there is very little natural swing in the pace makes instruction difficult for the rider, and enables the horse to resist easily. This situation confronts the rider with many difficulties during the course of training. In order to overcome them, the best method is not to start the schooling with a detailed elaboration of the walk, but to couple it with the work at a trot and canter.

Fig. No. 1

One stride at a walk.

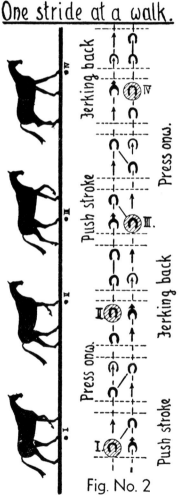

Fig. No. 2

The horse's silhouette while walking shows an almost level bearing (see Fig. No. 1), while the slight raising and sinking of its neck and head, to the rhythm of the lifting movements and hoof-falls of its forelegs, give the impression of nodding.

With regard to the sequence of steps in the walk, Fig. No. 2 gives a detailed explanation. By reading the diagram from left to right, the whole system of locomotion can be analysed.

It can be seen that in the walk the horse moves each leg at a different time, giving four separate hoof-beats. The step of either of the hind legs is always followed by the forward move-

Key to Fig. Nos. 2, 9, 15 and 20.

⊕ Foot-fall and support
∩ Support; forward thrust
♠ Thrust-off
↑ In the air; forward swing.
⋔ Before foot-fall.

ment of the foreleg on the same side, the motion of the foreleg being succeeded by the step of its diagonal hind leg (see Figs. Nos. 3 and 4).

## Succession of the steps:

2 ∩ ∩ 4

1 ∩ ∩ 3

___

## Left diagonal

∩ ↑

↑ ∩

In support:
  off hind
  near fore
In the air:
  the other two

## Left pair

∩ ↑

∩ ↑

In support:
  near fore
  near hind
In the air:
  the other two

Fig. No. 3

This series of movements can be analysed in detail as follows:

As a starting point, the phase of the right diagonal support (1—4) is created when, in the sequence of steps, the off-hind leg thrusts itself off the ground. This motion can be recognized by the fact that at the same time the left shoulder is half-way on its forward-directed movement, and the right shoulder half-way on its backward-directed movement.

This phase is followed by the left pair-support (1—2) at the moment of the thrust-off by the off-foreleg. Meanwhile the off-hind leg is half-way through its forward-swinging movement, and the near-hind leg on the half-part of its support position. The characteristic of this phase

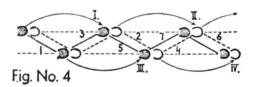

Fig. No. 4

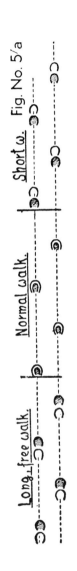

Fig. No. 5/a

Short ω.

Normal walk

Long, free walk

is that the right shoulder begins its forward movement, and the left its backward-directed movement.

The next stage is the left diagonal-support (3—2) at the moment of the thrust-off by the near-hind leg. The right shoulder is half-way on the forward, and the left half-way on the backward-directed movement.

Finally, the series of movements is completed by the phase of the right pair-support (3—4) with the thrust-off of the near-foreleg. Meanwhile, the near-hind leg is half-way on its striding forward motion, and the off-hind leg on the half part of its support position, in order to reach again the 1—4 phase of the motion. The left shoulder then begins the forward, and the right the backward-directed movement.

Within the above series of movements, the change of role of the pairs of legs is a slightly prolonged process, and there is a moment (between every diagonal and pair-support change) when the horse has three legs on the ground at the same time.

From the foregoing it can be seen that in the walk:

there are always at least two and, during the phase of support change, three legs on the ground;

there is no moment of suspension; and

the changing movements of the pairs of legs follow each other with a difference of a half time.

In examining the prints made by the hoofs (see Fig. No. 5a) it can be observed, that:

all these hoof-prints are evenly separated from each other by approximately 3 feet 6 inches (one metre); and each print originates from two legs on the same side (see Fig. No. 4).

In an extended walk, the hoof-prints of the hind legs slightly precede those of the forelegs. In a collected (shortened walk), they are lagging behind (also when the horse moves lazily).

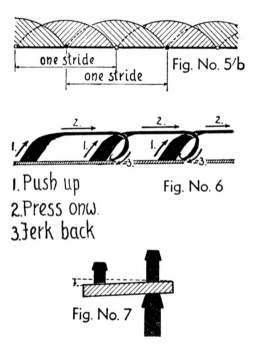

one stride

one stride

Fig. No. 5/b

1. Push up
2. Press onw.
3. Jerk back

Fig. No. 6

Fig. No. 7

The strides do not follow each other in space, but halve each other because the horse steps with its hind legs into the hoof marks of the forelegs (see Figs. Nos. 4 and 5b).

While the horse is using its legs in this manner its body conveys to the rider the following series of sensations (see Fig. No. 6):

At the change of the support position of the two hind legs, the sinking movement of that leg which comes into support, and the raising movement of that which thrusts off causes the horse's croup to make a sudden movement which gives the rider a sensation of a definite push-stroke. This movement of the croup, while the seat remains motionless in the saddle, slightly pushes up the buttocks.

While the stroke affects both buttocks, careful observation will show that the sensation is slightly more emphatic on the right side while the right hind leg steps, and vice versa.

During the phase of diagonal support, while the horse brings its hind leg forward, the buttocks become pressed forward and, at the moment of the simultaneous lifting and dropping movement of the two forelegs, the forehand, by a jerking kind of movement, pushes back the buttocks to their original position.

The series of the above alternating movements gives the rider a certain rocking sensation, demonstrated in Fig. No. 7.

Bearing in mind the described features of the movement, it will not be difficult to appreciate the degree of its regularity. It can be said that the better arranged and the more distinct the strides, the more clearly is felt the movement of the horse through the seat. If the animal happens to walk in a disjoined manner, the sensation of the push-strokes becomes blurred and indistinct, and this tends to prove that the strides are defective.

As the walk is the pace at which the horse's movements give the slightest push-strokes, it requires much more care to judge correctly the regularity of strides. There are numerous riders who neglect the work of walking on account of the insignificant sensation which it offers.

## THE TROT

The trot is the most rhythmical and most even pace of locomotion, and for these reasons it is the most suitable for covering long distances reasonably quickly and with relatively little exertion.

In the trot, the animal proceeds by making identical and simultaneous movements with its diagonal legs. In this way the pace, by its simple grouping of movements, and by its natural balance and swing, facilitates the teaching work of the rider and the learning of the horse. Therefore, this is the pace which plays the main role in the horse's schooling.

Upon examining the animal's silhouette, one can observe that it shows in the trot the highest natural bearing, and while proceeding the horse keeps its neck and head evenly in a quiet position (it does not nod, see Fig. No. 8).

Let us now consider the details of the movements which make up the trot (see Fig. No. 9 and the key to it in Fig. No. 2).

As a consequence of performing the steps by the diagonally paired legs, the horse makes two hoof - beats during the completion of one stride.

By the simultaneous beat of the off-hind and the near-fore hoofs the left diagonal support (I) is created, and by the other two legs the right one (II). Thus the trot is a series of these interchanging support positions.

As a rule in the trot, there are always two hoofs on the ground, but in a more accentuated cadence, at the moments of diagonal changes, the horse gets into a position of suspension. The hoof-marks on the ground are similar to those of the walk (see Fig. No. 5a).

The strides, as in the walk, do not follow each other in space, but appear to be interlocked by halving and interweaving with each other (see Fig. No. 5b).

The push-strokes which the steps convey to the rider are produced at the moment when the exchange of the diagonal support position takes place. Namely, when the forward-swinging hind leg leaves the ground, and by doing so, raises the horse's croup. The stroke tries to lift the upper body of the rider out of the saddle, and at that moment when the force of the stroke ceases to act, the seat jolts back into

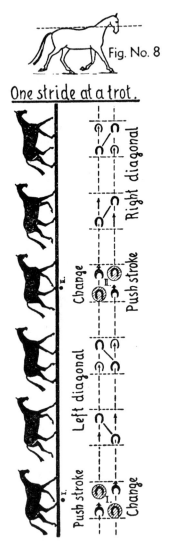

Fig. No. 8

One stride at a trot.

Fig. No. 9

its original position, due to the law of gravity. These two coupled movements recur at each diagonal change, thus giving the rider an impression of joggling (see Fig. No. 10).

It is easy to ascertain which diagonal movement is being performed at any moment by observing the horse's shoulder movement. When the animal is in the phase of left diagonal support (the near-hind leg and the off-foreleg are swinging forward), the right shoulder shows the forward and the left shoulder the backward-directed movement. In the case of the right diagonal support, the above position will give the reversed appearance (see Fig. No. 9).

As far as the identification of movements by sensing is concerned, it must be pointed out that the sensations are different,

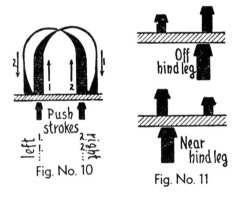

Fig. No. 10

Fig. No. 11

depending upon whether the jogs of the pace are balanced out by a sitting trot or evaded by riding of a rising trot.

When using the sitting trot, the sensation from which one can deduce the forward thrust of the hind legs is, that the push-stroke caused by the rising movement of the croup is more apparent on the right buttock when the horse changes from the left to the right diagonal movement, and vice versa (see Fig. No. 11). Simultaneously, the buttock of the opposite side—where the hind leg is at the moment of its hoof-fall—seems to sink a bit.

Another method is to recognize the movements of the hind legs when the rider imitates the process of rising trot (but only in his imagination, without actually rising from the saddle), and judges them according to the sensations derived therefrom.

In order to be able to apply this method, it is necessary to know the theoretical background of the process of a rising trot. In this connection it will now be useful to discuss in some detail the motions involved in the rising trot.

The actions performed by the rider in a rising trot are designed to economize his own energy and to offset the jogging effects inherent in the horse's movement. The energy which the rider requires for this latter purpose is obtained by making use of the strokes so characteristic of the trot (see Fig. No. 9).

Each movement of the rider in a rising trot is the result of the pushing effects of the two succeeding diagonal changes, and of the

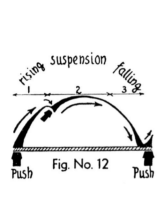

Fig. No. 12

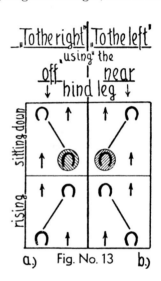

Fig. No. 13

law of gravity. The movement as a whole consists of three phases (see Fig. No. 12), which are:

- a distinct and rather sudden rise (the result of the upward-directed effect of the first stroke);
- an extended suspension (produced by the lifting force of the second stroke meeting the downward pull of gravity and, for a moment, counteracting each other); and
- a calm descent back into the saddle (the force of the second stroke being exhausted, the pull of gravity draws the rider naturally back into the saddle).

The rising trot can be carried out by using the directions to the right and to the left, just as the rider with his rising (lightening) and sitting down (burdening) movements accommodates himself to the motion of the horse's hind legs.

In referring to the direction of the rising trot, one can choose between two methods, depending upon whether the hind leg which is at the moment in its support phase

is burdened by the rider's sitting down movement; or

lightened by his rising movement (i.e. the rider burdens that hind leg with his sitting down movement which is in the forward swinging phase of its locomotion).

Throughout this book I have chosen to apply the first definition, so that a rising trot ' to the right ' means that the animal's off hind leg is burdened by the seat, i.e. the rider is ' using ' the right hind leg (see Fig. No. 13a). Conversely, in ' using ' the left hind leg, the rising trot is carried out ' to the left ' direction (see Fig. No. 13b).

In a rising trot the ' inside ' is the side of the ' used ' hind leg; the opposite one is the ' outside '.

In order to adopt the rising movement on a desired diagonal the rider, while trotting should first observe the movement of the horse's *outside shoulder*, and then select the moment of the *rising* so that it coincides with the phase of its forward-swinging movement.

In the beginning, a certain amount of practice will undoubtedly be necessary before the rider is able to recognize this movement, but later on he will have no difficulty in setting himself into the desired direction by sensing the horse's motion, without even having to look at its shoulders.

If the rider wishes to ascertain the direction he is using while in a rising trot, he should glance at the horse's shoulders. The *opposite* direction is used to that shoulder which swings forward simultaneously with the rider's rising movement.

The foregoing points also offer a solution to the problem of recognizing certain leg motions of the horse by sense while proceeding in a rising trot. Each stroke which results in rising from the saddle indicates the start of the forward-swinging motion of the inside hind leg. Each stroke which can be felt during the phase of suspension is the starting point for the forward-swinging motion of the outside hind leg and the inside foreleg.

The movements of the animal while trotting should convey the following sensations to the rider:

the push-strokes should be distinct and the strides easily distinguished from each other;

the strokes should follow each other forcibly and rhythmically.

In a sitting trot, the horse, in spite of its strokes, should carry the rider smoothly on its back. In a rising trot, it should throw him elastically upwards and then, after the rising moment, give him ample time to sit down again. If the strokes are uncertain, blurred and unrhythmical, the horse's movement will be disunited. If the strokes are stiff and clumsy, they prove that the animal does not use its back while moving and therefore has not enough swing.

### Canter and Gallop

In these two kindred types of pace, the horse carries out its movements by different muscular operations of all four legs.

The co-ordination of the various movements into actual strides can take two different forms, depending upon whether the near- or the off-foreleg is leading. In this sense, one can speak of cantering or galloping to the left (on the left rein, near fore leading), and to the right.

In these paces the side of the direction used denotes the ' inside ' of the horse.

The leading foreleg is that leg which does not take part in the motion of diagonal support, and, observed from the ground, it gives the impression that it always moves before the other foreleg. In the whole course of the locomotion, this leg exerts the most energy by lifting the entire weight of the horse into the phase of suspension.

The outside hind leg, when it reaches the ground after the phase of suspension, has to carry the entire weight of the animal for a moment and then push it forward into the diagonal support position.

In the canter or gallop it is possible that one, two, or three legs are on the ground at the same time. During the phase of suspension, none of them is in touch with it.

While in progress, none of the legs steps into the hoof-marks of the others, each one leaving its separate print.

THE CANTER

The canter is a soft, rhythmical pace, and its rocking-like movements can be followed agreeably by the rider. Among all the paces, the swinging movement of the horse's back is most pronounced in the canter. Because of this natural quality, the canter can be of substantial help during the horse's schooling in developing its back action.

When using this pace as a means of conveyance, only its extended form should be taken into account, as this ensures a reasonable speed and at the same time economizes the horse's energy.

In the canter the horse takes up a certain collection on its own initiative, and consequently it assumes a somewhat higher bearing. The holding of the neck and head is accompanied by a slight nodding, caused by the rising of the neck at the moment of the thrust-off of the leading foreleg, and the sinking of the neck with its foot-fall (see Fig. No. 14).

Fig. No. 15 shows the leg actions during one stride of the canter to the right (see key in Fig. No. 2).

Within one stride of the canter the horse gives three hoofbeats:

    I. The simultaneous hoof-beat of the inside (leading) hind leg and the outside foreleg.

    II. The hoof-beat of the inside (leading) foreleg, and

    III. After a brief suspension, that of the outside hind leg.

If the canter should give a sound of four hoof-beats, the whole performance must be very defective.

During the execution of each stride the following characteristic movements can be observed:

After landing on the outside hind leg, the inside hind leg and both forelegs are in a forward-swinging movement, while both shoulders perform a forward-directed movement.

Within this action, the forward-swinging movement of the inside (leading) foreleg is more distinct than that of the outside foreleg, and because of this the hoof of the inside foreleg tends to appear in front of the (inside) shoulder after the completion of its forward-swinging movement.

The appearance of the inside hoof roughly coincides with the hoof-fall of the inside hind leg, and then it is succeeded by the hoof-fall of the leading foreleg.

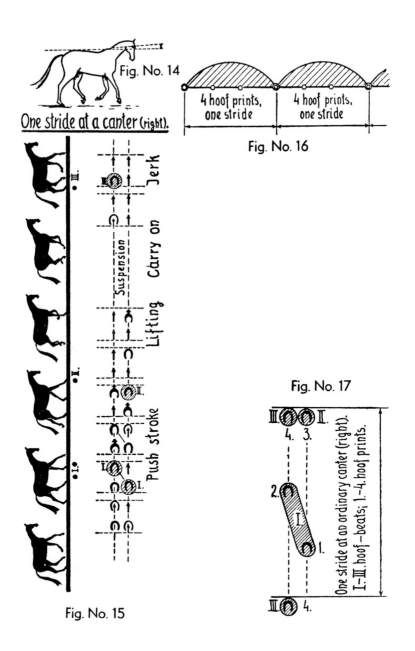

Fig. No. 14

One stride at a canter (right).

4 hoof prints, one stride | 4 hoof prints, one stride

Fig. No. 16

Jerk

Carry on

Suspension

Lifting

Push stroke

Fig. No. 15

Fig. No. 17

One stride at an ordinary canter (right). I.–III. hoof–beats; 1.–4. hoof prints.

An illustrative arrangement of the sequence of canter-strides at an ordinary canter is shown in Fig. No. 16, and the position of the hoof-prints in Fig. No. 17.

These features of the pace differ slightly in a short and in an extended canter, due to the different degree of suspension involved. Namely, in an ordinary canter there is a short suspension, in a short canter it does not appear at all, and in an extended form of the movement it is distinct. From this one can conclude that the pattern of the hoof-prints is influenced by the speed.

In the canter, the rider feels, instead of simple strokes, a rhythmic movement composed of four beats, which gives a pleasant sensation of rocking. The sequence of these beats can be described as: . . pushing . . . lifting . . . carry on . . . jerk . . ., which appear during a stride in the following manner:

At the thrust-off of the outside hind leg, the push-stroke is felt by the sudden lifting of the croup which tends to dislodge the rider's seat from its original position.

Fig. No. 18

In the following phase, the thrust-off of the leading (insides foreleg gives the impression that the horse wants to ' press ' it) shoulders under the rider's thighs and lift him upwards.

Then, in the ensuing phase of suspension, accompanied by the ' lifting up', the rider feels as if the horse's back is tending to ' prop up ' his entire seat more markedly, and to carry him forward in a close cohesion.

Finally, at the moment when the outside hind leg touches the ground, thereby suddenly terminating the suspension, the rider can feel a forward-directed jerk, which completes this particular series of sensations.

In a correct canter, the rider should be able to sit deep on the horse's back, but he should distinctly feel the above details of the movement in his seat, all the time presenting a general impression of smoothness and elasticity (see Fig. No. 18).

In order to sense the direction of a canter, whether using the sitting or the forward position, the following characteristics of the movement should be observed:

The movements of the animal tend to push forward the rider's hip on the leading (in-)side, and to suck his opposite leg in to the horse's side. Along with this sensation, the rider can also notice that the use of his inside leg is easier than that of the other.

In order to ascertain by sight the direction used, the rider should glance at the horse's shoulders. He will see that the movements of the inside shoulder precede those of the outside, giving him the impression of being in a more brought-forward position than the other.

The appearance of the hoof in front of one of the shoulders also indicates the leading direction.

### THE GALLOP

The gallop is the pace at which the horse shows the most extended and flattest form of its bearing (see Fig. No. 19). In this pace, the animal proceeds with fairly ground-gaining strides, using great muscular energy and considerable exertion of its lungs. Thus the use of this pace can only be recommended for relatively short distances.

Fig. No. 20 reproduces the leg actions of the gallop to the right (see key in Fig. No. 2). In comparing this diagram with that of the canter, one can see a relationship between the two paces, but also certain differences in their character.

In the gallop one can hear four hoof-beats (as against three in the canter). The first (I) is that of the inside hind leg. The second (II) is given by the outside foreleg (in a canter these two fall together). The third (III) hoof-beat is given by the inside (leading) foreleg, which is followed after its thrust-off by an extended suspension. Then the horse lands on its outside hind leg, giving the fourth (IV) hoof-beat.

The manner in which the gallop strides are linked together can be seen in Fig. No. 21. The greater the speed the longer will be the phase of suspension, and as a consequence the hoof-prints of the leading foreleg and the outside hind leg will be farther apart.

The detailed arrangement of hoof-prints is sketched in Fig. 22b. It illustrates at the same time the difference between the canter and gallop strides, and also shows that the horse is able to perform both canter and gallop actions at the same speed (about 350

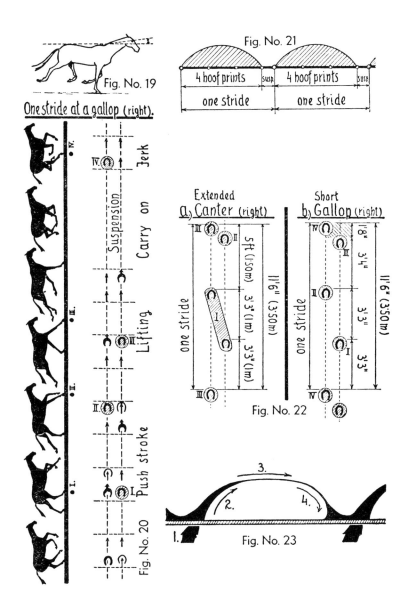

Fig. No. 19

One stride at a gallop (right).

Fig. No. 21

| 4 hoof prints | susp. | 4 hoof prints | susp. |
| one stride | | one stride | |

Jerk

Carry on

Suspension

Lifting

Push stroke

Fig. No. 20

Extended
a) Canter (right)

5 ft (1·50 m)

3'3" (1m)

3'3" (1m)

11'6" (3·50 m)

one stride

Short
b) Gallop (right)

1'8"

3'4"

3'3"

3'3"

11'6" (3·50 m)

one stride

Fig. No. 22

3.

2.

4.

I.

Fig. No. 23

yards, or 300 metres per minute), and to cover an equal distance with one stride of these paces (about 11½ feet, or 3.50 metres).

In contrast to the canter, the gallop movements are accompanied by the alternate appearance of *both* fore-hoofs in front of the horse's shoulder during the stride action, noticeable during a rather long moment. This characteristic is due to the fact that, after the landing on the outside hind leg, the movements of the forward-swinging forelegs are very vigorous. Within their joint motion, the movement of the outside leg precedes that of the inside (leading) leg, and therefore it appears first to the rider.

The sequence and character of the sensations caused by the gallop action are, in their four-beat rhythm, almost analogous to those of the canter. The only difference can be found in the strength and duration of the effects produced by the movements involved. This is especially true in the ' carry on ' phase, as the extended suspension tends to make the sensation more intense (see Fig. No. 23).

If the movement, as a whole or in part, gives a blurred, indistinct sensation without any character, or if it resembles a clumsy hustle, then the gallop cannot be regarded as acceptable.

Generally speaking, the horse always changes over from canter to gallop, since at least one or two canter strides have to be made before the attainment of the gallop pace. By increasing the speed and consequently lengthening the phase of suspension, a moment occurs when the simultaneous hoof-beats of the inside hind leg and the outside foreleg suddenly separate from each other. This is the moment when the horse actually changes into a gallop, and the outside hoof appears suddenly, without any gradual transition, in front of the shoulder.

The reduction of the pace from gallop into canter is indicated by the disappearance of the outside hoof, and by a sudden and pronounced jolt which is felt at the moment of change.

For the sake of the execution of these particular changes, the rider cannot exercise any definite influence on the horse, and therefore the selecting of the moment of change must be left to the animal.

THE JUMPING STRIDE

In order to acquire a deeper insight into the technique of jumping, it is necessary to examine closely all those movements of

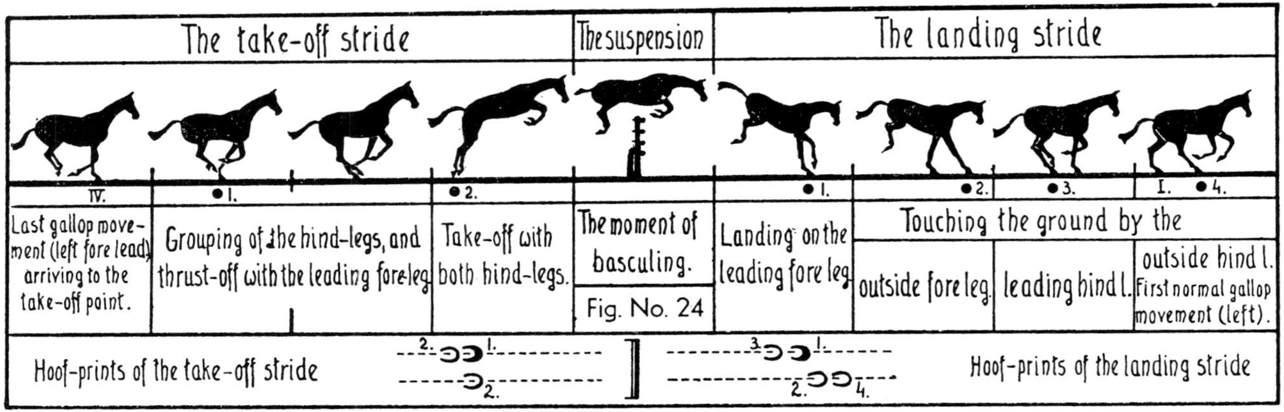

Fig. No. 24

It should be pointed out that:

all movements shown in front of the obstacle occur at the
same spot, marked by dot 2 (on the take-off side); and

all those which are drawn after the phase of suspension take
place in succession at dot 1 (on the landing side).

the animal which it makes during the performance of a jump (see Fig. No. 24).

### The approach to the obstacle

It occurs generally out of a canter or gallop, therefore we will examine the problem in connection with these paces.

When the horse approaches the obstacle it should proceed with even strides, giving three hoof-beats in a canter and four in a gallop.

### The take-off stride and the actual take-off

When the horse arrives in front of the obstacle, the last hoof-print of its leading foreleg—performed within the course of the regular strides—is also the spot of the take-off (see mark 1). Whenever the animal performs this critical hoof-beat, it simultaneously takes the energy needed for the thrust-off from this particular leg. This leg carries out the actual lifting of the forehand, and thus commences the take-off phase of the jump. The strength of the thrust-off also determines the height of the whole jumping motion.

Immediately after the thrust-off, both hind legs step in the vicinity of the hoof-print of the leading foreleg, thus grouping themselves for the take-off (see marks 2 and 2). In the ensuing second they, too, thrust off, and by making the horse's entire body airborne, complete the take-off phase.

In the above motion, the outside foreleg plays no active part. Without leaving any hoof-mark on the take-off side, it merely swings forward in the air.

### The landing

Here, the leading foreleg is the first to touch the ground, followed by the outside foreleg.

The inside hind leg treads in the path of the leading foreleg, whereas the hoof-fall of the outside hind leg treads in front of the hoof-print of the outside foreleg. At this moment the regular sequence of strides in the canter or gallop (ev. in trot) recommences.

To sum up, the last hoof-beat of the leading foreleg (mark IV) before the take-off, and the first hoof-beat of the outside hind leg (mark I) after the landing, coincide with the beats of the regular strides.

## THE RIDER'S IMPROVEMENT IN RECOGNIZING THE SEQUENCE OF STEPS

In order to recognize the sequence of steps involved in the stride action, the rider should, at the beginning of schooling, note carefully what sort of sensations certain movements produce in him, and be continually on the watch for these details. When he becomes aware of the sensations, he will be able to recognize immediately and instinctively whether the sequence of steps is correct or not.

In the early stages of schooling, if the rider is unable to recognize the difference between the good and bad sequence of steps in the walk or trot, he ought to place six or eight bars on the ground at a distance most suitable to the length of the horse's striding action (about 3 feet to 3 feet 8 inches, or 0.90 metre to 1.10 metres). He should ride over these bars at a lively pace natural to the horse, while sitting calmly in the saddle, and take careful note of the push-strokes caused by the movement. The bars force the animal to take regular, determined steps, and they also accentuate the sensation which the rider experiences on account of the higher shape of the movements.

In the canter this check does not seem really necessary because the motion itself is pronounced enough for the rider to form an opinion as to its quality, and the bars could make the horse lame.

However, it is necessary to emphasize that working exclusively with bars which are placed on the ground will never develop a lasting regularity in the horse's locomotion. The animal gets used to them in a very short space of time, and finally will just stumble over the bars with irregular steps.

# CHAPTER THREE

# The Means of
# Communication with the Horse

THE means by which the rider conveys his will to the horse
are the signals and aids. Generally speaking, the descriptions of riding problems do not differentiate categorically
between them. In fact, the distinction is often hazy, and can
cause some confusion in the rider's mind and in his activities,
the consequence of which is opposition on the part of the horse.

It is not merely by chance that this distinction is expressed in
the riding terms of every language. The old masters of equitation,
to whom the origin of these terms can be ascribed, were led by
experience to speak of both signals and aids. They recognized
the fact that it is of substantial importance to make a definite
distinction between these two ideas, and consequently, between
the activities which are their physical expression. However, this
distinction, both in essence and in practice, has become somewhat
blurred in the general method of riding and instruction, so that
the meaning of signals and aids is now almost identical. I will
endeavour to correct this flaw in the rider's understanding, as far
as possible, by dealing with the subjects separately.

To complete the information it is advantageous to examine the
performance of signals and aids, also according to whether they
are conveyed to the horse from a sitting or forward position. The
reason for this is, that the seat in the forward posture lacks a
certain amount of its aiding qualities, which can be of such great
assistance to the horse. Nevertheless, even in this position, the
animal has to be provided with the necessary assistance in an
absolute sense, and therefore one must find the ways and means
by which the loss of efficiency can be compensated.

With regard to the application of signals and aids the following
questions arise: What purpose do they serve? How can they be
carried out? And where must they affect the horse?

With practice, the horse's response to signals and aids should become almost automatic, and it is safe to say that the animal has adopted their ' meaning ' when the scale (strength) of execution can be reduced without any loss in the effect produced. Whenever the horse's response to a certain signal or aid becomes more and more apathetic, or if intensified vigour is required to maintain its effectiveness, then it is certain that the animal has not yet grasped its meaning. The reason for the apathy can probably be found in the rider himself. He may have applied the particular signal or aid in a faulty manner, or perhaps he did not give it sufficient emphasis to have a real effect upon the horse's performance.

SIGNALS (HINTS*), AND THE AGENTS OF THEIR EXECUTION

Signals and hints form the alphabet of communication between the rider and horse. By setting the letters of the alphabet into words, the ideas to be communicated acquire the necessary forms. But in order to be able to write words and sentences, it is first of all important to become acquainted with the letters, i.e. to learn to perform the basic motions which make up the signals, and practise them individually.

The agents of giving signals are:
     the legs (probably supported by the whip and spurs);
     the hands (by means of the reins and bit); and
     the seat (through its connection with the horse's back).
We shall now review their motional features one by one.

THE LEGS AS AGENTS OF COMMUNICATION (Table No. 1)

The correct positions of the legs are shown in Figs. Nos. 35–37, and 38/a-b (in Table No. 3) according to the methods of riding (sitting or forward position).

In order to endow the legs with the necessary influencing faculty, the rider must keep them in their entire length close to the horse's side in the region of the girth.

At the same time the knees—with their inner surface facing the horse—should cling smoothly but firmly to the saddle, hugging it so tightly that the rider feels perfectly secure on the horse's back.

To satisfy this demand the position of the thighs has an important role. The rider should *turn them to the inside* right

---

*Hints are also signals, but they are given with a special purpose of stimulating the attention and interest of the horse. They are applied chiefly by the use of the legs or the whip in a slightly firmer manner than normally.

from the hip-joints, and retain this position permanently. He should adopt this posture from the beginning of his training, so that it should become a second nature to him. Generally, persons who walk and sit instinctively with feet turned to the inside have less difficulty in achieving this aim than do others.

By turning the thighs in this position the strain of the tailor-muscles in keeping the knee-grip becomes reduced, and the appearance of stiffness lessened. This position of the thighs makes it possible for the legs to bring about considerable effect with the employment of little energy.

If the thighs are turned to the outside the knees become turned away from the saddle, and instead of the whole legs only the heels are in touch with the side of the horse. All strain in ensuring the knee-grip falls to the tailor-muscles, which can be easily over-strained. The effectiveness of the legs is very limited.

Furthermore, it is a point of the correct position of the legs that the heels should be moderately pressed down. In this position the thighs are drawn firmly to the saddle and the muscles of the legs become taut, which enable the rider to use the legs in a determined and, if necessary, energetic manner.

The legs, as agents of communication, are used for the following purposes:
the driving leg urges the horse to strive forward;
the lateral-moving leg requests him to make some movement in a lateral direction; and
the leg for take-off impulsion impels the animal (just in front of the fence) to take off at the desired moment.
Besides the above application, the legs—meant in their whole constitution—are engaged in two further activities, namely:
by exercising pressures with the thighs they support the effect of the driving leg; and
by transmitting pressures on the stirrups they respectively supplement and replace the taking function of the seat.

*The driving leg* (Figs. Nos. 25/a-b)
The aim, as the name suggests, is to give the signal to the horse to move forward. The characteristic action of this leg function is a touching-like movement against the horse's side on the girth. The strength of this action should depend upon the sensitivity of

Table No. 1    ILLUSTRATIVE OUTLINE OF BASIC LEG-ACTIONS

| at a walk and trot to both directions. | The driving leg | | | | The lateral moving leg | | The leg for take-off impuls. |
|---|---|---|---|---|---|---|---|
| | | at a canter | | | at all paces ; at moving | | at all paces. |
| | right fore leading. | left fore leading. | | to the right. | to the left. | |
| Alternative short touches by the legs. | Short touches by the leg on the leading side. | | | Breathing-like pressures by the outside leg. | | Simultaneous knock of legs on both side. |
| Fig. No. 25/a | Fig. No. 25/b | | | Fig. No. 25/c | | Fig. No. 25/d |

the horse, but it must never surpass a moderate scale.  One should strive from the very beginning of training gradually to reduce the 'touch' or 'knock' to a mild short press.

During the execution of the driving signal the rider must release the weight resting on the stirrups.

The action of the driving leg must have two significant features:

It should always be applied in a decided manner which will give confidence to the horse.  The application of the legs in an uncertain, tentative, or irresolute manner will produce a tickling effect on the animal.  This is bound to upset its nerves, and may easily result in its escaping from the controls by running away.

The touch should be exercised possibly on the same side of the horse as the hind leg by which it is expected to thrust its body forwards.  This is the very moment when the animal is in support position with that particular hind leg, and therefore it is *able* to exert an increased energy in its forward thrust, just at the moment it receives the signal.  The significance of this becomes even more obvious when one imagines the start from a position where the horse is not standing on all fours.  For example, if the near-hind leg is in a brought-forward position when the driving signal is given by the rider's right leg, the horse will step out with the off-hind leg, but its body will not move at all.  Only its leg steps forward, without any motional energy.  If the signal is given on the side of the hind leg which is already in a brought-forward position, then the horse, in order to execute an action, is compelled to push its body forward by the touched leg while it is in the support position.  Although, in this case, the challenged leg has not left its original position, it has moved and set the body in motion by employing useful energy.  This is the principle behind the right starting point for the move-forward in the course of locomotion.

When the aim of the signal is to correct the animal's position while it is stationary, it is necessary to make the horse carry out a mere leg-motion (without starting off).  In this case, the hind leg which has remained behind needs to be reminded, just as it has been described in the first part of the above example.  The horse due to the ensuing action, will not set its body in motion but will simply step forward with the leg which was left behind, and place it next to the other one.

In view of the fact that the horse does not use both its hind legs simultaneously during the onward move, it seems logical to assume that the simultaneous use of both legs in giving driving signals must be confusing to it. Although such a primitive signal will undoubtedly give some impetus to the animal to move forward in one way or another, such a performance cannot satisfy the good rider, since his horse's forward action ought to be correct. The use of this imperfect method has only one advantage, namely, that the rider does not need to be careful about the details of his action. This is why its application is so widespread.

Action of the driving-leg in walk and in trot (Fig. 25/a in Table No. 1)

The horse, both in the walk and trot, performs identical movements with its hind legs and makes its steps in the same way. The steps of both hind legs participate equally in promoting the horse's forward movement. When the aim is to accelerate its movements in these paces, it is necessary to speed up the movements of both hind legs equally. To achieve this effect, the driving signals have to be applied alternately to both sides. For instance, a short light pressure or knock of the rider's right leg for the desired movement of the horse's off-hind leg, and a touch of the left leg for the movement of near-hind leg, and again by the right leg for the off-hind leg, and so on.

The action of the driving leg in the canter and gallop (Fig. 25/b in Table No. 1)

The method of giving drive-on signals in canter and gallop differs from that in walk and trot. The root of the difference lies in the fact that in these paces each of the horse's four legs has a certain function in thrusting the body forward, and they perform this function by different movements.

This distribution of functions of the legs provides several equally valid possibilities for the application of signals, each of which has its particular advantage. Since it is impossible to exploit jointly these advantages, no definite opinion can be expressed as to where and when the signal is the most effective. It is a matter of individual taste as to which method is used, but *one* of them must be adopted and applied consistently.

From my own point of view, the best method in the canter and gallop seems to be to give the signal on the inside in a touching-like manner, by which the forward-thrust of the inside hind leg is animated. (To strike off into canter, see page 136.) The driving effect of the leg-action applied on the outside is perhaps more impressive than that of the inside, but this advantage is counterbalanced by its tendency to promote crookedness. That is why the application of the inside leg deserves priority.

Thus the drive-on signal (executed with the inside leg) should be applied in the canter at that moment when the hoof of the inside foreleg appears in front of the particular shoulder, and in the gallop when the hoof of the outside foreleg appears in front of the shoulder.

The execution of the touch by the inside leg is quite simple, as the movement of the horse is actually inviting this action.

*The lateral-moving leg* (Fig. No. 25/c, in Table No. 1)

The horse's hind quarters are chiefly controlled by the legs. Whenever it is necessary to push them away from the straight line, to adjust them into a certain position, or to avoid their undesired displacement (evasion), the lateral-moving leg-function is used.

In order to achieve these effects, one of the legs has to exert a pressure-like force against the horse's side. In carrying out the function, the rhythm of breathing should act as a guide: while inhaling, the leg should be pressed against the horse's side, and while exhaling, the muscles should relax without removing the leg from its position. In this manner, the leg will maintain contact with the horse's side, and the signal will not become a constant squeeze, but a living indication.

If the quarters have to be pushed to the left, or if an evasion to the right has to be counter-balanced, then the right leg should exercise the function just behind the girth, and vice versa.

While exercising the lateral-moving leg-pressures, the rider may increase the weight resting on the stirrup on the identical side. This additional function is the main difference between the driving and lateral-moving leg-effect.

*The leg in increasing take-off impulsion* (Fig. 25/d in Table No. 1)

In certain cases it is necessary to urge the horse to take-off. In order to achieve the needed effect, it is advisable to use a special driving-like signal, by which the animal will understand without a doubt the particular intention of the rider.

The horse, to complete the take-off action, makes a simultaneous thrusting movement with both its hind legs. This identical movement of the hind legs indicates that the simultaneous use of both the rider's legs is best suited to giving the take-off signal.

THE SUPPLEMENTARY TOOLS OF THE LEGS AND THEIR FUNCTION IN GIVING SIGNALS

The legs, as a means of communicating signals, are often unsatisfactory, especially in expressing the degree of emphasis attached to a particular signal. So, in order to increase the effect of signals, the legs are supplemented by the use of the whip and spurs.

*The use of the riding whip*

Generally speaking, the whip is used chiefly as a medium of warning, and is employed to increase the liveliness of the horse's hind legs. Therefore it is necessary, especially during schooling, for the whip to be long enough to enable the rider to touch the horse just behind his (the rider's) leg.

Skill in using the whip is just as important to the rider as is his skill in the use of the legs. Therefore the use of the whip must be thoroughly schooled. This schooling of the rider, unfortunately very neglected in general practice, deserves great attention.

The rider should reach the stage where he is able to exercise the tap of the whip without altering the original position of his hand (especially in a backward direction). He should be able to vary the strength from a slight touch to a pronounced biting hit, and to repeat each movement in quick succession.

By using the whip skilfully, the rider gives his activity a quality of determination, and even the most nervous horse learns its real meaning in a very short space of time, accepting the effect without becoming frightened.

The whip should be carried by the hand on the same side as the least sensitive side of the animal, or that which is handicapped by stiffness. The rider should immediately change it over to his other hand, whenever necessary. This change should be carried out with a firm and open movement, in order to avoid frightening the horse. However, a horse which has learned to look upon the whip as a means of support and not one of torture, will always regard it with confidence. Concerning the handling of the whip, the following recommendations can be made:

In the case where the horse does not respond to the signal given by the driving leg, then a light flick with the whip should be applied behind the leg, simultaneously with the touch of the leg. I would like to draw the rider's attention with special stress to the necessity of the *frequent* application of this flick. The horse perceives the biting touch of the whip together with the touch of the leg and so, after a few repetitions, it does not differentiate between their effects. It only remembers that the flick and the touch are felt jointly, and readily attributes both of them to the leg.

The signal by the whip produces a sudden stinging sensation in the horse. This results in a quick movement of its hind legs which, due to the rapidity of the movement, swing irresistibly under the body.

The whip should never be used to give a driving signal on the horse's shoulder, because such a hit will divert its attention, and will not give any impetus to move forward in a straight position.

Taking the second case, where the animal does not respond to the pressing function of the leg, the rider should give a tap of the whip to the horse's side behind the leg in function. Then, still maintaining the pressure of the leg, the rider should keep the whip on the horse's side for a short while. This procedure should be repeated in a breathing-like cadence as long as the animal does not yield to the signal and moves aside from the line.

If the horse objects to the pressing action of the legs, application of the leg should be omitted for the time being, and only the whip used as a means of giving the signal. At the same time, the leg should remain motionless, calmly resting on the horse's side instead of conveying pressure. If such a horse is not unduly forced to put up with the pressure of the leg, it will soon express its readiness to accept it and will respond to the pressure with obedience.

In the third case, where the animal is not inclined to respond to the take-off signal given by the two legs, the whip should be applied with a firm stroke on the horse's side behind the girth, with a simultaneous knock of the legs. It must be emphasized that the stroke should be synchronized with the movement of the horse, otherwise it may confuse instead of animate the animal.

However, a properly-schooled horse does not lose its liveliness, and, if urged with confidence towards the obstacle, it is not likely to need added encouragement by the whip except in unusual circumstances. In practice, one often sees a rider use his whip at every take-off. This is a very bad habit, and the proof of the rider's ignorance as well as of his failure to safeguard the animal's liveliness while approaching to the obstacle.

There is a further function exercised with the whip which can be very helpful in the relaxation of a certain stiffness in the horse's state. For this, exercise some mild trembling touches, without any biting effect, with the long elastic whip on the tiffened side or shoulder of the animal. The trembling on the kin creates a pleasant sensation in the horse, and inspires it to lax the muscles touched upon.

### The use of the spurs

The reason for using the spurs is first of all to sharpen the horse's sensitivity to leg-actions, and only secondarily to increase the effect of the legs. In this sense spurs can replace the use of the whip.

When riding insensitive, rough or clumsy animals, one need have no hesitation in resorting to the use of the spurs, but with noble, highly-bred horses (chiefly mares), one must consider their application very carefully, since their effect can be the reverse of that expected (e.g. instead of urging forward they may cause backing, kicking, etc.).

On the whole, it is best to school the horse in such a way as to make the use of spurs unnecessary. However, if the rider finds it useful during competitions to employ a more effective agent, *just to set his mind at rest*, he should select a type of spur which is one grade milder than that which he had in mind. In general it is best to choose spurs which have short, blunt and big-headed stems. They are meant rather to increase the hardness of the boots than to inflict sharp and painful pricks.

While jumping there are two main disadvantages in the use of spurs. Firstly, a suddenly inflicted kick coupled with pain may cause a spasmodic jerk in the muscles of the ribs, and as a consequence, the horse may become confused. Secondly, inexperienced riders like to make the seat firm with their legs, and if they are wearing spurs, they can cause severe damage to the animal's side.

THE ' PRESSING DOWN ' ACTION OF THE THIGHS (Fig. 41 in Table No. 3)

In order to carry out this very important action, the rider must exercise a pressure with his thighs on the muscles of the horse's withers, over a rather wide area.

By this action the rider affects that part of the animal's body which, from a riding point of view, is most important, namely, where the two main parts of the spinal column (the cervical and the spinal vertebrae) meet. This particular centre is bound together by a network of strong muscles which spread forward, backwards, and downwards.

By applying a pressure to these muscles, it is possible to exert influence smoothly both on the back and the neck of the horse, and to affect directly even its shoulders. In this manner, the pressing-down action of the thighs becomes an essential part of those combined operations which are:

the co-ordination of the movements of the above parts of the horse's body (neck, back, shoulders);

increasing the animal's suppleness and forward impulsion, as well as making the cadence of the movements more elegant; and

improving the ground-gaining quality of the motion, especially in a canter and gallop.

In order to learn the technique of this action, let us review the subject according to whether the rider is using the sitting or forward position.

The pressing down action of the thighs in a sitting posture (Fig. 41/a)

For the performance of the action do some deep inhaling and exhaling exercises. Then, when one of the *exhaling* movements nears its completion, stop the expiration of air. At this moment, while keeping the remaining volume of air in the lungs, try to execute a movement similar to that of lifting a heavy weight.

As a result of this exercise it can be noticed that the spine becomes somewhat arched, making the pelvis turn slightly more backwards and the upper body bend somewhat forward. In this arched position, the thighs are pressed downwards so that they are capable of increasing considerably the pressure on the saddle, even of their own accord.

It should be mentioned that, during the pressing action, the muscles of the thighs become somewhat expanded due to the exertion involved in the action and causing the seat-bone to be slightly lifted out of the saddle. This lifted position is of great value in increasing the effectiveness and the smoothness of the drive-on, because of its lightening effect. On the other hand, it is liable to decrease the close contact by which the seat keeps the back of the horse under control.

In order to maintain this important control, one has to perform the action in a breathing-like manner. That is to say, the actions of pressing down the thighs and of lowering the seat-bone must be connected by smooth transitions, starting from and returning to the ready position of the seat.

The rider should not overdo the practice of this pressing down action at first, in order to avoid overstraining the muscles of the inner side of his legs (tailor muscles). However, the fact that the action must be carried out with intervals of relaxation, as it will be seen later on, facilitates the gradual strengthening of these muscles.

As soon as the rider has acquired sufficient skill to perform the action in a resolute manner, he should try to combine the pressing-down action of the thighs with the driving action of the legs, because in practice these two actions are usually applied jointly.

The pressing-down action of the thighs in the forward position (Fig. 41/b)

In exercising this action the rider must lean the upper body slightly forward from the ready position, and exert a firm pressure on the thighs, starting from the waist, loins, and partly from the vertical muscles.

The control over the horse's spine is safeguarded by executing the thigh function in the aforementioned breathing-like manner and interchanging it with the pressures on the stirrups.

In both cases (sitting and forward position) the knees are preventing the pressure from being transmitted downwards to

the stirrups. For this purpose they are exercising, simultaneously with the pressure of the thighs, an increased
squeezing action.

Simultaneously with the application of pressure, the rider
should *ease his leaning on the stirrups*, and draw the thighs (starting
from the calves) more strongly to the saddle. This will considerably increase the effect of the entire action.

THE RIDER'S GRAVITATIONAL WEIGHT AND HIS PRESSING DOWN
ACTION ON THE STIRRUPS (Fig. 40/b in Table No. 3)

The significance of the effect produced by the load on the
stirrups is seldom emphasized in general riding instruction, and
the employment of this effect is greatly neglected in general
practice. This makes it necessary to deal with this extremely
important subject with special care.

The load by which the stirrups are burdened can result from a
gravitational weight being put on them, from some special action
exercised by the rider, or from a combination of these
two elements.

The effect thus produced is transmitted to the horse by the
front part of the saddle through the leathers and their points of
suspension. The transmitted effect manifests itself in a pressure
affecting the animal over a very narrow area just behind the
withers, where the back and the muscles are especially sensitive.

As this particular pressure is concentrated on a rather limited
surface, its effect is considerably greater than that of a pressure
exercised by the same weight or energy over a wide area on the
horse's back. Thus there is a big difference between the effects
produced when the rider uses the stirrups for the support of his
weight, and when he is resting with his seat and thighs on
the saddle.

Bearing in mind these considerations, the rider will find that
the pressure on the stirrups can become a very useful means of
communication, although it can also be the cause of the animal's
resistance. If this pressure is continued, it can arouse a stiffness
and opposition in the horse such as follows a continuous pulling
on the reins or rigid bracing with the seat. Therefore, the rider
should choose the measure of the weight with which he burdens
the stirrups very carefully, and always be ready to adjust it to
the particular situation. He should do this with the same care

as that with which he decides the strength of any of his other actions. With this mind, he should occasionally put a certain load on the stirrups, easing it when required, and ceasing altogether when the pressure produced is no longer necessary.

These considerations are of great importance in connection with the forward seat, and they should never be neglected even when the bulk of the rider's weight is resting on the saddle (in the sitting position).

For keeping the basic load on the stirrups the rider should weigh rather lightly on them, and use the stirrups only as far as is absolutely necessary to support his weight and ensure his safety in the saddle. He may support the rest of his weight and balance by taking advantage of the knee-grip.

To increase the burden on the stirrups relax the knee-grip and rest firmly on the stirrups by allowing free course to the falling weight.

To decrease the load: increase the knee-grip and rest more heavily on the thighs, thus stopping the downward course of the weight. In this posture, the touch on the stirrups is a groping-like function by which they are kept under the feet as desired (either in the middle or at the heel).

To emphasize the load on the stirrups, a mechanical function is necessary. This may be called the *pressing-down action of the stirrups*. In carrying out this action, first move the upper body slightly backwards from the ready position; and

> press on the stirrup(s) in the same manner as pressing on the brake of a motor-car;
> keep the stirrup(s) for a time (which is usually brief) under pressure; and then
> by relaxing the engaged muscles take up the basic posture again.

Further easing of the load is brought about in the same manner as described above for decreasing the gravitational weight.

To acquire the necessary strength and skill in the execution of these functions, the following exercises are recommended.

First of all, ride without stirrups, and improve your position in the saddle so that it becomes safe, flexible and absolutely independent of the support of the stirrups. During these exercises develop the muscles (knee-grip) by an equal amount of work in the sitting and forward positions (including rising trot and jumping over small obstacles). Take care, however, not to overstrain the muscles engaged, and therefore include frequent resting periods by riding in complete relaxation. It has to be mentioned that these exercises have also many advantages in the general improvement of the rider's knowledge.

When stability and ease in the saddle have been acquired, use the stirrups for the next exercise, which should be practised both in the sitting and forward positions.

To begin with, practise the functions in question individually (maintaining the basic load; varying the load by the regulation of gravitational weight; emphasizing the burden by the pressing-down action and by the combined function). During the course of these individual exercises

at first alter the burden equally and simultaneously on both stirrups in the following manner: starting with the basic load, increase and then decrease the weight, returning again to the basic load; next

learn to vary the load on the two stirrups independently of each other and with different weights.

After successful practice in performing the functions individually, the rider should practise several successive weight changes, and continue the exercises until he can perform all the functions in quick rotation.

The action of applying or withdrawing varying loads on the stirrups is usually employed in combination with other activities of the rider. For example:

during retardment, the rider should exercise alternating pressures on the stirrups, synchronized with the alternating taking functions of the hands. These stirrup-pressures support the alternating lateral-moving leg-pressures involved in the retardment, and thus become an effective part of this action;

during the drive-on, the rider should ease the load on the stirrups at the same time as he exercises the pressing-down action of the thighs;

during the combined application of drive-on and retardment, the pressures and their relaxation are employed in harmony with the other functions of the rider;

during the execution of the lateral-moving leg action, and that of the swing-improving action of the seat, the effect produced can be augmented by simultaneous pressures on the stirrup(s);

during the regulation of the horse (loosening the stiffness of the shoulders, withers and back muscles), and while balancing it in its adjusted position, the alternating pressing and easing functions (carried out in a light drumming-manner on the stirrups) are very effective due to the vibration produced.

From the various possibilities mentioned above, one can conclude that great advantages are afforded by the application of stirrup pressures. Therefore, the rider should not underrate the importance attached to them, but try to improve his use of them as much as possible. After becoming sufficiently skilled, he will find their effectiveness especially evident in the ease with which the horse can be directed.

### THE FUNCTION OF HANDS (REINS) IN GIVING SIGNALS

The hands themselves can best perform their functions when they are kept in a *straight prolongation* of the forearms (i.e. not pressed backwards or pulled inwards by bending the wrist). In this position they should be turned slightly inwards *by the forearm* so that the rider can just see the nails of his firmly clenched fingers.

The forearms and hands should form together a straight continuation of the reins, while the upper arms are kept smoothly close to the rider's body, in a line slightly more forward than vertical.

As far as the height of the hand and forearm position is concerned, this depends upon the horse's bearing and the posture used by the rider. It is generally higher when riding in the sitting than in the forward position.

While using the latter position, the hands should gradually drop lower and lower, in co-ordination with the bending forward of the upper body, and in proportion to the increase of speed. At a gallop and in jumping, the hands are already resting lightly on the sides of the horse's neck, preferably in front of the upper part of the shoulders. This particular form of carriage of the hands adds to the stability of the forward position. However, one has to be careful not to press the hands stiffly to the neck, as such a posture may result in causing stiffness in the rider's entire riding form.

When riding with a snaffle bridle, the reins should be kept divided between the two hands and placed between the ring and small fingers. (Concerning the double bridle, see page 260.)

The reins act on the most sensitive part of the horse's body, that is, on the mouth, and therefore the rider's skill in handling the reins is of paramount importance. By abusing the reins, he can cause considerable pain to the animal and even spoil it altogether.

The actions performed by the reins in passing on signals to the horse are derived from two basic movements, namely:

the pulling = taking with the rein; and

the yielding = giving with the rein.

As the reins have to convey to the horse a great number of different demands, it is obvious that the two basic actions, while retaining their character, must have a number of variations. By their application a multitude of helpful signals can be conveyed to the horse without any coercion on the rider's part, thus enabling the animal to respond in a light and supple manner.

The basic principles of applying these two basic rein functions are that

while using the hands, one should pull on the reins and not on the horse's mouth; and

one should yield with the reins and yet not lose contact with the mouth.

Bearing in mind these principles, let us see how the taking (pulling) and giving (yielding) functions of the reins can be performed in their main variations. The question is examined in Table No. 2/a, therefore it is recommended to study the details of this table before reading the next paragraph, which describes the various rein-functions. The movements shown by the figures in the table and identified by the accompanying text are the elements of these functions.

THE MAIN REIN FUNCTIONS IN CONVEYING SIGNALS (Table No. 2/b)

The rein functions in conveying signals are illustrated by Figs. Nos. 29-34 in Table No. 2/b, and discussed separately in the next paragraphs.

In studying the figures it is necessary to take into account those points which have been reviewed in connection with Figs. Nos. 26-28/3 in Table No. 2/a. The diagrams depicting the various rein functions should be studied from the top downwards, following the lines representing the reins. These lines show changes of the rein actions from the point of maintaining contact

## Table No. 2/a

### THE MOST CHARACTERISTIC FORMS OF MOVEMENTS IN REIN ACTIONS

The diagrams accompanying the text demonstrate the formation of power-effects exercised by the rider's hands, starting from and returning to their relaxed state. They are transmitted through the rein and the bit to the horse's mouth during the execution of signals.

The thickness of the lines indicates the intensity of the effect produced by the hand, according to continuity in time and in relation to the starting position.

The diagrams should be studied from left to right by following the line which shows the continuity of the entire procedure.

Even pulling-effect in short repetitions (for retardment).

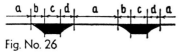

Fig. No. 26

(a) Basic posture in which the horse keeps contact.
(b) Short gradual transition towards the pulling-effect.
(c) Evenly distributed pulling-effect (short).
(d) Short gradual transition towards stopping the effect.

Even pulling-effect in prolonged form (for turning).

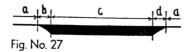

Fig. No. 27

(a), (b) and (d) as above.
(c) Evenly distributed pulling-effect (prolonged).

Action successively increasing and decreasing in strength (for lateral moving).

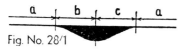

Fig. No. 28/1

(a) Basic posture.
(b) Pulling-effect accomplished during an extended period of transition and with increasing strength.
(c) Ceasing of the pulling-effect, accomplished by an extended transition and decreasing strength.

Action with successive increase in strength and sudden decrease (for loosening).

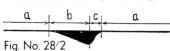

Fig. No. 28/2

(a) Basic posture.
(b) As in the previous case.
(c) Ceasing of the pulling-effect carried out by sudden transition.

A knock-like sudden action (jerk on the bar of the mouth with disciplinary purpose). Its application is extremely limited, very delicate, and only permitted in experienced riders with self-control.

Fig. No. 28/3

(a) Basic posture which suffers sudden disrupture.
(b) *Calmly* exercised jerk with the rein which has a knock-like effect of slight or moderate impact on the mouth.

If the action shown in Fig. No. 28/1 is executed simultaneously with both hands (in an advanced stage of education only) it has the effect of collecting the horse.

The jerking action (Fig. No. 28/3) should never be exercised simultaneously with both hands, or with the purpose of making the mouth softer. A jerk only on the stiffened side, instead of relaxing the opposition aggravates the situation. Thus, in case of its employment it should always be an interchanged action.

to the return to the starting position.  In order to make the
rein functions more understandable, the diagrams also show
with shadowed space the side of the animal's mouth on which
pressure is exercised by the action.

### The rein for maintaining contact (Fig. No. 29)

The rein in maintaining contact, i.e. an uninterrupted smooth
connection between the bit and the horse's mouth, is *of very light
tension*.  It must neither pull nor be loose, either in a stationary
position or in motion.  Without this basic form of its application
no rein function can be executed correctly.

The rider must acquire the skill by careful practice in keeping
the reins evenly in this particular state, otherwise he will alternately jerk on the horse's mouth and lose contact.   In doing so,
he confuses the animal and arouses its opposition (see also page 16).

### The retarding rein (Figs. Nos. 30/a-b)

The retarding movement, i.e. the pull on the rein, is a definite,
but never hard, taking action, which has not yet been completed
when the pulling terminates.   It is concluded when the hand
completes the process by *returning to its original position*.   In this
way the pulling action is an intermittent one.  With practice the
rider should become skilled in exercising the retarding action in a
manner that he carries out the ' pull ' by tightening the hand and
arm muscles only, and performs the yielding part of the function
by the relaxation of these muscles.   Thus the total action is
completed without actual (visible) movements.

This yielding element of the retarding signal is especially
important for the effectiveness of the entire action.  It is the
'power' in it!  Without this yielding, the slightest retarding
signal is a harmful pulling and affords no assistance to the horse.
But due to its yielding phase, the intermittent action exercises a
loosening effect on the horse and helps it to perform the desired
retardation in a submissive manner.

The retarding signal should be applied against the forward-
thrusting movements of the hind legs.   For this reason those
pulling actions of the signal are most competent which act on
the side *opposite* to the forward-thrusting hind leg.   A checking
action applied to the hind leg which is in the air (i.e. with the
rein of the identical side) has no effect.   Consequently, it is

Table No. 2/b     ILLUSTRATIVE OUTLINE OF BASIC REIN EFFECTS

| The simple leading rein. In all paces. | The retarding rein. | | The turning or directing rein. In all paces. | The counterbalancing or lateral moving rein. In all paces. | The loosening rein. In all paces. | The counter deviating rein. In all paces. |
|---|---|---|---|---|---|---|
| | In walk and trot. | In canter and gallop. | | | | |
| left — right | left — right | left — right | left — right | left — right | left — right | left — right |
| Both reins keep equally the contact and follow smoothly the horse's movements. | Alternatively executed interlocked pulling and yielding action by the hands. | Interlocked pulling and yielding action by the hand which is opposite to the leading direction. | Mild pulling action by the hand on the turning side. | Equally in-and-decreased pressing actions by the h. which is opposite to the wanted moving dir. | Short pressing actions with sudden yielding by the hand which is on the side of stiffness. | Combined turning and loosening rein action by the h. which is on the opp. side of deviation. |
| Fig. No. 29 | Fig. No. 30/a | Fig. No. 30/b | Fig. No. 31 | Fig. No. 32 | Fig. No. 33 | Fig. No. 34 |

possible for only one rein to provide the retarding effect at any given moment. From this one can conclude that it is *not advantageous* to give retarding signals by the use of the reins *simultaneously on both sides*. Therefore, while pulling on one side of the rein, the other must keep the contact only, and should neither pull or ' support ' the acting rein nor become loose.

(At the beginning of the practice, the short pulls should follow each other at somewhat longer intervals, leaving one or two leg motions unaffected between each composing part of the signal. Later on one can increase the trend of the movements, but without becoming hurried in the performance.)

The actual number of pulling actions depends largely upon the sensitivity and the degree of rideability of the horse. A well-educated horse will respond satisfactorily to retarding signals of two to four slight pulls. However, in its advanced stage of education, the horse should perform the retardation mainly in response to the signal given by the seat or stirrup pressure.

The function of the retarding rein in the walk and trot
(Fig. No. 30/a)

Both in the walk and trot, the hind legs have an equal share in the forward movement of the horse. In order to slow down this motion, it is necessary to put the brake on both legs separately. Therefore, the pullings on the reins, as signals, have to be applied *in alternate succession*. In practice it operates in the following manner: the right rein pulls (slowing down the near-hind leg), and then it yields . . . the left rein pulls (slowing down the off-hind leg), and then yields . . . the right rein pulls again . . . and so on.

This method of using the reins is by no means identical with the so-called 'sawing' movement, because each of its part-actions start only at that moment when the previous one has been completed *by yielding*.

In carrying out the hand actions alternately, instead of simultaneously, the main advantage is that the rider produces twice as many of the yielding functions which complete the individual signals as in the case of the simultaneous hand actions. The increased amount of yielding greatly increases the smoothness of the procedure and, consequently, the effectiveness of the actions. Thus the animal can respond with greater ease and the rider, owing to the ease in the horse's reaction, can profit from the advantage of this method.

The function of the retarding rein in the canter and gallop (Fig. No. 30/b)

The stride motions of these paces make it necessary to give the signals only on one side (see page 43).

If the inside hind leg is to be curbed, only the outside rein should be used. The rhythm of the procedure can be illustrated in the following manner: the outside rein takes . . . yields . . . takes . . . yields . . ., etc.

*The directing or turning rein* (Fig. No. 31)

The basic rein signal for turning consists of the simple pulling of the rein on the side to which the turning is directed. This action is continued until the horse has turned to the desired degree. However, as we will see later on, it is never a long-lasting pull. The strength of the signal depends upon the sensitivity of the horse and upon its rideability.

While pulling on the turning rein, the opposite hand should yield just as much pressure as is represented by the pulling. As soon as the horse has completed the turning movement desired, the pulling and giving effects should cease.

*The counter-balancing and lateral-moving rein* (Fig. No. 32)

The purpose of these rein-functions is to cause the horse to make a lateral movement with its forehand or shoulders, or to prevent it from doing so on its own accord.

The counter-balancing and lateral-moving rein functions are quite identical, but despite this it is necessary to make a certain distinction between them in order to facilitate the explanation of their application.

*The counter-balancing rein* is used in co-operation with other actions to prevent the horse from abandoning a desired bent position or from taking on a crooked posture.

*The lateral-moving rein* co-operates with the rider's other actions which are applied to create and maintain a desired bent position, or a lateral movement, and to help eliminate crookedness.

These tasks are performed by applying the signals only to

one side.  Consequently, the signals are transmitted by only one of the reins.

To create the desired effect, the rider applies to the rein a series of breathing-like pulls, incorporating similar pressures from the muscles of the hand.  The intensity of these consecutive functions is gradually increased and decreased, in a movement similar to that of squeezing and releasing a soft rubber ball.  The involved pulling should be directed towards the rider's hip on the opposite side.

The entire sequence of actions should be carried out harmoniously, with strength, smoothness and a sense of refinement. As to the amount of strength involved, this is determined by the extent of the desired lateral movement, or by the degree of the horse's tendency to become evasive or crooked.

The number of counter-balancing or lateral-moving rein functions corresponds roughly to four to six consecutive pressures. This series can be repeated two to three times.

During the procedure, the rein which is on the opposite side of the acting rein constantly maintains contact and follows the movement of the horse.

Furthermore, it is essential that the rider's leg which is on the opposite side of the rein action should take care of the hind quarters.  The animal is apt to seek an escape from the pressing effect of the rein, and to this end its most convenient tactic is to make way with the quarters in the opposite direction.  At the same time the rider's other leg keeps up the liveliness.

### The collecting rein

The action of the hands is the same as that for producing the lateral-moving effect (see Fig. No. 32), but has to be employed simultaneously with both hands.  It should be practised only in highly advanced stage of education.

The rider's aim in utilizing this rein function is to give a signal to the horse to *increase* its already established state of collection just before undertaking an exerting task, e.g. a take-off.  It has to be emphasized that this function is by no means suitable to *produce* collection (see more details on page 323).

### The loosening rein (Fig. No. 33)

This rein function is used for the release of stiffness in the lateral muscles of the horse's neck. It is characteristic of this stiffness that it appears only on one side of the neck. Therefore, the loosening rein can operate only on that side where the stiffness has been observed.

The action is composed of two parts, namely, of a taking and a giving element. The pulling of the rein should be started in a gentle manner and then, by gradually increasing the pressure, the rider successively enforces its effect. The yielding part, however, should be performed by a sudden movement which emphasizes its essential element, i.e. the loosening effect of the action.

Within the procedure, the gradually increased pulling and the sudden giving should follow each other in a smoothly continuous manner, and the two composing parts can be repeated several times. The entire function should be executed by the rider by means of tightening and relaxing the muscles of his arm and hand.

When employing the loosening rein the hand holding the other rein must remain in contact with the horse's mouth, and smoothly follow its movements.

There is another method of accomplishing the loosening process. According to it, the rider, while performing the action of sudden yielding, with his same hand (without opening the fist), pats the horse's neck. In this method

the horse, feeling the sudden yielding of the rein, tends to loosen that basis which it created during its stiffness in order to support its improper balance;

by patting, the rider can make the horse sense, psychologically because of its rewarding effect, and physically because of its jogging or trembling effect on the muscles, what he wishes it to do.

The hands themselves can also bring about very successfully a loosening effect on the horse's muscular system. For this, take the reins in one hand. Place the other in front of the saddle on the withers in a position where the thumb is on the one and the fingers on the other side. Exercise with them alternately drumming-like touches on the withers. The vibration thus produced relaxes the stiffness of the muscles, and at the same time the procedure calms the horse by the pleasant trembling sensation caused. Make good use of this simple means of loosening, especially during the daily loosening exercise (see page 266), and when schooling young horses.

There is also another useful hand movement for calming and relaxing the horse. While keeping the reins in the hands, strike up and down once with the one fist and once with the other over the mane. Apply these strokes rather often during the ride, especially when the rein-contact has already been established, and even when the horse is in a collection. The sudden relaxation of the contact, coupled with the pleasing stroke, produces the effect desired.

### The counter-deviating rein (Fig. No. 34)

This rein function is a combination of the directing and the loosening rein. The action of the hands consists of slight pullings diverging from the rider's body (sideways and backwards), which are combined with some yielding movements.

The brief pullings of the rein should be carried out in close succession, similar to the way in which a rubber band can be tightened up slowly and then abruptly released. After each pulling and yielding movement, a brief (one or two seconds) interval should be allowed before starting a new action.

### Passive tension with the hands (reins)

The term 'passive tension' describes a certain state of the rider in which he remains neutral, without exercising any active or yielding function. Thus, it is the maintenance of an existing posture against any possible event which may upset it.

The passive tension of the hands is employed against the horse's pushing action by which it tries to pull the reins out of the rider's hands. The animal can exercise this undesired action very often and with varying intensity. Therefore, the rider must be constantly prepared to display his passive function in accordance with the horse's behaviour.

The necessary tension involved in the function is created by pressing the fingers and fists, and by tightening up the muscles of the upper arms and the shoulders. At the same time, however, so should the mildest, as well as the firmest, tension be blended with a definite, though externally unnoticeable, vibration of the tightened muscles.

The state of tension is mostly a very short one, and must be cancelled out before any actual reaction is felt by the rider. This yielding part of the function is most important, since it is that which effects the relaxation of the animal's resistance.

The cancellation of the passive tension is brought about by either a sudden or gradual relaxation of the engaged muscles. Afterwards, the hands should keep up the continuous contact with the horse's mouth with the sensation of pushing the reins forward (see page 76).

In order to perform the above movements of the function, the reins should be kept at their adjusted length (see page 104) in the hands, near to each other and well in front of the body. Only with such a hand-position can the rider perform the functions without delay, and display his interchanged muscle-functions with refined feeling and varying intensity.

The passive tension of the hands together with its relaxation is a most important function of the rider. Its sensitive performance is a great help in riding, but its incorrect execution arouses increased resistance in the horse. Therefore, the rider should improve his ability to perform the function at the highest possible level. The practice of pressing a rubber ball with varying intensity is a very useful means of improving his physical skill.

When the horse exerts some resistance, the passive behaviour of the hands may sometimes give the impression of a pulling action. In such a case the rider should be careful not to produce this harmful effect, and should curb any tendency towards it. If the rider notices that the effect of the passive tension is not sufficient, instead of pulling, he should yield at first for a moment, and out of this relaxation (mostly a quick one) introduce a retarding action terminating in a renewed yielding (see page 111).

THE SEAT AS AGENT OF COMMUNICATION (Table No. 3)

The seat, together with the thighs, and enforced by the knees, is the rider's connection with the horse's back. There are two main forms of seat to be considered: the seat for school riding (Fig. No. 35), and the seat for forward posture (Figs. Nos. 36 and 37 on page 71).

Whatever the position of the seat, it must be free from stiffness! The rider must keep his entire muscular system in a state of suppleness coupled with refined mobility, and not force his body to safeguard a strictly defined external shape of the seat.

He should sit comfortably in the saddle, for an uncomfortable seat will result in stiffness of the body which is certain to be communicated to the horse, and it will in turn become stiff. The comfortable seat, however, must be close, firm and flexible in its stability.

The seat, in its general meaning, is close when the thighs, knees, and legs are firmly connected with the horse (in the sitting posture the seat-bone also). To satisfy this demand the turned inwards position of the thighs has an important role.

The correct position of the thighs, combined with heels pressed down, is the main stabilizing factor of the seat. As a result of turning in the thighs and pressing the heels down, the upper body will show a balanced carriage (will not dangle uncontrolled), and the position of the knees will be stabilized (will not slide). At the same time the independent mobility of the rider will be secured, both in sitting and in forward postures, as well as during the performance of jumps.

A seat in which the thighs are turned to the outside, and the heels pulled up, always reveals signs of stiffness, instability and ineffectiveness since it is 'open'.

Using either the sitting or the forward posture, the rider can be in a normal (relaxed) state, or in a position ready for exercising influence on the horse.

In the normal position, by keeping up the form of the seat adopted, the bearing of the rider shows a relaxed easiness. In this state, however, the seat is not adapted to immediate communication with the horse.

In order to increase its action readiness it is necessary to bring the seat from its relaxed (normal) state into a more collected state. For the sake of clarity, this particular form of the seat will be referred to in the following explanations as the 'ready position' of the seat. Since it is the starting and finishing point of all the rider's activities, it plays a very important role in conveying commands to the animal.

In the ready position the rider is able to carry out his various actions by the seat, thighs, and legs without delay, and he is enabled to interchange them with one another in accordance with his intentions. Furthermore, he can perform the functions equally in the most refined and firmest manner within the exactly limited bounds demanded by the actual situation.

In this position the hands 'get near' to the horse's mouth, giving them every opportunity to perform their functions clearly, and to 'push' the horse forward by the reins (see page 76).

In using the seat the rider must acquire the ability

constantly to appraise the varying conditions which are conveyed to the seat by the muscles of the horse's back and by its locomotion;

to follow with complete suppleness the entire trend of the motion;

permanently to maintain his own balance in relation to the balance of the horse, but also

to be able to alter smoothly his balance-position and the pressure on the horse's back in order to achieve respectively an alteration in the motion and a loosening effect on the muscles of the back.

We shall now examine in details the employment of the seat, separately in its sitting and forward posture.

THE SEAT FOR SCHOOL RIDING (Figs. Nos. 35 and 38/a-41/a in Table No. 3)

The purpose of the seat for school riding (sitting posture) is to ensure a continuous direct contact with the horse's back. Riding

The seat for school-riding.
(In walk, trot and canter.)

Fig. No. 35

in this form of seat greatly facilitates the task of the rider, but not that of the horse. Since its use creates some difficulties for the animal, the sitting position can only be employed when the horse has outgrown its green stiffness and begins to 'bear' itself.

### The normal position of the seat for school riding (Fig. No. 38/a)

The seat in its normal position must be a deep one, meaning that the rider must sit 'in' the saddle and not 'on' it. He should keep his upper body in a supple, erect bearing, with a slightly concave carriage of the waist and with a vertical pelvis.

The weight of the body is evenly divided between the buttocks and the seat-bone, which should be situated as near as possible to the first pommel, thus resting (through the saddle) mainly on the bundles of muscles linked to the withers of the animal. The thighs should lie tightly on the saddle, enclosing an angle of about 50° with the horizontal. With the thighs in this position, the knees are automatically placed correctly.

When adopting this position the rider should 'drop' the entire weight of the body, by the force of gravity, through the buttocks, thighs and legs, right down to the heels.

### The 'ready position' of the seat for school riding (Fig. No. 39/a)

Actually, this position is nothing else but a combination of the French relaxed position and the German braced position,* utilizing the ease of the former and the influencing capacity of the latter.

The over-all picture which the rider presents to the observer while sitting in the ready position can be summed up in the following manner:

His head is erect, with the chin slightly drawn in;

the upper body leans slightly behind the vertical line (5°-10°);

the chest is slightly vaulted, with an erect bearing of the spine;

the lower part of the spinal column is somewhat bent forward, making the buttocks turn slightly forward, while the seat-bone is placed deeply into the saddle;

the thighs, knees and legs are kept in their normal position.

---

* Braced position: the rider, by bracing certain parts of his back, waist, and the muscles of the loin, creates in the structure of his seat a certain elastic tension. By leaning slightly backwards, he pushes forward the lower part of the spine, so that the buttocks become set forward, whereas the seat-bone presses strongly into the saddle. This tension of muscles cancels the slight concave position of the waist, and makes the spine take up a straight form.

There is not a vestige of stiffness in the rider's muscular system, and the tension in his bearing is no more than necessary to maintain the above position.

The ability to assume the ready position, together with the recognition of the sensations by which it is maintained, can easily be mastered by the following simple method:

Starting from the normal position, the rider should slightly draw in his chin, and

while inhaling deeply, bend his upper body a little backwards from the hip-bone, simultaneously pushing forward the lower part of the spine.

The drawing-in of the chin has an important bearing on the procedure, since it produces a small degree of tension which, due to its effect on the muscles of the rider's back, prevents him from hollowing the waist and pushing forward the pelvis.

In order to resume the normal position of the seat, one has to employ the above procedure in reverse. In this way, the 'expiration' cancels the effect of the previous inspiration. After this change of position, the rider must be careful to retain the definite sensation of cohesion with the saddle, in a state of perfect balance.

*The taking action of the seat in the sitting position* (Fig. No. 40/a)

The taking action of the seat performed in the process of retardment is called the 'taking with the seat'. In exercising this action, the rider should bend his upper body a bit further backwards from the ready position, which causes his seat-bone to press down deeper in the saddle.

The pressing down of the seat-bone is carried out mainly by the muscles of the waist. However, the effect of the pressure becomes more pronounced due to the fact that the seat-bone cannot shift forward because the thighs, which cleave to the saddle and are fixed by the position of the knee, check any of its movements through the pelvis.

With the aid of the taking action of the seat, the rider can exert a downward pressure on the horse's back, which tends to decrease the swinging movement of its spine and results in slowing down the motion of the horse (see also page 69).

Ideally, the retarding effect of this pressure should be brought into operation when the undulating movement of the spine is at its peak. This can be roughly identified by the push-strokes caused by the stride-action of the horse.   At the same time this means that the pressure should never be a long-lasting function.

## Table No. 3

### ILLUSTRATIVE OUTLINE OF BASIC POSITIONS
### AND ACTIONS OF THE SEAT

| Normal (relaxed) position | Ready position | Pressing down action of the | |
| --- | --- | --- | --- |
| | | seat-bone or stirrups (taking action) | thighs (animating and collecting action) |
| a.) while using the seat for school riding (sitting posture) | | | |
| | | | |
| b.) while using the forward-seat (in forward position) | | | |
| | | | |
| Fig. No. 38 | Fig. No. 39 | Fig. No. 40 | Fig. No. 41 |

41/c.

*The 'swing-improving' action of the seat*

It is used, in contrast to the taking action of the seat, in order to *increase* the swinging movement of the horse's spine, and it should be performed in the following manner:

At the trot, take up the ready position, and without employing any body tension, sink the seat deeply into the saddle, establishing a close and continuous contact with it; then

when the spine comes to one of the lowering phases of its motion enforce the gravitational sinking movement of your body by a short pressure on the horse's back. Relax it, however, immediately when the motion of the spine gets into its upward swinging phase.

The pressure thus exercised increases the lowering motion of the spine, and the accumulated force of the pressed-down spring automatically increases its upward motion, provided that the rider ceases in time the pressure exercised by his seat. These coupled functions, carried out in rotation, result in the increased swinging movement of the back.

The rider can best understand the meaning of this motion and execute it most correctly if he imagines himself riding in a rising trot without, however, actually performing the rising and sitting-down movements, but only 'feeling' them, while keeping his seat continuously in the saddle.

The use of these movements is highly effective in gradually improving the swing of the horse's back. However, it must be borne in mind that the exercise should not contain more than five to six swing-improving movements in succession. If it is desired to have a longer period of exercise, it is advisable to separate the practice of these movements by periods of rest.

In order to employ the swing-improving action of the seat while using the rising trot, one should add more stress to the sitting-down motion (in this case, of course, actually performed).

If the rider's aim is to slow down the swinging movement, he should start the rising movement with a slight delay by which he exercises a pressure on the horse's spine just when it starts to swing upwards.

*The passive tension with the seat*

This function of the seat is similar in essence to the passive tension of the hands, and its application is based upon the same principles.

In performing this function, the rider, starting from the ready position, changes the lightness of the seat-contact to a firm one, and by constantly retaining this firmness, keeps the horse's back under strict control.

As a rule, the passive function of the seat is carried out jointly with the identical function of the hands, and for the same purpose.

THE SEAT IN THE FORWARD POSITION (Figs. Nos. 36, 37 and 38/b-41/b in Table 3)

The characteristic external feature of the forward position is, that the rider, by elevating his seat out of the saddle and carrying his upper body in a bent-forward posture, is no longer in a direct contact with the horse's back through his buttocks and seat-bone.

The internal characteristic of this position is its inherent stimulating influence on the animal's forward motion.

*The purpose of the forward position*

It is to ensure balance during extended movements, and to provide the horse's back with complete freedom of movement.

In order to maintain the mutual balance of the rider and horse, even when riding at great speed or while jumping, it is necessary for the rider to arrange his own centre of gravity so that it precedes the animal's centre of gravity in the trend of the motion. He can achieve this by leaning forward with the upper body (see page 86).

The horse often requires considerable freedom of back and neck in the course of its work, particularly while performing broad and vigorous movements (with a colt, this manifests itself in awkwardness of movements). The forward position enables the rider to avoid hindering these broad actions, and at the same time permits him to accommodate himself to them with small and neat movements.

These are the reasons why, in racing, the American style of seat has developed and, in jumping, the jumping-seat introduced by Captain Caprilli.

After sufficient practice, the forward seat can offer the same stability as that provided by the actual sitting position, where the seat is firmly supported by the saddle.

*The normal position of the forward seat* (Fig. No. 38/b)

Although the diagram is self-explanatory, it is necessary to mention some additional points which merit consideration.

The rider should hollow his back slightly and bend the upper body forward. In this posture, the angle at which the upper

## The seat in the forward position.

Fig. No. 36

In trot (ev. in walk).

In canter, gallop, and jumping.

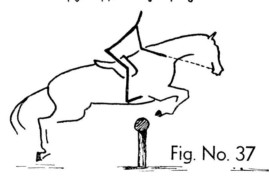

Fig. No. 37

body and thighs meet should be about 100°-110° in the walk, trot and slow canter. In proportion to the increase in speed, and in accordance with the horse's actions, the rider should bend the upper body more and more forward, but without changing the basic structure of the above position (see more details on page 86).

It is incorrect to arch the waist instead of bending the lower part of the spine forward, as in so doing the rider's seat is pushed out of its correct position both backwards and upwards. In such a posture the seat loses all its influencing possibilities and the rider, though he may lean forward as far as he can, will always remain 'behind' the horse.

Straightening the thighs from the knees is equally wrong, as it deprives the seat of its elasticity and stability, as well as its influencing capacity. By leaning forward in this position, the rider gets 'ahead of' the animal instead of being 'with' it.

The thighs should be in contact with the saddle chiefly with their inner, and partly with their lower muscles, in the half-length towards the knees. Through the thighs, the upper body should weigh flexibly upon the area of the saddle which lies laterally from its longitudinal axis and slightly lower than the vertical axis. While maintaining this position, the rider must take care not to protrude backwards with his seat. He can prevent this by pressing the buttocks forward. In such a posture, a bump on the horse's spine can only be caused by the faulty dropping back of the rider.

In order to determine and become accustomed to the exact extent of elevation required in the saddle, and to acquire the characteristic sensation, certain exercises are recommended as described below. (For these exercises, one should make the leathers two to four holes shorter than in school-riding, and take the stirrups right to the heels.)

*In the walk:* Place a few poles on the ground at irregular distances of 3-5 yards (metres) apart. Ride over these poles while freeing the animal's back from the seat by assuming and staying in the forward position. The irregularly-placed poles will force the rider to remain in the above posture in order not to fall back on the horse's back.

*In the trot:* Ride at a rising trot, which will produce the bending forward of the upper body, together with the required extent of elevation in the saddle. After a while, *at the beginning of one of the sinking-down movements*, stop the motion and continue to ride in this arrested position.

*In the canter:* Maintain *permanently* the normal forward position.

*While jumping:* Increase the forward bending, but take care not to 'stick out behind' with the seat.

It must be emphasized that, in all four cases, the rider should not stand in the stirrups. He should use the stirrups only as supports but also cease from time to time leaning on them altogether during the exercise.

The forward position is used: when riding in extended paces; for the loosening exercises in the canter; while riding young horses in order to provide more facility for free going (in all paces); while riding in the country; when jumping (also out of the trot); and when signs of resistance are felt and the animal's ambition for free going needs to be refreshed (in all paces).

### *The ready position of the forward seat* (Fig. No. 39/b)

The general significance of this posture is the same as described in connection with that of the seat for school-riding.

The form of the ready position corresponds roughly in appearance to the normal posture of the forward seat. There is a slight difference in the holding of the rider's back, the spine being straight instead of slightly hollowed. The thighs sink a bit nearer to the saddle, while the knees, legs and heels retain their original position.

To assume the ready position, the rider should follow the same method which has been recommended for the procedure in the sitting form of riding. As a result

the buttocks become pressed forward and the seat-bone downwards;

the upper body, from the joints of the hip, exercises a pressure on the thighs which tends to keep the seat in its elevated position;

the effects of the elevating function of the thighs and the pressing-down force of the upper body counteract each other and produce an elastic tension in the seat, which is thereby endowed with the necessary action-readiness and stability.

### *The seat actions in forward position*

When the rider is using the proper form of the forward seat, the basic techniques for influencing the horse can be applied just as well as when sitting in the saddle, and at the same time the free movement of the animal's back is ensured.

In this posture, too, the starting point for executing the various seat actions is the ready position of the seat. Therefore, it is of special importance to riders who have to perform in the forward seat to master thoroughly the ready position.

*The taking action* (Fig. No. 40/b)

In performing this action, lean a bit backwards from the ready position, and exercise some firm pressures on the *stirrups* (as described on page 50).

The pressure, by affecting the horse's spine over a *narrow area*, provides a definite signal for retardment. The horse learns very quickly the meaning of this action.

*The swing-improving action and passive tension of the forward seat*

The swing-improving action corresponds in essence to that which has been described in connection with the seat for school riding.

The function of passive tension is executed by fixing the thighs and keeping the weight prolonged on both stirrups.

In practising all the above functions of the seat (with the exception of the swing-improving action), the exercises or experiments should start from a stationary position. Then the rider can successively increase his demands on the horse by gradually increasing the animal's motion.

### THE AIDS AND THE MEANS OF THEIR APPLICATION

The aids, in a general sense, are the rider's *mental activities associated with his physical actions* in giving signals. By backing up the physical functions with intellect, the entire communication is endowed with a real guiding quality. Thus, the aids not only transmit orders to the horse, but also *actively assist* the animal, and show it the best way of carrying out its tasks.

### THE PHYSICAL FUNCTIONS IN THE SERVICE OF PROVIDING AIDS

The physical functions by which the rider can aid the horse are the 'giving' (yielding) and the 'following' functions performed by the agents of communication, and the 'levelling function' of the rider.   Since their execution is almost identical, in both the sitting and the forward position, they can be reviewed jointly for both cases.

*The 'giving' (yielding)*

The giving is a function in which the activity of the muscles created by the application of energy (for signals, passive tension) is stopped by relaxation.   In this sense, relaxation means the gradual diminution of muscle tension down to the state of complete suppleness.   This particular state can also be achieved by certain effective movements of the hands, seat and legs.

The 'giving' function of the hands

Their giving function can best be illustrated by the following practical example:

Take a soft rubber band and stretch it from the thumb of the left hand to the index finger of the right hand.   In this position, the rubber band represents the bit and the rein, the thumb the horse's mouth, and the index finger the hand of the rider.

By holding the rubber band between the two fingers neither tightly nor loosely, one has the same impression as when taking up the rein-contact with the horse through the bit.   By pulling the band, a pressing sensation will be felt on the thumb.   If one wishes to relax this pressure *without losing contact* with the thumb, the band cannot be abruptly released, but the pulling must be gradually decreased until it is completely stopped.

Repeat the above procedure with the rubber band a few times, and it will give a clear picture of the sensations which the muscular action creates in the rider when the muscles are tightened for pulling and relaxing for 'giving' (yielding).

The rider has to acquire this facility for yielding with the hands by his sense of feeling.   While yielding, the hands must never lose contact with the horse's mouth, even at the moment of complete 'giving', so that the horse remains in constant 'use' of the bit.

The 'giving' function of the seat

This function expresses itself in the relaxation of all tension in the structural form of the seat after the completion of a positive action. The transition to the ready position during the process of giving must be carried out gradually, and with the same feeling as in the case of the hands. In this way the seat is able to remain in constant contact with the horse's back (in the forward position through the stirrups).

In order to endow the giving function with real aiding ability, it is important that the yielding with the seat and that of the hands should be smoothly synchronized.

The 'giving' function of the legs

The giving function of the legs is very limited, and consists of maintaining contact with the horse's side and awaiting its motion in a passive manner, after having completed a certain signal.

This condition can be most clearly demonstrated by referring to the function of the leg in which it exercises a lateral-moving effect on the horse's side. Within this procedure, it first carries out a positive action, i.e. a pressure, after which it adopts a state of passivity by relaxing the engaged muscles. The moment at which the leg ceases to exert its pressure represents the giving function of the legs.

*The following function*

The function of following is the rider's conduct in pursuing the movements of the horse in a smooth manner, inspired by a go-ahead spirit. The rider should enter wholeheartedly into this pursuit, engaging his entire will power in the process. When he is determined to adopt this attitude (and only then!) he will be able to discharge the motional part of the function without difficulty.

The 'following' is a continuation of 'giving', and therefore it is linked directly to the finishing phase of the giving.

The following function of the hands

In the course of following the horse's movements, the hands have a gentle, shoving-like function to perform, as if they were pushing the horse forward through the reins. This feeling is a peculiar combination of physical and mental motives which each rider has to recognize for himself.

The sensation involved in the shoving, i.e. the following function of the hands, is rather similar to that of pushing a wheel-

barrow.   Here, the weight of the wheelbarrow represents the
strength at which the horse 'rests' on the bit, the handles are the
reins by which the rider maintains the contact, and the action by
which the wheelbarrow is pushed forward symbolizes the go-ahead
spirit of the rider.

Just like the wheelbarrow, which does not roll forward without
the application of a pushing force directed through the handles,
the horse is blocked in its movements when it feels that the reins
wobble in their giving and following functions.

From the rider's go-ahead spirit, expressed in his pushing-like
conduct, the animal acquires facility in its motion and confidence
in its master.   This inspires it to submit to the rider's will and
obey him with pleasure.   The rider in the meantime is in full
control of every situation, regardless of the strength of contact,
since he is in position to 'push' the horse forward, or to curb it
at any moment.   When the rider is unable to bring this pushing
feeling into the reins, then even the lightest rein contact will have
an element of pulling.   Thus it is the basis for the maintenance
of contact and of the easiness in handling the reins.

Aside from its abstract qualities, the rider's following activity
also comprises certain physical manifestations, namely:

When the horse yields (both in retardment and collection), it
    does not drop the bit, but carrying it further forward keeps
    the reins in a state of light tension;

when the rider 'gives' with the hands, pushing them slightly
    forwards, the horse—by maintaining uninterrupted contact
    —follows this movement smoothly, preventing the reins
    from slackening.

These reactions give the rider the sensation of the bit being
linked up to the horse's mouth and the reins possessing a physical
hardness.   He seems actually to push the animal forward through
the 'hard' rein and through the mouth.

The rider must also acquire the skill in performing correctly
the transition from an action to yielding, up to 'pushing' the
horse.   This should be carried out with the feeling as if, after
pulling the wheelbarrow backwards on a very slight slope uphill
(without stopping in between), he smoothly changes his action
to pushing the wheelbarrow forwards on the same slope downhill.
During this procedure, the 'heaviness' of the action disappears
gradually, the wheelbarrow becomes light in the hands and is

rolling nearly by itself, with only a slight push to ensure its forward motion.

The full realization of these sensations depends largely upon the horse keeping its hind legs well under the body. Therefore, the support of the driving legs is very important in creating the conditions which produce them.

### The following function of the seat

In following the horse's motion, the rider must have a light hovering sensation in a state of balance, the whole animated by an attitude of absolute striving forward.

The upper body takes the form of the ready position, in which the rider's muscles are relaxed. In this state of flexibility, the seat should smoothly follow the movements of the horse's back and comply with its strokes, so that the rider could safely carry a full glass of water while in the saddle. The general appearance of his bearing should radiate ease, skill and elegance.

### The following function of the legs

This function manifests itself by a state of passivity in which the legs after the phase of yielding remain in a relaxed state and *in touch* with the horse's side. The legs should, in spite of their apparent passivity, transmit the rider's forward intention to the animal. The horse will sense this, just as it senses the slightest restriction or uncertainty on the part of its master.

In conclusion, it can be said that the 'giving' (yielding) and 'following' functions and their joint application are the factors which ensure the atmosphere of mutual forward-striving between the horse and rider. They constitute one of the most important secrets of success, and those who ignore their importance will find it almost impossible to develop a reliable and well-educated horse.

### THE LEVELLING FUNCTION

This is a combined function of the rider which incorporates fractions of his various basic activities in a harmonious, smooth, but not definitely arranged combination.

The component elements of the function are the minute pressures of the thighs, legs, seat (buttocks) or stirrups and reins, as well as the slight oscillating movements of the upper body.

All these actions, however, are complete only with the immediate relaxation of the previously engaged muscles.

While combining these minute indications with one another, the only reservation is that they should never act against each other during their simultaneous or interlocked application.

The levelling function, by its manifold changes in quick rotation, produces effects combined in longitudinal and lateral direction of an all-round loosening—animating—initiating feature. Thus, it has an exceptional aiding quality, by smoothing and polishing both the activities of the rider and the horse.

In spite of its inherent values, this function is not elucidated in general practice on its own merit, but is only used instinctively by the masters of riding, thereby making their activities spectacularly smooth and effective. There is no separate term for its denomination in use, and therefore I have tried to choose an expression which best approaches its characteristic feature. I hope to have found it in the term employed in the headline of this paragraph.

The performance of the levelling function occurs according to the typical variations listed below, and illustrated in Table No. 4 (variations 'a'–'e', each by a series of five diagrams). The successive explanations indicate at the same time the graduations according to which the rider must do his exercises in order to acquire the necessary skill to execute the function correctly.

Variation 'a'

To begin with, execute these basic elements of the function individually in rotation, so as action + yielding + action + yielding +, etc.

Variation 'b'

Perform two to four slight pressures by the thighs *interchanged* with those of the seat-bone (buttocks). These produce interlocked, minute drive-on and retarding effects, promoting the horse's suppleness and increasing its liveliness. Thus, they produce a pure longitudinal effect.

Variation 'c/1'

Make slight lateral changes in the position of the upper body by bending from the knees (and not from the hip only) in an

ILLUSTRATIVE OUTLINE OF THE VARIATIONS IN THE LEVELLING
FUNCTION

## Table No. 4

| Variation | Starting & finishing posture | Function in the succession of its composing elements. | | | |
|---|---|---|---|---|---|
| a. | Ready position | The particular action plus yielding in rotation. | | | |
| b. | | | | | |
| C/1. | | | | | |
| C/2. | | | | | |
| d. | – ‖ – | – ‖ – | Pressure by the thighs | – ‖ – | Pressure by the thighs |
| e. | | | | | |

The shaded parts in the diagrams, showing the rider, indicate the pressure (or its diminution) exercised by the particular agent of communication. The black dots show the position of the centre of gravity, and its trans-positioning in accordance with the lateral bending movement of the upper body.

The rhythmical changes within the function may succeed according to the performing ability of the rider in 1-3 stride-action.

oscillating manner between the right and left direction and thus alter in rotation the position of your centre of gravity. Perform these oscillating movements of the upper body with the feeling, rhythm and swing, similar to those which develop during dancing a smooth waltz.

During this, when the upper body is bending from the vertical position towards the one side, exercise a gradually increasing pressure by the corresponding buttock on the horse's back and by the same leg on its side. Then relax the pressure when the upper body starts to return towards the vertical position, and immediately repeat the same procedure in the opposite direction.

The main purpose of the oscillating movements is to loosen the shoulders and making them mobile in lateral directions (see page 100). The result desired is achieved when the rider has the *sensation* of the horse making lateral shifting movements under his seat, rhythmically and always in the direction opposite to the momentary bending movement of his upper body. The rider should repeat these oscillating movements until the sensation of 'shifting' appears.

Version 'c/2'

Improve the former version by including interchanged pressures on the stirrups and their relaxations, synchronized with the pressures and relaxations of the legs.

The rhythmical changes of the static centre, supported by the pressures of the legs, promote the lateral mobility of the forehand. The additional interchanged pressures on the horse's back produce a loosening effect, and divert the animal from adopting one-sided stiffness and crookedness.

Both versions ('c/1' and 'c/2') are producing a purely lateral effect on the horse.

Version 'd'

Combine the versions 'b' and 'c' with one another. Take care, however, that in this combination the pressures of the thighs (driving effect) should not be exercised simultaneously with the pressures of the seat or those of the stirrups, since these are producing retarding effect on the horse's back.

This function, as a whole, produces by its combined longitudinal and lateral influence a general suppling effect on the animal.

Version 'e'.  The complete form of the levelling function

Extend the version 'd' by exercising a gradually increasing pressure by the rein on the bar of the horse's mouth, always on that side towards which the upper body is bending.  Then decrease gradually this pressure simultaneously with the change-over of the bending movement of the upper body, so that, in the moment when it is in erect position, all muscles are relaxed.

At this variation of the levelling function, in which the reins have an active role, it is especially important that the rider, while he is exercising a pressure on the one side, should yield with the rein on the opposite side.

The rein pressures, accompanying the interchanged pressures of the buttocks, legs and stirrups, and being synchronized with the bending movements of the upper body, should by no means dominate the over-all function.  Used to excess they would spoil the general effect of the procedure, and arouse the horse's opposition.

In their essence, these rein pressures are slight *leading-functions*, executed with the aim of emphasizing the lateral movement of the shoulders which is brought about by the bending movement of the upper body.  This feature of the pressures is the criterion of their correct execution.  Otherwise, the rider is simply pulling down the animal's head and neck, which must be avoided under all circumstances.

The rider should blend all his activities by the levelling function, filling them with an 'inner vibration'.  In fact, it is the most characteristic inner vibration of the rider, endowing his activities with 'feeling'.  This, by releasing the horse from its mental and physical impediments, prevents the animal from developing irregularities, and helps the rider to overcome them.

The rider's function of passive tension can also be blended in certain cases by the rein pressures involved in the levelling function.  In this way the effect of the tension can be increased without upsetting the smoothness of the function.  Such a reinforcement of the passive tension becomes necessary if the rider wishes to provide it with some regulating or collecting effect.  By this means the function checks the pushing action of the horse against the bit, and reminds the animal to retain its state of collection whenever it has an intention to stretch its spring-system or throw about the head and neck.

COMPREHENSIVE ILLUSTRATION OF THE RIDER'S GENERAL 'FEELING' AND STEERING ACTIVITIES DURING THE PERFORMANCE OF THE LEVELLING FUNCTION

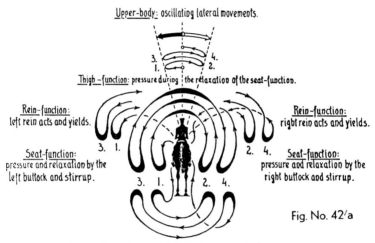

Upper-body: oscillating lateral movements.

Thigh–function: pressure during the relaxation of the seat-function.

Rein-function: left rein acts and yields.

Rein-function: right rein acts and yields.

Seat-function: pressure and relaxation by the left buttock and stirrup.

Seat-function: pressure and relaxation by the right buttock and stirrup.

Fig. No. 42/a

Leg-function: interchanged (left, right) pressures and relaxations.

The diagram may inspire the rider by revealing the feeling by which the physical movements involved in the function should be directed.

The pleasantly swinging lines show the character of this feeling which endows the activities of the rider with smoothness and rhythm, and interlaces the effects of the diverse part-functions into an harmonious unity.

As the waves, radiating from a centre, surround the point of their origin, so the effects, brought about by the " inner vibration " latent in the levelling function, embrace the mentality of the horse by their persuasive power, resulting in the pliant readiness of the animal to co-operate with the rider.

The diagram visualizes also the feeling necessary for the smooth performance of any of the rider's activities, since the levelling function, with its inner vibration, should always be latent in each of them, even in the " motionless " state.

The thickness of the lines in the diagram illustrates the intensity of the part-functions, starting from the relaxed state, and back to the phase of yielding again. One can clearly see the comparatively long duration of the *yielding* phases, making effective and smooth the actions connected to them.

The figures in the diagram mark the succession of the rider's activities. Functions marked by identical figures should be executed simultaneously.

Beside its general advantage in preventing and overcoming difficulties, the levelling function can also produce, according to the intensity of the elements involved, definite alterations in the motion of the horse in longitudinal or lateral directions. Bearing this in mind, the ultimate aim of the rider should be, that the horse may react submissively to these effects; increase or decrease the speed, change the direction of the course of riding, and collect or relax itself whenever desired. These reactions will always be free from stiffness and full of impulsion, enabling the animal to perform movements of the highest elasticity necessary for the execution of difficult tasks.

ILLUSTRATIVE REPRODUCTION OF THE LEVELLING FUNCTION IN ITS LONGITUDINAL DIRECTION, AND THAT OF THE FORWARD TENDENCY IN THE CHARACTER OF THE RIDER'S FUNCTIONS

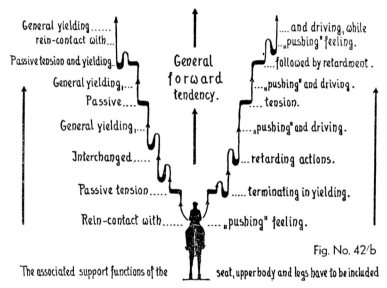

General yielding......
   rein-contact with...

Passive tension and yielding..

General yielding,...

Passive....

General yielding,...

Interchanged.....

Passive tension.....

Rein-contact with......

General forward tendency.

....and driving, while
..."pushing" feeling.

....followed by retardment.

...."pushing" and driving.

.... tension.

..."pushing" and driving.

...retarding actions.

......terminating in yielding.

...."pushing" feeling.

Fig. No. 42/b

The associated support functions of the       seat, upper body and legs have to be included

Remark: The text on the left and on the right side of the diagram should be read together.

The greatest advantage of the levelling function, however, lies in the fact that it brings horses of quite different natures *to the same level*, and thus *simplifies* the task of the rider in each situation during the course of riding.

In acquiring the knowledge to perform the levelling function, the difficulty appears more in developing that particular feeling which directs the rider in choosing the most appropriate combination of the function and the intensity of the elements involved, rather than in improving the physical skill necessary for its execution.   But by observing carefully the reactions of the horse, this difficulty will disappear during a few months' practice. With regard to the motional part of the function, it is best to perform the movements very distinctly at the beginning of schooling.   Later on, however, they should become almost invisible and exist only as an inner vibration in the activities of the rider.

THE RIDER'S WEIGHT IN MAINTAINING HARMONY OF BALANCE AND PROVIDING AIDS

In a regulated form of locomotion and in a spontaneous display of energy, the principal task of the rider is to maintain the correct state of balance.   In order to achieve this correct balance, the location of the centre of gravity of both the horse and the rider must be in harmony with each other and adapted to the pace and rate of locomotion.   The proper location of the rider's centre of gravity greatly facilitates the animal's task of safeguarding its own balance, making it easier to perform its motion and display of energy.

In advising the rider how to ensure an harmonious state of balance it is impossible to draw up definite rules, and the matter can be dealt with only in terms of general principles.   In fact, the rider has to create and maintain the joint state of balance between himself and the horse by instinctive feeling, just as he ensures his own balance by subconscious actions while standing or moving on his own two legs.

In the early stages of training, the rider should, for the sake of practice, at first simply shift his weight on the horse from its normal position to any other place.   While doing this, he should carefully observe the animal's reaction.

Later on, he should observe the horse's actual movements and behaviour prior to the shifting of his weight, and only then execute the transposition.   While doing so, he should carefully study the reaction of the animal.

During these exercises the rider will ascertain that he can very often exert a considerable amount of influence on the horse merely by changing his centre of gravity.   He will also realize that, by centralizing his weight at a certain place, the way in which the animal performs its locomotion will become more pleasant and regular, whereas in another position it will be defective.

The moment the rider is able to recognize the difference which a change of position of his weight may create in the animal's locomotion, he has established the basis for improving that particular skill with which he can also make good use of the possibilities mentioned above. From then on, the rider's only aim has to be to acquire a routine by which he can instinctively synchronize his own centre of gravity with that of the horse, in accordance with the particular situation.

Let us now examine the possibilities for recognizing and exploiting the proper balance positions of the rider in order to aid the animal.

### In stationary position

Broadly speaking, the horse's centre of gravity falls in that vertical plane which bisects the back at its lowest point.

Consequently, the rider's centre of gravity must fall in the same plane in order to safeguard the horse's balance. Therefore he has to sit fairly near to the pommel.

### In motion

As soon as the horse moves off, it changes its state of balance, and the rider has to adapt himself to this change.

While moving forward

Although the horse's centre of gravity remains in its original position, the rider has to place his own in front of that of the horse, in order to facilitate its locomotion.

Up to a speed of about 220 yards (200 metres) per minute, this act of bringing the centre of gravity forward can practically be neglected, but it should take the form of a decided go-ahead spirit on the part of the rider.

The more the rate of speed is increased, the more the rider has to bring his upper body, and thus his centre of gravity, forward. Therefore:

At an extended trot, he has to change over definitely to the rising movements;

at an extended canter, he has to lean forward with his upper
body, even when using the sitting position; and

at the gallop or jumping, he has to adopt the forward position
under all circumstances.

The greater the speed, the more it is necessary to lean forward
with the upper body, so that at a racing speed or in jumping
high obstacles, the bearing can be almost horizontal.

It must be emphasized that the leaning forward or taking back
of the upper body cannot increase or decrease the speed.  It is
possible, however, to facilitate by these means the action-potential
of the horse.  Doing so, one contributes to the alteration indirectly by creating a situation in which the animal can increase or
decrease the speed easily on its own accord.

While performing lateral movements (bends, flexions, turns,
sideways)

The horse always transfers its centre of gravity towards the
direction of its bending.  Consequently, the rider too has to
transfer his own in the same direction.  (This also explains why,
in the shoulder-in movement, when the horse proceeds in a
direction opposite to its bending, the rider does not place his
centre of gravity in the direction of the motion.)

There is but one exception from the above rule which, however,
is a very important one.  Namely, in the finishing phase of that
often used adjusting procedure the aim of which is the amendment
of the horse's faulty shoulder position (see page 173), the rider's
centre of gravity should be kept shifted in the direction of the
desired shoulder movement and not in the direction of the flexing
function involved.  By this means the execution of the shoulder
movement aimed at becomes facilitated for the animal, and as a
consequence of it, its resistance will disappear.

In performing sideways, the extent of the transposition of the
centre of gravity (both on the part of the rider and the horse) is
rather insignificant, in fact hardly noticeable to the observer,
but in spite of this the rider must always accommodate himself to it.

The shifting of the rider's centre of gravity towards the sides
has a considerable influence on the animal, since the horse follows
such a change by a lateral motion in order to maintain its own

state of balance. By exploiting this reaction of the animal, the rider can successfully influence it for turning or bending.

THE BALANCING ATTITUDE OF THE RIDER IN CONVEYING HIS DEMANDS

The crown of aiding the horse is that conduct of the rider by which he 'balances' the animal in the completion of its various tasks.

The means of 'balancing' are the signals and aids supplemented by the levelling function of the rider, and the different forms of reward and punishment employed in a harmonious combination according to the need indicated by the actual situation. They should free the horse from its impediments, ensure its being in the appropriate position, and support it in the execution of the movements in a supple manner. One cannot satisfy these demands by the application of single functions, since they will become in their execution long lasting, and by this fact upset the balance of the animal.

The motional part of balancing the horse is described in the next chapters, in connection with the methods of communication.

THE RIDER'S INTELLECTUAL PARTICIPATION IN PROVIDING AIDS

The mental activity of the rider in selecting the best possible method for influencing the horse helps the animal considerably in complying with his demands. Bearing this statement in mind, the possibilities described below should be considered.

*Choosing the appropriate moment (situation) for giving signals*

The significance of selecting correctly the particular moment for giving signals is decisive when, in the performance of a complete task, the aim is to endow the applied signal with a real 'aiding' value.

In order to achieve this aim, the rider has to take into account the degree of the horse's education, its transitory attitude, keenness of attention, and state of nerves. For example, when the horse is crooked or shows signs of stiffness, when the environment attracts its attention or when it is in the middle of some sort of exertion, etc., these circumstances may perplex the animal in responding to the signal. If the rider ignores these and similar impediments and neglects the proper moment for giving signals, the signals will be ineffectual at best, or (which is more likely) they will arouse an opposition in the animal. Thus the rider's action, lacking the important aiding value, will by no means result in the desired reaction from the horse. On the other hand, signals applied at the right time will lead to satisfactory results in performance, and produce a pleasant effect on the horse.

At the beginning of schooling, good use should be made of the *situations created by the horse* in order to teach it the meaning of the signals. Therefore the rider has an advantage in giving the signal for the performance of a certain task (e.g. for a motion on two tracks, a short turn, or to strike the horse into a canter, etc.) when the horse has, by chance and on its own initiative, taken up the position which is appropriate to the execution of the desired movement.

Later on, the rider himself will be able to create the most suitable situations for the horse's acceptance of the signals he intends to give.

Finally, as the standard of education increases, and the horse becomes more and more supple and obedient, it will readily and easily accept any sort of signal at any time.

*The application of supplementary signals in an organized manner*

There are certain circumstances in riding when the application of a single signal does not seem to express exactly the rider's intention. In such cases, the particular main signal should be supplemented by others, so that the animal will clearly realize what the rider desires.

Generally speaking, the use of combined signals can be applied in the following forms:

Several signals of different kinds applied at short intervals (in succession);

application of several signals consecutively, without interruption; and

simultaneous application of several signals which are not in contradiction with each other (some forms of these are called 'diagonal' signals or aids).

In fact, the expression of 'diagonal aid' means a combination of signals in which the right hand (rein) and the left leg are used simultaneously for an identical aim.

The main principle of application is, that the component signals should not counteract each other! This means, that in driving on and in retardment it is not possible to use diagonal aids or signals. On the other hand, one can use the lateral-moving leg simultaneously with the diagonally-applied leading, turning, lateral-moving or counter-balancing rein.

### INSTILLING THE RIDER'S 'WILL' AND 'FEELING' INTO THE SIGNALS

The mere performance of certain physical actions is not enough in giving signals, as they are only poor and spiritless movements. They have to be enforced by the rider's will, coupled with his feeling, in order to endow them with live and aiding power.

The 'will' is the rider's determination to execute his plans. This determination must be firm and resolute, and the signals must clearly reflect this spirit when demanding that a certain task be fulfilled.

The horseman's 'feeling' is the aptitude which permits him to identify the animal's various intellectual manifestations, and which enables him to follow consciously its physical movements.

It is important that he should be able to recognize the motives of every movement of the animal, and adapt accordingly his decisions and actions. In this sense, he must incorporate into every single action the 'feeling' which is most apt to promote and help every movement of the horse, and at the same time he must infuse his own actions with a similar feeling, in order to be able to check the animal's defective or malicious movements.

It can be stated in conclusion that in all riding, and especially in providing aids, it is not the mastering of the physical movements that is difficult, but the acquisition of those feelings which inspire the entire functioning of the system by which the will takes shape in actions.

The rider's capacity to pass on his 'will' and 'feeling' to the horse, and accommodate himself to it in using them, is the clue to mastering the art of riding.

### THE RIDER'S VOICE AS AN AID

The voice is of considerable value in riding, since the rider can attract the animal's attention by speaking to it and thus divert its curiosity from the surroundings.

The tone of voice in which the rider talks to his horse should create a warm and friendly atmosphere, and should give the animal a feeling of confidence and protection. Thus the horse will feel that no harm can come to it, and every task demanded will be undertaken as a pleasant form of pastime.

Therefore, the rider's voice must be calm and soothing. If it is rough and agitated, it will create nervousness and confusion in the animal. A pleasant sounding voice definitely affects the horse and assists it greatly in its tasks.

Words, as a means of communication, are of rather limited value so far as instruction and guidance are concerned. However, if the rider in the frequent performance of basic exercises constantly uses the same words together with the proper signal, the horse becomes familiar with them and will eventually obey the verbal order.

In these words, it is the rhythm and the articulation of their sound that are important. By these means some words can transmit in a fairly comprehensive manner certain demands to the horse. For example, in order to urge the animal forward, one should use in quick succession the short tone *go . . . go . . . go . . .*, and for slowing down that of *ho . . .ho . . . ho . . .*, just as the horse has to execute the movement demanded in a quick, lively leg-succession. By saying slowly *gooo*, or *hooo*, it is inspired to execute the alteration of its motion just as slowly as is indicated by the articulation of the used word. For calming down the proper articulation is *ho . . . hooo . . . ho . . . hooo . . .*, for the strike-off into canter *can' . . . te' . . . on . . . can' . . . te' . . . on . . .*, rein-back can be indicated by *back . . . back . . . back . . .*, etc. Thus, when choosing a word as a means of command, the essential requirement is that it should offer the possibility for an articulation which expresses the sense of its employment.

But the voice alone is not effective enough to explain more detailed actions, and the 'conversation' must be conducted by the use of signals and aids.

THE REWARD AS A MEANS OF COMMUNICATION

Reminding the horse of its merits, in one form or another, is of great psychological value and yields an abundant return. Therefore, the rider ought not to be sparing, but generous, in his praise.

The best recompense the rider can give his horse during the execution of a task is in his 'giving' conduct, both with the reins and the seat. After the completion of the task demanded, he can reward the animal by dropping the reins and freeing its back. By these means the horse is given a chance to stretch itself and to recuperate from its exertion, thus invigorating its muscles.

Patting on the neck is also a means of reward. It is not only a simple dalliance since it has a positive effect on the horse. Namely, the touches, exercised in quick succession, produce a pleasant trembling sensation in its muscles which delights and calms the horse. Just in this effect lies the rewarding value of patting (see also page 61).

It is a useful practice to present the animal with some sort of delicacy after a good performance, such as a lump of sugar, piece of bread, carrot, etc., or a few oats. In riding in the open country, one can allow the horse to take a bite of grass.

The greatest and most effective reward is simply dismounting. With this in mind, the rider should finish the daily routine work with a certain task, and after its successful performance, dismount.

PUNISHMENT AS A MEANS OF COMMUNICATION (see also page 273)

Punishment of the horse is one of the most delicate problems in riding, and therefore it must be applied with the utmost care and knowledge.

The only occasion upon which punishment is justified is when the rider is *convinced of the animal's malice*. Occasional opposition is no reason for imposing it in any form. In the event of some sort of repeated resistance, the best solution is to seek the counsel of an experienced rider, or failing that, to make a thorough analysis of the symptom, and try to overcome it by calm schooling.

Before blaming the horse, the rider should make a careful check *on himself*, since 90 per cent. of the opposition may rise from *his own* mistakes.

A frequent mistake of the rider is his failure to make it possible for the horse to carry out the task, or his making demands which are beyond the maturity and intelligence of the horse. Much of the animal's opposition may also be traced to some physical pain or fatigue, which prevents it from obeying the demands or paying enough attention to them.

Obstinate resistance, which appears at a later stage, can be ascribed to the fact that at the beginning the teacher, instead of exploiting the methods of schooling, accustoming, curing, etc., employed punishment as a 'corrective', proving the validity of the maxim that *when the knowledge of riding comes to an end, abuse begins*. If the rider loses his temper, he will not emerge from a difficult situation with credit. 'Patience brings its own reward', and by being patient, punishment can in most cases be avoided.

However, when it is necessary to resort to punishment, the rider must be firm and calm. Before undertaking any action, he should smile or whistle to ensure that there is indeed no anger in his mood. By this simple means, he can very successfully control and check himself, and thus endow his measures with real educational value, which, after all, is the purpose of the punishment.

The main instrument of the punishment is the riding whip. In practice, it should only be applied to the horse's side. Its application should never reach as far as the animal's thighs, not to mention its head. To use the whip in this debasing manner is unworthy of any horseman.

After the application of two to three energetic strokes of the whip, the rider should calmly continue the routine work of schooling. If the punishment was justified and correctly administered the horse will show readiness to obey; if not, it will aggravate the situation.

In the case of spoilt or, in a mental sense tautly-resisting horses, on exceptional occasions it is permissible to exert with great care and *calmness* some slight or moderate jerks on the bars of the mouth. The purpose of these jerks is to remind the animal by the pain caused to relax its *mental opposition*. They should never be applied for making the mouth 'softer'. This is impossible (see page 145).

It is necessary to emphasize, however, that such jerks can only be employed by knowledgeable riders, and then only as supplementary means of secondary importance interlocked with the *methodical* procedures. Whoever tries to 'correct' the horse by these means only will spoil it totally, and experience great disappointment.

It is unwise to use the reins for exercising some general punishment. As a result of such inconsiderate treatment, acute stiffness in the horse's back may ensue, and the work of schooling, which has been carried out with such trouble, will have a disagreeable setback for weeks.

After our thorough study of the animal's system of locomotion and the various means of communication, we shall now see how to make good practical use of this knowledge in exercising influence on the horse to obey our demands and to complete tasks imposed upon it.

PART TWO

# The Methods of
# Communication with the Horse

# CHAPTER ONE

# Basic Conditions of Communication with the Horse

THE communication between the rider and the horse is a bilateral process in which each performs a definite rôle. The rider's function is to convey his will considerately, whereas the horse's is to obey it. The former desires, and the latter fulfils. The desire should never be reckless, and the fulfilment never forced. In this partnership the rider represents the superior mentality and therefore he must choose the most psychologically suitable ways and means of making the horse understand and obey his wishes; and be able to maintain a harmonious relationship by influencing the animal's will or by accommodating himself to it.

It is therefore important that every action should first be foreseen, if only very rapidly, by instinctive feeling. The aim of this consideration is to discover the best means by which the rider should convey his will to the animal, and the best method by which he can convincingly impose his will on his partner.

In complying with these conditions, the rider must always remember that the horse, with the exception of certain rare cases where malice is the origin of the trouble, will respond as it has been taught to the *actual actions* of the rider. If the action of the rider is not one suitable for producing the desired effect, the animal will not comply with his demand; instead, by obeying an order issued by the wrong action, the horse may 'disobey' the rider *through no fault of its own*. This characteristic of subordination in the animal is a valuable asset to the rider, for without it the horse would not respect his well-executed actions either, but act always in accordance with its own will.

Hence, if in the course of giving signals and aids, the rider fails to produce the expected response on the part of the horse, or if he senses any opposition from the animal, he should consider it a warning that he is directing the horse by wrong actions.

The explanation, guidance and expression of the will are most effective when conveyed by words which are supported by perceptible means. In communication with the horse the force of the words can only be depended upon to a very limited extent (see page 90). Therefore it is necessary to express the essence of words by signals and aids.

The rider should accommodate himself in conversation as far as possible to the 'language' of the horse (see page 1). It is necessary in such conversation that the *manner* in which the signals and aids are applied shall be chosen to suit the mentality of the animal. The physical means of application is of secondary importance.

## Basic Features of the Rider's Functions in Conveying His Demands

### THE COUPLED FORM OF INDIVIDUAL ACTIONS

*Each action of the rider must be completed by the immediate relaxation of the engaged muscles.* This means that the rider must cease exercising the physical functions, involved in a given signal or aid, *before* the horse has actually responded to the demands. The execution of the particular task should occur during the yielding phase which completes all the rider's activities. The reason for this is that only during the phase of yielding can the horse react with smoothness to a conveyed demand.

If the first attempt in giving a particular signal fails to produce the reaction desired, it should be repeated in entirety, including the yielding phase, until the horse obeys. During the horse's education the active and yielding phases of the rider's signals will blend more and more together, and eventually the animal will respond almost instantaneously. However, even though the two composing elements of the signal may seem to be fused into one breathing-like function, each phase must remain distinct in the activities of the rider.

The rider should acquire the skill to change over *automatically* to yielding from any exercised action. To achieve this, it is advisable to instruct the pupil right from the early stages of his schooling to perform his signals in their coupled form. Riders who are schooled, but not accustomed to giving signals in this manner, have to concentrate on it at the beginning. In a short time, however, led by the pleasant reaction of the horse, they will soon acquire the feeling necessary to execute the movements involved.

### THE COMBINED APPLICATION OF SEVERAL ACTIONS

*The horse should be directed in each situation in a 'balancing' manner,* and not be 'forced' rigidly by single and long-lasting actions to complete a particular task.

In reality, the rider's actions depend on each other and so in the application of the main actions the supporting elements have always to be present, if only for a matter of seconds, in a warning-like manner; e.g. during a retardment the rider must apply the alternate support of several driving actions and during a drive on the support of several retarding actions is necessary.

In this sense, 'balancing the horse' means that the rider conducts it in each situation by combined functions, like balancing a cane on the tip of a finger. As the cane cannot be kept erect with an absolutely steady hand, so the horse will become upset when the rider tries to direct it by single, passive functions during the completion of a certain task.

As we could see in Part I, already the basic movements of the agents of communication with the horse are executed in the sense of the above consideration (e.g. the retarding signal by interchanged hand actions with their interlocked yielding elements; the lateral moving effect of the hand or leg by breathing-like pressures, etc.).

The execution of the more improved functions and procedures occurs in the same balancing manner. This is described in the following chapters.

The main advantages which result from the application of the balancing conduct of the rider are as follows:

By this means the rider can supply the explanatory words so badly needed during the communication with the horse, but which the animal could not understand. He will really 'aid' his mount, and not only demand something from it, such as the execution of a certain task, the correction of some irregularity, the abandonment of any form of resistance, etc.

The frequent changes involved in the procedure prevent the mental opposition of the animal and the stiffness of both the rider and horse by their general loosening effect.

Their employment has also an indirect advantage to the rider. When he makes an incorrect action during the course of his conducting activities this will not last long, and thus will not press the animal into a stiff opposition. Before this could occur he has already changed it, and immediately the situation is improved.

In acquiring the skill to apply the method here recommended, the rider should carry out the following exercises:

At first perform the basic functions individually in their coupled form.

Then practise interchanging them (one by one) smoothly with one another.

Next vary the diverse functions gradually in series up to a stage when changes can be performed in long and quickly alternating rotation.

These exercises develop the rider's general suppleness. The frequent changes in his muscular functions prevent the rider from becoming stiff. In this way the rider avoids one of the greatest impediments to riding.

Furthermore, these changes combine the various activities of hands, seat, legs flexibly together, and enliven their effect. This vitality ensures that the actions will remain smooth and powerful, no matter whether they are employed with the slightest or with increased energy.

The rider should develop a natural aptitude for this method, and employ it regardless of the form of seat used by him.

If the rider trains the horse conscientiously by means of this balancing conduct, in the course of time it will retain its balanced state automatically. At this stage the animal will react to simple hints if they are applied with the vitality mentioned. Thus

the maintenance or increase of speed and liveliness can be indicated by the legs and thighs;

the renewal of collection, control or correction of the lateral mobility of shoulders, and the adjusted position of the horse by means of the reins;

the shortening of speed by the seat and stirrups;

the stirring of the horse in lateral directions by the transference of the centre of gravity.

This refined sensibility of the horse becomes of paramount importance when performing in competitions.

The effects lost by simplification can be replaced by the creation of increased liveliness in the animal's supple motion and the application of the hints in complete accordance with its actual position.

BASIC CONDITIONS OF THE HORSE'S STATE FOR THE SMOOTH EXECUTION OF ORDERS

Having emphasized the importance of the rider's balancing conduct for *transmitting* his will in a comprehensive manner we will now show the conditions which enable the horse to *receive* orders easily and execute the allotted tasks smoothly. Since this subject plays an important rôle throughout our study, it is necessary to deal with it before commencing further examinations, in spite of the fact that there are some details involved the discussion of which will not occur until later.

## The lateral mobility of the shoulders and steadiness of quarters

The basic condition in the general state of the horse for receiving orders and executing tasks unobstructed is the lateral mobility of its shoulders and the steadiness of its quarters.

They are closely connected with each other, since neither the mobility of shoulders nor the steadiness of quarters can be satisfactory without the other.

The lateral mobility of the forehand denotes the willingness and ability of the horse to make supple movements with the shoulders in both directions from its longitudinal axis.

The steadiness of quarters refers to that condition of the animal in which it *retains* its straight or bent position, both during the motion and in a stationary position, without any forced displacement of the croup.

The chief characteristic of this particular state is that the horse can execute smoothly the *turn on the haunches* movement (see page 212) at any time and in either direction.

Only in the state of pliability described above can the horse be balanced easily on a straight course, led smoothly on a bent line, struck off with determination into canter. Furthermore, it is necessary for the execution of a correct take-off, and at any time when the regularity of the animal has to be restored.

To assist the horse to assume this state and use it instinctively, its schooling for the execution of prompt and smooth lateral movements by the forehand should be carefully carried out. This should be done with the same care as occurs in its improvement for the execution of transitions in longitudinal direction.

In connection with this particular schooling, the rider must know that the horse is inclined to oppose the lateral movement of the forehand by stiffening itself and omitting or withdrawing the participation of the shoulders in the movement (see details in Table 5). In doing so it fixes the forehand, and instead of the desired lateral movement it performs a short turn round the shoulders (perhaps round the centre), i.e. an evasive movement by the quarters.

This form of evasion is a serious defect in the general behaviour of the animal. It can spoil many movements during the course of riding. Therefore the aim of schooling is to free the forehand by the establishment of its lateral mobility and fix the quarters by the forward engagement of the hocks. This can be achieved in the following manner:

First establish the suppleness of the horse in longitudinal direction according to the recommendations described on pages 146 and 160. Then the procedure necessary to achieve the direct object follows.

During this the basic movements concerning the horse's motion and the activities of the rider correspond to those of the turn on the haunches.

Bring the animal to a standstill. Then make some oscillating movements by the forehand while the quarters are fixed. One step in the one direction, and one in the other direction.

If the horse, by showing resistance, gets stuck either at the start or during the exercise, cease operations and make some loosening movements in a longitudinal direction.

Thus, by interchanging several times these two parts of the exercise, the animal will become supple and ready to complete the oscillating side-steps with equal readiness in both directions.

A further improvement is to let the horse make the movements described above while in motion. The performance is correct when the horse reacts to the rider's lateral leading function by striding immediately *out of the shoulders* in the direction indicated. To overcome difficulties interchange the exercise with that in a stationary position

By continued schooling the horse should reach the stage when it reacts under any circumstances to the slightest indication of the rider, such as a slight oscillating movement of his upper body. From this moment onwards the rider is able to direct the animal easily in each situation. At this stage checking the existence of the lateral mobility of shoulders, and even the restoration of this mobility, should be carried out by the levelling function.

CONTACT BETWEEN THE RIDER AND THE HORSE

Contact is a state of relationship between the rider and the horse in which their wills are united and the complementary parts of their bodies brought into touch with each other. Thus it involves a mental as well as a physical element. The former makes communication effective through physical means and by its aid the animal can be guided by simple functions which are hardly noticeable.

In order to establish mental contact, introduce the daily work (after the loosening exercise) by patiently executed alterations in rather quick but smooth rotation. For this purpose the walk, connected with minute halts and short trotting motions, is the most suitable pace. During the procedure emphasize the yielding element of the functions involved and in answer the horse will sooner or later also yield. The mental contact between the partners arises in this moment of their mutual yielding (see also pages 16, 133 and 146).

After having created the mental contact by which the horse's attention is attracted to the rider, its existence should often be checked and its dissolution prevented during the whole course of riding. With this aim employ similar functions as suggested above; they can, however, be executed in an abridged manner on a greatly reduced scale and at any pace. The application of the levelling function is also of great assistance in ensuring the permanent state of this contact.

The same procedure should be employed whenever the reestablishment of the mental contact becomes necessary or before the immediate correction of an irregularity is commenced (see page 146).

The physical contact—that is, the actual touch between the rider and the horse—has to be taken up on those points where the effects of the actions between the two partners are conveyed and received.

The act of establishing and maintaining physical contact must arise from mutual resolution. This mutual resolution is translated into the physical actions of the rider and the horse, resulting in the external form of the contact. If the physical touch is the result of a one-sided resolution, it cannot be called 'contact' in its true sense. For instance, the fact that the rider is sitting on the horse's back, or keeps the bit by pulling on the animal's jaw with the reins, or lays his legs to the horse's sides, does not mean that contact has been established; the rider is merely in touch with certain parts of the horse, not with the whole organism.

The physical contact has to be established and maintained at three particular points: between the rider's hands and the horse's mouth, his legs and its sides, his seat and its back.

THE REIN-CONTACT

This denotes a state in which the horse is in smooth contact with the rider's hands through its mouth (by the bit and reins).

Taking up rein-contact must not be mistaken for the collection of the horse. The animal should keep this contact already before it can be collected, regardless of the shape of its neck-carriage.

The rein-contact has a dual purpose:

it creates the means of mental communication between the two partners and it provides physical help to the animal.

The latter function manifests itself in two forms:

by giving a frontal support to the horse's spring system it promotes the development of the harmonious swinging movement of this system (see page 69); and

by limiting the animal's tendency to extend towards the front it determines the frontal end of the frame according to the measure of collection desired (see page 244).

From the beginning of schooling a considerable part of the communication has to be conveyed by the use of the reins in one way or another. Therefore, it would be desirable to acquaint the novice horse with the creation of the rein-contact during the first days of its training. Unfortunately, this is not practicable due to the difficulty of the process, and therefore taking up rein-contact must be taught gradually in combination with other types of work.

The rider's first job is to educate the horse so that it should take up the contact willingly; later on it will seek it instinctively with complete confidence as soon as it has been offered by getting in touch with its mouth. It must feel genuine assistance from this touch, since only such an understanding will produce the true state of contact.

The animal's confidence can only be won if contact does not cause it any inconvenience. Therefore, the rider must be able to keep the bit in easy and uninterrupted touch with the mouth, i.e. to 'balance' it on the jaw smoothly following the natural movements produced by the horse's locomotion. The rider who has acquired this skill will never joggle or jerk with the reins, but will handle them with a refined mobility. Exercises producing lightness (see page 13) are also means of improving this particular skill. Furthermore, it is very useful, while keeping contact with the horse's mouth, to make often broad but smoothly swinging gesticulating movements with the hands and arms. In doing so, attention should be concentrated on the maintenance of the established contact. These rounded-off movements, by their inherent smoothness, automatically relax the tension of the hands and arms which can easily become stiff and joggle in a fixed position. Later on, by decreasing gradually the magnitude of the movements, the rider will have no difficulties in 'balancing' the bit also with 'steady' hands on the jaw, without interrupting the continuity of the light rein-contact.

In order to exercise a control over the bit while it keeps contact, it is necessary to find the length of rein which is best suited to the length of the horse's neck in its natural bearing (see page 249).

In principle, this length of reins should be taken up as soon as the animal has become accustomed to having the bit in its mouth. At the beginning, however, it is often necessary to allow the horse a relaxation and reward it by dropping the reins. Merely lengthening is not enough, since it does not afford complete relaxation.

Teaching should be carried out in the following order:
while in the stationary position or in the walk take up the appropriate length of rein with the bit kept smoothly in touch with the horse's mouth so that the reins neither wobble nor pull; then
start off at a trot of moderate speed (the trot being the most suitable pace for this purpose) and pliantly follow the horse's mouth with the hands;
during the motion drive the animal forward with determination and show it the way to find the bit by *stretching the neck*

*forward and downwards.* If the bit does not cause any discomfort, the horse will soon start leaning on it.

As soon as this occurs cease your own effort to promote the contact and simply hold the reins, leaving it to the horse to maintain the touch that has been established. While trying to develop this aptitude in the animal, the rider should not interfere with its mouth by the activity of his hands. That is why, at this very early stage of schooling, it is advisable to practise retardments as rarely as possible.

After four or five weeks, when the novice has developed the habit of keeping a firm contact, practice of retardment actions can be gradually increased. At the same time an effort should be made to make the horse more and more aware of other signals and aids, and the application of basic regulating movements commenced.

In determining the strength of the rein-contact the decisive factors at this stage of the horse's education are the speed, the magnitude of the movements employed in the motion, and the extent of their swing. The higher the horse's education and the slower the speed, the lighter should be the pressure of contact. This indicates, at the same time, that the smaller the rhythmical movements in the motion, and the less muscular work required from the horse (because it will be supplied by the swing itself), the lighter the contact. However, in extended speeds or in jumping, when the movements and muscular exertion involved are greatly increased, the strength of the contact can be augmented, provided that the lightness* of the horse is assured.

To permit a stronger contact does not mean that the animal can fall on the bit, for such a position causes stiffness and this must be avoided by all means.

The slackening action of the reins (i.e. a sudden and pronounced giving movement) can be of great assistance in ensuring easiness. It is a form of action between a simple yielding and a complete loosening of the reins. Simultaneously with the slackening action, the horse should be driven forward (if necessary with the added

---

*The 'lightness' of the horse means the degree of willingness and readiness by which it carries out its tasks.

'Easiness' is the yard-stick of the strength which is produced by the rider or the horse in maintaining contact. What is light is not necessarily easy, and easiness without lightness is of no value in riding.

stimulus of a tap of the whip), and then contact with the mouth should be taken up again.

The less experienced the horse, or the stiffer its resistance, the more substantial must be the slackening movement of the hands, and the more often it has to be repeated. This is far more effective in 'breaking' the animal's resistance than pulling or stiff bracing actions which try to make the horse yield by sheer force.

As the animal becomes more sensitive the broad movements of the hands can be reduced until the slackening action becomes simply a sudden relaxation of the hand and arm muscles.

The slackening action should be used frequently to show affection for the horse; as a form of reward; or to emphasize the sense of the yielding function. Even the best schooled horse sometimes needs this momentary relaxation of the contact, which makes the rider's subsequent actions more vivid and ensures smoothness in their execution. Thus the usefulness of the slackening actions should always be borne in mind. They bring ease to the maintenance and—even though it may seem paradoxical—continuity of the contact.

We now wish to call attention to some further questions which are in one way or another connected with the subject of rein-contact. These are: the correct length of reins in keeping contact; the three main faults which cause difficulty in keeping the rein-contact; and the flexed position of the horse's head.

### The correct length of the reins in keeping contact

A reliable method for ascertaining the right length of reins is to bring the hands well forward in front of the upper body (see page 53) and by accommodating oneself to the *actual carriage* of the horse's neck shorten the reins so that they are almost tight.

At this length the reins can at any time be immediately employed with equal certainty in transmitting the slightest and more augmented effects.

In this position the hands can easily follow the horse's mouth, or exercise their passive function (see page 62) when the animal tries to pull the reins out of them.

The length of the reins which the rider adjusts to the natural (i.e. longest) neck-carriage of a young horse can be considered the longest one that is ever used in general practice. As the schooling proceeds and the horse's neck tends to become increasingly arched and held higher, the length of the reins should be correspondingly shortened.

There are certain circumstances in which the animal has to stretch its neck considerably in order to carry out a certain task (e.g. jumping, extension of paces, ascending slopes, etc.). This stretching movement of the neck has to be facilitated by following with the hands and arms, and *not* by lengthening the reins. The fact that it allows for this free movement of the hands and arms is one of the main reasons for the present form of the jumping seat.

THE MAIN FAULTS IN KEEPING REIN-CONTACT AND THE METHODS OF CORRECTION

There are three main faults in keeping rein-contact, such as

when the horse, by over-bending its neck and head, discontacts itself from the bit in a backward direction: it comes behind the reins (bit);

by throwing up its head it destroys contact in an upward direction: it gets over the bit; and

when opposing the contact by stretching or pushing the head and neck in a forward direction: the animal pulls or pushes against the hands.

In spite of the difference in the manifestations of the horses' resistance and in the manner in which it tries to escape from the influence of the rider, the method of curing the faults is similar in essence. This is so because in each case the irregularity is produced mainly by the horse's mental opposition, which must be overcome first of all.

To overcome opposition the best method is the repetition of *smooth* loosening functions with their dominating element of yielding. The application of energetic actions has only a very limited rôle. Consequently, the rider should not hesitate in the present case to repeat his functions, without increasing their strength, if necessary in long series.

The main reasons for the animal's opposition are that the rider uses his hands either simultaneously or more than necessary, without the inclusion of moments of yielding. He does not keep a smooth permanent contact, thus the bit alternately jerks on the mouth and loses contact with it;

he fixes his weight stiffly on the animal's back (either through the seat or the stirrups); and

fails to apply the support of his legs in driving the hocks under the body and ensuring the horse's liveliness.

Thus, in curing the defects the first step to be taken is the correction of the rider's faulty conduct.

In more acute cases, to amend the situation, in addition to this general measure, the following recommendations are suggested:

### If the horse is behind the reins

The essence of the correction is the drive-on by which the horse is urged forward *to the bit*. It is wrong to follow the animal's evasive movement by pulling the reins back, a very common fault of ignorant riders.

The procedure may be carried out in the following order:

At first drive the horse energetically forward while easing the reins in a slightly exaggerated manner. Then, in order to check the animal, make a half-halt (see page 133). If it resists, by over-bending its neck, stop instantly the retardment and drive it forward again. From this renewed onward urge repeat the half-halt and during its drive-on phase emphasize the 'pushing feeling' in holding the reins.

Repeat smoothly but with determination the procedure in a balancing manner until the horse, by giving up its opposition, keeps continuously a soft contact on the bit.

Thus, the rider's successive functions are: drive-on in relaxation . . . interchanged taking action . . . quick yielding plus expressed 'pushing' . . . drive-on . . . taking . . . yielding plus 'pushing', etc.

Incorporate into the procedure the levelling function.

### If the horse gets over the bit

Establish at first a smooth continuous contact, holding the reins with a 'pushing feeling'.

Relax the horse's opposition by the same loosening procedure as described in the former case. During this, however, change over with the hands into a *short* passive tension (see page 62), terminating in quick relaxation at the moment the horse by tossing up its head tries to pull the reins out of the hands.

The effect of the passive tension reminds the animal, by direct sensation in the mouth, to keep its head still, and the immediate relaxation of the tension encourages it to abandon its mental opposition. Without the general loosening procedure and the quick relaxation the application of the passive tension is both useless and harmful.

As a preventive measure it is advisable to employ the oscillating movements of the levelling function with its smooth *interchanged* rein-pressures on the mouth and with the leg-pressures on the horse's side.

Horses are more inclined to throw their heads about during the performance of transitions. Therefore, it is an advantage to introduce and underline them by the soothing and loosening movements of the levelling function. The slight changes exercised during the function divert the animal's opposition by their relaxing effect and keep the head steady.

As a supplementary means to this procedure, applied mainly in the early stages of schooling, it is of advantage to combine the functions of passive tension involved with one or more short but determined touches on the neck. This can be applied at the moment when the horse is tossing up its head and neck.

The touches should be exercised in a pushing-like manner, alternately in quick succession, by the clenched fists and be directed in front of the withers on the mane.

Since this immediate warning does not cause any discomfort to the horse, but produces a pleasant relaxing effect on the stiffened neck, the animal will soon realize its purpose. As the action is coupled with the essential part of the procedure, it helps the horse to identify its meaning (of the procedure). Thus, later on the animal will obey the rider smoothly without the application of this supplementary aid.

The execution of the action also benefits the rider. It prevents him automatically, by the inherent forward directed hand movement, from making attempts to correct the irregularity by pulling the reins.

The relaxation of the neck muscles can be promoted also by playing with the fingers on the withers, or striking over the mane from time to time during the procedure (see page 61).

*If the horse pulls or pushes against the hands (bit)*
Frequently the horse expresses its resistance by **pushing against**

the bit. This action of the animal is also the cause of many other difficulties which the rider encounters during his daily work.

Most horses are inclined to exercise from time to time a pushing action against the bit with *slight or moderate intensity*. This kind of opposition can occur—according to the animal's disposition— even after its advanced schooling.

There are, however, horses, mostly spoilt or uneducated, which show their increased resistance by *pushing hard* against the bit.

In both cases there are two characteristics of the irregularity, namely, when the pushing action is connected only with stiffness of muscles extending to the spring system; or when it (the pushing action) is aggravated by the increase of speed.

The slight or moderate pushing action is connected mostly with some kind of stiffness, without increasing the speed. This, in cases of improper treatment, results in nervous fidgeting or even rearing.

The hard pushing action is usually accompanied by an increase of speed. This, when treated incorrectly, can result in extreme cases in causing the horse to run away.

In either case the essence of correction (within the general recommendations given in the introductory part of the present paragraph) is the employment of *yielding* during the execution of the rider's actions.

By the yielding of the rider the hardest 'puller' becomes soft, while rigidity agitates the kindest of animals. The finer the horse and the stiffer the rider, the harder the resistance, giving the misleading impression of 'hardness' of the mouth.

A further common feature of these irregularities is that the distribution of the animal's weight is shifted to the forehand. The more its balance position is upset, the more the horse tends to push against the bit and lean on the hands of the rider, seeking a 'fifth leg' in order to safeguard its balance and prevent it toppling over on its nose. Therefore, during the process of correction, regulation of this particular defect should be included (see page 162).

The theoretical background of the procedure, the knowledge of which is necessary for its sensitive performance, is as follows.

The opposition of the horse produces stiffness, which spreads over its entire spring system. This becomes stretched and breaks its supporting frame by pushing away the bit in front, and by lagging behind with the hocks in the rear. In this posture the back cannot take up its swinging movement, the horse reacts negatively to seat and rein functions (see Fig. No. 43/a) and ignores the leg signals.

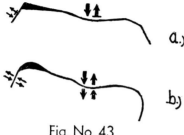

Fig. No. 43

On the other hand, when the horse is in submission, its spring system remains within the limits of its frame, and when it is in motion the flexibly spanned system is brought into an easy swinging movement. The animal smoothly absorbs the functions of the rider as conveyed by the various means of communication (see Fig. No. 43/b).

The rider's first task in correcting the irregularity is to cultivate the feeling by which he can recognize the horse's state of pliability, i.e. the appearance as well as the disappearance of the horse's opposition (see page 143). Then he should gradually improve his skill in carrying out the motional part of the regulation.

The performance of the corrective measures in question requires skilful horsemanship, since during their execution feeling and determination, energy and refinement must be co-ordinated harmoniously with one another.

It should be still mentioned that the pushing action of the horse must not be mistaken for stretching its neck and head after the bit when the rider lengthens the reins (at jumping, travelling at speed, proceeding on steep slopes, etc.). The rider should even promote this tendency of the animal by acting always in a 'forward' and never in a 'backward' sense.

Bearing in mind these general points, we shall proceed to examine the horse's defective pushing action according to its main variations, together with the remedy.

*Slight or moderate pushing (pulling) action against the bit*

The horse expresses this form of opposition usually in slower paces. While doing so it pushes itself with unengaged quarters during the motion instead of stepping freely forward.

The remedy for this irregularity is in the combined application of drive-on and retardment (see page 129) or half-halts, executed in a balancing manner and involving moments of passive tension.

During this procedure the successive activities of the rider and the ensuing reactions of the horse follow the order below

The horse: proceeds at the walk (or trot), showing the symptoms of a moderate resistance.

The rider: drives the animal forward determinedly (legs, tap of the whip, thighs) and completes his actions by a sudden yielding movement of the hands.

The horse: because of its resistance does not stride out, but pushes the neck and head against the bit.

The rider: immediately following his sudden yielding, drives the horse forward again by a quick, firm action in order to collect its hind legs under the body. This important motion can be best achieved by one or several taps of the whip applied behind his leg; immediately after this action he changes the bearing of his hands and seat by a sudden motion into passive tension in order to forestall the pushing action of the horse's neck and head.

The horse: still ignores the rider's activity and, instead of striding forward, repeats its pushing movement. This time, however, the push cannot become effective because the horse's mouth is bound by the bit, which is firmly fixed by the passive tension of the rider's hands.

The rider: after counteracting the pushing action of the horse, changes from his passive attitude to a renewal of the yielding function of the hands and seat.

He then repeats the series of actions described above in quick rotation until the animal abandons its resistance, and, accepting the frame determined by the rider, strides off without trying to push against the bit.

Thus the sequence of movements is as follows: drive-on . . . sudden yielding . . . quick drive-on . . . passive tension terminating in a sudden yielding . . . quick drive-on, etc.

The procedure is similar when the horse, simultaneously with its moderate pushing action, increases the speed slightly. In this case more emphasis should be given to the pressure of the seat or to that on the stirrups during the phase of passive tension.

If the tendency to increase speed is augmented, apply the method recommended for the correction of the next variation of the defect.

*The horse's hard pushing action against the bit*

This form of irregularity can appear either when the horse is in a loose state or when it is under the rider's control.

In the first case the animal drops its head near the ground in an attempt to reach the unsupported bit and push it away. When the rider tries to bring the horse under control it makes repeated pushing movements, mainly downwards to the ground, with its head and neck.

In the second case the horse exercises the same kind of pushing actions as in its free state, but it acts immediately against the bit by them. The strength of these pushes is usually fairly moderate in the beginning, but they become stronger when the animal is required to fulfil a demand.

This particular irregularity can become the source of great difficulties and therefore we should deal with its correction with adequate care.

*Correction of the horse's hard pushing action when it is not aggravated by the animal's tendency to increase speed*

*Method of correction if there is no malice in the horse's behaviour*

The procedure is similar to that discussed in connection with the former version of the defect except for the following:

Complete without delay each function of passive tension by a half-halt, terminating in a sudden yielding. Within this

the performance of the passive tension should be restricted to a very short time;

the execution of the likewise short half-halt should be demanded by energetic functions; and

the succeeding drive-on must be effected by substantial animation.

In the course of this procedure the pushing action of the horse is counteracted by the short but firm action of enforced passive tension. This produces a mild jerk on the horse's mouth and a slight bump on its back, and is consequently slightly punitive. Relaxation is achieved during the yielding and drive-on functions of the rider. Therefore, while changing over from retardment to drive-on during the half-halt, the rider must take special care that these actions do not coincide, in spite of the rapidity with which the change is made. Failing this, the horse will increase its resistance instead of becoming supple.

The series of actions can be summed up as follows: drive-on . . . sudden yielding . . . quick drive-on . . . minute passive tension coupled with a half-halt and terminating in a sudden yielding . . . quick drive-on, etc.

*Method of correction in the case of the horse's malicious behaviour*

The correct execution of this procedure calls for a great deal of horsemanship. Therefore an inexperienced rider should not practise it.

The characteristic element in this procedure is a quick warning and a simultaneous punitive action in the form of a jerk with the reins against the hard pushing action of the horse. This function can be carried out either in combination with the passive tension of the last but one case, or with the half-halt of the former version.

The effect produced by this jerk on the front part of the spring system is similar to that produced by the tap of the whip on the back part of this system. The effect of both actions is to quicken the horse's movements. The pain inflicted (as a means of punishment) is of secondary importance.

In order to intensify the effect of the function, it is better (just as in the case of the whip) to repeat the slight jerk rather than to increase its strength.

In its whole this is a very delicate operation to execute, in which the basic requirement is that the rider should be able to conceal his 'roughness' with refined feeling.

The order of the entire procedure is: drive-on . . . sudden yielding . . . quick drive-on . . . passive tension (or possibly a half-halt) enforced by the jerking function . . . sudden yielding . . . quick drive-on, etc.

If the application of this procedure becomes necessary, which is very seldom, it is desirable to execute it at a walk connected with half-halts. With sufficient practice, however, it is possible to make the alterations between a slow trot and walk.

Before resorting to this very delicate procedure, the rider should spend a *long time educating* the animal by means of the milder form of correction. He should make use of it only after a thorough consideration of the case.

*Correction of the horse's hard pushing action when it is aggravated by the animal's tendency to increase speed*

*Slowing down and controlling the rushing horse*

The horse's state and the sensations produced by it are in many respects similar to those described above. The situation, however, is aggravated by the horse's desire to increase speed, which can produce a feeling of helplessness in the inexperienced rider.

The secret of the success in mastering the situation lies in the rider's absolute *confidence* in his knowledge and in the effectiveness of his actions, regardless of the *immediate* reactions of the horse.

The application of sheer force is useless, since the 'power' of controlling the rushing horse is in the latent yielding functions which complete the actions. Thus the rider must *dare* to yield, instead of pulling toughly on the reins when the horse tries to run away with him. The uselessness of sheer force can be best demonstrated by the fact that a rider of moderate strength, but possessing the necessary feeling, can easily control horses which run away with much stronger riders who lack the necessary understanding.

Bearing this in mind, prior to the description of the method of correction, let us see how the rider can acquire his self-confidence and feeling in order to carry out the task.

Ride on a quiet horse—beginning with a walk and then up to a gallop. During these exercises make a series of retardments interlocked with drive-on phases. *Observe* the reactions of the horse to the functions involved. You will experience a slowing down tendency in the horse's bearing, setting in always during the yielding phase of the retardment employed. This is the first indication of getting into the desired feeling.

Repeat the same exercises and observations on a horse apt to push against the bit, but without intending to run away.

Next extend the observations while sitting on a horse of higher spirits and riding it at a gallop.

Finally, test yourself and your knowledge while riding one inclined to rush. Do this at first under quiet conditions and later on in more exciting circumstances.

By means of these gradually built-up exercises the confidence of the rider and his skill in controlling rushing horses will improve rapidly and the former difficulty will soon disappear.

We now can proceed to examine the details of the process of

correction following the rider's successive activities and the horse's ensuing reactions.

The horse: its forehand is heavily overloaded, pushes obstinately against the bit and increases the speed.

The rider: after the employment of a brief passive tension, looses the reins suddenly by a substantial yielding movement and drives the horse forward in order to get its hocks more under the body.

The horse: as a consequence of this sudden action, loses its false balance and its resistance becomes slightly undermined.

In response to the driving signal it strides more under the body, but at the same time it tries to restore its balance position by increasing the speed.

The rider: making good use of the weakness thus produced, gives a definite retarding signal, terminating in quick and substantial yielding.

The horse: does not show any noticeable inclination to slow down; it may even increase the speed, but subconsciously collects its hocks more and more under the body.

The rider: is not worried because of the apparent failure of his effort, but continues to repeat his functions with their dominating yielding element and without increasing the strength employed during the active phases of the retardments.

The horse: after a few repetitions of the rider's actions, suddenly changes its behaviour during the *yielding phase* of one of the involved retardments and starts slowing down.

The rider: is overtaken by an overwhelming feeling of superiority and his feeling of helplessness disappears on account of the sudden change experienced in the horse's behaviour, even if this change is for the time being only a small one.

He continues to repeat his functions.

The horse: its state of balance becomes adjusted and by decreasing its opposition shows willingness to submit itself to the authority of the rider.

It may still show a tendency to rush, but this can easily be checked by the rider.

The rider: reminds the animal from time to time by the same functions as he used before on the maintenance of its supple state. By this means he prevents the horse from renewing its opposition.

During the whole procedure described above it is very desirable to include in the various activities of the rider the levelling function with its manifold changes. The application of the inter-changed stirrup and thigh pressures in accordance with the retard-ing and driving (yielding) functions is extremely effective.

In the course of curing this bad habit in the animal it may be necessary in the early stages for the rider to execute in a more impressive manner the retarding element of the procedure. This can be reached by the application of firmer, but not longer, pulling effects. On such occasions, however, as more stress is put upon the retardment, the quicker and more substantial must be the yielding element in which the pulling actions terminate.

In cases of spoilt horses the process of persuasion calls for certain instructive exercises necessary until the animal realizes the intention of the rider. This period will not last long, since the 'new' method—in contrast with the constant hard pulling to which the horse was accustomed—will not cause pain or make him frightened. It leads the animal to adopt a much more comfortable and less strenuous situation. The horse, by its instinctive liking for comfort, quickly realizes the advantages of accommodating itself to the rider and responds with pleasure.

During these exercises accustom the horse gradually to using a high speed interchanged by slowing down phases. In this manner it will adopt the fast motion under soothing circumstances and become fond of it. As a result, the excitement caused by the speed will disappear and the rider will be able to check the animal at any time. This will affect its general attitude and ease the task of the rider.

In order to speed up the process the first exercises should be carried out quietly, preferably alone.

Later on expose the animal *gradually* to more and more exciting circumstances by riding it in company with other horses, up to the stage where the difficulty has started. When the rider retains his calmness and determination the animal will react soon and willingly also under the most 'exciting' conditions, such as hunting or racing.

*Flexed position of the horse's head*

The above term denotes the lateral position of the head-carriage in relation to the neck. This flexion, in one form or another, is a prerequisite of almost every riding activity. It is not necessarily connected with the bending of the neck or spine, but can be combined with them.

The procedure of flexing can be performed either from a straight position into a lateral one, or vice versa.*

In a straight position ('flexed' to the straight position) the horse's head and glance are directed forward and the rider cannot see either eye. In keeping the horse's head in this position, the reins must be in equal contact with the mouth on both sides.

The characteristic feature of the lateral flexion of the head is that the horse, even though it may be holding its neck straight, turns its head slightly sideways. Its glance is set in the direction of flexion and the rider is just about to see the eye which is on the side corresponding to the direction of the flexion (a stronger flexion is considered incorrect).

In order to move the horse's head into a lateral position, the rein on the side of the flexion desired should warn the animal by a slight pull to turn its head and to keep it in the desired posture. If necessary, this warning action can be repeated several times, but each action must be completed by a yielding phase.

If a horse is bent, the head must always be flexed in the direction of the bending, and any other head position is faulty. The purpose. of this head position is to emphasize the bending and to complete it in its forward direction. Furthermore, the process of flexion greatly facilitates the bending of the horse, since the turning of its glance in the desired direction automatically sets up the direction of its bending.

THE LEG-CONTACT

The leg-contact denotes the connection between the rider and the horse, in which the rider's legs and the horse's sides join each other effectively.

This form of contact is automatically achieved by the establishment of the animal's cadenced, supple and collected motion. Thus it accompanies that physical state in which the horse performs its motion, and is by no means an abstract matter. As soon as the animal starts to move in the manner indicated above the rider

---

*Directing the horse into the straight position should not be confused with adjustment to the straight position, as the first is the process of directing the animal from one correct into another correct position, whereas the second is to change an incorrect position into a correct one.

can feel its body attracted to his own like a magnet, and simultaneously it presses its sides to his legs. This pressure is distinctly felt on the inside of the upper part of the calves, clearly indicating the moment when the horse has taken up the contact offered by the legs.

From this instant the application of firm or articulated leg actions becomes unnecessary! It is a wonderful sensation for the rider who, from now on, can direct his horse by refined actions; indeed, even by his thoughts. The animal reacts immediately to the pressure of the calves by striding forward, whether the pressure is applied simply to animate the horse or to produce take-off impulsion. On the other hand, if the rider applies a mild pressure a bit longer, the horse reacts smoothly by performing the desired lateral movement.

Indeed, the horse is stepping 'with the rider's legs'.

### THE SEAT-CONTACT

The seat-contact refers to the connection between the rider's seat and the horse's back when unified in motion, action and feeling.

This form of contact evolves in a manner rather similar to that of the leg-contact and also accompanies the physical state of the animal's motion. Thus it can be said that both of them arise simultaneously.

The rider, whether he is using the sitting posture or the forward position, desires to sink deeply into the saddle, whereas the horse tries to cling to the rider's seat with its back.

From this moment of contact the sensation which overcomes the rider is that he is stepping in the locomotion through the horse's back with his own legs, while the animal reacts smoothly to any action of the seat. At the same time, the reins become of secondary importance as a means of regulating the speed.

In order to acquire the sensation and to master the skill of the seat-contact it is necessary first of all for the rider to be able to counter-balance any possible jolt or jerk which might upset its unbroken continuity. For this reason the following exercise should be practised, which is also useful for developing the rider's sense of balance.

Sit, without the use of stirrups, preferably on a calm horse, taken on the lungening-rein.

While riding, first at a walk and later on at a trot, lean backwards with the upper body at about 45 degrees, or even more, from the vertical position. Then, with the thighs held away from the horse's sides, the knees are raised up to the height of the withers (or even higher), leaving the legs, moderately bent from the knees, hanging downwards.

In this position the rider's entire weight rests on the animal's back through his seat-bone. In order to avoid falling off the horse and to maintain his position, the rider is constantly compelled to perform certain balancing movements, which are useful in improving the sensation and skill in question.

During the exercise, when the rider no longer has difficulty in safeguarding his balance, he should try to appreciate and memorize the sensation which is conveyed by the continuous close contact with the horse's back, and which radiates from the animal in motion while it virtually 'carries' him on its back. This is the same sensation by which the seat-contact must be maintained, and which enables the rider to influence the horse during the various operations of riding.

The special sensation by which the rider 'keeps' his seat on the animal's back while in forward position can be discovered by practising the following exercise:

When riding in a rising trot cancel the rising movements at one of the moments when the seat and the saddle are touching and retain the upper body in its leaning-forward position.

In this particular posture the seat-bone rests on the rear third-part of the saddle and is exceptionally sensitive to the push-strokes. In order to prevent the push-strokes dislodging the seat from its position, the rider should counteract them by gently pressing down the thighs.

Ride for a time in this posture and note the sensation which the seat-bone and the maintenance of the contact with the back convey, especially during the moments of the push-strokes.

In summarizing this chapter, it can be said that by the establishment of the triple-contact the rider enables the horse to exploit its abilities to the full, since it becomes collectible and consequently submissive in carrying out immediately his most arduous demands.

This is the ideal state, in which the horse is really kept between the legs and the hands and under the seat, and is by its whole attitude 'in front' of the rider.

Whoever can promote this ideal triple-contact with the animal adds wings to its motion. This is equally true in every branch of horsemanship, in dressage, jumping, racing, etc., and therefore it is of very great significance.

At this improved stage of education the horse almost resists hard and heavy actions of a rider, and perhaps this is the reason why a non-compliant rider cannot get along with a well-schooled horse.

# CHAPTER TWO

# Stirring the Motion of the Horse

THE object of this chapter is to deal with the problem of producing or ceasing the locomotion of the horse according to the rider's intention and to discuss what should be done when the rider wishes to exert some effect on the continuation or alteration of the stride actions he has produced.

We shall commence by describing the general features of transitions, since their correct execution provides the basis of all stirring functions of the rider and of the movements performed by the horse.

## TRANSITIONS AND ALTERATIONS IN GENERAL

The term 'transition' denotes a change in the extension of a particular pace, and 'alteration' means the change from one pace to another.

The start as well as the halt, and the extension as well as the reduction of motion (whether within a certain pace or during the change from one pace to another), must be accomplished by the horse in a lively manner, with definite but relaxed movements, which must not be vague or timid, and without hesitation. This quality of the horse's action also endows the change with smoothness being, apart from clarity and precision, the main demand for its correct execution.

In order to preserve the necessary mobility and suppleness of the horse, the rider has to 'shake it over' into the new motion or motionless state. This means that the main signals, which indicate the execution of the desired change, should always be blended by the levelling function, i.e. by manifold slight changes in the rider's position and muscular functions (seat, leg, stirrup and rein pressures). As a result of such conduct the animal will 'tread' into the changed motion, which is the issue of further correct performances. Therefore:

the extension of speed or pace must not be attempted by a continuous or more augmented driving, which results in the horse gradually 'pushing' itself into the increased motion and rolling away;

reduction of speed or pace must not be enforced by a continuous pulling-back, which arouses resistance and delay or causes the animal to lose its mobility and to 'fall' abruptly into the new motion required of it.

Thus the smoothness of the change cannot be compared with that of a train which is rolling on wheels. The horse must never 'roll', but it must remain distinctly pacing during the completion of the change.

In event of great differences between the used and the desired new motion and speed, it is possible that the horse will not be able to change over immediately. In such cases it is advisable to insert two or three intermediate (part-) changes, since this makes it more practical for the animal to perform the total change in a distinct and regulated manner. The part-changes should follow each other in quick succession, but each one must always retain its individual character.

With regard to exercising signals and aids, it should be noted that, especially at the beginning of schooling, they require a longer time at a higher speed than at a slower one. This means that they must be applied more *frequently* at a faster than at a slower form of locomotion. At the same time, it is not necessary to augment the strength of the signals employed.

A further consideration which has an important bearing on the performance of transitions and alterations is that the horse can only perform them elastically when—besides active quarters—its shoulder mobility, equally in longitudinal and lateral directions, is unobstructed. Therefore, this condition must always be maintained. Check, renew it, and prevent its abandonment by frequent applications of the oscillating upper body movements, accompanied with the smooth, interchanged leg and rein pressures involved in the levelling function.

The rider can easily prove whether the transition (or alteration) is correctly performed by the horse, since it produces during their most important *starting phase* a typical sensation in the rider.

During the transition into increased motion the rider has the impression that the horse suddenly 'steps out' from behind his seat in a forward direction. The animal produces this sensation by a pleasant jiggling movement.

During the transition into a slower motion (retardment) the sensation is as if the animal would pull back its body from the front with a short, jerking movement under the seat of the rider.

Each procedure connected with the change of the horse's speed and pace is carried out by certain combinations of drive-on and retarding actions. We shall now examine these activities, at first separately, and then extend the examination to their combined application.

### THE DRIVE-ON PROCEDURE

The force behind every drive-on is the rider's own impetus, his determination to strive forward. If he is able to convey his unswerving will to the animal by using the proper means of communication, he will also transfer his own forward impulsion to the horse and promote its 'forward-obedience'. This forward-obedience should be one of the principal goals which the rider endeavours to achieve!

The horse can strike-off best if it receives the command at a moment when its spring system is in a 'cocked' (collected) state. Thus, in order to drive the animal forward at first, urge it on (preliminary drive-on, to make the hocks tread under the body), then

> retard it out of this forward striding movement (cocking the spring system, i.e. collection), and

> at the moment of the horse's yielding complete the procedure by giving the effective drive-on signal for the execution of the forward motion desired.

In this way the spring system filled with energy provides the horse with the increased power required for a correct strike-off.

The driving part of this procedure is also a combination of activities, the elements of which are the actual drive-on and checking function of the rider. They operate in the following manner:

> give the drive-on signal by determined touches of the legs (depending upon the pace which is being used); simultaneously

> transfer the weight from the seat-bone (stirrups) to the thighs, and exercise with them a slight pressure on the animal's muscles around the withers. It is necessary to draw special attention to the condition that, during this phase of the

drive-on, the rider should not exercise pressure by the seat-bone or the stirrups on the horse's back. Riders, in their effort to succeed, may easily commit such faults which, by the counteracting effect produced, will confuse and upset the animal and rouse its opposition. *After* the drive-on signal alternate mild pressure of the thighs with a pressure of the seat-bone (stirrups) in order to exercise control over the horse's entire spring system.

The hands should contribute to the effect produced by the legs and seat by yielding, with the feeling of pushing the horse forward into the motion. While the seat is exercising its control function the hands may go over for a moment into passive tension, checking the animal's suppleness through the bit.

These activities should be repeated during the forward driving process until the horse is practically *swung* into the increased motion. This feature of the drive-on is of the utmost importance, since it endows the performance with smoothness, thus enabling the horse to obey in a supple and submissive manner and to carry out the forward movement with determination.

The dimensions of the functions involved should gradually be reduced as the horse shows improvement, but the procedure as a whole should always retain its original character.

For instance, when the horse has learned to take up the leg- and seat-contact, it is sufficient to replace the driving function by breathing-like pressures of the calves and knees and the checking function by a short passive tension performed by the seat and hands. Later on, when the final schooling has been completed, the rider should be able to produce the effect desired by exercising a mild giving action with his hands simultaneously with a slight pressure of the thighs.

Some horses, at the beginning of schooling, tend to be so timid with regard to the use of the legs that even a slight touch frightens and excites them. The rider can help such a horse to overcome this feeling of fright in a short time, without any particular interference, by keeping his legs calmly on the animal's sides.

In some cases this acceptance of the legs may be followed after a while by a certain degree of apathy, which is due to the fact that the horse has become accustomed to the presence of the legs.

In other cases the young horse feels no aversion towards the legs from the very beginning, and so its apathy, which in the former case was due to habit, is natural.

In any case, sooner or later every horse reaches the stage where its sensitivity in accepting and obeying leg signals must be developed.

The rider must not try to increase the animal's sensitivity by augmenting the strength of the knocks of his legs, as this will only result in a deeper apathy. But if mild touches of the legs are accompanied by a *flick of the whip*, the horse will realize more and more clearly the meaning of the leg signals in relation to the rider's actual intention. The moment the animal recognizes the leg effects as virtual signals its apathy toward them will cease. From this period onwards the strength of the leg effects can be gradually decreased without danger of a relapse in the horse's standard of obedience.

Obedience to the drive-on signal can be considerably improved by the reassuring tone of the rider's voice. In fact, it is often beneficial to make use of the voice, since its softness tends to give more ease and lightness to the movements of the horse.

In cases where the horse is too insensitive or inattentive to refined drive-on signals, the rider should not hesitate to apply an energetic 'shake-up' (a sudden animation by the legs or whip), even if it results in a momentary loss of regularity. But this firm 'shaking-up' should not be confused with a nervous roughness arising from impatience. It is an auxiliary measure only.

The 'shaking-up' should be carried out by a few biting flips of the whip on the horse's side in quick succession, with a strength suitable to its sensitivity, while allowing it complete freedom with the reins and letting it 'jump' a few strides forward.

### THE RETARDING PROCEDURE

In order to point out the special significance of the rider's and the horse's refined improvement in giving and receiving correctly the orders for the retardment, which is the key to the easy performance of any task during the course of riding, I may introduce the present paragraph by the following slogan:

Make the horse receive the retarding signal with pleasure, resulting in the smooth and quick change in its motion. Refine patiently its willingness to assume the signal until it is instantly accepted by its mind and does not arouse opposition against the physical actions employed.

Retardment is one of the most ticklish procedures in riding, since if wrongly applied it may easily confuse the horse or inflict unnecessary pain, provoking its stiff resistance.   It should be regarded, in contrast to one-sided pulling actions, as a combined procedure with interlocked yielding and driving phases.

Therefore, before administering the retarding signal, first drive on the horse and then give the direct indication for the reduction of the motion by the combined use of the reins, seat (stirrups) and legs.   Within this

the reins perform their yielding combined with taking actions; the seat or stirrups exercise pressure on the horse's back; and the legs convey alternately short pressing effects on the sides of the horse.

When the left rein pulls, the left leg acts, and vice versa.   In practice, this function of the legs supplements *very effectively* the retardment and greatly facilitates its execution.

Each of the activities described above should be completed by a moment of yielding.   Thus pressure by the seat-bone or stirrups should be changed to that of the thighs, while the rider simultaneously yields with the hands and eases with his legs.   This yielding attitude of the rider is followed by a brief driving phase, after which the whole procedure should be repeated several times.

When the horse receives the signals for retardment it will respond to them slowly or quickly, according to the stage of its education, and while reconciling them with the task imposed, it will decide to obey.   Its acceptance of the retardment function can be distinctly felt by the reins and the seat.   While the horse is still in the rhythm of its original motion the rider will notice a *sudden change* (though only for a few moments) in the sensation which is conveyed to his hands and seat.   The bit and the seat, which formerly felt like touching a hard surface, are resting now on a soft rubber cushion.

At this critical moment the rider should adopt an attitude of complete 'giving', even before the animal has accomplished the retardment.

As soon as it feels the yielding of the rider, the horse is stimulated to tread into the retardment in a soft and smooth manner, while maintaining its impulsion.   Theoretically, the action of retardment has been completed at this moment.   *The horse is still in motion, but has already been retarded!*

However, if the animal should happen to decrease its motion to a standstill without yielding, this means that retardment has not been completed. Although the whole process is finished, the stiff reduction of the motion has been due to compulsion and not obedience. *Although the horse has slowed down, it is not retarded!*

The horse's passive resistance against the retarding rein is a fault similar to its moderate pushing action against the bit. Therefore, the remedy for this form of opposition is in principle the same as described on page 112 for curing the pushing action.

In order to ensure the impulsion of the horse during the retardment, in addition to the interchanged functions involved, every reduction in speed or motion should be completed by a drive-on. The rate at which this is performed depends on the standard of the animal's education.

This means that in case of young horses the animal should be retarded into a speed which is slightly slower than the one desired and then urged into the speed originally intended by a drive-on action.

When dealing with schooled horses the extent of the component actions in the procedure can be reduced to a minimum.

The procedure of halting the horse is described on page 133.

In teaching retardment to a novice a beginning should be made with the soothing and slowing-down effect of the rider's voice. The horse will thus perform the retardment on its own initiative, and the rider should offer no interference with the reins, even if the transition seems to be too long.

As the horse becomes gradually accustomed to the feeling of the bit in its mouth, the rider can gradually teach it the actual retarding signals. Therefore, in addition to the use of the voice, he should introduce step by step the application of the reins, supported by the alternate pressures of the legs.

During this period it is of great importance that the bit should not cause the slightest pain in the horse's mouth. The animal must learn to accept the pressure of the bit with absolute confidence. In this way its resistance, resulting in its opposition and in the stiffness of the back, can be prevented (see page 163).

At a more advanced stage of schooling the rider should use the taking action of the seat and pressures on the stirrups, which reduce the intensity of functions to be performed by the hands. The horse is quick to react to these actions of the rider, especially when they are carried out in combination with the leg pressures.

At the end of the schooling it should be sufficient for the rider to resist slightly with his hands and exercise a mild pressure on the animal's back, in order to produce a satisfactory retardment.

It can be seen from the above description that each drive-on function includes certain actions of the retardment, and vice versa. This combination of actions is necessary because the horse is inclined to reduce its impulsion only if simple and continuous retardment is applied; likewise, during the drive-on it is apt to lose the swinging movement of its spring system if the drive-on does not contain elements of retardment.

It is the different proportions in which these two elements are employed that determine the final result, i.e. whether the horse will decrease or increase its locomotion. Thus it is evident that the drive-on and the retardment are fundamentally similar procedures, even though their results are quite opposite.

It is essential that the horse reacts to both the drive-on and the retardment *with the same refined sensitivity*. This means that it is of little value for the horse to react quickly to a retarding function if it cannot also accelerate its speed with the same rapidity, even when the acceleration is demanded immediately following a retardment. This readiness of the horse is particularly important in connection with jumping. Here the animal must be equally obedient in following the rider's demands for both the drive-on and the retardment in whatever sequence they may be given, in order to retain its impulsion or regulate, or alter, its stride action. Often such aids must be employed during the last strides before the take-off, especially when the obstacle produces a curbing effect in the horse. If the animal fails to submit at once to the rider's influence, its success in clearing the obstacle will be very doubtful. A fault is much more likely.

THE COMBINED APPLICATION OF THE DRIVE-ON AND RETARDMENT

The elements of this procedure are the drive-on, the retardment, and the yielding function of the rider by which the retardment is completed. By combining the elements in different ways the rider can produce a wide variety of effects and he will find that this procedure is one of his most valuable factors in riding.

The basic principle in applying the procedure correctly is that the drive-on and the retardment must be interlocked with one another like the links of a chain. They must *follow* and never counteract each other. This means that during the sequence of movements

> the drive-on should be linked to the yielding phase of the preceding retardment, and start with an easing-up on the horse's back by pressing down the thighs; and
>
> the retardment must be linked to the yielding phase of the previous drive-on, and start with the control influence on the spring system by pressing down the seat-bone or the stirrups.

These general principles apply equally to each of the three main variations, which we will now examine.

The basic form of the procedure is when the rider executes the drive-on and the retardment with the same intensity, while the transitions to and from the interlocked yielding function occur in a gradual manner. This is especially applicable in connection with the

> improvement of the horse's proper response to the drive-on and retarding functions themselves (page 131);
>
> establishment of mental contact with the horse (page 102);
>
> regulation of the stride-action (page 149);
>
> restoration of an equal balance of the body (page 162);
>
> loosening the stiffness of the back (page 163);
>
> increasing the animal's suppleness (page 146);
>
> development of the swing in its motion (page 242); and
>
> producing a state of collection (page 244).

The second combination of the drive-on and retardment consists of a determined retardment, whereat the transition to its yielding phase is performed by a sudden movement and followed by the drive-on action. It is especially useful for the creation of liveliness (page 150).

The third variation is when the retardment is executed from an energetic drive-on. It is employed for the collection of the horse while jumping (page 248).

If the yielding function is carried out by a sudden movement, this same procedure will promote the elimination of the horse's toughness in accepting the retarding rein function (page 56).

To assist the rider in acquiring the skill and feeling necessary for the proper execution of these combined procedures, the follow-

ing exercise is recommended, which—as it will be seen later on—
has additional advantages.

The exercise is based upon the effects produced on the horse
by a sloping ground.

Before entering a descent, the animal is inclined to slow down,
but on the slope it starts immediately to roll downwards to the
bottom.

When approaching an ascending surface it starts to rush uphill,
but on reaching the top it is inclined to slow down, having lost
its liveliness.

The aim of the exercise is to make the horse stride at an
absolutely uniform speed all the time. To succeed the rider must
control the animal from stride to stride by alternating his driving
and retarding functions in quick succession.

To carry out the exercise the rider should choose an area (about
200 to 250 yards or metres square) where the ground offers good
opportunities for riding back and forth in short laps over an
irregularly undulating surface.

At first the horse should walk over the area with dropped reins.
During this time the rider's control over the animal should be
restricted to preventive measures. According to the effect which the
ground formation may have on the horse, the rider should give it a
hint before reaching the critical parts of the course:

by a smooth and short 'touch' on the reins and a mild pressure on
the stirrups, which can be repeated a few times, the horse is
prevented from rolling off; and

by a mild knock or a short pressure with the legs, together with
the pressure of the thighs, it is prevented from slackening
speed.

When the horse walks quietly up and downhill in such a free
state the pace should be changed to a steady (rising) trot, while
leading and controlling the animal in the same way as during the
walk.

When introduced to the exercise in this way the horse learns
to react smoothly to the retardment and drive-on, because the
rider's influence is preventive and gentle. It may take a few weeks
to reach the stage when the animal is moving satisfactorily over
this undulating area, after which the practice of the actual exercise
can be commenced.

This should begin on each occasion with the loosening of the horse. Then the rider should take up the reins, establish contact with the horse according to the stage reached in its education, and then ride at a *steady trot*, safeguarding the liveliness of the motion.

During this ride the rider should exercise the retarding and driving functions at the critical sections of the course. It is likely that these actions will alter the speed of the horse in the opposite sense to its normal reaction to the ground formation. Therefore, the rider should immediately change his guiding activities in accordance with the altered situation.

Now the animal, inspired by the formation and supported by the rider's last act, will tend to change speed of its own accord, and this should be prevented by the rider's renewed counter function. Thus the horse should be guided from stride to stride by alternating drive-on and retarding activities all over the exercise area.

The correctness of the rider's guiding influence is shown by the reaction of the horse:

if it slows down on the critical sections, this indicates that it has lost its liveliness, proving that the driving function was insufficient or applied too late;

if it rolls away, this is a sign that the retarding function was incorrect, mainly because the rider has only pulled on the reins without completing the action by the necessary yielding.

During a correct performance the rider will have a distinct sensation that the horse is striding with his own legs in response to his demands.

Thus the exercise refines the rider in his actions and improves the animal in its reactions. It improves the suppleness of the horse, encourages its muscular development, and does more to increase the flexibility of its joints than any other single exercise. Furthermore, by the fact that the exercise produces many changes in a rather quick succession in the position of the horse while it is trotting steadily up and downhill, it (the exercise) improves considerably the swinging movement of the animal's back.

In order to encourage this improvement, the rider should keep the horse's back free from the pressure of his seat and the weight on the stirrups whenever he is riding up or downhill during the exercise. Therefore, he should take up the forward position even in a walk, and during the rising-trot he should not perform the sitting-down movements on the uphill or downhill sections of the course. This practice is also valuable to the rider by increasing his stability and flexibility in the forward seat, and especially for jumping.

The exercise should be practised as often as possible, not only during the period of the horse's education, but also later on, whenever its state of pliability renders it necessary. It might be performed in connection with the daily loosening exercise, or with gymnastic exercises for jumping training.

### The half-halt

The half-halt is derived from the combined operation of retardment and drive-on. It has an important regulating and refining effect on the horse, and that is why its application is frequent and very useful during the course of riding. Furthermore, by half-halts executed in smooth and quick rotation, the mental contact with the horse can be satisfactorily achieved.

The characteristic feature of the half-halt is that the retardment involved is carried out only to the point where the horse *mentally* accepts the function by its momentary yielding (the sign of its willingness to retard), whether or not the physical movement of retardment has been completed.

Bearing in mind this consideration, the half-halt is performed in the following manner:

As a preliminary to the procedure, the rider drives on the animal. Then he carries out the retardment, following which he completes the half-halt by a newly applied drive-on.

The extent of the retardment depends upon the sensitivity of the horse to the particular functions involved. At the beginning of schooling the horse may even be brought to a standstill, aiding it to accept the effect of the retarding function by yielding before being driven on again. As the animal's sensitivity to retardment improves, the dimensions of the motions can be decreased and the momentary yielding of the horse will gradually appear sooner and sooner. Finally, in more advanced stages of education it is sufficient for the rider to change his bearing to a passive tension of the hands and seat in order to bring about the horse's *willingness* to retard.

### THE STATIONARY POSITION AND THE TRANSITIONS CONNECTED

The transition into stationary position, the horse's behaviour in standstill and the move-off from there, as a whole performance, affords important evidence of the standard of education achieved by the rider and the horse.

Within the execution of the task the down transition is in principle a normal shortening of speed, which may eventually be completed by the insertion of some graduations. During this operation the rider should 'balance' the horse (see page 98) in a straight regulated movement and complete his functions by expressed yielding. In this way the horse is enabled to change over and tread with determination into the state of standstill from the motion. The smoothness of this transition results in the calmness of the horse during the next phase of the exercise.

The animal should halt on the straight line and squarely on all legs. While in the stationary position it should look straight ahead and keep an even rein-contact. It must not move either with the head or with the legs. To assist the horse to remain motionless the rider may employ slight hints produced by scarcely noticeable levelling movements of the seat. At the same time, the legs should be kept smoothly close to the sides of the animal, so that through them it can feel the soothing calmness of the rider. By these means he is keeping up the mental contact and the forward impulsion in the animal, so important in a stationary position. Any rigidity or force (especially by the reins!) will upset the horse and spoil the performance.

The move-off should be indicated by determined but smooth actions, introduced by the yielding of the hands and the driving signal of the legs. Then aid the horse in a balancing manner to stride out *straight forward* with resolute leg motion without losing its state of collection. This can be promoted if the rider 'plays' with the seat on the horse's back by changing slightly the pressure on it produced by his weight and keeps alive the lateral mobility of the shoulders by the performance of the levelling function. After such a start the horse will proceed in suppleness and complete the task to the satisfaction of the rider.

## Method of Schooling and Correction of Faults

Owing to the fact that during the exercise the motion must be reduced to a standstill and then renewed again, the horse has plenty of opportunity to resist the will of the rider and become evasive or restless. Therefore, right from the beginning the schooling has to be carried out with special care in the following stages.

Execute the retardment in the usual manner. The horse in the last phase of the procedure, when it loses the swing of the motion and the activity of the quarters, is inclined to oppose the retardment. It deviates from the straight line (mostly with the croup) and, after some fidgeting or rolling steps, falls stiffly into the motionless state.

To prevent this faulty behaviour interchange the retardment with minute drive-on phases. After the halt make the animal tread forward one to two steps, and only by a new retardment bring it to a standstill.

In order to accustom the horse to remain calm while in the stationary position, drop the reins and let it enjoy idleness and freedom.

When the animal has learned to remain quietly on the spot, begin with the correction of the foot position by the method described on page 42. During this it is a good practice for the instructor from the ground to touch with a whip the leg left behind. After this drop the reins. By consequent corrections the horse will halt automatically on all fours in a fairly short time, provided that the retardment is completed by yielding.

Next retain the rein-contact during the exercise, keep the head and neck straight, and prevent the horse looking about. This is a frequently noticeable fault. It is caused in most cases by the horse's opposition rather than by some 'interesting' or 'exciting' situation (see page 174). Thus, looking about must be forestalled mainly by attracting the animal's attention to ourselves. This should occur already before halting the horse (see pages 16 and 412), and then retained after the completion of the halt by the employment of the levelling function in its reduced form. If, however, this is not effective enough, obtain the horse's attention by some pulls on the rein opposite to the direction of the curiosity shown, interchanged with the forward animating effect of the legs (slight, short pressures).

While keeping the rein-contact, take care that the horse is not pushing against the bit or coming behind it. With regard to the correction of these faults see page 108.

The move-off should be undertaken on each occasion according to the general recommendations. In this way the horse learns to stride straight forward with resolute steps, neither becoming lazy nor rolling into the motion. A common fault is, when moving off, for the animal to toss its head and neck. In preventing this, besides driving on in a balancing manner, apply the method described on page 109.

SPECIAL INFORMATION RELATING TO ALTERING THE HORSE'S MOTION AT A CANTER

The canter starts with a striking-off action. The most appropriate moment for the strike-off is when the hind leg which is on the side opposite to the direction of the canter (the outside leg) and the foreleg which will 'lead' the movement (the inside leg) are in support position. This particular position occurs in walk and in trot during the corresponding diagonal phase of the pace (see pages 20 and 24). For instance, if the object is to bring the horse into a canter to the left, the signal for the strike-off should be given when the animal is in its left diagonal support phase.

In a stationary position the horse is completely supported by all four legs; consequently, it can start the movement immediately by striking off on either of its forelegs.

Owing to the fact that there are two diagonal support phases in the same stride, the horse has two opportunities to execute the strike-off during each stride, either to the right or to the left. In spite of this twofold possibility, it will never hesitate in its choice, but will *always* select for its action the direction which best suits the general *position* of its body.

Therefore, before making any attempt to execute the task, the rider should first place the horse in the position which corresponds to the direction of the canter action he wishes to perform. Thus the principal 'aid' for the execution of the action is to create the proper position. If the rider *aids* the animal into this position and then *signals* the action he desires, the horse will fulfil his demand accordingly and without hesitation. This is why it is impossible to propose the strict application of any special 'aid' for the purpose. There is only one rule, but it is most important: the horse must be *struck off* into canter, and not *driven* into it!

The position of the horse for the strike-off is correct: when it is straight, or bent in the direction of the strike-off action, and the lateral mobility of the shoulders is unobstructed.

In order to check the horse's position, the rider should first of all ascertain whether the shoulder connected with the leading foreleg, which starts the strike-off action, is free from surplus load. He can most easily discover this by performing some oscillating movements with the upper body, by which he encourages the animal to make slight lateral movements from the shoulders.

If the horse follows the rider's movements by performing lateral shoulder movements equally in both directions, it is in a state from which it can execute a definite strike-off action in either direction.

If the animal reacts in one direction only, it will eventually strike off in the direction *opposite* to its mobility.

A fairly well-trained rider can already ascertain this mobility, and the conditions required for the strike-off, without actually checking it, from the manner of the horse's general motion.

An experienced instructor can judge with certainty the situation from the ground, proving that these recommendations are based on facts visibly demonstrated by the horse.

In order to obtain the proper position for the horse, the oscillating movements mentioned should be carried out until the animal's shoulder mobility is expressed especially to the *outside*.

In more acute cases the rider should make the shoulders mobile by executing some turn on the haunches movements in an oscillating manner, such as one or two steps to the right . . . one or two steps to the left, etc.

When this basic condition for the strike-off has been achieved its execution can follow.

First of all, there is the (slight) bending of the horse (see page 196). The bending of the neck 'shows' the animal the direction which the strike-off should take.

Next, the rider should bring about the 'cocking' of the horse's spring system by the application of a half-halt (or half-halts).

Then he should eliminate the uneasiness caused by the lateral bent position of the forehand by yielding with the inside rein. At the same time, he should lighten the horse's inner side by moving the centre of gravity a little towards the outside and holding the leg on that side a bit more firmly to the horse's flank.

After all this preparatory work which ensures the proper position of the horse, the rider can apply the signal for the strike-off into canter. A driving touch of the *inside* leg, accompanied by pressure of the outside leg, seems to be the most effective signal. But it is perfectly correct to teach the horse to carry out the strike-off by any other signal; for instance, a more pronounced pressing of the outside leg.

A well-trained horse must be able to execute the strike-off while maintaining its *straight position*, at which only its head is flexed slightly in the direction of the action desired. In such cases the method of striking off is as follows:

Indicate the flexion of the head by the inside rein and simultaneously exercise pressure behind the girth with the outside leg. These two actions together have a certain collecting effect and, at the same time, they are increasing the freedom of the inside shoulder.

Then relax the effect of the inside rein and give the signal for the strike-off with the inside leg by exercising a brief touch on the girth.

Thanks to these 'aids', the rider can ensure the proper position and elasticity of the horse, and it will strike off into a canter in the direction from which the driving 'signal' has come.

With the improvement of the horse's schooling all these articulated functions, described above, become merged more and more into another, so that finally it is enough for the rider only to 'think' of the action and the animal will strike off instantly.

When the horse has struck off into a canter correctly it will maintain its proper position without any particular interference for a short time. But after a few strides it is bound to lose the correct form of movement if the rider does not intervene.

The responsibility for providing support falls mainly upon the rider's inside (i.e. driving) leg. This leg has to prevent that frequent fault of the horse in trying to get inwards from the straight line with the quarters. The leg can perform its dual function without difficulty, since the touches applied for the drive-on also serve as warnings to the horse to maintain its straight position. However, if this action of the drive-on leg does not prove to be effective, then it should also exert one or two lateral-moving pressures from time to time.

The outside leg should constantly maintain contact with the horse's side and be prepared to exert pressure if the animal should abandon the straight line with its quarters. This occurs quite rarely.

The duty of the outside hand is to keep the animal's outside shoulder in check and prevent the horse from trying to increase speed. This dual task of the hand is analogous to that of the inside leg.

The inside hand should prevent the shifting of the horse's forehand toward the inside by exercising a few lateral-moving pressures.

The levelling function, by which all these activities of the rider are blended, assists the horse in retaining its balance during the motion and in following the direction demanded by the rider.

If the lateral mobility of the shoulders became defective during the motion, one should avoid employing any lateral-moving rein effect against the connected pressing action of the horse (see reasoning and the method of correction on page 173).

The increase and decrease of speed at a canter are carried out according to the same principles as described in connection with the general considerations (see page 122).

The action of changing into lower paces is the reverse of that of striking off into canter. The horse is only able to carry out such a change when its leading (inside) foreleg gets into a support position joining the diagonal support phase of the opposite side. For instance, in the case of a canter to the left, this particular position occurs when the left foreleg gets into support while the inside (left) hind leg and the outside (right) foreleg are in the diagonal support phase.

The signal for the change of pace is the taking action of the *outside* rein, supported by the taking action of the seat and by the pressure of the rider's outside leg.

Teaching the Novice the Strike-off into a Canter

During the early stages of schooling the main object of this particular education is that the horse should perform the change without excitement and remain calm afterwards while cantering.

In the beginning of teaching make the changes at a trot while keeping the reins long enough to ensure ample freedom of action to the horse; and

give the drive-on signal according to its *observed* momentary position.

Because of the widespread fault in horses, their left-sided crookedness (see page 173), which reduces the shoulder mobility to the right, teaching the strike-off action to the left generally causes more difficulties than to the right. In order to amend the situation, the rider should make good use of any opportunity for striking it off into a canter to the left when the animal frees its left shoulder *on its own accord*.

With the increase of the horse's adjustability the rider will become more and more capable of achieving the appropriate position and make the horse strike off with equal certainty and easiness in either direction.

During this period of tuition it is of special advantage when the rider introduces the strike-off action by the oscillating movements of the levelling function. He should give the drive-on signal at the moment when the upper body has finished one of the bending movements towards the outside and *starts* to swing back towards the inside.

### The change of legs in the air at the canter

This term refers to that particular action of the horse whereby it changes the leading direction of the pace movement while in the suspension phase of the canter or gallop.

According to the present regulations for the three-day event, the presentation of this action is not required in the dressage test. Nevertheless, it is very useful to teach the animal to perform it at the rider's request.

The advantage of this training is particularly evident when riding a winding course with obstacles, for the rider will be able to bring the animal into the canter action which complies with each changing direction of the course. This affords the horse the best chance of approaching and jumping each succeeding obstacle in a regulated state, even if the fence should be situated on the curve of a turn.

The action of changing legs in the air is natural to the horse, so that it often makes the movement of its own accord. Therefore, the change will not cause the animal special difficulty, even if required by the rider.

If the rider is able to give the signal for the strike-off into a canter in the proper manner, and the horse can obey it while maintaining its straight position, it will also learn in a short time the signal indicating the change of legs in the air.

Just as in the case of the strike-off into a canter, the decisive factor in changing legs in the air is the establishment of the horse's appropriate position.

If the horse happens to change its position during the canter, it is apt instinctively to change over to the opposite direction, provided that it has sufficient impulsion. And so, in training the horse for this task, the first exercises should be designed to improve its facility to change its position without losing impulsion. For this reason the exercise should be carried out in the following order:

First ride in a slow canter on a long straight line and create a high degree of impulsion in the horse's stride action. At the same time, apply the levelling function to promote the lateral mobility of the shoulders and remove any surplus load from the outside shoulder.

Then change the flexion of the animal towards the outside by means of the outside rein and by pressing the inside leg *mildly* behind the girth. Do not apply any further actions in order to extract the change.

The change of flexion should be repeated while riding on the same straight line, always returning to the original position.

If the horse should lose its impulsion in the course of changing its position, the exercise should be interrupted, the animal brought into a straight position, its impulsion increased, and only then should the procedure be resumed.

After performing the above exercise a number of times, the horse will change the direction of its pace movement by itself, either simultaneously with the change of flexion or shortly thereafter.

In order to facilitate the horse's effort, it is of advantage to emphasize the oscillating upper body movements of the levelling function employed towards the inside. By this means the animal's outside shoulder becomes free and so, in the moment of changing the flexion, it (the shoulder) can easily take over its leading function.

After performing the change of legs the animal should be rewarded by a brief rest, following which the rider can repeat the entire exercise two or three times, but not more.

When the horse has become accustomed to changing legs after a simple change of position, the next step is to consolidate this particular association of ideas in its mind.

For this purpose the exercise should be performed on a large circle of 40 to 60 yards in diameter and the oscillating movement, together with the change of position, must be executed while the rider changes the direction of riding through the centre of the circle. However, at the moment of changing the position the animal should still be allowed to execute the change of legs by itself, without any prompting from the rider.

The next step is to teach the horse to perform the action in response to a given signal. In achieving this aim the following procedure is recommended, the execution of which should be carried out in a large circle.

After refreshing the lateral mobility of the shoulders, turn the horse inside from the circle and, at the same time, exert strong pressure by the *momentary inside leg* (which will become the outside leg in the new direction) behind the girth, indicating the necessity to change position.

While approaching the centre of the circle, increase the freedom of the new inside shoulder and apply a brief but firm drive-on signal by the *new inside leg* at the moment when the upper body *starts* to swing from the momentary leading direction in the new one. It is most effective when the application of this signal is synchronized with one of the phases of suspension of the stride action.

Immediately *afterwards* increase the animal's flexed position by the new inside rein.

It is most likely that the first attempts will fail to produce the result desired. The rider should not worry about the delay or alter his activities, since the horse will comply sooner or later, but in any case quite suddenly, with his demand.

There are horses which like to perform the change at first in two separate phases by starting with their forelegs and then taking one or two strides before completing the action with the hind legs. The rider should not try to correct this habit of disjointed performance, as the animal will eventually find the proper solution by itself.

With certain horses the change of legs stimulates them to rushing. Such an animal must be firmly halted after each performance and then calmed down by a brief rest.

After a few weeks' schooling the horse will perform the change of legs in the air satisfactorily even if required to do so when riding on a straight course. It should be noted, however, that the animal should not be expected to perform the task more than five or six times in the course of any one lesson.

When the horse has learned to execute the change of legs, the rider should pay particular attention to make sure that it does not do it of its own accord while riding on a curved line in counter-lead.

# CHAPTER THREE

# Regulation of the Horse's Motion

AN adjusted or regulated form of locomotion is one of the factors which increases the adaptability and performing capacity of the horse. Regulation also enables the animal to use its strength in the most economical manner and endows it with all the most desirable qualities which are necessary for good riding.

In order to acquire the feeling, knowledge and skill necessary to correct any possible irregularities in the horse's locomotion, it is important that the rider should know:

the factors which affect the general behaviour of the horse, its locomotion, and the state of its body;

recognize the various deficiencies which may cause resistance and irregularities in the motion; and

apply the proper methods for eliminating these defects.

He should also know that before the application of any special (physical) corrective measure the mental cause of the defect, the horse's resistance, must be eliminated by the re-establishment of the mental contact (see page 102) and by the creation of suppleness in its behaviour (see page 146).

FACTORS AFFECTING THE GENERAL BEHAVIOUR OF THE HORSE

RECOGNIZING THE HORSE'S EXISTING PLIABILITY

The rider's ability to appreciate the state of the horse's pliability and to make the animal supple is of the greatest importance. To acquire the necessary knowledge and skill is not a matter of being born with an exceptional gift; it can be achieved by every rider in due time. Once the rider has acquired this ability he will become enabled to achieve his aims quickly, and neither he nor his horse will have difficulty in performing any task within the limits of their talents and gained education.

The horse's pliability is shown in its readiness to obey in a supple manner, and its lack of pliability takes the form of stiff resistance to the rider's authority.

*Characteristics of opposition and submission and those of stiffness and relaxation (yielding)*

Opposition and submission are the results of the horse's mental functions. Stiffness and relaxation are evidence of its physical attitude. In their manifestations opposition and stiffness, submission and relaxation are closely related to one another.

*Opposition* gives the rider the impression that his signals are being ignored by the horse, especially *during the retardment*. This characteristic sensation is most pronounced during the execution of the last phase of the halt, when the animal continues to step slowly forward instead of completing willingly the halting movement. In response to the rider's yielding phase during the taking action, the horse stretches its neck and head forward and downwards, trying to pull the reins out of his hands.

The typical manifestation of *stiffness* is a sensation of tension conveyed to the rider *during the drive-on* by the horse's back. This can be most clearly felt during the first phase of drive-on from a stationary position, or during a half-halt, when the horse gives up the rein-contact and pushes itself into the motion with stiffened back muscles. This stiffness spreads over to the muscles of the ribs, making the animal's sides hard and insensible. Simultaneously, the rider feels that the horse is ignoring his driving signals, while the bit is lying on a hard bar and the seat on a beam.

Opposition and stiffness are mostly connected with some defect in the lateral mobility of the shoulders. Thus by checking this mobility, one can also detect the state of the animal's suppleness.

*Submission and relaxation (yielding)* manifest themselves commonly in the easiness and elasticity of the horse's reactions. The sensations felt by the rider are *the same during both the driving-on and the retardment*. These are:

The horse's back swings into the slowed-down motion and then into the increased one without rigidity. It is flexible and the muscles do not radiate any stiffness. There is none of that curious sensation of inner tension in the rider which is so characteristic of the horse's stiffness and resistance. It strides immediately out of its shoulders in either direction if the rider asks it to do so.

The change in motion is smooth, revealing the animal's willingness to accommodate itself to its master's desires. This can be best observed during the performance of half-halts.

The rider feels as if a pleasant swinging and jolting action were gently rocking his seat on a padded chair. He has the impression that the bit is lying on a soft rubber cushion and that his legs are touching an elastic surface.

The horse yields to the rider's yielding without stretching its neck or losing the contact during the retarding and driving actions.

*Acquisition of sensations characteristic of the horse's momentary state of pliability*

In order to ascertain the sensations in question, the rider should concentrate his attention mainly on the state of the horse's back (see page 163) and the animal's readiness to execute changes of movement.

The sensations felt by the hands should also be observed and taken into account, although they are only of secondary importance. It may be of interest to explain the reason for this in detail, since many riders attribute importance to the sensations conveyed by the mouth of the animal.

The hands, when engaged in an active or passive function, can detect the momentary state of the horse's pliability in the form of a particular sensation conveyed through the bit and mouth. This sensation is usually more impressive than that felt through the seat, in spite of the fact that the reverse should logically be true. The difference in the intensity of these two sensations can be misleading and may encourage the rider to attribute the sensations felt by the hands to the 'quality' of the horse's mouth. Such a mistake will be avoided if the rider realizes that this sensation is in no way connected with the sensitivity of the mouth (see page 110), for it is produced by the entire spring system and its effect is transmitted to the hands through the front part of this system, which ends in the mouth.

During the course of the rider's self-education it is desirable to experiment first with a horse that is already well schooled and inclined to be submissive. In doing so the rider can best identify the characteristic sensation of suppleness in the horse's bearing. The animal displays it most vividly during the alteration in its pace action (if it is not hampered by the rider), especially when changing the pace from a walk to a trot or vice versa.

For the sake of the experiment make good use of this phenomenon and carry out the exercise in the following manner:

While the horse proceeds at a walk, take up the rein-contact and sit smoothly in the saddle in the ready position. The reins should be kept rather short and held with relaxed muscles and a fairly stretched-forward carriage of the arms, since the sensations can be appreciated more fully in this position than with long reins.

After having established this position, drive on the horse, preferably by mild taps of the whip, from a slight half-halt into a slow trot. Then, starting from a slight animation, give retarding signals for changing the pace into a walk.

During the drive-on phase of this procedure the animal should be allowed to make a few steps forward; meanwhile, observe carefully the sensations which are conveyed to the seat by the horse's back and by the motion of its steps. For the time being it is probable that you will not be conscious of anything but stiffness and a feeling of an angular motion.

Then, starting from a slight animation, give retarding signals for changing the pace into a walk. During the retardment make similar observations as before. At the beginning it is most likely that the horse will offer resistance to the actions of the reins, seat and legs, creating a general sensation of hardness.

When this stiffness is felt (shortly after the commencement of the action), stop the retarding signals and yield with both the hands and seat by slightly exaggerated movements. Now, it is also quite probable that the animal will not respond to the rider's action by relaxation, but will continue to follow the trend of its movements stiffly with its back and try to pull the reins out of his hands.

To improve the experiment, repeat these two parts of the procedure, slight half-halt plus drive-on into trot . . . animation plus retardment into walk . . . sudden yielding . . . slight half-halt, etc., over and over again until the moment comes when a sudden sensation of softness and sensitivity is felt by the seat, hands and legs. This is created by the change-over to submission and is produced by the relaxation of stiffness in the horse's back.

The rider should not neglect to explore and memorize this sensation, since it is one of his most valuable aids in establishing and maintaining the supple state of the horse.

### Creation of suppleness in the horse's behaviour

The secret of producing suppleness is to obtain the horse's

understanding and willingness to obey, since the state of its body depends mainly upon the quality of its mental apprehensions. The more successfully the suppleness of the animal's mentality is attained, the more readily does it offer the suppleness of its body.

There is an interesting and convincing proof offered by the horse itself for the validity of this statement. Horses often give an *audible* sign when they are changing from opposition into sub-mission by starting to snort kindly. The rider can best recognize this phenomenon during loosening exercises or regulating pro-cedures at the moment when the change in the horse's general behaviour sets in. It is evident that this 'talking' is the expression of a mental function, thus the relaxation of the body, which the rider can perceive simultaneously with the snorting, must also be a direct result of the animal's mental function.

The mind of the horse can be best approached by means of frequent changes in the activities of the rider and in the motion of the animal. They are relaxing its instinctive opposition, 'shak-ing' it into and 'balancing' it smoothly in a supple state.

Changes in the rider's activities enable him continually to check the state of the horse's pliability by inserting during the per-formance of the main task minute demands for the execution of contrasting movements (e.g. during a drive-on, minute retard-ments, and vice versa). According to the animal's reaction to the control actions, he can, if necessary, immediately introduce suit-able corrective measures before he is confronted with an acute defect. With the aid of these control activities, the rider should check the submission of the horse to this drive-on and retardment and verify the permanent free lateral mobility of the animal's forehand (shoulders). The application of these activities of the rider is based upon the following considerations.

Horses, when displaying impulsion, are naturally inclined to relax resistance and by it the stiffness of the muscular and spring system during the performance of alterations of their own accord. The reason for this is that it is easier for the animal to change the pace action when it is in a relaxed state. Therefore, it is inclined to become supple for its own convenience during the alterations and two to three ensuing steps. Consequently use can be made of such changes to produce a state of suppleness in the horse. The rider must know, however, that

the horse is able to perform smooth changes in its locomotion

more easily in a slow motion than in a faster one; but
it is easier for the rider to keep up the animal's impulsion in
a more extended motion than in slower ones.

These conditions of opposite meaning make it necessary that the
rider (the superior partner) should satisfy the demands of the
more difficult claim and make easier the task of his mount.

Therefore, the horse should be allowed to proceed during the
procedure by the use of that limited motion at which it can still
react easily to the indications of the rider. This is at the beginning
of schooling a rather slow motion, performed at a similarly slow
speed. Then, in accordance with the improvement of the horse's
submission, the motion and the speed can gradually be increased,
by which the task of the rider becomes facilitated.

The liveliness of the horse, which can easily decrease during a
slow motion, should be kept alive by increasing its impulsion.
If the rider notices that the animal, in spite of his support, is
losing its impulsion during the exercise, he should restore it by
driving forward the animal for a while in complete freedom and
then resume the schooling at the desired speed.

The exercise itself should proceed in the following order:

After the loosening exercise, start the schooling by practising
alterations between a walk and a stationary position.

Then change over to a slow trot and make the alterations in
combination with a walk. This is the main part of the exercise,
which, if necessary, should be repeated in a very long series.

These two parts of the exercise serve at the same time the
purpose of taking up mental contact with the horse.

Later on (after the establishment of the mental contact) expand
the exercise to include transitions between a slow and a more
extended trot, then make changes to a canter and, finally,
transitions within the canter itself.

In some cases of a more taut nature it is a good practice to
perform the alterations between a forward motion and rein-back.
During this procedure reduce the forward motion gradually to a
halt; from there start immediately the backward motion for three
to five steps and adjoiningly, without the insertion of an effective
halt, drive the horse forward again. Repeat this procedure a
number of times, however, interchanging the backward transitions
from time to time with those of forward character.

This variation of the suppling-up procedures is very effective, but special emphasis should be put on the interlocking yielding phases. Otherwise it can easily produce a result opposite to the one desired and hurt the joints of the quarters. Its application is recommended for occasions when a quick regulation is necessary, e.g. during warming-up procedures before jumping.

There is a further variation of the procedure, applicable at a more advanced stage of education. Make the horse step very slowly at a trot. In such an exaggerated slow motion, when the animal loses its impulsion, it falls immediately into a walk. To prevent it doing so the rider must display in his bearing great easiness and interchange from step to step his smooth drive-on and retarding functions. By these changes he automatically preserves the impulsion of the slow motion and promotes the attainment of suppleness by the horse. During the exercise increase from time to time the speed for a few strides and after this relaxation resume the slow motion again.

This practice is specially important while teaching the horse to increase its liveliness and approach an obstacle in absolute suppleness.

It is desirable to introduce the daily routine work of even well-educated horses, after their general loosening, by one of these suppling exercises. By this means the liveliness of their motion can be easily achieved (see page 238).

When a horse has been trained from the very beginning according to these principles it will seldom display hard resistance, but will be willing and supple. Only very occasionally will the application of special corrective measures be necessary.

During the re-education of spoilt horses the alterations are the chief means of correction. In such cases, however, the rein-back variation can be more often employed in addition. The inclusion of substantial corrective measures for the elimination of special or acute irregularities will also be frequently necessary.

FACTORS AFFECTING THE SMOOTH FLUENCY OF THE HORSE'S MOTION

THE REGULATED SEQUENCE OF STRIDES

In a well-regulated sequence of strides the component steps are resolute, lively, even and progressive in their purpose to gain ground.

*Resoluteness* means that the strides are pronounced, clear, decisive and elastic. Each stride must be independent of the others by starting from and finishing in itself. By no means should they be blurred by the preceding or following strides.

*Liveliness* denotes the quickness or slowness of the sequence of strides in which the movements are performed (see also page 238). It depends mainly upon the pendulum which is represented by the natural length of the horse's legs (including humerus and femur). The length of this pendulum determines the normal liveliness of each individual horse. Furthermore, the liveliness depends upon the applied speed, and consequently in the case of an extended speed it is higher, and in a collected pace lower, than normal. The criterion of the right form of liveliness is the way in which the animal steps forward with its hind legs. If the horse does not tread under its body, then instead of proceeding in a high state of liveliness when performing fast movements it merely rolls off; instead of using a low speed, it moves late and lazily.

*Evenness* expresses that quality of locomotion in which the strides follow each other in a uniform sequence, rhythm and measure.

*Progressiveness* is based on the natural length of the horse's strides. It also depends upon the rider's particular demand. A well-schooled horse must be able to perform strides considerably longer or shorter than their natural length without losing their resoluteness or evenness.

PROCESS OF REGULATING THE SEQUENCE OF STRIDES

The main components of the process of regulation are the initiating and the decreasing of the motion, the common elements of which are the drive-on and the retardment, each one completed by its yielding phase and blended by the levelling function of the rider.

At the drive-on the rider must exploit the impulsion which he has created for the purpose of regulation. In actual practice the drive-on, owing to its inherent animating quality, can effect a regulation on its own, or it can be used as the starting point for a regulating action.

At the retardment its regulating value is found in its tendency to collect the horse and in its definite yielding effect, as well as

in the fact that it is the action from which the medium of regulation, namely, the drive-on, must be accomplished.

At the combined application of drive-on and retardment these
two basic functions are performed in rotation. By this means it is
possible to diagnose a great number of causes and consequences of
irregularity in the animal's motion and general bearing, and even
eliminate many of them without further interference.

For the regulation of the horse's stride action, by their inherent
qualities the above functions afford the best possibilities.
For example:

in the case of a horse which is rolling off, the regulating procedure consists of firm but smooth retarding and determined
drive-on elements interlocked by yielding phases with each
other;

in the case of sluggish horses, in the combination of the joint
function of drive-on and retardment the emphasis is on the
drive-on; however, the determination of the retardment is
also important.

In both cases these jointly applied functions should be repeated
until the rider feels that the animal's strides are becoming distinct
and gaining ground.

The method of correcting the irregularities which may appear
during the transitions and alterations is to recommence the
motion which has been wrongly performed. The improvement
provided by this method is based on the restoration of the starting
position, which, in other words, means that

in order to regulate the increase of motion, the horse has to be
brought into a position from which it is possible to set it in
motion; that is, it must be retarded; and

in order to correct the decrease of motion, the horse must be in
a position from which it can be retarded; that is, its motion
has first to be increased.

THE TENDENCY OF THE HORSE TO DEVIATION AND ITS OPPOSITION TO
FOLLOW THE COURSE INDICATED BY THE RIDER
(DIRECTING THE YOUNG OR SPOILT HORSE ON THE COURSE DESIRED)

During the course of riding the rider will notice that the horse
is bound to alter the course of progress when left unsupported and
cause difficulties when directed away from the direction taken.
There are two main reasons for this.

The first is the horse's instinctive effort to maintain its equilibrium or to preserve its momentary state of balance. There is no objection involved in this behaviour of the animal.

The second reason is the deflective instinct of the horse which urges it to follow a course independently of that of the rider's intention. In this case the animal comes into conflict with the rider, and this can culminate in its malicious behaviour.

### The natural tendency of the horse to deviation

In order to reduce instability of an unstable object or being, it must be balanced by some kind of motion, whether it is in the spot or while changing place. Compare the situation arising when carrying a fully filled tumbler or walking along the corridor of a running train.

The horse, to safeguard its balance, is acting in a similar manner by its instinctive wavy movements during its locomotion. These can become under certain circumstances one-sided, and thus divert the animal from the direction wanted, or obstruct it in obeying demands for the alteration of its established balance position.

In such situations the aiding activities of the rider have to be twofold. He must inspire and facilitate the horse to perform its instinctive balancing motion and direct and keep it in the direction desired.

Both requirements can simultaneously be achieved by the performance of slight oscillating movements of the rider's upper body. To enlighten the meaning of this function, and at the same time to make the task of the rider easier, the employment of two proved methods is recommended. By the aid of them he can already exercise a smooth guiding influence on the horse at the early stages of education.

The first method is designed to support the horse in maintaining its adopted state of balance while proceeding on a straight course.

For this purpose select a distant point as a target. Gaze firmly at it and try to keep the line by sheer force of will power and by remaining constantly with the upper body in the exact direction. This will cause the rider to change rhythmically the position of the upper body, always in opposition to the digressions of the horse's wavering motion.

With each change in the rider's gravitational state the animal changes the direction of the course. By successive lateral changes in his position the rider facilitates the balancing of the horse and at the same time the directing effect of the movements prevents it from substantial deviation. Thus, by the combined effect of this procedure, the horse will proceed in suppleness towards the selected target, i.e. on the line chosen.

In the beginning these oscillating movements of both parts are in evidence, but later they diminish with the improvement of the horse. Finally, they will continue as invisible inner reflex movements in the horse and rider.

During this procedure the reins should not be used. The stirring of the horse may be achieved by the function of the upper body, while the regulation of the speed is controlled by the seat (pressures on the stirrups) and the legs (thighs).

With regard to the second method, when the horse is ordered to change the direction the activities of the rider are very similar to those employed in the former case. The main difference is that the rider, instead of the distant target of the former case, follows the *curve to be taken* with his glance. Otherwise stirring and balancing the animal on the curved line occurs according to the same principles as described above. It is advantageous to put a slight 'swing' into the oscillating movement of the upper body when it bends from the inside to the outside, in order to prevent the horse from cutting the curve.

To sum up, the horse satisfies the aim of the rider in both cases by instinctive reflex movements. There is no harsh compulsion in guiding the animal and so its forward spirit and smoothness—so important in conducting young horses—is maintained.

The slight oscillating movements apart from keeping the shoulders mobile also produce changes in the pressure on the back, which produce a pleasant loosening sensation in the animal. These effects increase considerably the general value of the procedures.

By their inherent qualities these methods are adapted to *prevent* the horse from deviating from the intention of the rider. If, however, the animal causes difficulties and the aids mentioned are not effective, the rider must carry out a substantial correction.

### *The objection of the horse to keeping the course desired*

Unfortunately, it is impossible at the early stages of education (or re-education) to cure this irregularity by eliminating the causes which are producing it. Therefore it is necessary to employ subsidiary practices. By the aid of them it is possible to make riding fairly smooth before the final results of the methodical schooling are achieved.

The natural tendency of the horse to deviate may be aggravated by various effects conveyed to him from within and without, in which cases the rider finds himself confronted with objections on the part of the animal. They manifest themselves in more or less increased deviating movement from the line taken and in pressing away from the course when the rider intends to change the direction. The difference is to be found in the factors which produce the deviation.

The simple deviation is the result of an instinctive or physical compulsion. In the case of the turning difficulty the origin of the defect is the resistance or the obstinacy of the horse.

When the reason of the deviation is based upon instincts, such as the animal's 'will' (mentality), smooth progress becomes upset alternately in both lateral directions.

In the event of physical compulsion, however, which is caused by the natural or adopted crooked state of the horse (see page 167), the irregularity determines the direction of the deviation. On such occasions the animal, by following the impulse brought about by the crookedness, finds it easier to perform its motion in an oblique manner. It proceeds either towards the side which is identical with the displacement of the forehand (shoulders), or towards the side opposite to its shifted croup position.

The actions of the horse, by which it performs the deviating movement, are in their physical manifestations similar in both cases. Thus this defective motion can be put right, in any case, by the application of similar methods; it is only necessary to concentrate more on the persuasion of the horse's mentality when the defect originates from its 'will'.

The corrective procedure is a fairly short one. It is composed of two phases interlocked in quick succession. They are

the correction in longitudinal direction (loosening by half-halts);

the correction in lateral direction, consisting of the creation of weakness (one sudden lateral function) and elimination of the deviation of the motion (function of counter-deviation).

Less experienced riders are inclined to neglect the introductory part of the procedure and commence the correction with the immediate cure of the defect, the last phase of the operation. The consequence is a struggle with the horse, a frequent experience when an unskilled rider tries to keep a resisting animal on a straight line or on the curve of a turn.

In the first phase of the correction a loosening effect should be produced in order to shatter the resistance of the horse in longitudinal direction and to open the way to the lateral correction of the defect.

For this purpose it is necessary to make some definite half-halts, the number and execution of which should be co-ordinated with the stage of horse's schooling and the degree of its resistance. During their execution include the oscillating movements of the upper body and give ample scope to the yielding functions involved in the procedure, especially on the stiffened side of the animal. Riders are inclined to pull the rein on this side, increasing the resistance of the horse. The effective execution of this loosening procedure is the key to general success.

In milder cases this procedure is effective enough to eliminate also the lateral impediment of the motion. Failing this, the *drive-on phase of the last half-halt* executed should be interlocked with the next element of the operation.

In this a state of weakness in the horse's resistance, which affects harmfully its willingness to accept measures for lateral corrections, should be produced. For this purpose a quick change should be made in the form of a sudden turning action in the motion *towards* the direction of the horse's tendency to deviation, even if the situation is apparently aggravated for a moment. The hasty movement by which the animal reacts to this particular demand (since it coincides with its intention) acts as a side-blow on its static centre and upsets its balance. In this state of instability the basis of its resistance becomes undermined for a moment and the horse will show an inclination to submit itself to the further demands of the rider. In more acute cases repeat this function a few times in an oscillating manner, by returning after each attempt to the issuing direction.

During the execution of this phase of the procedure the rider may have a feeling of confidence in his actions similar to those described in connection with controlling rushing horses (see page 115). In the present case he should acquire confidence in the effect of his lateral actions, by means of which he persuades the animal to perform movements in the direction of its faulty inclination. These lateral functions correspond to the yielding and driving functions performed during the process of slowing down rushing horses. The actual control function corresponds to the retardment involved in the slowing down process.

Making good use of the state of weakness created, the elimination of the deviating movement can commence by interlocking the following phase of the correction in the substantial yielding unction by which the sudden turning action has been completed.

During this phase the main implement of the procedure is the rein by its counter-deviation function, employed in the direction opposite to the horse's deviating movement. Its effect is supported by the transfer of the rider's weight and his lateral moving leg pressures on the identical side.

The interlocked yielding moments of this rein function are of utmost importance, since the horse gives up its resistance in one of these moments. It strides *suddenly* out from its shoulders in the direction desired.

While the active rein exercises its function the other rein must not interfere with the mouth. It is preferable that the rider loses contact altogether rather than exercises its slightest pull or passive resistance. If the rider omits this relaxation, he challenges the opposition of the horse and makes the animal 'malicious'. Instead of promoting the correction, *he* aggravates the situation!

In the present phase of the correction the functions to be employed are similar in character, differing only in their intensity according to whether the deviation occurs in the direction of the horse's stiffened side or the opposite one. In other words, whether towards the same side from which the rider meets hard opposition against the rein function, or whether it is ignored by the horse by an evasive lateral movement of its neck and head.

In the case where the animal shows stiffness on its left side, the elimination of the deviating movement occurs in the following manner.

If the deviation coincides with the side of the stiffness:

the particular weakness is produced by a *slight*, short turning function and the counter-deviation by *moderate* functions.

If the deviation occurs on the side opposite to the stiffness:

weakness may be caused by *moderate* turning function and the counter-deviation function with *increased stress*.

If the horse does not react to two to three successive directing

Fig. No. 44/a

*Horse:* after giving up resistance proceeds straight forward

*Rider:* drives forward

*Horse:* strides out of its shoulders towards the direction opposite to the deviation
*Rider:* repeats the counter-deviation function. This can be preceded by refreshing the state of weakness
*Horse:* still shows inclination to deviation
*Rider:* Changes his activities and exercises counter-deviation functions

*Horse:* increases suddenly its deviating motion by which its balance becomes upset
*Rider:* exercises leading function towards the direction of the faulty motion (creation of state of weakness)

*Horse:* lessens its resistance and stiffness, continues a reduced deviation
*Rider:* exercises some half-halts to loosen the resistance and stiffness of the horse

*Horse:* proceeds in a stiffened position and deviates from the course of riding

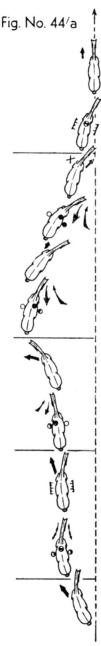

rein effects involved in one counter-deviation function, stop the process and refresh the state of weakness before a new attempt is made. It is most likely that after two or three repetitions of the overall procedure the animal will give up its resistance and by it the deviating motion.

Fig. No. 44/a illustrates (starting from the bottom upwards) the actions of the rider and those of the horse in that succession as they follow each other during the course of the procedure. One has only to complete the meaning of the functions recorded by the particular degree of their strength.

As a rule, the propensity to deviate manifests itself at the beginning of schooling, and especially when riding away from the stable. The young horse keeps striding forward in a wavering manner and by pulling off first to one and then to the other direction it tries to turn back towards home. There is no malice whatsoever in this tendency. It is instinctive, and therefore correction of the fault should be carried out gently.

The correction of the irregularity occurs according to the same principles described formerly. But one can omit the creation of weakness involved in the general procedure, since the animal tries to change the direction of progress of its own accord.

When the rider senses the animal's intention to deviate, which will most probably occur shortly after the start of the ride, the action of counter-deviation should be applied at once, taking care that it does not hamper the horse's locomotion.

The animal will almost certainly respond by changing over to a deviating movement towards the other side, and consequently the rider has to change the direction of his counter-action as well.

After a few attempts to make these wavering movements the horse will come to its senses and lessen its resistance, until finally it is resigned to the fact that the only agreeable course is to proceed forward. It will do this for its own convenience.

The procedure is illustrated in Fig. No. 44/b. It shows, at the same time, the method how the rider should direct the horse during its progress. First the expressed deviating movements are counteracted by substantial measures. Then, in accordance with the diminution of the resistance, the counter-measures

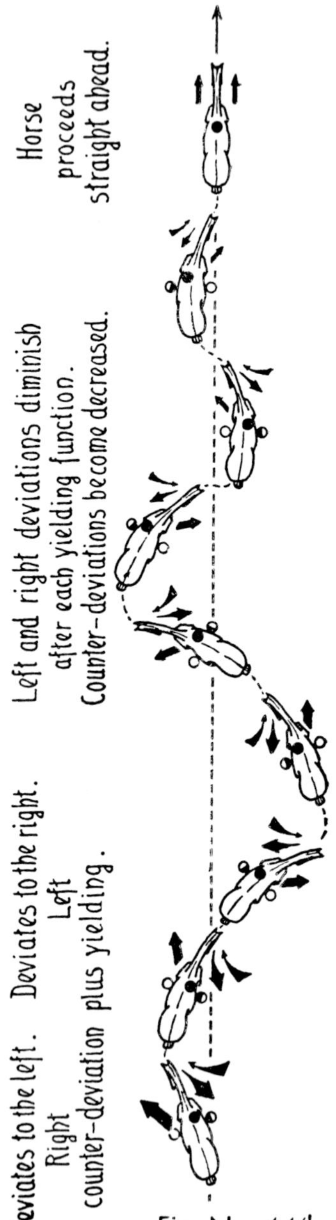

Horse proceeds straight ahead.

Left and right deviations diminish after each yielding function.
Counter-deviations become decreased.

Deviates to the right.
Left counter-deviation plus yielding.

Deviates to the left.
Right counter-deviation plus yielding.

Fig. No. 44/b

become more and more reduced, until they are living only as a thought in the conduct of the rider, expressed in his slight levelling function.

These minute functions, brought about ultimately by invisible inner reflexions, are the secret of smooth conduct and of a submissive determined forward motion full of impulsion.

If the horse turns suddenly away from the direction of riding, e.g. because it becomes frightened by something, refuses to jump an obstacle, etc., the first step to be made by the rider is a determined and, if necessary, most energetic counter-deviation action. He must bring the horse back by *this* means into the direction originally used and *never by continuing the animal's evasive movement on a circle.* It is necessary to draw special attention to the above statement, since many inexperienced riders try to correct the situation in the wrong manner mentioned. The result of this incorrect practice is most likely to be the horse's renewed opposition. After the counter-deviation action the correction of the situation occurs according to the cause which has produced the particular evasive movement (see the detailed explanations).

The activities of the rider described in the present paragraph produce a valuable loosening effect on the horse, which can often prevent the animal from taking up a stiff crookedness. Bearing this in mind, this particular conduct is closely linked with that combined operation, the aim of which is to correct the horse's acutely crooked posture.

FUNCTION OF THE HORSE'S BODY IN THE MOTION AND ITS REGULATION

The horse performs the actual movements of locomotion by its legs. However, the way in which the legs can discharge their duty depends upon the collaboration of the entire body. If the position of the body is regular, the performance will be efficient; otherwise, the body will hinder and obstruct the free movement of the legs and hamper the course of the horse's onward motion.

Correcting the possible irregularities demands a fair amount of skill on the part of the rider, but even more important is his sense of feeling, which can only be developed by careful observations and persevering work. The difficulty is that the irregularities may manifest themselves in a number of different ways and they may appear in all sorts of combinations; they may only slightly hinder the clarity of the animal's locomotion or destroy it completely.

In dealing with the various operations of adjustment, it is only possible to explain the main principles, but I shall endeavour to offer solutions to a number of specific problems which may arise in the course of practice. When the rider has become familiar with these basic principles it will be easier for him to develop an instinct for recognizing the situation and choosing the appropriate treatment in each particular actual case, as he will have a sound theoretical background.

The irregularities and their treatment can be best examined in two main groups, as they confront the rider in practice with problems, according to the position of the object.

In the first group we will deal with the general manifestation of the defects and their elimination, and in the second group with special cases.

### THE GENERAL MANIFESTATION OF DEFECTS IN THE STATE OF THE HORSE'S BODY AND THEIR CORRECTION

As a rule, the horse in a faulty state, due to either of the irregularities, produces a particular sensation in the rider. This is a curious feeling of tension in the rider's body, as if an inner force were trying to extend it. As soon as the horse becomes regulated and supple this odd sensation disappears instantly.

However, while the rider is in the throes of the sensation, it is possible for him to diagnose the various deficiencies separately in accordance with the method recommended for each particular irregularity.

If there is a common sensation produced by the various impediments of the horse's body, it is evident that there must be a similarly common method of adjustment by the application of which the horse's defective state can be, at least partly, restored.

The evolution of this method is based upon the fact that, whatever the nature of the defect, its origin is in the horse's mind and it takes shape in one way or another in its body, mainly in stiffness of the back or shoulders.

With regard to the mental background, the rider's aim should be to make the animal realize that the whole situation is most comfortable if it is in a supple state. In this persuasion his first task should be to prevent the development of impediments by recognizing and smoothly counteracting any defective intention of the horse. This is, at the same time, the best method of safeguarding the animal's regularity. For this purpose make good use of the general loosening exercise, without the employment of any active interference or of the execution of some mild suppling movements as described on page 266.

If, however, the rider fails to prevent the irregularity, or the loosening exercise is not effective enough, he should at first employ the following general method of correction, the essence of which is derived from the present discussion:

To begin with, relax the muscles completely and cease all activities previously exercised, since the cause of the defect may be due to their incorrect application.

Then, while in motion (best at a walk), execute some slight interchanging movements of loosening character in quick succession (various forms of the levelling function, touches on the withers, etc.). The aim is to produce a mild 'trembling' effect on the horse, which by its pleasant sensation stimulates the animal mentally to abandon its opposition and thereby loosen the stiffness.

If the result desired is not yet achieved, in order to produce the necessary suppling effect make half-halts eventually in long series, according to the recommendations given on page 146.

The rider, by the application of the method described above, will generally overcome the horse's opposition, while loosening any stiffness in its body. Therefore, before making any attempt to cure individually one or other irregularity by the employment of special means, the rider should introduce his corrective measures always by this general method.

SPECIAL MANIFESTATIONS OF DEFECTS IN THE STATE OF THE HORSE'S BODY AND THEIR CORRECTION

In curing acute or greatly improved irregularities it is necessary to employ special methods suited to the particular requirement of the actual case. This relates mainly to spoilt or obstinate horses and when teaching the animal for the correction of definitely ascertained defects.

In connection with the execution of the various procedures certain general considerations of practical importance should be mentioned.

At the beginning of the practice the procedures should be carried out at a walk and trot. Only when the horse has become fully conversant with their basic principles can the irregularities be treated in a canter. In theory, the procedures are the same in all three paces, but at the canter one must take into account the effect of the special nature of the pace action (see page 193).

The process of adjustment can be equally well accomplished when using either the sitting or the forward position.

Finally, the rider should take great care at the early stages of schooling, when substantial and firm regulating actions are necessary, not to overstrain the animal. During this period it is desirable to employ gaiters on the hind legs.

Having reviewed the general aspects of the subject, let us now examine each irregularity in turn.

### Natural crookedness

Natural crookedness originates from the region of the withers and shows a slight distortion in the continuity of the spinal line, causing a lateral shift of the quarters. Actually this is an inherent structural impediment of almost all quadrupeds and is most evident in dogs. Thus it is a direct consequence of natural causes.

The diagnosis and cure of this irregularity are carried out in exactly the same manner as is recommended for correcting the stiff crookedness of the body (see page 170).

### Unequally distributed balance of the body weight

The soundness of any posture, either in stationary position or in motion, depends upon the equilibrium in which it is maintained. In a proper state of balance the weight is equally distributed around the static centre of gravity, so that no part of the body is overburdened by an extra load. The unequal encumbrance would upset the whole posture of the body by shifting its centre of gravity.

Owing to the external load which may weigh heavily upon them, horses are inclined to distribute their own weight unequally in their bodies. The forehand in particular can easily become overburdened, resulting in an immediate adverse effect on the mobility of the shoulders.

With such an unequal distribution of weight the animal cuts into the ground with its forelegs, while its hind legs, which ought to thrust the body forward, cannot find sufficient support on the ground, since they do not carry sufficient weight.

In most forms of crookedness the force of the defect displaces the shoulders from their straight position. In such cases the shoulders, being already overburdened, become unequally laden. The surplus load weighs on the shoulder which is in the direction of their displacement.

The following symptoms can be of help in diagnosing the defect:

in its state of faulty balance the horse tries to find support from the reins, making the rider feel a strong tension in the hands;

the animal deviates from the straight line towards the direction of the more heavily laden shoulder;

while changing direction, it performs movements characteristic of the turn round the shoulders instead of round the quarters;

the horse tends to stumble, even on a slight unevenness of the ground, making this mistake mostly with its foreleg on the overladen side.

In order to restore the balance of the body, it is necessary to set the forelegs free from the ground, by which they obtain freedom to advance, and to shift the weight more towards the quarters, which facilitates the work of the hind legs in thrusting the body forward.

To succeed the best method is to use a continuous series of retardment and driving functions (half-halts). The yielding phases which join the two functions together provide the horse with the best chance of treading more under its weight with the hind legs, while enabling it to strike more forward, and thus to correct the overburdened state of its forehand.

### The stiffened muscles of the back

This particular irregularity is closely associated with the general impediments of the horse's body. Thus the recommendations given on page 160 are of special importance in connection with the present case.

In addition to the general causes, there are some other factors which bring about the stiffening of the muscles of the back. These are: carrying the saddle, tightening of the girth, the load, the hard touch or movements of the rider and pain.

An acute state of stiffness conveys to the rider the same impression as if the horse were trying to discharge its droppings. This sensation is greatly reduced when the back is only mildly stiffened, but the effect can still be distinctly felt. It is also clearly recognizable in the animal's reaction to the drive-on function (see page 145).

However, the sensation is most apparent in the seat, which feels a physical hardness both during the locomotion and in the stationary position. In most cases this sensation is not as strong on both sides of the back, since the stiffness usually affects them with unequal intensity.

As the stiffness can be felt mainly in the seat, this should be used for diagnosing the irregularity. For this purpose the rider should bring the seat into contact with the horse's back more closely than normally. He can do this by sinking it emphatically into the saddle during a series of stride actions. In order to ascertain at the same time the difference of intensity affecting the two sides of the back, the rider should create this closer contact in those moments when the back muscles on the critical side are firmly propped up by the support position of the identical hind leg.

The movements of the rising-trot are the most suitable for the proper execution of the formal part of the procedure and the development of the feeling required. The reason for this is that

each sitting-down movement establishes the needed closer contact with the animal's back, and

the establishment of this contact automatically occurs in those moments when one of the hind legs is in the support position.

By choosing the direction of the rising-trot the rider is certain that his seat will touch those side muscles of the back which he has decided to probe when they are in a propped-up position. If at the moment of lowering the seat the touch of the back conveys a pleasant elastic feeling, then the rider knows that the horse's side which is on the direction of the trot is in a state of suppleness. If the rider feels by his seat the same sensations alternately on both sides, this should indicate that the animal's back muscles on both sides are in equally supple state.

It is not only the rider but also the horse in which the action of the seat can arouse pleasant or unpleasant sensations, according to whether the movement touches its supple or its stiffened side. The difference in the sensation can stimulate both the rider and the horse to perform movements by which the sinking back into the saddle occurs while the hind leg on the relaxed side is in its support phase.

Thus, if the rider does not take care in choosing the direction *deliberately*, he will instinctively sit down during that phase of the motion which conveys the pleasant sensation; and

the horse, if the rider in sitting down happens to fall on the stiffened side of the animal, will make an effort by fidgeting to 'jog' the unobservant rider over to the use of the other direction.

In view of the fact that the majority of horses are inclined toward left-sided stiffness, it can be assumed that most riders execute the rising-trot to the right.

The procedure for loosening the stiffened back muscles should always start with, and probably be completed by, the general method for the correction of defects (see page 160).

In some isolated cases this general treatment will not result in the complete relaxation of the back muscles. Then the rider should resort to loosening them direct.

The motion of the rising-trot, with its burdening (taking) and easing (yielding) elements, is ideally suited to supplement the basic procedure or to be used in combination with it for producing the loosening effect. In order to demonstrate to the horse more plausibly the meaning of the functions employed, the rider should augment his sinking movements so as to touch the saddle in a bouncing manner.

In the case of one-sided stiffness choose for sitting down that side of the back which is affected by the impediment, which is generally the left side, and restrict the bump to the buttock on the inside; that is, where the stiffness is located.

The more the horse relaxes in reaction to the sharper touches of the seat, the more the rider should reduce their strength to the mild form of sitting-down movements which he normally uses.

When the animal has lost its one-sided stiffness the rider should reward it by changing the direction of his sitting-down movements, thus lightening the burden on that side of the back which was affected by the irregularity.

During the procedure it is desirable for the rider to reduce the sharpness of his action from time to time, either by sitting down in a smoother manner or by changing direction during a few strides.

The animal will realize very quickly that the locomotion becomes more pleasant if it meets the rider's sitting-down movements with relaxed back muscles. Therefore, prompted by its preference for convenience, it gives up its stiffness, thus fulfilling the desire of its master.

The effects produced by the movements of the rising-trot can also be achieved by using the sitting position. For this purpose the rider should exercise repeatedly stronger but short pressures of his seat on the saddle in conformity with the rhythm of the trot. For the cancellation of the pressures he should in similar rhythm relax the engaged muscles of his waist.

While riding at a walk the basic method for the elimination of the stiffness in question can be supplemented by the following procedure:

Move the upper body slightly *backwards* from the ready position and from this posture

exercise a pushing-like pressure with the seat-bone towards the animal's withers by moving the lower end of the spine and the buttocks moderately forward.

Maintain the above posture during two or three push-strokes and repeat the pressure of the seat-bone once or twice; finally,

take the upper body forward again to the ready position during two or three push-strokes, and then

repeat the whole procedure several times.

Horses are rather inclined to stiffen their back muscles *after* the completion of transitions. It is, therefore, prudent for the rider to apply preventive measures at these moments. For this purpose he should exercise repeatedly slight pressing-like movements of the seat on the animal's back by moving the lower part of the spine forward and downwards and then back to its original yielding posture. The same effect can be produced by short pressures on the stirrups or by interchanged pressures of the buttocks.

During schooling this method of checking should be carried out frequently when the horse, having been brought into a standstill position, responds to the drive-on signal by going into motion.

With horses which have reached more advanced stages of education this checking action is unnecessary; it is generally sufficient if the rider mildly braces his waist for a moment in order to warn the animal to maintain its suppleness.

THE DISTORTION OF THE NATURAL LINE OF THE SPINE

This form of irregularity occurs as an adjunct to the stiffness of the back muscles and may manifest itself in the following manner:

By affecting the back in a *longitudinal direction*, the effect distorts the natural line of the spine either

by arching it slightly into a convex shape, which is common; or

by making it concave, causing a stiff hollow back.

By affecting the back in a *lateral direction*, the stiffness produces a crooked posture of the horse, which can be traced either

to the counter-bracing of the stiffened back muscles, or

to their one-sided contraction.

### THE LONGITUDINAL DISTORTION OF THE BACK

*The convex distortion of the spine*

This irregularity manifests itself in the protruding of that part of the back which is covered by the saddle. Although this is hardly noticeable to the eye in most cases, the accompanying tension clearly reveals the trouble to the rider.

The distortion interferes with the free swing of the spinal column, causing stiffness in the entire system of locomotion. As a result the horse may display considerable resistance.

The rider can diagnose the presence of this irregularity by observing the horse's reaction to the retarding action applied from drive-on. During this the resisting back muscles aggravate the distortion, giving the rider the impression that he is pushed up by the back into an elevated and unstable position, while the horse is preparing itself for the execution of a buck. At the same time, the animal either jolts into a decreased motion or into a standstill. When driving it forward, the horse, instead of stepping out freely, pushes itself slowly into the motion.

Furthermore, due to the stiffness of the horse's muscles and spinal column, the convex back conveys a sensation of considerable hardness to the seat, which can be clearly ascertained by checking the swinging movement of the back.

The elimination of this fault should begin with the loosening-up of the back muscles, as described on page 165. If it does not yield satisfactory results, it will be necessary to employ the following measures:

While riding at a walk, take the upper body slightly *forward* from the ready position and simultaneously drive the horse on;

remain in this position during two or three push-strokes while *pressing down the thighs* on to the muscles in the region of the withers.

Next, take the upper body back again into the ready position, but not further backwards, as is the case in the muscle-loosening process, and exercise *with the seat* greater pressure over a *wide area* on the horse's back beyond the deepest point of the saddle. This produces a vertically downwards effect;

> while maintaining this position the pressure should last during one to three push-strokes, while passively resisting with the reins.

Finally, relax the muscles engaged in the action; and

> repeat the procedure a few times, starting with the action of taking the upper body forward.

The alternating effects will push the spine in a loosening manner into the right position and thus correct the convex distortion.

When the horse no longer resists and ceases its convex distortion the rider will feel a pleasant sensation of elasticity, which appears, as a rule, quite suddenly without any transition.

An alternative and equally effective method of eliminating this distortion is the application of the swing-improving function by the seat (see page 69).

If this procedure is employed, the rider should increase the adjusting effect of the sitting-down motion involved by performing the motion with greater emphasis while his seat touches the horse's back on a rather wide area through the back third-part of the saddle. Having completed the sitting-down motion, he should 'keep' the seat on the saddle for a moment and only afterwards raise the body again. With this short passive function of the seat the rider acts against the resistance of the horse's back.

In more acute cases carry out the above procedure with the following alterations:

> interrupt the rising movements and 'keep' the seat, while maintaining the forward position, continuously on the saddle during two to four push-strokes. During this period, at the moment of each push-stroke

> exercise (from the above position) a mild pressure with the seat against the horse's back and simultaneously

> change over to a passive tension with the reins, which should be discontinued as soon as the rising movements recommence.

Due to the rhythmical changes of position, this series of actions adds smoothness to the procedure in spite of the transitory passive tension involved and will *aid* the horse in abandoning the convex distortion of its back. If necessary, the entire procedure should be repeated without increasing the strength of the activities employed.

When the convex distortion appears in combination with a one-sided muscle contraction it is best first to correct the latter irregularity and afterwards undertake the treatment of the distortion.

Later on, when the rider has acquired some experience in dealing with these troubles, he can attempt to cure both impediments simultaneously.

### The stiff hollow back

In this particular physical state the horse's back shows the reverse form of the convex back. Its effect is partly to hinder the swing of the spinal column, thus making the entire locomotion stiff, and partly to help the horse to evade the influence of the rider.

The rider's sensation, apart from the stiffness felt in the horse's back, is the feeling that his seat is sunk deeper than usual into the horse. The animal tries to evade the action of the reins by getting over the bit and the rider's driving legs have difficulty in preventing the hocks from lagging behind and in urging them under the body. On the whole, the animal gives the rider an unpleasant impression of helplessness. It proceeds in a flurried manner with the forelegs, while dragging its hind legs after its body.

During the process of eliminating this defect the introductory muscle-loosening procedure is of great importance, and therefore its execution requires the most careful attention.

But the main responsibility rests on the rider's legs, which are used to drive the hocks energetically forward. While the legs are in action the hands have to maintain the contact in an especially refined manner. In this way the animal's spine is supported from the front, enabling it to take up the normal arching of the back. The rôle of the seat is to facilitate the horse in adopting this position by following the swinging motion of the spine without any resistance.

For the sake of promoting the arching of the back, the bascule-improving exercise (see page 291) is a valuable aid and its frequent practice is recommended.

## THE LATERAL DISTORTION OF THE SPINE, CROOKEDNESS OF THE HORSE

All experts on riding universally agree that the greatest difficulty in equitation is to keep the horse straight; that is, free from any faulty deviation from its straight position. I think it may be worth while analysing this problem in detail in view of its extreme importance.

Figs. No. 45/a-f show the characteristic differences between the horse's straight, bent and the various crooked positions.

Crookedness, defined more accurately, occurs when the straight or bent line of the horse's spine is broken by the distortion of its continuity. The distortion of the spine is most characteristic at its points of support, which are in the front between the shoulders, and in the rear between the hip-bones. Generally speaking, these are the focal points of stiffness and crookedness.

The cause of this irregularity is to be found in the horse's resistance (mental function), which results either in the counter-bracing of the back muscles or in their one-sided stiff contraction.

### CROOKEDNESS CAUSED BY COUNTER-BRACING

Crookedness is most frequently caused by the horse's function of counter-bracing, and this can be regarded as the most serious trouble which upsets the regularity of the animal (see Figs. No. 45/c-e).

In this state the horse tries to press away from the focal point of the stiffness, in the region of the withers, those parts of its body which are connected to it. According to the distribution of the effect produced by the counter-bracing, and the parts of the horse's body on which the effect is focused, the irregularity may manifest itself in three main forms:

the counter-bracing affects equally the forehand and the quarters, which is the most common case;

its effect is focused on the quarters, which occurs frequently; and the effect is focused on the forehand, which is comparatively rare.

The common manifestation of these defects is that the horse, if unaided, turns its neck, and sometimes its croup as well, in the direction opposite to the side of the stiffness. At the same time, the displaced shoulder stands hard against the stiffened neck (see Fig. No. 46/a), which is the main difficulty to adjustment.

## Table No. 5

### CHARACTERISTIC FORMS OF THE HORSE'S POSITION

| Adjusted horse | | Crooked horse | | | |
|---|---|---|---|---|---|
| in | | the crookedness is caused by | | | |
| straight | bent | counter-bracing | | | muscle contraction |
| position | | equally distributed | focused on the | | |
| | | | quarters | forehand | |
| | | | | | |
| Fig.No.45/a | Fig.No.45/b | Fig.No.45/c | No.Fig.45/d | Fig.No.45/e | Fig.No.45/f |

The position of the horse has a definite influence on its movements and reactions to the rider's demands. In order to clarify the practical meaning of this statement, we shall analyse the subject according to the

animal's straight and crooked positions, supposing that the crookedness is caused by left-sided stiffness;

by taking as examples three commonly used movements, the progress on a circle, the performance of turns and the strike-off into a canter;

detailed whether the execution of the particular movement occurs to the right- or the left-hand direction; and see

in which direction and why the horse reacts more easily or quickly, and why its reaction is more restricted when the execution of the same task takes place in the other direction.

### THE ADJUSTED, STRAIGHT HORSE

The shoulders and the croup of the animal are in the same line;
the load on its shoulders is equally distributed; and
its shoulder mobility is equally free in both directions.
The horse executes the tasks demanded with equal suppleness and readiness in each situation.

### THE CROOKED HORSE

*If the crookedness is caused by equally distributed counter-bracing or by that focused on the buarters.*

the shoulders of the animal are pushed slightly to the left and its croup pressed a bit to the right;
there is a surplus load on the left shoulder; and
mobility of the shoulders is free to the left side only.

Riding on a Circle
Riding on the left rein is easier, because
its direction coincides with the direction of the shoulder mobility and
preventing 'falling-in' requires counter-balancing actions only.
This is the reason why riders prefer riding by instinct on the left rein on a circle.
Riding on the right rein is more difficult, because
its direction is opposite to that of the mobility of the shoulders; and
the obstruction caused by this must be counteracted by substantial actions; and
the animal is inclined to resist the rider's corrective interference.

The Performance of Turns
Turning to the left is more difficult, because
the overburdened left shoulder and the direction of its mobility inspires the horse to fall hastily into the turn.
Curing this fault may arouse the animal's opposition.
Turning to the right is easier
in spite of the fact that the turn occurs in the direction opposite to the shoulder mobility, because
the main fault of turning, the falling-in, owing to the particular position of the horse, is automatically counteracted by the animal.

The Strike-off into the Canter
The performance is more difficult when asked for the left fore leading, because
the left shoulder, being overburdened, has no freedom of action and pulls the horse to the left.
Striking off with the right fore leading is easier, because
the right (leading) shoulder is free of surplus load and thus it is not hampered in its action.

*Situation when the crookedness is caused by counter-bracing focused on the forehand or by one-sided muscle contraction:*
in the first case the shoulders are pushed to the right, while the quarters retain their original position;
in the second case both the shoulders and the quarters are pulled towards the centre of the contraction;
in both cases there is a surplus load on the right shoulder, and the shoulder mobility is noticeable towards the right side.

Concerning the movements of the horse and its reactions to the rider's demands, the situation is in all details the reverse of those formerly discussed.

## *Equally distributed counter-bracing*

Due to the bracing power produced by the horse's resistance, the shoulders become pushed away from the straight position towards the side of the stiffened back muscles and starting from there

the neck and the croup—prompted by the characteristic counter-bracing function of the muscles—are pressed towards the side which is opposite to the displacement of the shoulders and, at the same time

the shoulder on the critical side becomes overburdened.

When in this posture, the horse deviates from the straight course slightly in the direction of the shoulder displacement, while the faulty position of the croup promotes this deviating movement.

For example, by left-sided counter-bracing, which is the most common case, the shoulders are pushed to the left, the neck and the croup pressed to the right, making the animal deviate to the left. The reason for this left-sided symptom is found in the fact that the natural crookedness of the horse induces it to exercise the counter-bracing in the same direction.

In diagnosing the irregularity the rider will note a peculiar sensation of tension in that half of his body which is on the animal's critical side, whereas on the other side he feels something akin to emptiness. At the same time he has the sensation that his seat-bone on the stiffened side of the horse is not elastically supported by its back.                    [*Continued on page* 174

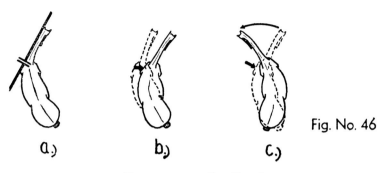

Fig. No. 46

a.)              b.)              c.)

EXPLANATION OF FIG. NO. 46

Diagram a)

The horse in its crooked posture props up from behind the stiffened neck and by *pressing* against the rein 'hangs' on it. The animal shows resistance towards any action executed by this particular rein, giving the impression of 'one-sided hardness of the mouth'.

If the rider, inspired by his faulty instinct, tries to eliminate the hardness by pulling the rein on this side, he will aggravate the situation with all its undesirable symptoms. All directing functions of this rein meet also resistance without resulting in the reaction desired.

Diagram b)

In order to remedy the situation, the critical shoulder must be first of all 'pushed away' from behind the stiffened side of the neck. This can be achieved by the *counter-deviation effect of the opposite rein* coupled with the oscillating movement of the upper body, or by the establishment of the lateral mobility of the shoulders.

In the beginning, when practising the procedure, it often happens that the horse shows a tendency to roll or rush away, or it does not react to the leading function of the rein opposite to its shifted shoulder position. These are common forms of resistance which can easily be overcome by some smooth but definite half-halts of loosening effect, interlocked in the general flow of the adjustment.

Diagram c)

The shoulder does not stand any more against the neck, the 'hardness of the mouth' disappears and the horse accepts with smoothness the effect of any rein function on its critical side.

In order to make more clear the meaning of the defect in question, we shall compare it with the pushing action of the horse (see page 109):

the former is connected with the animal's crooked position and its correction *starts* with *yielding* the rein;

the latter is produced by the horse's opposition and its correction *starts* with the function of *passive tension*.

*Conclusion: at any time when, as a consequence of stiffness in the shoulders, 'hardness' is felt through either of the reins, the rider may exercise lateral moving or loosening effect with the critical rein only after the shoulder is removed (by the aid of the counter-deviation rein effect) from its fixed and propping-up position.*

The previous satisfaction of this basic condition is supposed by the author whenever the application of the rein functions mentioned is recommended by him in the explanations below.

The irregularity can also be felt distinctly by pulling on the reins. A pull on the critical side meets resistance from the stiffened muscles in the horse's neck, propped from behind by the shoulder in its faulty position (see Fig. No. 46/a). The horse does not turn smoothly in response to the action of the turning-rein, but tends to fall stiffly into the new direction. While pulling on the other rein the rider's sensation is as if the pull ends in emptiness, and he has simultaneously the impression that, in order to bring about an effect by his hand, he is compelled to shift it over to the side opposite to its normal position. In response to the turning signal the horse, instead of performing a round turn, makes a movement similar in character to that of the turn on the forehand.

The difference in the reaction shown by the horse to the pulling effects of the rein may be the reason for the unjustified statements of certain riders, who declare: 'My horse's mouth is hard on the left side', 'My horse is left-mouthed', etc. In reality, no horse is stiff or hard in the left or right side of its *mouth*! In order to dispel this unpleasant sensation it is necessary to remove the stiffness from the muscles and discharge the shoulders from rigidity. This will eliminate the crookedness and by it the difference felt in the 'sensitivity' of the mouth.

As a help in diagnosing the sensation which is conveyed by the straight and the crooked position of the horse, and to emphasize the difference between them, the rider will find it useful to try the following practical experiment:

The experiment is based upon the bad habit common in horses of looking with distorted neck in the direction opposite to their stiffened side, as if attracted by some object of curiosity or fright. This reaction is prompted by their instinct of retention. Thus the animal which is inclined to become crooked by left-sided stiffness almost always tries to find a 'cause of fright' on the right side, and vice versa. The opposite side offers no particular interest to the horse, except when it observes a genuine cause for fright.

The rider can make use of this phenomenon by choosing a long, straight line, on one side of which is an object which can arouse the animal's interest more than the scenery on the other side (e.g. a stone wall, an edge of woods, a fence, etc.; see Fig. No. 47).

If the horse is inclined to left-sided stiffness and crookedness, it should first be ridden on the selected course with the attractive object on the right-hand side (Fig. No. 47/a).

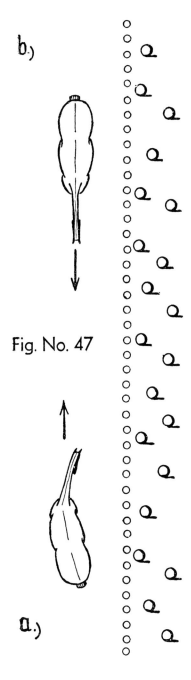

b.)

Fig. No. 47

a.)

In this case the horse will keep looking with great interest and with a strongly distorted neck to the right, towards the edge of the woods, and will show pronounced symptoms of left-sided counter-bracing. While it proceeds in this state the rider should analyse the sensation of tension which is conveyed by the crookedness of the horse and carefully memorize these impressions.

Then the horse should be ridden in the other direction, so that the object of interest is now on the side which is opposite to the animal's inclination to crookedness (Fig. No. 47/b). The change causes a conflict between its two different instincts, namely, that between

its curiosity, which urges it to look at the strange object by turning its neck towards the left and pushing its shoulders towards the right, and

its inclination towards left-sided crookedness, the characteristics of which are opposite to the above.

Because of the conflict of these two instincts, the contrasting effects cancel each other and the animal gets into a more or less straight position, thus arousing a particular sensation in the rider. He should concentrate on himself and try to analyse the sensations which are created by the horse's straight position.

Then, by riding up and down this course, he should alternate the two situations. Owing to the sudden change, the difference in character of the two sensations can be vividly appreciated.

As it has been stated already, the elimination of the irregularity should always be preceded by a suppling of the back and by correctly adjusting the distribution of the animal's weight. The more successfully this is completed, the more simple will be the task of eliminating the defect.

The special process of adjustment is composed of the following four elements:

1. The 'stirring movement of shoulders'; its purpose is to remove the shoulders from their fixed position by the counter-deviation rein function (see Fig. No. 46/b).

2. Creation of a state of weakness in the horse's resistance, shown in the stiffened muscles of the back.

3. A distinct (sudden) change of flexion and turning movement in the direction opposite to the 'stirring movement', with the aim of completing the release of the neck from the propping effect of the stiff shoulder (see Fig. No. 46/c), and the loosening of any remaining stiffness.

4. Counter-holding of shoulders for preventive purpose, executed towards the side opposite to the deviation, and a simple change of flexion for a renewed 'stirring movement'.

This process, with its interchanged movements, is a typical example of the method of how to 'balance' the horse (see pages 88 and 98). It is also a distinctly articulated form of the levelling function.

I have endeavoured to give an explanation of each movement in the form of questions and answers, the answer to each question being given both by text and by diagrams. By reading in succession the answers to the questions under b, a full account of the procedure of adjustment will be found.

This explanation takes as an example the most common problem —the horse which becomes crooked by left-sided counter-bracing. The operation is identical in the case of right-sided counter-bracing; only the particular sides involved in the explanation have to be reversed.

The key to the diagrams which accompany the text is shown in Table No. 6.

## Table No. 6

### KEY TO THE TEXT-DIAGRAMS

It illustrates at the same time as a summary the basic functions of the rider

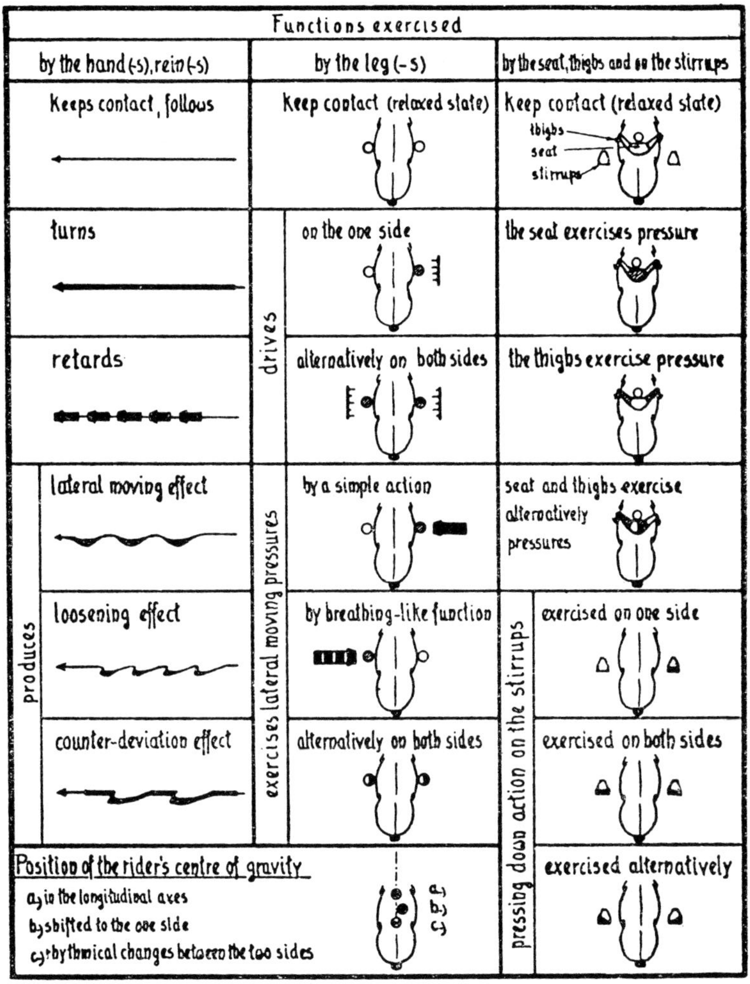
Functions exercised
by the hand(-s), rein(-s)
by the leg(-s)
by the seat, thighs and on the stirrups
Keeps contact, follows
Keep contact (relaxed state)
Keep contact (relaxed state)
thighs
seat
stirrups
turns
drives
on the one side
the seat exercises pressure
retards
alternatively on both sides
the thighs exercise pressure
produces
lateral moving effect
exercises lateral moving pressures
by a simple action
seat and thighs exercise alternatively pressures
loosening effect
by breathing-like function
pressing down action on the stirrups
exercised on one side
counter-deviation effect
alternatively on both sides
exercised on both sides
Position of the rider's centre of gravity
a.) in the longitudinal axes
b.) shifted to the one side
c.) rhythmical changes between the two sides
a.)
b.)
c.)
exercised alternatively

*Remarks:* Signs drawn at the same height on the two sides of a diagram denote *simultaneous* actions.

When two different kinds of rein or leg signals are drawn under or next to each other on the same side of a diagram it denotes that the particular actions follow each other in *succession.*

We shall now examine in detail how the procedure is carried out from phase to phase.

*Phase No. 1, the stirring movement of shoulders* (*Fig. No. 48/a-d*)
What is the horse's bearing? (Fig. a)

It proceeds at a walk and displays all the adverse effects of crookedness, produced by the equally distributed counter-bracing, by falling on its left shoulder and deviating slightly towards the left. The shoulder on the stiffened side stands hard against the neck, giving it a fixed background for exercising resistance.

What is the object to be achieved by the rider? (Fig. b)

His aim is to counter-balance the horse's deviating movement to the left by making the shoulders mobile and let the horse step from the shoulders in the direction opposite to the deviation (right).

At the same time, he desires to change the position of the quarters. This is achieved automatically, since one of the side-effects of his main function shifts the quarters to the left.
What is the rider's action? (Fig. c)

He conducts the horse to the right by a counter-deviation action of the right rein, while yielding with the left rein. He blends this process by the levelling function.

His right leg provides a lateral-moving effect and animates.

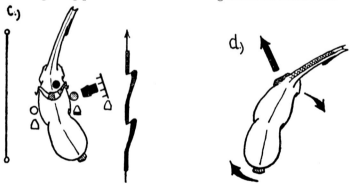

What effect has the rider's action on the horse? (Fig. d)

At first it gives no sign of yielding and, instead of turning smoothly, it drifts from its shoulders towards the left.

After a while it suddenly 'wobbles' with the quarters to the left, while making a pivot around the forehand towards the right.

*Phase No. 2, the creation of a state of weakness* (*Fig. No. 49/a-c*)
What is the object to be achieved by the rider? (Fig. a)

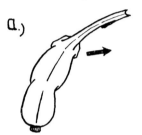

The unsuccessful attempt of the first phase is to be fortified by inserting an effective loosening element, in order to weaken the horse's resistance, and thus to quicken its inclination to obey.

What is the rider's action? (Fig. b/1-2)

While proceeding in the turn which is directed unsuccessfully to the right he

first retards the horse (Fig. b/1), and then

in the moment of its yielding to retardment he drives it resolutely in a pushing-like manner *towards* the direction of the stirring movement (to the right; Fig. b/2).

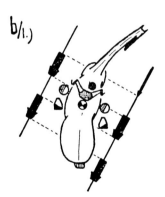
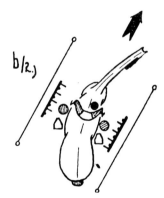

The interlocked retardment and drive-on, which can be repeated several times, create the weakness in the horse's resistance.

The involved levelling function increases the loosening effect of the procedure on the shoulders.

The pushing action of the rider, by obliging the shoulders to participate in the desired motion, promotes the shoulder mobility and by it makes a first step towards their adjustment.

What effect has the rider's action on the horse? (Fig. c)

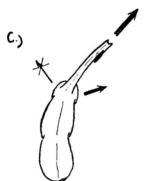

The horse tends to yield and to step forward to the right.

It ceases drawing to the left and the character of its motion to the right is that of the turn on the haunches.

The horse will not show this inclination immediately after the first trial, especially during the first weeks of schooling. Therefore, before carrying out the action of the following phase, it is necessary to repeat the actions of the first and second phases until their aim has been achieved. During this procedure, the course of which is illustrated in Fig. No. 50, the horse—by successive repetitions of the stirring movements (I) interchanged with the

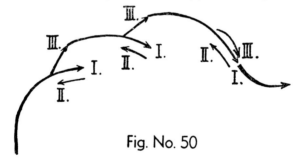

Fig. No. 50

interlocked retardments (II) and drives-on (III)—may perhaps make a half-circle or even greater turn, until the final drive-on action proves the presence of the 'state of weakness' by becoming effective in the direction desired (forwards to the right).

*Phase No. 3, the distinct, sudden change of flexion (Fig. No. 51)*
What is the object to be achieved by the rider? (Fig. a)

He attempts, after producing the state of weakness and the

mobility of the shoulders, to transfer the horse's shoulders to the
side opposite to their resisting position (to the right), and by this
to stop the adverse effect of the stiffened shoulder (left).   Sub-
sequently he intends to remove the remaining stiffness from
the muscles.

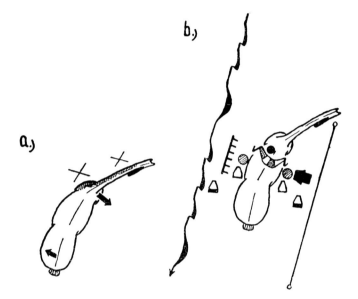

What is the rider's action? (Fig. b)

Making good use of the momentarily loosened state of the back
and the shoulders, he yields with the former leading rein (right)
and employs the opposite one (left) to lead the horse in the same
direction.   This change in the directing functions of the reins
must be carried out with an emphatic, sudden movement, but
*without a jerk.*   The emphatic effect in the change of flexion pushes
the shoulders to the side opposite to the original displacement (to
the right).

While the rider is executing this change of flexion he should
transfer his centre of gravity to the *outside* (right) in order to
promote the transposition of the shoulders.   This is a very important feature of the procedure, since the gravitational effect thus
produced obliges the animal to shift its shoulders and to stride out
of them in the direction in which their mobility has been restricted.

At the same time, this action enables the rider to exercise increased pressure with his outside leg on the horse's side, thereby prompting the adjustment of the quarters.

The rider can augment the effect of the change of flexion by exercising a definite pressure with the thigh on the inside (left) of the horse simultaneously with the lateral-moving pressure of his outside (right) leg.

When the horse yields smoothly to the change of flexion the emphatic action, which is characteristic of the procedure, must be stopped *immediately*. At the same time, the weight of the upper body should be brought slightly to the inside in order to establish the harmony between its position and the horse's flexed position. Furthermore, the inside (left) rein must be eased with special care, while the horse can take up a slightly stronger contact on the outside rein.

But the emphatic action must also ease *at once* if the function of the acting rein (left) encounters stiffness and resistance on the part of the animal. This reveals that the shoulders have not yet been removed from their fixed position. In this case the previous procedure should be repeated in order to achieve a state of pliability. Trying to accomplish an emphatic change of flexion in the face of stiff resistance is injurious, as *it works against the development of the horse's suppleness*.

After the successful emphatic change of flexion:

the directing action of the new turning rein (left) should be combined with some loosening functions and, if necessary, with one or two lateral-moving functions in order to retain the shoulders in their adjusted position; simultaneously

the rider's outside leg (right) keeps the quarters on the line by exercising lateral-moving pressures.

What is the effect of the rider's action on the horse? (Fig. c)

The animal, in its state of weakness, and on account of the sudden change of flexion, pushes its shoulders in the direction opposite to the initiating action of the rider. By this it promotes the relaxed flexibility of the neck, which is slightly bent in the same direction. The animal does not stretch longer against the left rein (Fig. c/1).

The hind legs step into the hoof-marks left by the forelegs and the horse follows the curve involved in the movement (Fig. c/2).

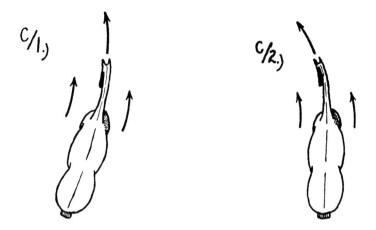

*Phase No. 4, the counter-balance of shoulders and quarters (Fig. No. 52)*

What is the object of the rider? (Fig. a)

In order to prevent the shoulders from becoming displaced again, and the critical shoulder (left) overburdened, the rider must see that they are kept to the right and the quarters on the line.

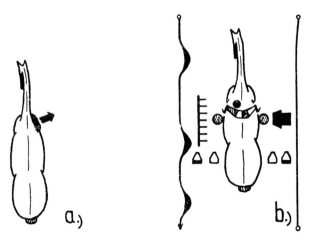

What is the rider's action? (Fig. b)

He exercises counter-balancing movements by breathing-like functions of the left rein.

His right leg keeps the quarters in line by exercising lateral-moving pressures.

In supporting the above functions he changes his weight position from the inside to the outside and back again in an oscillating manner.

His left leg animates!

What is the effect of the rider's action on the horse? (Fig. c)

During the first few strides it yields to the counter-balancing function of the left rein and rather tends to put weight on its right shoulder (Fig. c/1).

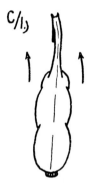 

Progress while in this position is unusual and tiring for the animal, since the bend it has assumed is opposed to its natural crookedness and these forces act against each other. The horse soon stiffens the muscles of its back again, shifts over the shoulders suddenly and puts the weight on the left shoulder. In the entire movement a sudden drifting to the left is felt, while the quarters 'wobble' over to the right (Fig. c/2).

From this moment the whole procedure should be repeated all over again.

The repetition of the procedure is also advantageous in milder cases, when the horse, after the completion of the fourth phase, does not abandon its adjusted position harshly. On such occasions, after the 'counter-balance of shoulders', the flexion of the animal should be changed by a smooth function in order to introduce the renewed 'stirring movement'.

*The maintenance of the adjusted position*

In order to maintain the horse's adjusted position, in addition to the application of the levelling function, the rider should fix its quarters against displacement from the straight line by the means of determined lateral-moving leg pressures and mild counter-deviation rein functions. This practice is the most simple way of safeguarding the general adjustment of a supple horse, since the functions involved automatically support the animal also in retaining its shoulders in the adjusted posture.

As a preventive measure, it is advisable to repeat from time to time the procedure which is described in the fourth phase of the adjustment. Concerning further recommendations, see page 188.

COUNTER-BRACING FOCUSED ON THE QUARTERS (FIG. NO. 45/d)

This is a reduced version of the irregularity caused by the equally distributed counter-bracing. Thus its character, recognition and elimination are very similar to those discussed in connection with the example above.

The main difference is to be found in a stronger displacement of the quarters, whereas the position of the forehand is approximately normal. Consequently, during the procedure of adjustment the replacement of the quarters and their fixing in the regulated position must be carried out with increased attention.

In this state the horse produces a distinct deviating movement towards the direction opposite to the croup position, the result of which is that the animal, if unaided, proceeds on a circle with its neck slightly distorted outwards, corresponding to the nature of the stiffness.

COUNTER-BRACING FOCUSED ON THE FOREHAND (FIG. NO. 45/e)

In this case the horse focuses the effect of its counter-bracing on the forehand, leaving the quarters practically unaffected.

In order to make further explanations more vivid, let us take the typical case of left-sided counter-bracing focused on the forehand.

The characteristic side-effect of the irregularity is that the animal pushes the forehand with its stiffened (left) shoulder and foreleg into a deviating movement (towards the right). The result of this is that the horse, if unaided, proceeds on a circle corresponding to the direction of the counter-bracing (to the right), while its neck is turned towards the inside of this circle. In an extreme case the circling can take the form of a stiff revolving.

First introduce the procedure by some half-halts of loosening effect.

Then the deviation in the motion must be definitely stopped by the application of the corresponding counter-deviating rein effect, supported by lateral-moving pressures of the leg on the same side (the left rein and leg) and the transposition of the centre of gravity (to the left). This should be interchanged with slight counter-movements of the same character, made in an oscillating manner.

When the horse *starts* striding out of its stiffened (left) shoulder in the direction of the counter-deviation (left), the rider should loosen the general stiffness of the animal by performing some half-halts again.

Then, in order to fix the forehand in its corrected posture, he should execute, during one of the yielding moments of the loosening procedure, a *mild* (not emphatic) change of flexion with the rein opposite to the one which has been used for effecting the counter-deviation (in this case the right rein). After the change of flexion this rein may exercise some mild counter-balancing effects.

During further progress the rider should repeat the overall procedure until correction has been completed. Concerning the execution of these repeated movements, the recommendations given on page 188 are equally valid.

CROOKEDNESS CAUSED BY ONE-SIDED MUSCLE CONTRACTION (FIG. NO. 45/f)

This irregularity is the result of the cramped contraction of the back muscles by which the horse generally resists the rider's harsh or incorrect rein actions or his improper attempts to bring the animal into a state of collection.

The stiff contraction originates from the region of the animal's withers, from the same point where the origin of the counter-bracing is found. Its effect, however, manifests itself in the drawing of the affected parts of the body *towards* the centre of stiffness, instead of pressing them away. Thus the horse pulls its head and neck on the one hand, and its quarters on the other, toward the inside of its stiffened back muscles by the means of muscular contraction. In this way the animal's body becomes crooked, showing a faulty bent position in which the lateral displacement of the croup is usually more marked than that of the forehand. If unaided, the horse never turns its neck in the direction opposite to the stiffness.

Generally, the animal changes over to this form of resistance from counter-bracing and retains its original one-sided stiffness. If the horse happens to start the irregularity from the straight position, it will produce it on the side of its natural crookedness.

Aside from a general sensation of stiffness, the rider can discover the irregularity by looking for the following symptoms:

Through his seat he can feel a slight twist on the side towards which the quarters are displaced, making his waist and leg press slightly forward, while his other leg tends to slide backwards on the animal's side.

Owing to the one-sided nature of the stiffness, the horse resists the actions of the rein on its critical side. Furthermore, while in motion, it is inclined to deviate slightly from the straight line towards the side opposite to the stiffness.

Among the sensations which this situation produces, the one-sided stiffness is the most unpleasant. The rider should not be misled by this sensation, however, since the major defect is the horse's mental resistance to external influence.

In order to correct the irregularity, the rider's first duty is to stop his own faulty activity. Then, to promote further progress in the correction, he should drive on the horse firmly and loosen the stiffness of its back by half-halts. After this introduction he should proceed with the execution of the special adjustment. For this

counteract the deviating motion of the animal by a definite counter-deviation action, which loosens the shoulders from their contracted position and indirectly commences the adjustment of the croup; then

in order to augment the effect of the straightening process, apply a mild change of flexion in the direction opposite to the contraction and simultaneously push the quarters to the straight line with the leg on the side of the contraction; if necessary, support this latter action by a tap of the whip;

as an additional measure, exercise from time to time some mild pressures with the leg on the critical side of the animal as a reminder to it to keep its straight position.

It happens quite frequently that, while the rider is correcting the position of the croup, the horse suddenly changes the contraction of the muscles to a counter-bracing and simultaneously takes up a deviating motion towards the opposite side. The rider should eliminate this new irregularity by the appropriate method of adjustment.

For further recommendations, see the next paragraph.

CHANGE OF CORRECTIVE MEASURES DURING THE PROCESS OF THE HORSE'S ADJUSTMENT

The horse is inclined to evade the rider's influence during the course of adjustment by suddenly changing over to some new form of resistance. Therefore it is necessary for the rider to comply flexibly with the new situation created by the horse and to alter his actions in accordance with the changing situation.

This can especially easily occur during those procedures the aim of which is to correct the faulty position of the horse caused by counter-bracing focused on the forehand and by one-sided muscle contraction. The reason for this is that the lateral-moving side-effect of the rein action, which performs the critical change of flexion, is apt to cause the animal to change its irregularity to equally distributed counter-bracing or to a counter-bracing focused on the quarters by pushing its forehand towards the side of its stiffened back muscles.

Bearing this in mind, one can conclude that the critical point during the procedure is the change of flexion, which, in its normal flow, follows after the 'creation of weakness' This is the point where the rider has to take care and employ his counter-measures. Here must he display special smoothness and increase the loosening effect of his activities in order to *prevent* a faulty change in the horse's behaviour.

According to this consideration, and by taking the case when the irregularity is caused by the horse's left-sided stiffness, the elements of the procedure can be summed up as follows:

a *definite* stirring movement to the left;

the creation of weakness by some half-halts;

a *mild* change of flexion towards the right;

a *mild* stirring movement to the right;

the creation of weakness by some half-halts;

a *mild* change of flexion towards the left; and then

repeat the whole procedure in the same sequence, smoothly and interlocked with yielding phases, until the horse takes up its straight position in absolute suppleness.

Apart from its own aim, the rider should employ this means of adjustment frequently, interlocked with the continuity of the basic forms of regulation, by which their smoothness and general loosening effect becomes increased; and for preventive purposes, in order to avert the development of various defects in the horse's behaviour.

By observing closely the movements and their succession of the above process of adjustment, and those of the levelling function, a definite relationship between them can be discovered. The effects produced by both are similar in character, the only difference being in the degree of the general effect and in the time necessary for their execution. The effect of the methodical procedure is more augmented, whereas the execution of the levelling function needs shorter time.

In the course of perfecting the horse's education it is of special importance to exhaust the possibilities latent in this similarity. The meaning of this statement is as follows:

Generally speaking, when the horse proceeds on a straight line there is ample time to forestall crookedness by the application of methodical measures. However, if the animal has to make a sudden turn, a jump, or other quick movement, the defect can appear so suddenly that the rider has no chance to prevent it by lengthy interventions.

In order to avoid such unpleasant situations, which prevent success in coming events (especially during competitions), the animal's obedience in effecting adjustment ought to be developed to the greatest possible degree. For this the best approach is to improve its sensitiveness, drilling patiently by both the individual and the combined method of correction discussed later, until they become unified in a 'fortified levelling function'. In this the normal effect of the levelling function becomes greatly increased and the length of the articulated process considerably reduced. In the end a short indication of the levelling function will represent in the horse's mind the manifestation of the whole process of adjustment to the straight position.

PRACTICES WHICH PROMOTE ADJUSTABILITY TO THE STRAIGHT
POSITION

In order to educate the horse successfully for its adjustability,
one has to employ every means which help, directly or indirectly,
to make it understand the meaning of the signals and aids involved
and, at the same time, facilitate the performance of the actions one
has demanded.

For this purpose the rider can make excellent use of the exercise
described on page 175, where the horse is taken to a long, straight
track, on one side of which is an object likely to attract its
attention (see Fig. No. 47).

First, let the horse proceed in the direction in which it volun-
tarily takes up a more or less straight posture and is most inclined
to obey the signals used to safeguard its straightness (Fig.
No. 47/b).

During this straight course teach the animal, by patient
repetitions, to accept the counter-deviation rein effect for the
stirring movement of shoulders and to obey the lateral-moving
leg pressures for the adjustment of its croup position. Exercise
these functions on the side where the particular object is located.

While turning away from the attraction, accomplish the fourth
phase of the operation, designed for the counter-balancing of
shoulders.

While riding in the reverse direction, drop the reins and let
the animal rest. Use a track rather far away from the main course.

Before turning back again, take up the reins and execute some
half-halts in combination with removing the shoulders from their
rigid position (creation of weakness, Phase No. 2).

During the turn, which should be rather wide, first for a short
time continue the former movements and then execute with
special attention the emphatic change of flexion (Phase No. 3).

After this repeat the whole process several times.

For further improvement it is useful to start the following
additional exercises at about the fifth month of schooling:

the shoulder-in and the turn on the haunches for suppling the
shoulders and improving their lateral mobility; and
the croup-in, for promoting an easier yielding of the quarters.

THE PRACTICE OF ADJUSTMENT TO STRAIGHT POSITION IN A
CONFINED SPACE AND WHEN SCHOOLING GROUPS OF HORSES

The process of adjustment in question can also be taught and practised in a confined space, even where the possibilities of various movements are severely restricted or where a number of horses and riders are being schooled at the same time. The following exercises are especially designed for these conditions.

*Riding through corners*

With a horse which is inclined to deviate to the left as a result of crookedness:

ride to the left direction in the riding arena;

when approaching a corner, lead the horse by the right rein directly against the corner (stirring movement of shoulders); then

perform one or two half-halts in order to create a state of weakness; adjoiningly in the corner

turn suddenly to the left with the left rein, thereby completing the emphatic change of flexion; and after passing through the corner

secure the horse's shoulders in their position to the right by exercising lateral-moving effects with the left rein (counter-balance of the shoulders).

The use of corners in the above manner is also an excellent means of making quick adjustments during the performance of a dressage test.

*Riding on serpentine lines*

The external form of the process of adjustment to straight position resembles in many respects a serpentine-like movement. Consequently, for teaching the horse and rider the task, the riding of a serpentine can be employed very effectively.

While riding the loops the leading function of the rider should be coupled with the adjusting movement which corresponds to the direction of the curve of the line.

*Riding on circles*

This exercise offers the best possibilities for practising and teaching the regulation of the horse.

Ride a circle (about 30 yards or metres in diameter) continuously to the right (four to six riders can be accommodated on the same circle) and use this ride as an introduction to the actual exercise by performing several half-halts (Fig. No. 53).

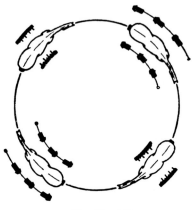

Fig. No. 53

After this commence the execution of the actual exercise shown in Fig. No. 54/a-d.

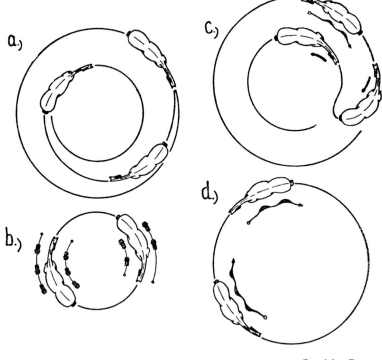

Fig. No. 54

Fig. a)  By leading the horse *inwards* with the right rein, reduce the circle (stirring movement of shoulders).

Fig. b)  While proceeding on the reduced circle, make some half-halts; during them execute the drive-on part energetically and push the horse's forehand forwards to the right (creation of weakness).

Fig. c)  After one of the drives-on, change over to the left-hand direction by suddenly turning the horse with the left rein towards the *outside* and continue riding on the big circle (distinct change of flexion; this movement should be executed simultaneously by each rider accommodated on the circle).

Fig. d)  Immediately after the change of direction exercise lateral-moving effects with the left rein in order to retain the shoulders in their adjusted position; that is, shifted to the right (counter-balance of shoulders). The whole exercise can now be repeated in the opposite direction.

ADDITIONAL REMARKS CONCERNING THE ADJUSTMENT OF THE HORSE AT A CANTER

The principles of regulation, which have already been described, are equally valid when the elimination of an irregularity takes place at a canter. The methods require a slight *formal* alteration only in those cases where the process involves a change in the animal's flexed position.

The reason for this is to be found in the conflict between the following demands:

at a canter the horse always has to be flexed (and during a turn also bent) towards the direction of the canter action, e.g. at a canter led by the near foreleg it must be flexed to the left;

in the process of regulation, however, certain part movements require a flexion and bending of the horse in the direction *opposite* to the pace action.

Therefore it is necessary to find a method which can satisfy these two conflicting conditions in a co-ordinated manner.

This particular problem can be solved by completing the necessary change of flexion or bending to the opposite direction *only to the extent of the animal's straight position.*

The curtailment in the aid given can be compensated for by the application of some interlocked half-halts carried out before the change of flexion and demanded with greater firmness, but without altering the direction of canter. The creation of weakness also has to be accomplished more emphatically, in order to achieve the necessary lateral-moving effect of the reduced rein function affecting the forehand.

STABILIZING THE HORSE'S LOCOMOTION IN ITS REGULATED FORM AND
THE PRACTICAL MEANING OF THIS TASK

When the horse has reached the stage of schooling where it has developed a sense of regularity and is perfectly obedient to the rider's regulating actions, it is desirable to give the animal a certain amount of time during which it has a chance to learn moving in regularity for longer periods without the constant assistance of the rider. One should devote the necessary time for this development separately at each pace, the length of which depends on the individual horse's progress.

At the beginning of this accustoming period it is important to practise each pace at the speed at which the animal is most responsive to retardment *and* drive-on without losing its liveliness. This speed is always a moderate one and can be called the horse's *working speed*.

In the first phase of the work in question it is sufficient to accustom the horse to maintain regularity while proceeding at its natural working speed. The training should be extended to each pace, but with stress on the canter.

During this early stage it will often be necessary to change the speed in order to restore regularity. Later on, however, the regulating actions will need to be applied less and less frequently, the period of regularity will become longer and longer and the rider's influence can be restricted to a slight interference for purely preventive purposes.

When the horse is able to perform a canter of two or three minutes in regularity without the support of the rider some further demands may be imposed. The first should be a change of speed in order to accustom the animal to maintain its new speed without regulation.

Difficulties will most likely be encountered during the transitions and also in maintaining the new speed, since it is no longer the natural working speed of the horse. The principles to be followed in overcoming these difficulties are as follows:

first of all try to prevent the development of an irregularity;
if prevention is not possible, carry out the regulation in the
*working speed* of the horse; and starting from this point
build up the exercise anew and repeat the entire process until
the desired result has been achieved.

Next, the horse can be taught to overcome some difficulties during the course of its progress without falling into irregularity. For this exercise one should employ obstacles of dimensions suitable to the used pace and speed and the horse's degree of education. For the same purpose one can carry out unexpected turns, confront the animal with impressive circumstances, etc.

If the horse loses its regularity during these exercises, one should revert to the basic position and, after renewed regulation, start the exercise all over again.

In the show ring or on a cross-country course it is very often necessary to ride the horse at a great speed. At such a speed the maintenance of regularity is difficult, but it is of vital importance. On such occasions the rider should always be aware of the necessity of maintaining regularity and he should prepare his horse accordingly.

The length of time which is necessary for establishing and strengthening the regularity of movement is approximately one to one and a half years, depending upon the skill of the rider and of the horse.

In the art of riding it is the adjustment of the horse which demands most of the rider's attention. He must have a well-developed 'feeling', be skilful in handling the reins, and familiar with the functions of his upper body, seat and legs when engaged in the various operations. The rider must blend the different effects of the above actions so that they supplement each other harmoniously, thus creating and maintaining the smooth regularity of the horse. The art of performing these fairly complex procedures skilfully is proof of the rider's knowledge. He who has mastered the processes of adjustment is almost certain to encounter no major difficulties in any field of riding.

Although the rider can profit greatly by using the seat for school riding during the operations in question, he must also be capable of accomplishing the desired actions while in the forward position. If the horse can be led to the proper solution of the tasks while the rider is in the forward position, the benefits will be very noticeable later on in jumping or in riding cross-country.

# CHAPTER FOUR

# The Basic Positions and Movements of the Horse

### THE LATERAL BENT POSITION

THE term 'bending' signifies partly a certain activity of the rider and partly a certain condition of the horse. Its meaning can be more easily visualized by carrying out the following experiment (see Fig. No. 55).

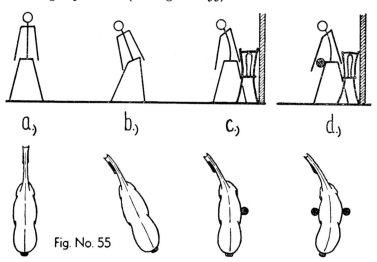

Fig. No. 55

**Fig.** a)   Stand with the upper body straight and the legs slightly apart. This posture may be compared to the straight position of the horse. It is 'flexed' to the straight direction and the motion proceeds forward on a straight line.

**Fig.** b)   By bending the spinal column from the waist towards the left the hip-bones will tend to move towards the right. Likewise, trying to bend the horse to the left by pulling the left rein or by exercising a lateral-moving pressure by the right leg will make it turn to the left, but its quarters will fall out to the right instead of becoming bent.

**Fig.** c)   Repeat the above exercise, only this time support the right hip with the back of a chair placed firmly against the wall. Now, when the spinal column is bent, the hip remains in position. Likewise, the horse's flank on the right (outside) must be supported by the rider's right leg so that it can bend its spinal column.

Fig. d)   To ensure that the hip does not move away from the chair due to a
strong lateral bending, and to prevent one's self from losing balance and
falling inwards, it is necessary that the inner side finds a support around
which the procedure can be completed.  In the case of the horse, this support is the rider's inside leg, which props it up against any lateral displacement caused by the action of the rein or the pressure of the rider's
outside leg.

The bending of the horse to the left (around the rider's left leg)
can be produced as follows:

while sitting in the ready position, transfer the weight of the
body to the left (inside);

exercise a mild pulling effect (pressure) on the left (inside)
rein, consisting of slowly and evenly accented breathing-like
movements similar to the action of pressing a soft rubber ball.
This function causes the horse's head and neck to become
flexed to the left; the left rein must also exercise intermittent
lateral-moving effects in order to prevent the horse's shoulders
from falling inwards.

now produce a lateral-moving effect by breathing-like pressing
movements of the right (outside) leg and keep the quarters
slightly to the left.  Thus this leg, in co-operation with the
outside rein, accomplishes the bending of the horse around
the inside leg of the rider.

the rider's left (inside) leg must be on guard to maintain the
horse's liveliness and its forward impulsion.  A secondary
task of this leg is to perform intermittent counter-balancing
effects whenever the horse shows a tendency to fall inwards
on account of the shoving effect of the outside leg;

yield with the right (outside) rein from the very beginning of the
procedure.  This rein performs only a few mild counter-
balancing effects, so that the outside shoulder does not fall out
(towards the outside).  Thus the right rein, supported by the
inside leg, keeps the horse on the straight line during the
exercise.

When the horse has become set in the bent position the reins and
the outside leg should cease their functions, but they should remain
in definite contact with the horse and be able to resume their
activities at any moment.

In teaching bending, or when practising it for gymnastic purposes, one can make good use of riding at a *trot* on a circular track.
These conditions compel the horse to bend its spine and conform

flexibly by either stretching or shrinking its back muscles, as required by the curve of the course (see Fig. No. 56).

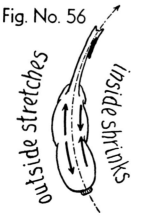

Fig. No. 56

outside stretches

inside shrinks

The exercise should always be commenced by riding on quite a large circle, which is gradually reduced (see Fig. No. 54/a) as the vigour of the movement is increased.

The same exercise will have the additional beneficial effect of improving the horse's suppleness if the circle, after being gradually decreased, is gradually increased again by following the pattern of a spiral line. Thus the increase of exertion is followed by a state of relaxation, which is readily appreciated by the animal as a momentary rest and as a reward.

By frequently changing the direction of riding on the circle, the elasticity of both sides of the horse is improved equally and it also prevents the animal from becoming indifferent or bored by the same routine.

However, the rider should always devote a greater amount of time to riding in the direction towards which the horse's correct bending appears to be more difficult (this is generally to the right).

Further means of developing lateral bending are certain gymnastic exercises, such as riding at a trot on serpentine lines or practising movements on two tracks.

THE DEVELOPMENT OF THE HORSE'S ABILITY TO TURN CORRECTLY

The horse's ability to turn correctly is extremely important, because the soundness of the motion in the new direction depends upon it. Therefore the action of turning must be light and smooth and the animal must constantly maintain its complete regularity. After a bad turn the horse loses its well-balanced state, and if it is then required to fulfil a task (e.g. a jump, etc.) the result is likely to be unsatisfactory.

The basic principle of turning correctly is that the horse should proceed *on the curve of the turn*, but the rider must guide the animal with that special kind of feeling that makes it remain on the 'outside' of the curve (Fig. No. 57). This means that one should imagine that the curve of the turn is not a single line, but a narrow strip of ground. While negotiating the turn one should retain the animal on the outer side of this strip and not allow it to pull to the inside or drift from there to the outside.

The object in achieving this conductiveness is that the horse may display free mobility in its shoulders. Consequently, before under-

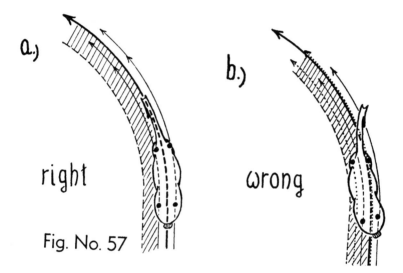

a.) right

b.) wrong

Fig. No. 57

taking any turn, the first task must be to satisfy this particular demand. Bearing this in mind, it is necessary to check frequently the shoulder mobility of the horse also without a definite turning intention and immediately amend a fault which may upset its easiness (see methods on page 98). In such a state the animal is able to make a turn smoothly at any time and in any direction.

The start of a turn will be correct when the sensation of 'shifting' felt by the rider during the checking or loosening procedure is expressed in the direction *opposite* to the intended turn.

But the correct start is not enough for the completion of a smooth turn; the rider must also support the horse in retaining its suppleness during the execution. For this purpose he should combine the levelling function with the act of turning and by it interrupt the straight continuity of his conduct. Thus he should employ the changes involved in the levelling function as a means of prevention even before he notices some deviation from the course of the turn and so 'balance' the animal while it completes the task.

In getting the necessary feeling the rider should perform turns by the application of the following method:

When starting the turn he should indicate the movement by a mild pulling on the inside rein and by shifting his weight to the same side. Then, for guiding his mount on the selected line of the turn, the rider should keep *watching* the track which he wants to cover and—without being specially concerned with the motional part of turning—transmit his will by suggestion to the horse. It will respond with surprising sensibility!

In support of this mental influence the rider should bend his upper body flexibly always in the direction opposite to which the horse shows a tendency to deviation. The application of these supporting movements will become necessary several times during the execution of any turn.

By practising these combined functions and observing the effects brought about in the horse's reactions the 'feeling' for the performance of the characteristic method of turning (see next paragraph) is improved. At the same time, the application of this suggestive method already makes the turning movement of the horse fairly smooth during the early stages of its schooling and greatly counter-balances its attempts to cut the curve off or abandon it to the outside. (See also page 153.)

Now let us examine closely, and with the inclusion of the above 'feeling', the technique by which the correct turning capacity of the horse can be achieved.

In order to give a clear idea of the process of turning, the explanation can be divided into two parts:

first, taking the exceptional case of the horse which is not inclined to crookedness, and then

dealing with the usual case of the horse that shows an inclination to crookedness during the turning process.

THE TURNING OF A HORSE WHICH IS NOT INCLINED TO CROOKEDNESS

Theoretically, the turning of a straight horse can be achieved by simply pulling the rein which is on the side of the turning until the animal has completed the desired action. In practice, however, this

simple continuous pulling and also the horse's turning movements
have to be altered to a certain degree, despite the animal's ideal
state of regularity.   The reason for this alteration is that the
pulling of the turning rein always tends to cause a mild shifting
of the horse's shoulders.   If the pulling action lasts for a considerable time, the horse may lose its well-balanced state and fall
out of the turn.   That is why, even under ideal conditions, certain
measures must be taken to prevent the animal's crookedness.   In
order to achieve this, it is best to divide the turn into separate stages.

The method by which the turning process can be broken down
into its component parts is illustrated in Fig. No. 58/a and
explained in the following text.

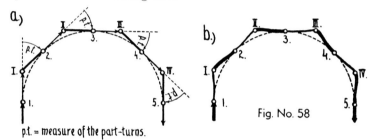

Fig. No. 58

p.t. = measure of the part-turns.

I-IV: 'Turning points'.
1-5: 'Touching points'.
Line between 1 and 5: Course of the 'total turn'.
Line between I and I (etc.): 'Counter-turn' to the 'turning point'.
Line between I and 2 (etc.): 'Part-turn' to the 'touching point'.
Line between I and II (etc.): Tangent to the curve of the 'total turn'.

As can be seen from the diagram, the course of the turn
consists of a number of short straight lines and several small
part-turns.   The straight lines always touch the curve of the turn
from the outside, so that they surround it in the form of a polygon.

In applying the above principle, however  one has to bear in
mind that the horse is a quadruped, and therefore it is unable to
perform the small part-turnings on one specific spot.   This is the
reason why the straight tangent lines and the angular part-turns
must become merged together as shown in Fig. 58/b.   The use of
this agreeable bent line can also be exploited for preventing or
eliminating crookedness, as will be seen later on.

We shall now consider, with the aid of Fig. No. 59, how this
technique works in practice.   (In order to emphasize the characteristic features of the procedure, the drawing has been greatly
exaggerated.)

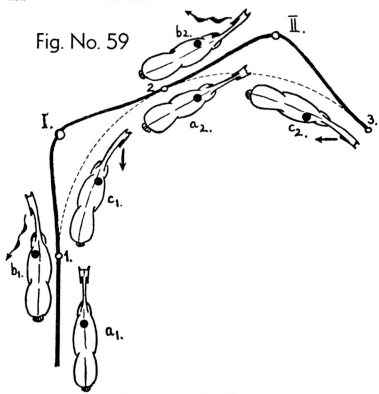

# Fig. No. 59

### EXPLANATION OF FIG. No. 59

$a_1$) The adjusted horse arrives at the starting point of the turn, which is also touching point No. 1

Here the procedure of turning commences: the rider flexes the animal to the outside direction (left) and leads it to turning point No. 1 by performing a *counter-turn*. During this movement the effect of the rein which leads the counter-turn (the left) should be blended with some mild lateral-moving pressures in order to free the horse's outside shoulder and to put a slight weight on the inner one. The aim of this process is to amass an excess load on the inside, which can be absorbed during the turning by the side-effect of the next turning-rein.

$b_1$) The horse during the counter-turn

When the horse has been brought into the above position one can assume that turning point No. 1 has been reached and the movement of counter-turning can be ceased.

At this point the rider changes the horse's flexion, after which he leads it inwards (right) to touching point No. 2 in order to execute the part-turn.

$c_1$) The horse during the *part-turn*

The animal can easily negotiate the part-turn without losing its regularity, since the slight lateral-moving side-effect of the leading rein can absorb the surplus weight which has been put on the inside shoulder during the previous phase. Thus the load of the shoulders becomes equalized.

While approaching touching point No. 2 the rider flexes the horse to the straight position.

$a_2$) The straight horse passes through touching point No. 2

From now on the rider repeats the above procedure of counter-turns and part-turns until the horse ($b_2$, $c_2$, etc.) has negotiated the entire turn.

The more educated the horse, the shorter will become the distance which lies between the touching points and the turning points. Consequently, the turning points will seem to become more numerous and to get nearer to the curve of the total turn, thus making it more and more consistent with the normal segment of the circle. Finally, the movements involved will merge together. However, the rider should always maintain the double character of his actions, although very subtly, as a form of preventive aid to ensure the horse's balance.

THE TURNING OF A HORSE WHICH IS INCLINED TO BECOME CROOKED

Horses will often show an inclination to crookedness during a turn or, in spite of the greatest precaution, they may take up a crooked position while turning by one-sided counter-bracing or by muscular contraction. When executing a turn with such a horse two specific requirements have to be satisfied:

the actual accomplishment of the turn, and

the prevention of crookedness.

In analysing the process of turning it is necessary to deal with the subject separately according to the horse's inclination to become crooked in one way or the other. In order to make the explanation more visual, we will take as an example a case where the particular irregularity originates from the left-sided stiffness of the horse.

Figs. Nos. 58 and 59 are useful as a detailed study also of the turning of a horse with defective inclinations. The analysis shows that the *course* which has to be followed during the process of turning is the same whether it involves a horse which is inclined to crookedness or a straight horse. The difference lies in the actions involved and not in the shape of the curve of the turn.

TURNING A HORSE WHICH IS INCLINED TO BECOME CROOKED BY EQUALLY DISTRIBUTED COUNTER-BRACING OR BY COUNTER-BRACING FOCUSED ON THE QUARTERS

Owing to the fact that the execution of the turn is usually made defective by these particular irregularities, the emphasis must be laid on these cases when studying the question of turning.

*Turning towards the direction of the stiffness (left)*

Under such conditions the horse does not bend its neck easily to the rein signal (left) which meets the animal's resistance and it 'turns into' (instead of towards) the new direction round the over-burdened shoulder (left). Furthermore, the animal falls inwards from the curve of the turning because of its one-sided shoulder mobility and the position of the quarters. The general impression of the rider is that the turn is carried out stiffly around the inside foreleg.

The process of turning (Fig. No. 60)

Phase No. 1, the counter-turn (Diagram a)

Lead the horse by the right rein towards the outside direction to turning point No. 1. This action also induces the animal to stride out from the shoulders to the right.

If necessary, a loosening action can be added by inserting a half-halt in order to create a state of weakness for the following change of flexion.

The left rein, while maintaining contact, 'gives' slightly and follows the horse's movements, but also participates actively in the above half-halt.

The rider's right leg ensures liveliness, while his left leg looks after the quarters to prevent them from falling out of line.

Phase No. 2, the correction of the position (Diagram b)

While taking advantage of the effect brought about in the previous phase, *and the horse steps out of its shoulders to the right*, the left rein suddenly changes the flexion of the horse to the left and by blending the flexion with lateral-moving pressures pushes the shoulders to the right. If necessary, the action of the left rein should be combined with some loosening movements.

The right rein gives, while maintaining contact, and defines the extent of the flexion to the left.

The rider's left leg ensures liveliness. The right leg holds the quarters in line by exercising lateral-moving pressures against the side-effect of the flexing rein.

Phase No. 3, the part-turn (Diagram c)

Lead the horse by the left rein towards the inside direction to touching point No. 2.

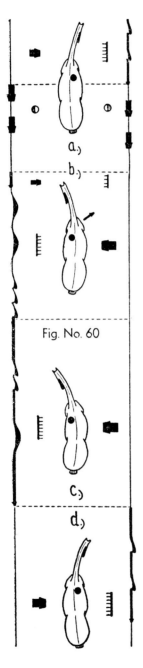

Fig. No. 60

In order to increase the counter-balancing side-effect of the leading rein, combine the leading action of this rein with some lateral-moving pressures.

The right rein maintains contact during this entire phase.

The rider's right leg provides energetic lateral-moving pressures, while his left leg takes care of liveliness.

Phase No. 4, change of flexion for the new counter-turn (Diagram d)

The right rein changes the flexion by a smooth movement to the right.

The left rein maintains contact and defines the extent of flexion to the right.

The rider's right leg ensures liveliness, while his left leg prevents the quarters from falling out of line.

Further phases

The previous phases should be repeated over and over until the turning has been completed.

*Turning in the direction opposite to that of the stiffness (to the right)*

In this case, while the rider is pulling the turning-rein (right), the horse's neck breaks-in without much resistance instead of bending. The animal 'turns over' to the new direction around the overburdened (left) shoulder and, caused by its one-sided shoulder mobility, the quarters tend to drift outwards from the curve of the turn.

The process of turning should be performed in a manner similar to the turning towards the opposite direction (left), but the part-turn and the counter-turn actions must be interchanged.

TURNING A HORSE WHICH IS INCLINED TO BECOME CROOKED BY COUNTER-BRACING FOCUSED ON THE FOREHAND

The turning of a horse in such a state needs the most care from the rider. The reason for this is that the animal not only presents all the difficulties of the other cases, but it also renders the turn more difficult by exercising concentrated pressure on the forehand. This condition affects the horse's movement of turning in the following manner:

If the direction of turning coincides with that of the animal's stiffness, it falls suddenly and sharply into the turn (to the right)
    if the turning occurs towards the direction opposite to its stiffness, the horse deviates strongly towards the outside (right).

The procedure of turning is shown in Table No. 7/a by a series of sketches which show the different stages of the process in a film-like manner. It has to be noted, however, that during the execution of the turn the component movements have to be repeated until they produce the effect desired. The next movement can only follow afterwards.

These sketches depict simultaneously the method of turning either to the right or to the left. The reason for this is that, the part-turns being greater than the counter-turns (which the sketch does not account for), the total turn is, according to the rider's intention, completed sometimes to the right and sometimes to the left.

TURNING A HORSE WHICH IS INCLINED TO BECOME CROOKED BY ONE-SIDED MUSCLE CONTRACTION

Since such horses show a marked inclination to resist the rider's influence, it is important that he should endow his actions with a high degree of smoothness and loosening effect. The contracted state of the horse affects the turning movement in the following manner.

    while turning to the side of the contraction it resists the rein action, whereby the crookedness of its position becomes more augmented. Instead of turning, it drifts towards the opposite direction (outside);

## Table No. 7/a

TURNING A HORSE INCLINED TO LEFT-SIDED COUNTER-BRACING
FOCUSED ON THE FOREHAND

| Phase | a.) Turn to the left. | Figures | b.) Turn to the right. |
|---|---|---|---|
| | Execution of part-turn, etc. as in Phase No.1. | | Execution of counter-turn, etc. as in Phase No.1. |
| 4. | Change of flexion to part-turn: introduced by transpositioning the centre of gravity; effected by repeated distinct rein actions and leg-support | | Change of flexion to counter-turn: introduced and effected according to Phase No.4. in column a.) |
| 3. | Execution of counter-turn: effected by repeated, smooth rein actions, and supported by the counter-balance of quarters. | | Execution of part-turn: effected and supported according to Phase No.3. in column a.) |
| 2. | Change of flexion to counter-turn: introd. by transp. the centre of grav. effected by smooth rein and counter-balancing leg actions, and followed by loosening the remainig stiffness. | | Change of flexion to part-turn: introduced, effected and completed according to Phase No.2. in column a.) |
| 1. | Execution of part-turn: introduced by transpositioning the centre of gravity; effected by firm and repeated counter dev. action, and followed by creation of state of weakness. | | Execution of counter-turn: introduced, effected, and completed according to Phase No.1. in column a.) |
| State of starting condition. | Horse adjusted to straight position. | | Horse adjusted to straight position. |

while turning to the direction opposite to the contraction, the animal shows less resistance and executes the turn with comparative ease, however, in a faulty bent position.

The procedure of turning is similar to that shown in Table No. 7/a. There are the following differences:

the counter-deviation rein actions should be performed towards both directions with gentle effects;

the change of flexion and the adjoining part- or counter-turn are executed with firmness towards the direction opposite to the contraction and with smoothness towards the other direction.

Bearing in mind the horse's increased inclination to resistance, the characteristic phases of the turning procedure must often be repeated before starting a following one.

During his activities the rider may perform from time to time a slight passive resistance; however, the main feature of this function must be the final sudden yielding.

During the execution of the task the rider's leg which is on the critical side of the animal must be active all the time in exercising firm lateral-moving pressures.

THE TURNING OF A HORSE IN A CANTER AND GALLOP (Table No. 7/b)

The development of the horse's ability to turn correctly when in a canter or gallop is of utmost importance, since the three-day event horse, the hunter and the show jumper have to discharge most of their duties while moving in these paces. It is therefore vital that the turn should be performed properly and that the animal's regularity before, during and after the turn can be easily maintained or restored.

The principles of the procedure involved conform with the techniques already described. Their execution requires only an adjustment of form, according to the considerations explained on page 193.

The best practice is first to acquaint the horse with the methods of turning at a walk and in trot. It is only after this that the correct turn should be taught at a canter and later on a gallop. Until this stage has been reached the rider's attention should be concentrated on not hampering the horse while taking a turn at a canter or gallop.

The details of the turning procedure can be found in Table No. 7/b. With regard to the execution of its component phases,

# Table No. 7/b

## TURNING THE HORSE AT A CANTER (OFF-FORE LEADING)

| Phase | | a.) To the right. | b.) To the left. |
|---|---|---|---|
| **5.** | During the course of the part-turn | horse bent to the right | horse „flexed" to straight position |
| **4.** | Before the part-turn | change of flexion and bending to the right; it can be carried out either with emphasis or by gentle movements according to the necessity of some adjustment. | change of flexion to straight position; |
| **3.** | During the course of the counter-turn | horse „flexed" to straight position | horse bent to the right |
| **2.** | Before the counter-turn | change of flexion to straight position; it can be carried out either with emphasis or by gentle movements according to the necessity of some adjustment | increasing flexion, bending to the right; |
| **1.** | (While proceeding on a straight line | the horse's head is flexed slightly to the direction of the canter-action (right) | |
| **Notes.** | The method of turning at a canter—besides the sharp restrictions in flexion, resp. bending—conforms with that of the general practice. | In counter-turn: the horse is „flexed" to straight position, and proceeds in the direction opposite to its canter-action. In part-turn: the horse is bent according to its canter-action, and the direction of the turn corresponds to that of its leading movement. | In counter-turn the horse is bent according to its canter-action, and the direction of the turn corresponds with that of its leading movement. In part-turn the horse is „flexed" to straight position, and proceeds in the direction opposite to its canter-action. |

the same recommendations are valid as mentioned in connection with those of the former cases.

TURNING THE HORSE BY THE OUTSIDE REIN

The term 'turning by the outside rein' signifies the procedure by which the horse is directed to turn through its shoulders by the rein opposite to the direction of the turn.

In theory the procedure seems simple, but it is not so easy in practice because its successful execution depends on the completely free and unobstructed shoulder mobility of the horse. This means that no attempt should be made in turning the animal by the outside rein before the rider has not satisfied the demands of this basic condition. Furthermore it is difficult for the horse, while under the dominating influence of the function of the outside rein, to accomplish the turning in such a manner that it can follow the turning with its lateral flexing. Owing to these difficulties, unprepared horses usually lose their regularity and by pointing to the outside they fall strongly into the turn or resist hard against its execution.

While turning the horse by the application of the method in question the outside rein provides a lateral-moving effect on the animal's outside shoulder. The rider's inside leg ensures the maintenance of liveliness, while the outside leg takes care that the horse does not fall out of the curve of the turn with its quarters. The function of the inside rein is to safeguard the proper lateral flexion (to the inside).

In conclusion one can state that the rider may employ this method of turning only after the animal's painstaking general schooling. In fact, the advantages of turning by the outside rein are, in contrast to the difficulties which may arise, very limited and therefore it is much better (except in the course of special dressage schooling) to omit its application altogether.

TURNING THE HORSE DURING THE EARLY STAGES OF ITS EDUCATION

The main instrument of turning a young horse is the transposing of the rider's weight towards the direction of the intended turn, coupled with the application of the suggestive method described on page 152.

Unfortunately, one cannot entirely avoid the employment of the reins, but the rider must handle them with utmost care in order to ensure the easiness of conduct. The main task of the reins is to prevent the animal from following its natural inclination to deviate. Their use for turning is recommended only as a supplementary means of secondary importance.

Until the horse does not show a tendency to deviate it will move under the rider's weight-influence at least roughly on the curve on which he wishes to complete the turn. If an intention to deviate is noted before or during the turn, the defect should be corrected by the employment of the counter-deviation rein-effect. The procedure of turning is shown in Figs. Nos. 61 and 62.

Turning towards the direction

corresponding | opposite

to that of the horse's tendency to deviation (left).

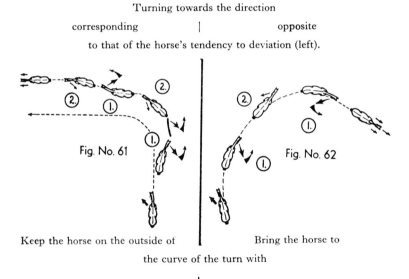

Fig. No. 61

Fig. No. 62

Keep the horse on the outside of | Bring the horse to

the curve of the turn with

enforced counter-turns (1.) enforced part-turns

effected mainly by the means of (eventually repeated) counter-deviation rein actions, terminating in yielding and partly by the transposition of the rider's centre of gravity.

Ensure the mobility of the procedure by interlocking

mild part-turns (2.) mild counter-turns

effected mainly by the horse's tendency to deviation and augmented eventually by the rider's gentle turning function.

THE SHORT TURNS

The short (narrow) turn is a special form of change of direction by which the turn is executed as nearly as possible at one precise point.

There are three forms of short turns, according to the particular point around which the movement takes place: the turn on the forehand (around the shoulder); the turn on the haunches (on the hocks or on the quarters); and the turn on the centre.

In executing the short turns the most important demand is that the horse should perform *each step* of the movement by clear-cut and lively leg motions, while keeping a light contact with the reins. It must not roll into the turn of its own accord. The rider should have the feeling that he can stop the horse's stepping at any moment by the application of the slightest control actions and that he can continue the motion just as easily if he wishes, either in the same direction or in the opposite one.

The prerequisite of this condition is that the horse should be absolutely obedient to the slightest retarding and driving signals. And so, before starting to perform any short turn, the submissive state of the horse must be firmly established. During the execution of the task the animal's state of pliability has to be checked from time to time by mild half-halting actions.

The moment the rider feels a sign of stiffness, either in the horse's back or on the reins, he should *immediately* ccase the exercise, insert a loosening action, and only after the horse's yielding should he resume the exercise by letting the animal *step* into the motion again. Without this condition a short turn can never be performed correctly. This recommendation also applies to the execution of the half-pass and the other movements on two tracks.

THE TURN ON THE HAUNCHES (Fig. No. 63)

The broad principles which govern the horse's turn on the haunches are similar to those of a regular turn. The main difference is that in the turn on the haunches the curve of the turning is reduced to zero. The motion is brought about by the lateral movement of the shoulders and it occurs virtually around the pivoting inside hind leg. The horse 'proceeds' with the forehand in the direction of its bent position while taking steps of varying lengths with each of its other legs.

The aiding activities of the rider can be summed up as follows:

The inside rein (which is on the same side as the direction of the movement)

flexes the horse's head and neck in the direction of the turning; and 'leads' the turn by a simple turning effect interspersed with moments of yielding. *Each* stepping action of the animal should be facilitated by such a yielding moment. This rein also counter-balances the horse's tendency to roll into the turn (which is frequently the result of a lengthy pull by this rein); it virtually has to *lead the horse step by step* around the turn. In this sense the inside rein leads and yields . . . counter-balances and yields . . . leads and yields . . . and so forth. (For the leading activity the rider can move his hand slightly sideways.)

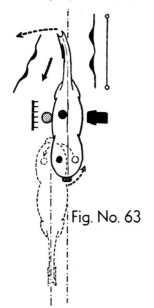

Fig. No. 63

The outside leg (which is on the side opposite to the direction of movement and is held on the girth)

promotes the turn by exercising breathing-like pressures; and,

as a secondary task, checks the quarters against any evasion which may be caused by the leading effect of the opposite rein or by the animal's resistance.

The outside rein

promotes the lateral movement of the forehand and also counter-balances the horse's tendency to hang back with the shoulders out of the motion by mild lateral-moving effects; and,

as secondary tasks, controls the maintenance of the proper flexion (the horse must not break-in the neck towards the direction of the turn) and checks the animal's forward stepping.

The inside leg (which is kept slightly behind the girth)

takes care of the horse's forward impulsion by determined

driving function, and prevents it from rolling into the turn, by means of counter-balancing pressures interlocked with the driving actions.

The seat

is in ready position and the rider's weight is brought slightly towards the inside.   It controls the horse's backward or forward stepping by exercising pressures either by the thighs or by the seat-bone.

When the turn has been accomplished it is necessary to resume riding at the same pace at which the horse was proceeding before the turn.

During the performance a slight stepping forward must not be considered as a serious fault.  In fact, since it helps to stop the tension affecting the pivoting hind leg, it should be tolerated, especially during the early stages of schooling.

On the other hand, stepping backwards, or a lateral evasion from the pivoting point, are serious faults and must be prevented from the very beginning.

If during the performance of a continuous turn the horse gets stuck and tries to overchange the motion to a turn on the forehand, or round the centre, increase a little the breathing-like pressures of the outside leg and those of the outside rein.  Simultaneously give emphasis to the yielding movements of the inside rein while it exercises (without increasing the strength!) the leading function originally used.  In the moments of yielding, which are indicating the counter-movements, transfer the centre of gravity to the opposite side, and from there bring it again into its original position, always in rhythm with the new leading action.   Such oscillating changes are very effective in loosening the stiffness which causes the difficulty in question (see also page 101).

Let us now examine how the turn should be performed during the schooling period (see also page 210).

Before commencing the exercise the rider should restore the horse's regularity and refresh the lateral mobility of its shoulders. By these means also the hocks become driven well under the body. Since the turn can be performed either from a stationary position or from a walk, the rider must, after the above regulation, create either one of these conditions.

Then the horse has to be flexed towards the direction in which he wishes to turn.

The next movement is the actual beginning of the turn, when the rider influences the horse to make two to three side-steps, with definite shoulder activity, by the lateral movement of the forehand (part-turn).

Now, after ceasing the turning action with a halt, the horse must be helped to strike off in the above manner towards the opposite direction (counter-turn).

These two movements should be carried out in an oscillating manner. The digression from the starting point should always be greater towards the direction of the desired main turning, so that the process will eventually lead to the completion of the turn. In this way it is possible to free the animal's inside hind leg from the tension caused by the pivoting and, at the same time, maintain its suppleness. This tension, particularly after three or four con-secutive side-steps, is apt to produce in the animal a very unpleasant sensation, which tends to make it step outside from the pivoting point.

Later on, as the horse's knowledge and sensitivity increase, the extent of the counter-movements will gradually decrease until the rider is enabled finally to replace his articulated functions, which support the effect of the leading rein, by slight rhythmical changes in his weight position.

THE TURN ON THE FOREHAND (Fig. No. 64)

During the turn on the forehand the horse, while taking steps of varying lengths with its legs, pivots around the inside foreleg (determined by the turning movement of the forehand) as it 'proceeds' in the opposite direction with the quarters. Thus this turn is the result of a bilateral-like movement, the centre of which is at about the front line of the withers, and divides the animal's body into two parts. The proportion between them is about four to six.

The rider has to accommodate himself to these conditions by a twofold activity, namely.

he has to *move* the part of the horse's body which is beyond the pivoting point in the direction opposite to the decisive turning movement and to the animal's flexed position; and

he must simultaneously *lead* the other part of its body towards the direction of the turn, which is the same as the direction of the flexed position.

The first activity renders the execution of the turn more difficult for the horse, but the second tends to make the movement easier.

The signals and aids used in the operation are the following:

The inside leg plays the most important rôle in executing a turn on the forehand:

it moves the horse's trunk in a lateral direction by exercising breathing-like pressures on the animal's side beyond the girth; whereat

its secondary tasks are to drive the horse during the turning movement and to prevent the forehand from falling inwards.

The inside rein

promotes the turn by a simple turning effect, leading the front part of the horse in the pivoting direction. This function of the rein must be interlocked with substantial yielding phases in rhythm with the horse's stepping action;

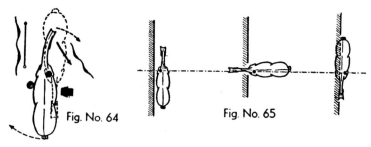

Fig. No. 64          Fig. No. 65

its further task is to co-operate with the rider's inside leg in preventing the horse from falling-in; and

it must check any intention the animal may have to push itself into the motion with its quarters. These activities of the inside rein produce a collective effect which augments the otherwise very limited value of the exercise.

The outside leg

is kept firmly to the horse's side, slightly in front of the girth;

it controls the front part of the animal in order to prevent a possible falling-out or stepping in the outside direction by exercising mild pressures;

its secondary task is to ensure that the horse strides step by step and maintains its lateral position by applying intermittent counter-balancing effects; furthermore, it must check any intention the animal may show to roll backwards.

The outside rein

supports the control action of the outside leg with a mild counter-balancing effect and checks the horse so that it does not stride forward. It also takes care that the animal does not over-bend its neck in a lateral direction.

The seat

supports the work of the legs and reins with appropriate actions of the seat-bone and the thighs, together with the transference of the rider's weight in the direction of the horse's bent position (inside).

The execution of the turn on the forehand is not a difficult task for the horse. As a matter of fact, the animal instinctively prefers to place the stress of its weight on the forehand, and this facilitates the movement of the hind legs around the shoulder.

As a rule, the exercise must always be performed from a stationary position; therefore, before starting the forehand turn, the horse must be brought to a standstill. Then the rider should flex the animal to the desired direction. Finally, the turning can be accomplished by the application of the function as described above.

While carrying out this task the horse must not be allowed to step forwards or sideways, for this would mar the whole performance. But a slight slip backwards is not a serious fault, since it is not contrary to the nature of the movement, which has somewhat the character of the rein-back.

In order to prevent resistance and evasion during the procedure, the rider should comply with each momentary situation by his flexible use of the functions of the legs, reins and seat. If preventive measures prove unsuccessful, he should stop the movement, regulate the horse, and only then recommence the turn (see also page 212).

With regard to teaching the turn on the forehand, the same principles apply as for the turn on the haunches. In this sense, the entire process of turning should be carried out gradually by part-turns and counter-turns, while special attention should be given to the stirring of the quarters.

The turn on the forehand can never be performed properly if the horse is standing at the side of the wall of a confined space. When the animal turns its neck and head on such a place they are bound to come into collision with the wall, whether it is an actual or a symbolic one (the enclosure of the arena), and after the accomplishment of a 180° turn the horse is liable to let half of its body drift outside the confined space (see Fig. No. 65).

Despite the impossibility of performing the task correctly under these conditions, certain dressage tests require the execution of such a turn along the wall of the arena. When the rider is confronted with such a task, the horse should be directed in the same manner as described above, the only difference being that the pivoting should take place around an imaginary point between the two forelegs. In the course of the performance these two legs move around the pivoting point on quite a small circle. After the completion of the 180° turn they will be in a position which is the exact opposite of their starting position. During this motion they will have to step quite slightly backwards; however, this is not a noticeable fault.

In case when the horse gets stuck during the turn, the principles of correction are analogous, as described on page 214 (turn on the haunches).

Interchange the continuity of the turning by slight counter-movements. Give emphasis to the yielding function of the leading rein when the turning leg exercises pressure, and increase its effect when the leg is relaxing during its breathing-like lateral-moving activity (see also page 82).

In more acute cases couple the repeated leg pressures with mild knocking effect. At the same time, the opposite leg, by exercising also lateral-moving pressures (on the girth), takes care that the horse's pivoting leg should not leave its position under the increased turning effect.

The turn on the shoulders is an exercise which can only be practised with real profit at an advanced stage of education. Its practice during the course of preliminary schooling is more injurious than useful to the horse.

One of the main objects of the horse's schooling is to free the forehand and improve its lateral mobility (see page 100). This mobility is largely restricted by the instinctive retention of the animal, since it prefers to overburden and fix the forehand in its unpolished state.

When the rider, in spite of the condition mentioned, attempts to teach the novice how to fix the forehand before it (the forehand) is absolutely free and mobile, he co-operates with the animal in developing its faulty instinct.

What is the importance of the exercise in comparison with its disadvantage? It has some collective effect on the horse, but this can only be useful when the animal is already free of rigidity in the shoulders. As a substitute for the exercise there are others (see page **W**) which do not fix the forehand artificially.

The exercise can afford certain aid in the development of the mobility of the quarters. But there are also exercises more suitable for this purpose (the croup-in, half-pass, and even the shoulder-in) which do not upset the improvement of the quarters in its position.

By the employment of the exercise during the period of advanced training the rider can prove whether the horse is able to fix the forehand and move the quarters at any time on demand.

With regard to the preparation of the horse for competitions, it is regrettable that the performance of this task (because of its apparent easiness) is only required in novice classes. Thus riders are compelled to teach something which is at the time harmful for the general development of the horse. Therefore they should be very careful not to spoil the animal by the force of this condition.

The practical significance of the turn on the forehand is evident chiefly in hunting and riding in the country, during which it is often used to open gates which *swing towards* the horse and rider. For this operation the horse should be brought into a position where it stands parallel to the gate, facing its opening side, and close enough to enable the rider to reach the latch either with his hand or with the crop.

In this position the rider can easily undo the lock; then, while performing the *turn on the forehand*, he pulls the gate open and, by stepping slowly, passes through it without difficulty.

When opening a gate which *swings away* from the rider the horse must make a *turn on the haunches* movement, starting from a position similar to that described above. While the horse is stepping, push the gate and after three to four steps swing it outwards and let the animal step quietly through the gap.

During the procedure prevent the horse, with the greatest determination, from swerving the quarters away from the pivoting point.

Both of the above procedures have an excellent educative effect on the animal. Therefore the rider should make good use of them during schooling and at any time when riding in the country.

THE TURN ROUND THE CENTRE (Fig. No. 66)

In this movement the horse, while turning around its centre, 'proceeds' equally with both the forelegs and the hind legs, though in opposite directions. Of all the short turns, its execution is the most natural to the animal and therefore offers no particular difficulties. If the horse yields readily to the influence of the simple turning rein and the lateral-moving leg, it may even carry out the turn without any previous practice at all.

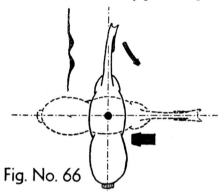

Fig. No. 66

The turn on the centre should always start from a stationary position, with the horse flexed towards the direction of the turning movement of the forehand.

During the execution of the turn the 'leading' is equally divided between the rein which is in the direction of the turn and the leg on the same side. The rein and the leg on the opposite side should be kept in readiness to exercise counterbalancing effects and to ensure that the horse steps properly in the movement.

It never becomes necessary for the animal to step slightly forward or backward during the turn, because there is no pivoting leg in the movement which might become tense, as is the case with the other short turns.

THE PIROUETTE

This is a turning movement on the spot resembling the short turns, with the difference that during the change of direction the horse retains its originally used pace. This means that during the execution of the task it is continuously stepping with all four legs and neither of them is pivoting. The animal does not halt, neither before nor after the completion of the turn.

The pirouette can be carried out either on the quarters or on the forehand or round the centre of the body.

*The pirouette on the haunches* (quarters) is the main form of such movements, since it is the most natural and it can be executed at the use of all three lower paces. During the turn the inside hind leg is stepping on the spot around which the outside hind leg describes a very small circular line, and both forelegs, by crossing each other, are also proceeding on a circular line. The characteristic feature of the movement is that of passing through a corner in croup-in position (see page 231).

*The pirouette on the forehand* can be performed either at a walk or at a trot. While performing the turn the inside foreleg is stepping on the spot, its pair proceeds on a very small circular line and the hind legs make similar movements to those made by the forelegs during the pirouette on the quarters. The characteristic feature of this turn is that of taking a corner in shoulder-in position (see page 229).

*The pirouette on the centre* can only be executed at a walk and it is the same movement as the turn on the centre with the reservation of keeping up the continuous leg motion.

In the dressage test of combined events the performance of pirouette movements can only be demanded at a walk. Their execution at a trot and canter belong to the tasks of special dressage schooling.

In order to carry out a pirouette, first increase the horse's collection and liveliness (not speed). Then reduce its forward movement by the application of half-halts almost to nil and immediately afterwards (in the moment of yielding) start with the turning movement. For its execution lead the horse by similar aids and signals as being used for the indication of that short turn which corresponds to the intended pirouette.

Regarding possible faults and their prevention, the principles discussed in connection with the short turns are equally valid also in the case of the performance of pirouettes.

THE REIN-BACK

The sequence of strides corresponds to that of a trot, but in a reverse direction, making the horse proceed backwards. The movement of 'trot' in a reverse direction may be confusing to the animal and therefore, before backing can be practised, this difficulty has to be overcome by schooling designed to prevent the horse's resistance. It is common knowledge that the horse can display its toughest resistance when asked to step backwards.

The horse must perform the movement with complete suppleness; while keeping an even rein contact it should step distinctly and simultaneously with its diagonal legs.

The signals and aids which are used correspond to those of the retardment as performed either at the walk or trot. However, within these signals stress is led on the interchanged leg pressures and the application of the reins should be reduced to the minimum. If the animal is inclined to be obedient to the retardment, it will probably learn to perform an unobstructed, smooth backing to the rider's almost *invisible* functions in a short space of time.

In executing the rein-back the horse's onward movement should first be stopped (retardment). Next, it is advantageous to keep the horse at a standstill for a while, since by this means one can avoid the appearance of a number of faults. Then the backward movement can be commenced by the application of the usual retarding signals. For example, pressure of the right leg and the seat simultaneously with a slight retarding function of the right rein . . . yielding . . . pressure of the left leg and seat together with the light pull of the left rein . . . yielding . . . and so forth. During this procedure it is important that the actions of the rider should always be stopped by relaxing the engaged muscles, but never losing either the rein- or the leg-contact.

When the rider feels that the horse is ready for backing, he should indicate the movement chiefly by the alternating leg pressures, supported by mild pressures of the seat, while the hands should simply follow the horse's backward movement with the feeling—even if it sounds paradoxical—of forward tendency.

The simultaneous signals which are performed by the legs and reins can follow each other in a slow sequence, because the stepping backwards of the horse is also a slow movement. If it is not slow, it is surely incorrect! Each aiding element of the procedure should produce one step from the animal.

When a horse that has already learned the appropriate signals for the rein-back fails to step backwards immediately when they are applied, the rider must not lose his patience over the delay. It is certain that the animal will yield sooner or later if he continues to apply the signals alternately without increasing their strength or changing their form.

The main faults in the rein-back can be divided into two groups, according to whether the horse resists the movement and comes over the bit, or whether it rolls backwards and comes behind the reins. The combination of these faults results in the animal's making only half-steps with one leg or the other (mostly with the near-hind leg).

The best way of avoiding the horse's resistance is for the rider to perform his aiding activity in the alternating manner described above. If, in spite of this, the animal resists, the rider should interrupt his functions and resume them only after the horse has performed some suppling exercises (half-halts) in forward motion.

The rider's legs should always be on guard to prevent or to stop the rolling back. At the slightest sign of such an intention on the part of the horse they should drive it energetically forward. Thus the rider must not fail to check *each step* and, if necessary, alternate his backing and driving activities in quick succession and in a long series. This intermittent procedure is the best cure for a faulty rein-back. It also makes the horse step equally with its legs and maintain the all-over regularity of its motion.

The method of teaching the rein-back can be outlined as follows:

Make the horse halt from a walk and then try to continue the retardment into backing. It is almost certain that the first attempts will not succeed, for the animal will probably resist the signals by stiffening its quarters.

In order to change this situation the hind legs have first to be moved in one way or another out of their position of resistance. Since the possibility of making the horse step forward must be temporarily discarded, and since success has not proved possible by a backward-directed action, let us see what happens when the stiffness is 'attacked' in the 'flank' by moving the quarters to one side. We will find that the horse willingly fulfils such a demand, and so the motion thus obtained produces the desired result and enables the rider to go on with the schooling.

To achieve this movement of the quarters exercise some lateral-moving effects with the leg, or taps of the whip, on the side opposite to the direction of the desired movement. At the same time, perform mild taking actions coupled with yielding moments, just as in a normal retardment, with the rein on the same side as the acting leg. While the horse is moving aside with the quarters it can be allowed to fall out of line with the croup by a step or two.

Then change the actions and push the quarters to the opposite side in the same manner as before.

After having carried out these movements four or five times in an oscillating manner, the process should be discontinued, the animal driven forward for a short while and then given some rest. Afterwards the entire exercise can be repeated.

When the rider has practised the exercise a few times he will notice that the horse starts to step backwards a little, while shoving its quarters to the side. Later on the lateral movement gradually becomes smaller and smaller, whereas the stepping backwards appears to be more and more distinct. After two to three weeks of practice a clear, continuous, straight backing can thus be achieved without encountering any resistance on the part of the horse.

### The Side-steps; Moving on Two Tracks

When proceeding by side-steps the horse moves off the normal track made by the forelegs and hind legs and steps on a new track with one or both pairs of legs. During this motion the legs which step on the new track cross each other.

Taking into account this characteristic feature of the movement, two main forms of side-steps can be distinguished:

when only one pair of legs, either the forelegs or the hind legs, step off the original track; and

when the horse abandons the original track by cross-stepping with both pairs of legs.

In the first case the animal's entire body is bent and a lateral movement is performed by the crossing legs, but, on the whole, the horse maintains the original direction of its course. In this form of side-steps there are four variations, namely:

the 'shoulder-in' (Fig. No. 67) and the 'shoulder-out' (Fig. No. 68), when the animal steps crosswise with its forelegs. In these movements the horse is bent in the direction opposite to its advancement. These side-step movements are especially useful for suppling the animal and for increasing its adjustability to the straight position;

the 'croup-in' (Fig. No. 69) and the 'croup-out' (Fig. No. 70), when the cross-steps are performed by the hind legs. Here the bending of the horse corresponds to the direction of the advancement. These forms of side-steps are suitable for improving the horse's turning capacity and also for increasing its readiness to be collected.

In the second general form of side-steps, when the horse crosses

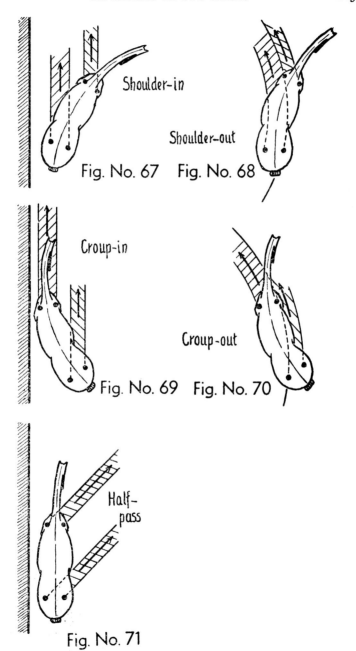

Shoulder-in

Shoulder-out

Fig. No. 67  Fig. No. 68

Croup-in

Croup-out

Fig. No. 69  Fig. No. 70

Half-
pass

Fig. No. 71

both its forelegs and hind legs, only its head is flexed slightly (towards the direction of advancement). Although the animal makes a forward-directed movement, it actually changes the direction of its course.

This form of side-steps consists of the 'half-pass' (Fig. No. 71) and, in its most extreme form, the 'full-pass'. These movements are very useful for improving the agility of the shoulders and haunches or developing their muscular strength and flexibility. In addition to these physical advantages they are also very useful for increasing the animal's aptitude for collection.

Considering their various beneficial effects, one can conclude that the side-steps should never be regarded merely as an end in themselves. They are important mediums, both for schooling the young horse and for developing a high standard of conduct in the horse which is already trained.

THE EXECUTION OF TWO-TRACK MOVEMENTS

The principles which govern the rider's guiding activities during the performance of all forms of two-track movements can be summarized as follows:

'Balance' the animal in its motion and blend the activities involved with the levelling function.

In leading the horse's forehand importance is centred on the reins as well as on the seat, whereas in directing the quarters it is focused on the legs, supported by the seat.

The rider should lighten the animal's movement by shifting his weight slightly in the direction of the horse's bent position.

The horse must not be forced into the exercise by the use of strong actions. On the contrary, it should be guided by the application of mild signals, which in case of need should be repeated. Later on, after the first indication by which the performance is commenced, the rider's following attitude and his animation will provide sufficient aiding power to lead the horse successfully and ensure its progress during the movement. However, care must be taken that the animal does not draw or pull itself into the motion of its own accord, or by the force of its crooked position. Doing so, its stepping action will become a sort of rolling or falling into the direction of the movement. Furthermore, it is necessary to draw special attention to the prerequisites (see page 173) on which the possibility of practising the recommended lateral moving rein functions depends. In case their employment, because of the horse's momentary resistance, is not eligible, one should substitute the particular function by the leading or counter-deviation effect of the other rein until the animal starts stepping out of its shoulders in the direction desired.

The rider's activities, which are described in the following examples of two-track movements, are the same whether the exercise is executed at a walk or trot.

A detailed examination of the shoulder-out and the croup-out is not included because they are unimportant during the education of jumpers. However, the rider who is interested can find some information on the subject by studying the relevant Figs. Nos. 68 and 70.

*The shoulder-in* (Fig. No. 72)

The execution of the movement consists of four phases (described in accordance with the 'right shoulder-in'):

Phase No. 1 (Fig. a)

The bending of the horse and leading its forehand towards the inside from the single track.

The rider leads the forehand with the inside (right) rein towards the inside from the straight track, just as if he were going to start a turn. However, at the same time he gives a more distinct flexion to the horse's head and neck towards the right.

In order to prevent the shoulders from falling out due to the bending action, the outside (left) rein has to exercise a counter-balancing effect.

The inside leg promotes and maintains the activity of the inside hock, which ensures the forward-thrusting movement. As a matter of fact, horses are very inclined to evade this activity.

The outside leg effects the bending of the quarters by lateral-moving pressures.

The seat follows the movement in the ready position and, at the same time, the rider transfers his weight to the inside (right).

Phase No. 2 (Fig. b)

The commencement of motion on two tracks.

When the rider gets into the position as shown on the diagram his activities are as follows:

The inside rein, together with the inside leg held on the girth, pushes the horse sideways by exercising a firm lateral-moving effect. This action compels the inside foreleg to cross in front of the outside leg and gets the forehand off the track of the hind legs. The outside foreleg then proceeds in the hoof-mark of the inside hind leg, or perhaps a bit more inside. Both hind legs occupy roughly the original track.

The outside rein controls the leading of the horse and prevents the shoulders from falling out by mild alternating counter-balancing effects.

The rider's outside leg maintains the horse's liveliness.

In the seat the rider's weight is kept transferred to the inside.

Phase No. 3 (Fig. c)

Proceeding in the shoulder-in position.

The inside rein and leg, by exercising lateral-moving pressures, compel the horse to stride on two tracks. Meanwhile, the inside rein also controls the flexed position of the horse (which must not turn its neck or look towards the outside direction!) and the leg supervises the activity of the animal's inside hind leg. The interlocked yielding movements of the inside rein are extremely important in promoting the motion.

The outside rein has the important function of leading the horse in the direction of the course, while his outside leg maintains liveliness. With both his outside hand and leg (the latter being kept slightly behind the girth) he controls the animal's outside flank by an occasional counter-balancing effect.

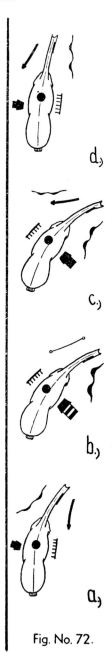

d.)

c.)

b.)

a.)

Fig. No. 72.

Phase No. 4 (Fig. d)

The resumption of the one-track movement.

While the inside rein pushes the shoulders to the opposite side, the inside leg ceases to exert its lateral-moving pressures and drives the horse onward.

The outside rein supports the activity of the hand on the opposite side by leading the forehand back to the straight line.

The duty of the outside leg is to keep the croup firmly on the track.

At the completion of the task the seat resumes its normal position (weight in the centre).

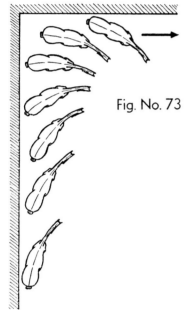

Fig. No. 73

Riding through corners in the shoulder-in position (Fig. No. 73)

Before reaching the corner the horse should be retarded slightly and, while the inside rein turns (leads) it, the inside leg provides a firm lateral-moving pressure behind the girth. On account of this activity the croup almost 'sweeps out' the corner, just as when making a turn on the forehand. (Actually, the turn on the forehand is also a shoulder-in movement.)

So, when the animal has reached the corner, the rider should let it make a movement similar to the turn on the forehand, whereby the forelegs can proceed on a very small circular line.

As soon as the croup has passed through the corner, the forelegs should be treading sideways again.

*The croup-in* (Fig. No. 74)

This exercise can be divided into the same four phases as the shoulder-in and it will be discussed in connection with the 'right croup-in'.

### Phase No. 1 (Fig. a)

The bending of the horse and bringing its croup towards the inside from the original track.

The rider should make a narrow turn towards the right so that it can be exploited first to achieve a more distinct flexion of the head and neck and secondly to promote the bending of the quarters.

During this movement

the inside (right) rein leads the horse into the turn and augments its flexion;

the inside leg maintains liveliness and may also exercise a counter-balancing effect;

the outside (left) rein yields to the turning, but also gives support to the shoulders to prevent them from falling out (to the left);

the outside leg seeks to enforce the bending of the quarters by exercising lateral-moving pressures behind the girth.

### Phase No. 2 (Fig. b)

The commencement of motion on two tracks.

When the horse has reached the position as sketched in the diagram the following signals should be applied:

the outside leg pushes the croup sideways by energetic lateral-moving pressures, thus compelling the horse's outside hind leg to step across in front of the inside leg and to get off the track of the forelegs. Both forelegs proceed on approximately the original track; meanwhile, the outside hind leg steps in the hoof-mark of the inside foreleg, or perhaps a bit further to the inside;

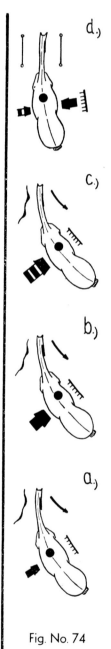

Fig. No. 74

the inside rein leads the motion and maintains the flexion;

the inside leg ensures liveliness; and

the outside rein counter-balances the shoulders to prevent any possible falling-out, and also resists occasionally in order to increase the effectiveness of the outside leg;

in the seat the rider's weight is shifted more to the inside.

In addition to the above activities, the rider safeguards the horse's shoulders in a straight position by pressing his inside thigh and knee to the saddle.

### Phase No. 3 (Fig. c)

Proceeding in the croup-in position:

the outside rein and leg force the horse to proceed on two tracks while the rein provides a counter-balancing effect against over-bending in a lateral direction, the leg exercises lateral-moving pressures;

the inside rein leads and maintains flexion (the animal must not look to the outside);

the inside leg counter-balances an excessive falling-in of the croup and maintains liveliness;

the position of the seat remains unchanged.

### Phase No. 4 (Fig. d)

The resumption of the one-track movement:

the inside rein decreases the flexion to the right (by 'giving') and keeps contact with the horse;

the inside leg moves the croup to the straight line (left) and safeguards liveliness;

the outside rein assists in flexing the animal back to the straight position;

the outside leg stops moving the croup inwards and provides a counter-balancing effect against a possible falling-out;

the seat resumes its normal position.

### Riding through corners in the croup-in position (Fig. No. 75)

The main feature of proceeding in the croup-in position through a corner is that the animal's forehand has to 'sweep out' the corner, as if it were making a turn on the haunches (the turn on the haunches is virtually a croup-in movement). Therefore, when the horse has reached the corner, it should perform a movement similar to the turn on the haunches, whereby the pivoting (inside) hind leg can proceed on a very small circular line. As soon as its forehand has passed through the corner, the hind legs must tread sideways again.

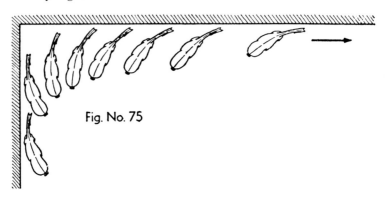

Fig. No. 75

*The half-pass (counter-change of hands on two tracks)*

This exercise is the crowning glory and the highest form of side-steps, not only because its actions have been developed from the previous exercises, but also on account of the striking beauty of its movements, which makes it, indeed, rank second to none. The energy, elasticity, rhythm, swing and gaining of ground are characteristics which distinguish this particular form of gait on two tracks from the others.

In performing the half-pass the horse must proceed between two parallel lines with a hardly noticeable flexed position of the head while stepping forward and sideways (Fig. No. 71).

The entire movement is led by the forehand, which is never preceded by the quarters. The outside legs cross in front of the inside legs. (If the half-pass happens to be performed from left to right, then the left legs cross in front of the right legs.)

The horse has to proceed simultaneously forward and sideways with a considerable swing while performing movements which are unusual to it, but, despite these difficulties, its locomotion must have an absolutely *forward tendency*. In order to endow the motion with this quality, the horse must perform its actions in a state of complete suppleness and ease. It must not fall into the sideways motion or oppose its execution.

Concerning the rider's attitude while aiding the animal to perform its movements in the desired manner, the 'feeling' discussed on page 235 and the general recommendations found on page 415 are of great importance.

We shall now examine the various signals and aids which the rider should give during the execution of the exercise. (Half-pass, performed from left to right; Fig. No. 76.)

The commencement of the half-pass movement (Fig. a)

It is important to note that, before commencing the half-pass, the rider should lead his horse straight on the line from which he intends to start the movement. He should by no means *turn* the animal into the direction of the half-pass movement. Aside from the fact that such a start would be regarded as incorrect, both the commencement and the execution of the movement are far more difficult from this undesirable position. To start with:

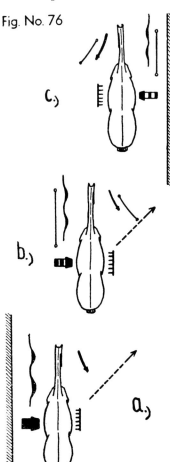

Fig. No. 76

c.)

b.)

a.)

the inside (right) rein indicates the direction of the desired movement and promotes a slight flexion of the head. During the action the hand can be kept slightly away from the body (towards the right);

the inside leg ensures the animal's liveliness a n d urges its haunches forward;

the outside (left) hand, with slight breathing-like pressures, provides a mild lateral - moving signal to the forehand;

the outside leg, by lateral-

moving pressures, signals the quarters to commence the proceeding on two tracks;
the seat shifts slightly over to the inside (right) and by this
position it determines the direction of the horse's stepping
under its body.

While proceeding in the half-pass movement (Fig. b)
the inside hand maintains contact in which the sensation of
following develops into a feeling of 'pushing' the rein. It also
leads the horse in the desired direction;
the inside leg safeguards the animal's liveliness;
the outside hand almost loses the contact and exercises only
from time to time a mild lateral-moving effect. Its function
is only a warning-like indication of the lateral movement
and must be applied with such a refinement that it does not
hinder the crossing movement of the legs;
the outside leg participates in maintaining liveliness and also
exercises from time to time some lateral-moving pressures
in order to prevent the quarters from evading the movement;
the upper body is held slightly in the direction of the motion
(inwards), and the seat safeguards the swinging motion of the
back in absolute unity with the saddle.

Resumption of the one-track movement (Fig. c)
The new inside (left) hand changes the horse's flexion and
follows the movement while keeping contact;
the new inside leg takes over the duty of animation;
the new outside (right) hand counter-balances any possible
falling-out of the shoulders;
the new outside leg keeps the croup on the straight line with
its counter-balancing effect;
the upper body and the seat resume their normal position.

*Teaching the two-track movements*

Two-track movements can only be taught when the horse is
capable of taking up the rein-contact, can be led while maintaining
it, and when it reacts submissively to the retarding and drive-on
signals and the lateral mobility of its shoulders has been improved.
A horse, the shoulder mobility of which is not equally free in both
lateral directions, cannot perform any two-track movement cor-

rectly. Therefore, one cannot possibly start teaching these movements in the earlier stages of the horse's education.

The rider's greatest aid in teaching two-track movements is his recognition of the sensations which he should feel when the movements are performed correctly. Thus

he must have the impression that he can drop at any time the rein opposite to the leading rein without any danger of the horse losing its state of balance or its bent position; and simultaneously

he must feel that his upper body is drawn by the force of the movement towards the animal's bent position.

If the rider does not have these sensations, it is certain that the execution of the movement is incorrect. It should be added, however, that the above sensations will not appear immediately when dealing with novice riders or young horses. In fact, the first impression will almost invariably be a sensation of stiffness.

With the inclusion of the above sensations the rider should employ during the schooling exercises the same signals and aids which have been recommended previously for the general execution of the particular movements. (See also page 226.)

The training should start with the shoulder-in, followed by the croup-in, and finally the half-pass may be taught after the horse's forehand and quarters have already been made agile by the preceding exercises.

In teaching the shoulder-in and the croup-in the first exercises should be carried out on a straight line (along a wall or fence) and only later executed on a circle. (The schooling of the shoulder-out and the croup-out should be carried out in the reverse order.) The half-pass should be practised between two straight parallel lines.

The tuition of the shoulder-in and croup-in can be facilitated if the rider starts the execution of the movement from riding on a small circle which touches the straight line along which the exercise is to be performed. In this sense the commencement of the shoulder-in movement should occur in that moment when the horse's forehand *leaves* the touching point, and that of the croup-in when the forehand *approaches* it.

In a short time this method of schooling will improve the animal's sensitivity to such a degree that a slight lateral-moving rein effect will be enough to bring its forehand off the original track, just as a slight lateral-moving effect of the leg will move its quarters off the track used before.

These two exercises automatically make the horse obedient also to the commencement of the half-pass, which, however, must occur from riding on a straight line. If, during teaching two-track movements the horse meets some difficulties, or at any time when their execution needs correction, the employment of the following procedure is recommended:

first of all, stop side-stepping; next

refresh the animal's obedience in longitudinal direction by some half-halts, and

restore the lateral mobility of its shoulders by some successive changes in the position of your gravitational centre (oscillating upper body movements);

in more acute cases, if the reaction expected fails to appear, supplement the above functions by the whole procedure of adjustment to straight position; and then

the moment the horse's suppleness thus has been created, the original exercise can be resumed again.

The rider should not neglect to interchange the side steps practised, often with his slight checking or definite corrective measures either with a preventive aim or at the first sign of the animal's resistance. With its improvement the reactions of the horse will gradually become more and more refined and the rider will be able to reduce the *dimensions* of his functions. At last the employment of the invisible levelling function will give enough impetus to the horse to retain its suppleness and perform the tasks demanded correctly.

# CHAPTER FIVE

# Increasing the Horse's Action Potential

IN the present chapter we shall examine the various techniques of endowing the horse with faculties by which it can refine and increase its performing capacity.

The means by which this aim can be achieved are the animal's liveliness and swing. Although these qualities are latent in the horse's natural motion, they must be developed to the highest possible degree by methodical schooling.

By making good use of the effects which are produced by the increased liveliness and swing, the horse can be brought into a state of collection which enables it to expend its energy in the most economical manner.

Since the motive power of all three qualities (liveliness, swing and collection) is impulsion, it may be useful first to examine more closely this important subject.

### THE IMPULSION OF THE HORSE

Impulsion is the horse's keenness in performing tasks either on its own accord (in freedom) or when demanded by the rider. It reflects the animal's striving to go forward and carry out with eagerness the actions required of it. Impulsion enhances the quality of the entire motion and even affects the animal's appearance in a stationary position. It gives real value to the collection of the horse.

When the horse is in motion impulsion increases its liveliness and swing. In a stationary position it intensifies the horse's energy, creating the impression that the animal is almost bursting with a desire to satisfy any demand that may be imposed upon it. In collection, impulsion is the natural driving power which endows the horse's movements with beauty and at the same time increases its performing capacity.

Impulsion is an inherent quality of the horse and depends upon the animal's individual temperament. While this may vary widely, impulsion can be developed to a fairly high level by proper education even in animals that are not favourably endowed. The main feature of such an education is the rider's ability to communicate his demands in such a way that he *always aids and never hampers* the horse in the execution of its movements. Further details are described on page 147.

The meaning of swing, liveliness and impulsion is often confused, so that it is desirable to compare their essential characteristics:

swing and liveliness are physical qualities inspired by impulsion; impulsion is a characteristic of the horse which manifests itself in the animal's keenness to perform.

Furthermore, impulsion must not be confused with running away. The former is a forward driving inspired by willingness; the latter originates in opposition.

(Concerning the importance of impulsion in jumping, see the information on page 325.)

## LIVELINESS AND ITS DEVELOPMENT

The liveliness which a horse displays in its movements is a measure of its actual mobility. Each horse has its natural degree of liveliness which is based on its individual physique and temperament. It is the aim of schooling to increase this individual liveliness as much as possible without upsetting the regularity of the natural sequence of strides.

The significance of liveliness lies in its practical value. It is liveliness which endows the animal with vitality, and actually enables it to accomplish the most challenging tasks.

In a general sense, the term is used to define the rate at which the horse keeps its legs moving in a rhythmical sequence of strides* (see also page 150). This definition, however, is very limited in its meaning, since it does not include the main demands and characteristics of a correct lively motion. These are:

---

*Liveliness—the number of steps the horse makes during a certain time.
Speed—the distance the horse covers in a certain time.

the submissive behaviour of the horse filled with impulsion (mental demands); and

the suppleness and swing of its body in performing the energetic leg actions (physical demands).

The limited extent of the general definition is likely to cause misinterpretation in reviewing and producing the horse's liveliness; therefore it is necessary to deal with the subject with special care.

The creation of the animal's basic state, out of which the correct liveliness can be achieved, is described in various paragraphs (see submission and suppleness on pages 144 and 160; impulsion on page 237; and swing on page 242). By these means the horse is made submissive, its body and muscles supple and relaxed. At the same time, they are producing elasticity and swing for the animation of the motion, if its spirit, the animal's impulsion, is promoted and not suppressed by the rider's functions.

Quickening of the horse's leg action is only an additional part of the introductory operation mentioned above. It can only follow *after* the introduction has been completed with satisfactory results.

In order to emphasize the proper trend of the procedure in question, it is necessary to draw special attention to two common faults which are often committed during its execution:

the first is when the rider forces his horse to assume a quick leg motion by senseless driving only;

the second is when he lets the animal step quickly in a state of resistance or agitation without establishing the horse's basic state for the performance of a correct lively motion.

The result is in both cases rolling, rushing with incited leg action, but not liveliness in its real sense. In its state of opposition the animal is stiff and does not react submissively to the rider's demands. All its movements are already in their basic element faulty and the energy displayed is deluding. Thus, concerning performing capacity, it is much more valuable at a somewhat slower motion if it is made in suppleness, since its quality can easily be improved by a simple animation, but the correction of a faulty liveliness needs substantial interference.

After establishing the horse's basic condition for the creation of liveliness, the development of it should start with practising transitions and alterations. Within their execution stress should be laid on producing resoluteness in the animal's supple reaction. This initial resoluteness will become expressed in a certain quickness of the leg motion which can easily be preserved and even increased later on.

The most suitable exercise for the purpose is the interlocked application of drive-on and retarding actions in quick succession. During this procedure the animating effect of the rider's drive-on activity can be enhanced if he taps the side of the horse with his whip at the same time as applying the leg signal. In response to the tap the animal will suddenly thrust its hind legs forward and this suddenness in the movement is the factor which helps the horse realize the aim of the rider and to comply with it.

By this means the horse will also learn to react to the driving signals in accordance with the rider's aim, either by increasing the speed or by quickening its leg motion. If the animal has learned to perform the transitions and alterations with resoluteness, the direct procedure of the animation should be carried out in the following manner:

> drive the horse on with determination; the animal's reaction to this will first of all be to increase the speed;

> let the animal proceed for a few strides at this increased speed and then make it slow down by applying a pronounced retardment action in which the stress is on the yielding phase;

> simultaneously with the yielding, repeat the drive-on signals in order to animate the horse again; and then

> repeat the entire exercise several times.

The essential quality of the procedure is the connection of the two parts: the quick drive-on and the sudden yielding moment of the retardment, which must be joined together with 'feeling'. The reason for

> increasing the speed is to generate sufficient force in the horse so that it will have a store of excess energy readily at hand in case it is necessary to accelerate the motion of its legs; and the reason for

> decreasing the speed is to cause the animal to alter the use of the same output of energy for transforming its long, ground-gaining strides into shorter but faster and perhaps slightly higher movements.

If the horse rolls off or becomes lazy instead of showing increased liveliness, the above exercise should be alternated with the correcting process discussed on page 150.

In general, sluggish horses are apt to be lazy and temperamental animals are more likely to roll off. As far as the work of animation is concerned, it is simpler to produce liveliness in a sequence of strides which has become sluggish than in a motion which rolls off. Consequently, it is easier to achieve a settled liveliness with lazy horses than with highly-strung ones.

After the creation of a state of liveliness this condition must be permanently maintained. In order to achieve this aim, the same basic procedure should be used for preventive purposes, but in a somewhat abbreviated and simplified form. As a preventive practice it is sufficient to exercise the taking action by the seat (pressure on the stirrups) and to replace the usual driving signal by one or two brief pressures of the legs and thighs. When performed in this manner the entire procedure is hardly noticeable.

There is another practical exercise which is bound to improve the animal's maintenance of liveliness. Horses are inclined to lose their liveliness when certain external influences produce resistance in their minds. For instance, if different surfaces of the ground contrast sharply with the surroundings (being darker, lighter, deeper, wetter, etc.), the horse may be unwilling to step freely on or into them. The rider can make good use of this phenomenon for educational purposes by practising the following exercise—preferably before the routine loosening procedure, when the horse's inclination for resistance is most pronounced.

Ride straight towards the piece of ground which offers some contrasting feature, and when the animal's intention for retention is felt give determined taps with the long riding whip behind the leg, while preventing any deviation from the straight direction. (It is harmful to give stronger leg signals than normal, since these will produce the reverse effect of the one which is desired.) The taps of the whip should touch the horse's side in a rhythm which corresponds to that of the desired liveliness. By means of these taps the rider should keep up the impulsion with the utmost resolution and prevent the animal from slowing down. While coming nearer and nearer to the contrasting surface the strength of the taps can be increased in proportion to the horse's increasing tendency to resist.

After a few attempts the horse will notice that nothing un-pleasant happens to it and, associating the drive-on signals with the necessity of retaining liveliness, it will be equally obedient when the signals are given by the legs alone and the punitive-like use of the whip can be discontinued.

The value of this submissive obedience of the horse in maintaining liveliness is most evident when riding up to unfamiliar obstacles of strange appearance, which otherwise would inspire it to hold back.

This exercise, in which the rider enforces the horse's liveliness stride by stride, is also an excellent means of improving himself. It will develop in him the feeling necessary to prevent the horse from refusing a jump, a descent into a ditch (quarry) or pond, etc., because he will be able to transfer his determined go-ahead spirit to his mount. A horse which approaches an obstacle with forward obedience coupled with liveliness will never stop in front of it.

It should be noted that this exercise will lose its educational value when the animal has become accustomed to the particular curiosity. Therefore, one should change the practice site as soon as the horse's lively approach is the result of habit and not of the rider's activities.

### THE SWING AND ITS DEVELOPMENT

The swing is the manifestation of a flexible easiness coupled with liveliness which radiates from the horse and is reflected in its every movement. This ease of deportment is the factor which endows the animal's movement with beauty and harmony.

In a physical sense, the swing originates from the horse' back, and it is expressed most visibly in the movement of the legs.

The rider can aid the horse to bring swing to its back (which is the main part of its spring system) by providing the system with a support at its two extremes, for no spring can swing when in a state of looseness. The support may be given partly

    by the bit, by establishing the rein-contact and thus keeping the front end in a smoothly fixed position; and partly

    by the hocks, by driving them well under the body and thus fixing the rear end of the spring system (see Fig. No. 77).

The swing of the back reveals itself in an elastic undulating movement. It is the horse's own motion which produces this swing and which eventually gives force to its whole being.

The swing manifests itself in the leg movements by giving the impression that the animal does not merely lift its legs during the locomotion, but uses them in such a manner that they simply bounce off the ground. This bouncing feature of the motion has a special importance during the take-off stride, since it augments the thrust-off action of the leading foreleg (see page 36).

With regard to the sensation created by the swing, the rider, either in the sitting or forward position, has the overwhelming impression that he is in complete harmony with the horse, while a delightful springy, rocking feeling pervades his body.

We shall now consider the ways and means by which this swing can be brought into the horse's movement.

The most suitable pace in which to improve the swing in the motion is the trot. Although the canter may seem to be better suited by its natural swing to develop the swing of the horse's back, the rhythmical movements of the trot prove to be more effective in accomplishing the desired results. However, considering the advantages of the canter movement, it is a good practice to include in the trotting work from time to time some exercises in the canter in order to refresh the swinging movement of the back by this natural means.

The first step in the process of developing swing is to regulate the sequence of strides and to remove the stiffness from the horse's back by the joint application of drive-on and retardment. The resulting suppleness of the back provides a suitable basis for the next and most essential part of the procedure.

Take the horse to the reins and ride it in a steady trot while keeping the seat in a close contact with the horse's back. Proceed in this manner until you have the sensation that the animal is virtually striding with your own legs.

Before arriving at this state the rider is frequently obliged to influence the animal by smooth drive-on and retarding actions blended by the levelling function (see Fig. No. 42/b) to retain the steady rhythm of its motion. These slight alterations which maintain the evenness and the permanent liveliness of the steady motion are the mediums which initiate the swinging movement in question. In particular the alternating mild pressing-down actions of the thighs and the seat-bone which are involved in the above activities have the effect of bringing about the desired swing at the same time as they control the regularity of the motion.

The next step is to increase the swinging movement of the back by the application of the appropriate seat action (see page 69) executed in a smooth manner.

When the back is swinging nicely the rider can spread the swing to the horse's entire body by changing the moderate speed into a faster one and then slowing down again in a rather quick rotation. During this process each part-action should be completed by a soft but brief transition. The softness of the transition is achieved by the yielding phase which completes every action of the rider.

While alternately striding quickly forward and slowing down again, the horse's movements gradually acquire more and more swing.

After a certain period of improvement it will be possible to maintain the swing permanently by following the same procedure as was used for creating it; however, the dimensions should be reduced to those of the levelling function. At the end of the schooling the animal will adopt the swinging movement of its own accord and the rider's only care will be to prevent the horse from abandoning it.

### The Collection of the Horse

The collection of the horse (meant as a procedure) denotes those combined activities of the rider by which he encourages the animal to display its talents to the utmost limit of its ability. In other words, the collection of the horse is the process of spanning elastically the animal's spring system so as to make it capable of producing more strenuous exertions and a higher degree of swing. In the state thus created it can respond immediately to the slightest activity of the rider's hands, legs or seat and it can be led with a minimum of effort.

The horse gives clearly visible evidence of its collected state. It raises its outstretched neck higher on account of the arched bearing, drops its nose more to the vertical, lowers its croup by treading well under its body, and its entire contact with the rider becomes quite light.

The great distinction of the horse's general appearance makes a striking impression on riders who neglect the serious work required to produce it. Instead, these riders will use various artificial measures in an attempt to impose upon their horses a bearing which somehow resembles that of an animal which is collected. This kind of interference must be condemned! Such measures neither increase nor preserve the energy of the horse, but, on the contrary, cause useless fidgetings which waste its power.

The basic principle which should govern the construction of the collecting procedure is that

the span desired in the horse's spring system must be created *by the animal itself*, using the inherent collecting power of its motion;

the rider's contribution is to inspire the animal for the performance of the necessary motion and to provide its spring system with support in the manner as described on page 242.

If the horse is in a loose state, its entire spring system (running from the mouth to the hocks through the poll, neck and back; see Fig. No. 77) gives the impression of expansion. When the rider

Fig. No. 77

wishes to make it cocked it is necessary to push the system together between its two extreme points, the mouth and the hocks. The higher the degree of the collection, the closer are these points shifted to each other. This shift in their position, however, must be achieved by pushing the hocks more and more forward to the mouth and by no means by pulling the mouth nearer to the hocks.

These conditions indicate that the state of collection cannot be produced by some sort of a simple signal or aid, but rather by a group of actions. If the rider does not succeed in collecting the horse, then it is better to let it move freely and get along on its own strength.

The process of collection, both in the course of schooling and when riding educated horses, has to be carried out gradually *on each occasion*. Failing this, it can easily happen that the spring system snaps or takes up a concave shape instead of becoming spanned. The more educated the horse, the more readily it will carry out the component parts of the process, so that with training the complexity of the whole procedure will eventually diminish.

However, while the component parts will take on a simpler form, and while the collection will be achieved in a shorter space of time, it will always be necessary to include all the various elements of the operation, even if they are only applied briefly.

The complete process of collection is composed of the following phases (in the order in which they should be executed):

the loosening exercise (see page 266);

the establishment of the mental and physical contact (page 102);

the regulation of the horse's motion (see page 143);

the creation of liveliness (see page 238), the performance of distinct alterations within certain paces, changes of paces (see page 122), and the execution of rein-back movements (see page 221);

the increase of suppleness by practising some short turns and movements on two tracks (see pages 212 and 224).

These are the introductory exercises which pave the way for the collection. If they are carried out properly, they will already create a certain degree of collection which can be finally completed according to the principles described below.

The motion by which the horse completes its state of collection is produced by the joint application of drive-on and retardment, coupled with an increase of animation. In order for the motion to exercise the necessary effect, it is important that the rider should imbue his aiding activities with a high degree of go-ahead spirit. He should carry them out with determination, but with smoothness, and he must not show the slightest sign of rigidity.

While the rider executes the *drive-on phase* of the procedure, he must do this with a very particular feeling as if he were trying

to drive the quarters with his legs—through the calves and knees—towards his thighs, and from there

to shove the quarters forward toward his hands by the pressure of the thighs, and finally

to 'push' the horse's entire body into the forward motion through the reins by the 'following' conduct of his hands.

*The retardment* should be performed with a particular feeling as if the effect of the reins does not stop at the horse's mouth, but is transmitted through the rider's arms, shoulders, hips, seat-bone (in forward position through the stirrups) to the back of the animal.

If the horse shows resistance during the operation, either by trying to pull the reins out of the rider's hands or by stiffening its back, the rider's collecting activities should be interchanged by a mild function of passive tension performed by the hands and the seat. At higher stages of education the effect of this interference can be reinforced by a simultaneously applied drive-on action terminating in complete relaxation of the engaged muscles.

Once the state of collection has been created it is a much simpler matter to maintain it, especially if the rider has mastered the application of preventive measures. However, if prevention has been ignored or neglected and a difficulty arises, then the rider will have to repeat the operation of collection all over again. The essence of maintaining the state of collection is to preserve the horse's forward impulsion and its liveliness.

The horse indicates its intention to give up its collected state and stretch out by slight fidgetings, and this is the moment when the rider should employ his preventive measures. For this purpose it is quite sufficient to warn the horse by small and hardly noticeable animating actions in a flexible manner and in rather quick succession. Within these actions the drive-on should be exercised mainly by the pressure of the thighs and the retardment be accomplished by the pressures of the seat-bone (stirrups). Occasionally the employment of a gentle but definite passive tension can also be useful.

It is very advantageous, also, without any positive reason, to check from time to time the pliability of the horse in its collected state in order to forestall the animal's slightest tendency to abandon it. For this purpose the levelling function shown in Fig. No. 42/b offers the best possibilities. During its execution the rider should concentrate his attention on observing the behaviour of the horse's back. If he senses in the moment of his first passive or taking action some resistance, he should continue the levelling function with its manifold minute movements (Fig. No. 42/e). These will loosen the stiffness, yet before it actually develops, and thus preserve the cleanness of the horse's collection.

### The collection of the horse while using the forward position

The general principles of collection are the same whether the process is accomplished in a sitting or forward position. The only difference lies in the technique by which the various actions of the seat are carried out. Needless to say, the effects of the seat which have been brought about by actions in the sitting position must correspond exactly in each phase of the operation to those which are accomplished in the forward posture.

The pressing-down effect of the thighs has to be supported by an increased pressure of the knees and calves, while the rider lightens his weight on the stirrups (see page 48).

The effect of the taking action of the seat has to be supplemented by a firmer pressure on the stirrups (see page 52).

In order to create the horse's collected state with the aim of making good use of it in forward position, the rider can lighten *his* task by using the sitting method of riding until the animal has been brought into a state of suppleness. However, to facilitate the work for the horse and refresh its sensitivity and forward impulsion, he should change over to the forward position as soon as possible.

### The collection of the horse when jumping

In jumping, when the horse has to move within a relatively wider sphere and the increased span of its whole spring system becomes indispensable, it is exceptionally important to increase the animal's energy by collection. In order to be able to provide the jumper with supplementary energy at any desired moment, and to restore its state of collection swiftly if it should spread out in front of the obstacle, it is important to develop its sense of collection to a very high degree.

The basic technique of collecting the horse for jumping is the same as the method that has already been described. However, the procedure by which the animal's *already existing collection can be rapidly increased* requires further special schooling. This can be undertaken only when the horse's collection by the normal procedure has reached a high standard.

The first task of this special training is to school the horse to react submissively, by increasing its state of collection to a retarding signal (firm, if necessary) applied from a determined driving-on. In other words, the horse's sensitivity must be developed so that, after the drive-on signal, a pressure on its back, coupled with a simple pulling action of the reins, is able to check it instantly right to the hocks *without breaking its swing*, thus augmenting the required span in its spring system.

Later on its sensitivity should be developed to such a point that finally the horse, while permanently retaining its impulsion and liveliness, will increase its collection at any desired moment in response to a rein-signal.

The rein action which the rider should employ for this purpose is a simultaneous pulling by both hands. This should be executed within a *brief space of time* so that its application and cancellation are carried through in a smooth transition (see page 60).

The strength of the pulling must be decreased as the animal increases its sensitivity for collection. The pulling itself must be determined (if necessary, severe), *but never jerky*, since this may upset the horse's forward impulsion, which is of special importance to a jumper.

In response to the above rein action, which prompts the compression of the spring system, the animal produces an increased span inspired by its forward impulsion. The principle of the action is that the horse is expected to increase its collection *from the rear* while receiving the actual signal through its mouth.

In conclusion, it should be noted that the rider will inevitably fail to reach his goal if he tries to simplify the process of the gradual schooling by neglecting to emphasize its main feature, the improvement of the horse's forward spirit, during the tuition. Instead of providing the horse with wings, methods in which the element of spiritless pulling dominates will take all the pleasure out of its jumping. With regard to the execution and application of the collecting function for jumping, see full details on page 332.

*The bearing of the horse and its maintenance*

While discussing the process of collection it is necessary to consider the animal's 'bearing', since this is a direct *consequence* of the collection. One often comes across foolish statements such as ' the adoption of the bearing of the neck and head is the process of collection itself'. Having already explained the correct method of bringing about the state of collection, perhaps this conception can be dismissed as inaccurate without any further comment.

No special work is required in order to get the horse to move with a well-formed carriage. In fact, any such work should be discarded as useless. The proper bearing of the horse must come as a result of the exercises which are designed to collect it. During the activities the animal should adopt the desired carriage without the need of any forcing device, for it will find that the movement is more agreeable when it is performed in a pleasant deportment.

The horse's voluntary co-operation will do more to create and maintain the correct form of bearing than all those novel devices which try to pull its head down by force.

In general usage the 'bearing' refers mostly to the horse's external appearance, in which its neck is highly arched and its head-carriage takes a position approximately 0-30° to the vertical. In accordance with the increase of collection the neck-carriage becomes higher and higher and more arched. Simultaneously, with the increase of the elevation the distance between the mouth and withers becomes shorter and shorter.

It is important to note that the rider cannot hasten the improvement of the neck-carriage by shortening the reins, but must adapt the length of the reins to the *horse's* improvement. The difference between following and initiating the shortening process is considerable. It is a bad practice not to follow this natural improvement, but it is even worse when the rider tries to enforce it by arbitrarily shortening the reins. From such an attempt originates the greatest fault in riding, namely, the forced compression of the horse.

However, the term 'bearing' in its fullest sense not only denotes an external deportment, but also includes the presence of all those invisible qualities which contribute to bring about such a state.

A superficial carriage reduces the horse's neck to an ingeniously shaped but empty 'shell' which is bound to fall to pieces at the slightest friction from without or within and lose its form altogether.

When the neck has taken up the correct bearing as a result of collection it is consistent with the continuation of the spine and elastically conveys its swing. In this case the neck will always maintain its well-arched form regardless of external influence (Fig. No. 77).

There may be some variation in the requirements so far as the extent of the arching of the neck is concerned, but it must have the intrinsic quality mentioned above. With regard to jumpers, three-day horses and hunters, the bearing should correspond with that lightly-arched neck and head-carriage most suitable to the balancing action while jumping. However, in the dressage test of the combined competitions the horse may carry its neck more arched and more highly set because of the more intense collection which is necessary for the accomplishment of the prescribed test.

When the rider has completed the process of collection, he has also succeeded in bringing the animal into the right bearing, which it will retain without any further actions for as long as it remains in collection. While the horse shows no intention of abandoning its state of collection, the rider should follow its trend of motion in absolute smoothness with the feeling of pushing it forward.

The animal is inclined to give up its collection and bearing quite suddenly when it loses its liveliness and lags behind with the quarters. The manifestation of this deficiency is a tossing of the head and neck or a hard, stiff pushing against the bit. The direct methods of eliminating these defects can be found in the section dealing with the faults in keeping rein-contact. The essence of their application is that the rider should act with the aim of preserving the *obedience* (mental contact and submission) of the horse, but not with the direct intention to safeguard the *shape* of its deportment, which is only one of the physical manifestations of its obedience.

Young riders very often fear to get rid of the attractive shape of an arched neck and head-carriage. In their anxiety they are inclined to apply certain 'preventive' measures with the intention of securing the 'troublesome' created bearing of the horse. This is an extremely bad habit which leads the rider to undo his constructive work by senseless pulling or resisting with his hands. The result of such interference is that the animal becomes fidgety and, in a display of perfectly justified opposition, it abandons its arched deportment, thus arriving at a result which is just the contrary to that at which the rider has been aiming.

As a rule, the greater the experience of the rider and the more refined is his feeling in guiding the horse, the less trouble he will have in safeguarding the animal's bearing. A skilled rider can even make broad, gesticulating movements with his hands, for as long as he concentrates his attention on the maintenance of the fine, gentle contact with the animal's mouth the horse will not alter its nicely arched deportment.

The case is quite different with those riders who try to pull the animal into a 'shape' by force, by stiffly pressed-down hands, by all sorts of 'magic bridles' and different types of strap mechanisms. It is possible that the horse will yield to the pain inflicted by such measures by taking up an arched neck-carriage, but after the slightest movement of the hands and the first feeling of freedom it will toss up its head and give up its apparent state of collection.

## The Function of Passive Tension and its Uses

The manual feature of this function of the hands and seat have already been discussed in the first part. Now we shall examine the subject with regard to the improvement of the rider's ability to apply this function properly and to the development of the horse's sensitivity in accepting the effects that they produce.

### IMPROVEMENT OF THE RIDER'S ABILITY TO APPLY PASSIVE TENSION

The rider must pay great attention to developing his ability to perform the function of passive tension of both the hands and the seat. All the activities which are connected with these functions must be kept under the strictest control, so that the passivity in the function never becomes an act of pulling with the hands or of pressing hard with the seat.

As a general rule, the strength of the passive tension is always determined by the degree of opposition displayed by the horse. It is a combined function, composed of resisting phases and moments of relaxation. If the horse shows tough resistance, the phases of tension can be longer (say, 4 to 5 seconds); in milder cases their duration can be reduced to 1 to 2 seconds.

The importance of the rider's interlocked yielding moments can be proved by the fact that the horse's own decision to yield always occurs during one of these moments. Therefore it is essential that the rider perfects his technique of changing from passive tension over to relaxation and vice versa without ever losing the contact with the horse's mouth or with its back.

### DEVELOPING THE HORSE'S PROPER RESPONSE TO THE FUNCTION OF PASSIVE TENSION

*In teaching the horse how to react to the function of the hands* the following method can be used:

while in motion, take up the rein-contact and keep the bit on the horse's jaw;

retard the animal to a standstill, and if it happens that it leans strongly on the bit or pulls against the reins exercise some definite resistance by the hands which, however, should be blended with the inner vibration of the muscles making the inherent passivity smooth.   In answer to this, it is certain that the horse will yield to the rider sooner or later and by releasing its stiffness the lower jaw will become mobile (the horse will start to champ the bit); next

relax the muscles and let the animal champ the bit softly while keeping contact; then

drop the reins and after a brief rest repeat the same procedure several times.

*In teaching the horse the acceptance of the seat function* the exercise should be performed in motion.  For this

take up a close contact with the horse's back and keep the seat in this position;

exercise passive tension by the seat as soon as the animal shows resistance to the contact by muscle stiffness or by a vertical distortion of its back; then

cancel the function of passive tension the moment the horse yields and let it rest by freeing its back; afterwards

repeat the entire procedure several times.

With regard to both the procedures described above, it should be mentioned that the particular functions become more effective and more instructive when the passive tension of the hands and the seat are executed simultaneously.  Therefore it is useful for the rider to perform the exercises first individually and then simultaneously.  In the latter case the exercise should be coupled with half-halt movements.

After a certain amount of practice the horse will realize the connection between resistance (its own and the rider's) and discomfort on the one hand and between yielding (its own and its master's) and a pleasant sensation on the other.  At this moment the animal has really learned the meaning of the passive tension and from now on it will accept it submissively, regarding it as a means of assistance for the sake of its own welfare.

THE EMPLOYMENT OF THE PASSIVE TENSION DURING THE HORSE'S EDUCATION

Passive tension should be employed mainly in the final stages of the horse's education.  The functions involved should refine the animal and increase its willingness for submission.  The proper application of these means can produce a great improvement in the horse, but they can cause a relapse or even harm if they are improperly employed.

The rider should perform the passive tension of his hands and seat during the various procedures in the same manner as described above for teaching the animal the acceptance of the function, but with the inclusion of more expressed yielding phases.

By the aid of the passive tension employed the rider can either promote the horse's lightness in its reaction to rein and seat signals or increase its sensitivity for obedience, depending upon whether or not the passive tension is accompanied by a simultaneous drive-on.

*In promoting the lightness* of the animal the procedure should be carried out in a stationary position (only rarely, and only at an advanced stage of education should it be attempted while the horse is in motion) in the following manner:

exert a force on the horse by exercising passive tension with the hands and seat; then

relax the engaged muscles and repeat the process until the horse yields; afterwards

drive it on and carry out the whole exercise several times.

During the employment of the passive tension *no driving action* is permitted. The necessary forward impulsion is achieved by slight pressure of the thighs and by keeping the legs close to the animal's sides.

The yielding of the horse is achieved when its entire muscular system adopts a state of suppleness together with the yielding of the lower jaw. A yielding only with the jaws (the horse comes behind the reins) is a form of evasion which has *immediately* to be cured by the means described on page 108. The state of suppleness manifests itself in an elasticity felt through the seat and a sense of easiness conveyed through the reins.

During the procedure horses are inclined to keep looking aside by turning the neck instead of yielding, or to evade the rider's influence by stepping backwards. When this form of resistance occurs the rider should cease the passive tension and, after yielding, either exercise a short but resolute pull on the rein which is on the side opposite to the turning of the neck or, in the second case, drive the animal energetically forward for a few strides.

*For increasing the horse's obedience* to the rider's authority the process is an advanced form of the one above, since it must be carried out by simultaneously applying the *passive tension and the drive-on*. The delicate compressing feature of the procedure produces a very strong effect on the animal, and therefore the rider must be especially careful with its employment.

The procedure should be carried out in motion (only very rarely and only at an advanced stage of education should it be performed in a stationary position), according to the following method:

first, carry out the former procedure a few times and when the lightness of the horse has been achieved

drive it on determinedly (use the tap of the whip), however, instead of the 'giving' which usually accompanies the drive-on; exercise passive tension with the hands and seat;

proceed for a few strides and during this motion shove the horse's entire body forward to the fixed bit by means of a drive-on; then

relax the engaged muscles and proceed for a few strides with a sensation of pushing the horse forward; after this

drop the reins and give the animal a rest; then

repeat the procedure a few times.

The motion should be endowed with a substantial amount of forward impulsion, which is ensured not only by the drive-on action, but also by the pulling and rigidity-free feature of the passive tension and by the very slight yielding moments involved in it. These latter elements give the animal a chance to release its resistance.

The disciplinary aim of the procedure has been reached when the horse, while retaining its lightness in the back and on the bit, obeys submissively the forward driving and steps well under its body.

While the exercise is in progress horses are inclined to increase the speed instead of treading forward to the bit, and instead of yielding they are apt to go over into a sort of lateral movement (perhaps even into backing) by twisting their forehand. If this should occur, one has to discontinue the exercise for a short while in order to remedy the situation by applying a determined retardment (drive-on) or an adjustment to straight position.

In both cases, whether the aim is to produce the lightness of the horse or to teach it to obey, the result appears on each occasion after a certain period of transition. Within this period of transition there are numerous moments when the animal seems inclined to yield and then exerts resistance again. The rider must be able to follow this process with refined sense of feeling. In answer to every yielding he must be able to respond with his own yielding, and at every new sign of resistance he must employ the appropriate measures in such a manner that the horse's forward impulsion remains completely intact.

The selection of the right type and grade of corrective measures also requires a refined sense of judgment on the part of the rider, since the method selected must be perfectly adjusted to the horse's prevailing reaction (to a ready obedience, the rider's response should be complete yielding; to a slight resistance, a mild regulation, etc.). Furthermore, he must be able to reconcile his actions with the horse's temperament in order to avoid the use of measures which might confuse the animal or render his actions totally ineffective.

### Pressing Function on the Frontal End of the Horse's Spring System

By the aid of the already known means of influencing the horse one can safely reach a very high standard in its education and conductibility. But the rider can still increase the effect of these means and the performing capacity of the animal by the temporary application of this additional function.

As one can see from the headline, the purpose of the function is to exercise a pressure on the frontal end of the horse's spring system. This can be achieved by communicating a pressing effect to this system through the jaw in such a manner that it (the pressure) should not get stuck in the mouth of the animal. This latter condition makes the execution of the function rather complex, since by ignoring it, the pressure becomes a senseless pulling which obstructs the horse only. Therefore, before its application the rider must acquire great skill and refined feeling in the execution of his activities.

The essential feature and significance of the pressure produced by the function can be best demonstrated by comparing it with the already known pressure exercised by the seat on the horse's back.

Both of them serve the same purpose of promoting the elastic span and swinging movement of the animal's spring system.

Both of them are short, repeated pressures of gradually increasing and decreasing nature. Their strength can vary according to the actual situation between that of a slight indication (passive function) and of a firm action, but whatever this strength, the pressure must *never break the forward impulsion* of the horse. In order to comply with this demand, they are in both cases supported by the rider's general animation, executed in combination with expressed yielding phases and practicable in motion only.

The characteristic difference between them is that the former affects the *frontal end* and the latter the *middle part* of the system.

Now let us see the details concerning the performance and the application of the function.

The function in its whole is the reinforced form of the last version of the levelling function. Thus it involves *interchanged hand actions* interlocked with yielding phases.

It is a physical aid the performance of which can only occur after the establishment of the rein-contact. There is a certain compulsive element in this function becoming effective on the jaw, the most sensitive part of the horse. Therefore, it should only be employed when the animal has already learned to accept the pulling effect of the rein with confidence, so that the pressure does not stir up opposition in its mind. Ignoring this prerequisite of the function, it will become the source of the horse's resistance, resulting in crookedness, increased pushing action against the bit or throwing about with the head.

The pressure itself should be produced mainly by the gradually increasing squeeze of the hand and arm muscles, and only in a limited scale by pulling on the rein. It should last for a short while (I say one to two seconds) and terminate in the gradual relaxation of the engaged muscles. It is important to emphasize that the pressure should *never be executed simultaneously with both hands*.

In order to prevent the pressure being evaded by the mouth (the horse gets beyond the rein) or rebuffed by it (the horse resists against the bit), the rider should animate the horse by filling the function with his absolute forward strive, being reinforced during the involved yielding phases by his determined but smooth driving activity.

Within its already mentioned general scope the aims of the function are:

to remind the horse occasionally for the maintenance of its 'cocked' spring system;

to increase moderately the elastic span of this system;

to overcome the animal's transitory opposition against the acceptance of the frame determined in the front by the established rein-contact; and

to support the horse in retaining its supple state during the completion of tasks demanding some change either in the used pace or speed, or in the display of energy and motion (e.g. while moving on undulating surfaces, approaching obstacles).

In order to acquire the feeling and skill for the correct execution of the physical actions involved, carry out the following exercise:

Take two small rubber balls and attach each of them (separately) to an elastic strap about 3 ft. (90 cm.) long (they replace the reins). Fasten the free ends of the straps to a fixed object (representing the mouth of the horse) at a height of about 2 ft. (60 cm.) and about 6 in. (15 cm.) apart from each other.*

Then, while sitting in riding position in front of this object, take the balls in your hands and stretch the straps so that they are neither loose nor stretched tight (taking up the rein-contact). Now, for a short while, squeeze with gradually increasing strength *on one* of the balls and simultaneously pull mildly on the same strap.   Then relax gradually the engaged muscles and afterwards carry out the same action with the other hand.

Repeat these actions in rotation; take care, however, that they should always be interlocked by the relaxing phase of the previously exercised 'pressure'.  Practise this exercise on several occasions, until the feeling and skill for the performance of the pressure is firmly established in your mind.

As we could see from the foregoing, the performance of the physical movements involved in the function is not particularly difficult.  It needs much more self-education and observation, the acquisition of the refined feeling and improved knowledge by which the rider can correctly judge the situation which justifies the application of this delicate function.

---

* This installation is also useful for the acquisition of the skill necessary for the smooth performance of any other rein-function.

# CHAPTER SIX

# Various Supplementary Means and Methods for Developing the Horse's General Education

## THE DOUBLE BRIDLE AND ITS APPLICATION

THE double bridle is the main headgear of refined dressage riding. In jumping and cross-country riding, where the extended movements involved make it difficult to handle properly, one should, if possible, avoid the use of this bridle. However, in hunting, where horses make each other nervous or agitated in the crowd, and where it is, nevertheless, necessary to control the animal somehow, one has to resort in many cases to the double bridle. Needless to say, under such circumstances (especially when the education of the horse and the rider is limited) the rider's control over the animal is based on the pain inflicted and not on a mutual understanding. Therefore, whenever possible, one should also omit the use of the double bridle when hunting.

During the period of preliminary schooling only the plain snaffle bridle with its smooth and instructive effect should be used. Afterwards, however, the horse should be mature enough to accept the double bridle—in fact, its use is compulsory during the performance of the dressage test of the three-day event.

The double bridle is composed of a jointed snaffle-bit and a stiff curb-bit in order to enable the rider to bring greater refinement to the art of riding. Thus, its aim is to refine the animal and not to 'break down' hardness, as is so often believed.

The purpose of the snaffle-bit part of the double bridle is to direct the horse and to produce lateral effects.

The purpose of the curb-bit part is to underline the leading actions of the snaffle-bit so that the horse can be led by almost invisible hand actions.

When the young horse has acquired a reasonably high standard of knowledge and sensitivity, the rider can commence the application of the double bridle. But the rider himself must also possess a high degree of training before trying to use it. Like a razor, which is very dangerous in the hands of someone who does not know how to handle it, the double bridle can cause great harm to the mouth of the horse and spoil all its performances by stiffness if it is used by ignorant or insensitive hands.

When using the double bridle, the reins can either be divided between the hands or united in one hand.

If the reins are divided between the hands, it is obligatory to hold the snaffle reins divided, but the holding of the curb reins is left to the rider's discretion and he is at liberty to keep them

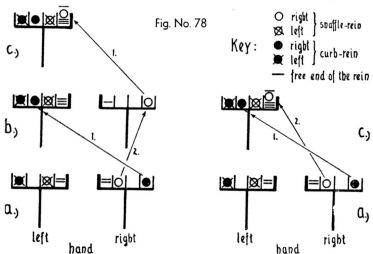

Fig. No. 78

Key:  ○ right } snaffle-rein
      ⊠ left
      ● right } curb-rein
      ▣ left
      — free end of the rein

left    right
   hand

left    right
   hand

either in one hand, or the left rein in his left and the right in his right hand.

Leading with reins which are equally divided between the hands (i.e. the two left reins in the left, and the two right reins in the right hand), creates an impression of apparent easiness, but if the rider is not master of the situation it can become the source of many troubles.

With regard to the technique of holding the reins between certain fingers, there are a number of practices which have been developed according to the special requirements of the dressage. A simplified arrangement which I personally recommend is shown in Fig. No. 78/a-c.

The diagrams reproduce the hands in that posture in which the rider, with a horizontal carriage of the under-arms and with the fists turned slightly inside, sees only the nails of the thumbs.

Diagram a:

shows the divided manner of holding the reins when the right reins are kept in the right and the left reins in the left hand. This technique is called the 'modern' or 'neo-classic' manner and forms the basis for further variations.

Diagram b:

illustrates the variation of divided reins when three reins are kept in the left hand and only the right snaffle rein is handled by the right hand. As it can be observed from the details of the diagram, this technique is not exactly the same as the so-called ‚'military manner', where the rider holds the left snaffle rein under the two curb reins.

Diagram c:

shows the form in which all four reins are kept in the left hand. This is a variation of the 'Fillis' method. In both cases the sequence of reins follows the same order, only their deployment between the fingers is different.

In all three cases, as it can be seen from the diagrams, the rider holds the left reins in the same place, enabling him to change from one manner to another by a simple movement.

The succession of movements while changing the particular manners, where the changing rein has to be placed in its new position, is indicated by arrows in the diagrams. The change of rein positions in the opposite sense should be carried out in the same way, only the actions involved must follow each other in reverse order.

When introducing the use of the double bridle stress should be laid on the snaffle-bit part. As the animal's knowledge and sensitivity improve, the curb-bit becomes more important, so that at the end of a special dressage schooling the horse is quite ready to be ridden solely by the curb-bit. However, this latter feature of the dressage does not come within the scope of this book.

During the first two weeks of accustoming the animal to the double bridle the curb-chain should not be employed. At this stage it is quite sufficient to ride on long, straight lines, while permitting the horse's mouth and tongue to become familiar with the two pieces of iron, and especially with the bar of the curb-bit.

After a certain space of time has elapsed the curb-chain can be attached to the bridle. To begin with, the curb-chain should be long, and only when the horse shows sufficient maturity in wearing it should it be properly adjusted to the animal's chin. As a rule, it is far better to attach the chain one hole too long than half a hole too short.

If during the exercises it is felt that the horse is not yet quite ready for the double bridle, the rider should immediately return to the snaffle bridle, or else he should hold the reins of the curb-bit very loosely, whether the curb-chain is loose or not. With the inclusion of such changes the rider should improve the horse until it has acquired confidence in the use of the double bridle and carries it with ease, reacting to its effect just as smoothly as in the case of the snaffle bridle.

In using the double bridle for giving signals and aids the principles are identical with those which govern the use of the plain snaffle. However, with regard to the execution of the movements, there are certain points to be noted, such as:

During the retardment:

the interlocking signals which are applied with the snaffle-bit become underlined by the curb-bit in the form of a mild pressure on the bars in the horse's mouth.

While turning the horse:

as the snaffle-bit of the bridle is the main instrument of the operation, the curb-bit is active only in the execution of its part actions, e.g. in the course of the inserted retardments (half-halts). Only highly schooled horses are able to obey smoothly and correctly the turning signals applied by the curb-bit.

In the adjustment to straight position:

it is advisable to refrain altogether from the employment of the curb-bit, as its sharp effect will increase the apparent stiffness and crookedness in the animal's bearing.

RIDING WITH REINS HELD IN ONE HAND

The principles governing this method of riding are equally valid in the case of the snaffle or the double bridle.

ILLUSTRATION PLATES

# Description of the Horses shown in the pictures

*(The data refer to the time when the pictures were taken)*

**Gipsy Love** (Flaminco—Night Haven), bay gelding, 6 yrs.

*Owner:* Her Majesty the Queen Mother.

The horse was previously trained for steeplechases. A most difficult animal to control; consequently went 'through' the fences or hit them. After schooling it became a reliable jumper, even when ridden in races by a strange rider.

**Kings Point** (Queen's Eyot—Steel Girl), chestnut gelding, 8 yrs.

*Owner:* Her Majesty the Queen Mother.

Horse in training for steeplechases. Present schooling during the mid-season. It has shown an acute opposition to the will and influence of the rider. This manifested itself in stretching out (instead of collecting) the spring system and in unwarranted expression of fright. Consequently it lost confidence in approaching the obstacle properly and stood too far back in taking off, which resulted in hitting the fences. After its sense of opposition had been overcome the difficulties immediately disappeared.

**Clarion** (Colorado Boy—          ), chestnut gelding, 5 yrs.

*Owner:* His Grace the Duke of Beaufort.

Horse unridden before its schooling started by the author. It has become one of its owner's favourite hunters.

**Sand Piper** (Sandiman—          ), chestnut gelding, 5 yrs.

*Owner:* His Grace the Duke of Beaufort.

Horse unridden before its schooling started by the author. It has shown difficulties by the extreme straightness of its natural back and neck line. After the establishment of its flexibility it became an excellent hunter.

**Rocky Marciano** (Earlstone—          ), brown gelding, 5 yrs.

*Owner:* His Grace the Duke of Beaufort.

Horse already ridden before its schooling was started by the author. Adjustment of the improper rein-contact (restless head and neck-carriage), elimination of increased inclination to left-sided crookedness and correction of the faulty jumping movement were the main objects of the re-education. It has become a keen hunter and good one-day event horse.

**Father Jim** (Sandiman—Mrs. Grandy), chestnut gelding, 5 yrs.

*Owner:* Mr. David Somerset.

Horse unridden before taken into schooling by the author. Lack of natural forward impulsion was the main difficulty to overcome. It has become a fine hunter and good performer in one-day events.

**Duhallo** (unknown), grey gelding, 8 yrs.

*Owner:* Mr. David Somerset.

Horse hunted several seasons before being purchased by the owner. Strong opposition, general stiffness and deviating motion have been the main defects to be cured, and willingness for determined take-off from a distant point had also to be improved. The aim has been achieved and the horse has become a first-class hunter.

**Pandur** (Gambrinus—Orso), bay gelding, 12 yrs.

Owned, trained and ridden by the author for five years. Died of influenza in 1937. Winner of six three-day events, fifth at the Olympic T.D.E. in Berlin, 1936. Winner of show-jumping competitions up to 5 feet (1.50 m.).

**Nefelejts** (Parsifal—Novella), bay gelding, 13 yrs.

Owned, trained and ridden by the author for 12 years. Taken away by the Russian occupation forces in 1945. Winner of three T.D.E.s and many prizes in show jumping, including puissances up to 6 feet 6 inches.

**Örvösgalamb** (Ossian—Pigeonette), brown mare, 12 yrs.

Owned, etc., as Nefelejts. Purchased from a racing stable as an uncontrollable horse. After education winner of various show-jumping competitions up to 5 feet.

**Keve** (Maxim—Csinos), bay gelding, 10 yrs.

*Owner:* Hungarian Olympic Committee.

Trained and ridden from beginning of its schooling by the author for seven years. Winner of many prizes in show-jumping competitions up to 5 feet 6 inches, including individual cup of Prix des Nations.

# The stationary position, and the walk

**1 Stationary position**
(' Father Jim,' David Somerset up)
Horse on all four legs, keeping
smooth contact. Horse and rider
relaxed, motionless

**2 Walk on flat with loose reins**
('Duhallo,' the author up)
Regular, free movement, horse and
rider relaxed

**3 Walk uphill with loose reins**
(' Kings Point,' the author up)
Lively, determined strides, rider
by bending slightly forward re-
lieves the horse's back.   Both
relaxed

**4 Walk downhill with loose
reins**
(' Rocky Marciano,' the author up)
Distinct, regular leg-succession,
freely swinging back-action, rider
follows the motion in relaxed state
and slightly forward bent position

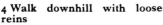

# The walk

**5 Ordinary walk on flat**
('Gipsy Love,' the author up)
Free, energetic motion of moderate speed. Four distinct hoof-beats in regular sequence. Rider keeps evenly a light rein-contact. Moderately arched head and neck-carriage

**6 Ordinary walk uphill**
('Father Jim,' the author up)
Increased action of the quarters ensures the free mobility of the horse. Otherwise as on flat

**7 Ordinary walk downhill**
('Sand Piper,' the author up)
Lightness of the even rein and seat-contact are the issue of the regular motion. Otherwise as on flat

**8 Collected walk**
('Clarion,' the author up)
Increased activity of the quarters and free mobility of the shoulders ensure the necessary energy of the pace at the somewhat slowed down leg-motion. Horse offering the treble contact elevates its arched neck-carriage, whereby its head is in almost vertical position. Rider in ready position and filled with an inner vibration ensures the lightness and forward tendency of his conduct

# The walk,
# and the rein-back

### 9 Extended walk
('Kings Point,' the author up)
Long, ground-gaining stride-action in regular sequence of steps. While keeping slightly firmer contact, the horse points its nose moderately forward

### 10 Turn with loose reins at a walk
('Duhallo,' the author up)
Rider 'balances' the horse in the turn by slight lateral changes of his centre of gravity between the normal position and the inside of the turn. Horse looks towards the direction of the turn

### 11 Turn at a walk while keeping r. contact
('Clarion,' the author up)
Horse slightly bent in its whole body (inwards), steps with free shoulders on the 'outside' of the curve of the turn. Rider conducts it in a balancing manner

### 12 Rein-back
('Duhallo,' David Somerset up)
Simultaneous motion of the diagonal legs (trot sequence in backward direction). Submissive, regular striding on absolute straight line. Rider keeps light contact, and is almost relaxed in his bearing

# The trot

**13 Trot on flat with loose reins**
(' Sand Piper,' the author up)
Regular, free movement at a rather
slow speed.  Horse and rider
relaxed.  Preferably rising-trot

**14 Trot uphill with loose reins**
(' Duhallo,' the author up)
In the free motion the horse
stretches its head and neck forward. Rider facilitates the engagement of the quarters by using the
rising-trot

**15 Trot downhill with loose
reins**
(' Gipsy Love,' the author up)
Horse, while using its working
speed, proceeds determinately
without rolling downwards. Rider
should stop the sitting movements
of the rising-trot before touching
the saddle with the seat. Otherwise see text to picture No. 14

**16 Turn with loose reins at a
trot**
(' Sand Piper,' the author up)
See text to picture No. 10

# The trot

**17 Ordinary trot on flat**
(' Father Jim,' the author up)
Rhythmical free action of medium
speed with swinging, energetic
motion. Horse keeping smooth
contact holds its neck and head in
a nicely arched carriage. Rider
follows the motion united with the
horse

**18 Ordinary trot uphill**
(' Rocky Marciano,' the author up)
Horse displays increased activity
of the quarters. Rider lightens the
task of the horse by using the rising
movement. Otherwise see text to
picture No. 17

**19 Ordinary trot downhill**
(' Clarion,' the author up)
Free and elastic shoulder activity
ensures the determination of the
downward motion. Otherwise see
text to picture No. 18

**20 Collected trot**
(' Rocky Marciano,' the author up)
By increased activity of the quarters and free mobility of the
shoulders the stride-action becomes higher in the slightly slowed
down but very energetic motion.
The steps are shorter and the
arched bearing of the neck and
head higher than in an ordinary
trot. Rider in full accordance with
the horse keeps a very light contact. See also text to picture No. 8

# The trot

**21 Extended trot**
((*a*)' Duhallo,' David Somerset up)
Highly active quarters and shoulders in complete mobility create the long, energetic stride-action which is full of swing. A short moment of suspension is included. Rider, by using the rising-trot, places his centre of gravity a bit forward. Horse taking slightly firmer contact points its nose in front of the vertical
((*b*) ' Rocky Marciano,' the author up)
Nice action. However, the horse could point its nose a bit more forward

**22 Turn at a trot while keeping r. contact**
( (*a*) ' Father Jim,' David Somerset up  (*b*) ' Mercur,' the author up)
(*a*) Horse, bent in its whole body towards the inside, proceeds smoothly and with free shoulders on the course. Rider directs the horse mainly by positioning his weight in a balancing manner. Otherwise see text to picture No. 17
(*b*) During the performance of the Dressage Test at the T.D.E. in Döberitz (Germany, 1935)

# The canter

### 23 Canter on flat with loose reins
('Gipsy Love,' the author up)
Relaxed, even movement of moderate speed. Horse feeling and enjoying freedom proceeds quietly. Rider by bending slightly forward increases the freedom of the horse

### 24 Canter uphill with loose reins
('Clarion,' the author up)
Rider by bending more markedly forward facilitates the free movement of the horse's back. Otherwise see text to picture No. 23

### 25 Canter downhill with loose reins
('Rocky Marciano,' the author up)
Horse, retaining its even speed, proceeds with regular, quiet stride-action. Otherwise see text to picture No. 23

### 26 Turn at a canter with loose reins
('Rocky Marciano,' the author up)
See text to picture No. 10

# The canter

**27 Ordinary canter on flat**
(' Rocky Marciano,' the author up)
Horse, at a rather slow speed,
moves rhythmically with energetic
actions in absolutely straight
position. It keeps an even and
light contact, and while its back is
swinging elastically the neck and
head are nicely arched. Rider,
united with the horse and its
motion, conducts the animal
smoothly, without any visible
actions

**28 Ordinary canter uphill**
(' Duhallo,' the author up)
Horse proceeds with energetic
activity of the shoulders and
quarters and displays increased
swing in the movement of the
back. Rider in forward position.
Otherwise see text to picture
No. 27

**29 Ordinary canter downhill**
( (a) ' King's Point,' the author up
(b) ' Gipsy Love,' the author up)
This motion, the characteristics
of which are rhythm, swing and
elasticity, needs a high degree of
balance and lightness both on the
part of the horse and the rider.
While keeping the rein-contact,
the rider facilitates the task of the
horse by the use of the forward
position. He prevents the animal
from rolling down by using slight
checking activities from time to
time

# The canter

### 30 Collected canter
(' Father Jim,' the author up)
Mobility of shoulders coupled with great activity of quarters bring about the cadenced, energetic stride-action of three hoof-beats in the slowed down speed. A highly arched neck and head carriage complete the general view of the horse. The rider ensures the maintenance of impulsion by his utmost lightness while conducting the horse

### 31 Extended canter on flat
(' Sand Piper,' the author up)
Horse lengthens the strides without quickening the stride-action. Remains calm and submissive. It lowers the arched neck-carriage and points the nose a bit forward. The rider allows a slightly firmer contact and bends his upper body just in front of the vertical

### 32 Extended canter uphill
(' Gipsy Love,' the author up)
Increased activity of the quarters and swing of the shoulders lengthen the stride-action. Rider, by using the forward position, lightens the motion of the horse. Otherwise see text to picture No. 31

### 33 Extended canter downhill
(' Father Jim,' the author up)
While performing the long stride-action during the downward motion, the maintenance of balance and rhythm is the key to success. Rider in forward position and keeping smooth rein-contact preserves the suppleness of the horse and prevents it from rolling down the slope

# The canter and gallop

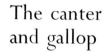

### 34 Turn at a canter while keeping r. contact

(' Clarion,' the author up)
Horse bent in its whole body to the curve of the turn, where it proceeds with free shoulders. Rider balances the animal smoothly on its course mainly by positioning his upper body. Otherwise see text to pictures Nos. 27 and 30

### 35 Counter-turn at a canter

(' Duhallo,' the author up)
Lightness and ease in the movement and conduct ensure the clear cadence while proceeding in the direction opposite to the leading-action of the canter. Rider 'flexes' the horse to the straight position and directs it mainly by his upper body

### 36 The hand-gallop

(' Pandur,' the author up)
This is a gallop (four hoof-beats) of slow speed. Horse proceeds relaxed with rhythmical stride-action. This picture was taken at the Olympic Games at Berlin as ' Pandur' passed the finishing posts after its clear round over the course of the speed and endurance test

### 37 The gallop

(' Wilchelmine,' the author up)
The most extended pace of the horse. Long, extremely energetic strides with four hoof-beats and prolonged suspension. In the picture ' Wilchelmine' is at the finishing post, winning the Great April Steeplechase in Vienna (1929)

# Movements
# on two tracks

**38 Shoulder-in at a walk**
(' Kings Point,' the author up)
While the hind legs remain on the
original track, the forehand is
brought inwards. Horse is moving
in a bent position opposite to its
progress. The rider promotes the
free shoulder activity by trans-
ferring his weight in the direction
of the horse's bent position and
easing the contact of the inside
rein. He is leading the animal by
the outside rein

**39 Shoulder-in at a trot**
(' Clarion,' the author up)
Beside the general demands above,
the increasingly swinging free
shoulder activity, promoted by
energetic activity of the quarters,
is the characteristic feature of this
movement on two tracks

**40 Croup-in at a walk**
(' Gipsy Love,' the author up)
While the front legs remain on the
original track, the quarters are
brought inwards from there. Horse,
in a bent position corresponding
to its progress, moves with energetic activity of the haunches.
Rider transfers his weight towards
the inside and keeps even contact
on the outside rein. He leads the
horse by smooth breathing-like
functions of the inside rein.

**41 Croup-in at a trot**
(' Rocky Marciano,' the author up)
Before starting this movement on
two tracks, increased impulsion and
energetic activity of the quarters
has to be created. Otherwise see
text to picture No. 40

# Movements on two tracks

**42 Half-pass at a walk**

(*a*) Seen from the front ('Gipsy Love')

(*b*) Seen from behind ('Kings Point')

Horse, slightly flexed towards the direction of progress, moves with free shoulders and supple quarters in an oblique direction parallel to its original course. The outside legs cross in front of the inside legs in regular sequence. Rider transfers his weight slightly to the inside. Inside rein and outside leg lead the horse, while the outside rein is almost loose

**43 Half-pass at a trot**

(*a*) Seen from the front ('Du-hallo')

(*b*) Seen from behind ('Sand Piper')

Increased mobility, swing and activity in the rhythmical energetic motion complete the demands described above

# Movement on two tracks, and short turns

### 44 Half-pass at a canter
('Father Jim,' the author up)
Horse in collection with slightly flexed head keeps very light contact and proceeds rhythmically at a slow speed in forward-and-lateral direction parallel to its original course. The leading activities of the rider are similar to those at a walk, only the lateral moving pressures of the outside leg are more augmented

### 45 Turn on the quarters
('Sand Piper,' the author up)
Horse keeping contact looks towards the direction of the movement and pivots round the inside hind leg while the outside foreleg crosses in front of its pair. Rider leads the horse mainly by the inside rein and outside leg (on the girth). He prevents the animal from stepping backwards or leaving the pivoting spot

### 46 Turn on the forehand
('Clarion,' the author up)
By pivoting round its inside foreleg, the horse completes the turning movement by stepping with the hind legs. Inside hind leg crosses in front of the other. While keeping contact, it looks towards the pivoting direction. Rider leads the horse by the inside rein and inside leg (behind the girth). He prevents it from stepping forward or leaving the pivoting spot in lateral direction

### 47 Turn round the centre
('Father Jim,' the author up)
Bilateral turning movement executed by simultaneous stepping of the front and hind legs in opposite direction. Horse looks towards the direction of the movement of the forehand. Leading similar as at the turn on the forehand, but the outside leg of the rider exercises also some lateral moving pressures

# The flat ditch

## 48 Crossing a flat ditch with loose reins

(a) Movement down the bank ('Rocky Marciano,' the author up)
(b) Movement up the bank ('Sand Piper,' the author up)

This exercise has an excellent loosening effect, both on the horse and the rider. It improves their mobility and flexibility by the continuous accommodation to quickly changing situations. The horse should proceed calmly up and down with regular sequence of strides, without altering its working speed. Rider remains permanently in a forward position (seat near to the saddle, without touching it). He directs the horse mainly by positioning his weight and changing pressures on the stirrups. The reins may only be used as supplementary means from time to time to check the speed. They have to be dropped instantly after their momentary employment.

## 49 Crossing a flat ditch in r. contact

(a) Movement down the bank ('Gipsy Love,' the author up)
(b) Movement up the bank ('Duhallo,' the author up)

This exercise serves gymnastic purposes, since it produces effects and motions similar to those necessary for the execution of a jump. The downhill movement collects the horse to the 'take-off,' the performance of which is substituted by the starting stride of the climbing. The movement uphill arches the back and the transition to the flat ground compels the animal to display the basculing action. The horse should stride at its working speed lively and energetically with regular sequence of strides. The rider, while in forward position and keeping rein-contact, may accommodate himself flexibly to the stretching and arching movements of the horse

# Elementary exercises

### 50 Stepping over miniature obstacles

(a) At a walk (' Gipsy Love ')

(b) At a trot (' Rocky Marciano ')

The application of the exercise is essential during the early stages of education, but its employment is highly recommended also for later on at any time during the daily loosening exercise. The horse should remain in its working speed and regular sequence of strides while approaching, stepping over and leaving the obstacle. It is, however, not improper for it to make calmly a small jump over the fence. The rider should lead the horse by loose reins in forward position (also at a walk), giving absolute freedom to the neck and back. It is advantageous to hold the mane or neck-strap to prevent the upper body from falling back into the saddle

### 51 Jumping over a very narrow obstacle

(a) Approach to the obstacle (' Gipsy Love,' the author up)

(b) Over the obstacle (' Father Jim,' David Somerset up)

The importance of the exercise lies in the fact that the rider is obliged to establish absolute easiness in the reactions of the horse and free its shoulders from any stiffness, otherwise it will unavoidably swerve away from the straight direction. The exercise should gradually be built up from the beginning by walking over the installation to its execution at a slow canter. It should be practised during all stages of the education, and its application during warming up procedures is also very useful

# Gymnastic exercises

### 52 Bascule improving pair of bars
(' Father Jim,' David Somerset up)
The elevated bar inspires the horse to make a close take-off, and that on the ground to arch its back and neck. To produce the gymnastic effect it is necessary to keep rein-contact and approach the installation at a fairly slow but lively trot. During the jumping phase, however, the rider must give ample freedom to the horse for the performance of its basculing action. Besides schooling, the exercise is very effective during warming up procedures. Its execution with loose reins has good loosening effect

### 53 The grid
(' Clarion,' the author up)
Besides schooling the correct jumping style, the main purpose of this installation is to improve the elasticity of the horse and in second place to increase the arching action of the back. This is achieved by the number of the composing elements and by the regulation of the space distances. The increase of height is not important. With regard to the execution of the exercise and its applicability, see text to picture No. 52, but it should not be practised with loose reins

### 54 Curtailed gymnastic double
(' King's Point,' the author up)
The main purpose of the installation is to increase the arching action of the back and in second place to improve the elasticity of the horse. Both aims are achieved by gradual curtailment of the space distance. The increase of height is not important. With regard to the execution of the exercise and its applicability, see text to picture No. 52, but it should not be practised with loose reins

# Jumping from a trot

a

**55 Jumping from a trot with loose reins**
(' Duhallo,' David Somerset up)
(a) Approach to the obstacle
(b) Over the obstacle
The exercise improves the rider's feeling of independence from the reins, as well as the confidence, calmness and self-determination of the horse for the performance of jumps. Horse should approach the obstacle calmly without increasing the working speed or breaking into canter. The rider should stop the rising-trot before reaching the take-off spot and, while remaining in forward position, let the animal take off on its own accord. Holding the mane is advantageous. It is best to start the exercise on each occasion at a height which the horse can step over and then gradually increase the height

b

a

**56 Jumping from a trot while keeping contact**
(' Gipsy Love,' the author up)
(a) Approach to the obstacle
(b) Over the obstacle
Jumping out of a trot is a schooling and refreshing exercise of basic importance, since the maintenance of regularity, which facilitates the task of the horse, is much easier at this pace for both partners than at a canter. The horse should approach the obstacle at a lively regular trot of medium speed. The rider, while in forward position (see text to picture No. 55) and keeping rein-contact, may concentrate his attention — while safeguarding the general regularity—on the free mobility of the shoulders. He should be prepared to follow the take-off movement at any circumstances with his upper body and hands. Falling back or pulling on the reins is a harmful fault. Losing contact is also faulty, but not harmful to the horse

b

# Jumping from a canter

**57 Jumping from a canter without reins**
(' Sand Piper,' the author up)
(*a*) Approach to the obstacle
(*b*) Over the obstacle
The exercise is an improved version, with increased educative values, of that performed at a trot (picture No. 55). When the horse gets confidence from jumping at a trot it will retain its calmness also when the approach occurs at a canter. Let the animal jump at first a few times from a trot and then execute the exercise in question. Take care of the upper body!

**58 Jumping from a canter while keeping contact**
(*a*) ' Gipsy Love,' the author up
(*b*) ' Father Jim,' David Somerset up
(*c*) ' Sand Piper,' the author up
(*d*) ' Duhallo,' David Somerset up
(*e*) ' Clarion,' the author up
(*f* )' Rocky Marciano,' the author up
(*g*) ' Kings Point,' the author up
See text on the next page

# Jumping from a canter

**Text to pictures No. 58 (a) to 58 (g)**
During the period of schooling the horse should approach the obstacle at a rather slow speed, with liveliness and complete regularity. To ensure the energetic stamp-off action of the leading foreleg the particular shoulder must be free of any impediment. Just before the take-off the rider may increase the span of the spring system for the jump by a smooth collecting action and then ask for the take-off, or leave its execution entirely to the horse, according to the stage of its education. During the take-off and the jump he should follow the movement of the animal flexibly with his upper body, arms and hands. At the moment of basculing special care has to be laid on the freedom of the back and neck. Therefore, at this moment (especially at bigger jumps) the interruption of the rein-contact is permitted

# Climbing exercises, the long, steep slope

### 59 Climbing ditch
(a) Descending ('Rocky Marciano,' the author up)
The horse should retain its calmness, step without hesitation on to the slope and proceed vertically downwards, according to the steepness of the formation, either at a canter or walk, or by sliding. Rider in the forward position gives ample freedom to the quarters, back and neck. The best support is to leave the animal acting and balancing down the slope on its own accord
(b) Climbing up ('Father Jim,' the author up)
The horse, by energetic climbing activity, ascends the slope in a vertical direction. After encouraging it at the bottom of the ditch, the rider's only duty is to ensure complete freedom of activity to the animal and keep it vertically to the slope. He may take hold of the mane or neck-strap

### 60 Long steep slope
('Sand Piper,' David Somerset up)
(a) Ascending the slope
Start from a vertical direction to the slope, from a distance of 20-30 yards (metres), at an energetic gallop. By the pushing power thus created the horse gains good ground uphill. After the exhaustion of this impetus keep the animal moving resolutely by energetic driving until it reaches the top. It does not matter if the horse slows down to a walk on the last section, but it should by no means halt. Otherwise see text to picture No. 59 (b)
(b) Descending the slope
See text to picture No. 59 (a) with the reservation that real sliding is excluded, since long slopes of such structure cannot be taken thus. On the last section of the slope control the horse, so that it does not roll down

# Bank exercises

a

### 61 Exercise for bank jumps

(' Gipsy Love,' the author up)
Liveliness in a regulated collected
state with active quarters and free
shoulders is the basic demand for
jumping up on to a bank. The
speed has little importance. Thus
only that speed should be used at
which the rider can satisfy the
basic conditions. The horse, in
its proper state, can jump on to
a very high bank at a rather slow
speed, but it will refuse the jump
or swerve aside if the rider tries to
solve the task by increasing the
speed only.

b

Jumping down from a plain bank
is more or less a question of
obedience and some skill, therefore it causes little difficulty
The above considerations give the
basis for the schooling of bank
jumps. For educative purposes
one can use any formation where
the horse is compelled to make a
jump in order to get from one level
to another
(a) and (b) Jumping up on to a bank
After the creation of the basic
conditions approach the bank either
at a trot or at a slow canter. Before
the take-off increase the action
capacity of the spring system by a
brief collection, and out of it let
the horse carry out the jump.
During this give freedom to the
back and follow the stretching
movement of the neck. On the top
restore the liveliness by energetic
animation

c

(c) and (d) Jumping down from the
bank
When reaching the take-off edge of
the bank don't allow the horse to
speculate, but by the application
of a firm driving signal increase its
impulsion for an immediate down-
jump. At the same time give complete freedom to the back and neck
of the horse

d

## 62 Use of casual opportunities

for accustoming the horse to surprising situations and for the improvement of its skill

For the purpose in question the rider should make good use of any opportunity offered by the country in great variety. It is not the magnitude of the particular obstruction which matters, but its surprising structure. Some examples are shown in the pictures (*a*) to (*e*).

(*a*) Jumping the fork of a tree (' Duhallo, David Somerset up)

(*b*) Jumping the fork of a fallen tree as a double (' Sand Piper ')

(*c*) Stepping into a pond with steep bank formation (' Gipsy Love ')

(*d*) and (*e*) Climbing on to a turned over tree trunk, then walking round on the 2 ft. 6 in. (0.75 m.) wide earth stripe supported by the parts of the broken off roots and stepping down from it on the opposite side (' Father Jim ' and ' Rocky Marciano ')

(*f*) Jumping a narrow water trough, standing freely in a field (' Clarion')

(*Top left*) **63 The pond** (splash). T.D.E., Budapest. Jumps freely without any hesitation and looks with confidence ahead. (*Top right*) **64 Slit trench and rail**, Olympic T.D.E., Berlin. Clears with swing and keenness the spread fence. (*Bottom left*) **65 T.D.E. Show-Jumping Test**, Olympic Games, Berlin. Fresh and bold jump after the strenuous endurance test. (*Bottom right*) **66 Brick wall**, show jumping, Vienna. Supple and precise jump in complete balance

(*Top left*) 67 **Spread obstacle**, at a show in Firenze. Harmonious movement, well-arched back-line, controlled leg action. (*Top right*) 68 **Upright obstacle**, at a show in Munich. Correctly in the trajectory of the jump. (*Bottom left*) 69 **The bank**, Nations Cup, Aachen. Well-taxed, powerful take-off for safe landing. (*Bottom right*) 70 **Big wall**, Puissance, Aachen. Typical moment of basculing

# Örvösgalamb, the author up

(*Top left*) 71 **Bank combination,** at a show in Luzern. Bold jump in an overwhelming manner typical of this mare. (*Top right*) 72 **Park wall,** at a show in Düsseldorf. In spite of an extremely energetic take-off, correct back-action. (*Bottom left*) 73 **Parallel-bars with water jump,** at a show in Warsaw. For clearing the spread the arch of the jump is high. (*Bottom right*) 74 **Simple upright obstacle,** at a show in Warsaw. The trajectory covers the exact height of the obstacle

# Keve, the author up

(*Top left*) **75 Parallel bars on the top of a bank**, at a show in Aachen. Free action with self-determination. (*Top right*) **76 Brick wall**, Nations Cup in Aachen. Calm, supple jumping movement. (*Bottom left*) **77 Water jump**, 16 feet (5 m.), at a show in Aachen. Perfect performance out of high liveliness (no speed). (*Bottom right*) **78 Sliding down**, slope 70°, 23 feet (7 m.), in Örkénytábor. See support action of the forelegs and engagement of the quarters

# Diverse Horses, the author up

(*Top left*) 79 **Papagaly.** Parallel bars, R●ma. Well-balanced precise jump. (*Top right*) 80 **Keve.** Puissance, Aachen. The little gelding gives his best. (*Bottom left*) 81 **Mercur.** Big water jump, T.D.E. Döberitz. This wonderful jump, giving the real sensation of flying, is the result of increased liveliness. (*Bottom right*) 82 **Gonosz.** Steeplechase, Budapest  Very distant landing after a calm but bold jump

83 The author starts to collect his experiences

. . . and now . . . he offers those to his dear readers

If the horse is submissively obedient to the rider's actions while riding with divided reins, it is certain that it will behave in the same way when he leads it only with one hand.

For the sake of practice, the rider should accustom the animal to this form of riding while performing the movements of the dressage test in combination with other exercises. In practising this technique the following recommendations may be useful:

the rider should change the manner of holding the reins when the horse is at a standstill (especially when the horse is in a double bridle);

then, during the ensuing movements, he should compensate for the loss of control

while turning the horse: by more definite changes in the distribution of his weight; and

while performing transitions: by more distinct seat (stirrup) and thigh actions.

When the horse can be conducted through its shoulders the indirect form of using the reins can be employed for the completion of turns.

Aside from these supplementary aids, the rider does not need to employ any other special actions while leading the horse with the reins held in one hand. He should conduct it in the same way as when the reins are divided between the two hands.

### RIDING WITHOUT THE USE OF THE REINS

When riding without reins the rider drops the reins on the horse's neck and leads it mainly by his weight influences. During the ride the animal does not suffer any interference with its mouth, but can enjoy the pleasure of motion in complete freedom. This has a soothing effect on its nature. In such an atmosphere horses soon learn this method of riding. Even a novice horse, or a more mature one with a tendency for running away, can be taught the technique within a remarkably short time.

Before dealing with the methods of teaching the animal we shall examine those activities which the rider has to carry out in order to exert the right sort of influence on the horse.

For keeping the animal on the straight course it is generally sufficient to give some slight warnings by the oscillating movements of the upper body (levelling function) when it shows an inclination to deviate from the established direction.

When the aim is to stir the horse in a lateral direction the rider has to alter his centre of gravity in accordance with the direction which he wishes to follow. The animal will respond by accommodating itself to the course indicated by the rider in order to maintain its own state of balance. To augment the effect of this aid it is much better to repeat the bending movement of the upper body in an oscillating manner than to increase its extent. If this should prove to be insufficient, the rider may resort to the use of the rein for one or two seconds in a warning-like manner. This short warning can be repeated if necessary, but must always start from and finish in the dropped position.

While turning, the rider should be particularly careful that the horse remains on the outside of the curve of the desired turn (in no case should it be allowed to cut in). He should lead the animal by counter- and part-turns and apply the necessary signals by altering alternatively the position of his upper body.

If the horse tries to increase the speed, this can be checked by applying the taking action of the seat or by pressures on the stirrups. If these are not effective enough, the rider should 'touch' the reins for a moment in order to reinforce the effect of the seat (stirrup) signal. If this touch needs to be repeated, it must always be carried out from the dropped position of the reins.

In the event of a sudden, unexpected movement (if the animal happens to make off or tries to run away, etc.), and the rider loses his balance, his best move is to grasp the mane or the neck strap. Only afterwards should he pick up the reins, and then only if he thinks that he cannot stop the horse by any other means. As soon as he has succeeded in controlling the horse he should give it its freedom again.

We shall next examine the method of accustoming the horse to move about freely without the interference of the reins.

Before starting the schooling remove the stable freshness from the animal by a quiet loosening exercise (see page 266); then

ride it on a large circle (about 60-80 yards or metres in diameter) with the use of the reins, both in walk and trot, until the horse has become accustomed to the surroundings (10-15 minutes); afterwards reduce the pace to a walk and drop the reins on the animal's neck. While proceeding on the circle, guide it only by the appropriate alterations in the position of the weight. When the circle has been completed in this manner several times

change over to a trot by a calm drive-on and continue riding without the use of the reins. When the horse has shown definite signs of obedience, stop and let it graze for a short while; then

repeat the whole procedure while riding in the reverse direction on the circle; next

change the direction of riding within the circle a few times by altering the position of the weight. During this ride alternate the pace between walk and trot, and halt several times in order to accustom the animal to perform transitions without the use of the reins.

Repeat the above series of movements on three to four consecutive days; and following this

extend the schooling further by including the pace canter (provided that the horse is already familiar with the method of the strike-off), in which the strike-off must be accomplished without taking up the reins; in the next stage of practice

ride the horse on freely selected lines and try to pass over, both in walk and trot, cavalettis and miniature obstacles up to 1 ft. 8 in. (50 cm.) set up at irregular distances.

If the rider gradually develops the teaching programme in this manner, there is a good chance that within a period of three to four weeks the horse will be able to be driven anywhere without the use of the reins in all cases where the task does not require collection.

Later on, in the course of the horse's general schooling and, in fact, during its entire career, riding without reins can be advantageously employed for increasing the value of the loosening exercises.

Riding without reins is also a useful practice for the rider, for

it endows him with stability and flexibility and, as a result, he no longer tends to grasp for the reins in order to safeguard his own balance, but feels absolutely independent from the reins (to the greatest satisfaction of the horse);

it gives him self-confidence and 'imbues' his hands with lightness, which is of great importance to all riders, and which results from his assurance in being able to control the animal perfectly without the aid of the reins;

it teaches the rider to diagnose both the physical position and the mental attitude of the horse and enables him to distinguish the constantly changing situations which occur during the course of riding;

it makes him realize in practice all those rather abstract 'sensations' which can be distorted or jumbled by the improper use of the reins.

When jumping (either for the sake of gymnastics or for the improvement of style), riding without reins offers the horse all the same advantages as when the exercises are performed in a loose lane (see page 313). In addition, it eliminates the disadvantage of the loose lane, which is that the horse, by jumping without the rider, develops its jumping technique under a state of balance different from when it has to carry the rider's weight.

### THE LOOSENING EXERCISE

The purpose of this exercise is to remove the horse's stable stiffness and steam, as well as to calm it down *without making it tired*. It is an essential part of the daily practice, since the success of the ensuing routine work depends largely upon the proper execution of the loosening process. In fact, by omitting the loosening exercise, one loses time instead of gaining it. The reason for this is that an unsupple horse will create considerable difficulties for the rider and will merely waste its own and its master's energy without bringing improvement into the quality of the daily routine work.

Therefore the rider should never fail to perform the loosening exercise, to which he should devote at least 15 to 20 minutes, in order to enable the horse to get rid of its stiffness. However, one can also replace the formal loosening exercise by the ride from the stable to the countryside.

The loosening exercise can advantageously be combined with all the exercises which are carried out with loose reins, namely:

riding without the use of the reins (see page 263);
stepping over miniature obstacles (see page 283); and
schooling on an undulating ground formation (see page 131).

Immediately after mounting, the rider should ride the horse with long reins and leave its back in a state of complete freedom. He should allow the animal to satisfy its curiosity without hampering its desire to keep looking to the right or left and should not demand any tasks requiring exertion. During this ride it is very advantageous when the rider exercises from time to time slight touches on the withers (see page 61), since those acts are pleasing and soothing to the animal.

During the loosening exercise one can use all three lower paces; however, the trot is the pace most suitable for the purpose.

The speed of the motion should be a steady one in which the horse can really loosen the stiffness of its muscles and joints. A hasty, hurried motion is likely to produce the opposite result.

During this ride it is desirable for the animal to negotiate a number of wide turns and to perform smooth transitions. At the same time, the rider can take advantage of the opportunity to warn the horse to give up its tendency for deviation, thus taking the first step towards regulating its motion.

While riding to the exercise ground the rider should always be on the look-out for all kinds of uneven features in the terrain which, in contrast to the uniformity of the road, offer some possibility of making different movements and, at the same time, give the horse a chance to collect experiences.

DRESSAGE-LIKE SCHOOLING ON SLIGHTLY SLOPING GROUND

After the loosening exercise it is a good method to start the dressage-like schooling on a slightly sloping (perhaps 6-8°) ground for about 15-20 minutes. One can choose for this purpose a tract of about 80 x 80 yards (metres) in area, where the routine work should be carried out in the same way as if the terrain were quite level.

The advantage of the sloping ground is that the horse's downward motion on a slight slope partially removes the irregularities which cause stiffness. The reason for this is that the horse, in order to maintain its balance, is compelled to adopt of its own accord a state of regularity, which is the chief aim of the dressage-like schooling. This relaxed state increases the animal's aptitude for learning during the practice session.

During the latter stages of the daily work, when the horse has taken up the triple contact and already moves in a light collection,

it is very useful practice to perform some exercises on the undulating ground surface as described on page 131.

### OVERCOMING THE HORSE'S NERVOUSNESS

As a general rule, the 'nervousness' of the horse is usually a
form of resistance by which it expresses its disapproval of improper
or reckless treatment and it is seldom attributable to the animal's
innate disposition.

Therefore, the remedy for nervousness can be found in the
application of correct methods of riding, which means that the
rider should influence the horse by the means which are most
appropriate to the tasks demanded of it. Aside from unsuitable
influencing methods, the most frequent forms of improper
handling are:

the neglect or incorrect execution of the loosening exercise;

the premature execution of exercises which overstrain the
horse;

failing to take into account its physical or mental condition.

If the rider's behaviour is correct while schooling the horse and
when performing, the animal will give up its resistance and consequently become calm and submissive.

In those exceptional cases where the nervousness is indeed an
innate deficiency of the horse, the key to its treatment is patience
and intelligence. The rider must never lose his patience! Instead,
he should communicate his own calmness to the horse by smooth
influencing activities, repeated as often as may be necessary. In
this sense the levelling function, with its all-round changing
feature, is directly designed for the purpose.

The horse's tendency to curiosity, as described on page 174, can
appear sometimes in a more developed form, giving the impression
of nervousness. The rider should not misjudge this undisciplined,
hasty looking about for nervousness. In order to amend the
situation, he should stop such movements instantly and determinedly by certain actions which attract the animal's attention to
himself. This aim can be reached either by a tap of the whip or a
short pull on the rein. As a result, the horse will quickly realize
that it cannot evade the authority of its master by such 'tricks',
and will give up its 'nervousness'. If the rider, instead of his
resolute interference, tries to 'calm down' such a resisting horse
by some uncertain pattings, etc., it will take this kindness as a

reward for its opposition and will increase its misjudged 'nervousness'.

In conclusion, it is safe to say that, in order to prevent or to cure nervousness, the rider must first develop in himself the real feeling of riding. But also, until reaching this ability, the young rider must be aware of this fact and by changing sensibly, correcting his own actions and filling them with *forward spirit*, he will overcome many difficulties which he might otherwise attribute to a weakness in the horse's temperament.

OVERCOMING THE HORSE'S TENDENCY TO BECOME FRIGHTENED

The way in which the rider should think when he wants to overcome the horse's fright is described on page 5, in connection with an example. Bearing in mind the previous information, we shall now examine the subject on its own merit.

Horses sometimes show an aversion to certain unfamiliar objects, as well as to a general environment if it is strange to them. Since the countryside can offer a great variety of things unusual to the animal, it is the best place in which to cure instinctive fright.

While riding out to the exercise ground the horse encounters on the road vehicles, often travelling at a fast speed, which produce the first sensation of fright. In the event of meeting such objects with a young, inexperienced horse it is best to come to a halt and, allowing as much freedom of the reins as possible, wait in a stationary position until the object has passed by. Because of the freedom from the reins, the animal will feel that its master has no interest in the approaching 'dangerous' objects, and thus will be convinced that they offer no cause for alarm. If the rider starts to pull or jerk the reins as a means of prevention, and tries to enforce calmness on the horse, the effect will be quite the reverse. His actions will serve as a warning to the animal that something dangerous is coming and that it must take care. Thus, instead of calming the animal, its fright is aroused.

While the horse is kept standing still the rider's attention should be confined mainly to preventing it from swerving suddenly. In order to achieve this, the rider has to keep in readiness the leg which is on the side from where the critical object is approaching, since the animal *always* tries to swerve with its croup towards that particular direction. If the rider should feel that the effect of his leg is not sufficient to check the swerve, he can reinforce it with some mild flips of the whip. At this moment (and not before) he can shorten the length of the reins and he can prevent the horse from deviating in the opposite direction with its forehand by the rein which is on the same side as the active leg. As soon as it is felt that the straight position of the animal has been preserved, the leg and the rein action can cease and the reins may be lengthened again. As a reward the horse deserves the conventional pat on the neck.

The procedure is similar when the object which is causing the fright is stationary and the horse should be led along or in front of it. The rider should pass by, keeping the reins long, without taking any notice of the object. If the animal tries to turn off with a sudden swerve, this can be prevented by the leg and the rein on the side of the object in question.

When, in spite of this assistance, the horse's aversion persists and it tries to escape from the object, the following method is likely to give the best and most lasting results. Its basic principle is to let the horse make the effort of overcoming its fright by itself, and it is certain that the animal will do this if it is not disturbed or coerced in its deliberation. This assumption is based on the fact that, aside from its reaction of instinctive fright, the horse also shows a considerable amount of *curiosity* in strange things. The rider can make good use of this by allowing the animal to overcome its fright while satisfying its curiosity.

This innate curiosity of the horse manifests itself by its proceeding slowly, perhaps even snorting, step by step, with its neck outstretched towards the frightening object. In its attempt to approach it, it will hesitate a moment, stop and start again a few times, but, urged on by its curiosity, it will gradually advance until it can smell the strange object. While smelling it may become frightened once or twice, step back and then approach again, but, realizing that no harm has befallen it, it will become more and more sure of itself.

During this procedure the rider's main aim should be to prevent the horse from turning sideways by smooth movements and, of course, to remain patient. He should support the horse virtually from step to step by *mild* animation of his legs. It is advisable *to stop the animal after each step* and let it stride out from a stationary position for just one step at a time.

If the object in question happens to be an obstruction which the horse has to pass over, and if it cannot come to a decision by itself, a certain encouragement on the part of the rider becomes necessary (a mild touch of the legs or a slight flip of the whip). In affording this assistance, the animal must not be interfered with by any action of the rein or seat. While the horse is pondering it should be given complete freedom; the rider may drop the reins and bend slightly forward with his upper body.

The horse clearly indicates that it has arrived at its decision by making a motion that resembles an intention to jump the obstruction. This shows that the rider's patience has won the struggle, despite the fact that the horse's decision is not followed immediately by an effective action. It is quite possible that the animal may still show some hesitation, but this can be overcome without difficulty either to the horse or to the rider. A flip or a little encouragement with the legs will dispel the rest of the hesitation and the animal, with a sudden movement, will throw itself over the obstruction or step into it, as the case may be.

Some horses show an aversion to *entering a horse-box* or similar vehicles. The following method of accustoming can be recommended for overcoming this fear.

Lead the horse with *loose (long) reins* to the horse-box. Halt in front of the ramp (covered with plenty of straw) and, without looking at the animal, or doing anything else, wait for a while. Then step on to the ramp and, retaining the loose rein, assume that the horse should follow you. If this does not occur (which is most likely), the instructor should take up position on the near-side of the horse's croup and encourage it to proceed *step by step* forward. For this purpose he may employ slight touches on the *back part of the hock* with an elastic whip until the animal steps on to the ramp. At the same time, in order to prevent it from swerving to his side, he should keep his free hand on the croup. Swerving towards the opposite side can be prevented by the application of straw bales, etc.

After the first step a brief rest should be given before a new encouragement by the whip follows. It is most likely that, on account of this, the animal will show no further resistance and enter the vehicle.

The main aiding feature of the process is the forward-driving effect of the tapping on the hock which the horse receives *from behind*, while in front its mouth is free from any interference.

## STUMBLING

Stumbling is a very unpleasant occurrence while riding and it can eventually become dangerous to the horse or rider. Therefore it is important that the animal should be trained to correct this defect.

The faulty movement resulting in a stumble happens mostly when the attention of the horse is diverted and it looks about instead of watching where to place its legs. In such a state of absent-mindedness the animal is bound to lose its balance and stumble if its hoof suddenly touches a protrusion on the ground, particularly if the going is hard.

On the whole, horses are more inclined to stumble with their forelegs than with the hind legs. Furthermore, the tendency for stumbling is more marked when it is the leg which is handicapped by the one-sided stiffness of the body that knocks against the ground. This is the reason why most horses stumble with their left legs. Some pain in one leg or the other can also be the cause of stumbling with that particular leg.

If the horse happens to stumble with its forelegs, the best remedy is to snatch up its head suddenly by a short, gentle jerking movement, which will pull the forehand after the head. It is useless to pull interminably on the reins, because they will give no assistance in restoring the horse's balance. On the contrary, such an action may confuse its instinctive movements by which it tries to prevent a fall. If the animal stumbles frequently, owing to its irregularity, it will be more effective to make it aware of its mistake at the moment of the incident by a tap of the whip. In response to the warning the horse will jump forward, and this sudden movement will fortify its lost balance. Thus, a slight punishment can provide an aid to prevent a fall, and later on the animal will overcome its difficulty in the same manner without, however, the warning of the whip. Nevertheless, the real remedy for stumbling is to ensure the regularity of the horse. A well-schooled horse, the regularity of which is kept alive, stumbles only very seldom.

If the horse stumbles with its hind legs, the rider must be careful not to fall back into the saddle. The animal's back is extremely sensitive at this moment because it has lost its support, and a bump can cause it considerable pain. Unfortunately, in such circumstances riders are very much inclined to fall back.

PUNISHMENTS AS A MEANS OF CORRECTING OBSTINATE OPPOSITION

Before the application of punishment the rider must make a quick check whether the opposition is indeed inspired by the horse's obstinacy. He must be convinced that the particular manifestation of it is not the result of an instinctive fear or of some objection against an improperly conveyed demand.

As a general principle, all punitive actions which are designed to break bad habits should be applied at the moment when the horse's opposition seems certain to prevail. It is bad to employ such measures too late, because the correction of a horse which is already in opposition is more difficult. But it is equally unwise to use the available measures without good reason for an imaginary 'prevention', since the horse may have been full of goodwill at that particular moment and will be at a loss to understand the reason for the punishment.

The most frequent cases of resistance which justify punishment are: rearing, stopping (not in front of obstacles), stubborn pulling away with the rider (napping), and objection to being mounted. Most other forms of opposition can be traced to these main manifestations of resistance.

It should be noted that in all these cases the use of the whip is not the only remedy. No, it is the last one! The rider's intelligence should contrive better measures than violence.

REARING

The rearing horse, by raising itself on its hind legs, creates a more or less helpless situation for the rider. At the beginning this may be due to mere mischief, or to its instinct to evade pain, but later on it may be the evidence of stubborn resistance to the rider. If he is not master of the situation, and if he indulgently tolerates the 'disorderliness' of the horse a few times, then the animal will quickly realize that rearing is a simple way of evading the rider's control and of enforcing its own will.

In breaking the animal of this habit, the best and least dangerous practice both to the rider and horse is to forestall any attempt to rear. However, prevention alone is not enough. To teach the horse that rearing is a disagreeable exertion the action must also have a punitive effect.

Before taking action against rearing it is most important to observe carefully whether the intention to rear has been enforced upon the horse. As it needs a considerable swing to rear, its intention can be detected in good time (it is often said, 'I noticed it from its ears'), and so the rider has ample opportunity to counteract the attempt.

As soon as he feels that the horse is on the verge of rearing he should pull *one of the reins* back so that the hand holding the rein is brought behind the seat and is pressed to the saddle bow (or he can sit on the hand), while the other rein is thrown to the horse. The animal's intention to rear is completely frustrated by these sudden movements, since its head is pulled into a position from which rearing is absolutely impossible. The action is not complete without its punitive effect. Therefore it is necessary for the rider, while keeping the rein in the position described above, to give some hard knocks on the horse's flank on the same side as the acting rein. This compels the animal to revolve, making a sharp turn around and around. This revolving procedure, which the horse is unable to oppose, should last until it becomes giddy (the rider has to be careful not to get giddy himself!), which can be easily recognized from the wavering movements of its turnings. Then the rider should suddenly release the rein from its pulled-back position and drive the horse energetically forward, if necessary with the whip.

This cure usually succeeds and after having tried a few of these turns the horse will find it most disagreeable to evade its work by rearing.

THE HORSE'S STUBBORN STOPPING (NOT AT OBSTACLES), REFUSAL TO START

If the rider feels that the horse *intends* to stop, the trouble can be avoided by applying a sharp tap with the whip and by setting it free from the reins. Any joggling with the legs or abuse of the whip will only aggravate the situation.

If the animal *has* stopped and declines to go ahead, it is first of all necessary to make its legs move somehow from their fixed position and then immediately to drive it forward with determination, while ensuring complete freedom of the reins.

In more acute cases the method of making some sharp turns can be applied, but in a more moderate form than when preventing rearing. When the revolving action sets the horse's legs in motion the pulled-in part of the rein should be suddenly released and the animal pushed forward by a firm drive-on action.

### STUBBORN DRAGGING AWAY WITH THE RIDER WHILE IN MOTION

Some horses fall into the habit of dragging the rider away by changing the course against his will. This habit can be associated with the horse's instinct to escape disciplinary actions or to find refuge, since such horses prefer to drag the rider to places where they hope to be protected from any unpleasant experience (in the shelter of trees, shrubs, buildings, walls, etc.).

The method of treatment is as follows:

take the horse to open ground (a stubble field or pasture land) where it cannot find a suitable place for 'refuge';

ride it there in the manner normally used for dressage-like schooling. Sooner or later the animal will become disobedient and will set out in a certain direction which it thinks will suit its own ends. At this moment

turn the horse around sharply (revolve) and then drive it forward by applying a few energetic strokes of the whip (this is the punishment); afterwards

perform some firm halts and starts (perhaps from trot and into trot) and complete the treatment by a brief walk with released reins.

After this rest work can be resumed, which will generally arouse renewed opposition. When it sets in the same corrective procedure should be repeated. After the third or fourth occasion, however, the rider, while allowing complete freedom to the animal, should return home. During this ride he must be careful not to impose any demand which will provoke fresh opposition.

As a result of this method the horse's bad habit can be broken within two to three weeks.

### OBJECTION TO BEING MOUNTED

In this form of resistance the horse tries to avoid being mounted by treading either aside or backwards and, rarely, by rearing. The origin of this opposition can in most cases be traced to improper treatment on the part of the rider, who, while mounting, either pulls on the reins, pokes the tip of his boot into the horse's side, or falls heavily on to its back, causing pain to the animal.

In order to mount such a horse, one should first try the normal routine for mounting a calm horse. If the animal opposes the rider's action

quietly take the reins off its neck and, while standing in front of it, make it tread backwards by giving slight pulls on the reins or a few light taps on the knees. The horse must continue backing until the movement becomes tiresome to it (four to six minutes); then

stop the animal, fix up the reins so that they are *loose* on its neck, and after this preparation try to mount again. If there is continued opposition, resume the backing procedure for one or two minutes more.

It is certain that the animal will become calm enough to be mounted after the second or third attempt. After a short ride stop it with relaxed reins and dismount. Then attempt once more to get into the saddle. In case of renewed opposition one or two minutes' backing can be resumed.

By applying this method the horse can be brought into normal condition within three to four days.

### 'Conquering' the Horse

During the course of its education every horse has to be 'conquered' by the rider from time to time in order to make it clear that it must accept his authority under all circumstances. When the animal has learned to submit to the rider's will it will be obedient when confronted with difficult tasks or when exposed to exciting situations, because the admonition administered while in its unconditioned state will have overcome the restrictions which might prevent it from complying with the rider's demands.

The process in question is not a means of momentary regulation or punishment, and therefore it should not be employed to overcome or to punish disobedience. It can be practised at most once in, say, every four to six months, and only by very experienced riders who can absolutely control their temper.

In order to carry out the procedure, the following conditions should be kept in mind:

Each horse has an individual imagination about certain objects, tasks, demands, etc., some of which are sure to raise occasional opposition in its mind (e.g. strange surroundings, a particular object, the performance of a certain movement, regulation of a particular irregularity, collection, etc.). The rider should carefully observe the horse, find out its weak point (which may change from time to time) and free the animal from its mental impediment by the application of methodical measures. As a result the horse will overcome its particular aversion or opposition, but the germ will still remain in its subconscious, even though the animal may react submissively to its master's supporting influence. At this stage the rider should employ the process described below for 'conquering' the animal.

He should first provoke the horse's opposition by demanding the performance of the particular task which inspires its resistance most easily. By this means he becomes justified in imposing punishment along with the necessary actions during the procedure.

The provocation can take the form of harsh actions, demands of an unusually high grade or in an abridged form before the proper loosening or introductory exercises, pushing the horse suddenly towards the disliked object, etc. This aggressive conduct will put the animal in a state of agitation and arouse its opposition, thus justifying retaliation by the rider.

The horse's resistance can manifest itself in extreme deviation, pronounced one-sided crookedness, muscle contraction, hard pushing against the bit, which is sometimes combined with a kind of jumping movement (lançade), rearing, stiff rolling backwards, etc.

Since most of these forms of opposition are expressed in the stiffness of the horse's back or in its crooked position, the animal can be most easily 'conquered' by enforcing the correction of these defects. The remedy consists of the interlocked drive-on and retarding actions and the adjustment to straight position.

During the interlocked drive-on and retarding actions reinforce the drive-ons by a few firm flips on the horse's side and the retardments by repeated jerks (without roughness); the interlocking yielding functions should be carried out by a sudden relaxation of the engaged muscles.

During the stirring movement of the adjustment to straight position the agitated horse is very much inclined to make a movement somewhat like a turn on the forehand, instead of striding out from its shoulder in the required direction. In this case apply some firm counter-deviation rein actions, supported by lateral-moving pressures of the leg on the same side. During the interlocked (suddenly started) yielding moments drive the animal energetically forward for a few strides (enforced quick drive-on) and introduce the next stirring movement by a firm half-halt. The 'conquering' should be achieved by means of these enforced stirring (counter-deviation) movements. When the horse reacts properly to them perform the ensuing change of flexion with increased stress and then repeat the entire procedure a number of times.

With regard to further conquering possibilities, the following recommendations may be helpful:

Execute some harsh retarding actions from a firm drive-on. If the horse starts rolling backwards as a result of this action, enforce the rein-back motion until the animal opposes it. Then continue the backing energetically for a few strides and, after a sudden yielding, drive the horse determinedly forward by applying a few hits to its side. During this harsh procedure the animal may fall back on its croup to the ground, and perhaps even turn over on its side. This accident, by causing a considerable shock to the horse, helps to obtain a successful result. But, in spite of this advantage, it is not admissible to provoke the fall deliberately.

In case of the horse's hard pushing action against the bit, apply the procedure described on page 113.

Enforced rearing should be punished according to the recommendations given on page 273.

During the procedure selected for conquering the horse a severe conflict takes place in its mind between its instinct to resist and its desire to obey. Sooner or later it will reach the stage where sweat breaks out on its body and it becomes foamy from one moment to the other. This is the sign that the animal has been conquered by its own intelligence, under the guiding influence of the rider.

From this moment onwards the horse will in most cases obey willingly. It will calm down and become dry as suddenly as it became foamy. After their surrender horses experience a pleasant change and very often give evidence of this by a kind of snorting (see page 147), as if to say to the rider: 'Very well, very well . . . I will accept your authority'.

If opposition should reappear after this first relaxation, the original conquering procedure should be applied again, but in a milder form. It is most likely that the horse will now surrender without much resistance.

If the horse should become gradually sweated during the treatment, this is proof that the rider has not proceeded correctly. He has merely been rough without feeling, causing the animal excitement and nervousness which progressively increases its opposition. The result usually is that the horse runs away with the rider helpless on its back.

### SWEATING CAUSED BY INNER EMOTION

At this point it may be worth while to comment on the occurrence of sweating which arises from the horse's inner emotions. This phenomenon is useful to the rider as an indication of the animal's momentary mental attitude.

This kind of sweating is caused mainly by the state of the nerves and only to a moderate degree by muscular exertion. It is most usually brought about by excitement, fright or opposition.

In case of opposition the horse stiffens certain muscle bundles, which cause it unnecessary and harmful physical exertion. As a result of its useless effort, the sweat breaks out more intensely on those surfaces which cover the stiffened muscles than on other parts of the horse's body.

This phenomenon gives the rider a visual clue as to the origin of certain difficulties. He can also ascertain which muscles have been engaged in the performance of a particular exercise during an especially strenuous work, and whether the identical muscles on the horse's two sides have been engaged equally during the exertion.

The stiffness of the horse is usually greater on its left side, resulting in a more intense sweating of this side of its neck, shoulders and loins. This fact is also an added proof that the cause of the 'hardness' so often felt on one side of the horse's mouth originates from the stiffness of those muscles which are on the stiffened side of the animal's spring system, and not from the mouth itself.

Horses very often break into a sweat in the stable after strenuous muscular work, substantial excitement, and particularly after having been conquered. In the first case the sweating is due to muscular exertion; in the other cases it can be traced to the mental function of the horse by which it remembers the agitation it has just undergone. On such occasions the moisture will appear at the same places as during the original incident, only to a lesser degree.

---

The foregoing information on the dressage-like education of the horse and the training of the rider completes the second part of this book.

At this point it must be evident that the varied demands of the different exercises must not be 'kneaded' into the horse by constant and lengthy drilling. It should be guided towards expedient solutions by sensible and frequent variations of the different movements. In this way the horse is gradually 'shaken' into the proper condition, thus establishing the basis of its submission. If it happens that the animal gets stuck in its work, a rest should be granted and the exercise resumed from the beginning. Frequent moments of relaxation will prove to be more beneficial than longer but fewer resting periods. This principle should be regarded as valid for every phase of riding, whether it concerns one particular task, one day's or one period's work, or the entire schooling of the horse.

Furthermore, it can be seen that the execution of the various actions and operations requires on the part of the rider a refined sense of horsemanship, considerable experience and skill. While the acquisition of these qualities may appear to be very difficult, any average rider can reach the necessary standard with sufficient practice. The rider endowed with his theoretical knowledge should first practice the various parts of the procedures separately, and only after he has acquired practical knowledge in carrying them out should he attempt to perform them jointly. The knowledge thus obtained will provide him with a sound foundation, not only to ride in a dressage-like manner, but also to undertake the jumping and the cross-country riding, which will be discussed in the next part.

# PART THREE

# Schooling of the
# Rider and Horse in Jumping

JUMPING can provide some of the greatest pleasures of all riding if the horse performs its task happily. The animal will show its happiness when it is permitted to execute the *motion of jumping* with ease, and thus develops a *liking for it*. Therefore, while schooling the horse in jumping the rider's most important duty is to improve in his mount a liking for this particular activity. If the animal enjoys it, it will approach obstacles with full confidence, while even a courageous horse will lose this precious confidence if its comfort during the jumping movement has been spoiled in some way.

The techniques of training the jumper are closely related to the methods discussed in the former parts. Consequently the fundamental dressage exercises, and the training for jumping, have to be carried out in conjunction with one another. The progress in basic dressage should provide all the essential means for the teaching of jumping, the development of which should be promoted mainly by routine exercises rather than by a clumsy repetition of the clearing of fences.

If the rider practises moderation in jumping during the horse's general education, he can both ensure its well-rounded improvement and safeguard the soundness of the horse. In this way the animal's mental and physical state will remain intact, so that it can start its career in fit condition to serve its master for many years.

It is not merely by an accident that certain horsemen and horses perform faultlessly in competitions. This result is achieved by persistent work and sound, careful schooling of both the rider and the horse, which culminate in the perfect harmony of their co-operation and faultless performance. Thus, riders the ambition of whom is to finish their performances in show-rings and over cross-country courses faultlessly and appear regularly at the presentation of prizes, should consider with special care the statement mentioned.

It should be noted that errorless jumping is also of great importance in hunting. Show-ring fences will fall when hit, thus preventing any serious harm to the horse. The case is quite different in the hunting field, where there are no carefully arranged and collapsible post and rails, gates, walls, etc. The horse is confronted with obstacles which are intended to contain or enclose and are often built strongly so as to defy hard use. Certainly these 'natural' obstacles were not designed in such a way as to minimize the consequences of the jumper's mistakes. Apart from the unpleasantness of falling, the horse may receive some very serious or fatal injury. Unfortunately, there are many hunters which bear traces of old injuries, not to mention those which, owing to such mishaps, are no longer in service. But, in spite of such obvious dangers, it is a common practice in training hunters to neglect their *schooling* over fences. One often hears a horse which scrambles over a low fence described as a 'good jumper'. Perhaps for those riders who ignore the pleasure of riding to hounds such a standard of 'good jumping' may be satisfactory. They have no ambition to stay with hounds wherever they go and will be better occupied in looking for open gates.

It is the aim of the present part to deal with all the problems which may be connected with the improvement of both the rider's physical skill and his competence for training the horse in performing keen and precise jumps.

# CHAPTER ONE

# General Schooling in Jumping and in Moving on the Country Track

THE teaching of jumping of an elementary standard and of the safe movement on the country track is part of the education of all riding horses, regardless of the particular duty which is to be allotted to them. The aim of this tuition is to improve the muscular system, the skill and elasticity of the animal and to develop capacity for obedience.

The horse, as part of its general education, must become accustomed to the idea that the objects which it encounters are neither to be feared nor regarded as impenetrable barriers. (This statement implies, at the same time, that the rider should refrain from intentionally placing an obstacle in the course of his horse which the animal could not be expected to deal with confidently.)

Within this preparatory work the training can be split up into the following periods of instruction:

stepping over miniature fences or cavaletti; *

teaching gymnastic exercises;

jumping small obstacles at a trot;

introduction to jumping at a canter;

introducing the novice to jumping under strange conditions; leading to

the further education of horses selected for the three-day event and show jumping.

### THE PERIOD OF STEPPING OVER MINIATURE FENCES

At this stage of education the purpose of the training is to accustom the animal to step over minor obstructions calmly and with freedom of movement. One can start as soon as the horse has become familiar with the idea of somebody sitting on its back and is willing to proceed quietly with its rider. To begin the exercise, place six to eight bars of natural colour on the ground, without any particular spacing (see Fig. No. 79), and ride over them 15-20

* "Cavaletti" is the plural of the word.

minutes at the walk and trot before completing the daily routine.

As soon as the horse has overcome these small 'surprises' during a few days' practice, the existence of the bars will not cause any embarrassment to the animal and the work can be carried out as if the bars were not there.

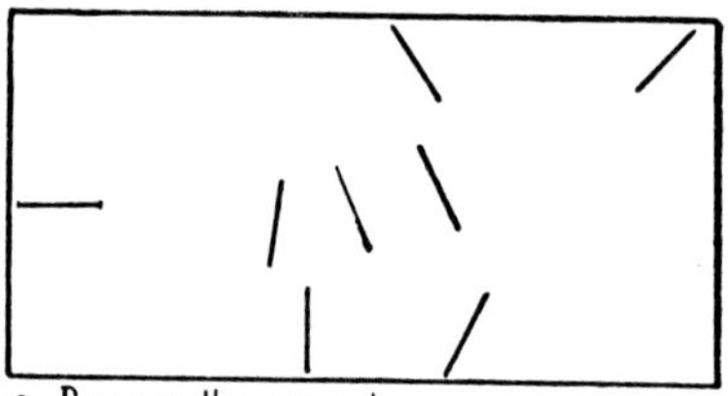

After two or three weeks employ the bars at the beginning of the daily work and let the horse step over them during the execution of the loosening exercise.

When the standard of the novice has improved so much that it can be ridden at a greater distance from the pilot horse, the bars can gradually be raised to 10-12 inches (25-30 cm.); they can gradually be replaced by cavaletti or other miniature obstacles (small logs, brush fences, walls, etc.). It will take about three weeks before all the bars on the ground can be exchanged for these substitutes.

These, however, should not be regarded as 'fences', since they are not designed for jumping, but only for loosening, familiarizing, and in a small measure for muscular development.

a) Bars on the ground.

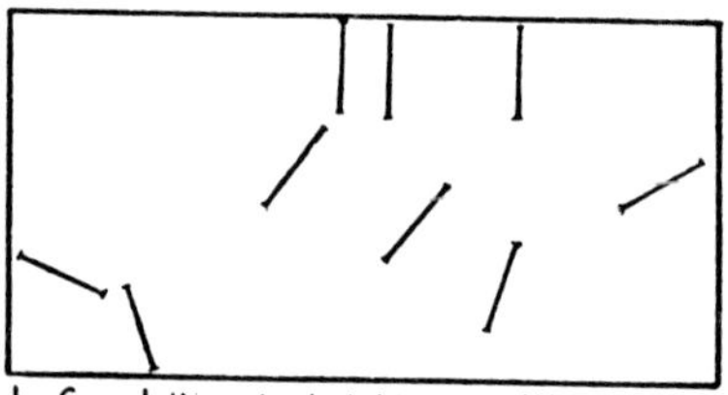

b) Cavalettis at a height up to 1'4"

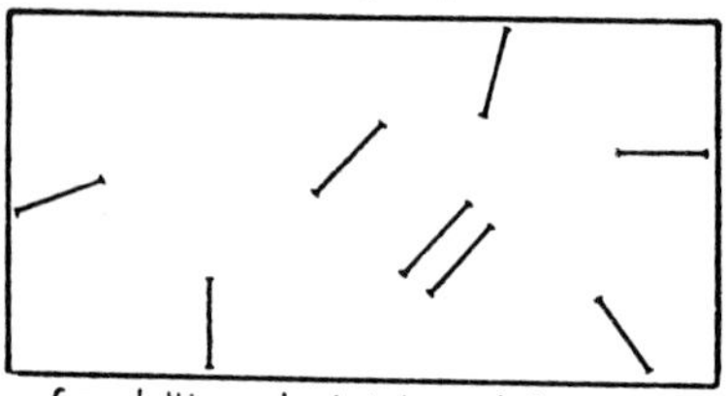

c) Cavalettis and miniature obstacles (1'6").

Fig. No 70

During the exercises in question take care not to confuse the horse and concentrate only on guiding the animal in the direction desired. While the horse is stepping over the obstructions use the forward position (even at a walk) and keep the reins loosened. Take them up only for a short while in cases of need.

Already at this stage of work the rider should employ the neck strap, which is so important a tool while schooling the horse in jumping. Even the best rider may occasionally experience an unexpected, sudden take-off in which his upper body gets 'left behind', so that he falls back into the saddle. This can be avoided by gripping the neck strap (instead of the reins), so that the horse is protected from pain and discouragement.

If the horse happens to be timid instead of calmly stepping over one of the obstructions, then it is best to make a firm halt in front of it, drop the reins and remain still. The rider need not concern himself with the horse, but should only prevent it from turning away. Sooner or later the animal will get tired of standing and eventually will step over the fence by itself. However, the procedure can be speeded up if there is somebody on the other side of the obstacle holding a small basket or bag of oats.

If the horse stands quietly in front of the obstacle, but shows no willingness to step over it, the rider can apply a few *slight* taps with the whip behind his leg. Here, too, care must be taken to prevent the animal turning away and the rider must be ready to follow any sudden movement of the horse at any time.

By the application of the above method the novice will gain the confidence required in later work for jumping.

## TEACHING OF GYMNASTIC EXERCISES

When the horse's capability in obeying the retardment and drive-on has improved sufficiently and it takes the rein-contact, then the preparatory work for jumping can begin.

The foundation for this work is the gymnastic. The exercises involved are necessary to ensure that the horse will adopt the right style in its technique of jumping. Therefore all means used for this purpose must be selected and employed in such a manner that they require such motions and movements of the horse as are desired.

In helping the animal, through mechanical aids, to perform its movements correctly it is still necessary to exercise control over the horse *by guiding it* during the performance. By this guidance we mean that the animal should be ridden with rein-contact, its liveliness established and its obedience to retardment and drive-on checked during the approach.

The gymnastic exercises can be carried out either on suitable natural formations of the ground or with artificial devices.

The best expedient for teaching, because it ensures ease, is the natural formation of the ground, and the particular schooling should utilize such an area whenever possible.

EXERCISES CARRIED OUT WITH THE AID OF NATURAL GROUND FORMATIONS

There are two main types of appropriate formations: the area with ascending planes and the shallow (flat) ditch. Neither of them is rare in the countryside, thus it is unlikely that the rider cannot find at least one of these formations for his exercises.

The exercises have some things in common in their employment with those carried out on an undulating ground formation (see page 131). Within the description of these latter exercises the principles of the rider's activities and the reactios of then horse are explained. It still remains necessary to discuss some additional details which have a special importance on the present case.

Furthermore, it should be mentioned that it will be useful to revert to the gymnastic exercises with the aid of ground formations later on when the horse has reached the stage of actual jumping. They will always provide a change of work for the animal and also help to relieve moderate stiffness without causing any strain.

*The track with ascending planes* (Fig. No. 80)

The most suitable formation is a moderately sloping surface, as shown on the diagram. The slope should include one or two short but steeper planes ('a' and 'b') in its average slant.

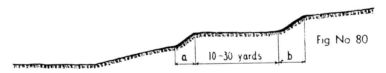

Fig No 80

In carrying out the exercise at the beginning, ride up the slope at a trot, and later at a canter. Make certain that the horse maintains its regularity and does not rush at the steeper places. As soon as one feels that the horse tends to increase its speed (this is the usual case), retard it, if necessary, to a halt. Then, at the moment of the animal's yielding, drive it forward again. If the horse tends to slow down while ascending, drive it forward with determination.

It is helpful to make occasional retardments and animations at various points of the slope in the manner described above.

At the top of the hill the reins may be dropped and the horse can rest while walking down the slope.

In riding up the slope, which can be repeated six to eight times, the starting point of the trot or canter should be varied. Once before turning towards the area, then during the turning, or at some time at the beginning of the slope, etc. In this way the horse will not perform the exercise in a stereotyped manner or rush towards the slope on its own initiative.

The advantages of this exercise, which facilitates the work of the rider in educating the horse, can be summarized as follows:

The rider can train his horse to approach and overcome obstacles without jumping, since the act of driving uphill on a sloping formation requires the same movements and muscular efforts from the animal as jumping. Thus it is possible to develop the horse at a stage when actual jumping would be harmful.

The slope helps to develop a smooth retardment, since the inherent braking tendency of the slope increases the effect of the rider's actions. The renewed start, on the other hand, is a real test of the horse's obedience to drive forward at a signal, for the slope requires a marked increase in strength.

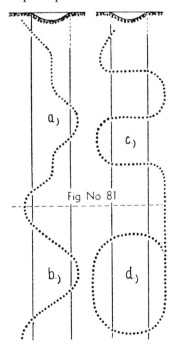

This exercise is very suitable for horses which tend to rush and teaches them to approach and overcome obstacles calmly.

(For further advantages, see page 132.)

*The shallow ditch* (Fig. No. 81)

This is a natural formation, just like the hillside already described, and it has a similar value and purpose. The gymnastic use of it consists simply of descending into the ditch, and then climbing out of it.

At the beginning of the exercise the horse should be brought into the ditch at an oblique angle, and after proceeding 5-10 yards or metres along the bottom it should climb up on the other side

Fig No 81

at the same angle used in descending. The ditch should be traversed in such a manner a few times in a serpentine-like course (see 'a' section of the diagram).

If the animal proceeds calmly, then the length of the course can gradually be shortened until it forms a continuous serpentine ('b').

After practising this movement 10 to 14 occasions, the sectors of the serpentine traversing the ditch can be reduced, so that the riding in and out crosses the ditch vertically ('c').

When the rider has reached this stage he can select a further section of the ditch where crossings are provided at two points close to each other (25-50 yards or metres), so that his track becomes a continuous circle or ellipse ('d').

At the beginning the rider should keep the reins loose and cross the ditch first at a walk and then a trot. If the horse shows sufficient calmness on a long rein, the rider can take up the rein-contact and thus exploit the real gymnastic value of the exercise.

Regarding the duration of the exercise, it is sufficient if the animal crosses the ditch eight to 10 times at a walk and the same number at a trot on one occasion.

### EXERCISES WITH THE AID OF GYMNASTIC DEVICES

The structures in question can be erected at any place where the rider wants to school his horse.

Their prime objects are:

to wind the animal's spring system, i.e. to collect the horse in the first phase of the exercise, and then

to unleash the compressed system, i.e. extract a jumping movement.

Their secondary objects are:

to emphasize the take-off spot;

promote the lifting action of the forehand and the thrust forward of the quarters;

enforce the forward stretching movement of the neck together with the arching of the back; and

improve the horse's bascule during the jump.

The constructions which can bring about the above effects are: the grid (Fig. No. 83); the pair of bascule-developing bars (Fig. No. 82); the combination of the former structures (Fig. No. 84); and the short gymnastic double (Fig. No. 85). Fig. No. 87 shows an example for laying out various gymnastic constructions

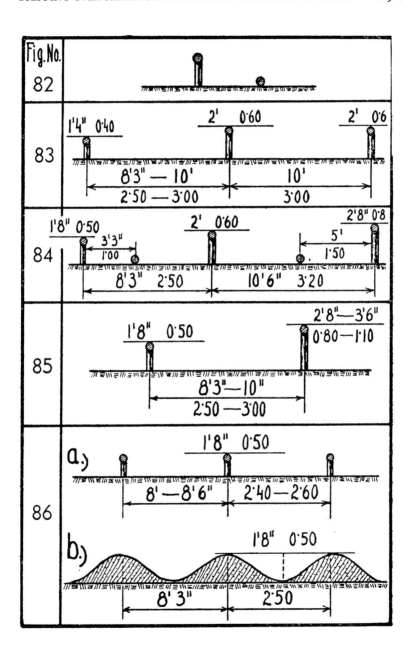

in a course (they can also be erected on a straight course, where the different elements should be situated 20-30 yards or metres apart from each other).

### The grid (Fig. No. 83)

This gymnastic consists of three to six bars placed in succession on low uprights. The height of the bars and their spacing must be determined for each individual horse (see below).

The purpose of the *first bar* is to bring about a pure jumping movement with no further demand regarding style.

The *second bar* is the essential part of the gymnastic. It should be put at a height about 4-6 inches (10-15 cm.) higher than the first one and erected at an average distance of about 7 feet 6 inches or 15 feet (2.25 or 5 m.) when approaching the grid at the trot. For use at a canter the distance should be 10 or 20 feet (3 or 6 m.). However, in determining the distance the stress should not be laid on the measuring rod, but on the horse itself, and the distance adjusted to the individual animal's length of stride.

The second bar—by virtue of its position—first checks the horse's motion, which produces automatically all the coiling (collective) effects mentioned above.  Then it extracts a new jumping movement which is already performed by the horse in the desired style.

The erection of the *third bar* and further bars follow the same principle which determines the position of the second bar in relation to the first one.

The main purpose of the third bar is to restrain the horse after its 'unleashing' in such a manner that it retains its elasticity and does not flatten out (i.e. does not lose the collection produced by the second bar, even after the jump).  Otherwise the purpose of this bar is the same as that of the second bar.

If the composition of the grid includes more than three elements, the additional bars serve the same purpose as the third bar.  The employment of additional elements gives more opportunity to acquire the correct feeling of performing the action.

This gymnastic device is not to be used for practising jumping over greater heights.  However, the task can be rendered more difficult, first by *decreasing* the spaces between the bars, and only secondly by increasing their heights.  Concerning height, it is advisable not to put the bars higher than 2 feet 8 inches to 3 feet

(80-90 cm.). If the bars are erected above 2 feet (60 cm.), the most suitable distance between them is about 21 feet 6 inches (6.60 m.).

As a rule, the first element of the grid should be approached at a trot, after which the horse can be allowed to jump the further elements at a canter.

Grids can also be erected permanently. In this case the supporting posts are sunk into the ground and the bars firmly fixed to them. They should be built so that they can be approached from both directions. Here, too, the number of bars is not more than five to six, placed equally at a distance of 9 feet 3 inches (2.80 m.) or 18 feet 6 inches (5.60 m.), and fixed also equally at a height of 1 foot 4 inches, 1 foot 8 inches or 2 feet (40, 50 or 60 cm.) per grid (the height of each bar of the same grid should be identical).

A permanent grid is a great convenience to the rider, as he has no problems in replacing the elements, but it has the disadvantage that the distances between the bars cannot be altered in order to satisfy the horse's special requirements.

Before concluding the discussion about the grids we should refer to a similar installation called the 'undulating course'. The structure of this can be visualized by imagining that two or three bars of a grid are covered with earth and graded smoothly to valleys midway between each pair of bars (Fig. No. 86/b). The surface of the earth can be made more durable by covering it with bricks placed edgewise.

The undulating course, traversed at a walk or trot, is a very good means of developing the proper motion of the horse's back and neck for jumping, since the same movements are required, though in a slower manner. This 'slow motion' provides the horse and the rider with an excellent opportunity to acquire the right bearing for jumping.

Both the grid and the undulating course can be beneficially employed before commencing actual jumping. They can be negotiated three to five times, preferably in conjunction with other gymnastics.

*The pair of bascule-developing bars* (Fig. No. 82)

This installation consists of two bars which work together. One of them is slightly raised and the other placed on the ground. The ratio in the position of the two bars is about one unit in the height to two units in width, e.g. 1 foot 6 inches (45 cm.) in height and 3 feet (90 cm.) in width.

The installation is always jumped from the higher side, and *only at a trot*.

The purpose of the higher bar is to force the horse to jump whereas the ground rail prevents it from standing back too far and produces the essential effect of the gymnastic.

The horse during the take-off stride, while accommodating itself to the close take-off situation, brings the hind legs well under the body and performs the thrust-off action of the leading foreleg with increased determination. At the same time the position of the ground rail requires the animal to complete the take-off by a very energetic action of the hind legs, to arch its back strongly during the jump, and to perform a clear basculing movement.

For the sake of avoiding the slightest interference with the horse's mouth, which could hamper the free development of basculing, it is advisable at the beginning to carry out this particular gymnastic exercise with loose reins.

It is most practical to erect this gymnastic in such a way that the rider can jump it continuously while riding on a large circle. The beginning ratio between the bars (about 1 foot or 30 cm. in the height and 2 feet or 60 cm. in width) can be increased gradually so that it reaches 2 feet to 4 feet (0.60-1.20 m.) after two to three months' practice. One must not attempt to exceed the above maximum measurements, since they are quite enough to arch the horse's back considerably. If the difficulty of the exercise is increased by broadening the bars only, one runs the risk that the horse may land on the ground rail and injure itself.

In the case of young horses, this exercise should be left till the end of the daily routine work. They can negotiate the gymnastic 15 to 20 times with interpolated resting periods.

In the case of more advanced horses, it is better to use the bascule-improving bars before the actual jumping, clearing them four to five times. This gymnastic may also be employed before competitions for warming up the horse and reinforcing the correct style.

An exercise which shares the same benefits is jumping an obstacle with a height of 1 foot 6 inches to 2 feet (45-60 cm.) while trotting downhill on a gentle slope (10°-15°). Here the ground itself serves as the ground rail, while the slope will encourage the horse to stretch its neck and arch its back.

*Combination of the grid and the bascule-developing bars* (Figs. 84 and 87)

This structure consists of three elements. The first is the bascule-developing bars, which promote arching of the back; the second is a simple bar which by virtue of its position gathers up the horse's spring system, which will be released at the subsequent take-off. (The narrower the distance between the bar and the first element, the greater will be the effect of the gathering.) The third element is also a pair of bars, but the pole on the ground is placed on the take-off side. This element serves as a reward after the effort necessary to overcome the first two elements. Its inviting formation also helps to increase the horse's buoyancy.

It is best first to build only the first element of the combination and jump it a few times alone before adding the other elements.

As a rule, this gymnastic should be approached at a trot, thereafter permitting the horse to perform its movements freely.

*The short gymnastic double* (Fig. No. 85)

This device consists of two elements, a bar placed at a height of about 1 foot to 1 foot 6 inches (30-45 cm.) and a second bar at a somewhat greater height. The latter can be raised during the exercise from 2 feet (0.60 m.) up to 3 feet 6 inches (1.10 m.). The distance between the two bars should be about 9 feet 6 inches (2.80 m.), which may be shortened to 7 feet 6 inches (2.25 m.).

The first bar makes the horse jump without any gymnastic compulsion. The second bar acts like the second pole of a grid, but the effect produced by it is considerably intensified.

In order to improve the arching movement of the horse's back, the distance between the two bars should be reduced during the exercise. The amount of take-off thrust and the height of the jumping action can be increased by raising the second bar.

The use of this gymnastic is generally suitable for horses which are more advanced in their jumping education. Its employment is especially useful before jumping a higher single obstacle or before performing a course.

The short gymnastic double should be approached at a trot. It is sufficient to jump it three or four times on one occasion. During this the severity of the task can be gradually increased.

## Example for the combined application of gymnastic installations.

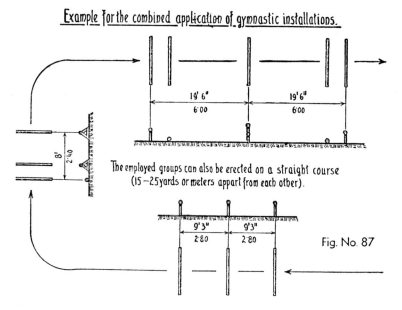

19' 6"  6·00   19' 6"  6·00

8'  2·40

The employed groups can also be erected on a straight course (15 –25 yards or meters apart from each other).

9' 3"  2·80   9' 3"  2·80

Fig. No. 87

### PERIOD OF JUMPING SMALL OBSTACLES (2 FEET TO 2 FEET 4 INCHES OR 60-70 CM.) AT A TROT

Jumping at a trot is a fundamental means of the horse's (but also of the rider's) training. On account of the slow approach the horse gets confidence in itself and in the obstacle. It learns to remain calm for the execution of the take-off and becomes fond of the jumping movement. Furthermore, its practice improves and refreshes the animal's skill and develops considerably its muscular system.

As soon as the horse reacts submissively to the drive-on and the retardment at a trot, and is capable at this pace of turning smoothly, jumping from the trot can commence along with the gymnastic exercises.

The structures which have been described up to this point are exclusively employed for loosening the horse or providing it with gymnastic exercise and thus should not be regarded as actual fences. The stage has now been reached when it is appropriate to confront the animal with a small but real obstacle.

The obstacle should be approached with a loose rein at a lively, rhythmical trot. It is not necessary for the rider to look at the fence. On the contrary, he should look far beyond it and concentrate principally on maintaining the horse's regularity of cadence.

If the horse tends to accelerate in its approach, the remedy is to make a halt right in front of the obstacle or circle away from it. Generally this measure can be applied whenever it is felt that the horse's approach is unsatisfactory. There is no need for the rider to fear that the frequent halts and turns will teach the horse to stop or run out. The contrary is more likely to happen, since few horses will 'refuse' an obstacle which can be stopped smoothly at any moment in front of it. The reason for this is that the horse which responds to the retardment submissively will also obey the driving aids if the idea of stopping should enter its mind (see also page 302).

At this stage of schooling the animal will frequently lose its regularity and it will be necessary for the rider to halt or turn away in front of the fence more times than he continues and jumps it. The rider must be patient in correcting the approach whenever necessary rather than making a succession of poor jumps.

During this early stage of education it is not wise to exercise any direct influence regarding the take-off. The emphasis should be placed on familiarizing the horse with the way in which the obstacles 'emerge' as it approaches them, since it must learn to judge for itself the most suitable place for the take-off. The rider should regard this part of the work as a means of providing the animal with its basic foundation of experience and allow it sufficient time to develop its knowledge.

At the same time, the rider should train his own eyes to judge the point of take-off while approaching obstacles. During the jump all his efforts should be to prevent confusion and to avoid causing the slightest discomfort to the animal.

If the horse slips back into a faulty style of jumping, it is advisable to return to the gymnastics and go over them a few times before a fresh attempt is made to jump independent fences.

SPECIAL SCHOOLING OVER ARTIFICIAL OBSTACLES

Obstacles used in the first stages of teaching jumping should not frighten the horse by any unusual shape, colour or setting. They should be attractive and inviting, so that they will prove sources of encouragement and pleasure to the animal. The obstacles should be placed in a way that helps the horse to judge the right take-off distance (see diagrams 'b' in Figs. No. 93-101).

Bearing in mind the above points, any type of obstacle may be used, provided that its height is appropriate to the horse's stage of schooling (2 feet to 2 feet 4 inches or 60-70 cm.). In jumping spread obstacles the width should not exceed 2 feet (60 cm.) and ditches should not exceed 5 feet (1.50 m.) in width.

Jumping double or treble obstacles should take place towards the end of this period of teaching, when the horse has learned to perform simple jumps correctly. While jumping small combinations the rider should approach the first element as if nothing followed it. After the first jump, however, the horse should be allowed to continue at a canter. At this stage of training the distance between the fences of a double should not be more than 21 feet 3 inches (6.40 m.). In the case of a treble, the distance between the second and third element may be increased to 22 feet 6 inches (6.80 m.).

Despite thorough schooling, a correct approach and a well-arranged fence, it still may happen that the horse will stop. When this occurs the animal should be held for 8-10 seconds facing the fence. Then it can be turned away and a fresh attempt made as if the former incident had never happened. There is no need to take precautionary measures after a single refusal other than ensuring complete liveliness of the animal, since usually it will jump the fence without hesitation at the second attempt.

However, should the horse stop again, a few taps (not hits) can be applied on its side with the whip while halted in front of the obstacle. During the procedure the horse must not be allowed to turn away in any direction. This action should be repeated three to four times, with an interruption of about 4-5 seconds.

If another person is on hand, instead of using the whip in the above manner the assistant should swish a few times towards the horse from behind, but without actually touching it. The rider continues only to keep the animal facing the obstacle.

Following this, the horse should be turned away and a fresh attempt made to jump the fence at a lower level.

In the event of repeated stops the rider can become more active with the tap of the whip. (The whip in the hand of the assistant can also slightly touch the horse.) It must be emphasized, however, that the whip should only be used to educate the animal, and not to punish it. The essence of the corrective measure lies in lightening the task until the horse can complete it. Afterwards the demands can be increased progressively back to the point where the difficulty occurred.

*The 'star obstacle'*

A combination of obstacles in a star-like arrangement, as shown in Fig. No. 88, can be used with advantage during the present

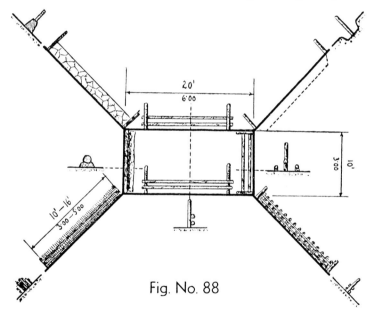

Fig. No. 88

period. It is a practical device which only takes up a small space, yet offers a good deal of variety. It can be erected anywhere for some particular occasion or constructed permanently.

The advantage of the star is that in riding around it, whenever the rider finds a moment when the horse is prepared to jump, he is always facing one of the composing fences, thus avoiding long detours to reach an obstacle. During such a detour the animal can easily lose its preparation and the rider must start all over again.

Riders are often inclined to neglect corrections while approaching an obstacle and thus fail to prepare the horse for the jump. They want to jump regardless of the animal's state of preparation, only because they have already decided to do so. The star obstacle, by virtue of its particular construction, is helpful in checking this harmful impatience.

If the components of the star obstacle are set at quite a low level (1 foot to 1 foot 6 inches or 30-40 cm.), they can also serve as loosening devices (miniature fences).

### INTRODUCTION TO SURMOUNTING HINDERING CONDITIONS ACROSS COUNTRY

During the present period of training the horse can already be asked to make small jumps while proceeding through the country-side. A small ditch, low hedge, an odd tree trunk or similar obstacle can be found almost anywhere.

Further object of the training is to give the horse the basic skill in proceeding smoothly and evenly on moderately sloping surfaces at a walk and trot. The aim is achieved by the execution of loosening exercises, tuition and gymnastics on the country track.

The rider should also try to climb some steeper slopes or cross brooks whenever such natural obstructions come his way. He should take advantage of all the possibilities which the country offers, but only to an extent that will not strain the horse (see some of them in pictures No. 62/a-f). The purpose of such exercise is to teach by 'fun and games', ignoring the magnitude of the accomplishment.

In this sense the selected slopes should not be steeper and longer than those which can be taken either up or downhill at a walk (see page 303), and the jumps up or down from surfaces of different level should not exceed the height of 2 feet 6 inches (75 cm.).

The detailed explanation of accomplishing the various tasks and the description of the particular obstacles takes place in conjunction with the examination of the later stages of the horse's training. At this point we will only deal with the horse's *introduction* to jumping ditches.

*Introducing the novice to jumping ditches*

Ditches are the most truly natural obstructions of the country and are part of the everyday life of a horse which has to move in such a terrain. The horse should know ditches in all their peculiarities and deal with them confidently even if they look imposing. Thus the rider should take great care to inspire confidence and willingness in developing the animal's abilities over these jumps. He should begin on a simple and modest scale, as most difficulties lie in overcoming the mental fear of the appearance of the obstacle. Demands should be increased gradually until the apprehensive attitude disappears. If the horse became familiar with jumping a small ditch in the earlier stages of its education, there will be sufficient time to develop its ability during the later periods.

For the first attempts a dry ditch should be selected, not more than 5 feet (1.50 m.) wide, but where the steep formation of the banks forces the animal to jump in order to get to the other side.

In approaching the ditch the horse should be ridden at a walk and directed vertically towards it. On reaching the edge it must be permitted to stretch its neck and 'smell' the ditch with its nose. There is no need for concern if the horse stops in front of the ditch, as it can easily jump more than 7 feet (2 m.) from a standing position.

The rider must show a resolute will, free of reservations, to cross the ditch and go with the animal's movements. These are the main factors which create the impetus in the horse to decide for itself.

The only physical action which the rider can use is a simple driving signal. Most horses, after a few seconds' hesitation, decide to 'get over' and throw themselves to the other side of the ditch. During this sudden action it is very important that the rider should not interfere with the horse's movement (he should grip the neck strap).

If the horse cannot make this decision, the driving signal of the legs can be emphasized by a tap of the whip behind the leg. In the meantime, the rider must be careful that the animal does not turn away or step back. If necessary, the horse should stand still for 5-10 minutes or even longer in front of the ditch. Should the horse get to the verge of jumping, but then decline, it should be patted a few times and allowed to come to a fresh decision. The rider must never lose his patience, but must wait, without inflicting punishment, until the jump is completed. The horse will jump, sooner or later, if the rider does not hinder it with confusing actions.

At the second attempt the right result will be achieved in a shorter space of time. Gradually the situation will improve, so that the horse is ready to clear the ditch with pleasure and without hesitation.

Occasionally resistance will start at some distance from the ditch. In such cases the horse should be halted and ridden to the edge of the ditch step by step. During this approach it must not be allowed to step sideways or backwards. Once the edge of the ditch has been reached the procedure is the same as in the previous case.

If the horse, after much hesitation and shivering, decides to jump, gets ready, but holds back again, the best remedy is to tap its side gently and *continuously* for a while a few times with the whip. Eventually the animal will regain its courage from the rider's determination and push itself over the ditch.

While teaching the horse to jump ditches the rider should bear in mind as a general principle that he must not turn away from the ditch if the horse stops in front of it. The animal should be urged gently until it jumps over from a stationary position. (This is unlike the practice used for erected fences.) This principle also applies to horses which tend to 'run away' while jumping ditches. They should be stopped in front of the ditch and made to jump it from a standstill. Turning away from a ditch can be recommended when the distance to it is more than 10-12 yards (or metres).

Furthermore, it should be emphasized that the rider must give plenty of freedom to the reins during the accustoming procedure. He should use them only occasionally for short moments when counteracting the horse's turning intention becomes necessary.

Introducing the Novice Horse to Jumping at a Canter
(Obstacles from 2 feet to 3 feet 3 inches or 0.60-1 m.)

When the horse is performing its regular work at a canter satisfactorily, in addition to gymnastics and jumping at a trot, jumping at a canter can be commenced. Even at this period it is not the height of the obstacle which matters, but the development of the style which has already been established by the work done before.

Since the horse's most natural pace is the canter, the rider is not likely to encounter any particular difficulty, provided the training in previous periods has been correctly carried out. One may then ask, 'Why not start teaching jumping at a canter?' The answer is that the key to jumping is in the approach rather than in the actual performance of the jump. It is far easier to ride the horse correctly and regulate its stride at a trot than at a canter. This is why the jump as a whole is easier for an untrained horse at a trot than at a canter.

A detailed explanation of riding towards the obstacle, as well as that of the rider's and horse's bearing during and after the jump, can be found on page 324.

Since the action of jumping at a canter begins with *striking off* into this pace, it is necessary for the horse to execute this act precisely and definitely before an attempt is made at jumping.

While the animal is cantering its response to the retardment and drive-on, its shoulder mobility and its smoothness in turning should be checked. When the rider is satisfied with these requirements, and the horse is holding a speed slightly below the average, then, and only then, can he look for the obstacle. (The star obstacle can be of great help in this early stage of schooling.)

If in approaching the obstacle the horse tends to accelerate, the remedy is either to turn aside or make it halt altogether. It is advisable to employ these two actions alternatively until the animal is able to approach the fence calmly. In most cases the cause of running into the obstacle is that the rider is pulling the reins. Therefore he should take care of his hands and 'balance' the horse during the approach. By doing so the rider can avoid many troubles and superfluous work.

If the animal shows resistance in front of the obstacle, a simple driving signal by the legs is the best means of assistance. (In case of need this can be reinforced by a tap of the whip applied beyond the leg.) It is desirable, however, if there is sufficient time after the application of the driving signal, to retard the horse for a moment and to reach the take-off spot by *repeating the driving signal from retardment once more* (animation).

In both kinds of disobedience the most successful cure is in practising the combined retardment and drive-on on a slope, as illustrated in Fig. No. 80.

Generally speaking, the rider should still not try to take any initiative in determining the point of take-off. The fences used in these exercises are not difficult and the take-off can best be left to the animal.

However, if the horse begins to develop a habit of trying to take off 'under' the fence, occasionally a take-off signal can be applied, provided that the *right take-off point* happens to come up at the right place. But generally the horse must learn to ascertain the correct take-off distance itself, for this is an important quality, especially for the three-day event horse or a hunter.

If the animal should refuse at a canter, it is best to repeat the approach at a trot (for this the fence can eventually be lowered) or make a few gymnastic jumps before a renewed attempt at jumping in the canter. Any 'pressing' or forcing of the horse with the seat or the whip towards the obstacle should be avoided (see also page 325).

The main kinds of work which should be done and the types of obstacles which should be used during the present period are described in the following paragraphs.

### The work for jumping

In the schedule of work two to three days weekly should be allotted to jumping at a canter. On each occasion loosening and gymnastic exercises carefully carried out may precede the jumping. This should also include practices without the use of reins.

For selecting artificial obstacles the same recommendations apply that were given for the work at a trot. The application of the star obstacle is highly advisable. The distances between the elements of a combination should be fixed at about 23 feet (6.90 m.) or 33 feet (10.20 m.).

For cross-country practice also the same types of obstacle used in the previous period should be employed, but their height can be increased to 3 feet 3 inches (1 m.). In addition, the training should be extended to include:

small fences placed on a gentle slope;

ditches, both dry and with water, and with varying types of banks (up to 8 feet or 2.50 m. in width);

shallow pools of water, which the horse can be asked to jump into and out of.

It should be noted that not more than three to four such exercises may be included in the training schedule for a single day.

*Improving the horse's skill on uneven surfaces*

The horse has already learned the foundation for moving safely on uneven surfaces through the loosening exercises, its lessons in regulation and the gymnastic exercises. Now it should be ridden in the open country over undulating ground at a canter as well and practise negotiating steep terrain formations.

Cantering over *mildly sloping ground* is done as it would be on the flat. There should be no difference in speed whether the animal travels uphill, downhill or on the level. As soon as the evenness of speed is upset the horse must be immediately regulated (see page 143).

The method of riding over *steep inclines* depends on whether the ground is ridden uphill or downhill.

When the horse is *descending a steep slope* it keeps its balance with its forelegs, but it carries almost the full weight of the body by bringing its hind legs under it. To perform this motion freely the horse must stretch its neck forward and downwards and the rider must lengthen the reins to maintain the contact with the animal. At the same time, he should lift his seat and bend forward with his upper body in order to free the quarters of his burden.

When the condition of the ground is satisfactory, riding down a slope of up to 25° can be performed in all three lower paces; above this steepness the descent should be taken at a walk. On a slope of over 55° the horse must slide down. Even in this case the rider must bend his body well forward (see picture No. 78).

The technique of *ascending a steep slope* coincides roughly with that of descent. In order to ease the exertion of the animal, and to ensure its free movement, it is necessary to allow it to stretch its neck well forward and to use its back freely.

In riding up a slope which is not steeper than 30° all three paces can be used; from 30° to 45° the ascent should be carried out at a walk or canter; and above 45° it should be performed only in a canter (which is already climbing).

Riding up a slope of 600-900 yards (500-800 m.) with moderate steepness (up to 30°) both in a walk and trot is a very good exercise for the horse's muscular system.

A short steep slope of about 45°, especially on sandy ground, can develop the lungs in addition to the muscles.

Moderate slopes have the advantage that work can be carried out without unduly straining the tendons and joints of the animal. This has a special importance during the horse's conditioning if the going is too hard for intensive work at a gallop.

However, riding up or downhill on a slope which is steeper than 30° incurs considerable strain, especially with young horses, and should be practised with great moderation.

### INTRODUCING THE NOVICE HORSE TO JUMPING VARIOUS SIMPLE TYPES OF OBSTACLES UNDER STRANGE CONDITIONS

The aim of this period is to complete the general education of the horse and give it opportunity to consolidate its basic knowledge. Furthermore, it should get some experience in jumping various kinds of obstacles under strange conditions.

This period of schooling may start when the animal's obedience for adjustments has become established.

If the horse has learned during previous periods the right style of jumping, and has taken a liking to it, it will always be willing to jump any kind of obstacle, even under circumstances unfamiliar to it. In order to reach such a stage of knowledge, it is necessary to *educate* the animal in jumping and not only to drill it over certain fences.

If somebody tries to 'school' his horse by the latter method, he may succeed in making it jump those particular obstacles, but such a horse will probably fail immediately when confronted with circumstances which are new, and thus the rider will always have new difficulties to solve.

In completing the general education the following method can be recommended.

### The schooling in jumping

Before jumping an unknown obstacle let the horse in the beginning have a look at it, facing squarely at the fence. During this 'inspection' do not permit any deviation from a straight position and tap the horse's side slightly with the whip. As a result of this stimulation it will suddenly reveal a forward inclination, showing its willingness for the completion of the task. This is the moment when *the rider can ask* the horse to turn away from the obstacle.

Then approach the fence at first at a trot and the second time at a canter from a fair distance. This is necessary in order to have time during the approach to establish the animal's regularity, on which the success of the jump will depend. There is no need to take further precautions, as it is unlikely that the horse will make any difficulties in a regulated state.

After having made the novice acquainted with some new obstacles in the above manner, it will gain confidence to jump novelties also without previous introduction.  The rider should check its obedience several times during the period by confronting the animal with fences never used before.  During these exercises it is useless to exceed the limit of moderate demands in jumping. Patience and tolerance will yield better and *quicker* returns.

At this time the horse may undergo its first instruction in improving its galloping action, developing speed by lengthening rather than accelerating the stride.  This must be achieved by the animal itself through the regulation of its motion.

The relevant recommendations can be found on page 427.  For the time being it is enough to use a speed of 500 yards (450 m.) per minute, increasing to 650 yards (600 m.) per minute.  The distance can be gradually increased from 600 yards (550 m.) to 900 yards (800 m.) during the course of the exercise.

The secondary aim of this part of the training is to improve the animal's lungs.  Alternative methods for this purpose are climbing a short steep slope, trotting or cantering up a long, mild hillside or proceeding at the same paces in deep sand or soft plough.   By these means the work carried out during the present period can help condition a horse for hunting, so that it will be fit for the opening meet.

After completing this period of the general education (altogether about one and a half years), horses which are designed to become hunters can begin their career equipped with a sound knowledge and a well-conditioned physical structure.

However, before they can be regarded as real hunters, they must acquire a lot of experience.  This object can be achieved during the first hunting season if the rider gives the animal every chance to further its knowledge gradually.  Thus the first season for the novice hunter should be regarded as a continuation of schooling.

THE FURTHER EDUCATION OF HORSES SELECTED FOR THREE-DAY EVENTS AND SHOW JUMPING

The standard which has been reached after the period of general education should not be regarded as sufficient preparation for the special training required by three-day event horses or show jumpers. Therefore it is necessary to continue their schooling for some time along similar lines in order

> to consolidate the results of previous training and improve the elasticity of the animal;
>
> to further develop the muscular system; and
>
> to improve the technique of jumping.

The starting condition of the period is that the horse can maintain regularity during the motion without the rider's constant support.

### Consolidation of previous schooling and improvement of elasticity by gymnastics

Even after the most thorough schooling it is necessary to continually refresh, by constant repetition and practice, the knowledge which has already been acquired. This practice serves not only as a reminder, but also consolidates and refines knowledge already gathered.

In regulating procedures the retarding and driving actions, and those lateral functions which produce the mobility of shoulders, are the dominant features. When these actions are alternated they also produce a virtual oscillation, as in longitudinal so in the lateral sense, of the animal's muscular system. This oscillation adds considerable value to the procedures, by which they can also be regarded as supplementaries to the gymnastics.

During the continuity of the daily work the actual gymnastic exercises can either be combined with the dressage schooling or inserted between that and the jumping exercise.

### The development of muscles by long canters

In developing the muscles used in jumping it is advantageous to employ long canters. This work can be done as follows:

Before commencing, the horse's muscles should be relaxed; every bit of stiffness and its cause should be removed. Then the cantering can take place.

The animal at this canter should proceed at a moderate speed, about 360 yards (330 m.) per minute, with ground-covering strides.

The canter should last until the rider feels that the horse's muscles are becoming tired. This will be marked by a need of more frequent warnings to keep up impulsion and eventually the start of sweating.

During the canter the leads should be changed about every five minutes, so that the muscles can become evenly developed on both sides. It is also advisable to start the canter on a different lead each time.

At the beginning one can devote about 10 minutes to cantering at one stretch, and this may be gradually increased to 20 minutes in three months' time. Longer cantering will probably not be necessary.

After the canter the horse can be relaxed by five or six minutes of trotting.

This work should be done once a week.

### Developing the horse's technique in jumping

Improving the animal's skill and experience

This item of the training occurs by style-improving routine exercises and by exercises under unfamiliar conditions. The height of individual obstacles involved can be up to 3 feet 9 inches (1.15 m.); and of simple combinations up to 3 feet 3 inches (1 m.).

Some recommendations regarding this aim ha e been given already and the detailed discussion of it appears in part four.

### Making the animal familiar with increased heights and spreads

After thorough general schooling the horse is now ready to learn the meaning of the height and breadth in jumping. For this purpose, *towards the end* of the present period the rider may attempt to jump obstacles of easy structure up to a height of 4 feet 3 inches (1.30 m.) and a breadth of 10 feet (3 m.). An explanation of this work can be found in connection with the special training of jumpers (see page 531).

If the horse has been properly prepared and schooled up to now this greater height and breadth should not cause any particular difficulty. During this period the rider should try to ensure that the horse will have pleasant memories of these first attempts to jump over larger obstacles. The most important factor is to ensure suitable take-offs for the animal. This is achieved by a balanced approach and by arriving at the right take-off spot. (For this latter purpose the take-off regulating devices can be of great help, see page 309.)

*Introductory work for jumping courses*

In competitions both the three-day event horse and the show jumper have to jump fences in sequence. Therefore it is not enough to school only over separate obstacles; the animal must learn to jump series of fences, i.e. a course ('parcours').*

During the schooling period the number of successive obstacles is determined by the horse's capacity to maintain its balance. The more capable it becomes of maintaining perfect equilibrium, the more fences it can jump in sequence. This condition of jumping fences in succession determines the basic principle of teaching, but also of riding courses in general. That is, that in completing the task the main problem is to negotiate the *obstacles* of the course and not the *line* on which they are erected. This means that the rider should readjust the horse after each jump and 'look' for the next fence when the animal is properly prepared. Consequently it is better to abandon a jump during the teaching period rather than 'chance it' under adverse circumstances.

In order to ensure steady progress it is advisable to begin schooling with the star obstacle in the following manner:

The horse should canter quietly around it and when the rider is satisfied with the regularity of his horse he can jump the nearest fence of the star. While continuing the canter he should check the regularity again and if it is still in order, or has been restored, he should attempt the following jump. At the beginning of training the horse should be given some rest after performing three or four successive jumps. Then the practice should be repeated in the other direction.

In the next stage of this work, after the performance of two to three successive jumps, the horse should be directed at one of the inner fences of the star. After this jump the rider may change direction (perhaps with a few trotting strides) and make two or three jumps in the new direction. This exercise should be carried out not more than twice on the same occasion and the horse must be allowed a brief rest between the two performances. For this exercise the height of the fences should not exceed 2 feet 4 inches (70 cm.).

---

*Each country has its own expressions for describing the various degrees of courses in addition to the general definitions of the F.E.I. In order to avoid misunderstanding, I will denote the standard of a particular course in the following explanations by a figure indicating the average height of the obstacles involved.

Once the animal proceeds smoothly and pleasantly around the star obstacle, four or five obstacles can be set up in an open space as a short course. The line connecting the obstacles should be simple and provide easy turns. The individual fences should be placed far enough apart from each other for the rider to be able to correct his horse in between. The obstacles themselves should look inviting and be of a sloping or ascending type, but not too broad. At this early stage of training combinations should not be included.

The series of jumps should be performed at a comfortable speed and under conditions affording pleasure to the horse, for their aim is to give the animal a liking for jumping courses. As schooling advances the distances between the obstacles can be decreased and the turns shortened by setting the fences closer to each other.

The height of the obstacles of these elementary courses should be about 6-8 inches (15-20 cm.) lower than the maximum height of single obstacles which have been jumped up to that point. The breadth of the fences should not exceed 2 feet (60 cm.). Thus, the average height of the course which can be aimed at for the end of the present period is 3 feet 7 inches (1.10 m.).

During the performance the rider's attitude must be one of firm determination, calmness and ease. He should not suggest doing something 'extraordinary', but follow the horse's movements skilfully and exercise control smoothly. If he is unable to satisfy these requirements, either the horse or the rider is not yet ready for the performance and the demands of the work should be reduced.

SUPPLEMENTARY DEVICES FOR SCHOOLING IN JUMPING

There are two devices which the rider can use to develop the horse's jumping abilities. These are the 'take-off regulating devices' and the 'loose (or jumping) lane'.

TAKE-OFF REGULATING DEVICES

The point of the animal's take-off has a dominant influence on the quality of the jump and it is obviously of great importance in approaching the obstacle to bring the horse to the spot most suitable for the take-off. In achieving this, especially during the period of schooling, two simple devices can be recommended: the device for fixing a turning point and the pair of cavaletti.

*Device for fixing the turning point* (Fig. No. 89)

The method of establishing the take-off by fixing a turning point is based on the following observation. If a horse always turns towards an obstacle at the same spot, it will always arrive at the same take-off point in front of the fence, provided that the speed is approximately the same on each occasion.

It is possible to employ this phenomenon by fixing a definite spot for the horse's turn towards the obstacle. The turning point can be marked by an upright or any other appropriate object.

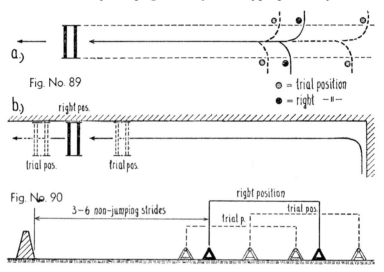

Fig. No. 89

○ = trial position

● = right — " —

Fig. No. 90

The procedure for determining the right place for such a turning point is carried out as follows:

place the selected object in line with one side of the obstacle to be cleared at a distance of about 30-50 yards (25-40 m.), as shown in Fig. No. 89/a (as the first attempt is to see where the horse will arrive for the take-off, the obstacle should not be higher than 3 feet or 90 cm.);

approach the turning point from a direction at right angles to the obstacle and, passing it, turn the horse towards the fence;

if the actual take-off point proves to be wrong, move the device nearer or farther from the fence and make a new attempt until one finds the most suitable spot.

When the turning point has been fixed the height of the obstacle can be raised as desired and jumped two to four times as required.

An exact take-off point can similarly be achieved when the turning point is already fixed by moving the position of the obstacle (this can be done in a manège or other confined place, see Fig. No. 89/b).

*The pair of cavaletti and their application* (Fig. No. 90)

The second method of regulating the take-off distance is the use of cavaletti. Their use is governed by the following considerations:

When the horse approaches an obstacle, however insignificant, it instinctively tries to adapt its stride to it so that less effort will be needed for the jump. Consequently the animal either maintains its original stride or changes it in order to fit the ensuing take-off spot to the position of the obstacle. By the use of a small fence, such as a cavaletti, this 'stride-changing' instinct can be employed to bring the animal to the right take-off spot. Since one cavaletti alone may not be sufficient to bring about the desired change in stride, it is advisable to use two, placed a short distance apart. While the horse is passing over cavaletti thus arranged, the first one effects a rough shift in the canter strides and the second completes the regulation.

These two cavaletti together form the second type of take-off regulating device. The height of the bars should be approximately 1 foot 6 inches (45 cm.). Their distance from each other is fixed by the length of the animal's stride at the intended speed, by allowing for one or two non-jumping strides between the two cavaletti.

After a preliminary estimate of the right distance between the cavaletti they should be placed 24-36 yards (20-30 m.) from the front of the obstacle (as shown in the diagram) set at a low level. Then the first attempt at jumping can be made.

According to the actual take-off, it may be necessary to adjust the position of the cavaletti in one direction or the other. The distance between the cavaletti, however, must always remain the same once it has been fixed.

After one or two further attempts it will be possible to place the cavaletti so that a correct take-off is ensured. When the point of the take-off has been fixed the height of the obstacle can be set at the desired level and the work carried out as planned.

In comparing the use of these two types of regulators, the former is more simple and requires less space, but the latter is more beneficial to both the rider and the horse. In practice, however, the rider is often obliged to employ the aid of the first method.

### THE LOOSE SCHOOL, LOOSE LANE OR JUMPING LANE (COULOIR)

The most suitable shape for a loose school, its measurements and construction are shown in Fig. No. 91/a-b.

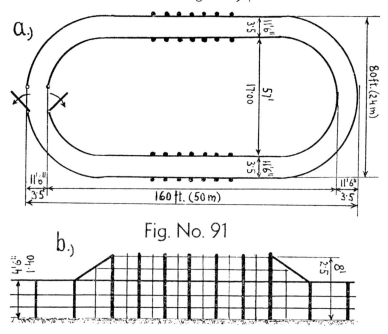

Fig. No. 91

The height of the outside frame is about 8 feet (2.50 m.).
The height of the inner frame is about 4 feet 6 inches (1.40 m.), but this height is increased at the dotted sector to 8 feet (2.50 m.). At this sector the posts are fitted with holes suitable to support poles or other obstacle elements.
Fig. b) shows the schematic outline of the inner frame at the dotted sector.

It is possible to erect the installation in different forms, but at a risk of rendering the exercise defective. For instance, a loose lane in the shape of a square would disturb the continuity of the horse's movement, while one smaller than the size recommended will greatly complicate the task of the animal. If it consists only of a straight course (not oval), then the use of various obstacles will be rather limited.

The loose lane should be used in the following manner:

When the horse has been led into the loose lane, remove the bridle or head collar and permit the animal to run around a few times on the empty course.  In most cases there is no need to urge the horse, but, if it refuses to move, a swish or crack with a long whip is usually sufficient.

When the environment has become familiar to the horse, the gymnastics or obstacles can be erected on the course and the animal allowed to clear them quietly of its own accord.  The distances between the elements of the gymnastics should be longer at the beginning and gradually decreased in accordance with the progress of the work.  This technique can help teach a free horse to acquire the right style of jumping.

The loose lane can also be used:

for practising jumping with horses with sore backs (after lameness horses must not be exercised in a loose lane);

for renewed gymnastics after a long rest with horses which have become 'sour' and disheartened with jumping;

for 'warning' notoriously careless horses by the use of fixed obstacles, thus making them liable to a fall, which will serve both as education and punishment;

for ascertaining the horse's jumping ability.

Finally the loose lane can be employed if the rider, lacking time or experience himself, still wants his horse to practise jumping.

The value of the jumping exercises carried out in a loose lane is limited, since the exercises, though useful, are not indispensable.  The horse cannot be taught jumping by the use of such exercises alone.

---

The knowledge which both the rider and horse can acquire through carrying out the programme outlined in the present chapter is sufficient to satisfy most ordinary requirements in jumping.  However, this level of knowledge is not enough for those riders who aim at the more difficult and intricate fields of jumping.

In order to provide the rider with the proper knowledge to satisfy higher requirements, a close examination of the more advanced methods of jumping will be dealt with in the next chapter.

# CHAPTER TWO

# Advanced Methods of Jumping

THE act of jumping should always be carefully prepared both during the period of the horse's schooling and in its finished state. The preparation should not be confined to those activities which occur just before the execution of the jump, the description of which is the main subject of the present chapter, but must include the whole process of establishing the horse's regularity as well. Thus it embraces the application of the entire system of education explained in the second part, for it is only in this way that the horse and rider can achieve a high standard with their mutual efforts.

We shall now consider one by one the essential factors which govern the execution of a jump.

### The Effect of Speed on the Horse's Stride and Jumping Movements

Speed influences the length of the canter (gallop) and thus has considerable bearing on the jump itself. The knowledge of this influence is important, both in planning and in executing the jumping performance.

The relevant statistics, showing the length of the stride at various rates of speed, are set forth in Table No. 8/a. An examination of these figures shows that a simple change of speed considerably alters the length of strides, and by this often one or two shortened or lengthened strides are enough to avert disaster even in the most critical situations.

From the table one can also see the extent to which the horse shortens its strides after the landing for two or three strides. This knowledge will be especially needed for planning and jumping combinations.

### THE ROLE OF SPEED IN APPROACHING AND CLEARING OBSTACLES

The speed used in approaching obstacles is conditioned by the particular demands of the competition and the height and width of the fence. The lower limit of speed (the minimum speed) is determined by the dimensions of the obstacle, whereas its upper limit (the maximum speed) depends on the ability of the rider and the horse in maintaining regularity.

Some approximate data regarding minimum speeds are given in Table No. 9. Three sets of figures are given, depending on whether the obstacle is upright (without spread), wide (without height), or is both high and wide.

## Table No. 8/a

### Relationship between speed and stride length

| General Characteristic of the speed | Rate of the speed in yd. per min. | Length of strides in ft. | | Rate of the speed in m. per min. | Length of strides in m. | | Application of the speed |
|---|---|---|---|---|---|---|---|
| | | on the flat course | after landing (2-3 strs.) | | on the flat course | after landing (2-3 strs.) | |
| Slow | 300 | 11′ 4″ | 11′ | 275 | 3·45 | 3·35 | Slow parcours |
| | 325 | 11′ 8″ | 11′ 4″ | 300 | 3·55 | 3·45 | |
| | 350 | 12′ | 11′ 8″ | 325 | 3·65 | 3·55 | |
| Medium | 380 | 12′ 4″ | 11′ 10″ | 350 | 3·75 | 3·60 | Average parcours |
| | 400 | 12′ 6″ | 12′ | 356 | 3·80 | 3·65 | |
| | 415 | 12′ 10″ | 12′ 4″ | 380 | 3·90 | 3·75 | |
| | 437 | 13′ 4″ | 12′ 8″ | 400 | 4·10 | 3·85 | |
| | 450 | 13′ 7″ | 12′ 11″ | 410 | 4·15 | 3·95 | |
| Fast | 492 | 14′ 9″ | 14′ 1″ | 450 | 4·50 | 4·30 | Fast parcours and cross-country |
| | 500 | 15′ | 14′ 4″ | 460 | 4·55 | 4·35 | |
| | 550 | 16′ 3″ | 15′ 5″ | 500 | 4·95 | 4·70 | |
| | 600 | 18′ | 17′ 2″ | 550 | 5·50 | 5·25 | |
| Steeple-chase | 656 | 19′ 6″ | 18′ 8″ | 600 | 5·90 | 5·65 | Steeple-chase |
| | 700 | 21′ 4″ | 20′ 4″ | 650 | 6·50 | 6·20 | |
| | 750 | 23′ 6″ | 22′ 6″ | 700 | 7·20 | 6·90 | |

The details of the table are ascertained according to the motion of a horse of good average action.

The heavy figures show the average main values within the particular groups of speed. In general practice it is best to work with these data.

## Table No. 8/b

**Additional shortening in the length of strides which follow the landing in cases when the 'basic height' of the obstacle (see Table No. 11) is more than 4 feet (1·20 m.), or the width of a ditch is over 10 feet (3 m.)**

| At a basic height of | 4' 3" 1·30 m. | 4' 6" 1·40 m. | 5' 1·50 m. | 5' 6" 1·65 m. | 6' 1·80 m. | 6' 6" 2·00 m. |
|---|---|---|---|---|---|---|
| At a width of | 11' 3·30 m. | 12' 3·60 m. | 13' 3·90 m. | 14' 4·20 m. | 15' 4·50 m. | 16' 4·90 m. |
| the additional shortening is | 4" 0·10 m. | 6" 0·15 m. | 1' 0·30 m. | 1' 4" 0·40 m. | 1' 8" 0·50 m. | 2' 0·60 m. |

There is an additional shortening in the length of strides after the landing when *a ditch appears on the landing side of an upright structure* and its width exceeds the landing distance belonging to the existing height.

The amount of shortening can be fixed as 6 inches (15 cm.) for each foot (0.30 m.) difference between the spread and the normal landing distance.

## Table No. 9

**Relation between the dimensions of an obstacle and the minimum speed**

| Obstacle | | | | Minimum speed | | |
|---|---|---|---|---|---|---|
| With height | | Without height | | yd. per min. | m. per min. | Obstacle with height and width |
| ft. | m. | ft. | m. | | | |
| 4' | 1·20 | 8' 6" | 2·50 | 275 | 250 | The minimum speed indicated for the height should be increased by about 25 yd. (m.)/min. for each 2 ft. (60 cm.) of spread |
| 4' 7" | 1·40 | 11' 6" | 3·50 | 300 | 275 | |
| 5' | 1·50 | 13' | 4·00 | 340 | 310 | |
| Further: | | | | 380 | 350 | |

The horse can clear the heights and widths shown above at an even lower speed, but this would subject it to unnecessary strain. A similar waste of energy occurs when the jump is performed at an unnecessarily high speed.

To sum up, the key to utilizing the horse most economically in jumping lies in the choice of the appropriate speed coupled with right impulsion (liveliness). This is particularly important in jumping whole courses.

Under certain circumstances, e.g. steeplechases, 'time' classes and jump-offs, the speed factor is of special importance. In such cases the rider has to relate the speed of his approach to the particular requirements of the competition, but only within the limit of knowledge mentioned above.

*Improving the rider's ability at estimating his riding speed*

It is not enough for the rider to realize the importance of speed; he must also learn to estimate the speed at which he is travelling so that he will be able to select the speed which is most appropriate to the task at hand. This is of paramount importance in jumping, particularly in riding into combinations. Furthermore, the rules of competitions often oblige the rider to maintain a stipulated speed, since there are time limits both in the combined tests and in the show ring. How can the rider meet these demands if he is poorly trained at judging speed? He will either waste his horse or be penalized on his score card for his ignorance.

From all this one can realize how important it is for the rider to acquire skill at judging speed. Fortunately, the development of this capacity is not particularly difficult and can be facilitated by the methods described below.

To begin with, select three distinct speeds for use while cantering. One should be slow, one medium and the third faster; it is best if these speeds correspond to rates of about 360, 440 and 520 yards (330, 400 and 475 m.) per minute.

During daily exercises at a canter employ these selected speeds and maintain their uniformity during the ride. In order to verify the rate of the selected speeds it will be necessary to check them on several occasions. This can be accomplished by establishing a distance of 150 or 200 yards (metres). Bring the horse up to the desired speed before reaching the marked course, so that it can maintain a uniform speed between the starting and finishing points. Measure the elapsed time with a stop-watch and derive the speed (see the calculation on page 320).

Besides the above exercise, take every opportunity of verifying, either directly or indirectly, the speed of the horse, e.g. take a secondary road along which the horse can canter on soft going (grass, sand, stubble-field, etc.). Be accompanied on the road by a motor car or bicycle equipped with a speedometer and driven at the speed intended. In the second stage of these exercises the driver should verify whether the rider has used the speed intended by him.

(300 yards per minute is equal to 10.3 miles per hour. For each 50 yards per minute increase, the speed increases 1.75 miles per hour.)

[Continued on page 320]

## Table No. 10

### Register of time requirement

Time required for covering the distance shown in the head-line

| Speed | 5000 | 4000 | 3000 | 2500 | 2000 | 1500 | 1000 | 900 | 800 | 700 | 600 | 500 | 400 | 300 | 200 | 100 | 50 | 25 | 20 | Speed |
|---|---|---|---|---|---|---|---|---|---|---|---|---|---|---|---|---|---|---|---|---|
| 210 | 23' 47" | 19' 2" | 14' 17" | 11' 54" | 9' 31" | 7' 8" | 4' 46" | 4' 17" | 3' 48" | 3' 21" | 2' 52" | 2' 23" | 1' 54" | 1' 26" | 57" | 29" | 14" | 7" | 6" | 210 |
| 220 | 22' 44" | 18' 11" | 13' 38" | 11' 22" | 9' 6" | 6' 49" | 4' 33" | 4' 6" | 3' 38" | 3' 12" | 2' 43" | 2' 16" | 1' 49" | 1' 22" | 55" | 27" | 14" | 7" | 6" | 220 |
| 230 | 21' 45" | 17' 24" | 13' 4" | 10' 52" | 8' 41" | 6' 32" | 4' 21" | 3' 55" | 3' 29" | 3' 3" | 2' 37" | 2' 10" | 1' 44" | 1' 18" | 52" | 26" | 13" | 7" | 5" | 230 |
| 240 | 20' 50" | 16' 40" | 12' 30" | 10' 25" | 8' 20" | 6' 15" | 4' 10" | 3' 45" | 3' 20" | 2' 55" | 2' 30" | 2' 5" | 1' 40" | 1' 15" | 50" | 25" | 13" | 6" | 5" | 240 |
| 250 | 20' 0" | 16' 0" | 12' 0" | 10' 0" | 8' 0" | 6' 0" | 4' 0" | 3' 36" | 3' 12" | 2' 48" | 2' 24" | 2' 0" | 1' 36" | 1' 12" | 48" | 24" | 12" | 6" | 5" | 250 |
| 262 | 19' 5" | 15' 16" | 11' 26" | 9' 33" | 7' 37" | 5' 43" | 3' 49" | 3' 26" | 3' 3" | 2' 40" | 2' 17" | 1' 54" | 1' 32" | 1' 9" | 46" | 23" | 11" | 6" | 5" | 262 |
| 300 | 16' 40" | 13' 20" | 10' 0" | 8' 20" | 6' 40" | 5' 0" | 3' 20" | 3' 0" | 2' 40" | 2' 20" | 2' 0" | 1' 40" | 1' 20" | 1' 0" | 40" | 20" | 10" | 5" | 4" | 300 |
| 330 | 15' 9" | 12' 7" | 9' 6" | 7' 34" | 6' 4" | 4' 33" | 3' 2" | 2' 44" | 2' 25" | 2' 7" | 1' 49" | 1' 31" | 1' 13" | 55" | 36" | 18" | 9" | 5" | 4" | 330 |
| 350 | 14' 17" | 11' 25" | 8' 34" | 7' 0" | 5' 43" | 4' 18" | 2' 51" | 2' 34" | 2' 17" | 2' 0" | 1' 43" | 1' 26" | 1' 9" | 51" | 34" | 17" | 9" | 4" | 3" | 350 |
| 361 | 13' 51" | 11' 4" | 8' 19" | 6' 56" | 5' 32" | 4' 9" | 2' 46" | 2' 29" | 2' 13" | 1' 56" | 1' 40" | 1' 23" | 1' 6" | 50" | 34" | 17" | 8" | 4" | 3" | 361 |
| 380 | 13' 9" | 10' 32" | 7' 54" | 6' 35" | 5' 16" | 3' 57" | 2' 38" | 2' 22" | 2' 6" | 1' 51" | 1' 35" | 1' 19" | 1' 3" | 47" | 32" | 16" | 8" | 4" | 3" | 380 |
| 400 | 12' 30" | 10' 0" | 7' 30" | 6' 15" | 5' 0" | 3' 45" | 2' 30" | 2' 15" | 2' 0" | 1' 45" | 1' 30" | 1' 15" | 1' 0" | 45" | 30" | 15" | 8" | 4" | 3" | 400 |
| 415 | 12' 3" | 9' 40" | 7' 14" | 6' 2" | 4' 50" | 3' 37" | 2' 25" | 2' 10" | 1' 57" | 1' 41" | 1' 27" | 1' 12" | 58" | 43" | 29" | 15" | 7" | 4" | 3" | 415 |
| 425 | 11' 46" | 9' 26" | 7' 5" | 5' 53" | 4' 42" | 3' 32" | 2' 21" | 2' 7" | 1' 53" | 1' 39" | 1' 25" | 1' 11" | 56" | 42" | 28" | 14" | 7" | 4" | 3" | 425 |
| 440 | 11' 22" | 9' 6" | 6' 49" | 5' 41" | 4' 33" | 3' 24" | 2' 16" | 2' 2" | 1' 49" | 1' 35" | 1' 22" | 1' 8" | 55" | 41" | 27" | 14" | 7" | 3" | 3" | 440 |
| 450 | 11' 6" | 8' 53" | 6' 41" | 5' 34" | 4' 27" | 3' 20" | 2' 13" | 2' 0" | 1' 47" | 1' 33" | 1' 20" | 1' 7" | 53" | 40" | 27" | 13" | 7" | 3" | 3" | 450 |
| 460 | 10' 52" | 8' 42" | 6' 31" | 5' 26" | 4' 20" | 3' 15" | 2' 10" | 1' 57" | 1' 44" | 1' 31" | 1' 18" | 1' 5" | 52" | 39" | 26" | 13" | 6" | 3" | 3" | 460 |
| 475 | 10' 32" | 8' 25" | 6' 19" | 5' 16" | 4' 12" | 3' 9" | 2' 6" | 1' 54" | 1' 41" | 1' 28" | 1' 16" | 1' 3" | 51" | 38" | 25" | 13" | 6" | 3" | 2" | 475 |
| 492 | 10' 10" | 8' 8" | 6' 6" | 5' 5" | 4' 4" | 3' 3" | 2' 2" | 1' 50" | 1' 38" | 1' 25" | 1' 13" | 1' 1" | 49" | 37" | 24" | 12" | 6" | 3" | 2" | 492 |
| 500 | 10' 0" | 8' 0" | 6' 0" | 5' 0" | 4' 0" | 3' 0" | 2' 0" | 1' 48" | 1' 36" | 1' 24" | 1' 12" | 1' 0" | 48" | 36" | 24" | 12" | 6" | 3" | 2" | 500 |

| Speed | 20 | 25 | 50 | 100 | 200 | 300 | 400 | 500 | 600 | 700 | 800 | 900 | 1000 | 1500 | 2000 | 2500 | 3000 | 4000 | 5000 | Speed |
|---|---|---|---|---|---|---|---|---|---|---|---|---|---|---|---|---|---|---|---|---|
| 520 | 2″ | 3″ | 6″ | 12″ | 23″ | 35″ | 46″ | 58″ | 1′9″ | 1′21″ | 1′32″ | 1′44″ | 1′55″ | 2′53″ | 3′50″ | 4′48″ | 5′46″ | 7′41″ | 9′37″ | 520 |
| 550 | 2″ | 3″ | 6″ | 11″ | 22″ | 33″ | 44″ | 55″ | 1′5″ | 1′16″ | 1′27″ | 1′38″ | 1′49″ | 2′44″ | 3′39″ | 4′33″ | 5′28″ | 7′17″ | 9′6″ | 550 |
| 570 | 2″ | 3″ | 5″ | 11″ | 21″ | 32″ | 42″ | 53″ | 1′3″ | 1′14″ | 1′24″ | 1′35″ | 1′45″ | 2′38″ | 3′31″ | 4′23″ | 5′16″ | 7′1″ | 8′47″ | 570 |
| 600 | 2″ | 3″ | 5″ | 10″ | 20″ | 30″ | 40″ | 50″ | 1′0″ | 1′10″ | 1′20″ | 1′30″ | 1′40″ | 2′30″ | 3′20″ | 4′10″ | 5′0″ | 6′40″ | 8′20″ | 600 |
| 624 | 2″ | 2″ | 5″ | 10″ | 19″ | 29″ | 38″ | 48″ | 58″ | 1′7″ | 1′17″ | 1′27″ | 1′36″ | 2′24″ | 3′12″ | 4′0″ | 4′48″ | 6′24″ | 8′1″ | 624 |
| 656 | 2″ | 2″ | 4″ | 9″ | 18″ | 28″ | 37″ | 46″ | 55″ | 1′4″ | 1′13″ | 1′22″ | 1′31″ | 2′17″ | 3′3″ | 3′49″ | 4′35″ | 6′6″ | 7′37″ | 656 |
| 675 | 2″ | 2″ | 4″ | 9″ | 18″ | 27″ | 36″ | 44″ | 53″ | 1′2″ | 1′11″ | 1′20″ | 1′29″ | 2′13″ | 2′58″ | 3′42″ | 4′26″ | 5′55″ | 7′25″ | 675 |
| 690 | 2″ | 2″ | 4″ | 9″ | 17″ | 26″ | 35″ | 43″ | 52″ | 1′1″ | 1′10″ | 1′18″ | 1′27″ | 2′10″ | 2′53″ | 3′37″ | 4′20″ | 5′47″ | 7′15″ | 690 |
| 700 | 2″ | 2″ | 4″ | 9″ | 17″ | 25″ | 34″ | 43″ | 51″ | 1′0″ | 1′9″ | 1′17″ | 1′26″ | 2′9″ | 2′52″ | 3′35″ | 4′18″ | 5′43″ | 7′9″ | 700 |
| 720 | 2″ | 2″ | 4″ | 8″ | 17″ | 25″ | 33″ | 42″ | 50″ | 58″ | 1′7″ | 1′15″ | 1′23″ | 2′5″ | 2′46″ | 3′29″ | 4′10″ | 5′34″ | 6′57″ | 720 |
| 740 | 2″ | 2″ | 4″ | 8″ | 16″ | 24″ | 32″ | 41″ | 49″ | 57″ | 1′5″ | 1′13″ | 1′21″ | 2′2″ | 2′43″ | 3′23″ | 4′4″ | 5′24″ | 6′45″ | 740 |
| 750 | 2″ | 2″ | 4″ | 8″ | 16″ | 24″ | 32″ | 40″ | 48″ | 56″ | 1′4″ | 1′12″ | 1′20″ | 2′0″ | 2′40″ | 3′20″ | 4′0″ | 5′20″ | 6′40″ | 750 |
| 755 | 2″ | 2″ | 4″ | 8″ | 16″ | 24″ | 32″ | 40″ | 48″ | 56″ | 1′4″ | 1′12″ | 1′19″ | 1′59″ | 2′39″ | 3′19″ | 3′59″ | 5′18″ | 6′37″ | 755 |
| 775 | 1″ | 2″ | 4″ | 8″ | 15″ | 23″ | 32″ | 39″ | 46″ | 54″ | 1′2″ | 1′10″ | 1′17″ | 1′56″ | 2′35″ | 3′14″ | 3′53″ | 5′10″ | 6′27″ | 775 |
| 790 | 1″ | 2″ | 3″ | 7″ | 15″ | 23″ | 30″ | 38″ | 45″ | 53″ | 1′1″ | 1′8″ | 1′16″ | 1′54″ | 2′32″ | 3′10″ | 3′48″ | 5′4″ | 6′20″ | 790 |
| 800 | 1″ | 2″ | 3″ | 7″ | 15″ | 22″ | 30″ | 37″ | 44″ | 52″ | 1′0″ | 1′7″ | 1′15″ | 1′52″ | 2′30″ | 3′8″ | 3′45″ | 5′0″ | 6′15″ | 800 |
| 825 | 1″ | 2″ | 3″ | 7″ | 15″ | 22″ | 29″ | 36″ | 43″ | 51″ | 58″ | 1′5″ | 1′13″ | 1′49″ | 2′25″ | 3′2″ | 3′38″ | 4′51″ | 6′4″ | 825 |
| Speed | 20 | 25 | 50 | 100 | 200 | 300 | 400 | 500 | 600 | 700 | 800 | 900 | 1000 | 1500 | 2000 | 2500 | 3000 | 4000 | 5000 | Speed |

The recorded values are equally applicable, whether the calculation is made in yards or in metric system. In the yard system the figures shown in the head-line mean distances in yards and the figures registered in side columns mean speeds in yards per minute rate. When using the metric system the registered distances represent lengths in metres and the figures in the speed columns refer to metres per minute rate.

The time necessary to cover an intermediate or longer distance as registered can be obtained by addition of part values.

Fractions involved in the data are rounded up to the nearest whole number.

The formula for the calculation is: divide the distance by the speed and multiply the dividend achieved by 60. The result gives the time in seconds. For example, the time necessary for covering 1280 yd. at a speed of 750 yd./min. is: 1280 ÷ 750 = 1.707 ; 1.707 × 60 = 102.42 seconds( 1′ 42″).

(300 m. per minute = 18 km. per hour. Each 50 m. per minute
increase means 3 km. per hour acceleration.)

With practice you will find that your results become more
and more consistent, indicating development of the required sense
of judgment.  In the early stages of practice it is enough to be
sure of the three basic rates of speed, since this will be sufficient to
prevent serious blunders.

The rider's next aim should be to learn the intermediate rates of
speed, as well as some of those which are below or above the
used limits, and identify them with certainty.

METHODS OF CALCULATION FOR FIXING THE USED SPEED AND THE
NECESSARY RATES

In order to complete properly the horse's training and to be able
to draw up a correct riding plan, the rider must have knowledge
in ascertaining:

the necessary speed; and

the amount of time during which a certain distance must be
covered by the use of a stipulated speed.

*What is the speed when the time and the distance are fixed?*
*(What speed should be used for covering a fixed distance in a given
time?)*

Divide the distance in yards (or metres) by the seconds measured
(or required); then

multiply the result thus obtained by 60, which gives the actual
rate of speed.

In other words, this figure indicates the distance in yards (or in
metres) which the horse covers in one minute (60 seconds).   For
instance, if it has covered 1,000 yards in 133 seconds, then

$$1,000 \div 133 = 7.5 \text{ and } 7.5 \times 60 = 450$$

Thus the horse has shown a speed of 450 yards per minute if the
distance has been measured in yards and 450 m. per minute if
measured in metres.

*How much time is needed to cover a measured distance at a given
speed?*

Since the calculation is more complicated than the former one,
Table No. 10 has been compiled in order to facilitate the rider's
work.  From this one can immediately work out the time needed

for covering a certain distance by the use of the more important rates of speed.

### THE SENSATIONS OF JUMPING AS FELT BY THE RIDER

In order to teach the horse the proper way to jump, it is indispensable for the rider to be aware of those sensations which the movements of the jump convey to him. In fact, a knowledge of these sensations affords considerable accuracy in judging the quality of the actual jump, and thus this faculty of judgment is most useful in recognizing the kind of work that should be emphasized in the horse's schooling.

The sensations conveyed by the jumping movement will be described for both a correct and a defective jump. The defective jump will be illustrated by two extreme forms so that the rider can identify those cases which fall in between.

### *The sensations of a jump performed in the right style*

At the approach to the obstacle

The well-educated horse conveys a sensation of a conscious determination and certainty, coupled with a resolute forward impulsion. This sensation counteracts any uncertainty the rider may have as to the spot where the horse will take off. He feels sure of himself and it is quite irrelevant to him whether the take-off occurs too far or close, as he will always be able to follow the movements correctly. Thus the rider is possessed by a distinct sensation that the horse can take off with determination even if it is left alone. At the same time, he must be confident that if he should initiate the take-off himself the horse would obey and carry out the task with equal determination.

At the thrust-off and the take-off

When the horse thrusts off with its leading foreleg and completes the take-off by the action of its hind quarters it creates somewhat the same impression as the first phase of the galloping stride, during which the horse lifts the rider up by pressing its shoulders under the thighs (see page 31).

In the phase of suspension

While the horse is rising into the air it makes first an upward movement and then, while balancing, a forward movement with its neck. The rider can follow these movements of the animal smoothly, since it will seem to him that his upper body is linked up closely with the horse and with the trend of its movement.

At the apex of the jump, while the animal is basculing, the arching of its back becomes most distinct and the rider feels as if he is being lifted higher and further than anticipated. There is no push in this sensation, but a pleasant swing forward.

At the landing

In the descending curve of the jump, especially at the moment of touching the ground, the rider feels that the horse is drawing him back to itself through its movements, so that he can follow it smoothly without difficulty.

To summarize, the correct action in jumping is an elastic thrust off the ground, flowing into the jump itself, which seems a smooth continuation of the initiating movement. As such it produces a distinct and agreeable sensation in the rider, a feeling that he is one with the horse while passing over the obstacle. The jump becomes a common undertaking. During the whole series of movements there is no tug, push or jolt; the action gives a delightful sensation of flying together with the horse.

*The sensation of the jump with hollow back, soft or stiff*

Some horses when jumping tend to hollow their back by slackening the muscles and in consequence the usual arching of the back fails to appear. This occurrence is generally known as a hollow soft back.

The hollow stiff back appears when the back of the horse becomes concave by contraction of the muscles.

Both forms adversely affect the jump and reduce its quality, even though a few horses have performed well despite a stiff hollow back.

Generally speaking, the cause of the hollow back is lack of schooling, but it can also be traced to external interference, such as the rider's falling back into the saddle, overburdening the animal, stiff resistance or pulling with the hands at the take-off and landing.

The sensations felt at a jump being performed with hollow back are as follows:

At the approach of the obstacle

While riding towards the fence the horse shows a desire to go forward, but it cannot express the sensation of determination and certainty, so that the rider feels that his mount is uncertain regarding the take-off. Such a horse particularly needs support from the rider, but its physical deficiency hampers its movements and reduces the readiness to obey orders.

At the thrust-off and take-off

If these actions happen to be far from the obstacle, the horse seems to jerk its body with a sudden, forward-directed movement into the jump, producing the sensation of a hard forward pull.

If these actions happen too close to the fence, the rider's sensation is as if the animal had jumped off all four legs at once.

If such a horse lacks determination to go forward, the sensation of uncertainty can increase to such an extent that even an experienced horseman may find himself 'left behind'.

After the thrust-off this horse also drops behind the bit and, as it does not stretch its neck forward, there is nothing for the rider to follow with his hands.

In the actual phase of the jump

During this phase the rider feels that the animal simply throws itself over the obstacle. He has no impression of lifting and at the top of the trajectory he feels that his body has a tendency to fall back.

At the landing

After a jolt the horse tends to rush, either ignoring the bit or pulling, and the rider will find it very difficult to follow the animal's awkward movements.

*Sensation of the jump in a stretched posture*

When the horse's spring system is not collected and not 'wound' enough for the action, but instead is stiffly stretched out, the jump will be performed in a stretched posture. Under these circumstances the horse is incapable of executing a distinct thrust-off and take-off.

There may still be a continuity of movement during the jump, but the animal with insufficient thrust-off will make a very flat trajectory instead of arching over the fence. Such a jump gives the rider a certain 'flat' sensation, as if the horse wished to brush through the obstacle.

Such a horse generally pulls, not only while approaching the fence, but also, after landing, when moving away from it.

## THE CORRECT PERFORMANCE OF THE JUMP
### THE APPROACH TO THE OBSTACLE

The horse should proceed in a cadenced and supple state, maintaining contact with the reins, thighs and the rider's legs and obeying their signals submissively. In this state the rider can easily keep the animal between his hands, thighs and legs without disrupting its motion. Thus he is always able to 'cock' the horse's spring system (increasing its collection) and release it (for the take-off).

In order to achieve this aim the rider should concentrate on the easiness of his mount (see page 13), the impulsion and liveliness of its action (see page 237) and the freedom of its shoulders, especially on the side of the leading foreleg (see page 100). In such a state the horse is enabled to move energetically and elastically in a quick cadence, bringing its energies to life. The creation of these qualities in the animal's motion should occur during its general preparation for jumping.

In addition to this general information, we shall now examine each of the demands mentioned, with special regard to the present subject.

### The easiness of the horse during the approach

Throughout the approach the horse should display a high degree of easiness in keeping rein-contact and retain its submission to the rider's demands.

The stronger the contact, the more the horse must bring its hocks under the body. In this connection one can state that the more the hocks support the body, the lighter the forehand, which reduces the strength of the contact. Thus a strong contact is usually a sign that the animal does not support itself with its hocks and is not collected for the jump. If, in spite of conveying a light sensation of contact to the rider's hands, the horse ignores the retarding signal or tries to resist or evade it (i.e. the animal does not obey), it is also sure to ignore the rein signal for collection and the leg signal for the take-off itself. In this case both the take-off and the jump will be uncertain. (Regarding strength of contact, see page 105.)

### The importance of impulsion and liveliness in jumping

Impulsion 'draws' the animal to negotiate the jump; liveliness 'lifts' it over the fence. Without impulsion the horse refuses the jump; and without liveliness it cannot clear the height properly. The combination of these two forces is essential in order to perform the jump correctly.

As a means of reminding the animal that it must preserve its animation when approaching the obstacle, the rider should support his leg actions by taps of the whip. If they are properly exercised, the hand movements involved will not alter the continuity of the rein-contact. However, it will facilitate exercising these movements if the rider uses a long whip as described on page 46.

The biting effect of the tap stimulates the horse's liveliness, which is already sufficient to push the animal over the obstacle. Repeated taps mitigate the resistance which puts a brake on the horse's impulsion and simultaneously increases its liveliness. Thus they aid the horse to overcome the obstacle.

In certain cases the rider should apply the tap or taps when he is still rather far away from the take-off spot. This may be necessary when he observes a loss in the impulsion and liveliness, or he may do it for preventive purposes, in order to accumulate surplus energy which the horse may need if it is confronted by a particularly impressive obstacle. In this way the rider will enable the animal to overcome its impediments in advance and to arrive at the fence in a state of complete readiness for the execution of the jump.

A hit by the whip may also be applied at the last moment before the take-off, but only for the purpose of increasing the horse's impulsion. It is a very delicate action, since it can hinder as much as it can support the horse in jumping. This is due to the facts that

by changing the position of the reins and hands the continuity of the rein-contact becomes suddenly upset. The horse then loses its balance at the last moment, when the need for balance is greatest;

the rider cannot execute his last collecting action (see page 332), which is so important in promoting the clarity of the jump;

in carrying out the change he is obliged to make certain more or less lengthy preparations, during which the animal slips out of control. In such an uncontrolled state it will jump only when it already has an ample amount of natural impulsion. If this is the case, the use of the whip would be superfluous and unjustified. On the other hand, if the animal does not have any natural impulsion, it will (being out of control) swerve away from the obstacle in spite of the hit of the whip.

Therefore this method should only be used by skilled riders who are able to preserve the continuity of the rein-contact and maintain control over the horse during the manipulation of the whip—and then only in exceptionally critical cases.

During the schooling period it is desirable for the instructor (from the ground) to ensure impulsion for the take-off by supplementing the stroke of the whip by a switch towards the horse. He should make the switching movement at the first sign of resistance, a few strides before the take-off, or just at the starting moment of the action.

### The freedom of shoulders during the approach

A free position of the shoulder on the leading side facilitates the engagement of the leading foreleg both during the approach and in executing the take-off stride. When the shoulder on the critical side is free the leading foreleg can perform its thrust-off action undisturbed and elevate the forehand from the ground more determinedly.

In conclusion, the rider should teach his horse from the early stages of training to approach obstacles in the manner described. This is necessary so that the animal will move correctly by instinct when it becomes confronted with a more serious task requiring all its energy and skill.

### THE LAST STRIDES BEFORE THE OBSTACLE

The last four or five strides in front of the obstacle should be used to reach an appropriate take-off spot and for the preparation for the take-off.

The location of the take-off spot has a major bearing on the execution of the jump. Therefore it is important for the rider to develop his skill in finding the proper take-off spot to the highest possible degree. The accomplishment of this depends on two main conditions:

first, the rider must be able to judge, from a distance of three or four strides in front of the obstacle, the place where the horse will take off if he does not alter its speed; and

secondly, the horse must respond to the slightest guidance from the rider.

If the rider sees, during the last strides, that the horse will arrive at a poor take-off spot, he can alter the length of the strides enough to provide a better one. Altering the length of strides can be achieved in the following manner:

by lengthening the last one or two strides and letting the horse spurt forward from a momentary collection (see page 124); or

by shortening the last one or two strides, ending with drive-on to ensure the maintenance of impulsion.

The data shown in Table No. 8/a clearly indicate the effect which change of speed has on the position of the take-off spot. The knowledge of these figures will dispel any doubt as to whether or not it is possible to make substantial corrections within a short distance. But the rider must also recognize that unnecessary interference, even if it seems insignificant, can easily spoil a propitious situation. Unfortunately, habitual 'checking' is common, especially in the case of inexperienced riders. In their ignorance they habitually break the horse's stride at a considerable distance from the obstacle without any definite reason. The result is aimless checking, because even the normal cadence of the animal is upset by it.

To sum up, it is permissible for the rider to change the speed, and thus alter the length of the stride, but only when such alteration is absolutely necessary. Indiscriminate 'checking', carried out long before reaching the obstacle, is proof of two conditions:

either the rider is unable to control (animate or retard) the horse smoothly by discreet signals, revealing that the horse is not sufficiently schooled for the task;

or he is incapable of judging the take-off spot accurately from a distance of three to four strides (40-50 feet, 12-16 m.). In this case the rider is not far enough advanced for the task.

From the above comments it can be deduced that

the maximum rate of speed which should be used in approaching an obstacle is one in which *the horse can respond* to the

rider's aids promptly and obediently. The lower the standard
of obedience, the slower the speed must be, and the smaller
the dimensions of the obstacles that should be attempted;
the rider should select a speed at which *he can clearly judge* the
situation.

It is true that even the best rider can misjudge a situation and
not realize his error until it is too late. Such cases, however, must
be exceptions and the rider must strive for consistent soundness
of judgment.

### Learning to ascertain the proper take-off spot

In developing a sound technique for ascertaining the proper
take-off spot a knowledge of the following features of the animal's
jumping mechanism will prove useful.

The take-off point is identical with that spot where the horse
executes the thrust-off with its leading foreleg in the last normal
canter (gallop) stride before leaving the ground. In other words,
the take-off starts with the thrust-off of the leading foreleg.

Thus, in establishing the proper spot for the take-off, the rider
must 'arrange' the animal's strides while approaching the fence so
that the particular thrust-off shall occur at a spot which lies at a
good take-off distance from the obstacle.

Furthermore, the rider must realize that in the take-off stride,
just as in the canter (gallop) stride, suspension begins when the
horse thrusts off with its leading foreleg. The only difference is
that before a jump the thrust-off of the foreleg is preceded by the
setting of the two hind legs for the completion of the take-off.

In each stride at a canter *only this* particular phase (prior to
suspension) is appropriate to the execution of the take-off.
Consequently, using an average length of stride, the possible
take-off points will appear in about every 12 feet (3.60 m.). How
appropriate this phase of the stride is in relation to the obstacle
determines whether the take-off will be too close, good or too long.

If the horse misses the take-off from a certain point, a regular
take-off cannot occur until the same phase of the next stride (i.e.
after covering of 10-12 feet or 3-3.75 m., according to the
actual speed).

With this understanding of mechanics of the take-off let us see
how the rider can improve his knowledge in practice.

His first task is to learn to anticipate, at a canter or gallop without jumping, the spot where the horse will make its next thrust-off action. Having acquired the sense, the rider should further improve his judgment, so that he learns to anticipate the thrust-off spot for two, three and eventually four strides away. In this way he will develop skill in seeing the take-off spot from a fairly long distance.

In the next phase of training the rider should execute the following exercise:

Select a fairly large area and lay some narrow marks ($1$-$1\frac{1}{2}$ feet or 30-40 cm. wide) on the ground at irregular distances, placed crosswise to the direction of the course of riding. The simplest and most practical marker is some loose straw. The markers represent the obstacles.

Ride over the course at a calm canter and comment loudly on the position of the take-off whenever approaching a marker. At the beginning of the practice it is sufficient to make the comment about one stride from the marker. Later on, when one's judgment has improved, increase the distance so that with practice one can estimate the take-off point with certainty even from a distance of about four to five strides.

The correctness of one's judgment can be verified by the markers in the following manner:

if the horse is too near to it at the moment of thrust-off of the leading foreleg, or has stepped on it, it shows that the spacing of the strides would not afford an appropriate take-off;

on the other hand, if the spot of the thrust-off falls about 5-6 feet ($1.50$-$1.80$ m.) from the marker, the spacing of the strides would by synchronized for a jump.

Since the present exercise serves principally to improve and check the rider's sense of judgment, it would be premature to attempt any alteration in the position of the 'take-off'.

When, however, a degree of accuracy has been achieved in the judgment, one can begin to experiment with the regulation of the 'approach', still using the markers.

Besides these introductory exercises, which do not involve actual obstacles, the rider should use every opportunity, while approaching even the most insignificant fence, of developing his judgment. He should always correlate the beats of the hoofs taking the horse towards the jump with the position of the obstacle. This practice will effectively sharpen the rider's judgment.

*Familiarizing the horse with different take-off possibilities*

Just as the rider must learn to appreciate the importance of the position of the take-off spot, and the possibilities which can arise in various circumstances, so must the horse.

Natural instinct will help most horses to find a good spot for taking off. Led by this instinct the animal will try to adjust its last strides while approaching the obstacle so that it can arrive on a spot from which the execution of the jump will be facilitated. But instinct alone is not sufficiently reliable. The horse's sense of judgment must be developed during the early stages of its training, when the execution of small jumps means no special exertion. Work over miniature obstacles during the loosening exercises or any other jumps which are carried out with loose reins (see pages 265 and 283) are indicated for the purpose.

During the later schooling for jumping the animal must become familiar with jumping from take-off points which are somewhat longer or shorter than normal. In achieving this aim the take-off regulating devices will prove of considerable assistance. With their aid the rider can exercise a certain amount of control over the horse's actions and can create whatever take-off positions are desired. As the rider knows in advance what sort of situation he has arranged, he can maintain a feeling of certainty which is passed on to the horse.

The crux of the method is frequently to alter the take-off distance with the aid of the regulator and thus face the animal with a variety of different situations. In executing the exercise the rider must give his take-off signal exactly at the desired point so that the animal will learn to accept and obey it at any time. Thus, between the regulating effect of the device and the assistance of the rider, the horse's knowledge of various take-off possibilities and its self-confidence can be greatly improved.

There are some horses which instinctively prefer to take off from a longer and others from a shorter distance. Such tendencies should be compensated for by placing the emphasis on the kind of take-off which appears to be more difficult for the horse.

During its more advanced stage of schooling the horse should get confidence in standing back while the approach occurs at a slow speed and taking off close to the obstacle when it proceeds at an increased speed. This confidence will inspire the animal to act with determination also in situations of most critical nature, and its determination will help it in overcoming encountered difficulties with success.

Carefully executed and often practised exercises for the achievement of the first aim are especially important. Carry them out at the beginning at a trot and later on at a slow canter (height of the obstacle about 2 feet to 3 feet 3 inches, or 0.60 to 1 m.). To begin with, make the animal supple and then, while maintaining complete lightness, approach the fence at a rhythmical, lively, but slow speed. If it happens that the horse reaches the fence at an odd take-off spot, animate it to stand back mainly by your unrestricted forward strive and partly by a take-off signal. During the take-off and the consecutive phases of suspension and landing the rider's complete following attitude is of utmost importance. *This* is what inspires the horse at the next attempt at making a distant take-off and establishes in due time its confidence in standing back at a slow speed. (The application of the take-off regulator can be of great assistance.)

*The horse's final preparation for the take-off*

The phase of the jump in which its final preparation takes place is confined to the last normal galloping stride before the take-off and the starting moment of the take-off stride.

Before the moment of the thrust-off and take-off a final collection and cocking of the animal's spring system must occur in order to ensure sufficient velocity. The timing and execution of the necessary functions is described and illustrated in Fig. No. 92.

The strength of the involved function depends on the horse's actual state of education. Nevertheless, it is important that the rider's initiative should be followed immediately by the horse. If energetic actions are needed, and can be applied without confusing the animal's mind, the rider can avail himself of these. However, only riders with great experience will succeed in collecting their horses by such actions, and only then if the animal has a great natural impulsion. In general, it is far more profitable to school the horse a bit longer than to risk spoiling it by employing such energetic actions incorrectly.

With practice the execution of the collecting function must become *quite invisible*, and this is the state when its application is indeed correct. Reaching this stage in the education of the rider and the horse, clear jumps will become routine and faulty ones exceptions.

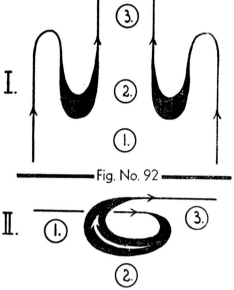

Fig. No. 92

1. During the last normal canter (gallop) stride:
   rein maintains contact with 'pushing feeling';
   animation, mainly by thigh pressure.

2. During the take-off stride:
   a) in the moment of the hoof-fall of the leading foreleg:
      brief collecting rein action with short but smooth transitions, executed with elastic muscle functions; the hand action shows a mainly downwards (only slightly backwards) directed movement.

   b) in the moment of the hoof-fall of the hind legs:
      take-off signal (animation) by the legs and thighs.

3. During the suspension (after the take-off):
   contact maintained in 'pushing feeling', hands follow the stretching movement of the neck.

Diagram I shows the function of both hands seen from above.

Diagram II shows the function seen from the side.

In order to acquire the necessary feeling and skill for the execution of the collecting function make the following exercises:

First, ride over an undulating course or continually recross a shallow ditch. (These ground formations extract from the animal similar movements in a slowed down succession to an actual jump.) While riding at a trot, give a driving signal each time the horse performs its last stride before reaching the ascending plane of the course. Adjoining to this, in the moment just before it is stepping on to the slope, execute the coiling function of the hands, terminating in complete 'following' while the animal is ascending the bank.

If the horse reacts to the procedure with a smooth half-halt ending in an *energetic stepping forward action*, the functions employed were correct.

On reaching this stage make the same exercise at a slow canter.

Next take two cavaletti, set at 20-21 feet (6-6.30 m.) apart from each other. Approach the first one at a trot and, while keeping rein-contact, let the horse perform the jump without any further aid. After the jump remain cantering and during the non-jumping stride give the driving signal. In the next moment, when the leading foreleg touches the ground, execute the collecting function.

This exercise, by its clearly articulated indication of the exact moments for the performance of the rider's involved actions, is an excellent means for his improvement.

The execution is correct when the take-off in front of the second cavaletti is energetic and the horse performs a well-arched jump over it.

Practise the above exercises often and in long series so that the execution of the movements involved becomes instinctive to you.

When the rider has acquired the necessary feeling by the means of the recommended exercises he can start practising the collecting function also in front of individual obstacles.

It must be emphasized, however, that before reaching the correct performing ability it is better to omit the application of the collecting function both during the horse's schooling in jumping and during competitions.

THE THRUST-OFF AND THE TAKE-OFF

Linked to the moment of the 'coiling' of the horse's spring system, the thrust-off and the take-off take place.

In these actions the will of the rider and the horse must become united. If the animal is gradually trained for its task in an atmosphere of mutual understanding, this aim can be achieved.

In order to encourage the animal and increase its determination, the rider should, immediately *after* his collecting function, make a synchronized squeeze with his legs to signal the take-off. His hands must not disturb the horse's balance, not even by suddenly loosening the reins. In this way the animal can maintain the collection necessary for the increased exertion required to lift the body into the air.

During this phase of the jump the rider should bend his upper body more forward, lift his seat a bit more from the saddle and ease the pressure on the stirrups, so that he does not hinder the arching of the back. In this position he is able to follow the movements of the horse's head and neck flexibly with his hands and arms and maintain contact with the mouth.

As we could see in the foregoing explanations, the rider must execute, during the short time of the last normal stride and during the take-off stride, various functions and movements with a

definite timing and in a very quick succession. Acquiring the
necessary performing ability needs perseverance with the recommended exercises. The effort is not in vain, especially in view of
the solution of more critical tasks. These arise mainly when the
rider fails to bring the horse to a good take-off spot and the animal
must take off either too near to, or too far from, the obstacle.

In order to provide the horse with the basis of a determined and
energetic take-off in such difficult situations, the application of
the collecting function has a great importance. In such cases the
rider must decide during the last but one stride with a reflex sense
on the intended solution and act *resolutely* according to this
decision for the collection and the extraction of the ensuing take-off
action of the horse. If the rider can weigh up reliably the meaning
of the actual situations, if he can impose his will on the horse and
this obeys his demands, the partners can overcome situations that
seemed hopeless.

The rider's decision will depend largely on the animal's individual abilities. If the horse is capable of executing the take-off
from a long distance, the animation, collection and the giving of
the take-off impulsion should occur one stride earlier than in the
case of horses which prefer a closer take-off.

If the horse should act against the rider's decision and stand back
instead of making an additional stride, the rider must avoid with all
his power remaining behind the horse's movement and pulling on
the reins. In critical situations it is best to give the reins altogether
to the horse and let it complete the jump quite freely.

In the other case, when the animal after its collection makes an
additional stride instead of taking off, the situation is not very
critical because the horse, due to its collected state, is enabled to
make a highly-arched jump. But the situation can become very
critical if the rider, by the confusing effect of the sudden change
in the anticipated movement, loses the continuity of the contact
with the horse. Riders can easily make this fault of dropping the
reins when the horse makes its additional stride after the collection.
Then, during the take-off and the jump, they remain behind the
movement, pulling simultaneously the reins. The result is that
the arching in the jump cannot develop and the horse's quarters
become pressed down on to the fence (especially if it is a spread
one). Thus such riders, instead of facilitating the horse's effort,
hamper it in the execution of its difficult task.

Riders who are still not prepared for the correct execution of the collecting function should also restrict their supporting functions—in addition to their complete following conduct—in critical cases only to preserving the horse's impulsion and liveliness. The animal should choose between the alternatives and act on its own accord. Therefore it is important to retain and improve the horse's ability to decide for itself.

### The preliminary phase of suspension

This immediately follows the moment of take-off and is the beginning of the ascending phase of the trajectory. During this short phase it is still possible to give the horse another signal for collection, which is effected by a *gentle* pulling of the reins and by a co-ordinated pressing with the legs.

By this collecting action the animal will tuck its legs closer to its body, enabling it to clear a greater height without increasing the lift of its body. However, the rider must be very careful about the timing and strength of the signal. If it is applied too late or too vigorously, it may easily spoil the bascule.

During the early stages of schooling, while jumping low and simple obstacles, it is not necessary to employ this action, which should be reserved for moments of greater need.

### The phase of basculing

In this phase the rider should ensure ample freedom for the horse to stretch its neck considerably forward, enabling the head to perform its balancing movement freely during the jump. For this purpose the rider should increase the angle of his forward position and sensitively follow the horse's mouth with his hands. He must pay special attention to the moment of basculing when the horse, at the top of the arch of the jump, tips over from the ascending phase into the descent. Here it does not matter if contact is momentarily disrupted. The main thing is to permit the animal complete freedom.

#### THE LANDING

The horse's movements in the landing phase of the jump must be followed smoothly by the rider so that he does not fall roughly against the horse's back. In order to save the animal from discomfort, he should also avoid falling on to the stirrups in this critical moment. At the same time, the hands should not interfere with the characteristic upward directed movement of the head and neck, since otherwise they can, by the pain caused, easily break the swing of the back. If rein-contact has been interrupted, its re-establishment should occur when the animal has already made up to three strides after the landing.

After landing, the regularity of the horse should quickly be restored. It must be firmly prevented from turning of its own accord and not allowed to hurry or slow down. A joyful buck, however, should not be restrained instantly.

A pleasant sensation of landing increases the animal's enjoyment and keenness in jumping; any discomfort spoils its ambition for the performance of the next jump. Therefore the rider must improve his skill in following and supporting the horse during landing with the same care as he practises steering the animal during the previous phases of the jump.

## Take-off and Landing Distances and Factors Affecting their Measurement

### NORMAL TAKE-OFF AND LANDING DISTANCES

(With special reference to measurement of distances in combinations)

We have already described methods which help the rider and horse to identify suitable take-off distances and also means of bringing the horse to the right point for taking off. We have not yet discussed, however, what the actual take-off distances are as expressed in figures. Since this is an important matter, we will deal with it in some detail.

Because of the close relationship between the take-off and landing our examination will include the measurement of landing distances as well. A graphic representation of these distances is in Fig. No. 93.

*The normal take-off distance* refers to the particular take-off point from which the horse can perform the jump with a minimum of extra strain or exertion. In practice the animal can enjoy such conditions within the area which starts about one-eighth (12.5 per cent.) before and extends about one-eighth (12.5 per cent.) beyond the calculated correct take-off distance.

GRAPHIC REPRESENTATION OF THE TAKE-OFF AND LANDING AREAS

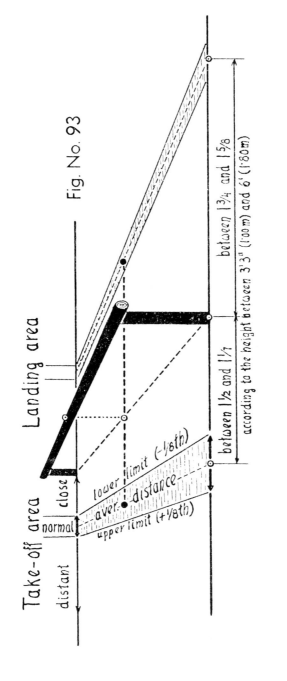

Fig. No. 93

At a slow parcours speed (see Table No. 8/a) the average length of the take-off and landing distances should be reduced by 7·5 per cent, and at a fast parcours speed increased by 15 per cent. The increase at a steeplechase speed is sometimes 50 per cent. or more.

*The landing distance* is regarded as the distance from the landing side of the obstacle to the spot where the horse touches the ground after the jump.

Generally speaking, the rider will be less concerned with its regulation than with that of the take-off distance, since it tends to remain reasonably uniform irrespective of the manner of the preceding take-off. The rider can, however, exercise some influence on its length by regulating the speed and degree of liveliness employed for the jump.

### DETERMINING THE NORMAL TAKE-OFF AND LANDING DISTANCES

The basic lengths of normal take-off and landing distances are based on a jump over a vertical obstacle which has no spread. These basic values, adjusted for various heights and the three main speeds, are shown in Table No. 11. In applying these distances compensation must be made for:

the 'type' of the obstacle (it affects mainly the take-off distance, except in so far as spreads are involved) and its basic height;

the position of the ground-line (which affects mainly the take-off distance);

the breadth of the obstacle (which influences mainly the landing distance, but, depending on the type of the obstacle, may also have a bearing on the take-off distance as well);

Let us now examine the above points, seeing how they apply to various obstacles and how they influence the performance of the jump.

### *The type of the obstacle and its influence on the basic height*

The type of a particular obstacle, as far as the take-off and landing conditions are concerned, is determined by their decisive heights and spread and the proportion between these elements.

Bearing this in mind, the following different types can be enumerated:

vertical (upright) obstacles without spread;

obstacles with sloping frontal plane (without spread);

obstacles with ascending structure;

upright obstacles with spread;

spread obstacles without height (ditches); and

combinations of the above types in the same obstacle.

## Table No. 11

BASIC VALUES OF THE NORMAL TAKE-OFF AND LANDING DISTANCES

| Height of the obstacle | Take-off distance | | | Landing distance | | | Figures, in accordance with the main average speed. |
|---|---|---|---|---|---|---|---|
| | Proportion to the height, and actual measurement according to the three main speeds. | | | | | | |
| | slow 350y/min | main average 415y/min. | fast 492y/min | slow 325m/min | main average 380m/min. | fast 450m/min | |
| 3'3" 1·00m | 1½ | | | 1¾ | | | (1.) 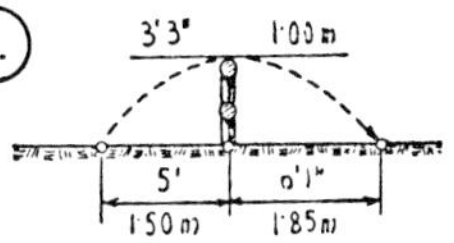 |
| | 4'7" 1·40m | 5' 1·50m | 5'9" 1·75m | 5'7" 1·70m | 6'1" 1·85m | 6'11" 2·10m | |
| 3'11"(4') 1·20m | 1⅓ | | | 1⅖ | | | (2.) 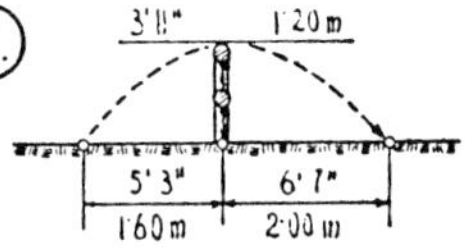 |
| | 5' 1·50m | 5'3" 1·60m | 6'1" 1·85m | 5'11" 1·80m | 6'7" 2·00m | 7'5" 2·25m | |
| (4'7")4'6" 1·40m | 1¼ | | | 1³⁄₇ | | | (3.) 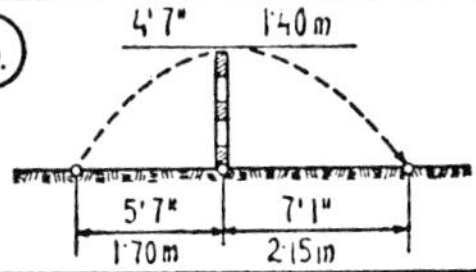 |
| | 5'3" 1·60m | 5'7" 1·70m | 6'5" 1·95m | 6'3" 1·90m | 7'1" 2·15m | 7'11" 2·40m | |
| 5'3" 1·60m | 1⅛ | | | 1⅜ | | | (4.) 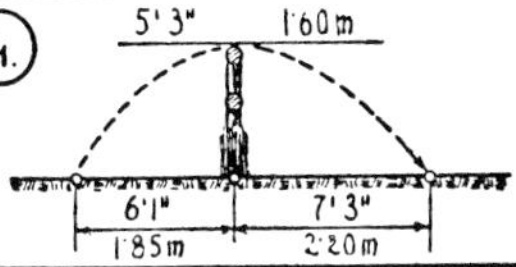 |
| | 5'7" 1·70m | 6'1" 1·85m | 6'9" 2·05m | 6'7" 2·00m | 7'3" 2·20m | 8'1" 2·45m | |
| (5'11") 6' 1·80m | 1⅛ | | | 1²⁄₈ | | | (5.) 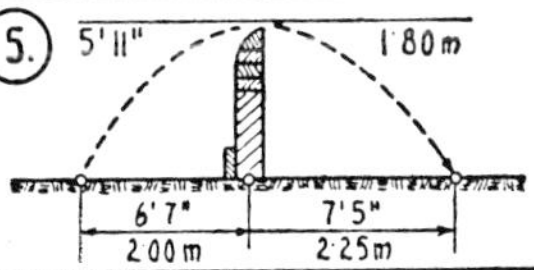 |
| | 6'1" 1·85m | 6'7" 2·00m | 7'7" 2·30m | 6'9" 2·05m | 7'5" 2·25m | 8'5" 2·55m | |

The data are assessed with special regard to combinations. In cases of single obstacles, however, they can be increased up to a height of 5 feet (1.50 metres) by ¼ (25%); at 5 feet 6 inches (1.65 metres) by ⅕ (20%); at 6 feet (1.80 metres) and over by ⅛ (12.5%) of the particular value indicated in the Table.

When making calculations for ascertaining take-off and landing distances those values should be employed from the present Table which comply with the 'basic height' of the obstacle.

The '*basic height*' of the obstacle is determined by the *addition* of the height indicated by the 'type' of the fence (it is either its actual or a calculated medium height, see Table No. 12) and the value of the '*spread coefficient*' being 1½ inches (3.5 centimetres) for each foot (30 centimetres) of the existing spread (including ground-line) between the take-off side and the highest part of the obstacle.

## Table No. 12

### THE OBSTACLE TYPES AND THE CALCULATION OF THEIR 'BASIC HEIGHT'

| Type of obstacle | Decisive proportion | Calculation of the „basic-height" | Figures with take-off & landing dists. acc.to T-s No. 11-15. |
|---|---|---|---|
| vertical (upright) without spread | $\frac{1}{1}$ <br> $4'+0'=4'$ <br> $\frac{0'+0'=0'}{4'}$ <br> $4/4=\frac{1}{1}$ | the actual height of the obstacle. <br> $4'$ (1·20m) | |
| sloping | betω.½ and $\frac{1}{3}$ <br> $4'+2'=6'$ <br> $\frac{2'+2'=4'}{2'}$ <br> $2/6=\frac{1}{3}$ | the height of the top plus spread coefficient <br> $4'+3''=4'3''$  1·20+0·07=1·27m <br><br> The front element must be regarded as a ground-line. | |
| ascending | betω.⅓ and $\frac{1}{6}$ <br> $4'+5'=9'$ <br> $\frac{1'8''+5=6·8'}{2'4''}$ <br> $2'4''/9=\frac{1}{37}$ | medium height between the top and middle element plus spread-coefficient <br> $3'6''+8''=4'2''$  1·05+0·18=1·23m <br><br> The front element must be regarded as a ground-line. | |
| moderately — upright with spread | betω.⅙ and $\frac{1}{16}$ <br> $4'+4'=8'$ <br> $\frac{3'+4'=7'}{1'}$ <br> $\frac{1}{8}$ | average of the take-off and landing sides plus spread-coefficient <br> $3'6''+6''=4'$  1·05+0·15=1·20m | |
| substancially — upright with spread | over⅟16 up to equal height | height of the landing side plus spread-coefficient <br> $4'+6''=4'6''$  1·20+0·15=1·35m | |
| spread without height (ditches) | only the spread has importance | no height | |

They all can appear with or without ground-lines.

The description of banks, drop jumps, obstacles on slanting surfaces will be found separately along with the discussion on the technique for jumping them.

The proportion which determines the type of the obstacle is arrived at by the following calculation:

First add the length of the spread (including ground-line) to the height of the element on the landing side on the one hand; and then separately

add the measure of the spread to the height of the front element; deduct the latter sum from the former;

the ratio between this result and the first sum shows the proportion which defines the 'type' of the obstacle:

e.g. at heights of 2 feet and 4 feet and a spread of 2 feet the calculation is: 4 feet + 2 feet = 6 feet, and 2 feet + 2 feet = 4 feet; 6 feet – 4 feet = 2 feet; thus the type proportion is: 2 to 6 = 1/3.

The same in metric system calculated:

120 + 60 = 180 and 60 + 60 = 120; 180 – 120 = 60; 60/180 = 1/3.

The relevant details regarding the types of obstacle mentioned, together with their decisive proportions and the method of determining their 'basic height', can be found in Table No. 12.

*The ground-line and its bearing on the take-off*

In riding terminology the ground-line defines the frontal base of the obstacle, or an additional element placed on the take-off side, either at ground level or slightly higher. If the front of the fence is not marked by such a line on the ground, one says that it has no ground-line or only an imaginary one.

The front element of an obstacle can also be regarded as a ground-line if, by its position and height, the fence becomes of sloping or ascending type. Generally, this is the case when the height of the element in question is halfway or less to the top of the obstacle.

The ground-line can be situated in the same vertical plane as that in which is the top element of the obstacle on the take-off side, i.e. in the frontal plane or further back. In this sense the position of the ground-line is fixed by its distance from the mentioned vertical plane. This distance is called the ground-line distance'.

## Table No. 13

### INFLUENCE OF THE GROUND-LINE ON THE NORMAL TAKE-OFF DISTANCE

| Position of the ground-line | The effect | Figures. |
|---|---|---|
| in the vertical plane of the obstacle | there is no particular effect | 4'  1·20 m<br>5'3"<br>1·60 m |
| moderately set back to a distance less than ½ the height of the obstacle | lengthens by ¾ of the ground-line distance | 4'7"  1·40 m<br>2'  0·6<br>¾<br>5'7" + 1'6" = 7'1"<br>1·70 m + 0·45 = 2·15 m |
| considerably set back — to a distance between ½ and ¾ the height of the obstacle | lengthens by ½ of the ground-line distance | 4'3"  1·30 m<br>3'  0·90<br>½<br>5'5" + 1'6" = 6'11"<br>1·65m + 0·45 = 2·10 m |
| considerably set back — to a distance between ¾ and the whole height of the obstacle | lengthens by ¼ of the ground-line distance | 5'  1·50 m<br>4'8"  1·45 m<br>¼<br>5'9" + 1'2" = 6'11"<br>1·75m + 0·35 = 2·10 m |
| substantially set back to a distance more than the height of the obstacle | the take-off distance can be fixed by general values, independently from other measurements of the obstacle, according to the main speeds : up to medium speed: 1ft (0·30m) at a fast parcours sp.: 1'6"(0·45m) at a steeplechase sp.: 3ft (1·00m) measured from the ground-line. | 4'  1·20 m<br>1'  7'<br>0·30  2·10 m |

The calculated distances must be measured from the projection of the top of the obstacle on the take-off side.

For the sake of clarity, the heights given in the Figures should be regarded as the 'basic height' of the obstacle.

The material of which the ground-line is composed has no particular significance so far as the take-off is concerned. However, in constructing artificial obstacles, the planner can greatly improve the attractiveness of the fence by using the most stylish and tasteful material for marking the ground-line.

The relationship between the position of the ground-line and the obstacle has a considerable psychological influence on the animal while deciding where to take off. Indeed, it is of great assistance in performing the entire action of the jump, as it aids the horse both in assessing the proper position of the take-off and in estimating the height of the obstacle.

An obstacle without an actual ground-line causes a feeling of uncertainty and tends to lead the horse to take off rather close.

If the ground-line is part of the frontal plane of the obstacle (see Table No. 13, Fig. No. 1), it guides the animal in appraising the situation, but also entices it to a close take-off.

The ground-line which is 'moderately set back' (up to a distance of about half the height of the obstacle, see Table No. 13, Fig. No. 2) is still regarded as part of the front of the fence, giving it a *sloping character*. It generally facilitates the performance of the jump, causing the horse to take off farther and farther back, depending on its placement.

When the ground-line is brought back even farther (up to a distance equal to the height of the obstacle, see Table No. 13, Figs. Nos. 3 and 4) it becomes independent of the front of the fence, giving it an *ascending character*. Such a ground-line draws the attention of the horse by itself, but still encourages a distant take-off. The position of such a ground-line can be regarded as 'considerably set back'.

The ground-line is 'substantially set back' when its distance from the obstacle exceeds the limit mentioned above (see Table No. 13, Fig. No. 5), changing the character of the obstacle to a spread. This distance requires the horse, while preparing for the jump, to appraise both the width and the height of the fence. Owing to this dual appraisal, the ground-line draws the animal to itself and encourages a take-off near to it.

It is important for the rider to know these details about how the position of the ground-line influences the horse's decision. Such knowledge enables him to assist the animal to accept favourable conditions or to overcome others. It is especially invaluable in critical moments when the horse shows doubt in choosing the right spot for the take-off. It is the rider who must take the initiative at such moments, resolving the animal's indecision.

For instance, if the horse happens to arrive out of stride at an obstacle which has a ground-line moderately set back, the rider should demand a distant take-off. If the fence has no ground-line at all, a near take-off will provide the right solution, because that is what the obstacle itself encourages the animal to do.

In certain cases, however, the ground-line adversely affects the horse's taking off. For example, a vertical obstacle with no ground-line, or one lying in the frontal plane of the fence, would encourage the animal to approach it closely, whereas a take-off from farther back would be more favourable.

In jumping high spread fences with a set-back ground-line it is sometimes better to respect the force which suggests a distant take-off. Thus, instead of a near take-off, which would seem to be indicated by the spread of the obstacle, a distant take-off may be demanded, according to the inspiration of the ground-line, if the horse is capable of such a big jump.

In all such cases the choice depends on the rider's knowledge and instinct, taking the horse's capabilities and the immediate situation into account. In order to make such snap decisions accurately the rider must be familiar with the possible solutions which exist in various critical situations. Once in possession of this knowledge he needs only practice, based on his observations, to be able to find instinctively the proper solution for the problem in hand.

*The influence of the spread of the obstacle on the normal take-off and landing distances*

The spread of the fence shortens the length of both the take-off and landing distances calculated according to the 'basic height' of the obstacle.

The reduction of the take-off distance

This reduction becomes necessary if the spread of the obstacle (including ground-line) is over 4 feet (1.20 m.). The extent of the reduction (regardless of the height) is recorded in Table No. 14. The calculated take-off distance (according to the basic height of the obstacle and the position of the ground-line) should be shortened by the appropriate value taken from the table.

## Table No. 14

REDUCTION OF THE TAKE-OFF DISTANCE IN THE CASE OF SPREAD OBSTACLES

| At a spread of | 4' 6"<br>1·40 m. | 5'<br>1·50 m. | 6'<br>1·80 m. | 7'<br>2·10 m. | 8'<br>2·40 m. |
|---|---|---|---|---|---|
| the reduction is | 6"<br>0·15 m. | 10"<br>0·25 m. | 1' 3"<br>0·40 m. | 1' 9"<br>0·55 m. | 2' 3"<br>0·70m. |

Reduction of the landing distance

The extent of the reduction is determined by the proportion of the height to the spread (including ground-line). The numerical meaning of the reduction is shown in Table No. 15.

The spread which appears beyond the top of the obstacle has no significance, unless it exceeds the length of the landing distance calculated for the top element (see Table No. 15, case No. 5).

THE MAXIMUM AND MINIMUM TAKE-OFF DISTANCES AND THEIR IMPORTANCE

The horse can take off successfully short of the normal take-off area and also beyond it. However, the expenditure of energy involved will considerably exceed that which the clearing of the obstacle actually requires.

### The minimum take-off distance

Taking off from a point past the suitable take-off area will render the jump rather difficult and, at worst, places the horse at a point from which it is unable to elevate fast enough to perform a faultless jump. The critical point past which this occurs deter-mines the limit of the minimum take-off distance. Its position depends on three major factors: the height of the obstacle, the speed at which it is approached and the skill of the horse.

In routine cases the minimum take-off distance corresponds to the ascertained basic height of the fence, provided that the medium speed of 415 yards (380 m.) per minute or a lower one is used for the approach.

If the horse goes past the minimum take-off distance at speed, it will not be able to achieve the necessary height before reaching

## Table No. 15

### THE INFLUENCE OF THE SPREAD OF THE OBSTACLE ON THE NORMAL LANDING DISTANCE

| Proportion between the height and spread (including ground-line). | The effect | Figures. |
|---|---|---|
| The spread is less than ½ of the height of the obstacle | shortens by ½ the length of the spread-distance | |
| The spread is between ½ and the whole height of the obstacle | shortens by ¼ the length of the spread-distance | |
| The spread is between the whole and 1¾ times the height of the obstacle | shortens by ⅙ th the length of the spread-distance | |
| The spread is over 1¾ times the height of the obstacle | shortens by ⅛ th the length of the spread-distance | |
| The spread appears beyond the erected structure and its measure is longer than the landing distance belonging to the element in front of it. | there is no shortening. If the calculated distance is shorter than the spread the difference must be overcome by increasing the liveliness (not the speed!) while approaching the fence. | |

The calculated distances must be measured from the projection of the top of the obstacle on the landing side.

For the sake of clarity, the heights given in the Figures should be regarded as the 'basic height' of the obstacle.

the erect part of the obstacle and will hit it. Failure is equally certain if the rider decreases his speed too much; the animal will lack the momentum necessary to overcome the spread of the fence and consequently will fall into it.

### The maximum take-off distance

The other limit of the take-off distance is represented by the line short of which the horse is unable to clear the obstacle. The distance of this line from the front of the fence gives the maximum take-off distance. In relation to the suitable take-off distance the maximum offers wider latitude than the minimum take-off distance.

The position of the maximum take-off distance, like that of the minimum, depends on three factors: the width of the obstacle, the speed of the approach and the jumping capacity of the horse.

A jump performed from a take-off point outside the upper limit of the distance will show a discrepancy between the curve of the jump and the cross-section of the fence, and consequently the animal must make a fault.

### DIFFERENT TYPES OF OBSTACLES AND HOW TO CLEAR THEM

We shall now proceed to consider prevailing types of obstacles and how to clear them, whether in schooling or after education is completed.

There are two main groups of obstacles: artificial fences and natural obstructions. Generally speaking, artificial fences are those which exist only to provide facilities for jumping. Natural obstructions are those which exist naturally in the country or are created there by man in order to enclose certain areas.

#### ARTIFICIAL OBSTACLES

Both in the schooling and at the shows jumping almost always involves the employment of artificial fences. Therefore it is necessary to have a clear idea of their general appearance and construction.

The basic origin of any artificial obstacle must derive, either in its natural form or stylized shape, from something which might be encountered while riding in the open country.

In regard to their structure, artificial obstacles must not only be jumpable, but also attractive. The neatness of an obstacle absorbs and even invites the horse to jump and increases its standard of performance without additional strain. Perhaps a comparison of the fence to a painting can most vividly illustrate the factors which determine the general aspect of an artificial fence. In this comparison

the structure of the fence represents the theme of the picture;

the wings provide a frame for it; and

the setting of the obstacle in the area in which it is erected can be compared with the surroundings in which the picture is placed.

In combining the various elements, just as in the case of a picture, it is not sufficient if they are attractive individually. They must be selected and composed in such a manner that they result in a unit of complete harmony. This is really a matter of taste, coupled with expert knowledge and painstaking interest.

The general points concerning the construction of obstacles are as follow:

Those parts of the obstacle which are likely to be hit by the horse should be fixed firmly so that they will fall or turn over only if hit by a real rap rather than a light touch.

However, the obstacles as a whole should not endanger the animal's soundness even in case of a serious blunder. Therefore they must be of collapsible construction.

Certain parts of most artificial obstacles are fixed on uprights. These must by no means dominate the general picture of the fence. If an upright does not completely suit the rest of the fence, it should be replaced with standards which are less conspicuous.

Usually only a limited number of obstacles, uprights and wings are available for schooling. These, however, should be carefully selected and the best utilization made of them. Although in practice one will encounter a great variety of obstacles, it is not necessary to try to duplicate them in schooling. All these variations can be traced to a few basic types and it is sufficient to train the horse over those alone.

During the horse's schooling fences should be adjusted from lesson to lesson, and even from jump to jump, in such a way that they furnish the horse with visual clues to the correct method of jumping. This is much more effective than installing a big store of obstacles for schooling purposes.

The term 'single obstacle' denotes structures that confront the horse with only a single task in approaching, jumping and moving on.

In courses, however, the term has a more limited meaning. In accordance with the regulations of the F.E.I., whenever the distance between two fences exceeds 39 feet 4 inches (12 m.) they are regarded as single obstacles. During the period of the horse's schooling, when its obedience is the decisive factor in laying out distances, this limit need not be taken into account.

We shall now consider the main types of single obstacles.

*Vertical (upright) obstacles without spread* (Table No. 12, Fig. No. 1)

This category includes all those obstacles the elements of which are theoretically in a single vertical plane. Although in practice there may be a slight spread involved, if it does not exceed the following ratios between the height and depth: at a height of 3 feet 3 inches (1 m.), not more than 1 foot (0.30 m.); at 4 feet (1.20 m.), 1 foot 3 inches (0.40 m.); at 4 feet 3 inches (1.30 m.), 1 foot 6 inches (0.45 m.); at 4 feet 6 inches (1.40 m.), 1 foot 9 inches (0.50 m.); and at 5 feet (1.50 m.) height, not more than 2 feet (0.60 m.).

The faultless jumping of a single bar is a most difficult task, though it can be simplified by filling up the empty space between the bar and the ground. In the course of teaching, an obstacle of this type can be made more attractive to the animal if these lower elements are placed in front of the vertical plane so that the fence appears to have a slightly sloping shape (see Figs. Nos. 94-98, facilitated form).

In jumping vertical obstacles the absence of any 'take-off' element makes judging difficult, and the horse requires every possible assistance from the rider. While approaching the fence the horse must respond readily to any action the rider initiates, which is best accomplished if the rein-contact is kept as light as possible.

In jumping such fences it is best to ask for a relatively long take-off, since the fence has no depth and a long arc can cover it. The situation becomes more difficult if the horse gets too near to the obstacle. In such cases great impulsion is necessary;

Examples for making obstacles easier or rendering them more difficult without the alteration of their essential height or breadth.

| No. of the Figs. | Form of the setting | 94 | 95 | 96 | 97 | 98 | 99 | 100 | 101/1 |
|---|---|---|---|---|---|---|---|---|---|
| | normal | | | | | | | | |
| | facilitated | | | | | | | | |
| | aggravated | | | | | | | | |

Water-jump Fig. No. 101/2 — normal: — facilitated: — aggravated:

with its help the horse can bounce itself into the air almost vertically. The best example of this can be found in a figure practised in the Spanish school called the 'Capriole'. Here, owing to overwhelming impulsion (generated by the 'Piaffe'), the horse is capable of jumping up to a height of 5 feet (1.50 m.) from the spot.

With horses which tend to rush it is necessary to maintain an easy contact on the reins. As such horses are inclined to become flat, the rider should avoid pulling, which only aggravates the situation. Instead of this, arching the jump should be achieved by coiling the spring system during the approach.

With horses inclined to be sluggish stress should be laid on keeping up impulsion; maintaining the necessary light contact will not cause special difficulty.

Thus the fundamental points in jumping upright obstacles are regularity, impulsion, a light contact on the reins and prompt obedience to the aids for collection and extension.

In training it is advisable to use vertical obstacles in their easier (sloped) form at first. This aid can gradually be decreased, so that at the end of the course the horse is jumping completely vertical fences (see Figs. Nos. 94-98, normal and aggravated form).

At the beginning, until the animal becomes familiar with the peculiarities of the vertical fences, the take-off regulator can be employed with advantage. At this stage every effort should be made to encourage a distant rather than a short take-off by appropriate positioning of the device in question.

*Spread obstacles with height* (Table No. 12, Figs. Nos. 4 and 5)

All obstacles in this group are of three dimensions. Their spread, in relation to their height, is considerable and both the rider and the horse must pay special attention to this fact.

The greater the height of the take-off side is in relation to the height of the landing side, the more difficult the jump becomes (see Figs. Nos. 99 and 100). If both sides reach the same level, the character of the obstacle becomes similar to an upright obstacle without spread, but it is a more difficult fence, since its landing side lies in a 'deep' position. These facts themselves suggest the correct technique of jumping.

A relaxed mechanism, which makes it easier for the animal to elevate its body, is the essence of jumping spread obstacles. This must, of course, be coupled with increased impulsion, sufficient to enable the horse to overcome the spread.

Many riders try to jump broad obstacles with an unreasonable increase of speed. This is wrong, since it is not the speed, but the impulsion and liveliness in the motion that matters. No greater speed should be used than that at which the rider experiences no difficulty in maintaining regularity (details on minimum speeds are to be found in Table No. 9).

The main point is that the horse must learn to jump broad obstacles with confidence, thus gaining instead of losing heart while jumping. In jumping broad obstacles the effort of the animal is facilitated by the fact that the arc of its jump more or less conforms to the shape of the fence. In addition, the horse is able to extend its arc by a simple stretching and balancing movement of its head and neck.

When the take-off and landing sides of a spread fence are at approximately the same level the horse must realize that it must jump the increased height of an imaginary element in the middle plane of the obstacle. This height must be actually attained at the peak of the horse's arc if the existing elements of the obstacle are to be cleared. After considering the breadth and the height of the fence, the height of the imaginary element (which will be the 'basic height' of the obstacle) can be established at about 4-9 inches (10-20 cm.) higher than the measured or calculated medium height.

During the teaching period the imaginary element can be marked by a light bar to help the horse to judge the necessary height of its jump.

As a part of this education, the rider should endeavour to teach his horse that, when wrong, it is safer and easier to jump broad obstacles by taking off from the closer rather than from the farther point. For this exercise it is best to use the parallel bars ('oxer'). The take-off regulator can be employed to bring the horse to a rather near take-off point, from which it can still execute the jump *conveniently* (if too short, it may result in a very distant take-off, which should be avoided).

*The sloping type of broad obstacle* (Table No. 12, Fig. No. 2)

The sloping obstacle is an intermediate form between the vertical and ascending type of fences. This is the easiest form of obstacle because of its pleasing and inviting form.

Since the structure of the fence includes a certain spread, it can easily be made more imposing without increasing the difficulty of the task. It is an extremely suitable medium for schooling. In practice these fences in their simple form can be used to start the teaching of jumping of both vertical and broad obstacles and also for training the animal to jump at speed.

*Ascending type of broad obstacle* (Table No. 12, Fig. No. 3)

The height of these obstacles is lower in front and higher on the landing side (the space between these two elements may be filled out by further elements).

Jumping this type of obstacle should not cause great difficulty, since the determination of the proper take-off spot is simple. Even a near take-off will give the animal time to get sufficient elevation without making a mistake. A too distant take-off can be more troublesome, since it may prevent the horse from over-coming the width of the fence.

*Broad obstacles* (ditches, Table No. 12, Fig. No. 6)

Strictly speaking, the expression 'broad obstacle' refers to clean ditches, since no height is involved.

As a matter of fact, ditches can be regarded as the classical form of broad obstacles. This is even true when a small brush or any other object of insignificant height is placed in front of them, though this additional element marking the ground-line provides them with a slight height.

However, such fences can also be classified as broad obstacles, in which the spread dominates the height.

In discussing the various types of ditches which appear in the country or the show ring a distinction can be made between flat and deep ditches.

Flat ditches are those which have little visible depth, since they are mostly filled with water. These are generally called water ditches or water jumps.

Deep ditches are visibly deep and have steep banks. They are called dry ditches. As a rule there is no water in them, but they retain the character of a dry ditch even if a little water collects in the bottom.

The method of jumping ditches is exactly the same whether a
flat or a deep ditch is involved, since in both cases a certain spread
must be overcome. If in practice differences appear, they will
derive from the method of introducing the horse to these two types
of ditches, since the difference in appearance will create different
problems. In the case of a wet ditch the fear caused by the sight
of the water, and in the case of a dry ditch the fear caused by the
depth, must be overcome (the method of overcoming these fears is
described on page 299).

Having reviewed broadly the characteristics of ditches, we shall
now consider the actual methods of jumping them.

As a rule it is best to ride at a lively but rather slow speed
towards the ditch. It is wrong to assume that the jumping of a
ditch necessitates great speed. This is not the case. What is
needed is not speed, but liveliness generated by impulsion.

In approaching the ditch a steady rein-contact must be maintained. It does not matter if this contact happens to be slightly
firmer than usual, because it will not impair the quality of the
take-off.

With horses which are inclined to rush it is advisable to let
them adopt a somewhat greater speed while approaching the ditch.
In order to assist such a horse in the jump, it is of special importance to increase their collection by making a brief retard
before the take-off.

In the case of horses which are inclined to be sluggish, one
should increase their collection and liveliness at a distance of six
to eight strides from the ditch and from there proceed to the
take-off point with an energetic drive-on.

Just as the single bar is the most difficult fence among vertical
obstacles, so the plain ditch among broad obstacles is the most
likely to cause trouble. The reason is that horses have more difficulty in selecting the right take-off spot than they do with high
jumps; most horses are inclined to take off too far away from the
ditch. Since this is bound to produce a shorter landing, the
animal is likely to hit the inside of the far edge of the ditch. The
relatively unimpressive record of long jumping, which is only
27 feet 3 inches (8.30 m.), can perhaps be attributed to this fact;
when jumping over fences, horses have often achieved a distance
of 33 feet (10 m.) or even more between the points of take-off
and landing.

In order to jump a ditch successfully, the most important point is to bring the horse to the proper take-off spot, which is close to the edge of the ditch.

If the rider's legs (especially with sluggish horses) are not strong enough to effect the take-off satisfactorily, it is advisable to enforce their action with a flick of the whip.

Jumping ditches of up to about 13 feet (4 m.) does not strain the animal and if the rider does not upset it in making its effort no particular difficulty will arise.

### SCHOOLING IN THE JUMPING OF DITCHES

The method by which the novice can be acquainted with the simple ditch and accustomed to clearing it is described on page 299. For the sake of the animal's further improvement, the particular schooling should be extended

>to acquainting the horse with the appearance of different types of ditches (water surface, depth, combined forms);

>to the manner of approaching the ditch so that the animal will not be afraid to come close to the edge from which the take-off will be carried out; and

>to the faultless clearing of the ditch.

### Simple water jumps and deep ditches

As the sight of water or depth can often be strange and frightening, it is advisable to jump ditches as often as possible, but not more than a few jumps at a time.

In encouraging the horse to approach close to the ditch, which is the crux of the proper take-off, the regulator can be employed with advantage.

In teaching the animal to jump water ditches faultlessly, a useful method is to place a bar over the middle of the ditch about 1 foot 4 inches to 1 foot 8 inches (40-50 cm.) above the level of the water (see Fig. No. 101/2). The bar will compel the horse to make the kind of arc which is necessary for clearance.

Such an aid is not necessary for deep ditches, since the sight of the depth itself will encourage the horse to make a sufficiently arched jump.

With proper schooling the animal can be taught to jump ditches easily in a short time, but an improvised, unsystematic attempt will often discourage it for ever.

*Combined ditches*

Both in the country and the show ring ditches are often combined with obstacle elements. These additional structures may be placed in front of, beyond or above the ditch. So altered, the obstacle cannot be regarded as a ditch in its classical form, but will belong to the group of high and spread obstacles.

There are two main groups of combined ditches, depending on whether the added structure is combined with a flat, water ditch or with a deep ditch with steep banks, generally without water.

Combined water ditches

These ditches are very picturesque and thus are very popular with show organizers. Their attractiveness has an inviting effect on the horse also. Such fences are pleasant to jump, no matter what sort of structure has been added to it, if the horse is familiar with the sight of the water. Nevertheless, in order to prevent the animal from a sudden surprise, it is necessary to practise such obstacles during the period of schooling.

The procedure to be followed in training the horse to jump combined water ditches is similar to that used in practising ordinary jumps.

Combined deep ditches

A deep ditch combined with an obstacle element is more likely to cause concern than the jump over a combined water ditch.

The 'novelty' of the obstacle which causes the horse's concern results from the position of the bars, which are usually placed over the middle or landing edge of the ditch. Thus the horse, in attempting to measure the height of the bar, is tempted to use the bottom of the ditch as a basis rather than the level of the surrounding ground.

Having misjudged the height, the animal may be impressed by the exaggerated dimensions and consequently be frightened. Therefore it is important to practise this jump frequently in order to teach the horse to judge the height correctly.

It is best to increase gradually the demands of this exercise. In making it more severe stress must be laid on increasing the depth of the ditch; increasing the height of the superstructure and the width of the ditch are of secondary importance.

COMBINATIONS

Combinations are series of two or more individual fences placed in sequence with intervening distances which do not exceed 40 feet (12 m.).

Within this limit there is no further restriction; the actual spacing of fences in combinations is left entirely to the discretion of the course designer. This freedom is also a matter of confidence, however, and those who wish to undertake the task must be fully acquainted with both the technique of planning the obstacles and the method of jumping them.

The actual setting of combinations entails a number of points which require special attention from

the planner, who has to design it;

the rider, who must prepare his jumping plan; and

from the horse, which is to perform the jumps involved.

PLANNING COMBINATIONS AND DETERMINING THE DISTANCES BETWEEN THEIR COMPONENT FENCES

In planning combinations it is important to establish distances between the composing obstacle elements that will provide the kind of challenge intended.

The general, but rather stereotyped, practice is to fix these distances (measured from the middle to the middle of the component fences) as follows:

at the learning stage (the novice course):

25 feet (7.60 m.) or 35 feet 6 inches (10.80 m.);

at the intermediate stage (the medium course):

26 feet (7.90 m.) or 36 feet 6 inches (11.10 m.);

in speed competitions:

27 feet (8.20 m.) or 37 feet 6 inches (11.40 m.).

These measurements should never be rigidly applied, since they are not necessarily suitable for the more intricate cases. In order to accomplish our task more precisely, let us consider the various points which have a bearing on designing the 'blueprint' for combinations.

In considering the distances at which the fences should be set

the planner exercises a definite influence on the success of the class by arranging distances that suit the speed prescribed for the particular competition;

in this way he can assist competitors who use the prescribed speed and make the task more difficult for those who ignore it;

he can also examine the jumping capacity, skill and obedience of the horse and test the horsemanship of the rider by employing distances which demand the skilful co-operation of both.

The calculation involved in planning combinations should be carried out according to the following explanation.

The total value of the intervening distance is composed of three elements:

the length of the landing distance following the first jump;

the length of the non-jumping stride (or strides) necessary to arrive at the take-off point; and

the length of the take-off distance at the next jump.

To make the calculation these three components have to be determined one by one in accordance with the speed intended (slow, medium or fast) in the following manner:

First, determine the basic height of each of the component obstacles, taking into account their spread and type (see Tables Nos. 11 and 12).

Then the calculation of the three components follows.

*To get the landing distance:*

take the normal landing distance (according to basic height and speed) from Table No. 11; from which,

in case of spread obstacles, *reduce* the amount indicated in Table No. 15.

Measure the distance achieved from the top element of the fence on the landing side.

*To get the length of the non-jumping stride(s):*

take the length of stride (after landing) from Table No. 8/a (according to the speed intended); from which

*reduce* the amount shown in Table No. 8/b if

the basic height is over 4 feet (1.20 m.);

a ditch is wider than 11 feet (3.30 m.); or

the landing side of the obstacle is far beyond its top element.

Measure the achieved length between the landing and take-off points.

*To get the take-off distance:*

take the normal take-off distance (according to basic height and speed) from Table No. 11; alter this length by

*adding* to it the value of the lengthening effect of the ground-line (see in Table No. 13); and in the case of a spread over 4 feet (1.20 m.) by *reducing* the amount indicated in Table No. 14.

Measure the distance achieved from the top element on the landing side.

Finally, the sum of these three component distances constitutes the correct intervening distance between the two fences of the combination.

It is useful to work out these calculations with the aid of actual examples as a means of practising the use of the tables mentioned above.

In the diagrams of these examples the obstacles are jumped from left to right.

EXAMPLES FOR PLANNING COMBINATIONS TO PROVIDE ADVANTAGEOUS JUMPING CONDITIONS

*Example No. 1*

The planning of a double for seasoned horses in a competition where the maximum height of the obstacles is fixed at 4 feet 3 inches (1.30 m.) and the speed at 415 yards (380 m.) per minute.

The obstacle to be employed is shown in Fig. No. 102 which also includes the results of the calculation made.

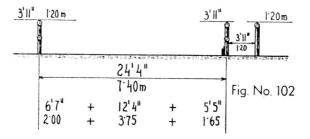

Fig. No. 102

CALCULATION OF THE INTERVENING DISTANCE

| Objects to be ascertained | | The calculation | | |
|---|---|---|---|---|
| | | Component elements and their tot-up | Numerical values | |
| | | | ft. | m. |
| Basic height | First obstacle: Vertical, 3′ 11″ (1·20 m.) high without spread | Decisive height (actual height) +Spread coefficient | 3′ 11″ — | 1·20 — |
| | | Total: | 3′ 11″ | 1·20 |
| | Second obstacle: Vertical, 3′ 11″ (1·20m.) high with 4′ (1·20 m.) spread | Decisive height (actual height) +Spread coefficient | 3′ 11″ 6″ | 1·20 0·14 |
| | | Total: | 4′ 5″ | 1·34 |
| Landing distance Take-off distance | According to the basic height and the alterations indicated in Tables Nos. 13-15 | Whole length —Reduction for spread (Table No. 15) | 6′ 7″ — | 2·00 — |
| | | Total: | 6′ 7″ | 2·00 |
| | | Whole length —Reduction for spread (not over 4′) (Table No. 14) | 5′ 5″ — | 1·65 — |
| | | Total: | 5′ 5″ | 1·65 |
| | Non-jumping strides according to the speed intended | 1 stride (medium speed) —Stride reduction (Table No. 8/b) | 12′ 4″ — | 3·75 — |
| | | Total: | 12′ 4″ | 3·75 |
| | Space distance | Landing distance +Non-jumping stride +Take-off distance | 6′ 7″ 12′ 4″ 5′ 5″ | 2·00 3·75 1·65 |
| | | Total: | 24′ 4″ | 7·40 |

*Example No. 2*

Planning a treble for a course of 5 feet (1.50 m.) height.

Speed is fixed at 437 yards (400 m.) per minute, thus the medium parcours speed is taken into account.

The desired combination is shown in Fig. No. 103 together with the results of the calculation made.

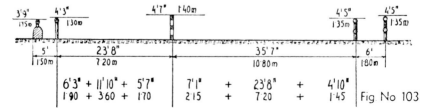

Fig No 103

CALCULATION OF THE INTERVENING DISTANCES

| | Objects to be ascertained | Component elements and their tot-up | Numerical values | |
|---|---|---|---|---|
| | | | ft. | m. |
| Basic height | First obstacle: Mod. upright, 4′ 3″ (1·30 m.) high with 5′ (1·50 m.) spread | Decisive height (medium speed) +Spread coefficient | 4′ 0″ 7″ | 1·22 0·18 |
| | | Total: | **4′ 7″** | **1·40** |
| | Second obstacle: Vertical, 4′ 7″ (1·40 m.) high without spread | Decisive height (actual height) +Spread coefficient | 4′ 7″ — | 1·40 — |
| | | Total: | **4′ 7″** | **1·40** |
| Take-off distance / Landing distance | According to the basic height and the alterations indicated in Tables Nos. 13-15 | Whole length —Reduction for spread (one-sixth of spr. d.) | 7′ 1″ 10″ | 2·15 0·25 |
| | | Total: | **6′ 3″** | **1·90** |
| | | Whole length —reduction for spread | 5′ 7″ — | 1·70 — |
| | | Total: | **5′ 7″** | **1·70** |
| | Non-jumping strides according to the speed intended | 1 stride (medium speed) —Stride reduction (Table No. 8/b) | 12′ 4″ 6″ | 3·75 0·15 |
| | | Total : | **11′ 10″** | **3·60** |
| | Space distance between the first part of the treble | Landing distance +Non-jumping stride +Take-off distance | 6′ 3″ 11′ 10″ 5′ 7″ | 1·90 3·60 1·70 |
| | | Total: | **23′ 8″** | **7·20** |
| Basic height | Third obstacle: Vertical, 4′ 7″ (1·40m.) high with 6′ (1·80 m.) spread | Decisive height (actual height) +Spread coefficient | 4′ 5″ 9″ | 1·35 0·22 |
| | | Total: | **5′ 2″** | **1·57** |
| Take-off distance / Landing distance | According to the basic height and the alterations indicated in Tables Nos. 13-15 | Whole length —Reduction for spread (Table No. 15) | 7′ 1″ — | 2·15 — |
| | | Total: | **7′ 1″** | **2·15** |
| | | Whole length —Reduction for spread (Table No. 14) | 6′ 1″ 1′ 3″ | 1·85 0·40 |
| | | Total: | **4′ 10″** | **1·45** |
| | Non-jumping strides according to the speed intended | 2 strides (medium speed) —Stride reduction (Table No. 8/b) | 24′ 8″ 1′ 0″ | 7·50 0·30 |
| | | Total: | **23′ 8″** | **7·20** |
| | Space distance between the second part of the treble | Landing distance +Non-jumping strides +Take-off distance | 7′ 1″ 23′ 8″ 4′ 10″ | 2·15 7·20 1·45 |
| | | Total: | **35′ 7″** | **10·80** |

*Example No.* 3

Planning a double for a speed competition. A speed of 492 yards (450 m.) per minute is taken into account.

The structure of the obstacle is shown in Fig. No. 104.

Special attention must be given to the second element of the combination, which has a substantially set-back ground-line. Here the take-off distance can be taken as 1 foot 6 inches (0.50 m.), as indicated in Table No. 13, case No. 5.

Otherwise the calculation follows the former examples.

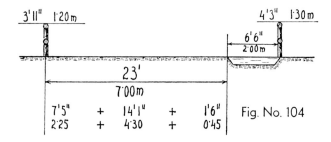

Fig. No. 104

*Example No.* 4

Planning a treble for a course with conditions complying with Olympic standard. The speed is fixed at 437 yards (400 m.) per minute.

The desired combination is illustrated in Fig. No. 105.

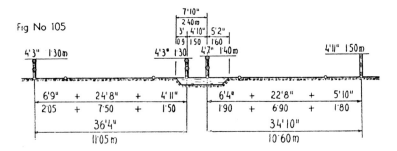

Fig No 105

In this example the calculation of the middle element needs special attention. It is an upright obstacle with a 5 feet (1.50 m.) spread and with a considerably set-back ground-line (the take-off side of the ditch).

Taking these data into account, the basic height of the fence is:

|  | ft. | in. | m. |
|---|---|---|---|
| medium height of the superstructure .. | 4 | 5 | (1.35) plus |
| spread coefficient (eight times).. .. | 1 | 0 | (0.28) |
|  | 5 | 5 | (1.63) |

On this basis the *take-off distance* is:

| | ft. | in. | m. |
|---|---|---|---|
| length according to Table No. 11 .. | 6 | 2 | (1.90) plus |
| effect of the ground-line (Table No. 13, Fig. No. 4) .. .. .. .. | 1 | 0 | (0.30) |
|  | 7 | 2 | (2.20) minus |
| reduction for spread, 8 feet or 2.4 m. (Table No. 14) .. .. .. | 2 | 3 | (0.70) |
|  | 4 | 11 | (1.50) |

The *landing distance* is:

| | ft. | in. | m. |
|---|---|---|---|
| length according to Table No. 11 .. | 7 | 4 | (2.20) minus |
| reduction for spread (Table No. 15, Fig. No. 4) .. .. .. .. | 1 | 0 | (0.30) |
|  | 6 | 4 | (1.90) |

In connection with the non-jumping strides it should be noted that there is a reduction (according to Table No. 8/b) of 8 inches (0.20 m.) in the first intervening distance and 2 feet 8 inches (0.80 m.) in the second one.

Otherwise the calculation can be completed in the normal manner.

Figs. Nos. 106 and 107 show two further examples in which the ditches must be regarded as ground-lines.

*Example No. 5 (for a slow competition, novice horses)*

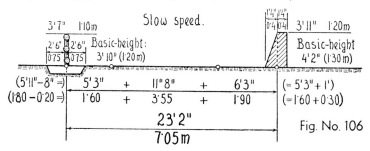

Fig. No. 106

*Example No.* 6 (*for a* fast *competition*)

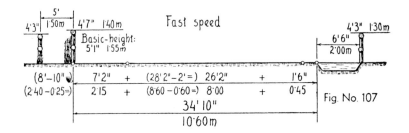

Fig. No. 107

THE ANALYSIS OF A COMBINATION BY THE RIDER AND THE PREPARA-
TION OF HIS RIDING PLAN

In drawing up the riding plan for clearing a combination the
following method can be of assistance:

measure by paces the distance between the obstacle elements;
and

estimate their type and basic height; as well as

the effect of the existing ground-lines and the spreads involved.

Assess with a quick glance the approximate length of the landing
and take-off distances, taking into account the medium parcours
speed (415 yards or 380 m. per minute), and

deduct the estimated sum from the total intervening distance.

Conclude from the result:

the necessary number of non-jumping strides (one to three) and
the speed (slow, medium or fast, see Table No. 8/a) at which
they have to be performed.

The proper interpretation of these latter data is the essence of
the correct plan.

Let us now examine this procedure as applied to various
examples. In these the problem is given by diagrams which show
the form and measurements of the combinations in question. They
should be approached from left to right.

In selecting the problems our chief aim has been to furnish the
kind of complicated problems which generally cause trouble.

*Task No.* 1

The situation given:

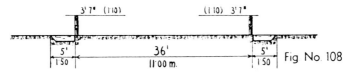

Fig No. 108

| Objects to be estimated | Process of estimation | | |
|---|---|---|---|
| | Component elements of the calculation and their tot up | Numerical values | |
| | | ft. | m. |
| Obstacle type and basic height | First: Vertical with 5′ (1·50 m.) ground-line | 4′ 3″ | 1·30 |
| | Second: Vertical, spread beyond | 3′ 7″ | 1·10 |
| Total distance needed for landing and take-off | Landing distance (Table No. 15) | 6′ 0″ | 1·80 |
| | + Take-off distance | 5′ 1″ | 1·60 |
| | Total: | 11′ 1″ | **3·40** |
| Remaining space for non-jumping strides | Distance given | 36′ 0″ | 11·00 |
| | —Above distance needed | 11′ 1″ | 3·40 |
| | Total: | **24′ 11″** | **7·60** |
| Chance to perform by comparing either two cases | Actual length of non-jumping strides | 24′ 8″ | 7·50 |
| | —Remaining distance | 24′ 11″ | 7·60 |
| | Total: | **3″** | **0·10** |
| | Situation given | 36′ 0″ | 11·00 |
| | Situation calculated* | 35′ 9″ | 10·90 |
| | * 11′ 1″ + 24′ 8″ = 35′ 9″ (10·90 m.) | **3″** | **0·10** |

*Conclusion:* With regard to the minor difference, the calculation corresponds to the demands of the problem.

*The plan:* To ride at a medium parcours speed and reach the second element in two non-jumping strides.

This particular obstacle was used in the course of the three-day event at the Berlin Olympic Games; it was the source of most of the faults, in spite of its simplicity. A possible reason for these failures is the fact that the riders, by misjudging the effect of the two ditches involved, tried to solve the problem by considerably exceeding the necessary medium parcours speed. In this way the non-jumping strides became rather long; the horse got too close to the second element of the obstacle and hit it. The author himself suffered this penalty, the only one (including the endurance test) during the competition and as a consequence lost the Olympic Silver Medal; this would not have happened if he had drawn up a jumping plan of this combination in the manner described above.

*Task No.* 2

Situation given:

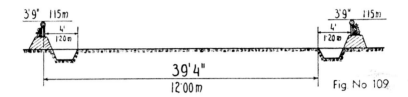

Fig No 109

DRAWING UP THE RIDING PLAN

| Objects to be estimated | Process of estimation | | |
|---|---|---|---|
| | Component elements of the calculation and their tot-up | Numerical values | |
| | | ft. | m. |
| Obstacle type and basic height | First: Sloping | 3′ 9″ | 1·15 |
| | Second: Substantial ground-line | — | — |
| Total distance needed for landing and take-off | Landing distance | 6′ 5″ | 1·95 |
| | +Take-off distance (Table No. 13) | 1′ 0″ | 0·30 |
| | Total: | **7′ 5″** | **2·25** |
| Remaining space for non-jumping strides | Distance given | 39′ 4″ | 12·00 |
| | —Above distance needed | 7′ 5″ | 2·25 |
| | Total: | **31′ 11″** | **9·75** |
| Chance to perform by comparing (either, or) | Remaining distance | 31′ 11″ | 9·75 |
| | —Actual length of non-jumping strides | 24′ 8″ | 7·50 |
| | Total: | **7′ 3″** | **2·25** |
| | Situation given | 39′ 4″ | 12·00 |
| | —Situation calculated* | 32′ 1″ | 9·75 |
| | * 7′ 5″ + 24′ 8″ = 32′ 1″ (9·75 m.) | **7′ 3″** | **2·25** |

*Conclusion:* The calculated situation does not solve the problem, because the difference (7′ 3″ or 2·25 m.) is long for a distant take-off and short for an additional non-jumping stride.

Let us see the solution of the problem using the considerably faster speed of 550 yards (500 m.) per minute, and letting the horse make two non-jumping strides, or when using a rather slow speed of 325 yards (300 m.) per minute with the performance of three non-jumping strides between the two elements of the combination.

| **Fast speed** Objects to be estimated | Process of estimation | | |
|---|---|---|---|
| | Component elements of the calculation and their tot-up | Numerical values | |
| | | ft. | m. |
| Obstacle type and basic height | First: Sloping Second: Substantial ground-line | 3′ 9″ — | 1·15 — |
| Total distance needed for landing and take-off | Landing distance +Take-off distance (Table No. 13) | 7′ 3″ 1′ 6″ | 2·20 0·45 |
| | Total: | 8′ 9″ | 2·65 |
| Remaining space for non-jumping strides | Distance given —Above distance needed | 39′ 4″ 8′ 9″ | 12·00 2·65 |
| | Total: | 30′ 7″ | 9·35 |
| Chance to perform by comparing either of the two cases | Actual length of non-jumping strides —Remaining distance | 30′ 10″ 30′ 7″ | 9·40 9·35 |
| | Total: | 3″ | 0·05 |
| | Situation calculated* —Situation given | 39′ 7″ 39′ 4″ | 12·05 12·00 |
| | * 8′ 9″ + 30′ 10″ = 39′ 7″ (12·05 m.) | 3″ | 0·05 |

*Conclusion:* In view of the minor difference the calculation corresponds to the demands of the problem.

*The plan :* To ride at a rather fast speed and reach the second element in two non-jumping strides.

| **Slow speed** Objects to be estimated | Process of estimation | | |
|---|---|---|---|
| | Component elements of the calculation and their tot-up | Numerical values | |
| | | ft. | m. |
| Obstacle type and basic height | First: Sloping Second: Substantial ground-line | 3′ 9″ — | 1·15 — |
| Total distance needed for landing and take-off | Landing distance +Take-off distance (Table No. 13) | 5′ 9″ 1′ 0″ | 1·75 0·30 |
| | Total: | 6′ 9″ | 2·05 |
| Remaining space for non-jumping strides | Distance given —Above distance needed | 39′ 4″ 6′ 9″ | 12·00 2·05 |
| | Total: | 32′ 7″ | 9·95 |
| Chance to perform by comparing either of the two cases | Actual length of non-jumping strides —Remaining distance | 33′ 0″ 32′ 7″ | 10·05 9·95 |
| | Total: | 5″ | 0·10 |
| | Situation calculated* Situation given | 39′ 9″ 39′ 4″ | 12·10 12·00 |
| | * 6′ 9″ + 33′ = 39′ 9″ (12·10 m.) | 5″ | 0·10 |

*Conclusion:* In view of the minor difference, the plan for three non-jumping strides can be carried out successfully.

In order to decide whether the problem should be solved by using two or three non-jumping strides, the individual qualities of the horse are decisive.

The above example clearly shows the bearing of the speed on the length of the strides and thus on the whole method of preparing the riding plan for jumping combinations.

*Task No.* 3

Situation given:

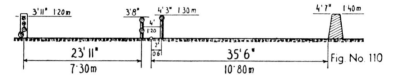

Fig. No. 110

DRAWING UP THE RIDING PLAN

| Objects to be estimated | Process of estimation | | | | | | |
|---|---|---|---|---|---|---|---|
| | First part of the treble | | | Second part of the treble | | | |
| | Component elements of the calculation and their tot-up | Numerical values | | Component elements of the calculation and their tot-up | Numerical values | | |
| | | ft. | m. | | ft. | m. | |
| Obstacle type and basic height | First: Sloping<br>Second: Vertical with spread | 3′ 11″<br>4′ 5″ | 1·20<br>1·35 | Second: Vertical with spread<br>Third: Sloping | 4′ 5″<br>4′ 7″ | 1·35<br>1·40 | |
| Total distance needed for landing and take-off | Landing distance<br>+Take-off distance | 6′ 7″<br>5′ 7″ | 2·00<br>1·70 | Landing distance (including reduction)<br>+Take-off distance | 6′ 5″<br>5′ 7″ | 1·95<br>1·70 | |
| | Total: | 12′ 2″ | 3·70 | Total: | 12′ 0″ | 3·65 | |
| Remaining space for non-jumping strides | Distance given<br>—Above distance needed | 23′ 11″<br>12′ 2″ | 7·30<br>3·70 | Distance given<br>—Above distance needed | 35′ 6″<br>12′ 0″ | 10·80<br>3·65 | |
| | Total: | 11′ 9″ | 3·60 | Total: | 23′ 6″ | 7·15 | |
| Chance to perform by comparing (either, or) | Actual length of non-jumping strides<br>—Remaining distance | 12′ 4″<br>11′ 9″ | 3·75<br>3·60 | Actual length of non-jumping strides*<br>—Remaining distance | 23′ 8″<br>23′ 6″ | 7·20<br>7·15 | |
| | Total: | 7″ | 0·15 | *incl. 1′ (0·30 m.) reduction | 2″ | 0·05 | |
| | Situation calculated*<br>– Situation given | 24′ 6″<br>23′ 11″ | 7·45<br>7·30 | Situation calculated*<br>—Situation given | 35′ 8″<br>35′ 6″ | 10·85<br>10·80 | |
| | *12′ 2″ + 12′ 4″ =<br>24′ 6″ (7·45 m.) | 7″ | 0·15 | *12′ + 23′ 8″ = 35′ 8″<br>(10·85 m.) | 2″ | 0·05 | |

*Conclusion:* In view of the minor difference, the calculation corresponds to the demands of the problem.

*The plan:* To ride at a medium parcours speed, reach the second element in one and the third in two non-jumping strides.

## Task No. 4

### Situation given:

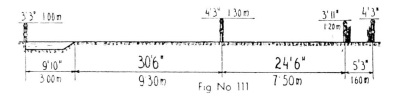

Fig No 111

### DRAWING UP THE RIDING PLAN

| Objects to be estimated | Process of estimation | | | | | | |
|---|---|---|---|---|---|---|---|
| | First part of the treble | | | Second part of the treble | | | |
| | Component elements of the calculation and their tot-up | Numerical values | | Component elements of the calculation and their tot-up | Numerical values | | |
| | | ft. | m. | | ft. | m. | |
| Obstacle type and basic height | First: Upright with spread beyond<br>Second: Upright without spread with ground-line | 3' 3"<br><br>4' 3" | 1·00<br><br>1·30 | Second: Upright without spread<br>Third: Upright with spread | 4' 3"<br>5' 2" | 1·30<br>1·55 | |
| Total distance needed for landing and take-off | Landing distance<br>+Take-off distance | 8"<br>5' 5" | 0·20<br>1·65 | Landing distance<br>+Take-off distance (including reduction) | 6' 10"<br>5' 3" | 2·10<br>1·60 | |
| | Total: | 6' 1" | 1·85 | Total: | 12' 1" | 3·70 | |
| Remaining space for non-jumping strides | Distance given<br>—Above distance needed | 30' 6"<br>6' 1" | 9·30<br>1·85 | Distance given<br>—Above distance needed | 24' 6"<br>12' 1" | 7·50<br>3·70 | |
| | Total: | 24' 5" | 7·45 | Total: | 12' 5" | 3·80 | |
| Chance to perform by comparing (either, or) | Remaining distance<br>—Actual length of non-jumping strides (including reduction) | 24' 5"<br>22' 8" | 7·45<br>6·90 | Remaining distance<br>—Actual length of non-jumping strides (including reduction) | 12' 5"<br>11' 10" | 3·80<br>3·60 | |
| | | 1' 9" | 0·55 | | 7" | 0·20 | |
| | Situation given<br>—Situation calculated* | 30' 6"<br>28' 9" | 9·30<br>8·75 | Situation given<br>—Situation calculated* | 24' 6"<br>23' 11" | 7·50<br>7·30 | |
| | *6' 1" + 22' 8" =<br>28' 9" (8·75 m.) | 1' 9" | 0·55 | *12' 1" + 11' 10" =<br>23' 11" (7·30 m.) | 7" | 0·20 | |

*Conclusion:* The distance in both parts of the treble is a little long.

*The plan:* Ride into the treble at medium parcours speed, reach the second element in two non-jumping strides and ask for a distant take-off. After landing keep up the impulsion and reach the third element in one non-jumping stride.

*Task No.* 5

Situation given:

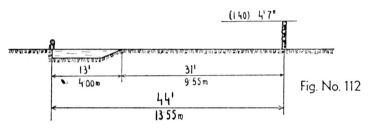

Fig. No. 112

DRAWING UP THE RIDING PLAN

| Objects to be estimated | Process of estimation | | |
|---|---|---|---|
| | Component elements of the calculation and their tot-up | Numerical values | |
| | | ft. | m. |
| Obstacle type and basic height | First: Spread, without height | — | — |
| | Second: Upright, without spread | 4′ 7″ | 1·40 |
| Total distance needed for landing and take-off | Landing distance | 1′ 0″ | 0·30 |
| | +Take-off distance | 5′ 7″ | 1·70 |
| | Total: | 6′ 7″ | 2·00 |
| Remaining space for non-jumping strides | Space distance given | 31′ 0″ | 9·45 |
| | —Above distance needed | 6′ 7″ | 2·00 |
| | Total: | 24′ 5″ | 7·45 |
| Chance to perform by comparing (either, or) | Remaining space distance | 24′ 5″ | 7·45 |
| | —Actual length of non-jumping strides (including reduction) | 22′ 8″ | 6·90 |
| | Total: | 1′ 9″ | 0·55 |
| | Situation given | 31′ 0″ | 9·45 |
| | —Situation calculated* | 29′ 3″ | 8·90 |
| | * 6′ 7″ + 22′ 8″ = 29′ 3″ (8·90 m.) | 1′ 9″ | 0·55 |

*Conclusion :* The distance is rather long, especially if the horse lands close to the ditch.

*The plan:* To ride at a medium parcours speed and reach the second element in two lengthened non-jumping strides.

The horse's actual landing after the ditch will show whether the original speed for the non-jumping strides will have to be increased or decreased to ensure (without altering the number of the planned non-jumping strides) a good take-off distance for the second element. This verification is, of course, a general recommendation for the solution of each problem.

The rider often has very little time in which to prepare his riding plan. Thus he must learn to make fast calculations and acquire the skill of applying them swiftly while he is inspecting the course. For this purpose the rider should solve a number of similar examples as shown above. This will enable him to foresee most of the problems which will arise in jumping combinations.

PRACTICAL METHODS OF JUMPING COMBINATIONS

One of the most impressive sights in riding is the co-operation between a good rider and his horse in correctly negotiating a combination. The main characteristic of their performance is the limited possibility for the animal's substantial regulation from the first element to the last.

In order to jump combinations *with certainty and determination*, the rider must comply with the following demands:

he must be capable of making a sound plan; and

ride the horse according to it, but, if necessary, be able to alter the plan without hesitation to suit changes in the prevailing conditions; and finally

he must know intimately the capacities of his horse and its level of experience, for these factors must be considered in deciding the best choice between various possible plans.

The rider should pay special attention to the components of the combination in order to anticipate the possible effects they may have on the horse (e.g. impressive fences produce sluggishness, while very easy appearances encourage sloppiness, etc.).

He should also consider the kinds of assistance which the character of the fences involved demand. In making his approach the rider must decide, in addition to speed, the degree of liveliness to be maintained and the strength of the rein-contact to be permitted (whether firmer or very light, etc.).

Another important matter in jumping combinations is the physical and mental preparation of the animal for the task. Therefore, at least four to five strides before reaching the obstacle, the rider must attain his horse's

regulated gallop at a speed which is appropriate to the heights and distances involved;

condition of increased impulsion in order to accumulate the power necessary for several jumps in short succession; and

its responsiveness to the signals of the reins and legs.

Along with safeguarding the above conditions, the immediate task of the rider is so to concentrate his attention on the first element while approaching the combination as if for a single fence. He should ask the horse to negotiate it regardless of further elements, but just according to the actual situation.

If the rider is able to bring the horse to the first element of a combination in the correct mental and physical state, it is almost certain that the animal will clear the whole combination satisfactorily.

Once the horse has cleared the first fence the rider's main concern should be to maintain the collection, cadence and impulsion and to adjust the length of the strides (by keeping the speed) to the distance between the elements through discreet use of his hands and legs.

The position of the composing fences, in terms of the number of non-jumping strides that separates them, is of little importance, since there is no difference in procedure if the second element is one, two or even three strides from the first. However, longer distances tend to render the horse's task easier.

We shall next examine in detail the actual methods of jumping combinations, with special reference to the rider's activities. It is only necessary to discuss the technique of jumping trebles, for the jumping of doubles is essentially the same.

Having dealt with the methods of designing combined obstacles and preparing the riding plan, the reader will already surmise much about the method of executing this plan.

JUMPING COMBINATIONS WITH ELEMENTS SET AT EASY DISTANCES

*Jumping a combination consisting of three vertical fences without spread*

Fig No. 113

The vertical nature of the component fences demands both impulsion and ease on the part of the horse, supported by smoothness of contact maintained by the rider.

If the first take-off is normal

When the horse jumps the first element in a good arc the rider's only duty is to follow the movement with his entire being. An accurate first jump regulates the horse for the second and third.

If the rider fears that the animal, despite having jumped the first fence well, is tending to flatten out or hurry, balance should be restored by a brief collection lest the subsequent fences be spoiled.

In case of sluggishness or loss of cadence, the rider's legs must act to restore the horse's liveliness by making a firm drive-on terminating in brief collection.

If the horse has stood back too far from the first obstacle

The result of a long take-off is usually a landing close to the cleared fence, which in turn produces too long a take-off for the next element. In such cases the rider should lengthen the intermediate stride, using firm support of the driving legs. Thus he can shorten the second take-off distance and a brief collection will promote the development of the arc over the second fence. After this jump the horse will usually meet the third element normally again.

If the horse lands too deep over the first fence

In this case the rider may alternatively choose:

to ask the horse, by firm checking, to collect itself and shorten the non-jumping stride(s); or

in quite extreme cases to force a very long take-off for the second element, omitting one of the non-jumping strides.

The advantage of the first (normal) solution is the strong collection. This makes the horse jump the second element in a highly-arched manner, which itself acts as a regulator, so that there is not likely to be any trouble with the third fence.

The advantage of the second solution is that the animal will stand back from the vertical second element. Its disadvantage is that the third jump may thus become too flat. In any case, this solution can only be employed with horses of exceptional jumping ability.

If the horse gets under the first fence, and jumps from an almost stationary position, it should be allowed to make an extra non-jumping stride. Even so, the animal will have lost its cadence and will have to jump the second element by sheer force. In this case energetic support of the rider's legs will be needed to prevent a refusal and restore impulsion. The horse will meet with the same difficulty while negotiating the third jump. If this kind of difficulty is frequent, the animal cannot be considered sufficiently advanced for the allotted task and it is advisable to return to simpler exercises for a while.

*Jumping a combination consisting of one vertical fence without spread, one spread and another fence like the first*

Fig. No. 114

The approach to and jumping of the first element are identical with the previous case.

If the second element has a sloping front (Fig. a)

its sloping character will facilitate the task in several ways.
While performing the jump the rider should concentrate on maintaining the horse's collection, so that it will be able to overcome the spread without flattening out.   Sometimes a quick animation will be needed to maintain impulsion.

If the horse has become flat by the second fence, it should be checked, out of which the take-off for the third element can evolve.

If the second element is vertical with spread (Fig. b)

the method of jumping applied to upright obstacles without spread is employed, except that the second element is approached with increased liveliness.
In such combinations there is little danger that the horse will become flat for the third jump; it is more likely to lose cadence.

*Jumping a combination consisting of a spread obstacle, a vertical fence (without spread) and again a spread*

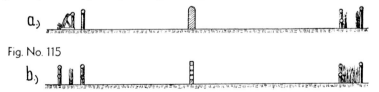

Fig. No. 115

This form of combination should be approached with increased collection because

if the first element is of sloping or ascending type (Fig. a), the collection will counteract the tendency of the fence to cause the horse to flatten out at the second jump and endanger its success;

if the first element is vertical with spread, so that both breadth and height have to be overcome, the horse can succeed only through collection coupled with liveliness.

In this type of combination the second element is the critical one. Therefore the rider must take special pains to retain or restore the horse's collection and liveliness after the first jump and to support it in this manner until the combination has been completed.

*Jumping combinations consisting of three spread obstacles*

Fig. No.
116

The difficulty of this task depends on the steepness of the elements. If they are of ascending type, the emphasis will rest almost entirely on maintaining impulsion. Consequently this condition must be established in the approach and safeguarded by the rider between the elements as well. A slight flattening out of the horse will not endanger a clear performance, unless the elements are very steep. In such circumstances the horse's lightness is very important.

JUMPING COMBINATIONS SET AT ODD DISTANCES

In order to clarify the problems which confront the rider while jumping such combinations, we shall examine the most difficult cases, in which the distances differ greatly from the horse's normal stride.

Execution of the combinations in question is a thorough test of the rider's skill, his knowledge of the lengths of the necessary strides and his ability to extract these strides from the animal by the right adjustment of speed.

For this task the animal must respond sensitively to strong

collection and yet respond just as submissively and promptly to the drive-on. If the horse is capable of satisfying such a standard of obedience, the satisfactory performance of even very difficult combinations will not cause too much trouble.

The main difficulty will arise when jumping that particular element of the combination which lies at an awkward distance from the fence cleared previously. Therefore, to find the solution of the problem it is necessary to consider how to make the jumping of this critical element easier.

First of all, a definite and well thought out riding plan is required. It should be borne in mind that

the take-off distance will deviate considerably from that which ensures a normal take-off; and

also the rate of speed will be considerably higher or lower than the normal one.

A knowledge of the animal's disposition and jumping capabilities will help to determine whether a long or short take-off should be employed. With horses which like to stand back, the first alternative should be chosen; with those which prefer a close take-off, the second.

As a general guide, it can be stated that if the first element of the obstacle is low (about up to 3 feet 9 inches or 1.15 m.) a slower speed is preferable; otherwise the higher the obstacle, the faster the speed.

With regard to the first solution (long take-off), it is important that the horse has sufficient experience in jumping at speed without becoming flat. In this case the shortest possible safe take-off at the first element will be of help. The usefulness of this method can be proved by the following facts:

the nearer the animal approaches the lower limit of the suitable take-off distance, the longer the landing distance that can be expected. Such a long landing distance will result in a more favourable take-off distance for the following element. With a fully-schooled horse it is possible to gain 3 feet 6 inches to 5 feet (1-1½ m.) and to overcome the difficulty of the situation.

Conversely, when the slow speed has been decided upon, it is better to demand the take-off at the first element from as far back as possible. This will bring the landing nearer to the cleared element and thus increase the ensuing take-off distance.

Having decided on his plan, the rider should follow it in every detail and not hesitate in front of the fence; only this decisiveness can overcome the horse's uncertainty.

When such an obstacle must be jumped even a well-schooled horse should be specially prepared before the performance.

In preparation it is advantageous to establish the desired take-off distance in front of the first element by the employment of a regulator. Thus it is possible to create a situation in which the critical take-off for the second element will occur exactly as planned.

*Solving the problem with a long take-off at the second element (increased speed, extended strides)*

The preparation

First, take a few individual jumps while riding at the desired speed, which is a rather fast one; then

jump two to three times an obstacle which corresponds to the combination in question. Although the elements can be arranged invitingly, the intervening distance must strictly correspond to that of the actual combination.

During this preparatory work the horse can, if necessary, be warned by mild self-rapping to prevent it from becoming careless while jumping at the greater speed.

The performance

In approaching the obstacle the aim should be to make the landing as long as possible.

If the horse happens to land well between the two elements, the rider needs only to maintain the rate of speed decided upon in his riding plan.

If the horse lands close to the first element, the rider must use all the means in his power to lengthen the non-jumping stride(s) and demand the take-off from a considerable distance. He must not allow the horse to make an additional non-jumping stride, since this would bring the animal so close to the second element that its clearance would become quite impossible from there.

*Solving the problem with a close take-off for the second element (low speed, short strides)*

The preparation

Make a few gymnastic exercises with the aid of the short

gymnastic double (Fig. No. 85) and, while performing the exercise, gradually shorten the distance between the component bars.

Otherwise the method is similar to the previous case.

### The performance

In approaching the obstacle the aim should be to make the shortest possible landing after the first element.

If this occurs as desired, the rider need only maintain the slow speed and the horse's increased liveliness in accordance with the plan.

If the horse lands too deep, the length of the following non-jumping stride(s) must be shortened energetically and a very close take-off must be demanded. The horse must not be allowed to omit any stride decided on in the plan. Otherwise the take-off will occur at a point too distant for the horse to clear the obstacle (presuming that this method is chosen because the distant take-off does not suit the horse).

*Schooling the horse to jump combinations*

The horse learns the first fundamentals of jumping combinations during the exercises performed with the help of gymnastic structures. Through such means the animal learns that it can perform several jumping movements in quick succession without any particular strain and gradually adapts itself to the special requirements necessary in jumping combinations.

In practice, learning to jump combinations can only begin when the horse knows how to jump simple obstacles and accepts regulation satisfactorily.

During the period of schooling the height of the combinations is always related to, but a bit lower than, the height of the single obstacles which the horse is working over. The proportion between these heights is set out in the following Table.

| Height of single obstacles | Proposed heights for | |
|---|---|---|
| | double | treble |
| 3' 3" (1·00 m.) | 2'8"—3' (0·8—0·9 m.) | 2'4"—2'8"—3' (0·7—0·8—0·9 m.) |
| 4' (1·20 m.) | 3'3"—3'6" (1·0—1·1 m.) | 3'—3'3"—3'6" (0·9—1·0—1·1 m.) |
| 4' 6" (1·40 m.) | 3'8"—4' (1·1—1·2 m.) | 3'4"—3'8"—4' (1·0—1·1—1·2 m.) |

In the early stages of schooling—when the animal is given every advantage—the practice combinations must be set to correspond to the strides of the horse at its most comfortable speed for jumping.

The exercise may be made easier by using a take-off regulator to ensure a correct take-off at the first element.

Furthermore, at first it is advisable to employ doubles of a very inviting appearance; the third element can be added later.

In choosing the various fences it is better for the first element to be an obstacle without spread, followed by a broad fence, rather than vice versa.

When the horse has shown satisfactory improvement in jumping simple obstacles and combinations in their facilitated forms, the demands can be gradually increased and the combinations made more severe.

This can be achieved:

by omitting the take-off regulating device;

by changing from the distances which are most comfortable for the horse and thus forcing it to use a speed which is faster or slower than the one it prefers;

by arranging the elements so that the alternations of types presents a greater challenge; and finally

when the horse has acquired more knowledge of jumping, occasionally setting up a combination at an odd distance.

## OBSTACLES OF NATURAL FORM AND THEIR TREATMENT

*General recommendations for building and jumping them*

The previous paragraphs have described the technique of building and of jumping artificial fences, ditches and their combinations. The rider will often encounter obstacles of these types in the countryside; whenever they occur the method of jumping is the same.

However, the most typical natural obstacles are those the main substance of which is the earth in natural or artificial formations, such as banks, deep and drop jumps, wide and deep ditches, jumps into the water (the splash), etc. The formation of the ground often necessitates dealing with various obstacles on a slanting surface and the variation of these obstacles, both natural and man-made, is infinite.

In the following methods, which are suggested for negotiating

the principal forms of these obstructions, the rider will also find
hints for solving the problems caused by their variations.

BANKS (Figs. Nos. 117-125)

The term 'bank' covers all obstacles in which the earth protrudes
above the level of the surrounding ground. The horse, in crossing
it, must either climb the ascending slope or jump to reach the top
of the bank; and in descending must either jump or slide down.

Banks can afford a variety of formations and are frequently used
both in cross-country courses and in the show ring.

The basic requirement in overcoming banks is increased
collection; no increase over a medium speed is necessary.

In considering the method of negotiating a bank, let us take first
the case in which the horse must jump to get on to the sloping side
or attain the top (see the left side of Figs. Nos. 117-118/b and
120-125).

The rising phase of the jump (including take-off), with all the
sensations felt by the rider, is exactly the same as that of a
normal jump.

The trajectory of the jump meets the surface of the bank either
at the end of the ascending phase or at the beginning of the
descending phase, depending on the shape of the bank. At this
moment a sudden jolt is felt in the horse's motion. Simultaneously
the animal, with its forelegs, grabs at the side or the top of the
bank and pulls its quarters to the same landing spot. While the
horse is executing this rather clumsy movement the rider must be
particularly careful to avoid falling back on to the animal's back.
If he is to facilitate the task of the horse, he must completely
follow its clinging and balancing movements.

The next action of the horse will be either further climbing, a
non-jumping stride or a new take-off, which may again involve a
rough sensation. At this moment the rider must restore the
forward impulse and liveliness of the legs, so that the horse will
have sufficient momentum to jump down from the bank with a
nicely arched, smooth movement.

The first one or two strides following the jump down will be
about a third shorter than those following a normal jump (see
Table No. 8/a). This becomes obvious when a fence must be
jumped soon after the drop.

When the rider and the horse have gained some experience in

# Table No. 16

## BANK FORMATIONS

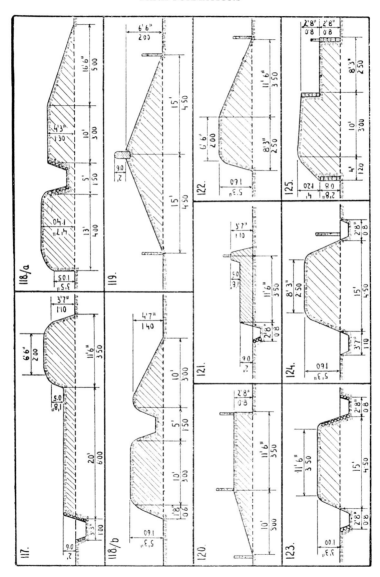

negotiating small and simple banks the bigger and more complicated formations, such as those mentioned below, will not cause
any particular trouble. In dealing with them the main point is to
make the animal preserve its momentum over the bank without
giving it a chance to speculate about the situation.

At flat and low banks an additional element is sometimes placed
above the wall of the take-off side. In such cases the jump on to the
bank must be regarded as a jump over a vertical obstacle without
spread. If the far side of the bank is altered by an additional
element, it must be treated as a drop jump. In such cases, if a
comfortable contact is maintained, the horse most probably will
not make a mistake.

When the additional structure is erected on a long flat bank, it
is generally better to allow the horse more freedom, so that it may
act on its own initiative (see Picture No. 75).

When the top part of the bank is only 6-10 feet (2-3 m.) wide
(see Fig. No. 124), and when the take-off for jumping down
immediately follows the landing on the top, the rider should
attempt to carry through the momentum of the initial take-off
on to the bank.

Often a ditch is present on the landing side of this kind of bank;
the rider must not allow the horse to 'explore' this unexpected
obstruction, but urge it to jump off promptly.

If the horse must jump over a high obstacle on to the sloping side
of a bank (see Figs. Nos. 119-120), it should be regarded as if the
jump were on a flat course.

(Regarding jumps over obstacles on the descending side of a
bank, see page 387.)

*Determining take-off and landing distances at bank jumps*
Jumping on to the bank

In jumping banks with vertical sides the take-off distance is the
same as for a simple vertical fence (Fig. No. 126/a).

If the take-off side of the bank deviates slightly from the vertical
(the slope is between 90° and about 60°), the calculation follows
that for a fence without spread with set-back ground-line (Fig.
No. 126/b).

If the slope is milder (about 45°), and especially if the height
of such a bank is over 5 feet (1.50 m.), the horse may climb up.

On the whole, it can be anticipated that the landing point on the

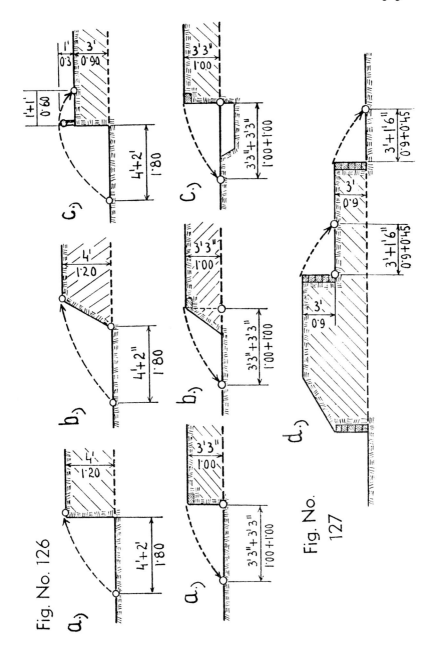

Fig. No. 126

Fig. No. 127

top of the bank will be near its edge (Fig. No. 126/a-b). However, when an additional obstruction (say a bar, or a low wall, hedge, etc.) is placed on the edge of the bank the landing distance can be assumed as twice the height of the additional element, measured from the upper level of the bank (Fig. No. 126/c). This calculation roughly coincides with the normal arc of the horse's jump.

Jumping off the bank

Here the take-off distance must be reckoned from the edge of the bank.

If the side of the bank is sloping, the horse can slide down instead of jumping off the slope.

However, sometimes an additional element, generally a low one, is erected on this side of the bank. In such cases the take-off distance will be twice the height of the additional element.

The landing distance is determined by the manner of the take-off. If the horse reaches the take-off point with unbroken momentum (mostly at flat banks, see Fig. No. 127/a-b), the landing distance can be taken as twice the descending height, but otherwise as only one and a half times the height. The latter ratio also prevails for very high banks, when the horse must climb while ascending (see Fig. No. 127/d).

The landing distance should be calculated from the edge of the bank from which the horse must jump off.

*Teaching the horse to jump banks*

In teaching the horse to jump banks an atmosphere must be created in which the animal gets real pleasure and gives its heart to the task.

Riders seldom have at their disposal real banks with which to school their horses. Fortunately, this is also not important because the training can be carried out successfully with the use of appropriate ground formations which require the animal to jump up or down from one level to another. During these exercises it is necessary for the horse to make the desired movement without hesitation; the rest will come from itself.

The horse's aptitude usually develops easily, since the actions involved are largely instinctive. Though it is not important to

concentrate on style, it is necessary to develop the muscles which
are needed in jumping banks.

In order to comply with this task, the best medium is a sandy
hillside 15-20 feet (4-6 m.) high with a slope of 35°-40°. Once
per week, before finishing the daily routine work, the horse
should canter up the slope once or twice. When such a hillside is
not at hand the same result can be achieved by taking a longer
canter (100-150 yards or metres) on a gentler slope, or by trotting
uphill on a course of 500-700 yards (450-600 m.).

DROP FENCES (Table No. 17)

Broadly speaking, drops can be regarded as the reciprocal forms
of banks. Thus, in jumping them the horse first moves downwards
and then returns to the level of the environment (Fig. No. 139/a-b).

### Table No. 17
#### VARIOUS FORMS OF DROP JUMP

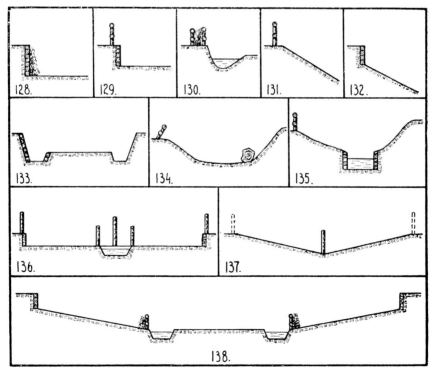

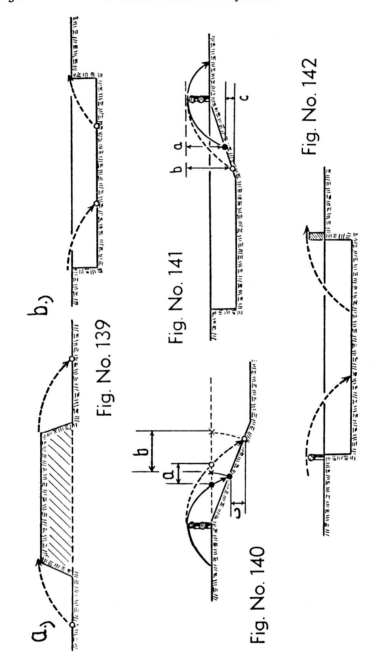

Fig. No. 139

Fig. No. 140

Fig. No. 141

Fig. No. 142

Although the general technique of jumping drops is identical with that of jumping banks, there are some special points to be considered separately.

If the drop involves jumping a fence and landing on a downhill slope, as in Fig. No. 140 (quarry, sand pit, etc.), the jump is executed as if it were a simple vertical obstacle. It is advisable to approach such an obstacle with increased liveliness, but at a *slow speed* and with quite a light rein-contact.

With horses which are unfamiliar with this kind of obstacle it is better to execute the jump from a trot, since it is easier to maintain the necessary regularity at this pace. Two additional arguments support the jumping of drops from a slow speed:

the sloping landing, as compared with level ground (see Fig. No. 140), causes both a lower landing ('c') and a longer one (see difference between the distances 'a' and 'b'); their increase tends to upset the horse's balance during landing;

with a slow approach the horse will not land so far and so deep on the slope (see dotted line) as with a fast one, saving its landing leg from becoming exposed to too much strain.

If the slope where the horse takes off in jumping out of the drop is accentuated by an additional fence at the top (see Fig. No. 141), the method of jumping will be governed by the following considerations:

The additional element in question, even if it is vertical without spread, can be regarded as an ascending type of obstacle (having also breadth); the slope itself requires it to be treated as such. As we have seen in jumping broad obstacles, it is desirable for the animal to thrust off from the lower limit of the suitable take-off distance, since this makes it easier to overcome the spread. This is even more important in the present case, since the longer the take-off, the greater the actual height (see dotted line on Fig. No. 141).

If both sides of the drop are sheer and marked by an additional fence (see Fig. No. 142), both elements should be regarded as vertical obstacles without spread.

### Teaching the horse to jump drop obstacles

Whenever during the work of schooling there is an opportunity to perform a drop jump, no matter how small, one should take advantage of it. It is easy to find in the country steep sides of ditches, low quarries, etc., where the horse, in order to keep going, must jump down.

At the beginning of the teaching period one should look for formations which have drops of no more than 1 foot 8 inches to 2 feet (50-60 cm.). Though the difficulty can be gradually increased by choosing deeper and deeper places, it is unnecessary to exceed a depth of 5 feet (1.50 m.). Even drops of over 4 feet (1.20 m.) should be performed only occasionally, since they place a real strain on the horse's legs. It is quite sufficient to make a jump of this depth only once or twice a month.

CLIMBING DITCHES (Figs. Nos. 143-147)

Though in general climbing ditches can be classified as drop obstacles, certain special conditions should be borne in mind in overcoming them.

These obstacles, which will be met with in almost every cross-country test and hunting field, are characterized by the breadth and steep formation (generally between 35° and 55°) of their banks. They are too broad to be jumped *in toto* and too steep to be traversed at a normal pace; thus the horse must resort to sliding down and climbing out again.

In competition there are no rules limiting the dimensions of the ditch, which must be taken in their natural formation. The measurements shown in Fig. No. 143 indicate the approximate dividing line between ditches that can be jumped and those that have to be climbed.

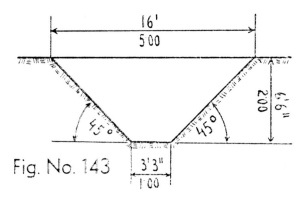

Fig. No. 143

Since the climbing ditch is one of the most common natural obstacles, a great number of variations is to be expected in practice. One ditch may be narrower or broader than another, shallower or deeper, or have steeper banks, etc. Moreover, the formation and composition of the ground will vary enormously, as the banks may be crumbling, slippery or uneven, and thus confront the rider with many different problems.

The method of negotiating climbing ditches may be divided according to the following conditions which they offer:

ditches which require only climbing (simple climbing ditches, see Fig. No. 144);

ditches which require climbing combined with jumping at the bottom (combined climbing ditches, see Figs. Nos. 145-148);

each of these types may appear with or without water.

*Simple climbing ditches*

If the bottom of the ditch is flat and wider than, say, 7 feet (2.25 m.), its negotiation will require no jumping and the obstruction can be regarded as a simple climbing ditch (Fig. No. 144).

In crossing such an obstruction the task rests almost entirely on the horse, for the rider will have little opportunity to help it in executing the necessary movements.

While the horse is descending the steep bank of the ditch it must proceed step by step to keep its balance, guided only by instinct;

when it has reached the bottom it gathers momentum for the climbing action, generally using canter motions.

In comparing the horse's work in the descent with the climbing out it will be noted that

the descent is aggravated by the mental hazards of the ditch and the motions involved demand a good deal of skill from the animal;

the climbing up is facilitated by the instinct of the horse to get out and the greater inherent stability of the climbing movement, even though more muscular energy is required than in the first phase.

Thus, on the whole, the descending phase of the performance is more difficult than the ascending one.

Once the horse has entered the ditch the rider's most important

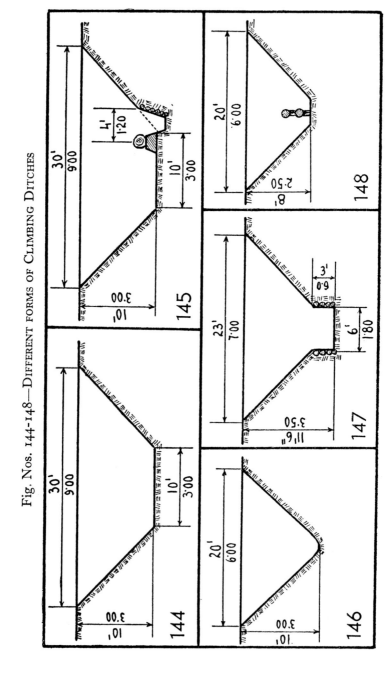

Fig. Nos. 144-148—Different forms of Climbing Ditches

duty is to avoid interfering with the animal's movements. Even though his assistance must be mainly passive in nature, he must still clearly manifest an overwhelming 'go-ahead' spirit.

When the horse reaches the edge of the ditch the rider can provide some encouragement with his leg or whip (mild taps) in order to make the entrance into the ditch more determined. If the animal's education has been properly carried out, it will not make any fuss about it.

After entering the ditch the rider should give the horse enough freedom to make the descent relying on its own skill. The necessary freedom is best provided by loosening the reins and bending the upper body well forward (this is valid both for descending and climbing). This position of the rider enables the animal to use its legs and back more freely.

During the descent the rider must ensure, by means of slight counter-deviation effects (with a long rein), that the horse does not deviate from a straight line, but proceeds downhill vertically.

When the horse has reached the bottom of the ditch impulsion should be increased to start the ascent;

during this, as in descending, the rider can leave the completion of the task to the horse, still making certain that the animal proceeds straight ahead.

While climbing upwards the rider should hold the mane (or neck strap) to facilitate his forward position. He should by no means pull or cling to the rein, this being a fault common to ignorant riders.

*Combined climbing ditches*

If crossing the bottom of the ditch requires a jump, more skill and energy are demanded from the animal and more assistance from the rider.

The simplest form of this obstacle describes a plain 'V'; there is no flatness at the bottom (Fig. No. 146).

This type of ditch serves as an intermediary between the two main types and thus helps prepare the horse to negotiate ditches which have an additional obstacle at the bottom.

In such cases the horse's actions are similar to those already explained, but before reaching the bottom it makes a small jump from one side to the other. The rider's only function is to urge the animal to cross this short distance.

When the bottom section of the ditch is deeply washed out, or
artificially shaped in this way (Fig. No. 147), or when an additional
fence is erected there (Fig. No. 148), the horse must make a bigger
jump across the bottom.   Jumping under such conditions is
exceptionally difficult, since the horse must take off while balancing
on the steep bank and must climb uphill immediately after landing
on a similarly steep bank.

The horse can only execute this laborious performance when it
possesses complete freedom.   The rider has nothing to do but
drive the horse forward and follow its movements smoothly.   The
reins should be slack to eliminate any interference.   The animal is
the best master of its own legs and the best aid the rider can give
is to forget about them.

If the sides of the ditch are deeply cut out at the bottom
(Fig. No. 147), many horses will be tempted to step into this
trough.   The rider must energetically prevent this, since the

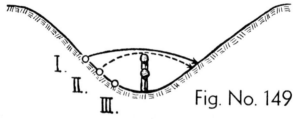

Fig. No. 149

animal can easily get stuck there.   Thus, while the rider must
still maintain freedom during the descent, he must also demand the
take-off most firmly.   The width of this jump, because of its
placement, may be considerable.   If the bottom part is, say 6 or
7 feet (1.80-2.10 m.) wide, the animal must make a jump of 12-14
feet (3.60-4.20 m.) in order to get from one bank to the other
with good momentum.   The momentum is particularly important,
for it must help the horse to climb out after landing on a sloping
surface.   With insufficient momentum the animal can easily slide
back to the bottom of the ditch.

When a fence has been erected at the bottom of the ditch (Figs.
Nos. 148 and 149) the horse should take off high enough on the
slope to be able to jump *across* without having to jump *up* (see
I in Fig. No. 149).   It is always easier for the animal to make a
wide, flat jump, even one 13-15 feet (4-4.50 m.) wide, than to
jump upwards from a steep slope (II).   If the horse should slide
under the fence, it will be completely unable to take off (III).

*Teaching the horse to negotiate climbing ditches*

As we have already pointed out, it is the horse which performs the whole task; accordingly it must be given ample opportunity to become familiar with the different types of climbing ditches and to develop through exercises the particular motions which are used in overcoming such obstacles.

This can best be accomplished by gradually increasing the dimensions and severity of the ditches and giving the horse as much chance as possible to gain experience. In this way the horse will learn to adapt itself to the different circumstances arising from a great variety of such obstructions.

JUMPING INTO WATER (THE SPLASH) (Figs. Nos. 150-152)

Obstacles of this type can be divided into two main groups, namely, those with mildly sloping banks, so that the surface of the water is almost even with the dry ground (Fig. No. 150); and those confined by steep banks, so that the water level is lower than the surrounding land (Fig. No. 151).

In competition both kinds of water jump are often made more difficult by fences placed where the horse enters or leaves the water. Less common, but not very tricky, is a fence in the middle of the water (Fig. No. 152).

Strictly speaking, jumping into water is an act of obedience involving no special skill or strength. The horse only needs to get used to the situation; once it has become accustomed to the presence of the water, and with the technique of negotiating it, there are rarely further difficulties.

The main support the rider can give is his own 'go-ahead' spirit, for the animal, like a sensitive seismograph, will adopt it and forget its own apprehensions about the obstacle.

Indeed, as far as physical support is concerned, the rider needs only to regulate the animal's motion in order to facilitate the act of jumping. To accomplish this he should collect the horse about eight to 10 gallop strides from the splash, so that it will arrive at the take-off point with a free forehand, straight and with a light contact. Before the take-off it is advisable to reduce the speed to about 380 yards (350 m.) per minute, because in landing the water tends to cut the horse's speed so suddenly that there may be danger of falling. The slower speed is even more necessary when the depth of the water exceeds $1\frac{1}{2}$ feet (0.50 m.).

Fig. Nos. 150-152—Different forms of Jumps into the Water (Splash)

When the horse must jump into a pond deeper than about 2 feet (0.60 m.), or the whole drop landing is more than 4 feet 6 inches (1.40 m.), as shown in Fig. No. 153, the pace should be changed a few strides before reaching the obstacle to a trot and the jump carried out at this pace.

In support of this technique in dealing with water jumps we might recall the three-day event at the Olympic Games in Berlin, when out of 35 competing horses 29 fell at such a water jump and only those which performed the jump from a trot were successful (the author was one of those).

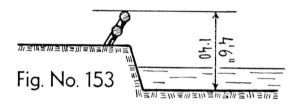

Fig. No. 153

At the moment of take-off the rider must encourage the animal by leg signals and a simultaneous freedom of rein. This freedom should be maintained even after landing until the animal can regain its balance in the water.

If the horse must jump again to leave the water, the rider should not interfere with the instinctive desire to get out.

*Teaching the horse to jump into a splash*

The preparation for jumping into water can be arranged as follows:

let the horse walk and trot several times into a splash which has no banks; then

at the edge of the water place a bar, hedge or trunk of a tree at a height of 1 foot to 1 foot 4 inches (30-40 cm.) so that the horse must jump while entering and leaving the splash; make this exercise at a trot;

as soon as the horse calmly performs the above exercises at a trot they can be repeated in a canter; after which

select a section of the splash where the bank is steeper, so that the water level lies slightly lower (about 1 foot to 1 foot 4 inches or 30-40 cm.) than the ground, but the landing depth should not be greater than 1 foot 8 inches to 2 feet (50-60 cm.).

Here, too, carry out the exercise first at a walk, then at a trot, and later on at a canter; after this

place a small obstacle at the edge of the steep bank, making the horse jump in or out of the splash, both at a trot and a canter.

In schooling it is not really necessary to increase the depth of the water or the height of the additional obstacle; the horse which learns to jump a small splash calmly and confidently will also perform a more serious splash jump without hesitation.

OBSTACLES ON GENTLE (15° OR LESS) SLOPES (Figs. Nos. 155-157)

Generally speaking, obstacles erected on a slope can be regarded as

vertical obstacles if the jump is executed while riding downhill; and

ascending obstacles if the action is carried out while riding uphill.

Thus the technique of jumping them is based on the methods discussed in conjunction with these types of obstacles and the techniques involved in the earlier exercises on undulating surfaces (see page 131).

Jumping while riding downhill

As riding downhill itself has a regulating effect on the horse, it is relatively easy to maintain it. This fact greatly assists in jumping.

It is an advantage to take off rather far back, since a stand back will reduce the height of the jump necessary to clear the obstacle (Fig. No. 158).

Jumping while riding uphill

Rising ground tends to upset the animal, making it irregular in its movements and inclined to rush. To prevent this the rider must be especially careful. He must not allow the animal to be distracted by the obstacle while approaching, but should assist it to take off regularly with increased liveliness.

It is very unwise to make the horse stand back too far, as a long take-off distance increases the height of the jump (Fig. No. 159).

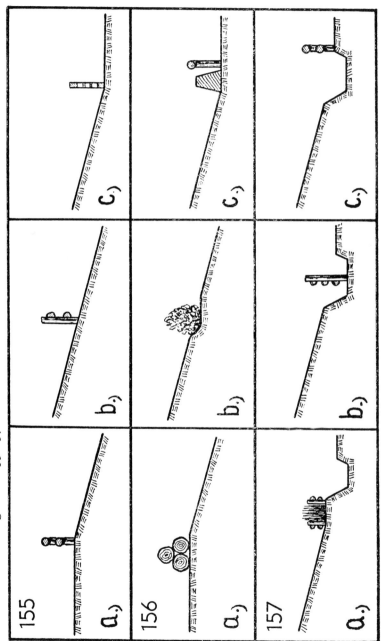

Fig. Nos. 155-157—Different Forms of Jumps on Slanting Surfaces

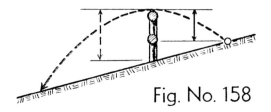

Fig. No. 158

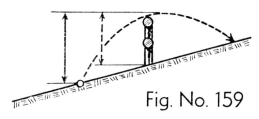

Fig. No. 159

### DESCENDING VERY STEEP SLOPES (SLIDING DOWN)

While riding in the country one may encounter slopes so steep that the horse cannot proceed in steps, but must slide down.

It begins to be necessary to slide on slopes of about 55°, and sliding is still possible on slopes of 75° (up to a depth of 10 feet or 3 m.) or 70° (with depths up to about 25 feet or 8 m.).

These very steep slopes are generally artificial, with firm clay texture (see picture No. 78). A slope of sandy material would soon lose its steepness and stony soil would soon ruin the animal's legs, especially its hocks.

In learning to slide down, the horse should be ridden at a quiet walk up to the edge of the slope. A loose rein will permit the horse to stretch its neck sufficiently and to step freely on to the slope with its forelegs. At this moment the rider must free the animal's back and help it bring the hocks under its body.

By this collecting movement the horse also brings its quarters on to the slope and, while 'sitting' on its hocks and propped by its forelegs, starts to slide down. In this first and most decisive phase of the descent it is most important to keep the horse straight; any deviation from a vertical slide may lead to an inescapable fall.

During the whole process the rider must keep his upper body bent forward in order to relieve the animal's quarters, which do most of the work.

Most horses will not wait until they reach the bottom of the slope, but, according to temperament, push themselves off at a height of 4-6 feet (1.20-1.80 m.) and jump to the ground. In order to compensate for the sudden jerk caused by this action, the rider must pay special attention to the following posture of his upper body.

Though slides are spectacular to watch, they usually cause the animal little concern. If the rider is sufficiently determined, the horse will proceed without hesitation. Resistance will occur only if the animal hurts its hocks in sliding and begins to associate sliding with a sensation of pain.

In teaching the horse to slide down steep slopes, practice over climbing ditches and drops affords the best foundation. If a horse has been properly schooled, it will slide down a slope of 70° and 20 feet (6 m.) deep without any elaborate practice.

### BUILDING 'NATURAL' CROSS-COUNTRY OBSTACLES

When planning cross-country obstacles one should mainly design fences of massive, solid appearance. Flimsy-looking obstacles belong more to the show ring, where limited space reduces the chances of creating authentic natural obstacles.

Any type of obstacle which is to be erected in the field must conform to the general character of the scenery. It is, therefore, necessary first to survey the site and only afterwards plan a suitable fence for the selected spot.

While surveying the possibilities of the area one will find all sorts of details which would escape attention when designing obstacles indoors. Furthermore, it is much simpler to decide on an obstacle in the field, where one can verify that it suits the country setting, than to try to adjust the countryside to an arbitrarily selected fence.

If the obstacle has been chosen and erected to co-ordinate with the selected site, it will not look odd. *It will be 'in' and not 'on' the scenery* (see also page 348).

### RECORD JUMPS

Although the obstacles used in record jumps are not of one special type, they merit attention because of their jumping characteristics.

Five different types of record jumping competitions can be

differentiated. They are: puissance; six bars competition; high jumping; long jumping; and high-and-long jumping.

As the first two types involve a series of obstacles, they will be dealt with later on when the technique of riding courses is discussed.

### High jumping

This kind of competition is performed over an obstacle which has no spread, but inclines at a slant of 55° (Fig. No. 160). The bottom of the obstacle is a brush fence about 4 feet to 4 feet 3 inches (1.20-1.30 m.) high, above which, on the slanting up-rights, the bars are placed with a gap between them of not more than 4 inches (10 cm.). The most suitable material for these bars is bamboo poles, covered by plaited straw. In raising the obstacle the number of bars is always increased.

During these competitions the horse must meet successively increasing demands; the rider can improve his chances for a clear jump by bearing the following considerations in mind:

In attempting very high fences it is especially important to bring the horse to the ideal spot for the take-off. The fact that in high jump competitions the same obstacle is jumped repeatedly facilitates the rider's task in this respect. In determining the spot for the take-off the simplest and safest way is to employ the method of the fixed turning point towards the obstacle (page 310).

During the training period it is first necessary to learn, within a space of, say, 40-80 yards or metres from the obstacle, the exact distance of a few turning points. Once in possession of these data the rider will be able at any time, and on any course, to fix the spot of the desired turning point and thus consistently afford his horse the best take-off possibilities.

As a practical method we suggest that the rider should measure the right distance before the competition and memorize the measured turning point in relation to some object on the course which he can always identify, or mark it by an inconspicuous but easily recognizable sign.

In warming up for the class the horse should practise using the necessary speed (400-500 yards or 380-450 m. per minute). Thus the rider can avoid surprising the horse by suddenly demanding a relatively high speed in front of the obstacle. Further details about warming up the horse are to be found on page 504.

Fig. No. 160

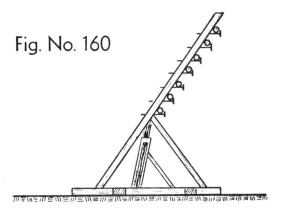

Fig. No. 161

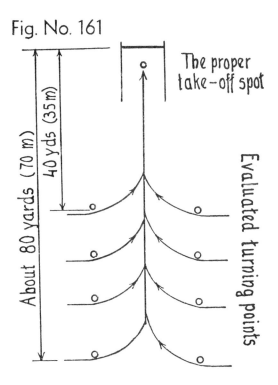

The proper take-off spot

About 80 yards (70 m)

40 yds (35 m)

Evaluated turning points

Executing the actual jump

Since during the approach the rider will be confident that his horse will meet the fence in stride, he will have no other concern than to keep the animal in free mobility and liveliness.

If while approaching the obstacle he notices the horse becoming sluggish or flat, he must restore its regularity by executing immediately—if necessary, in the most energetic manner—a collecting retard, followed by an equally energetic drive-on to restore the animal's elasticity. It must also be borne in mind that the retard may alter the original take-off point, which can be adjusted by lengthening the successive strides.

Hints on the horse's training in high jumping can be found on page 531.

### The long (broad) jump

The long jump is carried out over a water ditch some 16 feet (5 m.) wide, in front of which is a 1 foot 8 inch to 2 foot (50-60 cm.) take-off hedge (Fig. No. 162). The breadth of the ditch is increased

Fig. No. 162

by the gradual addition of more hedges to the original one; the row of hedges still gives the impression of being one wide, low hedge beyond which the surface of the water is visible.

In trying to achieve great breadth a correct take-off is even more vital than in high jumping. This will ensure that most of the length of the jump occurs on the landing side, so that the length which is officially measured will not be shortened by the wasted distance of a long take-off. The method of determining the proper take-off point and riding the horse to it is the same as described in connection with the high jump. As the fence is broadened, one must remember that the turning point—even when imaginary— must be moved backwards in proportion to the increased breadth.

In approaching the obstacle speed coupled with increased liveliness are very important factors, as the force of the accumulated momentum has a definite bearing on the length of the jump. However, the maintenance of the horse's regularity will put a limit on the speed.

The points mentioned in connection with the high jump are also valid both for schooling and riding the broad jump. While teaching, the water jump need not exceed 16 feet (5 m.).

Since broad jumping seldom appears as an item on the programme of a show, it is hardly worth while preparing a horse for this particular test alone.

## High-and-long jumping

This competition employs an ascending type of obstacle, the height of which corresponds to its breadth. The obstacle generally consists of a wide hedge, which indicates the breadth of the fence; beyond this are the bamboo poles on a sloping upright, determining the height of the jump. As the obstacle is enlarged the height and width are increased in the same proportion (about 4 inches or 10 cm. at a time).

As for the technique of jumping such an obstacle, the principles outlined for the high jump are valid in every detail.

This type of jump, as an individual competitive number, is very seldom included in the programme.

### OBEDIENCE FENCES

The principal characteristic of obstacles in this category is that normally—e.g. in hunting—the rider would never attempt to jump them.

Most frequently it is the narrowness of the obstacle and its wingless setting which causes the difficulty. The test of obedience can also be jumping a moving or noisy object (jet of water or anything which the human imagination can produce, e.g. dummies clad in gay coloured dresses, series of balloons fixed at a negotiable height, or burning torches stuck into the ground, etc.).

These obstacles do not really test the horse's jumping capabilities, but rather its capacity to obey. Just as in any other jumping task, it is important to approach these obstacles with complete regularity, but with increased shoulder mobility. The special importance of this point can be illustrated if we visualize an obstacle only 5 feet (1.50 m.) across. If the horse moves only one step to the side, it will miss the fence altogether. If the animal is not supple enough and the reins light, even a slight crookedness towards one side or the other will divert it from the right direction.

The horse should be prepared for such work by learning to obey through schooling and not by the customary random experiments. By habit the animal can learn to jump certain fences which are practised, but as soon as it is confronted with something new it is likely to fail if it lacks a high level of schooling. The higher the standard of the horse's education, the narrower the obstacles can be and more fantastic the things that can be used.

By jumping these kind of fences from time to time the animal's level of obedience can be checked.

Obedience jumping is seldom seen as an individual show competition. If the rider should encounter it, the proper education of his horse will afford his best chance to overcome the difficulties involved.

In submitting the foregoing explanations we have had a double purpose in mind:

First, to impress upon the rider the importance of schooling in relation to jumping and to guide him to the techniques by which the horse can be correctly developed. The possession of this knowledge will inspire the rider. He will always recognize the factors involved in the execution of a task demanded from the horse and be able to apply his efforts intelligently and productively. He will not make thoughtless demands upon the horse, but will truly educate it to perform the particular task in the form desired.

The second purpose has been to ensure that the horse, thanks to well-organized and pleasant schooling, will not only learn the various movements involved, but also come to enjoy them under whatever circumstances they have to be carried out.

When the horse has learned to enjoy the various movements involved in negotiating obstacles it has reached the stage when it can be truly called a jumper. Afterwards it only needs to get acquainted with show rings, cross-country courses or hunting fields in order to become the perfect fellow of its master. All this belongs to the period of continued training, which is the subject of the next parts of this book.

# PART FOUR

# The Three-Day Event

## Special Training and
## the Performance of the Test

THE three-day event with its varied challenges is the most beautiful and practical competition among the riding sports. The preparation for the test, comprising painstaking dressage, sound schooling in jumping and systematic training to develop the necessary stamina, demands considerable perseverance and competence from the rider as well as from the horse. However, the final performance of the test affords to both the greatest imaginable thrill.

While the individual parts of the three-day event are not too arduous, the complete test, with its long distances and fast speed requirements, demands an enormous display of energy and thorough preparation on the part of the horse. In order to meet these demands successfully, the animal must be of high quality both physically and mentally. A free, long, natural stride, enabling it to perform at speed without difficulty, a natural forward impulsion, and a keenness in overcoming obstacles are the basic qualities of a good three-day event horse.

Among horsemen the genuine three-day event rider is perhaps the truest idealist. The limelight provided by frequent appearances is of no importance to him; his ambition is to find satisfaction in the work itself, in training his horse to withstand even the hardest trials. The acknowledgment of his achievement, which he rightly expects, should come first of all from his comrade the horse, which with whole-hearted co-operation contributes its best performance to provide the rider with the very best sporting experience. Aside from keenness and courage, the most important qualification of the three-day event rider is the ability to judge correctly, from stride to stride during a performance, the state of the horse's strength and to adjust accordingly its output of energy to the demands imposed by the remaining part of the task. During the test it is important that he should use his partner's energy only to the extent to which it is *still profitable*. This means that it is just as great a mistake to undercut the time allowed by more than 5 per cent. rewarded by bonus points as it is to ignore the time limit. Unfortunately, this lack of horsemanship is not penalized by the regulations, although the horse well deserves such care for the sake of its soundness and in return for its efforts.

# CHAPTER ONE

# Tasks of the Three-Day Event Test and Subjects of the Training involved

THE special tasks for which the three-day event horse must be prepared are:
dressage test, as outlined in the prescribed regulations;
trotting over long distances (up to 4.35 + 9.32 miles, or 7 + 15 km.);
steeplechase (up to 2.48 miles, or 4 km.);
cross-country with obstacles (up to 4.97 miles, or 8 km.); and clearing a show jumping course (at a height of 3 feet 11 inches, or 1.20 m.).

The various techniques involved in the work of training supplement each other in many respects and by grouping them in the most suitable manner the health and energy of the animal can be safeguarded (see Distribution of Time and Work, page 517).

THE DRESSAGE TEST AND ITS REQUIREMENTS

The higher the level of the three-day event competition, the more important is the performance of the dressage test, since the rider's chances of putting himself in a position to win the cup are greatest in this particular phase of the event.

The endurance test, on the second day of the contest, forms the major struggle of the whole test. Every competitor naturally tries to obtain a horse which is particularly suitable for this task, and it can be assumed that on the second day the majority of the better horses will finish the competition in good condition. That is why, if the rider hopes to *win* the event, he must be prepared to post excellent results on the first day in the dressage.

The strategic importance of the dressage test should be kept in mind while practising the exercises recommended for perfecting the training, and even while performing the prescribed programme before the jury.

While practising the various movements in the course of schooling the rider must always remember that they are nothing more than different combinations of the actions which the horse has been taught during its preliminary education. If this has been carried out conscientiously, the horse will easily adapt itself to the various movements of the dressage test and the rider will reap the reward of his painstaking groundwork. But if the basic schooling has not been accomplished correctly, it is impossible for the horse to learn and perform the prescribed movements of the dressage test correctly.

Before examining in detail the requirements of the dressage test it is necessary to give a brief account of the different lengths of rein which are prescribed in the regulations. They may indicate three particular lengths to be used while performing the various movements:

the normal length, in which the horse keeps contact with the rider and shows an arched neck-carriage;

the long reins, in which the horse, while stretching its neck moderately, holds the bit through loosened reins;

the dropped reins, in which the rider holds the end of the reins, and where there is no contact with the horse's mouth.

THE PROGRAMME OF THE DRESSAGE TEST

The programme of the dressage test is designed in such a way that, aside from its competitive aims, it also tests the practical usefulness of the horse.

Basically, it is the quality of the schooling which is judged, since this determines the quality of the performance. In order to offer guidance as to how the horse should be prepared for the task and how it can best comply with the judging standards, it is desirable to recall the definitions of the F.E.I., which is the official authority on the subject:

'The object of dressage is to give the horse a pleasant ride, i.e. keen but submissive.

This double quality is revealed by:

the freedom and regularity of his pace;

the harmony, lightness and ease of his movements.

The horse thus gives the impression of doing what is required of him of his own accord.

Confident and attentive, he submits generously to the control of the rider.

His walk is regular, free and extended.

His trot is free, regular and with impulsion.

His canter is smooth, light and cadenced.

His quarters are never inactive or sluggish. They respond to the slightest indication of the rider, and thereby give life and spirit to all the rest of his body.

By virtue of a lively impulsion and suppleness of his joints, free from paralysing effects of resistance, the horse obeys willingly and without hesitation and responds to the various aids calmly and with precision'.

The order of the performance may change from time to time, but the movements involved will always remain more or less the same. If it happens that some new movements are demanded in a future programme, their basic features can still be found among the following recommendations and hints as to their execution.

In discussing the various movements of the test the most practical approach is first to describe the conditions which are applicable to all of them, and then to deal with their special techniques by grouping the movements according to the paces at which they can be performed.

### The horse's bearing, carriage of head and neck during the performance

Horses doing fast galloping work must not be burdened during their schooling by being made to adopt a highly arched neck and head-carriage, for the result of such an attempt may be stiffness. A moderate attractively arched deportment of the neck is perfectly sufficient and a properly schooled horse will adopt such a carriage automatically while in its well-balanced state. It will always retain this bearing, regardless of its pace or speed, if continuous rein-contact is maintained.

In order to keep the horse in its state of collection, 'play' during its motion, or while in the stationary position, with your muscles and position by performing the levelling function.

If a horse resists, don't try to pull down its head by the application of force, but amplify the above function by more augmented, interchanged animating and collecting elements (enforced levelling function, see page 189). As a supplementary means, it can also be helpful to exercise from time to time interchanged touches on the horse's neck (see page 109).

*The activity of the quarters and free mobility of the shoulders*

The greater the demands made upon the horse, the more important is the agility of the quarters and the free mobility of its shoulders. In performing any exercise or movement which requires collection or extended motion, this agility and mobility are especially important.

The agility of the quarters is produced by the collecting activities of the rider, performed with forward impulsion. Its development is encouraged by the rider's 'pushing feeling' in keeping the rein-contact and by the yielding functions involved in his activities.

The free mobility of the shoulders is a direct result of the former conduct of the rider. The key to its maintenance is the horse's obedience to regulations.

The rider should improve his feeling and determination, as well as his horse's obedience, up to a stage when he can perform the activities mentioned quite instinctively and the animal reacts promptly and submissively to them. By the improvement of this mutual readiness he can produce and maintain at any time the agility of the quarters and the mobility of the shoulders, which automatically ensure the correctness of the execution of the movements demanded. Thus the development of these qualities must be the main object of the preparation for the dressage test, and by no means the endless drilling of its prescribed 'figures'.

*Transitions, alterations and the halt during the performance*

Each change in the motion must be commenced or completed by the rider at a stipulated point of the arena. Therefore he should prepare the horse for the task in good time before reaching the particular point. This precaution is especially important with horses whose schooling is not yet perfected.

A change of pace can be demanded by the test in two particular ways, namely:

by a direct alteration, when the horse has to change its pace instantaneously (*e.g.* from walk into canter, or vice versa); or

by inserting an intermediate pace, or even paces (e.g. the alteration from rein-back into canter: first a brief halt, then after a few walking steps one or two strides of trot, followed by striking off into canter).

The latter form of alteration does not mean that the process should become a long-drawn-out show. This will not occur if the horse has a definite impulsion with submission.

The transitions within the same pace must be performed with elegance and ease. Therefore the rider should demand that the horse executes the transitions in a prompt and resolute manner. By doing so, not only are the conditions of the test being met, but at the same time the rider is exercising the best preventive influence on the animal to keep it supple and competent for the future demands of the performance. This is also the most reasonable and quickest means of forestalling the appearance of irregularity and preventing the horse from executing the prescribed exercises in a boring, monotonous and unimpressive manner.

As to practical recommendations for the performance of transitions, the following points should be kept in mind:

While shortening the speed or reducing the pace

> When decreasing the motion, first animate the horse in order to preserve its liveliness in the slower pace;
>
> during the change alternate the actions which indicate the desired movements with slight counter-actions, joined together each time by moments of yielding; then
>
> shorten the speed slightly more than is actually desired, so that the process can then be completed by a drive-on action in order to refresh the horse's impulsion. The transition thus executed has a further advantage, since emphasizing the shortening process adds to the beauty of the performance;
>
> after the change keep up the evenness of motion and the suppleness of the animal by retaining a swinging back and lively leg motion. For this purpose the application of the levelling function is the best means.

With regard to riding at a reduced speed, the main point to be borne in mind is that the slower the speed, the lighter the strength of the rein-contact must be.

While accelerating the speed or extending the pace

> introduce the change by a slight half-halting function in order to increase the horse's collection and thus enable it to strike off into the increased motion with determination and impulsion. This accentuates the beauty of a transition;

during the transition alternate the initial driving actions once or twice with a slight retardment instead of simply driving the horse ahead. By this means the animal can carry its full impulsion into the higher speed; it will not push itself into a rolling motion and will retain its calmness, these being such important features of a correct change in the motion;

after the transition the horse should proceed with cadenced and ground-gaining strides, during which the contact can be more pronounced. These conditions, however, except concerning the cadence of the strides, should be disregarded in cases when the alteration is carried out from a slow, collected pace into another one.

If the horse shows opposition during the above procedures, apply the same method of regulation described in connection with the pushing action against the bit (see page 109).

### The stationary position and the connected transitions

With regard to reducing the motion to a halt, the rider may consider whether the change has to be carried out directly from a given pace or by the insertion of an intermediate pace or paces. The higher the speed or pace from which the transition or alteration is to be performed, the higher will be the collection required on the part of the horse, and the more distinct the attitude of yielding on the part of the rider. The aim is to enable the animal to tread distinctly into a motionless state through a soft and fluid transition.

The rider must know by practice and observations the exact distance required by the horse and by himself for the smooth completion of the change, separately from each pace, into a stationary position. He should start reducing the motion in accordance with this limit of their performing capacity. It is a bad practice trying during the performance of a test to shorten the distance experienced. By doing this instead of halting correctly the horse will fall abruptly into the motionless state or, by displaying opposition, finish the movement beyond the prescribed spot.

Once in a standstill position, the animal must remain motionless, retaining the rein-contact and standing squarely on all four legs. The rider should also practise keeping this posture while holding the reins in one hand, since it may be necessary during the salute.

When moving off he should give the driving signal *determinedly* and simultaneously help the horse to perform the smooth but resolute strike-off, and the relaxed motion during the following steps, by the inclusion of the levelling function. (Regarding corrections, see page 134.)

The quality of the performance of transitions and alterations is evaluated and scored by the jury in combination with the scoring of those movements from and to which the change is executed. The main points of judging the performance are the smoothness, lightness and determination of the display and the maintenance of the horse's straight position during the execution of the task.

*Riding on the centre line*

Since the horse is not helped in its straight progress by the enclosure of the arena, riding on the centre line is a very suitable test as to whether or not the animal is able to proceed independently on a straight line. This ability is of great practical importance, and this is the reason why the performance of the task is required in all three paces. By this means the jury can gain sufficient evidence of the horse's schooling.

The important point in riding on the centre line is that the horse should proceed, with sureness and resolution, in a straight position and with a go-ahead spirit. It must never show the slightest sign of hesitation, nor deviate either with its forehand or quarters from the line marked in white in the arena.

In order to achieve these aims, ensure the horse's lightness and the freedom of its shoulders by the levelling function, while keeping a very light rein-contact and driving the hind legs determinedly forward. Don't try to force the animal to adhere rigidly to the line, because this will more likely force it away from there. During the ride look far beyond the judge's tent and, through your suggestion, the horse will automatically tend to maintain a straight line.

*The performance of simple turns*

On each curved line it is advisable to subject the horse to frequent but hardly noticeable counter-turns, so that its suppleness is always preserved. In this manner the animal will remain on the curve of the turn with both its forehand and quarters without making any deviation.

During the performance of the test the negotiation of turns can be excellently employed to make any slight adjustments in the horse's position.

Make the turns and negotiate the corners on a rather narrow curve, with the appropriate bending of the horse. Cutting off and looking outwards are serious faults. The quality of the turns performed has a considerable bearing on judging the general show of both rider and horse.

### The rein-back

The horse should perform this movement while maintaining a smooth and even rein-contact to invisible signals, producing a distinctly clear sequence of stride on an absolutely straight line. The steps should be of equal length and there should be no sign of rolling back or showing resistance. The performance of the motion should be carried out as described on page 221.

In order to perform the exact number of steps required it is best to count each backing step, but to *start* driving forward one step before the desired number of backing steps has been performed. Otherwise the horse will usually make one step too many.

After completing the rein-back the horse must remain standing calmly on all four legs, but it must also be able to step forward or backward immediately if required.

The manner in which a rein-back is performed is the best indication of a horse's submission, and so the execution of the task is always given special attention by the jury.

### THE COMPONENT MOVEMENTS OF THE DRESSAGE TEST

### The movements to be performed at a walk

The tasks in this group consist mainly of the execution of the different forms of the walk. However, the half-pass movement, the turn on the forehand and on the haunches may be included with them.

### The long, free walk (extended walk)

The horse should perform its strides with the utmost effort to gain ground, proceeding straight forward with a regular rhythm and cadence. Although it stretches forward its neck and head, it must not lose contact with the bit, unless the movement is required to be performed with loose reins.

In the event of breaking into a trot the fault should be corrected by a calmly applied retardment, from which the animal is then driven on with determination.

The ordinary walk

In this movement the horse should stride energetically with lively, regular steps, the length of which is determined by the natural length of its leg pendulum.

It must keep an easy rein-contact and proceed with a moderately arched neck-carriage. (Concerning the back action and impulsion, see the information on the collected walk.)

The collected walk

The steps are somewhat shorter and higher than in the ordinary walk and consequently the speed is slightly slower. In spite of these reductions, the stride action is full of mobility and more energetic than in the ordinary walk.

The bearing of the animal becomes higher and more rounded and it keeps a very light contact on the reins. The rider should follow the horse's movements almost to the point of pushing it forwards.

He should follow the swinging movement of the back with his seat and effect necessary corrections with mild functions of his thighs and seat-bone.

The vigour of the whole locomotion should be kept alive by the animating effect of the legs acting in co-ordination with the seat. If the horse is in a proper state of collection, the invisible pressures of the knees and calves will be sufficient to create the necessary impulsion.

The half-pass (counter-change of hand on two tracks)

In performing this task the horse must proceed in a hardly noticeable flexed position at an angle of 50° to the parallel lines of the arena, starting and finishing the movement at a prescribed spot.

The decisive point in the half-pass is the proper start away from the straight direction. Therefore the horse has to be led determinedly and without transition into the two-track movement, in which it should stride, without drifting, freely and with impulsion both forwards and sideways. The rider controls the movement mainly with the inside rein and his outside leg, while his centre of gravity is brought towards the direction in which the horse is moving. He should combine these basic functions with the oscillating effects of the levelling function.

During the execution of the task the employment of the lateral moving effect of the outside rein should be restricted to minute indications only, since under the influence of its firmer effect the horse is inclined to push the croup to the inside and turn its neck to the outside. Both results are grossly defective. It is necessary to emphasize the importance of this recommendation also in connection with that particular moment when the direction of the half-pass movement must be changed during the test.

The change of direction should be indicated by the rider, by the simple change of his leading activities combined with the transposition of his gravitational centre. There are no further aids necessary. On the other hand, the horse should execute a change in response to the rider's definite demand only and never act on its own accord, since a customary change can easily result in a stiff drifting or falling in the new direction.

Bearing this possibility in mind, it is wise practising the changing movement during the routine exercises in such a manner that the horse, after a ceased side-stepping phase, should never know in advance in which direction the next movement will occur. With this aim the rider should ask the performance of the half-pass in a repetition-like manner, interlocking the component parts of the exercise with short (one to three strides long) forward riding phases. During this he should start side-stepping several times in the same direction and demand from the animal an immediate change only occasionally and in a quite irregular succession.

The rider should direct the horse, right from starting the half-pass, by nearly invisible, light functions mainly by his suggestive power. He should avoid any forcing interference, which would hamper the animal only and make it resisting during the performance.

If the animal makes a mistake during the performance (changes its position in either direction, stops crossing the legs, breaks into trot, etc.), interlock one or two brief half-halts; from this let it make one or two strides forward and then start the cross-stepping anew. It is most unwise to force the horse to directly correct the situation from a faulty position. The occurrence of crookedness, stiff drifting, looking towards the opposite direction of the movement, are serious faults.

The turn on the forehand

This movement is included at the present time in the novice classes of one-day events.

The horse, while bent in the direction of the movement of the head, pivots around its inside foreleg. It must be prevented from stepping forward by the outside rein, and from deviating either side by pressures on the girth from the corresponding leg. A slight stepping backwards is excusable (see details on page 215).

The turn on the haunches

While approaching the spot where the movement has to be performed, check and refresh the lateral mobility of the shoulders by the slight oscillating movements of the upper body. Then, during the execution of the task, make certain that the inside hind leg does not move away from its pivoting point and the horse retains its correct bent position. A lateral shift from the pivoting point or stepping backwards is a serious mistake, but a slight forward step is excusable.

While carrying out both the turn on the forehand and the turn on the quarters, apply mild signals and let the horse perform the articulated side-steps under the effect of the rhythmical yielding movements of the leading rein. In case of need repeat the signals without increasing their strength.

In order to prevent, but also to correct, a faulty performance, the most effective method is to interlock a slight counter-movement (eventually only by the momentary transposition of the centre of gravity). This relaxes the tension in the pivoting leg, and by it forestalls the emergence of stiffness, which may create resistance on the part of the animal.

*Points in the judge's evaluation of the walk*

In judging the quality of the performance stress is laid upon:

regularity, rhythm, degree of impulsion and determination in the movement and the ground-gaining quality of the strides;

correctness of the horse's bearing (head- and neck-carriage) and its position (straight, flexed, bent); and the skill and obedience of the horse in executing the various figures.

### The movements of the test performed at a trot

### The ordinary trot

In this pace the horse should proceed straight forward with a free, lively, rhythmical and energetic stride action. The length of the steps must be long, but not extended. The hind legs should fall exactly in the hoof-marks of the corresponding forelegs. During the entire performance the animal should maintain a light and continuous rein-contact and display a nicely arched neck-carriage.

The use of both the rising and the sitting trot can be demanded.

### The collected trot

In comparison with the ordinary trot, the horse's state of collection is increased so that the animal adopts a higher head- and a well-arched neck-carriage; the strides become higher and shorter, so that the hoof-marks of the hind legs fall slightly behind those of the forelegs. Although the regular stride action becomes a bit slowed down, it remains energetic and radiates an impulsive mobility. Furthermore, the horse keeps a lighter rein-contact than in the ordinary trot.

In the course of the performance the rider should follow the animal's movements with his hands, seat and legs in the same manner as in the collected walk. His whole bearing must display an easy elegance, showing that he is united with his mount and with its motion. The rider is required to use the sitting position.

### The extended trot

In this pace the horse proceeds with considerably lengthened strides. The brilliance of the performance depends upon an energetic thrust-off of the legs and distinct forward-swinging movements of the shoulders. In its carriage the animal extends its neck and takes a slightly firmer contact on the bit. The hoof-marks of the hind legs precede those of the forelegs. The distinct execution of the transitions is of greatest importance (see page 410).

If the horse should break into canter while performing this movement, the most appropriate remedy is to retard almost to a collected trot and then make it strike off resolutely into the extended pace again. After such a drastic correction there is no need to fear that the horse will repeat its fault. However, if only a half-way measure is applied, it is quite likely that the animal will break into a canter again.

Certain horses are not naturally gifted enough to produce a really good extended trot. When such a horse has to be presented to the jury the best way to offset this lack of brilliance is to greatly reduce the speed of both movements which precede and follow the extended trot. By this means the difference in the rate of speed and in the animal's activity are accentuated. Generally the rising-trot is demanded.

*The circular figures (performed at a trot)*

The horse must be bent towards the direction of the curve followed in the course of the performance. While the animal is following the curve it must maintain its rhythm and cadence as well as a light rein-contact.

If the horse has been carefully schooled in taking turns, the rider will not encounter any difficulties in executing the various figures and will be able to 'draw' them on the ground of the arena with the animal's legs. He should balance the horse on the desired line and not try to control it by rigid forcing.

The circle, small circle and the volte

In the regulations of the dressage tests the description of these figures is given in the form of certain diameters which must be adhered to by the rider. In executing these movements it is advisable to remember that the smaller the circle, the more the speed must be decreased, and the more the 'hardness' of the hands should be relaxed.

(The volte is a circle with a radius corresponding to the horse's length: a diameter of 20 feet or 6 m.)

The circle in both directions (figure 'eight')

This is a figure in which two circles meet each other, ridden first in one and then in the other direction. While the horse is changing the direction the rider's concern must be that it should also change its bending. After having taken the first small circle of the 'eight' and having reached the dividing line, the rider should not proceed immediately to ride the second circle, but should make one or two strides forward on the straight line in order to give the horse a chance to adapt itself to the new direction. By doing this there is no danger of deviating from the figure 'eight', since the curve of the second circle does not leave the middle line immediately.

### The serpentine

This is a series of interlocking loops. It is similar to, though considerably easier than, the performance of the circle in both directions (which is also a serpentine line), since the animal has more time to adapt itself to the new direction by changing its bent position.

### The half-pass

In the execution of this task the same principles are valid as outlined in connection with its presentation at a walk.

It is at a trot that the half-pass movement offers the most attractive picture. The movement must be of swinging nature, generated by forward impulsion. Before starting ease the conduct and increase the amount of momentum. Then use the increased momentum to initiate the cross-stepping at the given spot.

All recommendations given for the performance of this movement at a walk are also valid for its presentation at a trot.

*Judging the performance at the trot*

The main points in judging the performance are:

subtlety and distinctness of the transitions;

liveliness, clarity, suppleness and determination of the strides;

correctness of the flexion, together with its changes; and

the turning ability of the horse and its aptitude to retain its balance while proceeding on curved lines.

*The movements of the test to be presented at a canter*

In general

During the performance the horse must go softly into its bridle and react submissively to the aids given by the legs or the seat, whether they are applied for the purpose of direction or for correction.

The difficulty of the performance lies principally in the problems posed by the more extended locomotion of the animal at a canter (in comparison with lower paces) and by the confined space of the arena. But if the rider can create a satisfactory state of pliability in the horse, he will find that even the limited proportions of the arena are large enough for the accurate presentation of the movements and figures demanded in the programme. Without pliability, however, the restricted space is likely to bring out all the defects which can be concealed in the lower paces.

Before striking off into a canter make sure that the animal is in the right position for the execution of the task. Then concentrate your thoughts on the performance of the action and give the signal in the yielding phase of the interlocking half-halt movement without any visible action. Strike off in an absolutely straight position.

When the horse is cantering on a straight line its body must be straight. Horses are frequently inclined to deviate towards the inside with their croup and special care is needed to prevent such a faulty position.

In a properly presented canter the sequence of hoof-falls must give three beats, otherwise the performance is grossly defective.

If the horse makes a mistake either at the strike-off into the canter or during the canter itself, correct the situation calmly and don't force the animal into a state of disorder by compelling it to make a hasty adjustment. For example:

if it strikes off in the wrong direction, retard it and recommence the action after a brief half-halt (increasing collection), coupled with the release of the inside shoulder;

if it happens to fall back into trot, ask it, after a brief collection, with calm but determined signals to adopt the canter again;

in case of changing legs of its own accord, retard it to a trot or walk and strike off in the usual way again in the proper direction. Don't try to enforce a change of legs in the air.

### The ordinary canter

The movements as a whole must be light and cadenced on account of the swinging action of the back. The strides should be free, with definite ground-covering character. The horse's bearing must show a moderately arched head- and neck-carriage and it should go softly into the bridle.

### The collected canter

Although the horse proceeds with short, slowed-down but higher strides, its swing and mobility are increased.  Its head and neck assume a more elevated and arched carriage and the contact on the bit becomes very light (see also collected trot).

The rider should follow the animal's movements with full contact and have a feeling of striding with his own legs.  His bearing must be quiet and proud.

### The extended canter

In this pace the strides become considerably longer than in an ordinary canter, without, however, accelerating the cadence of the stride action.  While proceeding, the horse must retain its calmness and the evenness of its strides.  It must show a definite responsiveness to the aids with which the rider may assist it and it should be able to carry out desired transitions promptly (the recommendations given on pages 122 and 412 are of special importance).  The animal may extend its neck moderately during the motion, but should retain a freely-arched carriage and keep an even contact on the bit.  The rider should bend his upper body slightly forward without, however, losing his seat-contact.

In order to avoid any difficulties during the performance of the extended canter, the following points should be given special attention:

before starting increase the collection of the horse and then let it *strike off* definitely into the extension (see page 411);

don't allow it to pull against the bit.  To avoid this, exercise definite passive resistance in the critical moments, followed immediately by an abrupt relaxation of the engaged muscles.  The latter function should be coupled with the pressing-down action of the thighs and the driving action of the legs;

while riding through the corners of the arena hold the horse on the curve of the turn by slightly alternating turning actions and ensure the maintenance of the correct bent position.  It is a serious fault for the animal to look outside while turning, since by doing so it shows stiffness.  It is also a fault if the rider decreases the speed while passing through the corners; this is a sign of deficiency in the horse's schooling.

Circular figures performed in a canter

While engaged in these movements the horse should be bent in the direction of the *canter action*. Otherwise the principles involved in performing these tasks are broadly identical to those described in connection with the trot.

Circles

The technique of performance is the same as in the trot.

The circle in both directions (figure 'eight')

Shortly before the completion of the first circle reduce the canter to a trot and ride straight ahead for one or two strides. During this change the horse's flexion and simultaneously make it strike off in the new direction.

The serpentine

When riding on a serpentine line the main point to remember is that the horse should proceed in a collected (short) canter while held on very light reins. If the animal has been schooled to canter smoothly in the above manner, the rider will have no difficulty in performing the loops required by the regulations. Therefore, during the course of schooling it is senseless to start making serpentines until the animal is supple and yields readily.

The turnings of the serpentine are accomplished in the normal way, using the right rein for the right turn and the left rein for the left turn. The horse must retain the direction of its original flexion during all the way on the serpentine line. Its bending alternates between that which corresponds to the inside leading curve of the loops and the straight position, when it proceeds on the curves leading to the outside. The rider should avoid changing the horse's bent position completely, since by doing so he not only makes a fault, but he can easily cause the animal to change legs in the air.

While negotiating the loops of the serpentine the rider's balancing conduct, coupled with his moments of general yielding (especially during the phases of counter-lead), is of special importance. This facilitates the task of the horse and ensures the smoothness and fluency of the whole performance. The rider should take care that the loops become of equal shape and size on both sides of the centre line.

Turning or riding through corners at a canter in counter-lead occurs in the same manner as described above in connection with the performance of serpentine lines.

### The half-pass in canter

This particular task figures in the regulations as an exercise demanding only a brief and slight lateral movement. The horse must proceed in a collected canter in the direction of the lateral movement. Its position must be straight; only the head should be flexed a bit. While the animal keeps a very light contact the quarters must be active and the shoulders mobile.

The half-pass should be conducted in the same manner in a canter as in a walk or trot. Since its execution is actually easier in a canter than in the other paces, the performance is not likely to present any special difficulty.

### *Judging the work at a canter*

The essential points can be summed up as follows:

The strike-off into the canter: easiness and distinctiveness of the horse's action and the correctness of its position.

The manner of moving: impulsion of the horse, evenness, rhythm and cadence of the motion and the ground-covering quality of the strides.

Proceeding on curved lines: adroitness, flexibility and state of balance; the horse's behaviour during movements in counter-lead; and the precision of the circular figures.

### *Riding with reins held in one hand*

Some regulations make it compulsory to ride during a short phase of the test with reins held in one hand. There is no special preparation necessary on the part of the horse or the rider, since only simple movements have to be performed during this particular phase of the test. The rider can easily compensate all the loss arising in his conducting possibilities by the application of the levelling function.

### THE RIDER'S PREPARATION FOR THE PERFORMANCE OF THE DRESSAGE TEST

The immediate requirement of the performance of the dressage test is that the rider should memorize the sequence of the movements involved so thoroughly that he can start it not only from the beginning, but also at any intermediate point.

An impeccable presentation depends very largely upon the rider's horseman-like behaviour and sense of style. Therefore, during the horse's schooling he should polish his own bearing and techniques by which he influences the animal. A reasonable method of checking the execution of the dressage-like schooling is to jump an obstacle of small dimensions (2 feet 6 inches to 3 feet, or 80-90 cm., with some spread) just after the routine work without inserting any additional jumping or gymnastic exercise. The quality of the jump will be a reflection of the work (see page 486). Or it is also a useful method of self-control when the rider, after having collected the horse, suddenly drops the reins. If the animal rolls away, it is shown that the procedure has been completed by force and not by correct actions.

Although these measures give some limited assistance, there is always a danger of being uncritical of oneself and becoming too self-compliant. This can result in mistakes which the rider fails to notice immediately, but rapidly diminish the standard of performance. Even the best riders cannot be exempt from this human weakness and, therefore, it is wise to ask someone of expert knowledge to make a periodic check on one's work during the time of preparation.

In order to improve and refresh the formal requirements of his general bearing (erect upper body, easy, natural yet correct seat, etc.), it is advantageous—even for an experienced rider—to ride without stirrups on the longe for 20 to 30 minutes every day for three to four weeks before the date of a more important test. During this exercise somebody should observe and correct the faults of the rider.

## The Speed and Endurance Test and its Component Parts

### THE ROADS AND TRACKS PHASES

In the speed and endurance test there are two phases during which the rate of speed is based upon the trot.

The first of these phases serves as the introductory part of the test; the second takes place between the steeplechase and the start of the cross-country.

In schooling the horse for this task the aim should be to make it lengthen its strides. This can easily be achieved by exercises which are specially designed for the suppling of the animal.

If the horse can proceed with long strides, it will require less movement to cover a certain distance and thus save energy. However, it is also true that *too* long strides, especially if performed protractedly, may cause considerable strain. Therefore, during the preparatory work the rider should determine the particular length of stride which exploits the animal's energy in the most efficient manner. A reliable guide can be found by observing the size of the pendulum formed by the natural length of the horse's legs, as well as the length and structure of the shoulders. As a result of this observation one should take as a standard the upper limit of the comfortable pendulum movement. On the average, horses using this length of stride will attain a speed of about 250 yards (230 m.) per minute.

Actually a speed of 262 or 240 yards (240 or 220 m.) per minute is demanded during the roads and tracks phases of the test. Furthermore, if the rider is anxious to arrive three to six minutes early at the beginning of the ensuing phase of the test in order to allow sufficient time to refresh the horse before its new start, he must demand a considerably faster speed in order to comply with the requirements.

This increase in speed would so intensify the rate of trot as to put an enormous strain on the horse. Therefore, the high average speed necessary must be attained by using the canter for certain sections of the course. The greater the difference between the stipulated speed and the normal speed of the trot, the longer must be the distance to be cantered. In working out the correct method of riding these phases of the test the following recommendations may be of assistance:

> if the prescribed speed is fixed at 240 yards (220 m.) per minute, then two-thirds of the distance should be covered at a normal trot (250 yards or 230 m. per minute) and one-third at a quiet hand-gallop (400 yards or 365 m. per minute);

> if the speed is fixed at 262 yards (240 m.) per minute, the length calculated for trotting should be a bit over the half of the distance (about 55 per cent.) and for cantering a little under the half of it (about 45 per cent.).

THE STEEPLECHASE PHASE

The purpose of this part of the event is to test the speed of a well-trained horse. The conditions under which the steeplechase is run are rather severe, the minimum speed demanded being 656 yards (600 m.) per minute.

The great exertion to which the animal is subjected during this test of speed will require a special programme of preparation. The horse must learn to move and jump at a speed required by the regulations even before the period of its conditioning commences and also to perform at an even faster speed over short distances.

The main goals of the preparatory training are:

to lengthen the strides at the gallop;

to accustom the horse to move at an increased speed; and

to familiarize it with jumping under such conditions.

While this hard training is being carried out the rider must ensure that the increased strain of the work is always in keeping with the gradual improvement of the animal's muscular system. By overreaching its limitations the horse can easily become overstrained, resulting in nervousness or even some form of physical breakdown.

*Lengthening the gallop strides and developing speed*

In order to develop speed, the horse must primarily lengthen, and only secondarily accelerate, its stride action.

For training purposes turf or sandy going (not too deep) are the most suitable. It is desirable to ride on long, straight stretches during these exercises.

In regard to the method by which the training itself is accomplished, the deciding factor should be the temperament of the horse. In any case, the animal's calmness must be maintained. Bearing this in mind

the horse should be at first acquainted with the course where the training takes place, so that nothing strange in the surroundings will divert its attention from its work; and

the rider should ride in the direction which best suits the horse's temperament.

A spirited, keen horse will be willing to strike off at an increased speed by itself. In such a case the rider's task is to calm down the animal's motion and restrain its nervousness. The simplest and best method of achieving this is to ride the course in the direction *away* from home, which will usually have a soothing effect on the horse.

A lazy or sluggish animal should be worked towards home. The feeling of approaching home, with all its familiar sights, will have a stimulating influence on the horse, so that it will readily increase its speed by itself.

In the case of very lazy animals a 'pilot horse' should be employed.

For the execution of the exercise the following plan is recommended:

at the start of the course strike off into a quiet canter at a speed of about 330 yards (300 m.) per minute and continue for a stretch of about 100-150 yards (or m.); then

gradually increase the speed over a long-drawn-out transition and lead the horse into a gallop. In order to be sure that the animal remains calm, allow it a generous amount of time to work up to the speed desired. This transition may represent a stretch of 150-250 yards (or m.), depending upon the individual animal.

To start with it is quite sufficient to use a speed of about 500-550 yards (450-500 m.) per minute. If the horse remains calm, this speed may be gradually increased. As a general rule, I would recommend an increase of about 50 yards (or m.) per minute after every three or four training rides. The speed can thus be gradually increased up to a limit of 800 yards (720 m.) per minute. Beyond this increases are quite unnecessary.

When the transition has been completed and the horse proceeds calmly with lengthened strides and balanced action at the required speed, it should continue at this rate for about 300-500 yards (250-450 m.), preferably on a straight part of the course. As this phase is the most important part of the exercise, great care should be taken to perform it correctly.

The method of decreasing the speed is exactly the reverse of that of increasing it. Thus the speed should first be reduced through a lengthy transition; then, while the animal proceeds at a quiet canter over a distance of, say, 100-150 yards (or m.), the pace can be altered to a trot and eventually to a walk.

While galloping the horse can take a firmer rein-contact, but it must retain its willingness to obey both the rider's driving and retarding actions. The rider should use the forward position and remain as passive as possible. However, he must follow perfectly the trend of the motion.

The aim of this exercise is principally the horse's schooling for the extension of its stride action and only secondarily the improvement of its muscular abilities; accordingly, emphasis should be placed upon the quality rather than the quantity of work. The work involved is not strenuous and it is unnecessary to devote a special day to its execution.

This practice in lengthening the strides provides an excellent opportunity for the rider to improve his ability to estimate speed by his sense of feeling. It is a good idea to use a stop-watch to measure the time taken to cover a definite, clearly marked distance (150-200 yards or metres) within the course, where the horse will be proceeding at top speed. The result obtained will inform the rider whether or not the exercise has been properly carried out and whether he has ridden the horse at the stipulated speed.

### Training the horse to jump at speed

As a first principle it can be stated that horses which have been properly schooled in jumping need only to learn to remain calm while jumping at speed. The execution of the actual jump will follow automatically.

It is unnecessary to acquaint the animal with the special fences employed on a steeplechase course. These are mostly of sloping types with a well-marked ground-line and permit the horse to brush their upper part. Even if an unknown obstacle is encountered on the course it is not likely to upset the animal, since, if well trained, it will jump the fence without hesitation. In addition to its obedience, the speed will help to overcome any reluctance.

When the horse approaches a jump at an increased speed it is of utmost importance that the rider should not worry about the obstacle itself, but merely dictate the speed and prevent the animal from hurrying or from slowing down the pace. Long before the obstacle he should fix his eye on the desired take-off point and drive the animal forward with all his will power concentrated upon arriving at the exact spot he has selected. This concentration of will, with its latent influencing power on the horse, has an enormous bearing on the successful performance of the take-off at a great speed. As the increased speed is likely to produce a long jump, it is desirable to stand back at the obstacle rather than to take off too close.

The method of training will depend upon the horse's attitude whether or not it is inclined to maintain the speed dictated by the rider; whether it offers resistance or tries to hurry. Whatever its attitude, the main purpose is to educate the horse so that it will immediately adopt and steadily maintain the speed demanded by its master.

In training a calm, obedient horse the rider has no problems and his only concern is to ensure that the work is carried out in conformity with the general recommendations.

If the animal shows a tendency to hold back, the best method is to work in the company of another horse. In this way the horse is likely to get the necessary assistance from its mate, both in maintaining the speed and in standing back far enough.

While training the horse in company the two horses should be ridden 'head and head' close to each other, since horses tend to take off simultaneously when jumping in pairs or in a close group. This indicates that, when riders neglect to approach the obstacle evenly, they can easily spoil the value of the exercise. Namely, if one of the horses lags behind the other, the first horse's long take-off will simply compel the other one to take off at the same moment from an even greater distance. In such circumstances it is quite possible that the second horse will be unable to make the obstacle from such a distance and will hit the fence and perhaps fall.

When satisfactory progress is observed during the training with a pilot horse an occasional attempt should be made without its employment. However, aside from these special checking-up exercises, it is desirable to do the fast jumping work with a pilot even during the period of the horse's final conditioning.

We shall now consider the animal which is inclined to rush while jumping at an increased speed.

With such a horse the training should not start until the animal has been taught to remain calm while lengthening its gallop strides. The most effective remedy is, and always will be, the rider's own calmness, physical as well as psychological. It is especially important that his hands remain quiet. They may keep up a firm contact, but be able to yield smoothly by relaxing the muscles; they must not pull or jerk nervously, as such actions are likely to increase the horse's speed (see also page 113).

A horse which is inclined to rush should be allowed to gallop at a high speed without much interference from the rider. He should be almost passive, especially 20-30 yards (or m.) before reaching the obstacle, so as to permit the horse to jump freely. If the speed has increased excessively, an adjustment should be made during the 50-80 yards (or m.) following the jump.

By allowing a certain amount of freedom to the animal (in not fighting for a slow speed) this method of teaching has a calming effect and after a while the horse will become obedient and respond to the influence of the rider. It is unlikely to take a long time to reach this goal. The confidence which the animal acquires in its master will always prove to be a source of calmness. In most cases it is not the horse's basic temperament which makes it rush and become restless, but the premature tackling of advanced work, or even pain resulting from over-strain.

When exercising, two or three sloping brush fences 3 feet to 3 feet 9 inches high (0.90-1.15 m.) should be used on the course, placed at a distance of 200-250 yards (or m.) from each other.

As a general rule, the training should begin with a speed of not more than 500-550 yards (450-500 m.) per minute, which should be gradually increased to 800 yards (720 m.) per minute over a distance of 600-800 yards (500-700 m.).

On one day when the horse has not yet jumped it is desirable to let the animal first make a few gymnastic jumps, followed by two or three jumps over a hurdle at a speed of about 450-500 yards (400-450 m.) per minute.

After a few minutes of rest the actual exercise can be commenced:

strike off at a quiet canter from a distance which, allowing for a lengthy transition, will permit the horse to attain the desired speed at approximately 100-150 yards (or m.) before arriving at the first fence; then

maintain this speed and ride the animal with resolute determination to each take-off spot;

after jumping the last fence reduce the speed very gradually, letting the horse slow down comfortably. Pulling up should take place, if possible, on a straight part of the course, since an attempt to stop on a turn involves great strain and may easily cause a bowed tendon.

During this exercise the stirrup leathers should be two or three holes shorter than usual. The rider's seat should be in the forward position and bent forward about 10-15° more than normally. In this position the rider's elbows will touch his knees, while the forearms form a straight prolongation of the reins. Thus the level of the reins and the forearms is more or less horizontal. The length of the reins is determined by this posture.

THE CROSS-COUNTRY PHASE

This phase of the endurance test demands a high degree of intelligence, intensive training and great ability on the part of the horse. It must be ridden at the minimum average speed of 492 yards (450 m.) per minute, which, however, may be considerably increased over certain sections of the course in order to make up the loss of time in other sections, e.g. when climbing, riding through woods, wading through water, etc. The course is long and its negotiation is aggravated by the employment of many obstacles.

In order to equip the horse with the qualities necessary for the successful completion of the task, its preparation should be carried out according to the following considerations:

its general schooling and elasticity must be improved (this occurs simultaneously with the dressage-like schooling and gymnastics);

it must be made familiar with natural terrain and its variations, therefore it should be ridden in the open country as much as possible;

it should be well acquainted with all types of natural obstructions and the means of negotiating them;

it must be absolutely obedient and have full confidence in the rider;

in critical moments the horse must be able to find satisfactory solutions swiftly on its own. Therefore certain facilities which are allowed during the preliminary schooling should be omitted while training. For instance, the rider should sometimes surprise the animal by suddenly facing it with obstacles of unfamiliar form;

it must be fully trained to gallop calmly and to jump at a considerable speed (up to 600-650 yards or 550-600 m. per minute). This part of the training is completed simultaneously with the horse's preparation for the steeplechase.

We shall now consider how these aims can be achieved.

*Training the horse to overcome obstructions of the cross-country course*

The variety of obstacles used on the course, both artificial and natural, is very great. Their size must not exceed 3 feet 11 inches (1.20 m.) in height (except those which permit brushing) and 14 feet 9 inches (4.50 m.) in width. To clear a simple obstacle of these sizes is not in itself a serious problem, but it can be made rather formidable if the structure, type and placement of the fences chosen are difficult. But the main difficulty lies in the fact that the horse has already exerted itself considerably during the previous part of the test.

During the preliminary schooling, discussed in Part Three, the horse has become familiar with various types of obstacles and obstructions. It has learned how to deal with them either by jumping or by some other means, depending upon the nature of the obstruction. The dimensions of these obstacles were, however, rather limited.

At the stage of special training one must improve the horse's skill, strength and experience by increasing both the dimensions and the variety of the obstructions. After the completion of this course of training their form, colour and placement should not cause the slightest difficulty to the animal.

The training in jumping obstacles on level ground can be carried out (without setting up an extra programme of work) simultaneously with the horse's improvement for jumping the parcours and completing the steeplechase. But, in order to increase their educating value with special regard to the present purpose, it is necessary to include at times in this work the jumping of one or two impressive and massive-looking obstacles. For instance, a pile of heavy wood logs, a broad hedge, the height of which can exceed the limitation of 3 feet 11 inches (1.20 m.), a natural water jump or other composition of ditches, etc., can be employed. Thus in selecting such training obstacles emphasis should be placed upon a broad and solid appearance in order to build up the courage of the horse in taking impressive fences.

If possible, the position of these obstacles should be changed from time to time and some variations made in their structure. The animal should not always jump the same fence at the same spot, since it will become so accustomed to it that the effect of developing its courage is lost.

Training the horse to overcome obstructions where climbing, sliding or dropping are required should be carried out by special exercises. All these actions demand efficient, regular and rather elastic movements, in which the horse must be thoroughly schooled.

During the previous periods of training the animal has learned in a playful manner how to use its legs while moving on undulating surfaces up and down on steep slopes. It has also learned to deal with small banks and drops and it is no longer an 'event' for it to step into a lake or stream.

In the course of the present special training greater demands are made, so that at the end of this period the horse is dealing with tasks requiring real effort and skill.

The rider must always bear in mind that the negotiation of many country-type obstructions requires a decrease in speed (when crawling, descending steep slopes, etc.). Therefore, while increasing the demands, he must also gradually urge the horse to deal with such time-absorbing obstructions with less and less loss of time. But the rider must be careful not to exaggerate his demands concerning speed, since this may upset the animal's balance in performing the particular task. The idea is to solve the problem at that fastest pace and speed which, in relation to the horse's training and natural stability, still permit the animal to execute the actions required with complete security.

In order to negotiate successfully climbing ditches or to carry out descents on steep slopes, it is essential to enter them properly. The speed and pace at which this can occur depends largely upon the steepness of the down slopes (see page 303) and, of course, the condition of the ground.

It is advisable to prevent the horse from overcoming climbing ditches at the expense of a big jump. There is no justification for such action either during the course of training or in the heat of competition. During the training the aim is to teach the animal sliding and climbing and not to subject it to severe exertion. There is no advantage in jumping climbing ditches during competition, since such big jumps take an enormous toll on the horse's energy and can result in falls which otherwise might be avoided. The risk involved in such a jump offsets any advantage it may offer in gaining time.

With regard to drop obstacles, it is advisable to limit the depth of any jump performed at a gallop. If the drop is more than 5 feet 6 inches (1.60 m.), taking it at a gallop may involve serious risks of injury to the horse's legs.

At the present stage of training the horse should be accustomed to jump a big obstacle as the first jump of the day without any preparation. For instance, from time to time the rider should jump a fairly wide hedge, a bulky tree trunk or a wide ditch, etc., during the loosening exercise.

The importance of this training lies in the fact that on the second day of the three-day event the steeplechase directly follows the road section, with no time allowed in between to warm up the horse for jumping. But this practice has also the advantage that it strengthens the animal's obedience when confronted with unexpected situations.

Natural obstructions, or the elements with which to construct them, can almost always be found in the regular exercise area. The ground, even if it is flat, will provide a great many variations in the form of obstructions, which the rider will discover if he rides with open eyes.

Making use of the ground is not only economical in avoiding unnecessary expense, but it also affords excellent opportunities for the rider to construct several real natural obstacles by himself. Later on, with a little work and material, he can adapt the available facilities to each new phase of training.

It is difficult to propose a detailed time-table listing the order in which the different obstacles should be jumped, since the available obstructions are in most cases widely scattered over the countryside. Bearing in mind that exercises over two or three different obstructions should take place during a particular daily lesson, it is best to train at each occasion over the obstacles which are close to each other, regardless of type. At each exercise the horse should be ridden over each of the obstructions selected no more than two or three times. The overall programme should be planned so that each type of obstacle is practised two or three times a month.

## THE SHOW JUMPING TEST AND THE SPECIAL REQUIREMENTS OF ITS SCHOOLING

The method of training the horse to jump the parcours is similar to the preparation of the show jumper. All the relevant details will be found in Part Five. There are, however, some additional points which should be especially considered when training the three-day event horse.

The various courses used in training should include several obstacles of surprising structure, without, however, being 'unfair'. For instance, a fence set up in an oblique way, so that the horse has to take it at an angle; an obstacle with its normally horizontal parts placed in a slanting position; the general appearance of certain fences should be altered by strident colour, such as a vivid blanket thrown over it; a smell of fresh paint, carbolic or mud should sometimes be employed, etc.

While practising the parcours the rider should occasionally include a few obedience tasks, e.g. opening a gate, or halting in front of the second element of a double, making a short turn and then jumping the first element again from the opposite direction (for such an exercise the space between the two elements should be equal to two or three non-jumping strides).

In training the three-day event horse, as compared to the show jumper, it is sufficient to devote half as many days to special schooling of jumping and do half as much parcours jumping in the scheduled work. This does not imply that the jumping schooling is less important to a three-day event horse, but rather that it is also partly accomplished by exercises carried out in other phases of the training. The increased galloping work, the preparation for the steeplechase and the cross-country, all provide an adequate training in jumping and a satisfactory development of the muscles —perhaps even to a higher degree than the work designed for a show jumper.

## The Importance of the Horse's Fit Condition

Having successfully completed the schooling programme as outlined above, the horse will have acquired sufficient *knowledge* and *skill* to enable it to take part in a three-day event competition.

It will have had ample opportunity to develop its musculature, to gain experience and acquire consistency in performance. As a result, the horse can be expected to obey its rider under all circumstances, to meet an emergency calmly, and to retain its composure when surprised.

However, while the work of schooling has technically prepared the horse for competition, it will still require additional training to bring it into a condition in which it can meet the great *strain* involved in the performance of the speed and endurance test.

Before dealing with this subject in detail it may be useful to explain some of the terms, such as 'condition' and 'conditioning', 'fast work' and 'galloping work', which are often used in connection with this special preparation of the horse.

### CONDITION AND CONDITIONING OF THE HORSE

The term 'condition', as used in riding terminology, denotes the working capacity of the horse and its physical state.

When the animal is fit for a certain competition it is 'in condition' to take part in that particular contest. When this working capacity has been raised to enable the horse to display its talent at the highest possible level it is said to be in its 'top condition'.

The work of developing the horse's capacity is called 'conditioning'. The object is to develop this working capacity to the standard required on the day of the competition. This means that the animal's condition must be perfectly fit for a certain short space of time.

The art of the trainer is to synchronize the demands of the test, the needs of the horse and the available time with the method of accomplishing all the preparatory work involved. He must be able to recognize the particular moment when the horse has reached the stage of perfection by observation alone without resorting to a preliminary trial. Putting the animal through such a trial might cause it to lose its 'condition' for the actual event.

Until the complete development of the horse has been achieved, and until it has reached its top condition, the animal should be confronted with increasingly difficult tasks. This means that until the horse has reached the top condition which is necessary to the performance of a three-day event of 100 per cent. Olympic standard it should first take part in competitions of lower degree. In this way the animal will be able gradually to develop its skill and capacity without becoming over-strained.  If the rider tries to 'rush' it without having gone through the stages of gradual improvement, he will only cause a senseless and premature exhaustion of his mount.

With the same consideration, if the rider's goal is to prepare his horse for an important international three-day event, during the preceding period it should take part only in competitions which are likely to improve its capacity and condition.

A horse in good condition is capable of learning new tasks and of improving itself even after its conditioning has been completed. Thus it is possible for it to learn a great deal during an actual performance, provided that the work of preparation has been soundly conducted.

Once a horse has been brought into condition for a competition its conditioning can be simply and quickly renewed after a short period of rest, even for a more severe test.  However, if the period of complete rest lasts more than six months, the conditioning programme must be repeated in its entirety.

THE MEANING AND IMPORTANCE OF THE 'FAST' AND 'GALLOPING WORK'

The horse does *'fast work'* when it travels at the highest speed of which it is capable. This work can also be called a 'sprint' or, according to its application, a 'pipe opener'.

Fast work is an important part of the horse's preparation, since it opens up the animal's lungs so that it will not run out of breath in the course of the speed and endurance test. Shortness of breath can undermine a performance even more than actual physical fatigue.

The effectiveness of the fast work can be judged by the fact that the horse is actually 'blowing' after its execution.  Thus the distance at which fast work is carried out should be between 800 and 1,300 yards (700-1,200 m.), depending upon the horse's fitness.

*'Galloping work'* signifies moving with well-extended long gallop strides.  This work of a three-day event horse is conducted at a

speed of about 650 yards (600 m.) per minute, while the rider feels that it still possesses a certain speed reserve.

The purpose of the galloping work is to improve the animal's muscles and to increase its stamina. It is of practical value to combine it with jumping over steeplechase obstacles. The relevant details for the application of the galloping work and the distances over which it should be executed can be obtained from the Distribution of Time and Work (see pages 520-521).

Fast and galloping work can replace the tedious routine of long, slow work in canter or slow gallop. They must not, however, be overdone, for, instead of improving the horse's condition, excessive demands will involve serious risks and exhaust the animal. It is better to perform these exercises more frequently on short distances rather than on longer ones at more substantial intervals.

In comparing properly employed fast or galloping work with a slow, long-drawn-out routine drill, experience has shown that the former brings the horse into fit condition, while the latter merely tires it.

# CHAPTER TWO

# Execution of the Three-Day Event Horse's Special Training

THE period devoted to the special training of the three-day event horse follows after its preliminary schooling. During this the animal's general knowledge (see page 283 and Table No. 18) is supplemented by 'professional studies' for its ultimate career.

Throughout this period of education the horse remains in a stage of development and, in spite of this fact, tuition is not restricted solely to the riding school or training fields. A part of the training is completed in show rings and courses, for solitary drill is combined with public appearances.

The object of these competitions is to enable the horse to acquire the experience and dexterity necessary for reaching the standard of a complete show horse for the fulfilment of 100 per cent. Olympic requirements.*

Accomplishing the preparatory work in the above manner offers a considerable advantage to the rider, since he can form an accurate opinion of his horse's capabilities in the light of different competitions. A clear understanding of the animal's capacity, reliability, physical strength, stamina, etc., will help to develop the rider's confidence in his mount. This confidence means 'half a victory' for the future.

Furthermore, gradual, systematic training affords the best guarantee that the horse, after the completion of its preparation, can be entered in the most important international contests with a reasonable chance of success.

---

* The percentages used to characterize the standard of the three-day event refer only to the length of the course and not to the size of obstacles or to the rate of speed. In the dressage test the entire programme must be presented in any event.

The general information for the execution of the training, as described on page 493 in relation to the training of the show jumper, is in an analogous sense valid for conducting the work of the three-day event horse.

Now we shall examine the principles under which the preparation of the horse should be completed. These recommendations will enable the rider or trainer to arrange the work properly and flexibly according to the actual demands of various situations.

THE NOVICE THREE-DAY EVENT HORSE AND ITS WORK FROM THE BEGINNING OF SPECIAL TRAINING UP TO THE PERFORMANCE OF A COMBINED TRAINING TEST (Table No. 19)

The work in autumn

After having finished preliminary schooling (see page 305 and Table No. 18) the animal should rest for a few weeks. Following this work can be resumed.

The exercises assigned to the autumn months are a continuation of the work done before. They should be practised, if possible, in open country, but at least out of doors. The data in Table No. 19 (first column) summarize the work to be done. We need only mention that during this whole period one must be careful not to strain the animal. In maintaining or refreshing its interest and impulsion it is better to vary the demands frequently than to resort to force. This latter statement also refers to the work executed during the further periods of the preparation.

Winter training

During the winter months it is usually necessary to work in a confined space or in a covered manège. However, if the weather and ground conditions permit, the rider should go into the country for a ride or participate in not too strenuous hunting in order to relieve the monotonous work of the riding school. Such rides will prevent the animal from losing contact with the country and make shorter the transition to the spring period of training. The distribution of work for this period can be found in the second column of Table No. 19.

Pre-spring period

In addition to the recommendations for work given in Table

No. 19 (third column) it is necessary to draw special attention to the following points:

As a result of the present training, which includes the final preparation for the horse's first competition in public, the animal must be able to clear with certainty courses of 3 feet 7 inches (1.10 m.) average height, including some simple obstacles of 4 feet (1.20 m.).

The appearance of the fences employed in these routine courses should be enticing and pleasing to the horse. It is a good practice to add to each parcours one or two obstacles which are new to the animal, but they, too, should be of an inviting type.

The horse's conditioning for its maiden competition is accomplished automatically through the exercises employed to open the lungs, lengthen the stride and improve skill in jumping at an increased speed.

### The first public performance and the work connected with it

About 10 days before the show the work of preparation should be restricted mainly to the regulation of the horse and bringing it under complete control. Jumping exercises should be reduced to gymnastics and once or twice at most to clearing some small individual obstacles (see details in Table No. 19, fourth column).

On the day of the contest, after the usual warming up, the horse will enter the show ring as a hopeful competitor in its first parcours. Suggestions regarding warming up and inspecting and riding courses are given in Part Five (Show Jumping).

In the first competition the rider's primary objective is to make certain that the horse behaves calmly and enjoys taking part in a contest. The best way of achieving this is to let the animal use the speed which it prefers. Looking towards the future career of the horse, it is important to ensure that the first test leaves a pleasant impression and to avoid creating frenzy or exhaustion by pressing it for a victory.

If the horse finishes the first parcours with ease, the rider can consider entering a second class at the show, though by no means on the same day.

If the performance has not been satisfactory, and the effort proves too much, the animal is probably not yet ready for the challenge; in such cases it is better to allow the horse more time for schooling and improvement. The rider must resist the temptation to make further public appearances for the time being, since the animal will never forget if it has suffered from the impatience of the rider during the course of education.

### The work during the late spring

For the further education of the three-day event horse it is advantageous to participate in a combined training test during the present period of training (see Table No. 19, fifth column). The animal will easily satisfy the demands laid down for the dressage part of this test, provided that it has had a sound preliminary schooling. Only the simple tasks involved must be practised with moderation. (It is advisable to use a snaffle bridle both in the preparation and presentation of the test.)

If there is no opportunity during this period to enter the horse in a combined training test, practice in clearing show jumping obstacles and courses should be reduced below the levels suggested in the distribution of work and more stress should be laid on overcoming natural obstructions.

A fairly reliable picture of the horse's general behaviour can be formed from its performance during the first show jumping competition and combined training test. The rider will see its reactions to travelling, to strange environments, unfamiliar stables, altered working conditions, music, noise and traffic, etc. But whatever this picture, the rider must remember that these tests are the first experiences of the horse and he must not be too critical. He should regard them as a means of teaching the animal to accustom itself to the conditions under which competitions are arranged. The experiences thus gained should be carefully analysed and taken into account during the next period of training.

### Finishing the novice horse's education for the first three-day event (with the inclusion of participation in one or two one-day events)

The 'knowledge' which the novice has acquired up to the present stage of training is still probably not enough for the performance of a three-day event. Therefore it is advisable to precede the work of conditioning with a period devoted to adding the finishing touches to its special education. This is particularly important, since during the period of conditioning the animal will have to perform such strenuous physical work that its energy must not be expended in learning new techniques.

The time allotted for the accomplishment of this work is about nine weeks, divided into three equal sub-periods, the details of which are shown in Table No. 20.

The work schedule for conditioning the novice three-day event horse for its maiden test can be found in Table No. 21 (including one or two one-day events).

Recommendations for the performance of the test itself follow in Chapter Three (page 448).

THE INTERMEDIATE (PROGRESSING) THREE-DAY EVENT HORSE AND ITS DEVELOPMENT UP TO A 100 PER CENT. OLYMPIC STANDARD

During the schooling period of the previous year the novice three-day event horse will have taken part in a few smaller jumping competitions and combined training tests, in one or two one-day events and in one three-day event requiring not more than 50 per cent. of the Olympic standard. The present year's work must complete the final preparation necessary to qualify the animal as a finished three-day event competitor. This can best be accomplished by competing in gradually increased tests of 50, 75 and 100 per cent. demands.

*Routine work during the season*

The characteristics of the routine work during the season will be:
the improvement of the horse's knowledge, together with the correction of particular weaknesses as they are exposed under the pressures of competition; and
the conditioning of the animal from event to event.

Since the horse will have been thoroughly schooled before its maiden test, the first part of the work can generally be restricted to refining and polishing its existing skill. Weaknesses should be corrected by means of intelligent schooling based upon thorough consideration of their origin.

The main concern of the rider will thus be concentrated on the progressive conditioning of the horse in order to improve its stamina in accordance with the increasing physical demands.

The distribution of work for this period of training is shown in Table No. 22/a-d. Regarding the educational work, the chart gives sufficient information. The work of conditioning, however, needs more detailed explanations, according to the stage of development.

*Conditioning for the year's first competition (possibly 50 per cent. requirements)*

The date of the first competition of the season provides the basis for scheduling the items of the conditioning procedure. This date varies according to the climatic conditions of different countries. For example, in England work can still take place outdoors during the winter months. This is why the date of the famous three-day event at Badminton is fixed so early in the year, at the end of April. In other countries riders are obliged to work indoors during the long winter season and start conditioning comparatively late.

Where the climate permits outdoor work in the winter the rider can budget his time in such a manner that he will complete his work of schooling and commence conditioning by the end of February. Otherwise conditioning will generally start in the middle of March.

If the horse has recently been in condition for its maiden test (50 per cent. requirement), the present work will be more or less a refresher and the achievement of its renewed condition is simple (see Table No. 22/a). However, if the maiden test and its conditioning were more than six months earlier than the start of the present conditioning, the method recommended in Table No. 21 must again be applied.

Regarding the first lung-opening exercises, it should be noted that in cases when ground conditions are unsuitable (frosty) on the days scheduled for the execution of sprints the work should be substituted by galloping uphill on a short, steep slope or trotting over a long, mildly rising road or track until the animal is blowing. In any case, it is advisable to carry out these lung exercises on calm, sunny days.

If no three-day event of 50 per cent. requirement is available for the introduction of the season, a one-day event can replace it, provided it includes a steeplechase course over a distance of about one mile (1,600 m.), or two one-day events if no steeplechase is included.

*Conditioning for the 75 per cent. test*

The actual work of conditioning starts with the preparation for the 50 per cent. test, which itself can be regarded as the main item during the horse's improvement in achieving the 75 per cent.

standard. Bearing this in mind, only a freshening-up process remains to be completed in the interval between the two shows (see Table No. 22/b).

There is no possibility of participation in a one-day event during this stage of the work, since its flow cannot be reconciled with such a task. It would mean an extra strain, which would adversely affect the animal's improvement.

### Conditioning for the 100 per cent. test

After the completion of the 75 per cent. event, which brought the horse into the necessary condition for the present test, it is of special importance that it should remain fresh and playful. In its high condition the animal is full of energy, which the rider should preserve for the performance of the next strenuous task. In this case the rider's only duty is to 'freshen up' the horse's condition (see Table No. 22/c).

In Table No. 22/d the reader can find some recommendations for conditioning the progressing three-day event horse when the procedure of its development cannot follow the gradual stages outlined above.

It must, of course, be a very exceptional case for the horse to be confronted with 75, or even 100, per cent. requirements without having participated in the lower grade tests. Such big gaps in the work can only be filled by lengthening the periods of education and conditioning so as to enable the animal to gather its skill and strength to comply with the great exertion. In order to avoid the danger of over-straining the horse during such a strenuous preparation, it is necessary also to insert some rests in its course.

If the horse in question has participated in show jumping or hunting a short time before the commencement of the special training, these factors should be taken into account during the preparation:

in the first case, the improvement of its dressage schooling and skill in passing over natural obstructions and an improvement of its speed, lungs and endurance will require the most attention;

in the second case, it can be assumed that the horse has its basic foundation of condition, produced by intense galloping, and will require only the 'sharpening' of the last gallop work.

Generally speaking, such horses will need more dressage-like schooling and careful preparation for stadium jumping.

The weaker the fundamental schooling and special education of the animal, the longer will be the period of work before conditioning. In any case, whether the horse has been prepared specially for the task or not, it is desirable to precede conditioning with a routine polishing and refreshing of its knowledge and skill (see Table No. 20).

### THE FINISHED (COMPLETE) THREE-DAY EVENT HORSE AND ITS WORK

Through rudimentary and special schooling the horse will now have acquired the knowledge necessary to fulfil the requirements of a most severe test. The gradually executed preparatory work, together with the three to four introductory three-day events in which it has competed, have equipped the horse with experience and improved its physical state. Without such a routine no horse can be regarded as a finished performer.

It would be, however, rash to conclude that once the work of education has been completed by all the efforts described above nothing more is left for the rider but to enjoy the reward of his endeavours. It is, indeed, important and essential to *maintain* the horse's knowledge from test to test and *refresh* its condition before each new performance.

At the beginning of each season even the experienced three-day event horse should probably take part in a 50 per cent. test. The preparatory work of this test corresponds to the work recommended for the springtime 50 per cent. event (see Table No. 22/a). This test can be replaced by one or two one-day events, as indicated on pages 445 and 476.

Aside from the introductory contest, the horse may take part within a season in three three-day events at the most, mixed of 75 and 100 per cent. requirements. Any further participation might prove harmful and could easily result in a complete breakdown.

With regard to taking part in other competitions, reference can be found on page 474.

The actual work of the finished three-day event horse is summed up in Table No. 23/a-c.

CHAPTER THREE

# The Performance
# of the Three-Day Event Test

IN connection with the performance of the test itself the rider
has many special duties and special kinds of preparation to
carry out. We shall explain these points in conjunction with
the various phases of the test.

## THE RIDER'S ROLE IN CONNECTION WITH THE DRESSAGE TEST

### BEFORE THE PERFORMANCE

The horse must be 'warmed up' for its performance.

The warming-up process should be introduced by loosening
exercises (see page 266), during which the horse should be led
with only snaffle reins.

After the loosening exercise and a brief rest the main part of
the warming-up process, establishment of mental contact and the
attraction of the horse's interest to the rider may begin (see
pages 16, 102, 130 and 146). This refreshes the animal's willingness to obey, makes it supple, restores its elasticity and the
regularity of the gaits and simultaneously introduces its collection.

Next the adjustability of the horse, its submission for the
execution of changes in the motion must be polished and its
collectability increased up to the stage when the rider feels that
the animal is reacting to his *thoughts* and stepping 'with his own
legs'. Within this work practice of individual movements of the
test can be useful, but the repetition of the whole programme
should be avoided.

The rider should not attempt to 'teach' the horse during the
warming-up process, since it is not a suitable occasion for such an
enterprise. 'Teaching' at this time tires and confuses the animal
and may also spoil its movements, in the performance of which it
has been excellent before.

[448]

Before riding to the collecting ring the rider ought to check the saddle, bridle and last, but not least, his own dress. The well-groomed appearance of the horse and rider readily attracts the spectators' attention and this interest may influence the jury's verdict in favour of the performer.

In the collecting ring the horse should be allowed to have a rest of five to eight minutes by walking around with loose reins.

When the rider is permitted to enter the area of the presentation he should ride there with loose reins, letting the horse look around in freedom. Then, still with loose reins, he should ride for a while at a walk and trot around the enclosure. After this brief calming and accustoming ride the rider can quietly collect the horse by making some half-halts and transitions with definite forward intention and in complete easiness. If there is time, he may repeat this procedure from interlocked relaxations instead of waiting lengthily in collection for the signal to enter the arena.

THE PERFORMANCE OF THE TEST

The rules of the F.E.I. contain certain general instructions with regard to the rider's behaviour during the presentation of the test. These are:

the use of the voice in any way whatsoever and clicking the tongue are strictly prohibited and are considered very serious faults;

the reins must be held in both hands, except where it is specified that only one hand should be used;

it is forbidden to carry a riding whip of any kind.

In addition to the above official instructions, the following recommendations should be given with reference to the rider's bearing during his performance. The countenance of the rider should reflect pride, giving the impression that he dominates his horse and is master of every situation. Nothing should seem to trouble his composure or to make him resort to coercion. His signals and aids should be invisible and he must make his public feel that he can execute all that is demanded of the horse with graceful ease.

When the start signal has been given the rider should take time for the horse's adjustment and collection and then ride, at the stipulated pace, from a rather distant point towards the entrance of the arena.  In this way he can best ensure that the animal will approach the saluting point on an absolutely straight line.

After the halt the rider must avoid the slightest rigidity during the preparation for and the execution of the salute.  This should be executed with lightness and elegance.  The necessary manipulations with the reins preceding and following the salute should be comfortable and relaxed.  Don't hurry.

Concerning the further presentation of the test, the main points have already been touched upon in Chapter One of the present part.  Nevertheless, it will be necessary to slightly elaborate on these points by describing some additional features which have an important bearing on the subject.  The key to the whole problem is to

*ride the 'horse' during the performance and not the 'test'.*

By this is meant that the rider's concern should be concentrated on maintaining the horse's submissiveness and regularity as it carries out its movements with a swinging back and well-cadenced leg motion.  While in motion the horse should give its rider the sensation that its back is united with his seat and it is striding with his legs.

The presentation should be one of ease, coupled with steady and continuous progress, while the prescribed movements are carried out exactly on the defined course.

The general picture of the animal's suppleness should be completed by the steady bearing of its neck and head in a well-arched carriage.  In order to comply with this demand, it is better to give the horse some freedom than to keep it too tight during the performance.

Whenever the horse shows some disunity in gait, or any kind of stiffness or crookedness, it can usually be assumed that the animal has lost its liveliness during too cautious performance of the 'test' being ridden instead of the 'horse'.  Thus, while performing it is important for the rider to remain natural and to ride with certainty and resolution.  This will encourage confidence and submission in the horse.

The rider can best avoid stiffness in his bearing by keeping his head erect and looking around unconcernedly during the performance, instead of observing only the horse's neck and head.  By doing so he can concentrate much more on the sensations conveyed by the animal and will notice the first signs of irregularities and prevent their development. In this way only minor corrections will be required and the smoothness of the performance will be safeguarded. When watching only the head and neck the rider is inclined to 'correct' the horse's carriage instead of its willingness to obey and by this means the movements of the animal. In consequence, the rider misses the proper moment for the real correction and spoils the horse's motion, as well as its bearing.

The rider should not worry about eliciting irregularities through a determined use of signals and aids. On the contrary, he must be sure that the animal will accept them and by their understanding it will be ready to obey. If signals are given in a tentative manner, the horse will either ignore them or become confused.

When some adjustment becomes necessary, some portion of the test should be used for its execution which is not of prime importance and which takes place in a fairly inconspicuous part of the arena. In order to be familiar with these possibilities, it is wise to study the regulations of the test in greatest detail.

## The Rider's Role in Connection with the Speed and Endurance Test

### THE INSPECTION OF THE COURSE

In a broad sense the speed and endurance test begins with the inspection of the course by the rider. It is very important, therefore, to take utmost care in this preliminary study of the course.

Generally the official presentation of the course takes place one day before the dressage performance. On this occasion it is handy to take along the map and diagrams which are specially issued by the organizer, together with a notebook in which remarks can be entered.

According to the regulations, the route of the cross-country test must be marked out so distinctly that it cannot be mistaken even at riding speed. This is truer in theory than in practice, however, and it is wise to get very thoroughly acquainted with the course and put down in the notebook all the relevant remarks regarding its peculiarities.

### The inspection of the roads and paths phases

During the tour of inspection these phases of the test are usually shown to the contestants by using cars.

The rider should keep his map and pencil at hand and mark down those sectors of the course on which it is possible to proceed at a canter or slow gallop. Notes should include details as to whether or not the first of these phases includes any small obstruction which might be jumped to help warm up the horse.

### The steeplechase course

The steeplechase course is presented to the competitors on foot.

While considering how to jump the obstacle the rider should mark down the most advantageous part of them with regard to turns and construction. Special note should be made of any obstacle which should be jumped at an angle for the sake of gaining time (in a turn).

It is important to mark on the map the sections at which the course ascends or slopes even in a slight degree, as this will assist ascertaining the desired speed (where the horse can proceed at an increased speed, where it must have some opportunity of relaxing, etc.).

### The cross-country course

This course is the main stage and the most complicated phase of the test. Therefore all its details should be carefully inspected, noted and memorized.

A rider who does not undertake this inspection seriously may easily become confused when travelling at great speed because of the many turns and obstacles involved. Therefore it is most important to memorize the features of the course where the direction changes. Confusion—even if it is a matter of a few seconds—means a loss of time, which can only be made up by increasing speed in a following section. Such correction wastes the animal's energy and eventually causes faults which could have been avoided. In order to facilitate the necessary preparation, the course is presented by walking it.

While inspecting the obstacles the rider should note and memorize all the features which might facilitate the horse's effort. It is useless to ponder whether or not the obstacle is a difficult one. The only relevant consideration is where it must be taken and the most suitable speed and direction for negotiating it.

At obstacles erected in an uneven or slanting area of the course first of all ascertain the spot which offers *the best possibilities for the take-off* and whether the formation of the ground is, at least during the one or two strides before reaching the spot, convenient for approaching the fence. Next analyse the landing conditions and, by bringing them into co-ordination with the take-off possibilities, decide upon the final plan for making the jump.

As a result the jumping of that part of the obstacle should be contemplated which lies between these two selected points. This can eventually necessitate jumping the fence at an angle or at a higher or wider sector than otherwise. In spite of these seemingly aggravated conditions, its clearing will be easier and safer than by ignoring the best take-off and landing conditions, and being guided only by the lesser dimensions when the rider is making his plan. The dimensions should only be considered in such cases as when they differ greatly in the same fence, and then only so far as the negotiation of which, even under perfect conditions, would require more effort from the horse than could be expected of it.

With regard to the course as a whole, attention should be paid to the condition of the ground (hard, soft, etc.) and to rising or sloping parts of the track (even if the deviation from the level surface is only very small). Furthermore, one should record in the map those sections in which real speed is possible and in which the reduction of speed is necessary. Separate note should be made of obstructions the negotiation of which takes considerable time because of the extreme reduction of speed or pace necessary for overcoming them. These particular notes may also include the anticipated loss of time (seconds).

### The run-in phase (cross-country on the flat)

This particular stretch does not require much attention in making the survey, since it is generally on a flat piece of ground with straight lines and without obstacles. Since there is no need to make any special plan, we will discuss the run-in only in connection with its performance (see page 471).

THE ANALYSIS OF THE STUDY OF THE ENDURANCE COURSE AND THE SHAPING OF THE RIDING PLAN

As soon as the rider gets back to his quarters after inspection he should glance through his notes and, if necessary, amend them while the survey is still vivid in his mind.

When the whole course with all its details is perfectly clear, then the rider can draft his plan. The essence of it is to prepare a schedule for the actions of both the horse and the rider in detail. Such a plan enables the rider to know beforehand his best approach in completing his performance.

In the heat of competition the rider can easily make an error in estimating speed. Therefore it is most important to determine within the plan the different speeds to be used during the performance. In this way, by forestalling all doubts, hurry and uncertainty, the rider will be prevented from over-straining his horse or unnecessarily exceeding the time allowed. (Methods of calculation can be found on page 320 and in Table No. 10.)

In drawing up the riding plan

the rider must have a definite plan for each separate phase of the course. Their preparation can be most reliably completed according to the following three items:

the drafting of the general project;

the composition of the timetable; and

the preparation of notes of reminder.

### The drafting of the general project

The object in drafting the general project is to ascertain the 'time aimed at', in which the particular phases of the course should be completed, together with the average speed this will require.

To estimate these data the rider must thoroughly know the capabilities of his horse, especially the maximum speed it can achieve without over-straining itself and how long it can withstand the strain. Thus these data are based mainly on the rider's 'feeling' and horsemanship. The connected calculations can be carried out in two ways:

first, one can determine the time aimed at and from that calculate the speed required; or

by the second method, when the calculation is made in the reverse manner.

For the roads and tracks phases the first method is more practical, while the second is more suitable for the steeplechase and the cross-country phases of the course.

In drafting the general project the rider has to consider:

how far the horse can satisfy the demands of the 'time allowed' for the particular phase and the speed necessary to achieve this time limit (these rates of speed and the times allowed can be found in the official conditions of the test); and

whether he can expect a surplus over the minimum requirement, and, if so, how large it might be.

By the latter anticipation the rider can estimate his chances of gaining bonus points, or of time for resting his horse between certain phases of the test.

When the situation has been considered in this manner the timetable can be drafted separately for each phase of the course.

### Composition of the timetable

Within the timetable the phase in question should be broken down into parts in which the horse can proceed under identical conditions and at a uniform speed.

As a result of the examination the rider will know that there are some sectors of the course

which are likely to permit the horse to proceed at the average speed best suited to achieve the time aimed at;

which require decrease in speed; and

which provide opportunities for an increase of speed.

In determining these sectors (accurate to within 50 yards or metres) certain terrain factors are decisive. These are:

the nature of the ground (normal, hard, deep, sandy, wet, etc.);

the formation of the terrain (flat, sloping, ascending, wooded, etc.);

the time-consuming obstructions (climbing, sliding, crossing of water, etc.). These must be scheduled in the timetable separately.

When the rider has completed the dissection of the particular phase into sectors and marked all the relevant details, he should then determine the rate of speed for each sector separately. For this purpose it is necessary to consider:

which part of the course is involved (the beginning, end, etc.);

what the horse has already accomplished before reaching the sector in question and how much remains to be done; and

in accordance with these considerations, whether the application of an increased speed would be difficult for the animal.

The next stage of the procedure is to ascertain the time required for covering each sector of the phase. For this purpose take out from Table No. 10 the time values corresponding to the distance of the particular sectors and to the speeds anticipated.

By adding up these values one obtains the actual amount of time necessary for finishing the particular phase of the course.

The average speed which belongs to the above total time can be obtained by the calculation as shown in page 320. The results thus obtained must approximately tally with those in the general project. Any discrepancy must be adjusted (usually by modifying the requirements of the general project).

If the time anticipated in the general project is smaller than that calculated in the timetable, the rider must examine the timetable and ascertain the most suitable sectors of the phase for increasing speed without placing undue strain on the horse. If it is not possible to adjust the timetable by the difference, the only solution will be to revise the average speed aimed at in the general project.

If the time in the general project is longer than that which is calculated in the timetable, the rates of speed scheduled in the table for the most strenuous sectors can be reduced.

Having carried out these amendments the timetable can be used as a basis for riding the course.

### Preparing notes of reminder

As a reminder during the performance of the test it is useful to have some small pasteboard cards (e.g. visiting cards) inscribed with the most important items of the timetable in a clearly visible manner.

The notes should be written in pencil or Indian ink (ordinary ink may become blurred if exposed to moisture) and abbreviated as concisely as possible.

We shall now consider, with the aid of an example, how a riding plan can be worked out in practice. In this example the distances and speed limits correspond to the requirements of a 100 per cent. three-day event.

PLANNING FOR RIDING OVER THE FIRST ROADS AND TRACKS PHASE

The distance of this phase is about 4.35 miles (7,650 yards) or 7,000 m. It must be performed at a speed of 262 yards (240 m.) per minute, so that the 'time allowed' is 29 minutes and 10 seconds. A shorter time is not rewarded by bonus points; lagging behind the 'time allowed' results in five penalty points for each commenced period of 5 seconds.

The drafting of the general project

The rider's object is to complete this phase 4 minutes sooner than scheduled in the regulations of the event. This would mean that the time 'aimed at' will be 25 minutes 10 seconds (29 minutes 10 seconds less 4 minutes).

Drawing up the timetable

Ascertain the following details:

the sectors which are to be covered at a trot and which at a canter; and

the speeds to be used during their negotiation in order to complete the phase in approximately 25 minutes 10 seconds;

the approximate times at which the rider will arrive at the desired checking points, which are roughly one-quarter, one-half and three-quarters of the length of the phase. By their aid he can control whether the calculated rates of speed were reached as planned.

In order to achieve the 'time aimed at', a bit less than half the distance (45 per cent.) has to be ridden at a canter (see also page 426). This proportion is acceptable in the case of our hypothetical example, as the terrain of the course allows for this amount of cantering.

With the aid of the notes made by the rider during the tour of inspection and of Table No. 10 the following timetable can be set out:

| | | | | | | | | | |
|---|---|---|---|---|---|---|---|---|---|
| 1. | Sector | 1,600 yd., | trot | 250 yd./min. | 6 min. | 24 sec. |
| 2. | ,, | 1,450 ,, | canter | 400 | ,, | 3 | ,, | 38 | ,, |
| 3. | ,, | 1,200 ,, | trot | 250 | ,, | 4 | ,, | 48 | ,, |
| 4. | ,, | 2,000 ,, | canter | 400 | ,, | 5 | ,, | 0 | ,, |
| 5. | ,, | 1,400 ,, | trot | 250 | ,, | 5 | ,, | 36 | ,, |
| | Total | 7,650 ,, | | | 25 | ,, | 26 | ,, |

The time calculated above is the same if the timetable is drafted in the metric system. *

By comparing the time of 25 minutes 26 seconds with the 25 minutes 10 seconds anticipated in the general project one can verify the correctness of the plan.

* From 7,005 m. 55%, 3,855 m. at a trot of 230 m./min... 16 min. 48 sec.
   45%, 3,150 m. at a gallop of 365 m./min.   8 ,, 38 ,,
   Total .. 25 ,, 26 ,,

If the calculated time exceeds that in the general project, it is better to lengthen those sectors where a canter is possible than to increase the speed of the comfortable trot projected.

If the ground conditions do not offer enough possibilities for cantering, it is necessary to calculate with shorter sectors for using this pace at a moderately increased speed, up to 450 yards or 400 m. per minute.

(If the conditions of the test should demand a slower speed than that mentioned above, say 240 yards or 220 m. per minute, then the time allowed to finish the distance would be 31 minutes 50 seconds. In order to achieve the 'time aimed at', being in conformity with our example, 26 minutes 50 seconds, it would be quite enough to cover only the third of the course at a canter.)

### PLANNING THE PERFORMANCE OF THE STEEPLECHASE

According to the rules of the event, a speed of 656 yards (600 m.) per minute is demanded in this phase. The length of the course in our example is 2.25 miles (3,934 yards) or 3,600 m. Thus it must be negotiated in 6 minutes ('time allowed').

Since the obstacles of the steeplechase course are generally uniform, they have no special influence on drafting the riding plan.

A bonus of two-fifths of each point can be gained for each metre per minute of speed faster than 656 yards (600 m.) per minute. Thus the maximum number of the bonus points is 36.

A penalty of three-fifths of a point is incurred for every commenced second taken in excess of the 'time allowed' up to the time limit beyond which elimination is entailed.

The goal of gaining bonus points should not lead the rider to over-tax the horse's capabilities, but he should calculate on that fastest speed which the animal can display without becoming over-strained, up to an average speed of 755 yards (690 m.) per minute.

### The general project

The rider, knowing the capacity of his horse, anticipates that it can cover the course (3,934 yards or 3,600 m.), together with its obstacles, at an average speed of 720 yards (660 m.) per minute.

At such a speed the required time is 5 minutes 28 seconds (see Table No. 10), which results in 24 bonus points (660 — 600 = 60, 60 × 2 = 120, 120    5 = 24).

Composition of the timetable

Attention should be concentrated on two special points:

the flat and sloping parts (jointly); and

the ascending parts of the course.

Estimate first these distances (within 50 yards or metres) from the survey sketch and add them together by groups.

Next determine the speed to be used on the flat and sloping sectors. On the ascending sectors it is not advisable to exceed the basic rate of speed (656 yards or 600 m. per minute); therefore

the average rate of speed (720 yards or 660 m. per minute) aimed at in the general project has to be achieved by increased efforts made on the flat and sloping sectors.

In our example, within the 3,934 yards (3,600 m.) long course, $350 + 250 + 200 = 800$ yards is the distance of the ascending sectors, so that the flat and sloping parts represent a stretch of 3,934 less 800 = 3,134 yards.

In order to cover the distance of 800 yards at a speed of 656 yards per minute, 1 minute 13 seconds are required (see Table No. 10).

This figure should be increased by 5 seconds, which is the time allotted to the horse for a breather. Thus the time which the ascending sectors would absorb amounts to (1 minute 13 seconds + 5 seconds =) 1 minute 18 seconds.

In order to ascertain the speed to be used on the flat and sloping sectors, by which the average speed of 720 yards per minute can be achieved, the calculation is carried out in the following manner:

deduct from the required total time of 5 minutes 28 seconds the consumed time of 1 minute 18 seconds; the difference is 4 minutes 10 seconds, or 250 seconds. This is the space of time left to cover the distance of (3,934 less 800 =) 3,134 yards);

calculating from the above time and distance one arrives at the necessary speed of:

$3,134 \div 250 = 12.53$ yards per second, i.e.

$12.53 \times 60 = 751$ yards per minute (see page 320).

Thus, in order to achieve the average speed of 720 yards per minute, the horse has to proceed on the flat and sloping sectors of the course at a speed of 751 yards per minute and on its ascending parts at 656 yards per minute. In this way it will cover the total course in 5 minutes 28 seconds and ensure the desired 24 bonus points.

The calculation is similar in metric system:

Out of 3,600 m. 280 + 250 + 200 = 730 m. are ascending and 3,600 less 730 = 2,870 m. flat and sloping.

The ascending sectors absorb 1 minute 18 seconds and the flat and sloping sectors require 250 seconds (explanation analogous to that for the yard system).

Thus the necessary speed for the flat and sloping sectors is:

2,870 ÷ 250 = 11.48 m. per second, i.e.

11.48 × 60 = 688 m. per minute (see page 320).

The results of both calculations are the same, since 751 yards equal 688 m.

From the above data the timetable can be set up as follows:

3,134 yards (2,870 m.) at 751 yards (688 m.) per minute
800     ,,     (730 m.) ,,  656   ,,    (600 m.) ,,     ,,

If the course contains so many ascending sectors that the speed on the flat and sloping parts has to be increased considerably in order to ensure the desired bonus points, their amount must be reduced and the timetable altered accordingly. The reduction of the demands can also be achieved by determining a slower speed than anticipated originally for the ascending sectors. As far as the reduction of the speed on the ascending sectors is concerned, it can become necessary mainly in cases when the horse's stamina is limited.

PLANNING RIDING ON THE SECOND ROADS AND TRACKS PHASE

There are three main points to be considered in planning the performance of this phase of the test:

the degree of exertion to which the animal has been exposed;

the length of the distance to be covered; and

the difficulty of the task awaiting the horse immediately after completing this phase.

Each of these considerations must be shown both in the general project and particularly in the timetable.

The distance of this phase in our example is 6.46 miles (10.4 km.), i.e. 11,360 yards (10,400 m.). It has to be accomplished at a speed of 262 yards (240 m.) per minute. The time allowed is 43 minutes 21 seconds.

The general project

After the steeplechase the rider should proceed possibly for 1 to 1.75 miles (1.5-2.5 km.) at a speed not more than 230 yards (210 m.) per minute. During this stretch the horse has a good opportunity to relax, the function of its lungs and heart calms down, and its muscular system enjoys a well-deserved relief. The remaining part of the phase should be completed at a trot of about 250 yards (230 m.) per minute and at a canter of about 400 yards (365 m.) per minute.

The aim is to arrive at the goal 5 minutes ahead of the time limit. This necessitates completing the course in (43 minutes 21 seconds less 5 minutes =) 38 minutes 21 seconds.

The drafting of the timetable

On the whole, the general points and explanations given for the first phase are just as valid for this second one.

Thus in the timetable of our example it will be sufficient to show the combined lengths of sectors to be covered at a uniform speed. These distances—except for the first one—can be split up into smaller sectors in accordance with the points mentioned in connection with the general project.

The items of the timetable would be as follows:

| | | | | |
|---|---|---|---|---|
| 2,200 yd. at 230 yd./min. | trot | 9 min. | 33 sec. |
| 4,050 ,, ,, 250 ,, | ,, | 16 ,, | 11 ,, |
| 5,110 ,, ,, 400 ,, | canter | 12 ,, | 48 ,, |
| 11,360 ,, | | 38 ,, | 32 ,, |

The result is the same when calculated in the metric system. *

PLANNING RIDING OVER THE CROSS-COUNTRY PHASE

In the example shown below the length of the course is 4.97 miles (8,745 yards) or 8,000 m. This stretch of course has to be covered at a speed of 492 yards (450 m.) per minute; thus the time allowed is 17 minutes 45 seconds.

A bonus of three-fifths of a point can be gained for each metre per minute of the speed faster than 492 yards (450 m.) per minute up to a maximum speed of 624 yards (570 m.) per minute. Consequently the maximum number of the bonus points is 72.

---

* From 10,400 m.

| | | | | |
|---|---|---|---|---|
| 2,010 m. at 210 m./min. | slow trot .. | 9 min. | 33 sec. |
| 3,710 m. ,, 230 ,, | normal trot .. | 16 ,, | 11 ,, |
| 4,680 m. ,, 365 ,, | hand gallop .. | 12 ,, | 48 ,, |
| | Total .. | 38 ,, | 32 ,, |

A penalty of three-tenths of a point is incurred for every commenced second taken over the time allowed up to the time limit, after which competitors are eliminated.

## The general project

The rider concludes from his inspection of the course that his horse is able to complete it at an average speed of about 550 yards (500 m.) per minute. This would result in gaining (500 — 450 = 50; 50 × 3 = 150; 150 ÷ 5 =) 30 bonus points.

In order to achieve this objective, the horse must complete the 8,745 yards (8,000 m.) long course in 15 minutes 56 seconds (see Table No. 10).

## The drafting of the timetable

Ascertain and list in chronological order the distance of each particular sector into which the course has been divided according to the factors which may have a bearing on the speed to be used on it (see page 455);

note at each sector the rate of speed in accordance with the estimates (see page 455) and mark the estimated loss of time at the time-consuming obstructions registered; then

work out the required time in which the sectors previously assigned can be covered at the selected rate of speed; and finally

sum up the calculated time values and compare this result with the 'time aimed at' in the general project.

In the following table an example is given to illustrate some of the possibilities which may occur on the cross-country course. For the sake of convenience, the results are worked out for both systems of measurement, showing the distances in yards as well as in metres.

As we can see, there is a difference between the requirements in the general project and the timetable, the latter being shorter than the former.

If the aim is to achieve the time value of 15 minutes 56 seconds, as anticipated in the general project, the total value of the timetable (16 minutes 14 seconds) will have to be reduced by the difference of 18 seconds.

Now the timetable should be carefully examined to find out

EXAMPLE FOR A TIMETABLE (CROSS-COUNTRY PHASE)

| Parts of lap | Nature of part distance | YARD SYSTEM | | |
|---|---|---|---|---|
| | | Distance from.. to.. or place at.. in yd. | Estimated speed (yd./min.) | Required time (Table 10) min. sec. |
| 1 | Flat with 8 flying jumps | Start-2,700 ——— 2,700 yd. | 600 | 4   30 |
| 2 | Climbing ditch (loss of time) | at 2,700 ——— — | — | 5 |
| 3 | Slightly elevated ground with 2 jumps | 2,700-3,000 ——— 300 yd. | 450 | 40 |
| 4 | Flat with 7 flying jumps | 3,000-5,200 ——— 2,200 yd. | 550 | 4   1 |
| 5 | Deep acre | 5,200-5,400 ——— 200 yd. | 350 | 34 |
| 6 | Jump into a splash (loss of time) | at 5,400 ——— — | — | 5 |
| 7 | Flat with 6 flying jumps | 5,400-7,100 ——— 1,700 yd. | 550 | 3   5 |
| 8 | Wooded land with 1 drop | 7,100-7,300 ——— 200 yd. | 400 | 30 |
| 9 | Slight slope with 2 flying jumps | 7,300-7,650 ——— 350 yd. | 650 | 32 |
| 10 | Flat with 3 flying jumps | 7,650-8,745 ——— 1,095 yd. | 500 | 2   12 |
| | Total time required | | | 16   14 |

## EXAMPLE FOR A TIMETABLE (CROSS-COUNTRY PHASE)

| Parts of lap | Nature of part distance | METRIC SYSTEM | | |
|---|---|---|---|---|
| | | Distance from.. to.. or place at.. in m. | Estimated speed (m./min.) | Required time (Table 10) min. sec. |
| 1 | Flat with 8 flying jumps | Start-2,500 ———— 2,500 m. | 550 | 4    33 |
| 2 | Climbing ditch (loss of time) | at 2,500 ———— — | — | 5 |
| 3 | Slightly elevated ground with 2 jumps | 2,500-2,800 ———— 300 m. | 400 | 45 |
| 4 | Flat with 7 flying jumps | 2,800-4,800 ———— 2,000 m. | 500 | 4    0 |
| 5 | Deep acre | 4,800-5,000 ———— 200 m. | 330 | 36 |
| 6 | Jump into a splash (loss of time) | at 5,000 ———— — | — | 5 |
| 7 | Flat with 6 flying jumps | 5,000-6,500 ———— 1,500 m. | 500 | 3    0 |
| 8 | Wooded land with 1 drop | 6,500-6,700 ———— 200 m. | 350 | 34 |
| 9 | Slight slope with 2 flying jumps | 6,700-7,000 ———— 300 m. | 600 | 30 |
| 10 | Flat with 3 flying jumps | 7,000-8,000 ———— 1,000 m. | 475 | 2    6 |
| | Total time required | | | 16    14 |

where the missing 18 seconds can be made up without causing harmful strain on the horse.

In the present case it appears to be most suitable to slightly increase the originally planned speeds at the Nos. 4, 5, 7 and 10 sectors of the course. In those where the course is of an ascending nature (No. 3), or where time-absorbing obstructions have to be overcome (like Nos. 2, 6 and 8), or where the speed has already been fixed at a considerable rate (like No. 1), the horse should not be further burdened by a faster speed for the sake of bonus points.

By taking into account the changes suggested above, the correction (with the aid of Table No. 10) will show the following results:

| No. of sectors in the timetable | The alteration in the timetable | | | | | | | |
|---|---|---|---|---|---|---|---|---|
| | Yard system | | | | Metric system | | | |
| | New speed | Time | | Gain of sec. | New speed | Time | | Gain of sec. |
| | | New | Old | | | New | Old | |
| 4 | 570 | 3' 52" | 4' 1" | 9" | — | — | — | — |
| 5 | 400 | 30" | 34" | 4" | 380 | 32" | 36" | 4" |
| 7 | 570 | 2' 59" | 3' 5" | 6" | 520 | 2' 53" | 3' 0" | 7" |
| 10 | 520 | 2' 7" | 2' 12" | 5" | 520 | 1' 55" | 2' 6" | 11" |
| | Total gain of time | | | 24" | | | | 22" |

This gain of time is sufficient to make up the deficit in the previous plan, 18 seconds. By replacing the original items of the timetable with the new data the plan is completed and can be carried out.

LEARNING THE RIDING PLAN

When the plan has been completed the rider should try to go through it by heart, just as he has plotted it out on paper. If he is satisfied that he knows it, he can appear in the test confident that he has done everything possible to ensure success.

There may be some riders who think that such minute preparation is superfluous and that it is absolutely impossible to keep to a scheduled timetable to the second. In this respect they may be right; however, the fact that the drafting of the plan enables the rider to examine the whole course in its smallest detail and thus become completely familiar with it offers him an advantage which should not be ignored. A thorough study of the details provides a valuable guide to the best and most economical method of accomplishing the task.

This knowledge endows the rider with decisiveness and certainty while riding the course, since he knows precisely where he must go faster and where he can relax. He is not likely to get agitated, to hesitate or make any grave mistakes. If he has memorized the details and is determined to achieve his objective, he is certain to follow the plan automatically.

Having done his best to estimate his horse's capabilities, the rider must stick to his plan during the performance. He should decline any outside advice (which, in any case, is forbidden) and not deviate from his plan in any way. There is no time to consider outside advice, nor to reconcile it with the prevailing circumstances. Accepting such an aid will only bring confusion and unevenness to the whole performance and may easily become the source of unnecessary faults.

## THE RIDER'S FUNCTIONS IN CONNECTION WITH THE ACTUAL PERFORMANCE OF THE SPEED AND ENDURANCE TEST

### Preparation for the start

Before discussing the actual riding of the course we shall describe briefly the rider's duties immediately before the start.

The first item is the weighing-in. The rider's weight is checked and, according to the regulations of the test, it cannot be less than 165 lb. (75 kg.). If it is under this limit, the balance must be made up by increasing the weight of the saddle. In such a case it is better to use a heavy saddle, even if lead is built in, rather than to employ one or more large weight cloths. Adding weight by weight cloths should only be used to balance small differences.

After the weighing-in special attention should be paid to saddling the horse. This process differs from everyday routine, as the horse has to be tacked in such a manner as to ensure the utmost security as far as the equipment is concerned. Thus it is necessary to fasten the flaps of the saddle by tying them down with a surcingle; a spare leather should be buckled on the horse's neck;

the stirrup locks should be fixed with a piece of wire so that they cannot spring open; on a rainy day a web rein can be buckled into the snaffle ring. If a bandage is used on the horse's tendons, it is advisable to sew it over after having tied it securely so that it will under no circumstances get disentangled. In the event of slippery going strong studs should be screwed into the horse's shoes.

The saddling and its check-up should be timed so that the rider can mount four to five minutes before the start.

In addition to careful saddling, the rider must also make sure that his personal equipment is in order. He should be provided with everything which facilitates riding and which is indispensable for the execution of his plans. Thus

the whip must be elastic enough and its handle should be fitted with a knob or a strong rubber ring to prevent slipping;

the spurs should be blunt, with a short stem, ending in a knob;

the little pasteboard cards which indicate the time and distance details should be fixed to the sleeve of his jacket (etc.), so that the card which refers to each particular phase of the course is easily visible and can be torn off after finishing the phase;

it is also good practice to wear a wrist stop-watch (duly adjusted to the official time), so that the speed can always be checked quickly and easily. (During the steeplechase phase, however, there is no time for such operations.)

While preparing for the start the rider should mentally review his plan for the last time.

### The first phase of roads and tracks

When the moment to start is approaching the rider should pull up calmly at the starting line and wait for the starter's signal. As soon as it is given the rider sets his horse and stop-watch in motion.

While proceeding at a trot he should use the rising method and while cantering sit in the forward position.

While trotting it is advisable to note which of the horse's hind legs is burdened by the sitting-down movement and to change to the other leg after each mile or so of distance (1.5-2 km.).

If the rider has noticed some sort of an obstacle during his inspection of the course, it is good practice to make a jump now at a steady speed.

At certain points of the course he should check his time against that which has been allocated in the plan.

After arriving at the end of this phase the rider should stop his watch, check the time and use the three to five minutes' spare time to give his horse a brief rest, to wash its mouth and to check up on the saddling.

### The steeplechase course

About one minute before the start the rider should take his position behind the starting line. According to the regulations, this can be crossed either by a flying start or from a stationary position.

In the first case, wait at a distance of about 25-30 yards (20-25 m.) behind the starting line. The starter announces the approaching moment by counting backwards . . . 5 . . . 4 . . . 3 . . . 2 . . . 1. As soon as '3' is called out strike off into a gallop and reach the steeplechase speed by the time you are breaking the tape and entering the course.

If the start is to take place from a stationary position, wait for the signal close to the tape. After the start accelerate the horse's speed within the shortest possible distance.

Either of the above methods will permit the rider to gain a bit of time and it may be the second thus gained that will prove to be decisive.

The steeplechase phase of the course should be ridden in forward position and the horse allowed to take up a firmer rein-contact.

With regard to speed control, the rider's attention must be concentrated on automatically changing over the rates of speed during the transitions between the particular sectors of the course.

While riding at high speed over the steeplechase course there will be times when the rider has a feeling that the horse's girth is about to burst. At such a moment it is necessary to let the animal give itself a breather for two to three seconds by relaxing the speed. Such a brief rest will refresh it, so that afterwards the speed can easily be increased again. If the rider overlooks the horse's need for this brief rest, or if he senselessly drives the animal on, he will not save the two to three seconds' loss of time, but may cause a considerable deterioration of strength.

Owing to unforeseen circumstances (a slip, stumble, bad take-off or misjudgment, etc.), even the best horse may make a fault without any intention of resistance. Likewise it can happen that even the very best rider may lose his balance and fall from the saddle because of some unexpected event. These and similar faults are accidents if they are not due to unpreparedness or ignorance.

In such cases the rider should not try to balance the penalty points by trying to earn more bonus points, as the intensified speed would only cause trouble without ensuring the result desired. His only course is to make up the *effective loss of time*. In order to justify this statement, consider the following arithmetical evidence:

When the horse swerves or stops in front of an obstacle the loss of time is about six to eight seconds and the fault is penalized by 20 points. This loss of time can eventually be made up and the number of good points originally planned may be achieved. But the only means of counterbalancing the penalty of 20 points would be to increase the average speed by 50 m. per minute, since each increase of 1 m. per minute results in $\frac{2}{5} = 0.4$ bonus points (20 being equal to 50 times 0.4).

If the original estimate in the riding plan for obtaining the desired number of bonus points is correct, the horse cannot be expected to produce a far greater increase of speed for the purpose of offsetting penalties.

The senselessness of increasing the speed applies even to horses which have no difficulty in performing at great speed. In this case the riding plan is based on the speed which ensures earning the maximum number of bonus points. This is the upper limit of the speed which is accepted by the regulations. Thus it is useless to drive the animal faster than necessary to make up the loss of six to eight seconds and by this means to reach again the upper limit of the awarded average speed. No speed over this limit can wipe out any penalty points.

Should the horse fall, or the rider be thrown from his mount, the result would be (if there are no further complications) 10 to 12 seconds' loss of time and a penalty of 60 points.

The 10 to 12 seconds' loss of time can perhaps be made up, but the 60 penalty points cannot possibly be eliminated, since, apart from other considerations, the maximum number of bonus points which the rider can gain in this phase is only 36.

*The second phase of roads and tracks*

While passing the finishing posts of the steeplechase course the rider simultaneously crosses the starting line of the succeeding phase of trot.

Entering this phase, he should let the horse slow down gradually from the great swing of the steeplechase by a long transition, so that after about 300-400 yards (m.) its speed has been reduced to a steady trot of about 230 yards (210 m.) per minute. It is a good idea at this point to have somebody on hand to pour a bucket of water over the horse's breast as it moves on in order to refresh it after the strenuous run of the steeplechase.

It is the practice of certain riders to dismount after the steeple-chase and run alongside their horse for a few hundred yards. This custom is not often justified by the results. If the rider is keen on running, and it does not cause him too great an exertion, there is no harm in affording pleasure to his horse by such methods. But if he dismounts and trudges along by the animal's side he will lose so much time that the horse will have to exert itself considerably later on to make up the delay.

During the following part of the course the same recommendations are valid as given for riding over the first phase of the test.

*The cross-country course*

In the cross-country test the rider must follow his plan most carefully. The necessity to change the speed frequently and within a very wide range can be a source of numerous errors and mis-calculations, especially if the rider has not previously made conscientious plans.

With regard to the execution of the plan, the following points should be noted:

The rider should take up his position a few yards (metres) away from the starting line. This will enable him to pass through it at a gallop at the starting signal. At the same time he should start his stop-watch in order to check the time occasionally during the course.

It is important to use the forward seat and, because of the increased speed and the fixed nature of the obstacles, to allow the horse to adopt a more definite rein-contact.

The animal's energy can be saved considerably and the time reduced if the rider follows the shortest possible line of the course and if he jumps the obstacles in a 'flying' manner (provided they demand jumping and not other actions, e.g. climbing, sliding).

This way of riding is the most effective for earning bonus points; however, it requires a knowledge of the course down to the most minute detail.

If the going is slippery, it is decisive that the horse should take off with complete determination. Any hesitation or attempt for the correction of the actual situation on the part of the animal will cause a long slide, bringing it under the fence and making the take-off very difficult or even quite impossible. In supporting the horse the determination of the rider, based on his sound judgment, is of paramount importance. According to the foreseen possibilities, especially if they seem to be disadvantageous, he should encourage his mount with resolution, but without altering its energetic stride action, to take off distinctly either from a distant or a close point from the obstacle. In critical cases, however, it is generally better when the rider asks the horse to stand back than to bring it close to the fence for the take-off. If the rider's conduct is filled with a spirit of unrestricted forward strive and his will transmitted with resolution, the horse will act without hesitation and thus it will avoid the harmful sliding.

With reference to faults, the points to be noted are the same as those discussed in connection with the steeplechase course.

It is true that in the cross-country phase the speed is less rapid and it would seem to be easier to gain time by an accelerated speed and by this means earn bonus points. This, however, is not quite true, since the scoring of bonus points is rendered more difficult by the fact that each three-fifths of a point requires that the speed be increased by 1 m. per minute. This means that, for example, to make up a refusal (which causes 20 penalty points) would require an increase in speed of 70 m. per minute.

*The phase of run-in (cross-country without obstacles)*

Upon completing the cross-country phase the rider automatically enters into this last phase of the endurance test.

There are no obstacles erected on the course and the speed demand is only 361 yards (330 m.) per minute. The regulation does not allow the earning of bonus points; however, exceeding the time allowed is penalized.

Owing to these conditions, this phase is designed to reduce the exertions which the miles and speed of the previous phases have placed upon the horse.

During the ride the rider should allow the animal to proceed comfortably with a freely swinging back, so that it can gradually calm down.

The speed is not important, since even a moderate hand gallop is sufficient to cover the distance within the time allowed and thus to complete the final phase of the second day's test.

### DUTIES OF THE RIDER AFTER THE ENDURANCE TEST

When the rider has arrived at the finish of the course he must not dismount until the steward in charge of the paddock has given him permission to do so. Then he should personally remove the saddle and, by stepping up on to the weighing machine, holding his saddle, verify that he still reaches the minimum weight of 165 lb. (75 kg.). If he has lost some weight during the test, he is entitled to add the weight of the bridle and perhaps the gaiters of the horse to the weight of the saddle.

After reweighing, the rider should join his horse again and remain with it until it has been groomed from sweat and mud. If there is a veterinary surgeon available, it is advisable to have him make a thorough check-up on the animal. First, its legs and tendons should be carefully examined to make certain they have not suffered any injury. The rider himself should ascertain that the saddle or the girth has not made the horse sore. Such a careful check-up will enable him to order the proper treatment immediately.

After this examination the horse should be sent home. If there is no horse-box available and stabling facilities are located at a great distance, the animal can be led home without the saddle after a rest of one to one and a half hours and a drink of chilled water. If sharp studs have been employed, they should be removed before the journey, during which it should be well covered according to the prevailing weather conditions.

Some hours after the test it is advisable to make a renewed check-up on the horse, preferably with a veterinary surgeon. At the same time also its gait should be examined at a trot. A slightly stiff movement should not cause any particular anxiety. This is the result of the severe effort and muscle-boundness.

Following this examination the animal should be taken out on a lead for about 40 minutes' walk in order to prevent the development of stiffness. Afterwards its legs (especially the tendons and hocks) should be sprayed with cold water and its muscles gently massaged with an embrocation of camphor solution.

If the horse has suffered a minor injury to its tendons, or if there is a slight sprain in some of its joints, or any other disability causing a slight lameness, cold (ice) compresses should be used or—if necessary—veterinary treatment should be given. The purpose of this is to enable the animal to pass on examination of its gait the next morning.

In the event of a more serious injury, veterinary consultation is unavoidable and it is better to be cautious and refrain from further contest. However, it can happen in important international competitions that national interests require that participation in the test should not be abandoned. In such a case one should try to give the horse the best veterinary treatment in order to bring it into a physical condition which will permit it to complete the test. However, the owner of the horse should bear in mind that such a demand is a very severe one and may cause further deterioration in the animal's health.

In the morning, whatever the physical state of the animal, its condition must be checked up again, its gait carefully inspected both at walk and at trot and its legs sprayed with cold water.

If the place of the examination is near the stable (five to 15 minutes' walk), the horse should be taken out on a lead for half an hour's walk after the morning check-up. However, if the distance to the place of the examination takes about three-quarters of an hour, this walk would be superfluous. On the other hand, if the examination should take place in the afternoon, the morning walk cannot be omitted, as its object is to remove general stiffness from the horse.

### The examination test of the horse

The purpose of the examination is to eliminate horses whose state of health might be seriously endangered by competing in the jumping test. Stiffness or a slight lameness do not constitute cause for disqualification.

The horse must be presented at the examination with the bridle or head collar only.

THE SHOW JUMPING TEST

Before the test the weighing-in of the rider is compulsory (minimum weight is 165 lb. or 75 kg.).

After this the preparation for the performance may commence with the inspection of the course and the consideration of the riding plan. Adjoiningly the warming-up process for the test follows.

During the process of warming up the rider must bear in mind that on the previous day the horse has undergone a severe exertion and therefore the restoration of its elasticity should be restricted mainly to gymnastic exercises and only to a few individual jumps. At the same time, it is advisable to arouse the animal's carefulness in jumping by mild self-rapping (see page 508). Such treatment is necessary in order to prevent the horse from jumping in too flat a manner, which it might have adopted during the previous day.

Otherwise, both in the warming-up process and during the jumping of parcours, the same principles apply as described for participation in jumping competitions (see Part Five).

PARTICIPATION WITH THE THREE-DAY EVENT HORSE IN SHOW JUMPING COMPETITIONS

The limited number of versatile competitions in which the three-day event horse can partake without endangering its health makes it possible for it to participate in a few jumping competitions as well. Such participation—if carefully selected—can improve its technique of competition and bring pleasure to the rider by enabling him to appear more frequently in public. If the horse's safety can be adequately secured and the rider can keep his passion for contests within reasonable bounds, participation in a show jumping test will result in the balanced utilization of the animal's knowledge and skill.

If the date of the selected show happens to coincide with the period of preparation for one of the three-day events, the show jumping can safely be regarded as a part of the preparatory work.

As a general rule, a horse in preparation for the three-day event should not attempt more than two complete courses in a show.

If a one-day event has been added to the preparatory work, it is desirable to avoid participation in any jumping competition at the same show.

Furthermore, it should be added that the novice three-day event horse should not start in courses with obstacles higher than 4 feet 3 inches (1.30 m.).     If it reveals brilliant capabilities at jumping higher parcours, and simultaneously proves to be less skilful in the cross-country or in the performance of the dressage test, it is better to change completely and train it to become a show jumper.     But if it displays promising capabilities both in the endurance and dressage tests, there is reason to hope that it will satisfy the requirements of the great international three-day events.     Such a horse can safely start in jumping classes during a longer interval between two three-day events which are higher than 4 feet 3 inches (1.30 m.), but care must be taken to conserve its strength for its main career.

# The Combined Training Test and the One-Day Event in the Light of Preparation for the T.D.E.

THE tasks which compose the programme of these competitions are chosen in such a manner as to test various aspects of the horse's skill and knowledge.

Since the tasks involved place gradually increasing demands on the animal, competitions can be of practical use in the systematic training and improvement of the three-day event horse. In this sense they should be regarded mainly as means of preparing the three-day event horse for its actual task and only secondarily as individual competitive objects. Bearing this in mind, their significance can be seen in the following points.

Both the combined training test and the one-day event are stages in achieving a level of knowledge necessary to meet the greater demands of the three-day event. When the three-day event horse takes part in these minor competitions it can adapt itself with relatively little exertion to the increasing grades of contests necessary for its mental and physical improvement. They can also provide the horse with ample opportunities to gain experience and learn show routine, which is so necessary, especially to a novice.

Taking part in these competitions can serve as a substitute for certain sections of the general training of the three-day event horse. For such a purpose, however, the date of the show must be co-ordinated with the programme of the overall preparation.

Finally, these competitions enable the rider to accustom his horse to varying conditions without having great expenses. They readily offer facilities to present a dressage test under unfamiliar circumstances and to jump obstacles which are unknown to the horse and which private individuals cannot afford.

### The combined training test

This is the simplest form of competition to test the standard of a versatile training. The test consists of a simple dressage programme which can be presented, if desired, in a snaffle bridle. It also includes a fairly easy jumping course (about 3 feet 7 inches or 1.10 m.) over a short distance, including certain obedience tasks. There is no speed and endurance trial in the test.

It can be usefully employed during the three-day event horse's special training, i.e. *before* the period of its conditioning, in order to replace the practice of jumping parcours at home.

### The one-day event

This test, as its name suggests, is a form of the three-day event with considerably reduced demands which also measures to a certain extent the horse's endurance and speed capacities. Owing to its limited demands, the entire test can be completed in one day. But, as there is no excessive exertion imposed by distance and speed, it cannot be considered a complete substitute even for the lowest (50 per cent.) standard of a three-day event.

The one-day event can be arranged at a show in three graduations:

for horses of novice standard (preliminary class);

for progressing horses (intermediate class); and

for complete performer (open class).

The prescribed tasks begin with a dressage test of preliminary, intermediate or F.E.I. requirements.

This is followed by a jumping course consisting of eight to 12 fences not more than 3 feet 6 inches, 3 feet 9 inches or 4 feet (1.10, 1.15, 1.20 m.) high.

The test is completed by performing a cross-country course of about $1\frac{3}{4}$, $2\frac{1}{4}$ or $2\frac{1}{2}$ miles (2,800, 3,600 or 4,000 m.) length, with about 16, 25 or 30 obstacles which are not higher than those of the jumping course. Ditches must not be wider than 11 feet (3.30 m.).

The inclusion of a short steeplechase course and road section is left to the discretion of the organizers of the event.

The above demands indicate the course which has to be taken for the schooling as well as for conditioning a horse to compete in a one-day event. Detailed instructions can be found on page 527. In addition to them, we shall now review the general principles of the horse's preparation, depending upon whether the task is regarded as a part of the three-day event horse's training or is considered to be a goal in itself.

### The one-day event as a part of the three-day event horse's preparation

The participation in a one-day event has three main advantages for the horse being trained for a three-day event:

it improves the animal's skill in performing the cross-country test;

replaces a part of its general conditioning programme for the anticipated three-day event; and

offers a convenient means of starting the season when there is not a 50 per cent. three-day event on the agenda (see also page 445).

The horse's schooling for the event (including jumping and cross-country exercises) should follow the same distribution of time and work designed for the three-day event horse (see Tables Nos. 19 and 20). In addition to this work, however, the special requirements of the particular dressage test should also be taken into account.

The horse will be brought into condition automatically by the routine work, since the participation in the one-day event becomes part and parcel of the general conditioning (see Table No. 21).

With regard to the date of participation in the one-day event, it is advisable to select a time which coincides with the long cross-country work scheduled in the course of the general conditioning (see Table No. 21, second and sixth weeks). If necessary, this course can be slightly altered to suit the date of the chosen one-day event.

### The one-day event as an individual competitive aim

The one-day event can be regarded as a goal in itself

when the horse being selected for the three-day event is unable to satisfy the endurance demands of the test; or

when the owner of the horse has neither the intention nor the opportunity to participate in more advanced three-day event competitions.

For the preparation of the horse the same training programme can be followed as recommended for a 50 per cent. three-day event with the following reservations:

> during the period of special education (see Tables Nos. 19 and 20) the special work designed for the performance of the dressage and show jumping tests should be brought in accordance with the particular requirements of the chosen competition;

> the work of conditioning should be followed up to that item of the training plan (see Table No. 21) where the recommended work can be substituted by the participation in a one-day event. This is scheduled in the second and sixth weeks' programme of the table mentioned.

The pleasure of participating in these competitions will repay the rider for the hard work spent on his horse's training. But, even so, he should not enter his horse in more than five to six one-day events during the season. However, in addition to these tests it may take part in a few show jumping competitions or combined training tests.

# PART FIVE

# Show Jumping

## Special Preparation and
## the Performance over Courses

SHOW JUMPING is a branch of riding in which the rider's art, skill and daring are combined with the horse's talent, dexterity and education to the highest possible degree. Mental and physical co-operation between the partners are of utmost importance in order to produce successful results.

The rider should practise his art primarily for the sake of the sport and the thrill of overcoming difficulties, and not merely for the satisfaction of appearing in public. He should consider the quality and not the quantity of performances, with the aim of trying to master the most intricate problems which the show ring may offer, and which often demand acrobatic skill from both rider and horse. This requires not only a great deal of enthusiasm for the sport, but also a sound background of knowledge which will enable the rider to guide and support his mount successfully under any circumstances. If he possesses these qualities, he will be able to prepare his horse and to employ it in competitions in such a manner that it becomes fond of them. The enthusiasm of the rider, combined with the pleasure of the animal, is sure to result in perfect achievement.

Show jumping is more popular among riders than the three-day event, since it offers more opportunities for the rider to appear in public. It is also easier to organize a jumping competition than a one-day event or three-day event and, as a result, jumping shows are more numerous than the other events.

The frequency of these competitions makes it possible to select jumping courses which are best suited to the individual horse. If the rider is careful in his selection, especially at the start, he can ensure considerable progress in his horse's development by systematically taking advantage of the most suitable opportunities.

The preparation of a show jumper consists of a special training programme and a conditioning process. The purpose of the special training is to provide the horse with the advanced skill and knowledge which are necessary before it can commence its jumping career (see page 305 and Table No. 18) and to improve it until it reaches the stage where it can be regarded as a finished show jumper. The conditioning brings the animal into a physical state in which it is able to perform the tasks without becoming exhausted by the exertion involved. With regard to the general importance of conditioning, see the details on page 437.

Aside from the routine work, a considerable part of this preparation occurs by participation in various competitions in which the horse is faced with higher and higher demands as its performing capacity becomes more and more developed. Finally, it should acquire a complete adroitness for top-class jumping almost by itself.

# CHAPTER ONE

# Subjects of Training during the Special Preparation of the Show Jumper

THE main subjects of the preparation are: schooling by dressage, gymnastic exercises, training in jumping, lengthening of the galloping stride, expansion of the horse's lungs and accustoming to varying conditions. We shall now discuss them in turn.

## Schooling by dressage

It is a well-known fact that the horse can only jump correctly and securely if it is ridden up to the obstacle in complete regularity. As the purpose of the dressage work is to improve the regularity of the animal's locomotion, this work is as important as the jumping practice itself.

During the period of preliminary schooling the horse will have obtained a high degree of knowledge which should enable it to jump correctly and with perfect confidence.

During the present period there is no need to teach the horse any *new techniques;* rather the rider should ensure by careful repetitions that it remains fully aware of the knowledge which it has gathered already. If the rider neglects the dressage work, the horse will revert to a stiff and crooked locomotion and, as a consequence of this, there will be a setback in all of its achievements, including jumping.

## Gymnastic exercises

In the course of special training the regular practice of gymnastic exercises is as important as the dressage work.

There are no new methods which the horse must learn. The same basic gymnastics which are already familiar to the animal are suited to its present needs.

During the training, however, the rider must choose intelligently those particular gymnastic devices or their combinations which best improve the suppleness and elasticity of the individual horse. If, for instance, the jumps are too stretched, it is advisable to use devices in which the distances between the component elements are diminished and enforce collection on the animal. If the swing of the jumping motion is lost, a suitable treatment is to carry out first the grid exercise with decreased distances between the elements and afterwards to jump a ditch or any low but rather wide structure in a setting as shown in Fig. No. 87. If the horse is well balanced, it is sufficient to use the simple grid in order to review the animal's elastic mobility.

It is advisable to continue the gymnastic exercises which are carried out on the country tract (see Figs. Nos. 79-81), as they are extremely helpful.

### Jumping

During the exercises devoted to jumping the aim should be:

to improve the jumping style of the horse;

to develop precision in clearing obstacles;

to familiarize it with all the typical forms of fences, singly and in combinations;

to practise jumping courses at a comfortable speed and later on at an increased speed.

Improvement of jumping style

A jump performed correctly will produce the best results while imposing the least exertion on the horse. Bearing this in mind, it is important to develop the animal's jumping style as far as possible by proper *instruction*.

The schooling should start on each occasion with some gymnastics designed to refresh the correct jumping movements of the horse. This should be followed by the essential part of the instruction, by the clearing of a specially selected obstacle, which should vary from time to time as to type and construction.

The rider must prepare each jump with the utmost care and enable the animal to reach the fence in perfect regularity. If he is careless, e.g. in creating the correct sequence of stride or the necessary collection and swing of the horse, the jump will fail and there will be a bad effect on the animal, which will suffer a setback in its training and may develop a dislike of jumping.

Four to five good jumps over the selected obstacle at the planned height can be considered sufficient exercise for one day. If the horse happens to have some difficulty, the severity of the exercise should be decreased and the work finished in a less strenuous form, so that the animal will always leave the schooling ground in a good frame of mind.

Developing precision in clearing obstacles

Correct style only is not enough for a show jumper. It must clear the obstacle completely and must not make a fault even by a slight touch. It is no exaggeration to assert that the horse must 'over-jump' the fence. In order to achieve such a standard of certainty, the best method is to educate the animal to use its back while jumping in a well-arched manner. This is usually accompanied by the legs tightly tucked under the body. The more tightly the legs are bent, the lower the body need be lifted to negotiate the obstacle. To make the horse arch its back good use should be made of the bascule improving device (Fig. No. 82) and the short gymnastic double (Fig. No. 85).

If the gymnastic exercises prove ineffective in making the horse tuck its feet under the body, and if it still touches the obstacle, more impressive corrective measures must be employed.

First of all fasten the bars of the gymnastic device so that when the horse touches one it receives quite a hard knock on its feet and this will serve as a warning to avoid making such mistakes again. In addition to this corrective effect, the device is of gymnastic value and will ensure that the exercise is carried out with a sufficiently arched back.

With regard to younger horses, the method mentioned is the most severe which should be applied. Older horses that have been imperfectly schooled and are accustomed to jumping without arching the back and with hanging legs will have to be subjected, in addition, to the methodical schooling to more severe methods of correction according to the following recommendations.

Occasionally place an iron rod at about 2 to 4 inches (5-10 cm.) over the second element of the short gymnastic double and then make the horse jump it. At the first attempts the animal will knock the rod off, causing itself some pain. Later on, as a result of the warning felt through its legs, it will pull them more and more under its body. By the help of this enforced gymnastic exercise the horse is taught to connect the tucking in of the legs with the arched use of the back. Another useful effect of the exercise is that it prevents the back from becoming hollowed after a hasty or hesitant take-off. This would occur if the iron bar were placed over a single obstacle.

When the animal has hit the iron rod two to three times the bar should be removed and an attempt made to jump the device without it. The last item of the daily work should be a jump over an individual obstacle (without an iron bar) with the aim of checking the result of the schooling and to reward the horse's efforts with a pleasant jump.

After a few treatments the iron bar can be discarded, at least for a certain time, as the animal will remember the pain suffered and will be careful with its legs. But as soon as it begins to drag its legs again the exercises with the iron rod should be resumed.

The chief purpose of this exercise is to teach the horse by mechanical means to accomplish the required motion in the correct posture. By repeating the motion a number of times the horse becomes accustomed to it and the whole concept of jumping becomes associated with the arched back and tucked-up legs. When the animal has reached this stage it can be said that it has learned the correct form of jumping.

It is necessary to emphasize that immense care has to be taken when using the iron rod. The intention is not to bang the horse's legs, since such a procedure is likely to cause sourness. Furthermore, horses which tend to hold back should never be trained with the iron bar, because it might produce in the animal a strong resistance to jumping.

Some further methods of warning the horse are described on page 507 (rapping).

Occasionally (about once a month) the rider should control the spontaneity and self-decision of the animal in clearing obstacles and ascertain whether the training has been carried out in the right manner. For this purpose he should ride the horse directly after mounting, without any warming up, to a rather wide fence about 3 feet to 3 feet 6 inches (0.90-1.10 m.) high and try to make it jump at a slow canter on its own initiative without any support. If the execution of the jump shows difficulties and restriction, or restlessness is observed, or if it has been performed without the use of the back, the demands of the training should be relaxed and efforts concentrated on correcting faults by renewed schooling and gymnastics.

Acquainting with various types of obstacle

The horse must be made familiar with all of the typical forms of obstacles and must learn how to jump them, both singly and in combinations.

The schooling over single obstacles should include practice in jumping ditches (with and without water, and these with and without superstructure) and negotiating bank formations in addition to various upright fences. The relevant details are described in Part Three.

Furthermore, during the practice of jumping single obstacles the horse may also be accustomed to the sight and jumping of increased heights and spreads. The general idea of this work is to first warm up the horse with gymnastics and then to work up gradually to the height or the spread of the jump desired. One of the take-off regulators can be employed to advantage in order to ensure the horse agreeable take-off conditions and by this means to increase its confidence in clearing the unusual height or spread. After having reached the standard desired the jump should not be performed more than twice on each occasion.

By practising jumping combinations of obstacles the horse should become experienced in clearing their varied and more intricate forms. It should also become skilled in jumping combinations set up at odd distances. During these exercises, when the horse has correctly negotiated a double of an irregularly increased distance, for instance, the same combination can be tried with the distance reduced. After a successful attempt the work for the day should finish. A slight mistake does not justify repeating the exercise, provided that the animal has jumped in the right form of movement. If the horse has difficulties and does not find the proper solution, the task should be simplified by altering the distance between the elements to a more convenient one. The original situation can then be gradually restored in two or three stages. (See combinations in Part Three.)

In addition to schooling over combinations, the horse should become familiar with jumping six-bars. For this task the animal must first be prepared by gymnastics in order to bring it into the necessary state of elasticity. At the same time, its liveliness should be increased to the highest possible degree. Then the rider can try to jump the bars at the desired setting. In case of a faulty performance the mistake should be corrected by renewing the entire original preparation (gymnastics, liveliness). The series of bars should not be jumped more than three or four times and each jump should be followed by a brief rest. With regard to the gradual improvement of the exercise, see more details on page 531 (Distribution of Work).

Developing skill in clearing courses

For this purpose one should use the courses involved in the routine work and those of the various competitions scheduled during the period of special education.

The small courses (with low jumps), which are used until the spring-time conditioning, can be treated more or less as a game, but they should also act as a check as to whether or not the animal is able to maintain its regularity while jumping a series of obstacles.

It is a good practice for the rider to omit the last parcours scheduled in the routine work just before a show and to replace it by an easy class at the show to serve as practice preceding the horse's participation in the important classes. While negotiating this small parcours the rider should not try to win it, but regard it rather as a suitable means of providing a useful 'school' for the animal. If it happens that the horse wins, the rider may consider it a generous gift. In comparison with the ordinary work at home, such a preparatory course is highly advantageous, as the experience and teaching effect is more marked owing to the fact that the jumping takes place under unusual circumstances.

The courses for competition should be selected according to the horse's increasing knowledge without, however, confronting the animal with tasks which lie beyond the limit of its momentary abilities. Such an improper trial would result in relapse instead of progress in the horse's improvement.

Improving the speed of jumping courses

As the standard of education progresses one can start employing exercises between the shows, which will help to improve the horse's speed in jumping courses.

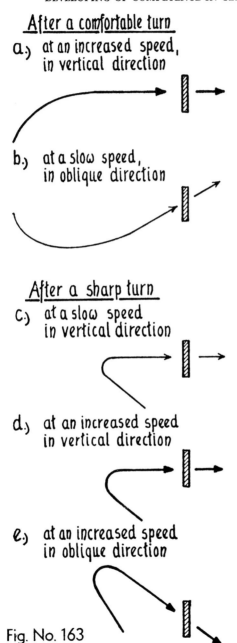

## After a comfortable turn

**a.)** at an increased speed, in vertical direction

**b.)** at a slow speed, in oblique direction

## After a sharp turn

**c.)** at a slow speed in vertical direction

**d.)** at an increased speed in vertical direction

**e.)** at an increased speed in oblique direction

Fig. No. 163

At the beginning of the special education the courses were ridden at a comfortable speed by taking wide turns and jumping the fences from a straight approach. However, when the animal can do this satisfactorily the demands can well be further increased. The finished horse must develop skill in making sharp turns at considerable speed and in jumping obstacles at an angle. The achievement of a respectable degree of skill in this, especially when the height of the parcours exceeds 4 feet 3 inches (1.30 m.), requires a most thorough education and a lot of experience on the part of the animal. The programme of these exercises can be outlined in the following manner (Fig. No. 163/a-e).

The first step is to introduce the horse to the execution of the task by:

jumping at an increased speed while approaching the fence from a vertical direction (straight approach, Fig. a) and

jumping at a comfortable speed while approaching the fence at an angle (Fig. b).

During the period of the intermediate show jumper's education it is enough to practise only these two exercises.

Next in order are exercises in training the animal to jump from a sharp turn. To start with

the horse should approach the obstacle at a comfortable speed in a vertical direction (Fig. c); then

the speed can be gradually increased (Fig. d).

Having completed these exercises satisfactorily, it should attempt to angle the obstacle at great speed after making a sharp turn (Fig. e).

It should be emphasized that the sharper the turn out of which the obstacle is approached the more care must be concentrated on keeping up the horse's shoulder mobility and the greater is the importance of the rider's balancing conduct while he turns his mount.

*Developing muscles and lungs and lengthening the galloping stride*

Any sort of exercise which improves physical strength can be used to encourage muscular development. For instance, the dressage-like schooling, if it is executed on slightly sloping ground or on undulating surfaces; exercises for the expansion of lungs (sprints, galloping uphill, protracted trotting uphill or in water); and exercises for the lengthening of the galloping stride. During the winter period long cantering (on soft going) produces very good results in physical culture.

With regard to lengthening galloping strides, the same method can be used as suggested for the three-day event horse (see page 427), with the reservation that it is not necessary to exceed a speed of 600 yards (550 m.) per minute.

The expansion of lungs can also be promoted with the same exercises recommended for the three-day event horse (see pages 305 and 429).

*Acquainting the horse with variations and alterations*

In the course of training it is very important to accustom the horse to changes in obstacles, both in their form and setting. The best trained horse, especially if it is of a nervous temper, is inclined to divert its attention from the actual task if startled by the sudden sight of strange surroundings (when entering the show ring, etc.). This, of course, can have a very adverse effect on the performance.

Therefore, from the very beginning of training every possible occasion should be used to get the animal accustomed to unforeseen events. The first step is to ride through urban areas and travel on highways. In this way the animal becomes more familiar with strange objects, sudden movements, noise and traffic. A further step is frequently to change the place of training so that the horse gets accustomed to working in strange surroundings. If the horse is usually ridden by itself, it will be advantageous to bring it into contact with other horses so that it may get accustomed to company. (Very often a horse which is unaffected by noises or the sight of machinery, etc., will become agitated when it sees another horse). Similarly, if the training is usually carried out in the presence of other horses, it is advisable occasionally to perform the work alone.

From time to time routine courses should be jumped in strange places by agreement with other riders in the neighbourhood. By such co-operation the training can be promoted very successfully.

As an immediate means of attracting the animal's interest the rider may give some slight flicks on its side at the moment when the horse's attention is diverted from him by the surroundings. This method can also be employed in show rings before starting the course.

Some further information on the subject can be found on page 269.

CONDITIONING THE SHOW JUMPER

The work of conditioning is carried out by sprints and by galloping up a steep sandy slope. This item of the show jumper's preparation requires less attention than in the case of a three-day event horse because the animal's physical engagement in the performance is less strenuous and thus the corresponding work becomes more simple.

The method of conditioning for the season-opening contest is shown in Tables Nos. 24 (for novice horses) and 26 (for intermediate and finished show jumpers). It need only be mentioned that if the rider is compelled to shorten the normal time of conditioning—because of the severity of weather—by as much as 10 to 14 days, or if it is apparent that the horse's condition is not yet satisfactory when the first scheduled show has arrived, the animal's first start should be postponed till a later date.

With regard to the horse's conditioning between two shows, the following points should be considered:

The horse's basic condition, which has been built up in the spring, can be maintained without any special work until the end of the season, provided the animal takes part in shows continuously at three to five weeks' intervals.

If the horse has difficulties with its breathing while negotiating a parcours, either during preparatory work or in a competition, it should carry out a pipe-opening exercise before its next performance (possibly one day before). For this purpose the most suitable practice is galloping up a steep slope, since it affects only the lungs and does not stretch the animal. If there is no suitable place for this exercise, however, a short sprint on a soft track or a 5-8 minutes canter in deep going can be substituted.

If more than two months intervene between two competitions the rider should proceed to the second, third and fourth week's work scheduled for training and spring-time conditioning. During this work the heights of the obstacles employed should correspond to those of the next show.

On the whole, it is satisfactory to include two lung-opening exercises, following each other at a week's interval.

# CHAPTER TWO

# Training the Show Jumper for Competitions

GENERAL INFORMATION FOR THE EXECUTION OF THE TRAINING

THE distribution of time and work for the show jumper's training is scheduled in Tables Nos. 24-26 and on page 529, according to the stages of its education. In addition, each of these stages is dealt with separately in the present chapter in order to elucidate the characteristics of the work recorded in the particular distribution. There are, however, some recommendations of general meaning, valid for the whole future of the show jumper, therefore we should introduce the special examination of the subject with their description.

*The horse's treatment after the completion of certain strenuous work until the time when its further methodical training or renewed engagement starts*

After the completion of each period of education and season of competitions the horse should enjoy three to five weeks' rest. During this time it can be turned out to grass or exercised in the same manner as recommended for three-day event horses (see Table No. 21, Remark).

The work between two seasons (during the winter period) should be arranged according to the experiences gained during the shows in which the horse took part in the previous season, proving its dexterity or any lack in skill, routine or education. Through their evaluation the rider should have a definite opinion about the possibilities which permit some relaxation in the further training and about the need of more intense schooling. The defects must be corrected now in the course of the present period.

During the winter most of the work must be done in a confined space or indoors. But when the weather and ground conditions

[493]

permit the horse should be taken outside for a ride in order to relieve it from the monotony of the riding school. It can also be hunted moderately with the aim of improving its muscular system and stamina. If, however, there is no chance for such outdoor work, the corresponding development of the animal must be promoted by protracted cantering indoors. This work is simultaneously the first step to the spring-time conditioning.

The general routine work during the winter and pre-spring period corresponds to that scheduled in Table No. 24, the only difference being that the height of the obstacles involved should be raised in conformity with the horse's particular stage of education.

Before the regular outdoor work starts horses which have been trained during the winter months on the soft sawdust of a manège must be first accustomed to natural ground. For this purpose, as soon as the milder weather sets in a week should be allotted during which the general work may gradually be increased.

Adjoiningly to the special preparation of the horse outlined above, its conditioning for the season-opening contest can commence. The distribution of the work involved is shown in Table No. 24, column three.

After the first spring show the horse should be allowed a rest of six to eight days, during which the work is restricted to riding at a walk and trot. This rest is necessary chiefly because of the exertion of bringing the animal into condition before the show. During the intervals between the following shows, if there is not much time, rest can be reduced to three to five days.

After the rest the horse's locomotion should be regulated by education, its obedience, mobility, turning capability freshened up and the jumping muscles improved by gymnastics (for this purpose the possibilities presented by the terrain may be useful).

Next it should receive the kind of tuition which will enable it to satisfy higher demands or correct established difficulties. In any case, the animal should be schooled and not over-trained through too strenuous work.

In this sense the improvement of the horse's jumping capacity should be promoted mainly by gymnastic exercises. Jumping of routine courses may be restricted and if it happens that the space of time between two shows is rather short, say three to four weeks, the practice of jumping courses can be omitted. Instead the rider should take a low parcours as introduction to the competition (see page 488).

If during the most recent show the horse has revealed slight difficulties or confusion, it is wise to relax the jumping exercises and omit clearing courses at least for two weeks. Stress should be put on careful education and gymnastics. On such occasions the rider may fall into the mistake of overdoing the corrective work instead of teaching the animal. This tends to make it sour. He should bear in mind that a little rest will provide the horse with more impetus than any amount of exaggerated work.

If the horse raises hopes by its performances in shows, but suddenly experiences a strong relapse, the cause may be both physical and psychological. In such cases the best remedy is a long rest. During this time the animal will forget bad impressions and lose the pains of fatigue which created its sourness. For a month or even longer the animal should not jump until it is felt that it is completely freshened up (the gymnastics should be reduced and those which remain be carried out by ground formations). Later on, when the horse shows definite freshness, jumping work can be resumed. As a response to the treatment the rider will feel the grateful reaction of the animal in showing its interest in, and knowledge of, jumping again.

Having outlined the general aspects of the show jumper's preparation for contests, we shall now discuss the details of the training according to the stages of its improvement.

THE NOVICE SHOW JUMPER AND ITS WORK DURING THE FIRST SEASON

*The work in general*

During this year of the training the educative work is already closely connected with competition. In planning the work the aim is to introduce the novice to shows and to create a liking for them.

Each of the shows in which the horse takes part must improve its knowledge and general education. Each show should lay the foundation for a further task of a higher standard.

There is no advantage in competing in too many shows in a season with a young animal. The result may be doubtful, without any improvement to him. The horse can display an excellent performance only if the natural means of development are provided. The demands should be increased gradually and with great care from classes of novice standard, so that at the end of the season the animal may participate once in a contest of middle standard (course of 4 feet 7 inches or 1.40 m. height).

It is true that the horse has not yet received any special coaching in mastering this height of parcours, but the systematic education and the gradual build-up of its improvement by participation in shows should have qualified it by now to face this new trial.

If, however, at the end of the season the novice is still not quite ready to compete in classes at 4 feet 3 inches (1.30 m.), it is a clear indication that it lacks some essential quality of a real show jumper.

*Particulars of the work to be done*

During the autumn months the animal should be taken out to the country tract as often as possible and its training carried on there. If the rider cannot spare the time for such excursions, the work can be completed in a confined space, but it should take place outdoors.

The work in the countryside should include practice in overcoming natural obstructions. These exercises serve the purpose of encouraging the horse to obey and jump in strange surroundings. When the animal passes over uneven ground it learns about banks and drop jumps; when it climbs ditches it accomplishes a fair amount of gymnastics; and when it jumps water or dry ditches it strengthens its aptitude for obedience. Furthermore, the experience and knowledge of the countryside will prove very useful while riding parcours. The constant change of scenery renders the horse relatively indifferent to the variations encountered in the show rings.

The information regarding the other work can be found in Table No. 24, first column.

During the winter period the training should be carried out in conformity with the general recommendations and according to the distribution of work shown in Table No. 24, column two.

In addition, it is necessary to draw special attention to the work of jumping courses, as this should be carried out in a really educative manner. The height of the fences should be gradually increased until they reach 4 feet (1.20 m.). If the animal loses form, eliminate the parcours from the work and substitute gymnastics for at least one to two weeks. It is also advisable to ease jumping and afford enough rest to enable the animal to recover. To force continuation of the work will produce disappointing results, as the horse loses pleasure and enthusiasm for its work.

The work of the early spring period is designed as preparation for the course of the horse's first show. At this performance it is advisable to participate in classes not exceeding 4 feet (1.20 m.).

During the previous period the novice will already have gained sufficient knowledge to jump courses designed for its standard. Therefore only the final touches remain for increasing the horse's dexterity. In addition to this, its conditioning must be carried out. After the completion of the work mentioned the novice can enter the show ring for its first competition.

Regarding the work before and during the days of the contest, see the information in Table No. 19, column four.

The first public test, whether of a three-day event horse or a show jumper, is always a landmark which indicates the completion of a long and arduous work. If the rider wishes to go further and win greater victories, he must continue the training based on results already achieved. The work from now on will often demand great perseverance, but it will also bring great compensations to the rider.

After the horse's maiden contest until the end of the season the work may be carried out according to the general recommendations and the distribution shown in Table No. 25.

THE INTERMEDIATE (PROGRESSING) SHOW JUMPER AND THE DEVELOPMENT OF ITS SHOW ROUTINE

When the novice horse has successfully completed its first season, during which it has had opportunity to gather some experience in competitions, it can be regarded as an intermediate show jumper.

In its next year the principal educative work is connected again with the participation in shows, the aim of which is to improve the animal's qualities by gradually increasing demands. As a result of this development it should reach, by the end of the season, a standard that will enable it to start once or twice in classes of 5 feet (1.50 m.) in height.

Methodical participation in shows will provide the horse with further useful experience and its knowledge will become firm and mature. Jumping courses higher than those mentioned should not be demanded during this season, since this might be too much for the animal. When it is gifted enough and settled in the routine of these medium high parcours, it is almost certain that in the following year it will negotiate the most intricate tasks in accordance with its capabilities and can also be started in difficult international competitions.

The distribution of time and work for the present season can be arranged according to the principles shown in Table No. 25, but the dimensions of the obstacles and parcours employed should be brought up to the actual stage of development.

An important item of the routine work is the improvement of speed in negotiating courses (for details see page 488). This should take place during the mid-season.

In deciding the class in which the intermediate show jumper may start in the opening contest the decisive factor is the quality of its performance at the close of the last season. If the animal has been successful in the classes of 4 feet 3 inches (1.30 m.) in height, it can safely be entered in such competitions. If it has encountered difficulties here, the rider should be content to start the season over courses not higher than 4 feet (1.20 m.).

THE FINISHED (COMPLETE) SHOW JUMPER AND THE DEVELOPMENT OF ITS PERFORMING CAPACITY UP TO THE LEVEL OF THE MOST INTRICATE TASKS

After successfully completing its second season the horse can be regarded as a complete show jumper even though its education is not yet finished. The skill of the horse in clearing courses is already of a high standard, but the quality of the performances must be refined. The work should aim at equipping the horse to start the following season in classes of every category which fall within its talents. This aim demands the perfection of the animal's regularity, the improvement of its muscles and elasticity, as well as familiarity with particularly large or solid obstacles.

The details of the routine work involved, with special reference to the first season at this standard, can be found on page 531.

In order to improve the horse's skill in jumping against time, some appropriate exercises should be included in the scheme of the first winter training. During the further years of the complete show jumper, when it needs more rest than work between the seasons, the number of the jumping exercises recorded ought to be reduced.

The finished show jumper should in its first season start the competitions possibly with a course of 4 feet 3 inches (1.30 m.), or at most 4 feet 7 inches (1.40 m.) in height. Later on the standard of the season-opening test can eventually be increased.

After the first show the demands imposed on the horse can gradually be increased, according to its abilities. This increase must, however, be carried out as in the previous year, from show to show, so that the impetus is provided by the competitions.

The limit of development is defined now by the talents of the horse. When it is evident that, despite its willingness, the animal cannot respond to further demands, it should not be pressed to do so. If the horse reveals some definite capacity in jumping high obstacles—such as puissance course, six bars jumping, both high and long jumping—in the second half of the summer period it can be entered in such classes. For these competitions the horse will not require any particular or elaborate preparation.

In the framework of the general training the animal may jump once or twice a height of not more than 5 feet 7 inches (1.70 m.), in six bars jumping 5 feet 3 inches (1.60 m.). Higher jumps take a considerable toll of the horse and it is a mistake to dissipate too much energy in the course of preparation.

It is impossible to teach the average horse to perform jumps in the region of 6 feet (1.80 m.) and over. For this a horse needs to be specially gifted. With a horse which has an inherent gift, and which has had the necessary schooling to employ its energy correctly, the heat of the contest will inspire it to make jumps never attempted before.

In performing such big jumps the animal can be supported best by the rider if he brings it to the proper take-off spot. This can be achieved most reliably by ascertaining the right turning point (see page 400). The turning point should be fixed so far from the obstacle that the horse, while approaching the fence, is able to acquire enough swing to execute the big jump. This, however, must be carried out by the horse itself, supported by the rider's resolute determination.

### CONSIDERATIONS GOVERNING THE EXTENSION OF DEMANDS

Any increase in the demands made on a horse should be

governed by the quality of the performance which the animal produced during its last competition. This performance should offer sufficient evidence regarding the height which the horse can achieve to suggest the kind of entries which the owner should make for the next show.

This appraisal of performance must be independent of the placing achieved by the horse in its last competition. This means, when it becomes apparent that the animal can maintain its ease in turns, proceed evenly in a regulated canter (gallop), take off courageously with the thrust-off filled with determination, it can be agreed that the horse is ready to enter a higher class.

If the rider is not absolutely certain that his mount is mature enough to participate in 'open' classes, he should be content, for the time being, to remain in a lower grade of competitions.

### HINTS ON THE DISTRIBUTION OF STARTS

A reliable estimate of the number of starts, and the classes to be chosen, can only be made after a thorough analysis of the horse. In the course of this analysis the animal's stage of education, natural talents, its general disposition, physical fitness and the question whether or not its legs can stand the strain should be taken into account. In the light of this consideration one comes to the following conclusion:

During the period of development (during the first two seasons)

the horse can participate in about eight and ten shows respectively. Within these shows it should not compete more than twice on three consecutive days or three times in four days. Several starts on one day should not be attempted, even if the animal could momentarily face the demand, since it may be the cause of repercussions in the future. According to this scheme the number of starts can be fixed at about 20 during the first year and at 24 during the second year.

While planning the entries one should include from time to time a class of moderately increased demands for the sake of the horse's development. The rider should make use of them even if the chance of a victory is slight.

During the first and the further seasons of the finished show jumper

it is possible to increase the number of shows gradually up to about 14 when the horse has reached its complete performing capacity. During these shows the number of starts can be, in comparison with the former periods, slightly increased and two starts on the same day can also be considered with moderation. In this sense the rider is enabled to participate in about 25 to 35 competitions during the season.

The nearer the horse reaches the completion of its special education, the more the rider should restrict entries to the more intricate classes in which it still has a reasonable chance to win. Thus, in choosing between different categories of test, preference should be given to the more difficult ones.

While riding a course with an older, more experienced jumper conditioned for the test, and for which the test is not any longer a part of education, it is advisable to give up the struggle immediately when the chances of winning have disappeared. In this case it is better to save the animal's energy for future occasions.

# CHAPTER THREE

# Riding the Show Jumping Course

IT is not only by riding properly that the rider can assist his mount; the following paragraphs call attention to a few other ways. In describing them it is intended to preserve the order in which the duties normally follow each other, from the act of entering the horse in the test to the final performance of the course.

*Entering more than one horse in the same class*

When the rider has more than one horse to start in the same class he should enter them in the order in which he wishes them to start. In this way the order of the horses will appear in the programme as the rider intends and it will not be necessary to apply for a change at the last moment.

In deciding the order the rider must consult his experience (concerning the nature of the horses) and consider his tactics.

As a rule, a horse which is still in the learning stage should start at first in the particular class. Horses which have more chance of winning, or need more care, should be left for the latter part of the competition. By doing so a novice, for which the main purpose of the test is to complete the course in one way or the other, will not have to leave the course after having made only a few mistakes.

An important reason for leaving the horse or horses with greater chances to the end is due to the fact that towards the end of the competition the situation becomes more clarified. The rider can weigh up the results which have been achieved by others and form a definite opinion regarding the necessity of improving his own performance. For example, by this time he will know whether or not it is necessary to aim at a clear round only or to lay emphasis on shortening the time, or after making a mistake whether he should retire and keep the animal fresh for another competition.

[502]

Regarding the order of starting, a further important factor is the temperament of the horse and the type of exercise necessary for warming up (see in detail page 507).

### Inspection of the course and shaping the riding plan

This scrutiny should start with a certain study of the official plan issued by the organizers. According to the rules it is compulsory for the rider to adhere to the lines (or to turning flags) laid down on the official plan of the course (with the exception of courses called 'take your own line').

As soon as the rider has memorized the features of the official plan (perhaps made a little sketch of it), he should make a survey of the course. It is advisable to inspect the obstacles first according to their sequence, ascertain their heights and shapes, and the distances between the combinations. Afterwards he should examine thoroughly the exact line of the course which he wishes to ride having regard to the prescribed limitations. Special attention should be paid (if it is a speed competition) to those places where time can be made and also to the obstacles which may be jumped at an angle.

In difficult courses it is advisable to measure the distances between the more critical obstacles. This helps the rider to anticipate the possibilities which the horse might face with its take-off. If this measurement suggests an unfavourable take-off distance, there is time and opportunity to ponder the best way in which the situation can be corrected, e.g. whether after the jump before the critical obstacle a brief retardment should be included, or if it is preferable to urge the animal to lengthen its strides. As by both interventions the length of the strides is altered, the position of the wrong take-off spot can be modified. A wrong distance can also be adjusted by the proper way of taking the turns. Here the rider must ascertain those turning points from which the convenient approach to the obstacle can be ensured for the horse.

In drawing up the riding plan for 'take your own line' classes use of the following order can be recommended:

divide the arena into two parts and connect the obstacles situated in these two parts of the show ring within their own group; then consider how to connect the two groups with each other and how to fit the whole course between the starting and finishing posts. This consideration will in most cases show that it is necessary to include in the plan one or two long lines without a jumping possibility. In order to make at least one of these long lines profitable, it is advantageous to draw up the riding plan in such a manner that the jumping of either the first or the last obstacle should occur in direct connection with the negotiation of that part of the selected course which is on the opposite side of the arena.

In determining the details of the plan the standard of the horse's education is decisive. The higher this is, the shorter turns can be included and the sharper jumping angles can be attempted.

In order to check any riding plan, it is of advantage, if there is time before the warming up, to watch a few horses jumping. For such control only reasonably orthodox horses' performances should be taken into account.

## Weighing-in

As in the second and third day of the three-day event, it is compulsory also in show jumping (except in record events) to conform to the prescribed minimum weight. This weight is 165 lb. (75 kg.).

In practice this weighing is often ignored, but the jury has the right to check the weight at any time.

There must be a scale for riders outside the course where they can ascertain their weight together with the saddle. In balancing the difference in weight the same methods can be applied which have been described in connection with the three-day event (see page 466).

If weighing-in is compulsory (Nations Cup, Olympic Games, etc.), it must be carried out exactly as has been shown with the three-day event.

## Warming up the horse

The object is to render the horse elastic without tiring it. The knowledge and energy of the animal must reach their peak during the performance of the course and not be wasted during the warming-up process.

Warming up must never be used as an occasion for teaching. Such an attempt will not succeed and only result in confusion, strain and nervousness. It must be borne in mind that the animal can display no more than the '*knowledge*' which it has already acquired during its routine work. It cannot be expected to expand this knowledge suddenly during the process of warming up.

However, this does not mean that the 'knowledge' acquired by the animal during the course of its education cannot be greater than that which the rider has ascertained by effective trials. It is quite possible that during the test the horse is able to produce a performance of greater value than at any time before, e.g. a horse which has never jumped higher than 6 feet (1.80 m.) may clear a height of 7 feet (2.10 m.) in competition. In this way experience gradually increases efficiency and leads the animal to a higher standard.

In the process of warming up, the first phase is the loosening exercise which precedes the actual work. It can be carried out at all three paces, while allowing complete freedom to the horse. If the stables are a considerable distance from the show ring and the horse covers this distance on foot, the extent of the loosening exercise can be reduced by taking this distance into account.

After the loosening exercise comes the actual work of warming up, which has to satisfy the rider on the following points:

refreshing the horse's willingness to yield to the rider;

improving elasticity and preparation for jumping;

practice in adopting the required speed (this work is specially important if the rider intends to adopt a greater speed).

The essence of the first task is the same as described on page 448 in connection with the dressage test. Within this special care should be laid on increasing the shoulder mobility of the horse and on refining its obedience to quick adjustments (half-halts, short turns, transitions, oscillating lateral movements, etc.).

Afterwards a few gymnastics are necessary to tone up the muscles engaged in jumping. The most suitable devices which can be erected anywhere are the pair of bascule developing bars (see Fig. No. 82) and the short gymnastic double jump (Fig. No. 85). In using these means begin with the first one. The horse should go over it a few times at gradually aggravated settings. Next comes the exercise with the aid of the second installation. This is the most important in the whole process of warming up. At the beginning of the exercise the distance between the two elements should allow the animal ample scope of movement, while their height can be set about 1 foot 4 inches (0.40 m.) and 2 feet (0.60 m.). The distance after two to three jumps can be somewhat narrowed and the height of the second element gradually increased so that it may reach the height of 3 feet 3 inches to 3 feet 6 inches (1-1.10 m.) after four to five jumps. When the excrcise has been completed a brief rest should follow.

The next stage of the warming-up process is jumping some individual obstacles. The height of these 'introductory' jumps should remain under the level of the course set out for the competition. Generally, if the height of parcours is fixed, e.g. at 4 feet 7 inches (1.40 m.), it is not necessary to exceed 4 feet 3 inches (1.30 m.).

If there is an extraordinary fence in the course, which is unknown to the horse, a simplified version of it can be erected and jumped once or twice. The rider may also erect the type of obstacle, in simplified setting, with which the animal has experienced most of its troubles, but the practice here should also not exceed one or two jumps.

As a general rule, it can be said that the more nervous the horse, the less it should jump in the warming-up process. The highly strung disposition of the animal should be calmed by a long, pacifying exercise with the inclusion of many smooth half-halts (mainly at a trot). This will relieve the resistance of the horse's mind and the stiffness of its muscles.

Warming up should be timed so that it is completed about eight to 15 minutes before the start. When the waiting time proves much longer than has been anticipated, it will be necessary to refresh the warming-up just before the start. This must not be more than a brief adjustment, a short gymnastic, and one to two jumps. If the horse should require any rapping, it should be applied then (see next paragraph).

The general method of warming up as described above must be adjusted if circumstances do not allow the rider to take the horse into the ring immediately after it has been prepared for the performance. This can happen when the rider wants to ride two or three horses in the same competition and the number of competitors is rather limited. In such cases there is not sufficient time left to complete the procedure by the normal method with each horse. This makes it necessary to carry out the warming up in two stages.

The first stage is a preliminary warming up, which is equivalent to a substantial loosening exercise, including all the work up to the gymnastics. Each horse must go through this work first separately, so that the horse which is scheduled to start first will remain last. In this manner the animal to be mounted last is able to start with uninterrupted work of preparation. The horse which by temperament or through limited education fusses with a partial warming up will benefit from this.

When the rider has finished performing with one of his horses and has mounted the next he can start on with the second part of the latter's warming-up process. This should begin with a brief adjustment, a few gymnastic exercises and finish from this stage onward in the normal manner.

During the warming-up process some riders may take the opportunity to rap the animal. Although personally we do not attribute great importance to this practice, we shall discuss it with the aim of affording some guidance in its application and thus providing some safeguard against its misuse.*

*The rapping (barrage)*

Rapping is a term used to indicate inflicting a smart blow on one or more legs of the animal. It is intended as a warning to the horse to intensify its attention in jumping the obstacle in a clear and distinct manner.

The effect of the knock varies according to its application:
a blow on the cannon-bone makes the animal raise its body. If it is inflicted on the forelegs, the horse is likely to lift the forehand, and the blow on the hind legs results in lifting the quarters;
a blow on the hoofs makes the horse pick up its affected feet more distinctly while jumping.

If any of the blows mentioned falls when the animal is in the ascending phase of the jump (before reaching the level of the obstacle), it acts as an inducement to a distant take-off, and if

---

*In Britain, raising the bar or using a rapping pole to hit a horse's legs on the show-ground is forbidden.

in the descending phase (on the landing side), it induces a near take-off. If the aim is only to raise the animal higher, the blow must be inflicted at the culminating point of the jump.

In the application of rapping, the rider must be very careful, since its abuse will cause much harm to the horse. Riders who venture to use it must have expert knowledge. Failing this, it is better to ignore it altogether, as its importance is limited and with most horses it is not necessary.

There are two main kinds of rapping, according to the way in which the blow is inflicted on the animal. In one the effect of rapping is obtained by setting the obstacle so that the horse, while jumping, hits itself (self-rapping). In the other the blow on the legs is inflicted by a person standing beside the obstacle (striking barrage).

Between these two forms of technique there is an intermediate method which is carried out by raising one end of a rail placed at a certain height on uprights. This is the simplest method of rapping and its effect the least injurious to the animal.

### Method of raising a bar

The instrument can be either the top bar of the obstacle itself (Fig. No. 164/a) or another pole which is placed there specially for the purpose of barrage (Fig. No. 164/b).

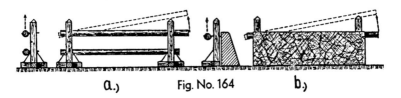

a.)          Fig. No. 164          b,)

The particular end of the bar should be lifted just at the moment when the horse's leg which requires the correction passes over it, so that the animal hits the pole.

Generally, such a dull knock with the bar will prove to be sufficient to make the horse aware of its carelessness.

### Self-rapping

The most simple technique of self-rapping is to jump a single rail without any facilities for judging (meaning that the obstacle has no ground-line). A horse which jumps carelessly will most certainly hit itself by knocking this bar off and cause itself some pain.

A more severe variation of the procedure is when a hollow iron

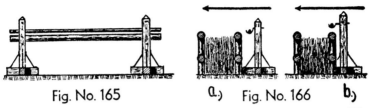

Fig. No. 165          a.)   Fig. No. 166   b.)

pipe is placed on or just above the rail (Fig. No. 165). The impact of the pipe, owing to its weight, inflicts a smarter blow on the animal's legs, which, together with the noise of the hollow metal, intensifies the effect of the warning.

Another method is to fix a light (but solid) iron rod about 2-8 inches (5-20 cm.) above the top rail of the obstacle, as shown in Fig. No. 166/b. The horse, while jumping the fence, will not take any notice of this thin and apparently insignificant bar and consequently it will hit itself by touching it. If after a few attempts the animal should become aware of the presence of the iron rod

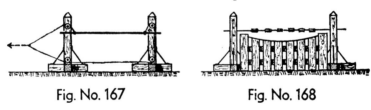

Fig. No. 167          Fig. No. 168

and try to evade it by jumping over it, the rod should then be fixed on the front of the obstacle so that it protrudes about 4-8 inches (10-20 cm.) from the fence (Fig. No. 166/a).

The installation can be made more effective by rendering the iron rod movable with the application of a cord mechanism running on pulleys (Fig. No. 167). This device has the advantage that the horse does not see the iron rod which is hidden behind the front view of the obstacle. It is also possible to manipulate the bar in such a manner that it can hit the animal's fore or hind legs as required.

With certain horses rapping can be most effective by making a specific noise like part of an obstacle being knocked off. Such a noise can be produced by stringing empty tins on a thin iron bar

(Fig. No. 168). The instrument should be placed either over or slightly before the front plane of the obstacle, as in the case of the simple iron rod. When the animal touches or knocks it off, the rattle of tins makes a loud and disagreeable noise very suitable for the purpose.

Barrage with the rapping pole

By this method the horse's leg is rapped by a person who has special knowledge of jumping and quick reflexes. This method is the most effective, but its application requires the utmost care and only experts should handle the rapping pole.

Compared with the other methods, this form of rapping has the advantage that the animal can be hit exactly on the particular part of its legs where it is most necessary and the effect of the stroke can be varied from a gentle warning to a severe punishment, according to the amount of force employed.

The bamboo cane is the most suitable for the purpose of a rapping pole, as it is hard and light and easily handled. But any kind of pole not thicker than a strong walking-stick may be used so long as it is not flexible. The length of the pole should be about 10 feet (3 m.).

While using the rapping pole it should be kept hidden and in a horizontal position behind the top rail or some part of the obstacle (Fig. No. 169). When the horse's legs are above the fence a hit

### Fig. No. 169

by the pole should be made on that particular leg or legs which the horse is not using properly.

The user of the pole must be very careful in placing the stroke on the stipulated place and with the necessary force only (the blow executed by an inexperienced person is in most cases greater than required).

Rapping as a means of the horse's education has been discussed on page 485. We shall now examine its employment in connection with the warming-up process only.

It should be left to the end of the process which ensures that the animal enters the ring with vivid impressions of the experience.

Horses which are too phlegmatic and careless can be warned by employing more rigorous methods of rapping, but even they must not suffer more than two or three hits.

A nervous animal should be warned by rapping only when it shows marked negligence, and even then the mildest form of warning should be employed (self-rapping). One or two blows are quite sufficient, as otherwise the horse will get confused and this will lead to mistakes.

Sticky, timid horses should not be rapped at all, since such punishment would only aggravate their difficulties. For such horses a light tap of the whip is more effective than the rapping pole.

*Waiting time before entering the ring (in the collecting ring)*

After the warming-up process it is advisable to make a thorough check of the saddle's position and the state of the rider's equipment.

Until admitted to the ring the animal should be kept walking with lively strides and dropped reins. During this time any positive action on the part of the rider must be avoided, since it is a period of rest for the horse. The lively form of walk ensures that the animal will not cool off and this is why it is not advisable to dismount.

Generally contestants experience some form of 'stage fright' while waiting their turn in the collecting ring. This is difficult to resist, but cannot be ignored. The rider who does not feel excited is not a real competitor, since the resolute will to win, and it is this which causes excitement, is the secret of victory.

However, this excitement must subside as soon as the contest begins and only operate subconsciously while the struggle is on. If stage fright originates from nervousness or becomes overpowering, it will cause confusion and have a hampering effect.

*Entering the ring and the start*

The show horse already knows what is going to follow during the warming-up process, but even more so during the waiting time in the collecting ring.  If it is well educated and competitions have been carefully selected and prepared (in accordance with its knowledge, capability, actual state of strength, etc.), it will possess vivid recollections of the experience.  Thus it will be pleased with the sensation which accompanies its appearance in the ring and will willingly enter.  On the other hand, if the ring has been the scene of exaggerated demands, great strain and pain, it certainly will produce fear in the animal and, as a consequence of such bad memories, it will resist entering the arena.

If the horse, in spite of this condition, has to take part in a show, it is best to have the animal led into the ring by the groom. (According to the regulations, as soon as it has crossed the entrance it must be set free.)  Without this aid the rider might easily become rough because of the provocation of the animal and this would only further aggravate the situation.

While entering the ring allow a few moments' complete freedom of the reins so that the horse can look round.  Meanwhile ride calmly to the saluting point.  There pick up the reins and salute with calm diginity.  Following this, approach the area of the start, regulate the animal, and strike it determinedly into a canter.  Then ride a circle, during which adopt the speed at which you wish to commence the course.

When the horse has accepted the correct attitude and speed the starting line can be crossed.

### The rider's concerns while riding the course

During the actual performance the jumping is the duty of the horse, but it is the rider's responsibility to support the animal by maintaining its regularity.  The more accurate the rider is in his conduct, the more distinct will become the horse's determination and self-confidence.  Ability to afford this aid is the real measuring stick of the rider's skill and the basis of his success.

The support of the animal should be exercised continuously in perfect harmony with its movements, thus keeping it in permanent balance.  In order to achieve this end, he should make good use of the oscillating movements of the levelling function while riding on the straight lines of the course, and of the more augmented part and counter-turning movements involved in the turning procedure (see page 202) while riding on its curved sections.

They will prevent the rider becoming stiff and long lasting in his actions as well as to act simultaneously with his hands, even if his smooth swinging movements are only indicated by an invisible inner 'intention'.

They preserve the submissive behaviour of the horse and by this the supple state of its body including the lateral mobility of the shoulders, which are prerequisites of the smooth performance of a course.

The slightly swinging 'serpentine line' which is produced by the conduct described, makes quick regulations practicable. It enables the rider to overcome difficulties which may hamper the animal in taking off, especially if the jump occurs shortly after a turn. The practical significance of the subject can be summed up in the following recommendation:

> if the horse, while approaching the obstacle is deviating to the *outside from the turn*, reach the take-off spot by getting it straight and jump from a '*part turn*' phase of the total turn;
>
> if it is drifting towards the *inside of the turn*, reach the take-off spot by getting the animal straight and jump from a 'counter-turn' phase of the turning procedure;
>
> if the horse is straight, reach the take-off spot from an indicated 'loop' the direction of which is opposite to its canter action.

The rider himself must be filled with a go-ahead spirit and must avoid any deliberate or involuntary action or movement which counteracts the valuable effects created by the unequivocal force of his spirit. If the rider possesses such an overwhelming determination and skill, his horse will also adopt this attitude and thus get wings for the jump.

While approaching the obstacle the rider should recollect the riding plan which he worked out for himself when inspecting the course and direct the horse accordingly.

The distance is about 50 feet (15 m.) from which an experienced rider can estimate the chances of his horse reaching the obstacle. This is the last moment when it is still proper to try and adjust the take-off distance if it seems to be necessary. This means that during the completion of the course the horse must not be taken out from its even and continuous *lively* striding merely for preventive purposes. Apart from other disadvantages (see page 326), this will result in a considerable loss of time.

Full details concerning the approach to the fence and the performance of the jump can be found in Part Three. With reference to slippery going, see recommendations on page 471.

If the horse happens to hit an obstacle, the rider must never look back. He may thus divert attention from balancing the animal on the line of the course and spoil the success of the next jump. The jarring of the fence and the noise caused do not necessarily mean that it has been knocked off and, in any case, looking back will not rectify the mistake. Such curiosity will only reveal a lack of self-discipline on the part of the rider. There is only one case when such behaviour is permissible and that is when the rider, to save his horse's energy, is thinking of giving up the struggle because it has lost the chance to win.

The completion of the course in a short time can be achieved mainly by the shortening of its line and to a considerably smaller degree by increasing speed. A higher speed generally demands that the turns are to be ridden on wider curves, which in contrast to the narrower ones means a loss of time. Therefore the standard of the animal's education and skill determines the basis of the harmonious balance between the narrowing of turns and extending the speed by which the horse can achieve its best possible result.

It should never be ignored, when the time factor is taken into account, that the rider may gain time even after he has jumped the last obstacle by passing the finishing posts at an increased speed.

After crossing the finishing line the animal should gradually be retarded and while riding an additional circle the pace should be changed to a trot. Then it can be driven towards the exit of the ring (possibly with loosened reins). Before reaching the exit, however, the animal should be retarded to a walk and allowed to look round again.

### The rider's rôle in jump-offs (barrages)

The single jump-off, when the time factor is decisive

In such a competition when several horses complete the course with a clear round or with an equivalent score a jump-off follows to decide their positions.

Regarding warming up for the jump-off, the rider must be guided by the horse's condition on how far it has cooled off since it finished the first round.

If the horse has taken part in the first half, or two-thirds of a well-filled class, one can count on at least an hour before the jump-off. In this case it is quite possible, as a rest for the animal, to remove its saddle. Then, about 40 minutes before the start of the jump-off, it ought to be replaced and the horse led in hand for about 10 minutes at a lively walk. Following this the rider can remount and after a brief adjustment make a few gymnastic exercises. Next comes the most important part of the warming-up process, the drill to accustom the horse to the faster speed which the rider intends to use during the performance.

The easier the jump-off and the more numerous the competitors, the faster will be the time which will win the test. However, this claim should not tempt the rider to over-drive the animal or demand more from it than it can afford. It is imperative to know exactly the maximum speed at which the horse can confidently negotiate the turns and clear the jumps. Use of this maximum speed should be practised during the warming up until the animal can repeatedly take up and maintain it at a short distance (150-200 yards or metres).

When the horse has adapted its movement to this particular speed two or three trial jumps should be made. The height of the jumps, however, can remain below the size of the obstacles on the course.

When the warming up has been completed the rider may dismount and look at the course from somewhere outside the arena (since it is not permitted to walk round the jump-off course). While doing so he should weigh up the requirements and possibilities of shortening the course so as to achieve a better time result. During this inspection and planning the horse should be kept walking at a lively pace, led in hand. When the rider has returned he may remount and await his turn at a lively walk.

In the event of a shorter space of time at the rider's disposal between the first round and the jump-off (which occurs mostly with those competitors who have started in the second half of the class) the main object of the warming-up procedure is to get the horse adapted to the desired speed. All other parts of the exercise can be curtailed, as the animal has not yet cooled off completely.

Successive jump-off

In puissance courses, record jumps or in the six bars competitions, when the rounds closely follow each other, the horse must be kept in a permanently warmed-up state. The principles of warming up for the first jump-off are the same as in any other case. Here the animal's preparation for faster speed serves the purpose of creating the necessary swing for jumping the higher obstacles which are included in these particular tests. For the second and successive jump-offs it is sufficient to bring the horse into swing by a brief process, enforced by one low jump and perhaps a mild rapping.

After each jump-off the rider should dismount as a sign of reward and leave the horse to gather fresh strength for its next performance.

### The duplicated round in the same class

In certain competitions, such as the Nations Cup team event, the identical course must be performed twice. In such cases warming up for the second round is only an abbreviated process which has to be carried out about 15-20 minutes before its start. (Brief adjustment, a few gymnastics and one or two low jumps.)

---

Participation in contests is a great pleasure for the rider especially if he becomes a successful contestant in big equestrian events. To achieve this goal he must be persevering both in his own and his horse's education. But, in order to retain his achieved position, the rider must also be able to withstand any temptation which may inspire him to part from his horse which has proved adequate to its chosen career during the long, painstaking work needed to bring it up to the required standard. Therefore he must try with all his means to remain in possession of his partner and protect it as much as possible.

To 'make' horses for business purposes and to educate them up for a promising sporting career are two different processes which can never be reconciled. The ambitious rider must abandon the quick material advantage and look for reward in achieving a more lasting success.

# DISTRIBUTION OF TIME AND WORK

FOR THE PREPARATION OF THE THREE-DAY EVENT (ONE-DAY EVENT) HORSE
AND THE SHOW JUMPER

FROM THE TIME OF TAKING THEM UNDER INSTRUCTION UNTIL REACHING
THE STAGE OF THEIR COMPLETE EDUCATION

The present distribution of time and work is compiled in order to provide the reader with a comprehensive picture of the overall trend of the horse's preparation. By using it, you will see the related application of the various subjects which have been discussed in detail, but whose interdependence and broad organisation have not yet been outlined clearly enough.

The data given in the distribution are based on results of the author's personal experience in successfully preparing a number of novice horses for three-day event and show jumping up to Olympic and Nations Cup standard respectively.

The distribution must not be regarded as rigid. It should only serve as a guidance to the rider in building up his manifold work. By the study of principles involved (arrangement, organisation, employment of necessary transitions and variations, etc.) the rider will always be able to accommodate himself to the special requirements of the horse. He will not run the risk of becoming absorbed by drilling away on minor details and thus losing continuity in progress.

In order to carry out adjustments in the programme it will often be necessary to 'consult' the horse also about the work to be done! The reckless perseverance in scheduled work, when the horse is confronted by difficulties, is an absolutely faulty method of education. It often leads to the roughness on the part of the rider which is the greatest danger in riding, and which is mostly the consequence of his ignorance. The rider's compliance, however, must reflect intelligence which is based on a highly sophisticated knowledge.

The more schooled the horse becomes, the rarer is the occasion when it expresses a different opinion, and the more one can accommodate oneself to the schedule.

In the present distribution the starting date for the education is the beginning of August. This proved to be most profitable, as one can adapt the necessary work best to the weather and ground conditions which are offered by the seasons involved. In this way also the finishing period of the preparatory work coincides best with the time when the horse can start its career.

## Table No. 18

DISTRIBUTION OF WORK DURING THE GENERAL EDUCATION OF THE HORSE UP TO NOVICE HUNTER STANDARD AND DURING THE ENSUING COURSE OF FURTHER EDUCATION FOR HORSES SELECTED FOR THREE-DAY EVENTS AND SHOW JUMPING

| Periods of training, their approx. duration and start | The work to be done within the | | |
|---|---|---|---|
| | Dressage-like schooling | Jumping exercises and on the country tract | Muscular, stride-lengthening, speed-improving and lung-developing exercises |
| **Stepping over miniature obstacles** — 2 months — When the horse already proceeds without being piloted | Riding freely on long straight lines (function of counter-deviation). Broad turns, mainly by weight transpositioning. Comfortable changes in the speed and of the pace. Conduct in expressed balancing manner with the inclusion of the levelling function. Acquainting with the rein-contact. | Stepping over miniature obstacles (cavaletti) up to 1 ft. 6 in. (0.50 m.) at a walk and trot. Walking over uneven surfaces, various but small obstructions of the country tract. | For muscular improvement execute dressage-like schooling on slightly sloping ground. Make exercises on undulating surfaces, ride uphill on long mild slopes (mainly at a trot). Special exercises for lengthening gallop-strides, increasing speed capacity and developing lungs are for the time being not recommended. |
| **Teaching of gymnastic exercises** — 1½ months — When moderate sensitiveness to drive-on and retardment is achieved | Increase turning capacity, confidence to the bit, and reaction to the drive-on and retardment. (Combined application of drive-on and retardment half-halts.) Introduce the regulation of the sequence of strides. Teach the rein-back, strike-off into canter to the particular direction desired. | Teach the right jumping movement by gymnastic exercises (artificial installations and ground formations). Ride on different surfaces of the country tract at a walk and trot. Overcome simple obstructions during this ride. | |
| **Jumping small obstacles** — At a trot — 2 months — When smooth reaction to drive-on and retardment at a trot is achieved | Improve the horse's dexterity in the tasks of the previous periods. Develop the swinging movement of the back, impulsion, lateral mobility of the forehand (turn on the haunches). Introduce the adjustment to straight position. Accustom the horse to riding without the use of the reins. | Improve the correct jumping style. Jumping at a trot (star obstacle) up to 2 ft. 4 in. (0.7 m.), ditches up to 6 ft. (1.8 m.). On the country tract, accommodate to ground conditions riding at all three paces, taking small obstructions at a trot, banks, drops up to 2 ft. (0.6 m.). | Make introductory exercises for lengthening the gallop-strides. |
| **At a canter** — 3 months — When smooth reaction to drive-on and retardment at a canter is achieved | Refine the knowledge achieved, ride narrower turns, smaller circles, serpentine lines at a trot. Teach the shoulder-in, croup-in at a walk, and extended movements at all three paces. Start with the moderate collection of the horse. | Introduce jumping at a canter up to 3 ft. 3 in. (1 m.), ditches 8 ft. (2.5 m.). On the country tract riding on undulating surfaces at a canter. Jump small obstacles at a trot and canter, cross simple climbing ditches and water surfaces. Banks and drops up to 2 ft. 6 in. (0.7 m.). | Exercises for lengthening gallop-strides at a speed of 500 yd. (450 m.)/min. on short distances, and for increasing speed capacity the same exercise over a distance from 700 to 1,300 yd. (600 to 1,200 m.). |

## Table No. 18—*continued*

| Periods of training, their approx. duration and start | The work to be done within the | | |
|---|---|---|---|
| | Dressage-like schooling | Jumping exercises and on the country tract | Muscular, stride-lengthening, speed-improving and lung-developing exercises |
| Introducing the novice horse to jumping under strange conditions 4 months When obedience to aids for adjustment is aroused | Consolidate the knowledge achieved, perfect the adjustability and suppleness of the horse. Improve its aptitude for collection.　Teach the shoulder-in, croup-in at a trot, half-pass at a walk, and the turn round the forehand. | Acquaint the horse with different simple obstacle types, easy doubles. Practise also in strange surround-ings.　Obstacles up to 3 ft. 6 in. (1.1 m.), ditches up to 10 ft. (3 m.), clear also easy combined ditches.　On the country tract extend the schooling to jumping on slanting surfaces, and to over-come easy combined climbing ditches. Banks and drops up to 2 ft. 8 in. (0.8 m.). | For muscular de-velopment proceed on short steep, and long mildly elevating ground, and make climbing exercises on very steep slopes.　Lengthening gal-lop-strides and in-creasing speed capa-city by combined exercises succes-sively from 500 yd. to 650 yd. (450 to 600 m.)/min. speed over a distance from 700 yd. to 1,300 yd. (600 to 1,200 m.). |
| Course of further education 4 months, weekly 2 days dressage-like schooling, 2 or 3 days schooling in jumping, 1 or 2 days exercises on the country tract. When adjustability of the horse and regu-larity of its movement has been achieved | Improve the general schooling.　Increase adjustability, supple-ness, impulsion, and obedience for collec-tion.　Practise short turns, as well as two tracks movements at a walk and trot, circular and serpentine lines at all three paces.　Carry out the school-ing interchanged on flat, slightly sloping and undulating surfaces. | Gymnastic exercises by artificial installations and ground formations at a trot and canter.　Schooling in jumping different types of single obstacles up to 3 ft. 9 in. (1.15 m.), ditches 9 ft. (2.8 m.), simple doubles and trebles up to 3 ft. 3 in. (1 m.).　Introduce the jumping of courses (parcours, 4-6 obstacles, star obstacle) up to 3 ft. 3 in. (1 m.). Practise this 2-3 times in a fortnight. Towards the end of the period make a few times jumps up to 4 ft. 3 in. (1.3 m.), ditch 10 ft. (3 m.) over well taxable obstacles of easy (slop-ing) structure.　On the country tract select the greatest possible variety in overcoming simple obstruc-tions in a comfortable manner, such as climbing ditches, jumps on slanting ground, drop-jumps, banks, jumps over and into water surfaces, etc. | Muscular develop-ment as above. Stride and speed improve-ment up to 760 yd. (700 m.)/min.　Start with jumping at an increased speed, up to 550 yd. (500 m.)/min. |

Table No. 19—DISTRIBUTION OF WORK DURING THE THREE-DAY EVENT HORSE'S SPECIAL EDUCATION UP TO ITS FINISHING TRAINING

Sub-periods of the training. Their weekly distribution and details of the work to be done

| | Winter time from middle of December to middle of March | Pre-spring (before the first parcours in public) until the end of April | Days of the first parcours in public about 8 to 10 days | Late spring during May |
|---|---|---|---|---|
| Composing sections of the education | 3 days for dressage-like schooling; 2 days for schooling in jumping; 1 day for muscle training | 2 days for dressage-like schooling; 2 days for schooling in jumping; 1 day for jumping courses; 1 day for overcoming country-type obstructions. | | As during the pre-spring period. During the last week eventually participation in a combined training test. |
| Dressage-like schooling | Increase the general knowledge; practise parts of the dressage test gradually up to the whole programme. The degree of the horse's suppleness determines the progress in the work. Horse in snaffle bridle; accustoming to the double bridle from time to time. | Refine the general knowledge of the horse with stress on perfecting its guiding qualities and adjustability. Practice of the dressage test can be reduced. Horse in snaffle bridle; accustoming to the double bridle from time to time. | Make exercises for bringing the horse under complete control (increase adjustability, suppleness, impulsion). | Start with light dressage schooling in snaffle bridle to restore regularity; then refresh the horse's knowledge in the performance of the dressage test, including that for the combined training test. The work interchanged in a snaffle and double bridle. |
| Training for jumping and overcoming country-type obstructions | Gymnastic exercises; jumping single obstacles up to 4 ft. (1.2 m.), combinations up to 3 ft. 7 in. (1.1 m.) courses gradually from 8 to 12 obstacles up to 3 ft. 7 in. (1.1 m.), in three weeks two times. Overcoming some obstructions of moderate dimensions, ev. during participation in hunting (about once a fortnight). | Gymnastic exercises mainly by the aid of ground formations; jumping single obstacles up to 4 ft. 3 in. (1.3 m.), combinations up to 10 ft. (3 m.), ditches up to 10 ft. (3 m.), courses gradually from 3 ft. (0.9 m.) up to 4 ft. (1.2 m.) including new obstacle structures. On the country tract refresh the knowledge and experience of the horse gained in autumn. | Gymnastic exercises; once or twice jumping small fences introduced by collecting exercises. Three days before the show: Clearing 4 to 5 obstacles of about 4 ft. (1.2 m.) in series. The day before the show: Light work, rest. With regard to the performance see page 502. After the show: Rest and light work for a few days, ev. schooling the dressage test of a combined training test. | Gymnastic exercises. During the third week (ev. the week before the contemplated C.T.T.): On one day a simple double (3 ft. 3 in. and 3 ft. 6 in., or 1 m. and 1.1 m.); after one day interval successive jumping up to 4 ft. 3 in. (1.3 m.) and the next day an easy course of 4 ft. (1.2 m.), including 1 to 2 inviting fences of 4 ft. 3 in. (1.3 m.) height. |
| Muscular, stride-lengthening, speed-improving and lung-developing exercises | For muscle training: Protracted cantering, gradually up to 20 minutes. This work can be substituted by hunting. | In weekly succession once: Opening of lungs by climbing or a short sprint; lengthening strides by a gallop at a speed of 500 yd. (450 m.)/min. over 800 yd. (700 m.); jumping at an increased speed over three hurdles on the above distance, once at 550 yd. (500 m.)/min. and once at 600 yd. (550 m.)/min. | | Lengthening of gallop-strides combined with jumping at an increased speed over 3 hurdles at a speed of 700 yd. (650 m.)/min. If the horse does not partake in a C.T.T. make this exercise twice, and overcome simple country-type obstructions of various forms. |

Table No. 20—DISTRIBUTION OF WORK DURING THE NOVICE THREE-DAY EVENT HORSE'S FINISHING EDUCATION (BEFORE ITS CONDITIONING) ACCORDING TO THREE WEEKS' SUB-PERIODS

| | Sub-periods of the training, their weekly distribution and details of the work to be done | | |
| --- | --- | --- | --- |
| | First 3 weeks | Second 3 weeks | Third 3 weeks |
| Composing sections of the education | 3 days for dressage-like schooling 1 day for schooling in jumping 2 days for training in overcoming country-type obstructions. | 2 days for dressage-like schooling 1 day for schooling in jumping 3 days for practice of overcoming country-type obstructions. | 2 days for dressage-like schooling 2 days for schooling in jumping and parcours 2 days for practice in overcoming country-type obstructions. |
| Dressage-like schooling | Make the horse used to keeping an even and smooth contact on the double bridle. Practise individual movements of the dressage test. During the third week practise eventually the programme of the combined training test in snaffle bridle. | The work is similar to that of the previous 3 weeks. Practise the dressage programme of the C.T.T. more intensively. | Develop the capacity of the horse gradually until it is able to perform the dressage test in three to four sections. The horse should become able to complete the dressage programme of the C.T.T. (ev.). |
| Training for jumping and overcoming country-type obstructions | Training for jumping comprises mainly gymnastic exercises by the means of surface formations and artificial installations in order to enhance the dexterity of the horse. Increase gradually the demand of overcoming the time-absorbing obstructions with less loss of time; stress is laid on those where the horse is labouring with difficulties. | Gymnastics. Dexterity exercises for clearing several single obstacles and combinations up to 4 ft. (1.2 m.) and a ditch 10 ft. (3 m.) wide. On the third week jumping an easy course of 3 ft. 3 in. (1 m.) average height. Training on the country tract requires the widest possible variation. On the same day negotiate in addition to some easier obstructions only 1 to 2 more difficult ones. Look for increasing swiftness in the performance. | During the first week: Jumping single obstacles and combinations up to 4 ft. 3 in. (1.3 m.) height, and a ditch 12 ft. (3.5 m.) wide. On the second week: A course with 8 to 10 obstacles 3 ft. 6 in. (1.1 m.) high (1 to 2 fences may be 4 ft. or 1.2 m.). On the third week: A course 4 ft. (1.2 m.) high, 1 to 2 attractive-looking obstacles 4 ft. 3 in. (1.3 m.) high. This item can be replaced by a C.T.T. Training on the country tract as during the previous 3 weeks, but choose more difficult obstructions and negotiate them in less time than before. |
| Exercises for increasing speed capacity and stamina | On the first week: Once a gallop uphill on a steep slope or 5 to 6 minutes' canter in deep going. On the second week: A gallop over 3 hurdles on a distance of 800 yd. (750 m.) at a speed of 600 yd. (550 m.)/min. A hand-gallop of 10 min. On the third week: A slow gallop (without obstacles) on a distance of about 1½ miles (2.5 km.) at a speed of 450 yd. (400 m.)/min. | On the first week: As during the previous sub-period, but increase the severity of the exercise by repeating or lengthening the climbing or prolonging the canter. On the second week: Gallop over 4 hurdles on a distance of 900 yd. (800 m.) at a speed of 600 yd. (550 m.)/min. On the third week: A slow gallop, reinforced by 6 to 8 easy jumps over a distance of 1½ miles (2.5 km.) at a speed of 450 yd. (400 m.)/min. | On the first week: As during the previous sub-period plus 12 min. hand-gallop. On the second week: Gallop over 5 hurdles on a distance of ¾ mile (1,200 m.) at a speed of 600 yd. (550 m.)/min. On the third week: A slow gallop reinforced by 8 to 10 moderate jumps over a distance of 1½ miles (2.5 km.) at a speed of 450 yd. (400 m.)/min. |

During these 9 weeks twice weekly the loosening exercise should comprise 30 min. ride at a trot at a speed of 240 to 250 yd. (220 to 230 m.)/min. After the completion of this period the horse must be rested for a week during which its exercise comprises 20 min. walk plus 20 min. comfortable trot plus 20 min. walk. If possible the horse should be led in hand from another horse. After this exercise it should remain in a shady paddock until feeding time.

## Table No. 21

DISTRIBUTION OF TIME AND WORK FOR THE CONDITIONING OF THE NOVICE THREE-DAY EVENT HORSE BEFORE ITS FIRST EVENT (50 PER CENT. TEST), WITH THE INCLUSION OF PARTICIPATION IN ONE OR TWO ONE-DAY EVENTS

| Week | Day | Details of the main work to be done |
|---|---|---|
| I | 1 | Schooling in a snaffle bridle; practise the O.D.E. dressage test; gymnastic exercises for jumping. |
| | 2 | Comfortable overcoming of simple country-type obstructions; practice of the O.D.E. dressage test. |
| | 3 | Schooling in a snaffle bridle; practise particular movements of the T.D.E. dressage test; gymnastic exercises for jumping. |
| | 4 | As on the second day. |
| | 5 | Pipe opener over 800 yd. (700 m.) or by climbing on a steep slope or cantering 5 minutes in deep going; schooling in a snaffle bridle. |
| | 6 | Gallop over 4 hurdles on 1 mile (1,600 m.) at 700 yd. (650 m.)/min. |
| II • | 1 | 3 miles (5 km.) trot (comfortably); jumping some individual obstacles up to 4 ft. (1.2 m.). |
| | 2 | Schooling in a double bridle; jumping in succession 5 to 6 obstacles up to 4 ft. (1.2 m.) in a snaffle bridle; 10 min. hand-gallop. |
| | 3 | Schooling in a snaffle bridle; practise the O.D.E. dressage test. |
| | 4 | Schooling in a double bridle; practise short parts of the T.D.E. dressage test, or in a snaffle bridle that of the O.D.E. |
| | 5 | Schooling in a snaffle bridle; rousing adjustability; gymnastic exercises for jumping; pipe opener. |
| | 6 | Gallop reinforced by 10 to 12 obstacles at 500 yd. (450 m.)/min. |
| III | 1 | Light exercise. |
| | 2 | Schooling in a snaffle bridle; rousing adjustability. |
| | 3-4 | Schooling in a double bridle; practise parts of the T.D.E. dressage test. |
| | 5 | Schooling in a snaffle bridle; gymnastic exercises for jumping. |
| | 6 | Some individual jumps up to 4 ft. (1.2 m.); schooling in a double bridle certain parts of the T.D.E. dressage test. |
| IV | 1 | 5 miles (8 km.) trot at 230 yd. (210 m.)/min.; schooling in a double bridle. |
| | 2 | Overcoming some moderate country-type obstructions (individually). |
| | 3 | Overcoming 8 to 10 bigger country-type obstructions in a swift manner (3 to 4 in succession). |
| | 4 | Schooling in a snaffle bridle; rousing adjustability; 12 min. hand-gallop. |
| | 5 | Schooling in a double bridle; practise parts of the T.D.E. dressage test. |
| | 6 | Schooling in a double bridle; practise the complete T.D.E. dressage test. |
| V | 1 | Schooling in a double bridle; practise the complete T.D.E. dressage test. |
| | 2 | Gymnastics; jumping a hurdle at an increased speed (3 to 4 times, individually). |
| | 3 | 700 yd. (650 m.) sprint with gradual transitions; schooling in a snaffle bridle. |
| | 4 | Gallop over 5 to 6 hurdles on 1¼ mile (2,000 m.) at 700 yd. (650 m.)/min. Long walk on the country tract. |
| | 5 | Schooling in a snaffle bridle; rousing adjustability. |
| | 6 | Schooling in a double bridle; practise the complete T.D.E. dressage test, or that of the O.D.E. in a snaffle bridle. |
| VI • | 1 | Overcoming 3 to 4 moderate country-type obstructions in a swift manner (individually). |
| | 2 | Schooling in a double bridle; practice of the complete T.D.E. dressage test, or that of the O.D.E. in a snaffle bridle; 12 min. hand-gallop. |
| | 3 | Gymnastics; jumping of a few obstacles individually, up to 4 ft. (1.2 m.). |
| | 4 | Gymnastics; jumping 5 to 7 obstacles in succession (course); ev. schooling of the O.D.E. dressage test. |
| | 5 | Schooling in a double bridle (or ev. in a snaffle bridle the O.D.E. dressage test); pipe opener. |
| | 6 | 2 miles (3,200 m.) gallop reinforced by 12 to 15 obstacles at 500 yd. (450 m.)/min. |
| VII | 1 | Light exercise. |
| | 2 | Schooling in a snaffle bridle; rousing adjustability. |
| | 3-4 | Schooling in a double bridle; practise parts of the T.D.E. dressage test. |
| | 5 | Gymnastics; some individual jumps up to 4 ft. 3 in. (1.3 m.). |
| | 6 | Course of moderate shape, 6 to 8 obstacles up to 3 ft. 9 in. (1.15 m.). Long walk on the country tract. |

Items marked with * can be replaced by an O.D.E. If an O.D.E. was included on the sixth week, jumping exercises indicated for the seventh week should be replaced by gymnastics and general schooling.

## Table No. 21—*continued*

| Week | Day | Details of the main work to be done |
|---|---|---|
| VIII | 1 | 6 miles (10 km.) trot at 230 yd. (210 m.)/min.; rousing adjustability (snaffle bridle). |
| | 2–4 | Schooling in a double bridle (ev. in unfamiliar surroundings); once overcoming 2 to 3 impressive obstructions. |
| | 5 | Schooling in a snaffle bridle; pipe opener. |
| | 6 | Gallop over 6 to 8 hurdles on 1¾ miles (2,800 m.) at 700 yd. (650 m.)/min. Long walk on the country tract. |
| IX | 1 | Light exercise; rousing adjustability. |
| | 2 | Schooling in a double bridle; practise the complete T.D.E. dressage test. |
| | 3 | Gymnastics; some individual jumps up to 4 ft. 3 in. (1.3 m.). |
| | 4 | Gymnastics; jumping a more severe course, 8 to 10 obstacles, up to 4 ft. |
| | 5 | 15 min. hand-gallop; schooling in a double bridle; practise the complete T.D.E. dressage test. |
| | 6 | A trial performance of the dressage test (ev. in unfamiliar surroundings). Long walk on the country tract. |
| X | 1–6 | Exercises interchanged in a snaffle and double bridle; once overcoming 2 to 3 moderate country-type obstructions and once a gallop over hurdles on ¾ mile (1,200 m.) at 700 yd. (650 m.)/min. |
| Competition | 1 | Long, quite loosening exercise (about 2 hours) including a short canter and some light gymnastics. |
| | 2 | A few individual jumps up to 4 ft. (1.2 m.); 10 min. hand-gallop. |
| | 3 | Schooling in a double bridle; practise the dressage test (moderately). |
| | 4 | Presentation of the dressage test to the jury; pipe opener. |
| | 5 | Performance of the speed and endurance test. |
| | 6 | Performance of the show-jumping test. |

On the 7th day of each week the horse should have a rest. Ride only ¾ hour at a walk.
After each strenuous gallop work let the horse walk in hand for ¾ hour in the afternoon.
After the test the animal must have a rest of 2 to 3 weeks. During this period its daily work should be restricted to 1½ hours' loosening exercise at a walk and trot (35 min. walk plus 25 min. trot plus 35 min. walk).

## Table No. 22/a

### DISTRIBUTION OF TIME AND WORK FOR THE GRADUAL DEVELOPMENT OF THE INTERMEDIATE (PROGRESSING) THREE-DAY EVENT HORSE UP TO 100 PER CENT. OLYMPIC REQUIREMENTS

| DISTRIBUTION FOR THE SEASON-OPENING CONTEST (50% REQUIREMENTS) | | |
|---|---|---|
| Periods of the work | Time | Details of the main work to be done |
| General improvement | November | The object of the work is renewed regulation of the sequence of strides, and making the horse's aptitude for adjustability more sensitive; gymnastics by ground formations. |
| | December | Practice of individual movements of the dressage test in a snaffle bridle. Gymnastics. Once per week a few jumps up to 3 ft. 7 in. (1.1 m.), and during the month jumping of two easy courses, one at a height of 3 ft. (0.9 m.), and the other at 3 ft. 3 in. (1 m.). |
| | January | Twice weekly dressage-like schooling in a snaffle bridle, practising first individual movements, later on parts of the test. Gymnastic exercises mainly by artificial installations. Twice per week some individual jumps, single obstacles up to 4 ft. (1.2 m.), combinations up to 3 ft. 7 in. (1.1 m.). Jumping courses three times, first two of 3 ft. 3 in. (1 m.) height, the third 3 ft. 7 in. (1.1 m.). Protracted cantering with 10 days' interval: once 10, and once 15 min. duration at 360 yd. (330 m.)/min. |
| | February | Twice weekly dressage-like schooling in a double bridle, practising first certain parts, later on the complete programme of the dressage test. Gymnastic exercises. Walks in the country-site. Twice per week practice of individual jumps up to 4 ft. 3 n. (1.3 m.), and medium combinations. Jumping courses four times, the last 4 ft. (1.2 m.) high. Protracted cantering with 10 days' interval, both of 20 min. duration. |
| | Intervening | Accustoming the horse to the country track (if necessary); the first lung-opening exercise and cantering on undulating ground. |

## Table No. 22/a—*continued*

DISTRIBUTION FOR THE SEASON-OPENING CONTEST (50% REQUIREMENTS)

| Periods of the work | Time | | Details of the main work to be done |
|---|---|---|---|
| Conditionng according to weeks and days | I | 1 | 4 miles comfortable trot; schooling in a double bridle, practising parts of the dressage test. Gymnastics by ground formations. |
| | | 2 | Overcoming easy country-type obstructions (possible climbing ditch, low drop-jump, water-jump, bank). |
| | | 3 | Schooling in a double bridle, practising parts of the T.D.E. dressage test, and in snaffle bridle those of the O.D.E. |
| | | 4 | 5 min. cantering in deep going or 10 min. hand-gallop; schooling in a snaffle bridle. |
| | | 5 | Gymnastics. 4 to 5 individual jumps over a hurdle at an increased speed. Rousing adjustability. |
| | | 6 | Gallop over 6 obstacles on 1 mile (1,600 m.) at 500 yd. (450 m.)/min. Schooling the O.D.E. dressage test. |
| | II | 1 | 4 miles (6 km.) comfortable trot. Schooling in a double bridle, practising longer parts of the T.D.E. dressage test. |
| | | 2 | $1\frac{1}{4}$ miles (2,000 m.) gallop (without obstacles) at 600 yd. (550 m.)/min. Schooling the O.D.E. dressage test. |
| | | 3 | Schooling in a snaffle bridle, rousing adjustability. A few individual jumps, single and combined up to 4 ft. (1.2 m.). |
| | | 4 | Schooling in a double bridle; practising longer parts of the T.D.E. dressage test. |
| | | 5 | 4 to 5 individual jumps at an increased speed. Schooling the O.D.E. dressage test. |
| | | 6 | Gallop over 6 hurdles on 1 mile (1,600 m.) at 650 yd. (600 m.)/min. Long walk on the country tract. |
| | III | 1 | Schooling in a snaffle bridle; rousing adjustability; practising the O.D.E. dressage test. Gymnastics. |
| | | 2 | Overcoming moderate country-type obstructions, at first individually, then 3 to 4 in succession. |
| | | 3 | Schooling in a snaffle bridle; practising the O.D.E. dressage test. |
| | | 4 | Schooling in a double bridle; practising the complete T.D.E. dressage test; 12 min. hand-gallop. |
| | | 5 | Gymnastics. A few individual jumps over a single obstacle up to 4 ft. 3 in. (1.3 m.), combination up to 4 ft. (1.2 m.). |
| | | 6 | Jumping a course 3 ft. 7 in. (1.1 m.) high, including 2 to 3 impressive obstacles. Long walk on the country tract. |
| | IV | 1 | 4 miles (6 km.) trot at 230 yd. (210 m.)/min. Schooling the O.D.E. dressage test. |
| | | 2 | Schooling in a double bridle; practising the complete T.D.E. dressage test. |
| | | 3 | Jumping individually 3 to 4 impressive country-type obstructions (including a bank) at 500 yd. (450 m.)/min. |
| | | 4 | Schooling in a snaffle bridle; rousing adjustability; practising the O.D.E. dressage test. |
| | | 5 | Pipe opener (about 900 yd. or 800 m.); practising the O.D.E. dressage test (moderately), or long walk. |
| | * | 6 | 2 miles (3,200 m.) gallop reinforced by 10 to 12 obstacles at 500 yd. (450 m.)/min. |
| | V | 1 | Light exercise. |
| | | 2 | Schooling in a snaffle bridle; rousing adjustability. |
| | | 3 | Schooling in a double bridle; practising the complete T.D.E. dressage test; 6 min. cantering in deep going. |
| | | 4 | Schooling in a snaffle bridle. Long walk on the country tract. |
| | | 5 | Gymnastics. 3 to 4 individual jumps over a hurdle at 700 yd. (650 m.)/min. |
| | | 6 | Gallop over 8 hurdles on $1\frac{1}{2}$ miles (2,400 m.) at 700 yd. (650 m.)/min. |
| | VI—VIII | | As during the IX—XI weeks shown in Table No. 21. |

*See remarks to Table No. 21.

## Table No. 22/b

| | DISTRIBUTION FOR THE PROGRESSING 75% TASK | | |
|---|---|---|---|
| Periods of the work | Time | | Details of the main work to be done |
| During the time between the contests | | | Improvement of the horse's knowledge by taking into account the experiences gained during the previous performance. If there is more than 3 months' interval between the two contests this preparatory work can occur according to the last 3 weeks sub-period scheduled in Table No. 20 (finishing preparation) with the addition of a few days light exercise. |
| Conditioning according to weeks and days | I | 1 | Schooling in a double bridle; practising parts of the dressage test. |
| | | 2 | Gymnastics. 3 to 4 individual jumps over a hurdle at 700 yd. (650 m.)/min. |
| | | 3 | Schooling in a double bridle; practising longer parts of the dressage test. |
| | | 4 | Pipe-opener (possible by climbing); schooling in a snaffle bridle. |
| | | 5 | 1¼ miles (2,000 m.) gallop over 6 to 8 hurdles at 700 yd. (650 m.)/min. |
| | | 6 | Schooling in a snaffle bridle; rousing adjustability. |
| | II | 1 | 5 miles (8 km.) trot at 230 yd. (210 m.)/min. Schooling in a double bridle; practising the complete dressage test. |
| | | 2 | Schooling in a snaffle bridle; practising the dressage test. |
| | | 3 | Schooling in a double bridle; practising the dressage test. |
| | | 4 | Gymnastics on the country tract; overcoming some country-type obstructions; long walk. |
| | | 5 | Pipe opener by a sprint. Schooling in a snaffle bridle; rousing adjustability. |
| | | 6 | 2 miles (3,200 m.) gallop over 8 to 10 obstacles at 500 yd. (450 m.)/min. Long walk in the country site. |
| | III—VI | | As VIII—XI weeks in Table No. 21 (novice 50% test). Alteration: Sprint in the last week 1,500 yd. (1,350 m.). |

## Table No. 22/c

| | DISTRIBUTION FOR THE PROGRESSING 100% TASK | | |
|---|---|---|---|
| Periods of the work | Time | | Details of the main work to be done |
| During the time between the contests | | | According to the recommendations given for the above case. |
| Conditioning according to weeks and days | I | 1 | Schooling in a double bridle; practising parts of the test. |
| | | 2 | Schooling in a snaffle bridle; rousing adjustability. Gymnastics. |
| | | 3 | Gymnastics. A few individual jumps over a single obstacle and a combination up to 4 ft. (1.2 m.). |
| | | 4 | Pipe opener (possible by climbing). Schooling in a snaffle bridle. |
| | | 5 | 2 miles (3,200 m.) gallop on undulating track at 500 yd. (450 m.)/min. Long walk on the tract. |
| | | 6 | Schooling in a double bridle; practising longer parts of the dressage test. |
| | II | 1 | 4 miles (6 km.) trot at 230 yd. (210 m.)/min. Schooling in a double bridle; practising the complete dressage test. |
| | | 2 | Gymnastics on the track. Overcoming some country-type obstructions (comfortably). |
| | | 3 | Schooling in a double bridle; practising the complete dressage test. |
| | | 4 | Gymnastics. 4 to 5 individual jumps over a single obstacle and a combination up to 4 ft. 3 in. (1.3 m.). |
| | | 5 | Gymnastics. Jumping a 3 ft. 7 in. (1.1 m.) high course (8 to 10 obstacles). |
| | | 6 | ¾ mile over hurdles at 700 yd. (650 m.)/min. |
| | III | 1 | 6 miles (10 km.) trot at 230 yd. (210 m.)/min. Schooling in a double bridle; practising the complete dressage test. |
| | | 2 | Overcoming individually some country-type obstructions in a swift manner. |
| | | 3 | Pipe opener by sprint. Schooling in a snaffle bridle; rousing adjustability. |
| | | 4 | Gymnastics. 4 to 5 individual jumps over a hurdle at 700 yd. (650 m.)/min. |
| | | 5 | 2 miles (3,200 m.) gallop over 12 to 14 hurdles at 700 yd. (650 m.)/min. Long walk in the country site. |
| | | 6 | Light exercise. |
| | IV—VI | | As in the above case during the last three weeks. |

# Table No. 22/d

DISTRIBUTION OF WORK DURING THE PREPARATION FOR HIGHER
REQUIREMENTS WITHOUT A GRADUAL ENHANCEMENT OF THE DEMANDS

| Task | | Work | Time (weeks) | Details of the main work to be done |
|---|---|---|---|---|
| **75%** | Without 50% | C'nditi'ning | During the gen. preparation | According to Table No. 22/a (' general improvement ') or according to Table No. 20 (9 weeks' programme). |
| | | | I—VI | According to the I—VI weeks' distribution in Table No. 21 (novice 50% preparation). |
| | | | VII | Light exercise. If not preceded by an O.D.E. include an easy parcours and 10 min. hand-gallop. |
| | | | VIII—XI | According to the III—VI weeks' distribution in Table No. 22/b (progressing 75% preparation). |
| **100%** | Preceded by 50% | C'nditi'ning | During the gen. preparation | According to Table No. 22/b (' During the time between the contest '). |
| | | | I—II | According to the I—II weeks' distribution in Table No. 22/a (progressing 50% preparation). |
| | | | III—IV | According to the I—II weeks' distribution in Table No. 22/b (progressing 75% preparation). |
| | | | V—IX | According to the II—VI weeks' distribution in Table No. 22/c (progressing 100% preparation). |
| | Without lower grades | Conditioning | During the gen. preparation | According to Table No. 20 (nine weeks' programme), or according to Table No. 22/a (' General improvement '). |
| | | | I—VII | According to the I—VII weeks' distribution in Table No. 21. |
| | | | VIII—X | According to the I—III weeks' distribution in Table No. 22/c. |
| | | | XI | Light exercise. |
| | | | XII | According to the III week's distribution in Table No. 22/c, but 2½ miles (4,000 m.) gallop over hurdles. |
| | | | XIII | General schooling; gymnastics; once a few individual jumps up to 4 ft. 3 in. (1.30 m.); and once an easy parcours. |
| | | | XIV—XVI | According to the IV—VI weeks' distribution in Table No. 22/c. |

# Table No. 23/a

DISTRIBUTION OF TIME AND WORK DURING THE PREPARATION OF
THE FINISHED THREE-DAY EVENT HORSE

| DISTRIBUTION FOR THE SEASON OPENING CONTEST | | | |
|---|---|---|---|
| **Task** | | Time | Details of the main work to be done |
| During the time between two seasons | | | During 1–1½ months after the conventional rest: Re-regulation; rousing adjustability; gymnastics. Then practice of the dressage test at first in a snaffle bridle, later on in a double bridle. Moderately employed jumping exercises (about twice a week) for clearing individual obstacles gradually up to 4 ft. 7 in. (1.4 m.), combinations also with odd distances; jumping courses about 5 to 6 times, from 3 ft. 3 in. (1 m.) up to one of 4 ft. 3 in. (1.3 m.) height. In fortnightly intervals a 10, 15, 20 and again a 20 min. slow canter. |
| Conditioning if the test is of | 50% | I—VIII | According to the distribution shown in Table No. 22/a. |
| | 75% | I—IV | According to the I—IV weeks' distribution in Table No. 22/a (progressing 50% preparation). |
| | | V | Light exercise; including an easy parcours. |
| | | VI—IX | According to the III—VI weeks' distribution in Table No. 22/b (progressing 75% preparation). |
| | 100% | I—II | According to the I—II weeks' distribution in Table No. 22/a. |
| | | III | According to the IV week's distribution in Table No. 22/a. Alteration: 1½ miles (2,400 m.) over obstacles. |
| | | IV | According to the V week's distribution in Table No. 22/a. |
| | | V | Light exercise, including an easy parcours. |
| | | VI | According to the III week's distribution in Table No. 22/a. |
| | | VII | According to the III week's distribution in Table No. 22/c. Alteration: 2½ miles (4,000 m.) over hurdles. |
| | | VIII—X | According to the IV—VI weeks' distribution in Table No. 22/c. |

*The application of the tables in case of the one-day event horse's preparation*

The special education of the one-day event horse can be carried out according to Tables Nos. 19 and 20. In this case the schooling exercises recommended with the use of the double bridle should be omitted, and it is enough to practise the movements and the programme of the dressage test required by the regulations of the one-day event and combined training test.

By the means of the fast gallop work the necessary conditioning of the horse is already introduced. Its completion occurs according to the distribution of work shown by the first six weeks programme in Table No. 21. Here, too, the exercises for the dressage test should include only practices for the one-day event.

It should be mentioned, however, that the participation in the one-day event scheduled for the sixth day of the second week should be regarded as an opportunity for the horse to gather experience. Therefore, the rider may complete it in a comfortable manner, and not try to press the horse hard during the cross-country phase of the test in order to gain bonus points. This test should be considered as the main item of conditioning for the second competition, scheduled for the sixth week's sixth day.

Thus, the Tables Nos. 20 and 21 (up to the sixth week's programme of the latter) show the distribution of work for the novice one-day event horse's finishing education and conditioning for its maiden test. This is, in its real sense, the competition scheduled for the sixth week.

The routine work during the mid-season can be carried out according to the recommendations summed up in Table No. 23/b. The reconditioning may be completed according to the principles outlined in Table No. 23/c (for the 50 per cent. task), and the preparation for the next season-opening contest according to Table No. 22/a (up to the marked one-day event).

In case of preparation for the three-day event the participation in both one-day events scheduled in Table No. 21 should be regarded as items of the conditioning for the horse's main task. Therefore, the rider should make good use of them in the light of this consideration, and not ask the animal to over-strain its performance to a degree that jeopardizes the trend of the general training.

## Table No. 23/b

| The work during the mid-season; valid for all cases shown in Tables Nos. 22,c and 23/c | |
|---|---|
| During the time between the last contest and the start of the renewed conditioning | After the completed test during 10 to 15 days light exercise (see remark in Table No. 21). Following this the knowledge of the horse should be improved according to the experiences gained during the last contest. Strenuous work should be omitted. After the season the horse should enjoy 5 to 6 weeks' rest (light exercise). |

## Table No. 23/c

| RENEWING THE CONDITION OF THE HORSE DURING THE MID-SEASON | | |
|---|---|---|
| The task for the condition-ing | Time (weeks) | The main work during the week With regard to details of other routine work (dressage, etc.) data of previous distributions can be applied in accordance with the actual training requirement |
| 50% | I | Overcoming some country-type obstructions (comfortably). 12 min. hand-gallop. |
| | II | Pipe opener. 1 mile (1,600 m.) gallop over 6 hurdles at 650 yd. (600 m.)/min. |
| | III | A few individual jumps over a single obstacle and a combination up to 4 ft. 3 in. (1.3 m.). A course of 3 ft. 7 in. (1.1 m.). |
| | IV* | 1¼ miles gallop reinforced by 10 to 12 obstacles at 500 yd. (450 m.)/min. |
| | V | Light exercise. 15 min. hand-gallop. |
| | VI—IX | As during the VIII—XI weeks shown in Table No. 21. |
| 75% | I | Overcoming some country-type obstructions (comfortably). 12 min. hand-gallop. |
| | II | Pipe opener. 1 mile (1,600 m.) gallop over 6 hurdles at 650 yd. (600 m.)/min. |
| | III | A few individual jumps over a single obstacle and a combination up to 4 ft. 3 in. (1.3 m.). A course of 3 ft. 7 in. (1.1 m.). |
| | IV* | 2 miles (3,200 m.) gallop reinforced by 14 to 16 obstacles at 500 yd. (450 m.)/min. |
| | V | Light exercise. 15 min. hand-gallop. |
| | VI—IX | As during the II—V weeks shown in Table No. 22/b. |
| 100% | I | Overcoming some country-type obstructions (comfortably). 10 min. hand-gallop. |
| | II | Pipe opener. 1,100 yd. (1,000 m.) gallop over 6 hurdles at 650 yd. (600 m.)/min. |
| | III | Pipe opener. 1¼ miles (2,000 m.) gallop over 10 hurdles at 700 yd. (650 m.)/min. |
| | IV | Practice without fast work. 12 min. hand-gallop. |
| | V | A few individual jumps over a single obstacle and a combination up to 4 ft. 3 in. (1.3 m.). A course of 3 ft. 7 in. (1.1 m.). |
| | VI* | 2½ miles (4,000 m.) gallop reinforced by 16 to 18 obstacles at 500 yd. (450 m.)/min. |
| | VII | Light exercise. 15 min. hand-gallop. |
| | VIII—XI | As during the III—VI weeks shown in Table No. 22/c. |
| | I | Overcoming some country-type obstructions (comfortably). 10 min. hand-gallop. |
| | II | Pipe opener. 1,100 yd. (1,000 m.) gallop over 6 hurdles at 650 yd. (600 m.)/min. |
| | III | Pipe opener. 1¼ miles (2,000 m.) gallop over 10 hurdles at 700 yd. (650 m.)/min. |
| | IV | A few individual jumps over a single obstacle and a combination up to 4 ft. 3 in. (1.3 m.). A course of 3 ft. 7 in. (1.1 m.). 12 min. hand-gallop. |
| | V* | 2 miles (3,200 m.) gallop reinforced by 14 to 16 obstacles at 500 yd. (450 m.)/min. |
| | VI | Light exercise. 15 min. hand-gallop. |
| | VII—X | As during the III—VI weeks shown in Table No. 22/c. |

The items marked by a * can be replaced by an O.D.E.

In such a case practise the programme of the dressage test involved also during the time before the conditioning.

In case of shorter intervals than 3 months between the competitions, the severity of the conditioning should be relaxed and the length of it shortened by excluding the weeks in which the long gallop over obstacles at 500 yd. (450 m.) and the 'light exercise' are included.

## Table No. 24—DISTRIBUTION OF WORK DURING THE SPECIAL EDUCATION AND ADJOINING CONDITIONING OF THE NOVICE SHOW JUMPER UP TO ITS FIRST SHOW

| Composing sections of the education | Period of the special education — Sub-periods, their weekly distribution and details of work to be done | | Period of conditioning, according to weekly and daily distribution | |
|---|---|---|---|---|
| | Winter period from middle of December until end of February | Pre-spring until middle of April | Weeks and days | Main items of the work in addition to dressage-like schooling and gymnastics |
| | 2 days dressage-like schooling | 2 days dressage-like schooling | I | If conditioning starts after indoor work: Accustoming to the open air and natural ground. Exercises on undulating surfaces. |
| | 2 days schooling in jumping | 2 days schooling in jumping | | |
| | 1 day jumping courses | 1 day jumping courses | | |
| | 1 day development of muscles | 1 day exercises on country tract | | |
| Dressage-like schooling | Refining and rousing adjustability. Improving smooth reaction to drive-on and retardment, as well as turning capacity. (Exercises in all paces.) | As during the winter, but with stress on the work at a canter and gallop. Exercises on slightly sloping and undulating surfaces. | II (1, 2, 4; 3) | Exercise on sloping and undulating surfaces. Jumping obstacles individually up to 3 ft. 7 m. (1.1 m.). |
| | | | II (5; 6) | Lengthening gallop-strides at 550 yd. (500 m.)/min. Jumping obstacles individually up to 4 ft. (1.2 m.). |
| Schooling in jumping | Increasing elasticity by gymnastics. Jumping individual obstacles up to 4 ft. 3 in. (1.3 m.) in height and 3 ft. 6 in. (1.05 m.) in spread. Moderate combinations up to 3 ft. 6 in. (1.05 m.). Courses gradually up to 3 ft. 9 in. (1.15 m.). Perform from time to time a jump without any previous preparation up to 3 ft. 7 in. (1.1 m.) in height and 3 ft. (0.9 m.) in spread. | Gymnastics by ground formations and artificial installations (reinforced ev. by the careful use of the iron bar). Jumping single obstacle up to 4 ft. 5 in. (1.35 m.) in height and 4 ft. (1.2 m.) in spread. Various combinations up to 3 ft. 9 in. (1.15 m.). Ditches up to 10 ft. (3 m.). Bank and drop jumps up to 3 ft. (0.9 m.). Courses up to 4 ft. (1.2 m.) including 1 to 2 inviting obstacles of 4 ft. 3 in. (1.3 m.). | III (1) | Practising some small bank and drop jumps (country). |
| | | | III (2; 3) | Lengthening gallop-strides at 550 yd. (500 m.)/min. Jumping obstacles individually up to 3 ft. 7 in. (1.1 m.). |
| | | | III (4) | Exercise on undulating surface. Jumping small ditch. |
| | | | III (5; 6) | Pipe opener by a sprint over 650 yd. (600 m.). Jumping obstacles individually up to 4 ft. 3 in. (1.3 m.). |
| | | | IV (1) | Practising jumps over ditches up to 8 ft. (2.5 m.). |
| | | | IV (2; 3) | Lengthening gallop-strides at 600 yd. (550 m.)/min. Jumping obstacles individually up to 3 ft. 7 in. (1.1 m.). |
| | | | IV (4) | Pipe opener by climbing. |
| | | | IV (5) | A few jumps up to 4 ft. (1.2 m.). |
| | | | IV (6) | Jumping a course of 3 ft. 3 in. (1 m.) height. |
| Exercises on the country tract | If weather and ground conditions permit, as in autumn (see Table No. 18, "Further Education"). | Dexterity exercises supplementing bank jumps, practices in clearing water jumps. | V (1) | Practising jumps over a ditch up to 9 ft. (2.8 m.). |
| | | | V (2; 3) | Lengthening gallop-strides at 600 yd. (550 m.)/min. Jumping obstacles individually up to 4 ft. (1.2 m.). |
| | | | V (4) | Pipe opener by a sprint over 800 yd. (700 m.). |
| | | | V (5) | A few jumps up to 4 ft. 3 in. (1.3 m.). |
| | | | V (6) | Jumping a course of 3 ft. 7 in. (1.1 m.) height. |
| Stride and muscle improvement | Development of muscles by protracted cantering gradually up from 5 minutes to 15 minutes. | Once a week as an addition to any work lengthening gallop-strides at a speed of 550 yd. (500 m.)/min. | VI | As during the Vth week; course 4 ft. (1.2 m.) high. |

Concerning the days of the first public performance see Table No. 10 (column four).

## Table No. 25

### DISTRIBUTION OF TIME AND WORK FOR THE IMPROVEMENT OF THE NOVICE SHOW JUMPER FROM SHOW TO SHOW

| Routine work between shows according to weekly distribution | Dimensions of the obstacles employed and the application of routine courses during the exercises between the shows |
|---|---|
| **2** *days per week dressage-like schooling:*<br>Rousing adjustability, improving suppleness, impulsion and turning capacity.<br>**3** *days per week schooling in jumping:*<br>Gymnastics mainly by ground formations, jumping individual obstacles and combinations, practising rudimentary courses.<br>**1** *day per week practices in the country-site:*<br>Climbing exercises, bank and drop jumps, ditches, both dry and with water.<br>If the horse shows satisfactory competence in contests the number of jumps involved should be reduced. | *During competitions up to 4 ft. (1.2 m.):*<br>Obstacles and courses as shown in Table No. 24 (pre-spring period).<br>*Before the start and during the participation in classes up to 4 ft. 3 in. (1.3 m.) height:*<br>Obstacles: Up to 4 ft. 9 in. (1.45 m.) in height and 4 ft. 6 in. (1.35 m.) in spread.<br>Courses: 6 to 8 days after the usual rest one with obstacles between 3 ft. 3 in. (1 m.) and 4 ft. (1 m.). This can ev. be repeated a week later. Then once weekly a course reinforced by 2 to 3 more difficult or new obstacles. 8 to 10 days before the show the course should include 3 to 4 fences of 4 ft. 3 in. (1.3 m.) height and a ditch of 10 ft. (3 m.).<br>*Before the start in classes of 4 ft. 7 in. (1.4 m.) height:*<br>Obstacles: Up to 5 ft. (1.5 m.) in height and 5 ft. (1.5 m.) in spread.<br>Courses: Arranged in the above manner but the mentioned heights should be increased by 4 in. (10 cm.) and the width of the ditch can reach the 11 ft. 6 in. (3.5 m.) mark. |

## Table No. 26

### DISTRIBUTION OF TIME AND WORK FOR THE DEVELOPMENT OF THE INTERMEDIATE SHOW JUMPER

| Work during the periods of education | | Work during the period of conditioning. Details of the main work to be done during the weeks (besides dressage-like schooling and gymnastics) |
|---|---|---|
| The educative work up to the conditioning for the season-opening contest occurs according to the principles laid down in Table No. 24.<br>The horse's development during the periods between the shows can be carried out in a similar manner as shown in Table No. 25.<br>In order to revise the work scheduled in these Tables in accordance with the more advanced knowledge of the horse, the data, referring to the dimensions of the obstacles, should be increased by about 4 in. (10 cm.). Furthermore, one should include exercises for increasing the speed of clearing courses. | I | If necessary: Acclimatization to outdoor riding; exercises on the country tract.<br>Pipe opener possible by climbing; individual jumps up to 3 ft. 7 in. (1.1 m.). |
| | II | Lung exercise by a short sprint.<br>Individual jumps: Single obstacle up to 4 ft. (1.2 m.), combinations up to 3 ft. 7 in. (1.1 m.).<br>Lengthening gallop-stride at 550 yd. (500 m.)/min. over 650 yd. (600 m.).<br>Overcoming country-type obstacle (ditch, bank and drop-jumps). |
| | III | Schooling in jumping up to 3 ft. 7 in. (1.1 m.), ev. with the iron bar.<br>Lengthening gallop-stride at 550 yd. (500 m.)/min. over 900 yd. (800 m.).<br>A few individual jumps up to 4 ft. 3 in. (1.3 m.). |
| | IV | Schooling in jumping up to 3 ft. 7 in. and over a water-jump 8 ft. (2.5 m.).<br>Individual jumps: Single obstacles up to 4 ft. 3 in. (1.3 m.), combination up to 4 ft. (1.2 m.).<br>Jumping a light course of 4 ft. (1.2 m.). |
| | V | Sprint over 700 yd. (650 m.); schooling in jumping as in the IVth week.<br>Individual jumps: Single obstacles up to 4 ft. 7 in. (1.4 m.), combination up to 4 ft. 3 in. (1.3 m.).<br>Moderate course of 4 ft. (1.2 m.) including 2 to 3 obstacles of 4 ft. 3 in. (1.3 m.). |
| | VI | The week of the competition: A short sprint, some gymnastics and a few jumps up to 4 ft. (1.2 m.). |

The data in the above part of the Table refer to the conditioning of the progressing horse's *season-opening contest,* but they show also the principles of conditioning for future stages.

*Distribution of time and work during the preparation of the finished show jumper. (With special reference to the work during the first season at this stage)*

The work during the winter and the early spring period.

The work should commence as soon as the horse has overcome the exertion of the previous season (after a rest of four to five weeks).

During the period lasting till Christmas the renewal of regularity should be the most important point in the work. During this time jumping can be ignored, and light gymnastic exercises may provide some variation in the work.

After Christmas jumping exercises can commence and three days per week can be devoted to this work in which the following objects of education should also be included according to the distribution as shown below.

On one day in every week:
    improvement of the style of jumping by schooling over different types of single obstacles.

On one day in every second week:
    practise jumping combinations; and
    accustoming the horse to high obstacles.

On one day every third week:
    practise jumping combinations set up at odd distances;
    introduction to jumping the six bars; and
    jumping parcours.

In incorporating the above exercises in the general volume of work the following example should afford some guidance.

First week:
    Improvement of style: Height of obstacle up to 3 feet 3 inches (1 m.).
    Combinations: Double jump up to 3 feet 3 inches (1 m.).
    Double with odd distance: Up to 2 feet 8 inches (0.80 m.).

Second week:
    Improvement of style: Height of obstacle up to 3 feet 7 inches (1.10 m.).
    Accustoming to high obstacles: Height up to 4 feet 3 inches (1.30 m.).
    Parcours jumping: Parcours up to 3 feet 7 inches (1.10 m.).

Third week:
    Improvement of style: Height of obstacle up to 3 feet 7 inches (1.10 m.).
    Combinations: Treble jump up to 3 feet 7 inches (1.10 m.).
    Introduction to jumping six bars: Four elements, from 2 feet 8 inches (0.80 m.) up to 3 feet 7 inches (1.10 m.).

Fourth week:
    Improvement of style: Height of obstacle up to 4 feet (1.20 m.).
    Accustoming to high obstacles: Height up to 4 feet 7 inches (1.40 m.).
    Treble jump with odd distances: Up to 3 feet (0.90 m.).

Fifth week:
    Improvement of style: Height of obstacle up to 4 feet (1.20 m.).
    Combinations: Double jump up to 4 feet (1.20 m.).
    Jumping parcours: Height up to 4 feet (1.20 m.).

Sixth week:
    Improvement of style: Height of obstacle up to 4 feet (1.20 m.).
    Accustoming to high obstacles: Height up to 5 feet (1.50 m.).
    Introduction to jumping six bars: Five elements, from 3 feet (0.90 m.)
       up to 4 feet 3 inches (1.30 m.).

Seventh week:
    Improvement of style: Height of obstacle up to 4 feet (1.20 m.).
    Combinations: Treble jump up to 4 feet 3 inches (1.30 m.).
    Double jump with odd distance: Up to 3 feet 3 inches (1 m.).

Eighth week:
    Improvement of style: Height of obstacle up to 4 feet (1.20 m.).
    Accustoming to high obstacles: Height up to 5 feet (1.50 m.).
    Jumping parcours: Height up to 4 feet (1.20 m.), perhaps with two to
       three obstacles of 4 feet 3 inches (1.30 m.) height.

Ninth week:
    Improvement of style: Height of obstacle up to 4 feet (1.20 m.).
    Combinations: Double jump up to 4 feet 7 inches (1.40 m.).
    Introduction of six bars jumping: Six elements, from 3 feet (0.90 m.)
       up to 4 feet 7 inches (1.40 m.).

In each exercise the emphasis should be laid upon painstaking preparation. The number of jumps involved should be kept as low as possible.

With regard to the other routine work (dressage-like schooling, muscular exercise, etc.), the recommendations given in Table No. 24 can be followed by taking into account the more advanced stage of the horse's education.

The conditioning for the season-opening contest occurs according to the data shown in Table No. 26. If the horse would start the season with a parcours over 4 feet 3 inches (1.30 m.) height, the jumping exercises during the last three weeks should be reinforced adequately.

The routine work during the periods between the shows can be carried out as that in the case of the progressing show jumper. The exercises, however, should include once or twice jumps gradually increased up to 5 feet 7 inches (1.70 m.), and clearing six bars up to 5 feet 3 inches (1.60 m.).

As a general recommendation for the routine work of the complete show jumper one should bear in mind that as its competence in jumping develops so less jumping exercises are necessary. Its legs should be saved, its mood kept fresh!

## CONCLUSION

We have now reached the stage when the schooling period has been fully completed, and the rider can feel that he has afforded all the knowledge and experience his horse may find necessary for a successful career.

With regard to the rider's personal qualities it is true to say that the best performances require the possession of inherent values which have been improved by study and experience. Nevertheless, it is open to anyone who will acquire the feeling and physical fitness for riding, coupled with endurance and instinctive courage, to achieve a high degree of excellence in his performances. Thus, such riders whose skill is not an exceptional gift but the product of systematic work may also become successful contestants in the greatest events such as in the Nations Cups or in the Olympic Equestrian Games.

A rider's good luck may contribute to his success, but it is by no means as important as is generally asserted. If the rider has acquired the right qualification, and has prepared his horse thoroughly, luck is likely to be on his side. Although everybody can be overtaken by misfortune, the absence of luck can mostly be attributed to gaps in positive qualifications. That is why it is a mistake to blame hard fate. In competitions the same riders and the same horses are, in most cases, to the fore, which proves that the role of chance is a minor factor.

It has been the aim of the present work to help the ambitious rider to become such a competitor whose success is not a mere stroke of luck, but the proof of a thorough education.

*All success to you my reader !*

# INDEX

Readers of this book who wish to be informed about new and forth-
coming publications on horses and horsemanship are invited to send
their names and addresses to:

J. A. ALLEN & COMPANY LIMITED,
1 Lower Grosvenor Place,
Buckingham Palace Road,
London SW1W 0EL.